Corporate Sustainabil
as a Tool for Improvi
Economic, Social,
and Environmental
Performance

Bartolomé Marco-Lajara
University of Alicante, Spain

Javier Martínez-Falcó
University of Alicante, Spain & Stellenbosch University, South A

Luis A. Millán-Tudela
University of Alicante, Spain

A volume in the Advances in Human Resources Management and Organizational Development (AHRMOD) Book Series

Published in the United States of America by
IGI Global
Business Science Reference (an imprint of IGI Global)
701 E. Chocolate Avenue
Hershey PA, USA 17033
Tel: 717-533-8845
Fax: 717-533-8661
E-mail: cust@igi-global.com
Web site: http://www.igi-global.com

Library of Congress Cataloging-in-Publication Data

Names: Marco Lajara, Bartolomé, 1970- editor. | Martinez Falcó, Javier, 1997- editor. | Millán-Tudela, Luis A., 1998- editor.
Title: Corporate sustainability as a tool for improving economic, social, and environmental performance / edited by Bartolomé Marco-Lajara, Javier Martínez Falcó, Luis A. Millán-Tudela.
Description: Hershey, PA : Business Science Reference, [2023] | Includes bibliographical references and index. | Summary: "Corporate Sustainability as a Tool for Improving Economic, Social, and Environmental Performance provides a guide for study, reflection, and critique to understand corporate sustainability while offering the basis for comprehending this phenomenon in different sectors of the economy. The book also sheds light on the new currents and challenges of the discipline. Covering key topics such as big data, ethical business, and strategic management, this premier reference source is ideal for business owners, managers, entrepreneurs, government officials, policymakers, researchers, academicians, practitioners, scholars, instructors, and students"-- Provided by publisher.
Identifiers: LCCN 2022056933 (print) | LCCN 2022056934 (ebook) | ISBN 9781668474228 (hardcover) | ISBN 9781668474235 (paperback) | ISBN 9781668474242 (ebook)
Subjects: LCSH: Social responsibility of business. | Sustainable development. | Sustainability. | Business ethics.
Classification: LCC HD60 .C6964 2023 (print) | LCC HD60 (ebook) | DDC 658.4/08--dc23/eng/20230118
LC record available at https://lccn.loc.gov/2022056933
LC ebook record available at https://lccn.loc.gov/2022056934

This book is published in the IGI Global book series Advances in Human Resources Management and Organizational Development (AHRMOD) (ISSN: 2327-3372; eISSN: 2327-3380)

British Cataloguing in Publication Data
A Cataloguing in Publication record for this book is available from the British Library.
All work contributed to this book is new, previously-unpublished material. The views expressed in this book are those of the authors, but not necessarily of the publisher.
For electronic access to this publication, please contact: eresources@igi-global.com.

Advances in Human Resources Management and Organizational Development (AHRMOD) Book Series

Patricia Ordóñez de Pablos
Universidad de Oviedo, Spain

ISSN:2327-3372
EISSN:2327-3380

Mission

A solid foundation is essential to the development and success of any organization and can be accomplished through the effective and careful management of an organization's human capital. Research in human resources management and organizational development is necessary in providing business leaders with the tools and methodologies which will assist in the development and maintenance of their organizational structure.

The **Advances in Human Resources Management and Organizational Development (AHRMOD) Book Series** aims to publish the latest research on all aspects of human resources as well as the latest methodologies, tools, and theories regarding organizational development and sustainability. The **AHRMOD Book Series** intends to provide business professionals, managers, researchers, and students with the necessary resources to effectively develop and implement organizational strategies.

Coverage

- Work-Life Balance
- Training and Development
- Personnel Policies
- Coaching and Mentoring
- Upward Feedback
- Workplace Discrimination
- Change Management
- Recruitment Process
- Disputes Resolution
- Job Enrichment

IGI Global is currently accepting manuscripts for publication within this series. To submit a proposal for a volume in this series, please contact our Acquisition Editors at Acquisitions@igi-global.com or visit: http://www.igi-global.com/publish/.

The Advances in Human Resources Management and Organizational Development (AHRMOD) Book Series (ISSN 2327-3372) is published by IGI Global, 701 E. Chocolate Avenue, Hershey, PA 17033-1240, USA, www.igi-global.com. This series is composed of titles available for purchase individually; each title is edited to be contextually exclusive from any other title within the series. For pricing and ordering information please visit http://www.igi-global.com/book-series/advances-human-resources-management-organizational/73670. Postmaster: Send all address changes to above address.

Titles in this Series

For a list of additional titles in this series, please visit: http://www.igi-global.com/book-series/advances-human-resources-management-organizational/73670

Handbook of Research on Dissecting and Dismantling Occupational Stress in Modern Organizations
Adnan ul Haque (Yorkville University, Canada)
Business Science Reference • © 2023 • 600pp • H/C (ISBN: 9781668465431) • US $315.00

Managing Technology Integration for Human Resources in Industry 5.0
Naman Sharma (Indian Institute of Foreign Trade, India) and Kumar Shalender (Chitkara University, India)
Business Science Reference • © 2023 • 294pp • H/C (ISBN: 9781668467459) • US $215.00

Leadership Perspectives on Effective Intergenerational Communication and Management
Fatma Ince (Mersin University, Turkey)
Business Science Reference • © 2023 • 289pp • H/C (ISBN: 9781668461402) • US $230.00

Examining the Aging Workforce and Its Impact on Economic and Social Development
Bruno de Sousa Lopes (University of Aveiro, Portugal) Maria Céu Lamas (School of Health, Polytechnic of Porto, Portugal) Vanessa Amorim (Porto Accounting and Business School, Polytechnic of Porto, Portugal) and Orlando Lima Rua (Porto Accounting and Business School, Polytechnic of Porto, Portugal)
Business Science Reference • © 2023 • 215pp • H/C (ISBN: 9781668463512) • US $225.00

The Experiences of Black Women Diversity Practitioners in Historically White Institutions
Tristen Brenaé Johnson (Moffitt Cancer Center, USA)
Information Science Reference • © 2023 • 330pp • H/C (ISBN: 9781668435649) • US $215.00

Handbook of Research on Acceleration Programs for SMEs
Inês Lisboa (Politechnic Institute of Leiria, Portugal) Nuno Teixeira (Politechnic Institute of Setúbal, Portugal) Liliane Segura (Presbiteriano Mackenzie Institute, Brazil) Tomáš Krulický (Institute of Technology and Business, České Budějovice, Czech Republic) and Veronika Machová (Institute of Technology and Business, České Budějovice, Czech Republic)
Business Science Reference • © 2023 • 575pp • H/C (ISBN: 9781668456668) • US $360.00

Developing Diversity, Equity, and Inclusion Policies for Promoting Employee Sustainability and Well-Being
Sónia P. Gonçalves (ISCSP-ULisboa, Portugal) Paula Cristina Nunes Figueiredo (Universidade Lusófona, Portugal) Eduardo Luis Soares Tomé (ULHT - Universidade Lusófona, Portugal) and José Baptista (ISCSP-ULisboa, Portugal)
Business Science Reference • © 2023 • 330pp • H/C (ISBN: 9781668441817) • US $240.00

IGI Global
PUBLISHER of TIMELY KNOWLEDGE

701 East Chocolate Avenue, Hershey, PA 17033, USA
Tel: 717-533-8845 x100 • Fax: 717-533-8661
E-Mail: cust@igi-global.com • www.igi-global.com

Table of Contents

Detailed Table of Contents

This chapter presents an overview of sustainable finance literature focusing on studies using environmental, social and governance (ESG) practices, and conducts a descriptive and comparative analysis of the Refinitiv ESG database worldwide. With increasing interest in ESG investing, it is common to integrate ESG factors into portfolio decisions. The authors first address the relevant literature to set the background for further studies. The chapter documents an increasing trend in ESG reporting and points out differences in ESG scores in terms of development level, region, industry, and legal origin for the period 2002-2019. Theoretical models and empirical tests, which integrate ESG factors into corporate performance, can only be established by a better understanding of ESG databases. Therefore, further research in the Refinitiv ESG database, as well as other ESG databases, is significant. This chapter contributes to this stream of research by explaining the Refinitiv ESG database with descriptive and comparative analysis, paving the way for new research on the subject.

Corporate sustainability is a topic that has gathered a considerable interest in the last years. Despite recent developments, some firms have led with changes in the environment for centuries to survive, being one of the tools used for corporate sustainability. This chapter analyzes how the most long-living companies in the world have carried out sustainable businesses through embeddedness and collaboration with the environment, mostly by the use of intangible resources and capabilities, in order to remain in the market. With a narrative perspective, the authors expose some of the practices developed by the abovementioned companies. The main conclusions extracted from those firms are aimed to be potentially applied to current companies and, thus, enhance corporate sustainability and survival through already proven mechanisms.

Saudi government pays high attention to the public sectors, such as Saudi Port Authority, in order to gain high level of competition in the global market. Saudi ports, which are considered as one of the busiest ports in the world, and the largest in the Middle East area. However, it has recently faced a severe problem of overstock of commodities. Although, the ports have significant contribution to the local economy, but, improper work environments and the heavy duty of the work has resulted in dissatisfaction and a low level of employees comments among cargo employees, which results in overstock of commodities at Saudi Ports Authority. Questionnaires were distributed to 365 government workers in the cargo sector, 285 were filled up. The outcomes of the study imply that work stress and working conditions may positively affect employee commitment, and that job happiness is an essential factor that workers can embrace in reaching their goals. On the other hand, workplace stress and working conditions might enhance commitment indirectly by giving job satisfaction.

This chapter aims to study how the New Energy Vehicle (NEV) industry is developing in the entrepreneurial ecosystem, under the Carbon Neutrality policy in China. This chapter explores the role of the Chinese Government, post the 14th Five-year plan period, in promoting sustainable development of new energy vehicles. This work also sheds more light on China's policies and how these institutions promote the development of environmental awareness in various industries. The overall effect on the environment of these developments, as well as the impact of China's environmental research and institutional changes of enterprises under the sustainable aims of carbon neutrality, will be discussed. This chapter also collates statistical information mainly on the carbon neutrality, carbon trading market, development of new energy vehicles and ESG investment. Cases from China are presented for deeper and funneled insights. The chapter also provides suggestions for the development of new energy vehicles and investment under China's environment-based ecosystems.

concept of organizational resilience confirms that the creation and development of an organizational resilience framework for structural construct can be supported by elements based on flexibility of organizational culture, organizational safety, and reliability, the promotion elements, and the deployment of organizational resources.

The aim of this chapter is to analyze the extent to which resource efficiency can be considered an economic opportunity to businesses, and to discuss the benefits and limitations of resource efficiency as perceived by companies. Based on established methodology, the authors performed literature review on benefits and limitations of improving resource efficiency, and opportunities resource efficiency could bring to businesses, and carried out interviews with six SMEs entrepreneurs. Results suggest the need to innovate in production and consumption and call for a more rigorous, science-based approach in decision making, especially when it comes to natural resources. International cooperation is seen as a means to making a transformation to resource-efficient future. The interviews also show that components most appreciated in promoting the efficient use of resources are (actual) financial aid and tax benefits, as well as education for sustainability and resource efficiency.

This study analyses the implications of organizational management variables in the enhancement of organizational citizenship behaviors. It departs from the assumption that management, motivation, commitment, leadership styles, innovation, and other relevant ideas have effects on the organizational citizenship behaviors. The method employed links the analysis, description, and reflection base on the theoretical and empirical literature review. It is concluded that organizational management variables enhance the self-efficacy of organizational members and the effectiveness of the organization involved in organizational citizenship behaviors.

Blockchains are currently recognized as a new area of digitization with difficulties in attaining sustainability. The research has not yet produced a unified framework for understanding the characteristics of blockchains that allow the development of financial trading markets over the long term. The topic of how blockchains support the growth of sustainable financial trading platforms and services still exists.

Preface

The world is currently witnessing a change in the business paradigm in which economic, social, and environmental variables are taken into account. In this sense, sustainable companies focus on the development of a profitability formula that, through the connection with stakeholders and the natural environment, operates in harmony with social and economic progress. In this sense, the concept of corporate sustainability refers to the attempt by companies to balance social, economic, and environmental objectives. It requires a strong orientation towards the future as well as an awareness of the need to preserve the existence and well-being of the human species. In this way, companies seek to ensure long-term business success while contributing to the economic, social, and environmental development of the territories in which they operate.

Corporate Sustainability as a Tool for Improving Economic, Social, and Environmental Performance provides a guide for study, reflection, and critique to understand corporate sustainability while offering the basis for comprehending this phenomenon in different sectors of the economy. The book also sheds light on the new currents and challenges of the discipline. Covering key topics such as big data, ethical business, and strategic management, this premier reference source is ideal for business owners, managers, entrepreneurs, government officials, policymakers, researchers, academicians, practitioners, scholars, instructors, and students.

The book is structured in 13 book chapters. Chapter 1 presents an overview of the sustainable finance literature focusing on studies using environmental, social and governance (ESG) practices and performs a descriptive and comparative analysis of the Refinitiv ESG database worldwide. The authors first address the relevant literature to lay the groundwork for subsequent studies. The chapter documents a growing trend in ESG reporting and points out differences in ESG scores in terms of level of development, region, industry and legal origin for the period 2002-2019. Theoretical models and empirical evidence, which integrate ESG factors into corporate performance, can only be established through a better understanding of ESG databases. Therefore, further research in the Refinitiv ESG database, as well as in other ESG databases, is important. This chapter contributes to this research stream by explaining the Refinitiv ESG database with descriptive and comparative analyses, paving the way for further research on the topic.

Chapter 2 analyzes how the world's longest-lived companies have conducted sustainable business through integration and collaboration with the environment, especially through the use of intangible resources and capabilities, in order to remain in the market. Using a narrative perspective, the authors present some of the practices developed by these companies. The main conclusions drawn from these companies are intended to be potentially applicable to today's companies and, in this way, to enhance business sustainability and survival through proven mechanisms.

Chapter 3 highlights that Saudi ports are considered one of the busiest in the world and the largest in the Middle East. However, it has recently faced a serious problem of commodity overstocking. Although the ports contribute significantly to the local economy, an inadequate working environment and heavy workload have led to dissatisfaction and low feedback among cargo employees, resulting in overstocking at the Saudi Ports Authority. Questionnaires were distributed to 365 government employees in the cargo sector, of which 285 were completed. The results of the study imply that job stress and working conditions can positively affect employee engagement and that job happiness is an essential factor that workers can adopt to achieve their goals. On the other hand, job stress and working conditions could increase engagement indirectly by giving job satisfaction.

Chapter 4 aims to study how new energy vehicles are developed in the business ecosystem under the carbon neutrality policy in China. This chapter explores the roles of the government after the 14th Five-Year Plan in promoting the sustainability of new energy vehicle development through policies (i.e., institutions). The authors analyze the impact of environmental research in China and the institutional changes of enterprises under the sustainable carbon neutrality goals. This chapter will conduct statistical and correlation analysis mainly on carbon neutrality, carbon trading market, new energy vehicle development and ESG investment. Cases from China are used for explanations, offering suggestions for new energy vehicle development and investment under China's environment-based ecosystems.

Chapter 5 aims to demonstrate women's empowerment through social entrepreneurship and to show the scope of social entrepreneurship and NGOs that analysts are currently unaware of, as well as to inspire those who have not yet studied this field and wish to conduct research on women's empowerment through NGOs. In this study, the author opts for a quantitative strategy and used the Scopus database to identify the research areas with the most significant research results, the initiation of research in the field of women's empowerment and NGOs, the source of the research, and the thematic area. This research focuses on 130 published papers in the field of women's empowerment in context with NGOs, which have been indexed in Scopus. The study demonstrates that bibliometric research on women's participation in social entrepreneurship can be carried out systematically and that a new scope of research on social entrepreneurship can be established.

Chapter 6 highlights that wineries can develop environmental management programs to save and reuse the resources they use. This represents a change of business paradigm in the wine sector that can be very beneficial, since, on the one hand, wineries that develop their environmental management can save costs and protect the environment, favoring the preservation of the environment to ensure the permanence of the sector in the territory and, on the other hand, such management can serve as a differentiating element in the market, allowing the winery to generate a competitive advantage. The objective of the authors is precisely to know what practices can be developed to ensure a correct environmental management. To this end, through a multiple case study, a decalogue of practices that every winery can develop to favor the preservation of the environment in which it operates is identified.

Chapter 7 aims to analyze socioeconomic sustainability in the post-pandemic era from an organizational structural construct based on a framework of elements for reliability, security and deployment of organizational resources. It is assumed that theoretical and empirical studies in organizational resilience have limited contributions on the concepts of high reliability organization applied to a diversity of entities and with a variety of characteristics. The method employed is the reflective analytic method of theoretical and empirical literature review. This study concludes that the emerging concept of organizational resilience confirms that the creation and development of an organizational resilience framework for the structural construct can be supported by elements based on organizational culture flexibility, organizational safety and reliability, advocacy elements, and deployment of organizational resources.

Chapter 8 aims to analyze the extent to which resource efficiency can be considered an economic opportunity for companies and to discuss the benefits and limitations of resource efficiency as perceived by companies. Based on the established methodology, the authors conducted a literature review on the benefits and limitations of improving resource efficiency and the opportunities that resource efficiency could bring to firms, and conducted interviews with six SME entrepreneurs. The results suggest the need for innovation in production and consumption and call for a more rigorous, science-based approach to decision making, especially when dealing with natural resources. International cooperation is seen as a means to achieve a transformation towards a resource-efficient future. The interviews also show that the most appreciated components to promote resource efficiency are (real) financial support and tax benefits, as well as education for sustainability and resource efficiency.

Chapter 9 analyzes the implications of organizational management variables in improving organizational citizenship behaviors. It assumes that management, motivation, commitment, leadership styles, innovation and other relevant variables have effects on organizational citizenship behaviors. The method employed links analysis, description and reflection based on the review of theoretical and empirical literature. It is concluded that organizational management variables enhance organizational members' self-efficacy and organizational effectiveness implicated in organizational citizenship behaviors.

Chapter 10 highlights that blockchains are currently recognized as a new area of digitization with challenges to achieve sustainability. Research has yet to produce a unified framework for understanding the characteristics of blockchains that enable the development of long-term financial trading markets. The issue of how blockchains support the growth of sustainable financial trading platforms and services remains unresolved. The authors conduct qualitative and iterative research to compile the basic concepts found in the literature and provide a conceptual framework with four sustainability themes and eleven types of affordances. The results are significant because they show how closely related these categories are, leading to conflicts between various sustainability-related concepts.

Chapter 11 aims to analyze a strategic transformational transition of green economy, green growth and sustainable development from the institutional perspective. The analysis begins by questioning the implications of the concepts and principles of green economy, green growth, and sustainable development from different perspectives in the transformational transition considering investment, trade and capacity building through the design and implementation of strategies and policies as well as measures from an institutional analysis. The methodology followed was the analytical review of the literature to derive inferences, challenges, proposals, and conclusions. It is concluded that the concept of green economy addresses current challenges by offering opportunities for economic development and multiple benefits for the well-being of all human beings.

Chapter 12 emphasizes that the establishment of high-tech zones (HTZs) is an important strategic measure for the development of high-tech industries in China. As knowledge-intensive areas, high-tech zones aim to improve networking, as well as the innovative and economic performance of enterprises and regions. There are extensive studies on the factors affecting the economic development of high-tech zones. However, some policy gaps remain on the topic of responsible research and innovation (RRI) of HTZs. This paper exposes the development status of China's high-tech zones and the obstacles to the practice of RRI in China, and then analyzes the cases of RRI in Shanghai Zizhu HTZ, Wuhan East Lake HTZ and Guangdong HTZ, and discusses how HTZs in the new era can succeed under the guidance of

RRI. Finally, some suggestions for the development of HTZs in China are presented, with the hope of perfecting the policy framework and promoting research and innovation in China's HTZs.

Chapter 13 aims to study the implications of digital transformation on Chinese enterprises. This chapter will seek to explore whether and how social capital can become a major driving force in designing a whole new digitally competent social fabric under the new normal in China. By analyzing the institutional impacts driven by the Chinese government, this chapter will explore how these impacts will succeed in generating any synergistic effects in bringing about digital transformation in business sectors. This chapter will use bibliometric analysis to conduct statistical and correlation analysis on cross-sector digital transformation. Cases from China will be used for comparisons. This chapter will provide suggestions for developing business ecosystems based on digital transformation in emerging economies in a sustainable manner.

The book aims to serve as a study guide, reflection, and critique to understand the benefits of the implementation of the Sustainable Development Goals by organizations. The book sheds light on the priority objectives that companies in certain sectors tend to adhere to, making it a must-read for academics and managers who want to deepen their understanding. The book could therefore become a thought-provoking work on the achievement of the Sustainable Development Goals, as well as the importance of corporate sustainability in achieving these goals.

Bartolomé Marco-Lajara
University of Alicante, Spain

Javier Martínez-Falcó
University of Alicante, Spain & Stellenbosch University, South Africa

Luis A. Millán-Tudela
University of Alicante, Spain

Acknowledgment

The editors would like to point out on this festive occasion the fact that this scientific book titled *Intellectual Corporate Sustainability as a Tool for Improving Economic, Social, and Environmental Performance*, published by IGI Global, is the result of the vigorous work and the sedulousness that characterized the activity and the actions belonging to the authors, to the members of the Editorial Advisory Board (EAB), and to the members of the Editorial Review Board (ERB).

Furthermore, the editors would like to express the deepest and the profoundest appreciation to the IGI Global team members, who were on top of the situation at every level and who turned this constructive collaboration into a wonderful scientific project that came to life in order to support hard work, creativity, dedication, knowledge, and education, in times in which the ability of organizations to promote sustainable development and foster environmental protection is a key feature for the survival and health of our Planet.

Editorial Advisory Board

Chapter 1
Corporate Sustainability:
The Use of ESG Scores in Finance Research

Naime Usul
https://orcid.org/0000-0002-8475-9887
Çankaya University, Turkey & Yıldırım Beyazıt University, Turkey

Işıl Sevilay Yılmaz
https://orcid.org/0000-0001-9499-5245
TED University, Turkey

ABSTRACT

This chapter presents an overview of sustainable finance literature focusing on studies using environmental, social and governance (ESG) practices, and conducts a descriptive and comparative analysis of the Refinitiv ESG database worldwide. With increasing interest in ESG investing, it is common to integrate ESG factors into portfolio decisions. The authors first address the relevant literature to set the background for further studies. The chapter documents an increasing trend in ESG reporting and points out differences in ESG scores in terms of development level, region, industry, and legal origin for the period 2002-2019. Theoretical models and empirical tests, which integrate ESG factors into corporate performance, can only be established by a better understanding of ESG databases. Therefore, further research in the Refinitiv ESG database, as well as other ESG databases, is significant. This chapter contributes to this stream of research by explaining the Refinitiv ESG database with descriptive and comparative analysis, paving the way for new research on the subject.

INTRODUCTION

For many years, finance theorists believed that individuals base their investment decisions on Bayesian techniques and come up with the optimal investment decision that maximizes their utility, which is the expected return with respect to risk. Thus, the expected return is considered the only benefit that is promised to an investor (Usul,Özdemir, & Kiessling, 2017). However, with the emergence of challenging ideas from psychology and decision-making literature (Kahneman & Tversky, 1972, 1979; Kahneman,

DOI: 10.4018/978-1-6684-7422-8.ch001

2003), other types of benefits are proposed such as expressive and emotional benefits. Yet, financial benefit retains its significance as utilitarian benefits and is perceived to be a part of total benefit (Statman, 2004). Social concerns in financial markets have been studied heavily in the literature, which produced the concepts of corporate social responsibility, socially responsible investing, ethical investing, sustainable investing, impact investing, and ESG (Environmental, Social, Governance) investing. Sustainable finance is considered an umbrella term for the above-mentioned concepts by researchers (Drempetic, Klein, & Zwergel, 2020). However, the initial attempts to explain such concerns were mostly "normative" studies that present "what socially responsible firms and investors should do". As various theoretical frameworks are continuously being developed in the field, the studies have evolved from being "normative" to "descriptive" (Leins, 2020). This chapter presents an overview of sustainable finance literature focusing on studies using ESG practices and conducts a descriptive and comparative analysis of the Refinitiv ESG database worldwide.

Sustainable investing is getting increasing attention both by researchers and by investors reaching $35.3 trillion across the United States, Canada, Japan, Australasia, and Europe as reported by the 2020 Global Sustainable Investment Review, published by Global Sustainable Investment Alliance (GSIA). This represents a 15% increase in sustainable investment assets under management from 2018 to 2020. Therefore, the sustainable investment appears to become a significant source of funding for those who are seeking to raise capital all over the world, shaping global capital markets. When the total assets managed under sustainable investment from 2018 to 2020 are considered, the US and Europe are the leading markets, representing more than 80% of the world's sustainable investing assets. The ratio of sustainable investment assets in the five major markets, namely Canada, Europe, Australasia, the US, and Japan are 62%, 42%, 38%, 33%, and 24% respectively in 2020 (GSIA, 2021). The report highlights that ESG integration stands out as the most common sustainable investment strategy.

Hence, the social motivations in financial decision-making, initially considered only in small niche markets, became a part of financial market activities as investors seek to find ways to invest morally (Dumas & Louche, 2016; Welker & Wood, 2011). The increased attention for sustainable investing is underlined by the increase in dedicated institutional investors, analyst coverage, and a decrease in the cost of capital of firms engaging in corporate social responsibility (Dhaliwal et al., 2011). In this context, Global Sustainable Investment Alliance reported that more than $30 trillion was managed under responsible investment criteria worldwide, manifested more in Europe yet rapidly growing in the United States in 2019. As ESG considerations started to become an important factor in investors' decision-making process, the companies voluntarily started to disclose related information in their annual reports or standalone sustainability reports (CFA, 2021). The increased tendency toward sustainable investing led to the development of various datasets quantifying companies' such concerns as environmental, social, and governance. The well-known sustainability datasets include MSCI ESG fund metrics, MSCI KLD scores, Moody's ESG issuer profile and credit impact scores, S&P global ESG scores, Bloomberg ESG scores, Morningstars Sustainability Ratings and Carbon Metrics, and Refinitiv ESG Scores. These datasets enable researchers to test the relationship between various corporate performance indicators and ESG factors. This chapter intends to describe Refinitiv ESG scores, which measure relative ESG performance for more than 9000 companies so that new studies could investigate the unexplored relationships using this dataset. The authors also present a comparative discussion on the main descriptive statistics related to ESG scores around the world for the period 2002-2019.

ESG refers to Environmental, Social, and Governance related concerns an investor may value while making an investment decision. The Environmental (E) dimension refers to companies' efforts to contribute to and be in synergy with the natural ecosystem such as decreasing pollution and waste, investing in carbon emission strategies, designing eco-friendly products and processes, using natural resources efficiently, etc. The Social (S) dimension covers companies' relations with the communities in which they operate. It includes satisfying customers with high-quality products while keeping them safe and putting employee health, safety, and loyalty in high priority so that they have a high-quality work environment. The Governance (G) dimension captures companies' fair management practices that are of best interests of their long-term shareholders. Such practices include fair and well-functioning boards and executive compensation plans, and avoidance of illegal practices (S&P Global, 2019, 2020; Matos, 2020). The governance dimension is dated back to the 1970s when Jensen and Meckling (1976) proposed the agency cost and Shleifer and Vishny (1977) overviewed the separation of ownership and control (the principal-agent problem) and presented differences in corporate governance systems around the world (Matos, 2020). Although there are concerns regarding a common measurement for corporate governance standards of companies (Bebchuk & Hamdani, 2009; Black, De Carvalho, & Gorga, 2012), quantifying governance success has always been of interest. Hence, ESG investing is not a "one size fits all strategy" but it is a way that allows investors to express themselves and companies to communicate their efforts for society. Investor analysts can develop investment plans that are compatible with their clients' prior concerns using ESG scores and their sub-sections. (Branch, Goldberg, & Hand, 2019).

The remainder of the chapter is organized as follows: Next section reviews the literature exploring the relationship between ESG concerns and several business dimensions. Then, the authors introduce the Refinitiv ESG Database and present the main descriptive statistics on ESG scores around the world. Next, future research directions and understudied areas of research are explored. Finally, the chapter concludes with a summary of the main findings and suggestions.

LITERATURE

With the introduction of the UN Sustainable Development Goals (SDG) in 2015, the ESG disclosure gained more significance for companies (Bebbington & Unerman, 2018; Li & Mckernan, 2016). From the investors' perspective, ESG investing was initially presented to be a negative screening process where investors passively avoid "sin stocks" as presented in the earlier studies (Kim & Venkatachalam, 2011). Nevertheless, it has evolved to be an active screening process whereby investors pay attention to some quality indicators about how -rather than what- the companies produce. (McQuillen, 2015; Renneboog, Ter Horst, & Zhang, 2008a,b). Observing its significance for both companies and investors, researchers develop an interest in sustainability and its implications for financial decision-making. There is a vast literature on the relationship between ESG (and related concepts such as CSR, SRI, and sustainability) and the corporate performance of the firms.

The findings of studies that compare the financial performance of ESG investment strategies with that of conventional ones -using different measures for ESG performance- are inconclusive. The initial studies in the field, which cover socially responsible investing (SRI) strategies, mostly report no significant performance differences between the SRI funds and conventional funds (Hamilton, Jo, & Statman, 1993; Statman, 2000; Kreander et al., 2005; Bello, 2005; Bauer, Koedijk, & Otten, 2005; Utz & Wimmer, 2014). Halbritter and Dorfleitner (2015) explore this relationship using various ESG ratings; ASSET4, Bloomberg, and KLD, and two different econometrical models; the four-factor model (Carhart, 1997) as well as Fama and Macbeth (1973). Although the four-factor model does not imply any significant differences between the returns by high vs low ESG score companies, Fama and Macbeth's regressions suggest a significant effect of some ESG variables on the cross-section. Nevertheless, the results are not robust to different subsample periods and ESG ratings; which underlines the importance of the database used in the research. Another study documents no significant differences between the financial performance of ESG indices provided by Thompson Reuters and that of conventional MSCI Indices (Jain, Sharma, & Srivastava, 2019).

Even though there are a few studies documenting higher returns for conventional investment alternatives, they conclude that these differences reverse with time or good screening by high ESG firms, which offsets the positive abnormal returns by conventional firms in aggregate terms (Bauer et al., 2005; Barnett & Salomon, 2006). An extension to this stream of research, which considers expenditure on ESG activities as contributing to inefficient resource allocation, presents evidence that high ESG spending negatively affects the position of the firm in the free and competitive market (Friedman, 1962, 1970; Sternberg, 2000). Moreover, this excessive cost will reduce firm profitability (Aupperle, Carroll, & Hatfield, 1985; Kim, Surroca, & Tribó, 2009). There are also studies showing that the sin stocks outperform portfolios with high CSR or ESG scores and conclude that controversial investment strategies may yield higher financial returns (Salaber, 2007; Hong & Kacperczyk, 2009; Fabozzi, Ma, & Oliphant, 2008).

On the other hand, there are numerous studies suggesting a positive relationship between ESG and firm performance. Mackey, Mackey, and Barney (2007) theoretically show that engaging in CSR activities maximizes the market value of the firm. Over 2000 empirical studies reviewed by Friede, Busch, and Bassen (2015), mainly document a positive relationship between ESG and financial performance. US and European investors are shown to increase their risk-adjusted returns along with the ESG rating of the portfolio, indicating a positive relationship between the financial and ESG performance of the firms (Kaiser, 2020). Likewise, there are several studies indicating positive abnormal returns for higher-ranked ESG portfolios in either CSR, sustainability, or ESG context (Orlitzky, Schmidt, & Rynes 2003; Derwall et al., 2005; Eccles, Ioannou, & Serafeim, 2014; Kempf & Osthoff, 2007; Statman & Glushkov, 2009). Further, Eccles et al. (2014) document a parallel finding using different data sources for ESG scores and confirm that higher-ranked ESG firms produce positive abnormal returns in the USA. The value of high ESG scores is also reflected in the merger and acquisition (M&A) process. Firms engaging in higher CSR activities realize higher M&A announcement returns and larger increases in post-merger long-term operating performance (Deng, Kang, & Low, 2013).

The literature also studies various dimensions of corporate performance other than financial returns in the ESG context. For instance, ESG activity disclosure reduces information asymmetry. Firms with higher ESG activity disclosure have higher leverage implying that ESG activity attracts debt financing (Hamrouni, Boussaada, & Toumi, 2019). Skousen and Sun (2019) study the relationship between employee performance and employee dimension in the ESG score. Results suggest a significant positive relationship between the rating and the performance measures which is robust to various empirical tests. Another study by (Aouadi & Marsat, 2018) finds that the positive effects of ESG are only significant for those firms that are larger, perform better, are located in countries with greater press freedom, are more searched on the Internet, are more followed by analysts, and have an improved corporate social reputation. Focusing on the accounting indicators, the literature finds a positive relationship between ESG score and operating performance using various accounting metrics such as return on asset (ROA), return on equity (ROE), and other profitability and efficiency measures (Russo & Fouts, 1997; Orlitzky et al., 2003; Derwall et al., 2011). Xie et al. (2019) report that the effect of ESG practices on corporate efficiency depends on the level of ESG disclosure. In particular, there is a strong positive relationship at the middle disclosure level, which is reversed at the low and high disclosure levels.

A strand of literature studies the effect of ESG on the cost of financing, namely the cost of debt and equity. In terms of debt financing, various studies reported lower costs of debt for companies engaging in better ESG practices (Chava, 2014; Goss & Roberts, 2011; Bauer & Hann, 2010). Moreover, this effect is more salient for firms with both high financial and social disclosure (Chen, Feldmann, & Tang, 2015; Ng & Rezaee, 2015). Dhaliwal et al. (2011) find that volunteer CSR disclosure has a positive effect on cost reduction and further suggest that it increases analyst coverage. In this context, Chauhan and Kumar (2018) point out that ESG disclosure is more valuable to standalone firms compared to business group firms. In a similar vein, for equity financing, the literature depicts a clear picture of lower costs for companies with higher ESG scores (Derwall & Verwijmeren, 2007; Sharfman & Fernando, 2008; El Ghoul, et al., 2011; Albuquerque, Koskinen, & Zhang, 2019). Thus, companies with higher ESG scores have lower financing costs. These findings can be associated with a lower risk of high ESG companies. Empirical evidence suggests that high CSR is a factor affecting the total risk of a firm, and it decreases idiosyncratic firm risk (Godfrey, Merrill, & Hansen, 2009; Goss & Roberts, 2011; El Ghoul et al., 2011; Bouslah, Kryzanowski, & M'zali, 2013). Thus, ESG is an addition to the risk factors identified in the previous mainstream finance literature such as size (Banz, 1981), price-earnings ratio (Basu, 1983), debt-to-equity ratio (Bhandari, 1988), book-to-market ratio (Fama & French, 1993), momentum (Carhart, 1997), and profitability (Novy-Marx, 2013). With this extension, promoting sustainability appears as a risk factor, denoting the social dimension of businesses, and shareholder wealth maximization is not the sole objective anymore.

These diverse findings in the literature are based on various datasets, which use different characterizations of ESG dimensions (Halbritter & Dorfleitner, 2015). Therefore, it is worthwhile to understand the methodology and the coverage of the datasets to interpret the results correctly. For this purpose, the next section introduces Refinitiv ESG Database and explores the ESG scores worldwide with respect to several dimensions, namely development level, region, industry, and legal origin for the period 2002-2019.

REFINITIV ESG DATA: COVERAGE, TRENDS, AND MAIN TAKEAWAYS

The authors compile Environmental, Social, and Governance (ESG) data from Refinitiv Eikon ESG (formerly known as ASSET4) database. This database presents percentile rank ESG scores for more than 9,000 publicly listed companies as of 2020 and dates back to 2002 for around 1000 companies based on company-reported data. The database collects firm-level ESG data by processing publicly available information such as annual company reports, company and NGO websites, stock exchange filings, CSR reports as well as news sources by their trained research analysts. Over 500 ESG measures are collected and standardized by these analysts on a continuous basis. To assure data quality, algorithmic and human processes are combined in the data collection process (Refinitiv, 2021). The initial indices covered were SMI, DAX, CAC 40, FTSE 100, FTSE 250, S&P 500 and NASDAQ 100 in year 2003. The coverage is improving each year and new companies from various indices all over the world are added over time. Finally, in year 2021, CSI 300 index is also included in the database with 950 new companies.

The database presents an ESG Combined score for which the calculation is based on the ESG controversies score and the ESG score. Figure 1 summarizes the methodology of ESG score calculation. The ESG score is calculated based on three main pillars, namely environmental, social, and governance scores. These pillars cover 10 main categories classified as resource use, emissions, innovation, workforce, human rights, community, product responsibility, management, shareholders, and corporate social responsibility (CSR) strategy. As depicted in Figure 1, the environmental pillar score encompasses resources use, emission, and innovation category scores which provides data regarding companies' commitment towards environmental issues worldwide. The Refinitive database defines environmental pillar score as "the weighted average relative rating of a company based on the reported environmental information and the resulting three environmental category scores". The social pillar score combines workforce, human rights, community, and product responsibility category scores which presents companies' attitudes towards employee and customer satisfaction. The Refinitive database defines social pillar score as "the weighted average relative rating of a company based on the reported social information and the resulting four social category scores". Finally, the governance pillar score is related to the managerial practices and rules enforced within companies. It combines management, shareholders, and corporate social responsibility (CSR) strategy category scores. The Refinitive database defines governance pillar score as "the weighted average relative rating of a company based on the reported governance information and the resulting three governance category scores."

Reported scores for environmental and social categories are benchmarked against the sector of the company while governance is benchmarked against the country. Thus, the database reports the relative ESG performance of companies. If the controversies score is also available in the given year, it is also included in the calculation of the ESG Combined score[1], otherwise, the ESG Combined Score and the ESG Score are equal. The controversies score is benchmarked against industry similar to environmental and social scores. Refinitiv also recognizes the variation in the materiality of each factor for different industries and puts weights on each metric for each industry on a scale of 1 to 10. The detailed definitions of calculated scores and category scores as well as variable titles and definitions are presented in Table 1. Refinitiv categorizes the companies into quartiles based on ESG score as given in Table 2 and orders the companies from poor to excellent relative ESG performance.

As of September 2020, there are 9,479 firms (69 countries) in the full sample. The status of 7,910 firms (from 68 countries) are active while 1,564 firms (from 48 countries) are inactive in the database. This chapter uses the data between 2002 and 2019. The ESG score is available for 922 companies in 2002 reaching 6,065 firms in 2019. Panel A and B of Figure 2 present the number of firms and mean ESG scores over time across developed versus emerging market economies, respectively. It is important to see the breakdown across these markets since developed countries pioneered the idea of ESG (Li et al, 2021) and understanding differences between development levels would help researchers in formulating their studies as well as interpreting the findings. The authors classify countries based on the S&P Dow Jones country classification of developed and emerging market countries[2]. In Panel A, the number of firms for all country groups is increasing over years and the increase is more pronounced for the US and emerging market countries after 2014, which is a reflection of the increasing interest in ESG reporting worldwide. In Panel B, the average ESG scores over years are increasing for firms from the developed market (excluding the US) and emerging market countries. However, the average score for the US companies decreased after 2014, as more firms are included in the database from the US. This divergence between EU and US can also be attributed to regulatory differences between these two regions starting from the UN Sustainable Development Goals in 2015. We expect the European Union to keep its leadership in terms of ESG considering the efforts by the European Comission to improve sustainability throughout the continent, specifically the EU member countries. Recently, Sustainable

Finance Disclosure Regulation (SFDR) is introduced in March 2021, to accomplish specific sustainability goals by enforcing companies to precisely disclose their practices.

Figure 3 reports the average ESG score and percentage of firms in each quartile (as explained in Table 2) per year for the full sample. The table reveals a decrease in the percentage of poor and satisfactory ESG performance firms over time while the percentage of good and excellent performance firms increases over time. In particular, the percentage of firms with poor ESG performance decreased to 23% of all firms in 2019 from 39% in 2002, and the percentage of firms with good ESG performance more than doubled (from 12% in 2002 to 27% in 2019) in the same period.

Figure 1. Refinitiv ESG methodology
Source: Refinitiv February 2021, Methodology

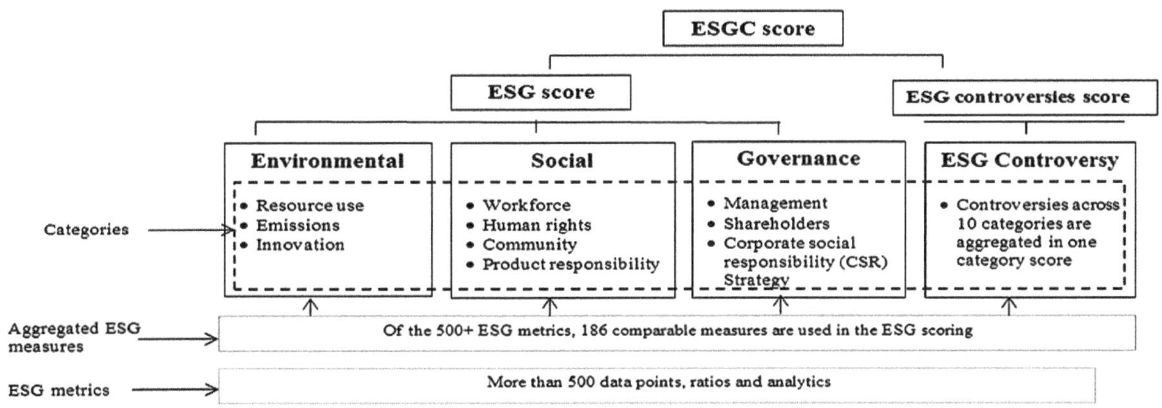

Table 1. Main ESG Scores & Definitions in Refinitiv ESG Database

Title	Description
ESG Score*	Refinitiv's ESG Score is an overall company score based on the self-reported information in the environmental, social and corporate governance pillars.
ESG Combined Score*	Refinitiv's ESG Combined Score is an overall company score based on the reported information in the environmental, social and corporate governance pillars (ESG Score) with an ESG Controversies overlay.
ESG Controversies Score*	ESG controversies category score measures a company's exposure to environmental, social and governance controversies and negative events reflected in global media.
Environment Pillar Score*	Refinitiv's Environment Pillar Score is the weighted average relative rating of a company based on the reported environmental information and the resulting three environmental category scores.
Governance Pillar Score*	Refinitiv's Governance Pillar Score is the weighted average relative rating of a company based on the reported governance information and the resulting three governance category scores.
Social Pillar Score*	Refinitiv's Social Pillar Score is the weighted average relative rating of a company based on the reported social information and the resulting four social category scores.
Resource Use Score**	Resource use category score reflects a company's performance and capacity to reduce the use of materials, energy or water, and to find more eco-efficient solutions by improving supply chain management.
Emissions Score**	Emission category score measures a company's commitment and effectiveness towards reducing environmental emission in the production and operational processes.
Environmental Innovation Score**	Environmental innovation category score reflects a company's capacity to reduce the environmental costs and burdens for its customers, and thereby creating new market opportunities through new environmental technologies and processes or eco-designed products.
Workforce Score**	Workforce category score measures a company's effectiveness towards job satisfaction, healthy and safe workplace, maintaining diversity and equal opportunities, and development opportunities for its workforce.
Human Rights Score**	Human rights category score measures a company's effectiveness towards respecting the fundamental human rights conventions.
Community Score**	Community category score measures the company's commitment towards being a good citizen, protecting public health and respecting business ethics.
Product Responsibility Score**	Product responsibility category score reflects a company's capacity to produce quality goods and services integrating the customer's health and safety, integrity and data privacy.
Management Score**	Management category score measures a company's commitment and effectiveness towards following best practice corporate governance principles.
Shareholders Score**	Shareholders category score measures a company's effectiveness towards equal treatment of shareholders and the use of anti-takeover devices.
CSR Strategy Score**	CSR strategy category score reflects a company's practices to communicate that it integrates the economic (financial), social and environmental dimensions into its day-to-day decision-making processes.

Note: * and ** represent Scores and category scores, respectively.
Source: Data Glossary, ESG Metrics in Eikon & DataStream by Refinitiv (As of August 2020)

Table 2. ESG scores classification

Score Range	Description	
0 to 25	First Quartile	"Scores within this range indicates poor relative ESG performance and insufficient degree of transparency in reporting material ESG data publicly."
> 25 to 50	Second Quartile	"Scores within this range indicates satisfactory relative ESG performance and moderate degree of transparency in reporting material ESG data publicly."
> 50 to 75	Third Quartile	"Scores within this range indicates good relative ESG performance and above average degree of transparency in reporting material ESG data publicly."
> 75 to 100	Fourth Quartile	"Score within this range indicates excellent relative ESG performance and high degree of transparency in reporting material ESG data publicly."

Source: https://www.refinitiv.com/en/sustainable-finance/esg-scores#company-esg-scores

Figure 2. Number of firms and average ESG scores over years across markets
Notes: Figure 2 graphs the number of firms and mean ESG scores by development level per year for the 2002-2019 period in Panels A and B, respectively.

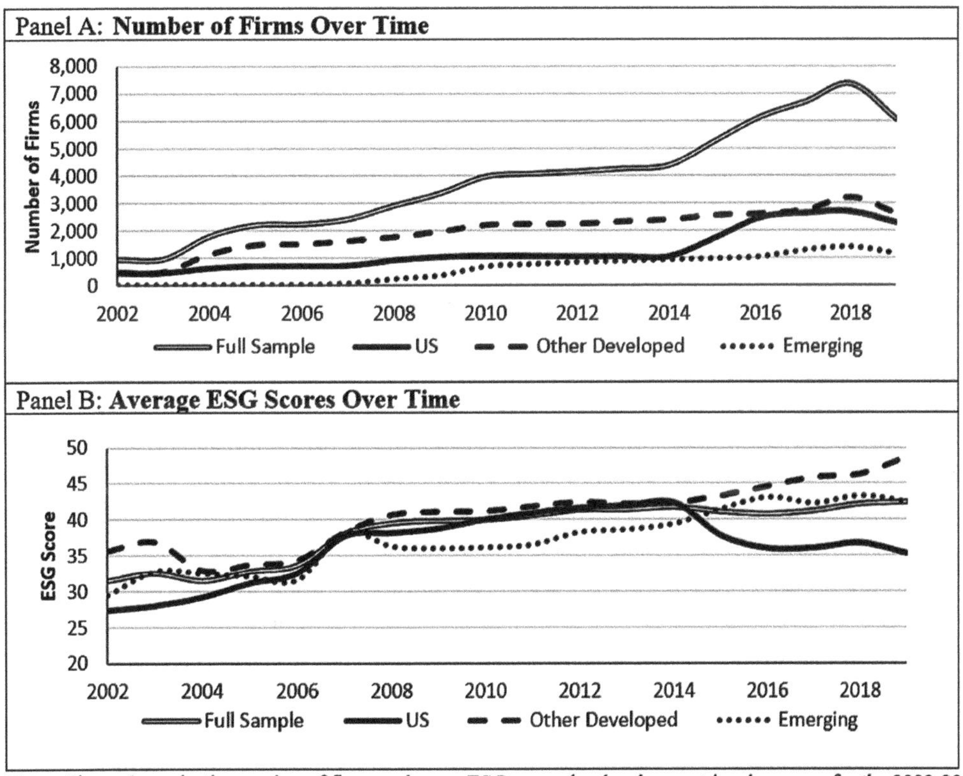

Notes: Figure 2 graphs the number of firms and mean ESG scores by development level per year for the 2002-2019 period in Panels A and B, respectively.

Figure 3. Percentage of each ESG score quartile over years
Notes: Figure 3 graphs the percentage of firms in each quartile (as explained in Table 2) per year for the 2002-2019 period.

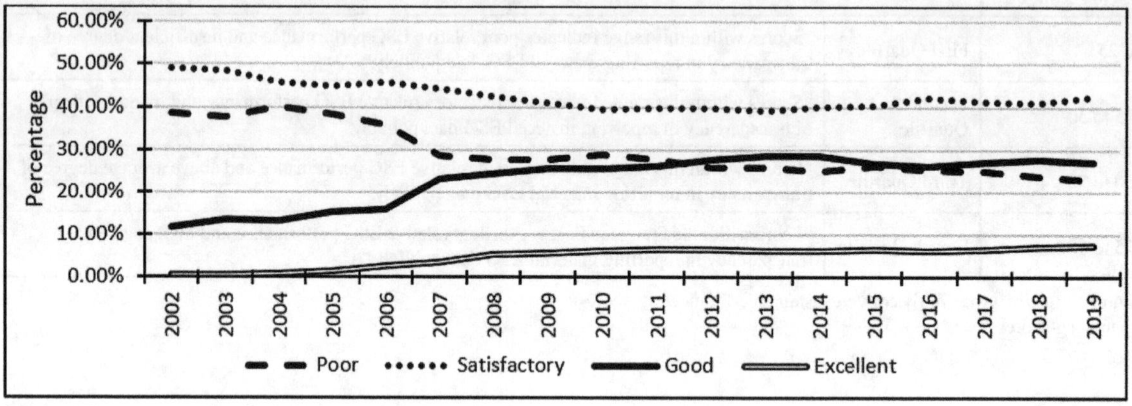

Notes: Figure 3 graphs the percentage of firms in each quartile (as explained in Table 2) per year for the 2002-2019 period.

Second, the authors describe the same data based on regional classification. Table 3 presents the regional classification over years. Firms are classified under 10 regions: Africa, America excluding USA & Canada, Canada, USA, Asia excluding Japan, Japan, Australia, Eastern Europe, European Union, and the Middle East. The first row for each year reports the number of firms from each region while the second row reports the average ESG score. In almost all years, we see that the mean ESG score for European Union countries exceeds the average scores observed in the rest of the world. The trend over years is increasing for all regions except for the United States. The divergence of the United States and European average ESG scores after 2014 could partially be attributed to the introduction of the UN Sustainable Development Goals (SDG), which are highly adopted by European firms leading to better ESG practices. Moreover, starting from December 2019, with the introduction of the EU Green Deal, this divergence may further increase as this deal introduces new measures for the member states of European Union in order to achieve the objective of becoming the first climate-neutral continent by 2050. The authors also observe that the lowest mean ESG scores belong to the Middle East. Though, the database coverage of firms from the Middle East is quite limited.

The third classification the chapter uses is industry classification. In Table 4, we document the industries covered. The table shows that 71% of the ESG data in the database belongs to industrial firms. This group is followed by banks, insurance, and other financial companies, which constitute around 19% in total, and the remaining 10% comes from the utility and transportation sectors. The overall ESG score is highest for the insurance companies (45.16%) while the lowest score belongs to other financial companies (36.57%). Figure 4 graphs the breakdown of the number of companies and average scores by industry over time. In Panel A1, the number of firms in each industry is visualized and the industrial sector dominates the whole database coverage in all years with an increasing trend. In order to see the trend in the rest of the industries, Panel A2 presents the number of firms in the industries excluding the industrial sector. The increasing trend persists in all industries. Similarly, the mean ESG scores are increasing for all industries, with a jump in 2007 as represented in Panel B of Figure 4. In almost all years insurance industry has the highest while other financial companies have the lowest mean ESG score.

Table 3. Regional classification and ESG scores over years

Year		Full Sample	Africa	America exc. USA & Canada	Asia Exc. Japan	Australia	Canada	Eastern Europe	European Union	Japan	Middle East	USA	Other
2002	N	922	1	2	8	7	18	50	372	27	1	436	0
	Mean (%)	31.54	50.63	48.05	27.03	41.53	39.01	32.20	35.47	36.63	22.60	27.30	
2003	N	936	1	2	8	7	18	50	382	29	1	438	0
	Mean (%)	32.60	56.65	59.97	27.61	52.64	41.38	33.73	36.64	36.19	20.37	27.96	
2004	N	1773	1	2	74	69	89	64	627	223	1	616	7
	Mean (%)	31.55	54.57	62.78	24.55	29.53	27.61	34.63	35.44	30.73	21.46	29.14	25.91
2005	N	2,186	1	2	89	81	103	72	755	386	1	686	10
	Mean (%)	32.82	50.69	45.58	25.59	31.95	28.64	35.14	36.62	31.04	25.20	31.08	28.58
2006	N	2,213	1	2	91	83	104	76	764	391	1	690	10
	Mean (%)	33.70	55.53	58.98	25.49	33.12	30.34	35.06	37.05	31.83	31.26	32.50	29.77
2007	N	2,400	2	19	133	87	170	89	780	401	2	707	10
	Mean (%)	38.05	38.14	43.04	30.99	38.78	31.73	39.43	42.69	34.18	24.59	37.66	33.85
2008	N	2,897	17	48	231	97	255	117	804	401	17	900	10
	Mean (%)	39.47	43.64	42.21	33.37	42.32	31.37	38.01	46.31	37.74	21.35	38.07	33.54
2009	N	3,336	23	74	341	202	263	133	834	409	29	1,018	10
	Mean (%)	39.79	43.84	41.11	33.52	34.71	33.05	38.86	47.54	39.65	26.72	38.71	35.19
2010	N	3,954	65	135	665	287	292	144	859	412	30	1,054	11
	Mean (%)	39.94	44.03	42.38	32.95	32.09	33.76	40.99	49.31	40.29	31.22	39.98	36.99
2011	N	4,054	95	145	719	299	282	143	876	409	29	1,045	12
	Mean (%)	40.54	41.41	42.73	33.42	33.21	34.82	42.06	49.71	41.08	32.14	40.87	36.90
2012	N	4,132	160	149	736	313	276	147	874	403	30	1,032	12
	Mean (%)	41.31	40.32	44.43	35.52	33.21	35.63	42.91	50.31	41.01	35.53	41.58	37.89
2013	N	4,243	157	157	770	357	289	150	875	411	30	1,031	16
	Mean (%)	41.34	40.85	44.22	36.06	32.46	35.31	43.36	50.69	40.80	36.53	41.89	36.50
2014	N	4,369	152	164	811	377	302	154	888	417	51	1,035	18
	Mean (%)	41.67	42.31	43.69	37.41	32.62	34.54	44.79	51.15	40.90	31.76	42.27	36.43
2015	N	5,265	148	169	844	374	311	158	991	426	89	1,705	50
	Mean (%)	41.04	43.90	45.55	39.68	34.34	35.46	46.46	51.34	42.17	29.23	37.70	28.89
2016	N	6,150	147	250	861	392	321	156	1,005	430	91	2,440	56
	Mean (%)	40.73	45.41	39.86	43.29	34.92	36.19	48.01	52.53	43.61	30.75	35.90	31.49
2017	N	6,710	148	274	1,113	398	318	174	1,088	433	92	2,611	60
	Mean (%)	41.17	45.65	41.37	42.46	35.39	37.19	48.86	53.35	45.14	30.99	35.98	34.00
2018	N	7,357	146	289	1,175	398	318	295	1,462	440	117	2,656	60
	Mean (%)	42.10	46.84	43.14	44.05	36.28	38.40	45.36	51.02	47.11	30.77	36.67	37.23
2019	N	6,065	119	117	1,116	356	192	206	1,222	375	55	2,254	53
	Mean (%)	42.35	49.51	45.94	42.82	38.64	38.04	48.04	53.42	49.25	30.40	35.22	38.56
TOTAL	**N**	**68,962**	**1,384**	**2,000**	**9,785**	**4,184**	**3,921**	**2,378**	**15,458**	**6,423**	**667**	**22,354**	**405**
	Mean (%)	**40.02**	**43.96**	**42.96**	**38.62**	**34.60**	**34.74**	**42.92**	**47.66**	**40.10**	**30.71**	**36.84**	**34.22**

Notes: Table presents the number of firms and average ESG Scores by region per year for the 2002-2019 period. Hence, United Kingdom is included in Eoropen Union countries in this table as United Kingdom left the European Union on 31 January 2020.

Table 4. Industries covered

General Industry Classification	N	%	Mean ESG Score (%)
01. Industrial	48,637	70.53%	39.59
02. Utility	4,727	6.85%	43.74
03. Transportation	2,141	3.10%	40.04
04. Bank/Savings & Loan	4,954	7.18%	42.69
05. Insurance	2,250	3.26%	45.16
06. Other Financial	5,992	8.69%	36.57
Not Available	261	0.38%	38.08
TOTAL	**68,962**	**100.00%**	**40.02**

Notes: The table presents the number and percentage of firms in each industry and average ESG Scores per industry for the 2002-2019 period.

Figure 4. Industrial classification and ESG scores over years
Notes: The figure presents the number of firms and average ESG Scores for each industry per year for the 2002-2019 period in Panels A and B, respectively.

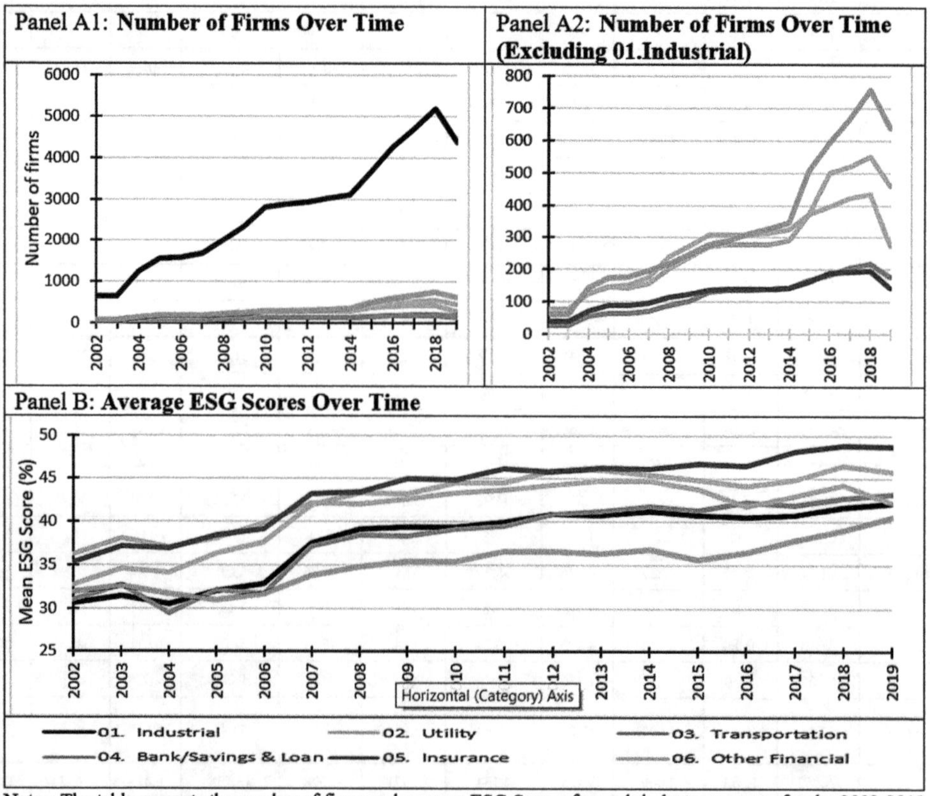

Notes: The table presents the number of firms and average ESG Scores for each industry per year for the 2002-2019 period in Panels A and B, respectively.

In the final classification, the authors take the legal origins of the countries in the sample into account. The countries are classified as "civil law" and "common law" countries as suggested by a series of articles published by La Porta and his colleagues in 1997, 1998, and 2008 (La Porta et al. 1997, 1998, 2008). These highly cited papers argue that the legal origin of the commercial law of the country has effects on many areas of economic and social life. In particular, common law countries whose law system has their origins in English law are more protective of investors than civil law countries whose origin dates back to Roman law and especially French civil law. By definition, the common law decision-making process is case-driven and unwritten principles play an important role in these countries while the civil law system court decisions are based on written law.

Literature on sustainability recently started to question how these different legal systems affect company sustainability and the relationship between company ESG practices and corporate performance. Liang and Renneboog (2017) reported a strong correlation between the legal origin of a country and the CSR rating of companies in that country. In particular, they find higher CSR ratings for firms from civil law countries than those from common law countries. Miralles-Quirós et al.(2019) investigate the effect of ESG performance on shareholder value creation and present the differences in this relationship between common law and civil law countries for a sample of 166 commercial banks from 31 stock markets during the period from 2010 to 2015. They report that there is a higher demand for CSR practices in common law countries represented by higher significant coefficients for social and environmental scores. They suggest that in civil law countries, where there are already strict government regulations related to CSR practices, a higher ESG score does not create additional value. On the other hand, in common law countries, where such practices and disclosures are mainly voluntary, a higher CSR score is valued highly in the market (Miralles-Quirós et al., 2019).

Similarly, Castillo-Merino and Rodríguez-Pérez (2021) report that legal origin is a significant determinant of sustainability performance based on a sample of 982 financial firms in 64 countries over the 2002-2018 period. They show that the ESG performances of financial firms based in civil law countries are higher compared to those of similar firms in common law countries. Figure 5 graphs the number of firms and mean overall ESG score by legal origins over the 2002-2019 period in Panel A and B, respectively. The increasing trend in the number of firms included in the Refinitiv ESG database is also presented in Figure 5 Panel A. Panel B shows that average ESG scores are higher in civil law countries compared to common law countries in all years. Thus, the findings in Figure 5 are in line with the previous literature which emphasizes the role of the country's legal origin in promoting sustainability policies and highlights the need to include regulatory differences into account in future ESG studies.

Figure 5. Legal origins and ESG scores over years

Notes: Figure 5 graphs the number of firms and mean ESG scores by legal origin per year for the 2002-2019 period in Panels A and B, respectively. The authors also conducted mean difference t-tests for each year and conclude that mean ESG scores are significantly higher for civil law countries each year in the sample period.

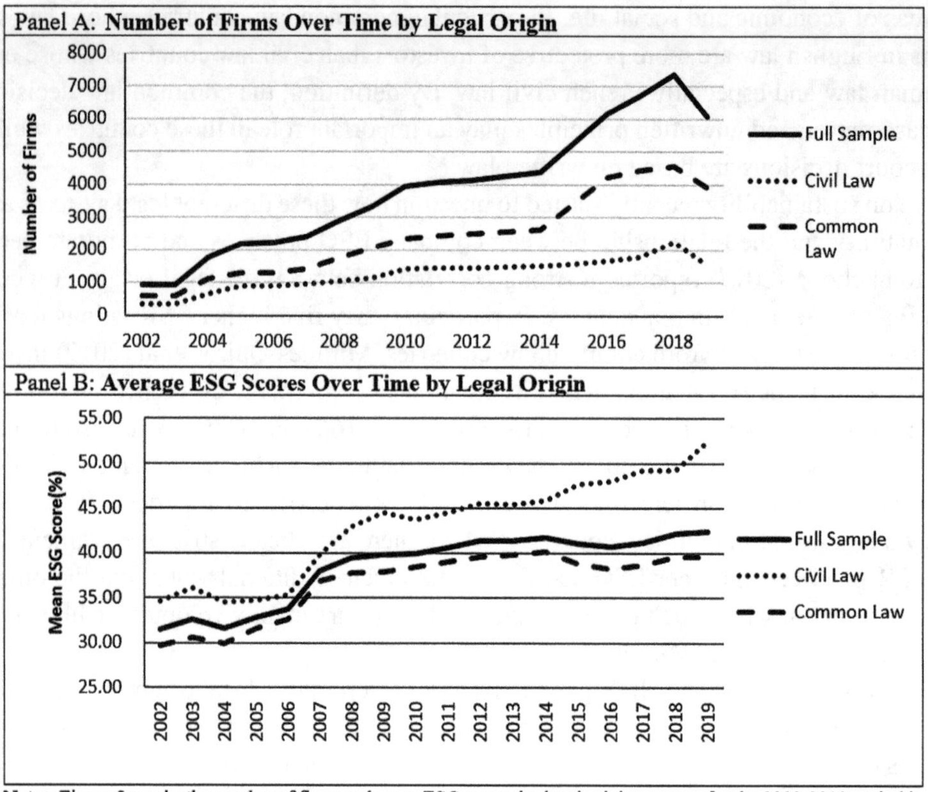

Notes: Figure 5 graphs the number of firms and mean ESG scores by legal origin per year for the 2002-2019 period in Panels A and B, respectively. The authors also conducted mean difference t-tests for each year and conclude that mean ESG scores are significantly higher for civil law countries each year in the sample period.

FUTURE RESEARCH DIRECTIONS

The relationship between ESG engagement and corporate performance is getting increasing attention from researchers as presented in this chapter. Yet, there is still much work to be done to increase our insight on this topic. First, theoretical models that incorporate ESG factors with corporate performance are required. Existing literature highly relies on "stakeholder theory" and "institutional theory" to develop a theoretical basis to integrate ESG into corporate performance (Li, et al. 2021). However, there are plenty of alternative theoretical settings such as social identity theory, signaling theory, agency theory, resource dependence theory, etc. which can be used in ESG studies. In addition, adopting an interdisciplinary approach and including psychological factors affecting financial decision-making as addressed by behavioral finance literature, would be beneficial to understand the social dimension better. Also, the behavioral approach would be significant to understand the investor side of the story and would relate ESG to not only financial but also non-financial returns such as "expressive" and "emotional" benefits

(Statman, 2004). Therefore, exploring these settings may lead to new theoretical models which would enhance our comprehension of ESG.

Second, having developed theoretical models, it is crucial to test these hypothesized relationships using ESG datasets. However, there are various datasets compiling ESG information of firms. This chapter introduces only one of them, namely; the Refinitiv ESG database. Previous research identifies significant variations in the methodologies of several ESG rating concepts. Besides, different characterizations of ESG dimensions lead to diverging findings in the literature (Gibson Brandon, Krueger, & Schmidt, 2019; Halbritter and Dorfleitner, 2015). As a consequence, it is significant to study one question using more than a single ESG data set. It would be interesting to explore different datasets, use them to answer the same question, compare the results, and dig up the methodology of datasets in order to explain any possible divergence. This would enhance our understanding of ESG scores and their interplay with different corporate performance indicators. Moreover, such efforts contribute to the promotion of the improvement in the ESG evaluation system which currently lacks uniformity (Li et al., 2021).

Third, there is scarce literature on the environmental and social dimensions of ESG compared to the governance dimension. Hence, the interactive relationship of environmental, social, and governance dimensions needs further improvement (Li et al., 2021). Additionally, the literature mainly concentrates on equity markets. Some studies are exploring different asset classes such as bond and real estate markets (Chava, 2014; Hoepner et al., 2016; Flammer, 2019; Baker et al., 2018; Eichholtz, Kok, & Quigley, 2010, 2013). Yet, there is still room for further research since other asset classes like hedge funds, private equity, infrastructure, etc. are highly understudied (Matos, 2020). Finally, existing studies highly investigate the ESG issues in the developed markets, specifically in the US market whereas it would be interesting to explore emerging markets for a global understanding of ESG practices. Hence, future studies on the interplay between different dimensions of ESG and its implications for different markets would enrich the sustainability literature.

CONCLUSION

This chapter presents a review of the current ESG literature and introduces a cross-country analysis of the Refinitiv ESG database which is a comprehensive database that covers 70% of the global market capitalization (Refinitiv, 2021). With increasing interest by researchers and practitioners in the field of sustainable investing, it is important to have a better understanding of the current literature and available databases. First, the authors contribute to the literature by providing a base for future research via reviewing the existing sustainable finance literature with an emphasis on ESG practices. Second, the chapter explores a well-known ESG database, Refinitiv, and presents a comparative and descriptive analysis of the database worldwide over the period 2002-2019. The authors document an increasing trend in terms of ESG reporting and point out differences in ESG scores in terms of development level, region, industry, and legal origin.

In particular, the average ESG scores are higher for developed countries, in which the idea of social responsibility first originated, compared to that for emerging market countries. The ESG scores worldwide, including in emerging market countries, may further increase by 2030, which is the stated completion date for the UN sustainable development goals. These goals are guidelines and not forced but highly promoted by the UN to encourage companies for sustainable business practices worldwide.

This will probably be reflected by higher ESG scores, which measure the performance of a company in terms of social, environmental, and governance aspects.

When the authors consider regional differences, firms from Europe (especially the ones from European Union) are associated with higher ESG scores each year for the 2002-2019 period. Moreover, the database coverage of firms from the Middle East is quite limited and the lowest mean ESG scores each year consistently belong to this region. Considering that the Middle East follows the sustainability idea behind, future studies may investigate the development in this region. In terms of industry classification, insurance companies exhibit the highest ESG scores over time. Firms from civil-law countries have higher average ESG scores in all years than firms from common-law countries. This finding is in line with the developing literature on the association of legal origin with sustainability and highlights the need to incorporate this variable into the analysis in future studies. Moreover, not only the ESG scores themselves but also the valuation of ESG practices in the marketplace is worth studying. For instance, a few previous studies report higher investor valuation for voluntary ESG practices of companies in common-law countries than in civil-law countries, in which the firms are already forced to better ESG practices by government regulations.

Hence, the findings will be a guideline for researchers in conducting empirical studies on ESG practices as the authors highlight differences in ESG scores across different economic development levels, regions, industries, and legal origins. The authors suggest that research in the Refinitiv ESG database, as well as other comprehensive ESG databases, is important since theoretical models and empirical tests which integrate ESG factors to corporate performance can be established by a better understanding of these databases. Therefore, this chapter adds to this stream of research by introducing the Refinitiv ESG database with descriptive and comparative analysis, paving the way for new research on the subject. This chapter intends to stimulate ESG research by depicting a general picture of the findings in the literature and providing fundamental knowledge regarding the Refinitiv dataset. In addition to researchers, the reported findings have also inferences for policymakers in introducing regulations to govern sustainability disclosure by companies.

REFERENCES

Albuquerque, R., Koskinen, Y., & Zhang, C. (2019). Corporate social responsibility and firm risk: Theory and empirical evidence. *Management Science*, *65*(10), 4451–4469. doi:10.1287/mnsc.2018.3043

Aouadi, A., & Marsat, S. (2018). Do ESG controversies matter for firm value? Evidence from international data. *Journal of Business Ethics*, *151*(4), 1027–1047. doi:10.100710551-016-3213-8

Aupperle, K. E., Carroll, A. B., & Hatfield, J. D. (1985). An empirical examination of the relationship between corporate social responsibility and profitability. *Academy of Management Journal*, *28*(2), 446–463. doi:10.2307/256210

Baker, M., Bergstresser, D., Serafeim, G., & Wurgler, J. (2018). Financing the response to climate change: The pricing and ownership of US green bonds (No. w25194). National Bureau of Economic Research.

Banz, R. W. (1981). The relationship between return and market value of common stocks. *Journal of Financial Economics*, *9*(1), 3–18. doi:10.1016/0304-405X(81)90018-0

Barnett, M. L., & Salomon, R. M. (2006). Beyond dichotomy: The curvilinear relationship between social responsibility and financial performance. *Strategic Management Journal*, *27*(11), 1101–1122. doi:10.1002mj.557

Basu, S. (1983). The relationship between earnings' yield, market value and return for NYSE common stocks: Further evidence. *Journal of Financial Economics*, *12*(1), 129–156. doi:10.1016/0304-405X(83)90031-4

BauerR.HannD. (2010). Corporate environmental management and credit risk. *Available at* SSRN 1660470.

Bauer, R., Koedijk, K., & Otten, R. (2005). International evidence on ethical mutual fund performance and investment style. *Journal of Banking & Finance*, *29*(7), 1751–1767. doi:10.1016/j.jbankfin.2004.06.035

Bebbington, J., & Unerman, J. (2018). Achieving the United Nations sustainable development goals: An enabling role of accounting research. *Accounting, Auditing & Accountability Journal*, *31*(1), 2–24. doi:10.1108/AAAJ-05-2017-2929

Bebchuk, L. A., & Hamdani, A. (2009). The Elusive Quest for Global Governance Standards. *University of Pennsylvania Law Review*, *157*, 1263–1317.

Bello, Z. Y. (2005). Socially responsible investing and portfolio diversification. *Journal of Financial Research*, *28*(1), 41–57. doi:10.1111/j.1475-6803.2005.00113.x

Bhandari, L. C. (1988). Debt/equity ratio and expected common stock returns: Empirical evidence. *The Journal of Finance*, *43*(2), 507–528. doi:10.1111/j.1540-6261.1988.tb03952.x

Black, B. S., De Carvalho, A. G., & Gorga, É. (2012). What matters and for which firms for corporate governance in emerging markets? Evidence from Brazil (and other BRIK countries). *Journal of Corporate Finance*, *18*(4), 934–952. doi:10.1016/j.jcorpfin.2011.10.001

Bouslah, K., Kryzanowski, L., & M'zali, B. (2013). The impact of the dimensions of social performance on firm risk. *Journal of Banking & Finance*, *37*(4), 1258–1273. doi:10.1016/j.jbankfin.2012.12.004

Branch, M., Goldberg, L. R., & Hand, P. (2019). A guide to ESG portfolio construction. *Journal of Portfolio Management*, *45*(4), 61–66. doi:10.3905/jpm.2019.45.4.061

Carhart, M. M. (1997). On persistence in mutual fund performance. *The Journal of Finance*, *52*(1), 57–82. doi:10.1111/j.1540-6261.1997.tb03808.x

Castillo-Merino, D., & Rodríguez-Pérez, G. (2021). The effects of legal origin and corporate governance on financial firms' sustainability performance. *Sustainability*, *13*(15), 8233. doi:10.3390u13158233

Chauhan, Y., & Kumar, S. B. (2018). Do investors value the nonfinancial disclosure in emerging markets? *Emerging Markets Review*, *37*, 32–46. doi:10.1016/j.ememar.2018.05.001

Chava, S. (2014). Environmental externalities and cost of capital. *Management Science*, *60*(9), 2223–2247. doi:10.1287/mnsc.2013.1863

Chen, L., Feldmann, A., & Tang, O. (2015). The relationship between disclosures of corporate social performance and financial performance: Evidences from GRI reports in manufacturing industry. *International Journal of Production Economics*, *170*, 445–456. doi:10.1016/j.ijpe.2015.04.004

Deng, X., Kang, J. K., & Low, B. S. (2013). Corporate social responsibility and stakeholder value maximization: Evidence from mergers. *Journal of Financial Economics, 110*(1), 87–109. doi:10.1016/j.jfineco.2013.04.014

Derwall, J., Guenster, N., Bauer, R., & Koedijk, K. (2005). The eco-efficiency premium puzzle. *Financial Analysts Journal, 61*(2), 51–63. doi:10.2469/faj.v61.n2.2716

Derwall, J., & Verwijmeren, P. (2007). Corporate governance and the cost of equity capital: Evidence from gmi's governance rating. *European Centre for Corporate Engagement Research Note, 6*(1), 1-11.

Dhaliwal, D. S., Li, O. Z., Tsang, A., & Yang, Y. G. (2011). Voluntary nonfinancial disclosure and the cost of equity capital: The initiation of corporate social responsibility reporting. *The Accounting Review, 86*(1), 59–100. doi:10.2308/accr.00000005

Drempetic, S., Klein, C., & Zwergel, B. (2020). The influence of firm size on the ESG score: Corporate sustainability ratings under review. *Journal of Business Ethics, 167*(2), 333–360. doi:10.100710551-019-04164-1

Dumas, C., & Louche, C. (2016). Collective beliefs on responsible investment. *Business & Society, 55*(3), 427–457. doi:10.1177/0007650315575327

Eccles, R. G., Ioannou, I., & Serafeim, G. (2014). The impact of corporate sustainability on organizational processes and performance. *Management Science, 60*(11), 2835–2857. doi:10.1287/mnsc.2014.1984

Eichholtz, P., Kok, N., & Quigley, J. M. (2010). Doing well by doing good? Green office buildings. *The American Economic Review, 100*(5), 2492–2509. doi:10.1257/aer.100.5.2492

Eichholtz, P., Kok, N., & Quigley, J. M. (2013). The economics of green building. *The Review of Economics and Statistics, 95*(1), 50–63. doi:10.1162/REST_a_00291

El Ghoul, S., Guedhami, O., Kwok, C. C., & Mishra, D. R. (2011). Does corporate social responsibility affect the cost of capital? *Journal of Banking & Finance, 35*(9), 2388–2406. doi:10.1016/j.jbankfin.2011.02.007

Fabozzi, F. J., Ma, K. C., & Oliphant, B. J. (2008). Sin stock returns. *Journal of Portfolio Management, 35*(1), 82–94. doi:10.3905/JPM.2008.35.1.82

Fama, E. F., & French, K. R. (1993). Common risk factors in the returns on stocks and bonds. *Journal of Financial Economics, 33*(1), 3–56. doi:10.1016/0304-405X(93)90023-5

Fama, E. F., & MacBeth, J. D. (1973). Risk, return, and equilibrium: Empirical tests. *Journal of Political Economy, 81*(3), 607–636. doi:10.1086/260061

Flammer, C. (2020). Green bonds: Effectiveness and implications for public policy. *Environmental and Energy Policy and the Economy, 1*(1), 95–128. doi:10.1086/706794

Friede, G., Busch, T., & Bassen, A. (2015). ESG and financial performance: aggregated evidence from more than 2000 empirical studies. *Journal of sustainable finance & investment, 5*(4), 210-233.

Friedman, M. (1962). *Capitalism and Freedom.* University of Chicago Press.

Friedman, M. (1970). A Friedman doctrine: The social responsibility of business is to increase its profits. *The New York Times Magazine, 13*(1970), 32-33.

Gibson Brandon, R., Krueger, P., & Schmidt, P. S. (2021). ESG rating disagreement and stock returns. *Financial Analysts Journal*, *77*(4), 104–127. doi:10.1080/0015198X.2021.1963186

Global Sustainable Investment Alliance. (2018). *Global sustainable investment review*. GSI. http://www.gsi-alliance.org/wp-content/uploads/2019/03/GSIR_Review2018.3.28.pdf

Global Sustainable Investment Alliance. (2020). *Global sustainable investment review*. GSI. http://www.gsi-alliance.org/wp-content/uploads/2021/08/GSIR-20201.pdf

Godfrey, P. C., Merrill, C. B., & Hansen, J. M. (2009). The relationship between corporate social responsibility and shareholder value: An empirical test of the risk management hypothesis. *Strategic Management Journal*, *30*(4), 425–445. doi:10.1002mj.750

Goss, A., & Roberts, G. S. (2011). The impact of corporate social responsibility on the cost of bank loans. *Journal of Banking & Finance*, *35*(7), 1794–1810. doi:10.1016/j.jbankfin.2010.12.002

Halbritter, G., & Dorfleitner, G. (2015). The wages of social responsibility—Where are they? A critical review of ESG investing. *Review of Financial Economics*, *26*(1), 25–35. doi:10.1016/j.rfe.2015.03.004

Hamilton, S., Jo, H., & Statman, M. (1993). Doing well while doing good? The investment performance of socially responsible mutual funds. *Financial Analysts Journal*, *49*(6), 62–66. doi:10.2469/faj.v49.n6.62

Hamrouni, A., Boussaada, R., & Toumi, N. B. F. (2019). Corporate social responsibility disclosure and debt financing. *Journal of Applied Accounting Research*, *20*(4), 394–415. doi:10.1108/JAAR-01-2018-0020

Hoepner, A. G., Oikonomou, I., Sautner, Z., Starks, L. T., & Zhou, X. (2018). *ESG shareholder engagement and downside risk*. ECGI Global.

Hong, H., & Kacperczyk, M. (2009). The price of sin: The effects of social norms on markets. *Journal of Financial Economics*, *93*(1), 15–36. doi:10.1016/j.jfineco.2008.09.001

Jain, M., Sharma, G. D., & Srivastava, M. (2019). Can sustainable investment yield better financial returns: A comparative study of ESG indices and MSCI indices. *Risks*, *7*(1), 15. doi:10.3390/risks7010015

Jensen, M. C., & Meckling, W. H. (1976). Theory of the firm: Managerial behavior, agency costs and ownership structure. *Journal of Financial Economics*, *3*(4), 305–360. doi:10.1016/0304-405X(76)90026-X

Kahneman, D. (2003). Maps of bounded rationality: Psychology for behavioral economics. *The American Economic Review*, *93*(5), 1449–1475. doi:10.1257/000282803322655392

Kahneman, D., & Tversky, A. (1972). Subjective probability: A judgment of representativeness. *Cognitive Psychology*, *3*(3), 430–454. doi:10.1016/0010-0285(72)90016-3

Kahneman, D., & Tversky, A. (1979). Prospect Theory: An Analysis of Decision Under Risk. *Econometrica*, *47*(2), 263–292. doi:10.2307/1914185

Kaiser, L. (2020). ESG integration: Value, growth and momentum. *Journal of Asset Management*, *21*(1), 32–51. doi:10.105741260-019-00148-y

Kempf, A., & Osthoff, P. (2007). The effect of socially responsible investing on portfolio performance. *European Financial Management*, *13*(5), 908–922. doi:10.1111/j.1468-036X.2007.00402.x

Kim, I., & Venkatachalam, M. (2011). Are sin stocks paying the price for accounting sins. *Journal of Accounting, Auditing & Finance*, *26*(2), 415–442. doi:10.1177/0148558X11401222

Kim, M., Surroca Aguilar, J., & Tribo Gine, J. A. (2009). The effect of social capital on financial capital. *INDEM Working Paper Business Economic 09-02*.

Kreander, N., Gray, R. H., Power, D. M., & Sinclair, C. D. (2005). Evaluating the performance of ethical and non-ethical funds: A matched pair analysis. *Journal of Business Finance & Accounting*, *32*(7-8), 1465–1493. doi:10.1111/j.0306-686X.2005.00636.x

La Porta, R., Lopez-de-Silanes, F., & Shleifer, A. (2008). The economic consequences of legal origins. *Journal of Economic Literature*, *46*(2), 285–332. doi:10.1257/jel.46.2.285

La Porta, R., Lopez-de-Silanes, F., Shleifer, A., & Vishny, R. W. (1997). Legal determinants of external finance. *The Journal of Finance*, *52*(3), 1131–1150. doi:10.1111/j.1540-6261.1997.tb02727.x

La Porta, R., Lopez-de-Silanes, F., Shleifer, A., & Vishny, R. W. (1998). Law and finance. *Journal of Political Economy*, *106*(6), 1113–1155. doi:10.1086/250042

Leins, S. (2020). 'Responsible investment': ESG and the post-crisis ethical order. *Economy and Society*, *49*(1), 71–91. doi:10.1080/03085147.2020.1702414

Li, T. T., Wang, K., Sueyoshi, T., & Wang, D. D. (2021). ESG: Research progress and future prospects. *Sustainability*, *13*(21), 11663. doi:10.3390u132111663

Li, Y., & McKernan, J. (2016). Human rights, accounting, and the dialectic of equality and inequality. *Accounting, Auditing & Accountability Journal*, *29*(4), 568–593. doi:10.1108/AAAJ-07-2015-2142

Liang, H., & Renneboog, L. (2017). On the foundations of corporate social responsibility. *The Journal of Finance*, *72*(2), 853–910. doi:10.1111/jofi.12487

Mackey, A., Mackey, T. B., & Barney, J. B. (2007). Corporate social responsibility and firm performance: Investor preferences and corporate strategies. *Academy of Management Review*, *32*(3), 817–835. doi:10.5465/amr.2007.25275676

Matos, P. (2020). *Esg and responsible institutional investing around the world. Literature review*. CFA Institute Research Foundation.

Miralles-Quirós, M. M., Miralles-Quirós, J. L., & Redondo Hernández, J. (2019). ESG performance and shareholder value creation in the banking industry: International differences. *Sustainability*, *11*(5), 1404. doi:10.3390u11051404

Ng, A. C., & Rezaee, Z. (2015). Business sustainability performance and cost of equity capital. *Journal of Corporate Finance*, *34*, 128–149. doi:10.1016/j.jcorpfin.2015.08.003

Novy-Marx, R. (2013). The other side of value: The gross profitability premium. *Journal of Financial Economics, 108*(1), 1–28. doi:10.1016/j.jfineco.2013.01.003

Orlitzky, M., Schmidt, F. L., & Rynes, S. L. (2003). Corporate social and financial performance: A meta-analysis. *Organization Studies, 24*(3), 403–441. doi:10.1177/0170840603024003910

Refinitiv (2021). *Environmental, Social and Governance (ESG) Scores from Refinitiv* (issue February). Refinitiv. https://www.refinitiv.com/en/sustainable-finance/esg-scores#methodology

Renneboog, L., Ter Horst, J., & Zhang, C. (2008). The price of ethics and stakeholder governance: The performance of socially responsible mutual funds. *Journal of Corporate Finance, 14*(3), 302–322. doi:10.1016/j.jcorpfin.2008.03.009

Renneboog, L., Ter Horst, J., & Zhang, C. (2008). Socially responsible investments: Institutional aspects, performance, and investor behavior. *Journal of Banking & Finance, 32*(9), 1723–1742. doi:10.1016/j.jbankfin.2007.12.039

Russo, M. V., & Fouts, P. A. (1997). A resource-based perspective on corporate environmental performance and profitability. *Academy of Management Journal, 40*(3), 534–559. doi:10.2307/257052

Salaber, J. M. (2007, November). The determinants of sin stock returns: Evidence on the European market. In *Paris December 2007 Finance International Meeting AFFI-EUROFIDAI Paper.*

Sharfman, M. P., & Fernando, C. S. (2008). Environmental risk management and the cost of capital. *Strategic Management Journal, 29*(6), 569–592. doi:10.1002mj.678

Shleifer, A., & Vishny, R. W. (1997). A survey of corporate governance. *The Journal of Finance, 52*(2), 737–783. doi:10.1111/j.1540-6261.1997.tb04820.x

Skousen, C. J., & Sun, L. (2019). Do employee dimension ratings reflect employee performance? Evidence from MSCI's ESG database. *Applied Economics Letters, 26*(14), 1182–1185. doi:10.1080/13504851.2018.1540843

Statman, M. (2000). Socially responsible mutual funds (corrected). *Financial Analysts Journal, 56*(3), 30–39. doi:10.2469/faj.v56.n3.2358

Statman, M. (2004). What do investors want? *Journal of Portfolio Management, 30*(5), 153–161. doi:10.3905/jpm.2004.442641

Statman, M., & Glushkov, D. (2009). The wages of social responsibility. *Financial Analysts Journal, 65*(4), 33–46. doi:10.2469/faj.v65.n4.5

Sternberg, E. (2000). The defects of stakeholder theory1. In R. I. Tricker (Ed.), *Corporate Governance* (pp. 391–400). Gower.

Understanding the. 'E' in ESG (2019). SP Global. www.spglobal.com/en/research-insights/articles/understanding-the-e-in-esg

Usul, N., Özdemir, Ö., & Kiessling, T. (2017). Affect-based stock investment decision: The role of affective self-affinity. *Journal of Behavioral and Experimental Economics*, *68*, 97–109. doi:10.1016/j.socec.2017.04.004

Utz, S., & Wimmer, M. (2014). Are they any good at all? A financial and ethical analysis of socially responsible mutual funds. *Journal of Asset Management*, *15*(1), 72–82. doi:10.1057/jam.2014.8

Welker, M., & Wood, D. (2011). Shareholder activism and alienation. *Current Anthropology*, *52*(S3), S57–S69. doi:10.1086/656796

What Is the. 'G' in ESG? (2020). SP Global. www.spglobal.com/en/research-insights/articles/what-is-the-g-in-esg

What Is the. 'S' in ESG? (2020). SP Global. www.spglobal.com/en/research-insights/articles/what-is-the-s-in-esg

Xie, J., Nozawa, W., Yagi, M., Fujii, H., & Managi, S. (2019). Do environmental, social, and governance activities improve corporate financial performance? *Business Strategy and the Environment*, *28*(2), 286–300. doi:10.1002/bse.2224

KEY TERMS AND DEFINITIONS

Behavioral Finance: Financial paradigm that studies financial decision-making incorporating irrationality of investors and inefficiency of the financial markets into account. This paradigm has an interdisciplinary assessment in the sense that it combines finance theory with psychological biases.

Corporate Social Responsibility (CSR): Financial perspective adopted by companies that place special emphasis on social, environmental, and governance concerns by considering that shareholder wealth maximization is not the sole objective of a business. High CSR companies take responsibility by promoting good social, environmental, and governance practices in their operations.

Environmental, Social, Governance (ESG) Score: Ratings produced by various data providers to assess the environmental, social, and governance performance of companies, which disclose related information.

Social Finance: Financial approach, which prioritizes investment alternatives better aligned to environmental and social objectives along with financial returns. This approach is significant in promoting projects with social impact, which struggle to raise capital.

Socially Responsible Investing (SRI): Type of investment strategy, which takes social, environmental, and governance concerns into account in investment decisions aiming for a more sustainable world.

Sustainable Development Goals (SDGs): Global goals introduced by the United Nations in 2015 to take action to protect the world and achieve a more fair, prospering, peaceful environment for all people by 2030. These goals are presented under 17 headings, which call for action in social, environmental, and economic sustainability.

Sustainable Finance: Type of finance that incorporates environmental, social, and governance (ESG) considerations into the financial decision-making process, which paves the way for a higher level of investments in sustainable projects with a long-term orientation.

ENDNOTES

1 Please visit https://www.refinitiv.com/en/sustainable-finance/esg-scores#methodology for the latest version of the methodology which is updated periodically. This study uses February 2021 version.

2 This study uses June 2020 S&P Dow Jones country classification. Countries classified as frontier market by S&P are classified as "Other" and included in total overall score but not presented separately in Table 1 since they constitute less than 0.6 percent of the sample.

Chapter 2
Corporate Sustainability and Long-Lived Companies:
A Lesson From the Oldest Firms in the World

Luis A. Millan-Tudela
https://orcid.org/0000-0003-3669-9960
University of Alicante, Spain

Bartolomé Marco-Lajara
https://orcid.org/0000-0001-8811-9118
University of Alicante, Spain

Javier Martínez-Falcó
https://orcid.org/0000-0001-9004-5816
University of Alicante, Spain & Stellenbosch University, South Africa

Esther Poveda-Pareja
University of Alicante, Spain

ABSTRACT

Corporate sustainability is a topic that has gathered a considerable interest in the last years. Despite recent developments, some firms have led with changes in the environment for centuries to survive, being one of the tools used for corporate sustainability. This chapter analyzes how the most long-living companies in the world have carried out sustainable businesses through embeddedness and collaboration with the environment, mostly by the use of intangible resources and capabilities, in order to remain in the market. With a narrative perspective, the authors expose some of the practices developed by the abovementioned companies. The main conclusions extracted from those firms are aimed to be potentially applied to current companies and, thus, enhance corporate sustainability and survival through already proven mechanisms.

DOI: 10.4018/978-1-6684-7422-8.ch002

INTRODUCTION

Corporate sustainability is a topic that has an increasing interest due to current problems in society. Pollution, climate change and inequalities have arisen to public discussions as threats that must be faced and defeated. In this sense, the role that companies play is crucial: as drivers of the economy, their actions have a high impact in the lives of every living being. In order to cover human needs, companies use the resources that nature grants. By doing so, the impact it has in the environment is considerable. In fact, the harm the environment (society, ecosystems, etc.) suffers is also returned to the companies themselves.

Through human history, crucial events have molded how the world is nowadays, having these events imposed radical changes in the way society is perceived. Despite those changes, some firms have overcome their own nature: fast mortality. Most of the firms hardly make it to 10 or 15 years of existence, but a few have achieved an incredible milestone: living for centuries, even more than a millennium in some cases. Given a first glimpse to those companies, the following question arises: has their relationship with the environment been determinant for survival? It is, have they been sustainable in a way that both the business and the environment have benefited?

To answer the prior questions, a qualitative, exploratory analysis of some of the actions taken by these companies has been developed. Specifically, the chapter is structured as follows: first, the background has been exposed. In this sense, a definition of corporate sustainability, derived from the definition of sustainability provided by the United Nations, has been given. Later, the oldest companies in the world have been identified, sorting them by the year of establishment and the economic activity they carry out. Following this identification, the main variables that are usually considered in survival studies have been exposed, as well as the direction of the relations between those variables and survival odds.

Once the above steps have been completed, the exploratory analysis has been developed. This analysis begins with the assessment on the influence the environment has in the likeliness of firm survival. More specifically, the culture distance model developed by Hofstede (1984; 2001) has been applied as a way of assessing the culture of the general environment the companies are in, as well as an analysis of the economic activities they develop. Once discovered that some patterns emerge, the features of the companies themselves have been studied. To do so, several secondary data has been considered (mainly corporate webpages and press articles). By doing so, the authors have been available to detect some actions carried out by the companies that have helped the preservation of the environment from a social perspective. More specifically, the strategic resources and capabilities of these companies have been identified, and through this discovering, the actions that have contributed to preserving the social environment and have been carried out by exploiting those resources and capabilities are exposed.

The final section presents the conclusions and a discussion derived from the explorative analysis developed by the authors. The main result that has emerged is that corporate sustainability has to be sincerely done by companies, fleeing false statements that are only intended to improve the image of the company. By doing so, better embeddedness in the environment is achieved by organizations and, thus, their ability to cope with the environment increases, gaining competitive advantages that make their survival more likely. To conclude, the limitations found during the development of this research are exposed: sample size and the lack of statistical test that confirm the assessments made emerge as the main ones. Despite existing some more, the authors are conscious and accept them as they considered that, in expense, a unique view (that is far from most of the research works that address the topic of business survival) is achieved.

BACKGROUND

Sustainability can be defined as "meeting the needs of the present without compromising the ability of future generations to meet their own needs" (United Nations, 1987). This definition, despite being extremely broad, makes it understood that it involves different dimensions. Following that definition, corporate sustainability may be defined by mixing the concepts of sustainability and entrepreneurial activity as the following: corporate sustainability is the commitment taken by companies that consists in satisfying the needs of the present by means of their economic activities without compromising the ability of future generations to meet their own needs.

According to the most recent data available, around 333 million companies were estimated to exist by 2021 (Clark, 2022a). Given an estimated population of 7.84 billion people that year according to the World Bank (2022), that leads to 1 company per 23.5 people. This single measure shows the relevance that firms have in our lives. What is more, things are even clearer from a qualitative perspective. Firms influence our daily life from almost all perspectives, involving economic, social, and demographic ones (Millan-Tudela, Marco-Lajara, Martínez-Falcó et al., 2022), among others as political, technological and ecological. Thus, sustainability practices carried out by firms around the world are crucial for human wellbeing.

However, most companies are not even sustainable for themselves. Taking the Spanish economic tissue as an example, only 43% of the firms make it to 10 years, what means that most of the economic organizations fail within their first decade of existence (Crédito y Caución, 2020), a fact that is reinforced by the estimation that, within the 1960-2020 period, 58.1% of Spanish companies perished (Millan-Tudela, Marco-Lajara, Poveda-Pareja et al., 2022). This is not something exclusive from this country. For example, Cefis et al. (2021) state from the works focused on other countries by Geroski (1995) and Caves (1998) that "new firms are the most exposed to risk of exit, especially in the first new years after entry" to the market. Despite the abovementioned, and according to the data given in the Statista database (Clark, 2022b), the are few firms that have faced threats and have persisted for centuries. Table 1 shows the most enduring firms in the world.

As can be seen, the 20 oldest living companies in the world were established between the 6th and 11th century. Those firms belong to a wide variety of sectors, being both manufacturing and service companies included.

A particular feature of this set of firms is that most of them are placed in countries characterized by a long existence and a deep culture. For example, 9 of those companies (45% of the firm set) are established in Japan, a country known by its defense of traditions. Another thing that stands out, despite being a bit obvious, is the fact that the economic sectors they are involved in can be classified as traditional. In this sense, the results are in accordance with the statements made by some authors. In the case of culture, Guerras Martín & Navas López (2016) defend that a strong internal culture has a deep influence in the behavior of a company. This conclusion may be applicable to the environment too (this is indeed assessed in the following section).

Another feature that may be present in most of these companies (or, at least, in their past) is their recognition as family businesses. According to Antheaume et al. (2013), family businesses are willing to sacrifice short-term benefits if it reduces their risk of exit and, to do so, they seek a common ground for family, business, and environment. This is in line with what Guerras Martín & Navas López (2016) call strategic fit, it is, the adjustment between a company's strategy (that reflects its culture) and the environment it has to deal with. However, Antheaume et al. (2013) also point out the need for prolonging the past and, at a certain point, breaking with it, as Colli et al. (2013) expose.

Table 1. List of most enduring firms sorted by year of establishment. Source: Clark (2022b)

	Company	Establishment Year	Location	Activity
1	Kongo Gumi	578	Japan	Construction company
2	Nishiyama Onsen Keiunkan	705	Japan	Hotel
3	Koman	707	Japan	Hotel
4	Hoshi Ryokan	718	Japan	Hotel
5	Genda Shigyo	771	Japan	Paper factory
6	Stiftskeller St. Peter	803	Austria	Restaurant (industry)
7	Staffelter Hof	862	Germany	Winery
8	Monnaie de Paris	864	France	Coin manufacturing
9	Tanaka-Iga	885	Japan	Religious goods manufacturing
10	The Royal Mint	886	England (UK)	Coin manufacturing
11	Sean's Bar	900	Ireland	Pub
12	The Bingley Arms	953	England (UK)	Pub
13	Nakamura Shaji	970	Japan	Construction company
14	Château de Goulaine	1000	France	Leisure
15	Ichimonjiya Wasuke	1000	Japan	Confectionery
16	Shumiya-Shinbutsuguten	1024	Japan	Religious goods manufacturing
17	Pontificia Fonderia Marinelli	1040	Italy	Bell casting
18	Weihenstephan Brewery	1040	Germany	Beer crafting
19	Weltenburger Brewery	1050	Germany	Beer crafting
20	Otterton Mill	1068	England (UK)	Water mill

Other features that define companies must be also considered. Literature on business survival recognize the effect that firm age and size exert on the odds of exit and survival. Regarding firm age, several studies have addressed its influence, concluding that the older a firm, the lower the odds of failure (i.e. the higher the probability of surviving) (Cefis & Marsili, 2006; Dimara et al., 2008; Fontana & Nesta, 2009; Talay et al., 2014; Ugur & Vivarelli, 2021). Similar conclusions are derived from the analysis of the influence firm size has on survival: the bigger the company, the less likely it is to disappear (Dimara et al., 2008; Fontana & Nesta, 2009; Talay et al., 2014; Ugur & Vivarelli, 2021). These behaviors may be explained by resource and capabilities allocation: if a company is big enough, it will have access to unique resources that are not available to all firms, it is, the firm will take advantage of the so-called heterogeneity and imperfect mobility (Guerras Martín & Navas López, 2016).

The role of innovation has also been deeply assessed on its influence in business survival. Several methodologies, definitions of innovation (radical vs. incremental, product vs. process, etc.) have been analyzed. In this sense, most of the literature converges in defining a positive influence being exerted by innovation in business survival, as Cefis & Marsili (2006), Dimara et al. (2008) or Banbury & Mitchell

(1995), just to give some examples. However, one of the conclusions Ugur & Vivarelli (2021) expose in their literature review is that there is no consensus regarding whether the relation firm innovation-survival is statistically significant and, if so, it the influence is positive or negative. The latter also state that this relation may be non-monotonic, and more specifically, an inverted U-shaped function. This would indicate that, in order to survive, a clear strategy regarding innovation should be defined. Otherwise, companies would face the risk of being "stuck in the middle", thus neither being able to differentiate from their competitors nor being able to face other companies through cost reduction.

It must be considered that most of the research developed in the field is based on quantitative analysis of medium and large samples. Thus, seldom has been attempted an individualized, qualitative research. The few examples that can be mentioned are similar to Antheaume et al. (2013), where they develop interviews with different managers from long-lived family businesses. As a consequence, authors believe that by analyzing the common features of the oldest companies in the world may lead to some interesting conclusions. By conducting an exploratory analysis, based on the use of secondary data (mainly companies' websites and press articles), results are expected to provide common conclusions among most of the firms considered. However, these companies reflect the most radical ones in terms of survival (by years in active), so the conclusions extracted from the work done in the following section must be considered as preliminary results, as it is needed for additional analysis that check whether conclusions can be extrapolated to a broader population.

LESSONS BROUGHT BY THE OLDEST COMPANIES IN THE WORLD

As it is stated in the previous section, one of the first remarkable things is that most of the companies are established in Japan. However, having a look at the rest of countries, we can also see that some of them have existed for a long time or, at least, the states that finally make them up. Regarding this discovering, it may be possible that the country, as a general environment, influences the fit of the firms and, thus, their survival odds. Indeed, authors like Guerras Martín & Navas López (2016) state that the relationship firm-environment is bidirectional, being the influence from the environment on the company way higher than the inverse relation. Thus, an interesting approach emerges from the study of the features that describe those countries.

The Influence of the Environment

In order to assess the environment influencing the company by their establishment in certain countries, the model of cultural distance firstly developed by Hofstede (1984) and later extended by himself 17 years later (Hofstede, 2001) is applied. This model uses six variables that, graded from 0 to 100, allow to describe in a broad sense the culture of a country. By comparing those variables among countries, it can be stated whether those countries are similar or different in cultural terms. Concretely, the model considers the following variables:

- Power distance: measure of power distribution. High power distance implies a more hierarchical culture.
- Individualism: assesses whether actions are directed towards autonomous or group work. The higher the individualism, the less the collaboration among people.

- Masculinity[1]: a higher masculinity is associated with more competition, while low values describe societies focused on consensus.
- Uncertainty avoidance: degree in which society accepts ambiguity and uncertainty. The higher this variable, the less risks people are willing to face.
- Long-term orientation: it measures the orientation towards tradition, money-saving and long-term results. The higher long-term orientation is, the more those behaviors arise.
- Indulgence: an indulgent society relates to leisure and fun, while low levels are linked to restrictive societies characterized by extended rules and prohibitions.

In order to assess the abovementioned variables, a web tool with a database that includes the results from Hofstede's model is used (Hofstede Insights, 2022). Results are shown in Figure 1.

Figure 1. Application of distance model developed by Hofstede.
Source: elaborated from Hofstede Insights (2022)

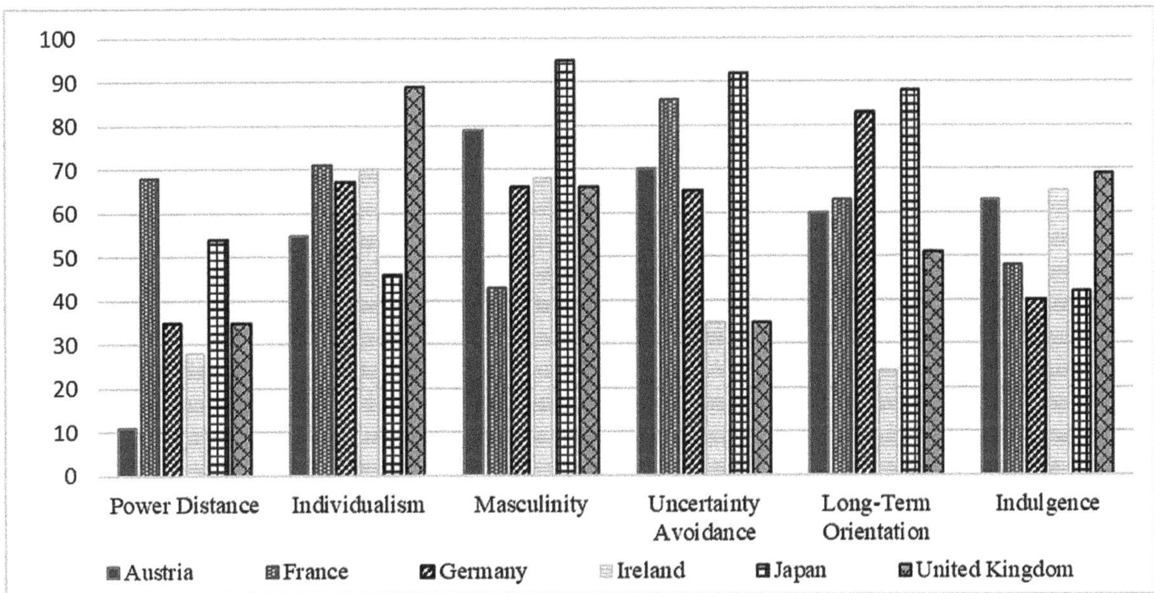

As can be seen, some variables diverge in values. In this sense, power distance, uncertainty avoidance and long-term orientation show different results, not establishing a certain pattern. Nor is the case of individualism. In this one, all countries show mid and high levels of individualism, what may indicate that societies that tend to collectivism create a more hostile environment in terms of survival. One possible explanation to that is effort reward. In the most collective societies, benefits are distributed among individuals (in economic terms, it can be linked to more social models). In "individualistic" societies, results are kept by those that generate the benefits (ignoring asymmetries in rent appropriation by power tenure). This, translated into microeconomic terms, is the so-known rent appropriation, stated as one of the conditions to consider that a company has strategic resources and capabilities (Guerras Martín & Navas López, 2016). In consequence, if society does not allow to rent appropriation, it will not enhance the generation and sustaining of competitive advantages (as companies will not enjoy their benefits), putting them in a lower position compared to companies from more individualistic countries and, thus, increasing their odds of failure.

Regarding masculinity, levels also tend to high values, being only a country with average score. Again, a society more focused in competition should enhance business performance as optimization is needed if firms want to reach a competitive advantage. A way to do so is through innovation. This is in line with hypothesis tested by many authors (Banbury & Mitchell, 1995; Cefis & Marsili, 2006; Dimara et al., 2008; Fontana & Nesta, 2009), who defend that, the higher the innovation, the higher the odds of survival. However, non-monotonic relations may also be possible. As stated in the previous section, a curvilinear effect may exist in the relation innovation-survival. However, other outcomes from being established in a competitive society (e.g. product differentiation, improvement of processes or optimizing resource allocation, among others) would theoretically place companies in a better competitive position and, consequently, improve their odds of survival.

Finally, we find that all countries show medium levels of indulgence. Low levels mean high restrictions. Environments like this may threaten business survival as certain activities would be restricted and, as a consequence, impede the development of certain resources. For example, extreme environments where rights of assembly or speech-freedom are controlled would impede the creation and sharing of knowledge, what is detrimental to business development. On the other hand, excessively tolerant societies (those that leave value creation on a second level compared to leisure and fun) would bring a chaotic environment, where unpredictability and lack of definition for certain aspects may trigger more uncertainty compared to more restrictive environments. Thus, societies with medium values that combine the benefits of indulgence and control may provide the best breeding ground for business development and, thereby, survival. It is, extreme values may threaten firm longevity.

Going back to Table 1, another analysis of interest is the evaluation of the products and services made by the companies considered. The first thing that draws attention is that there is no predominance of a certain set of activities. Goods (9 companies) and service production (11 companies) can be considered as equally distributed, so no differences emerge in this case. However, the products offered stand out as some of them are repeated across firms. For example, there are 3 hotels, all placed in Japan and established in the 8th century. The same happens for Japanese religious goods, English pubs (all created in the 10th century) and beer crafting in Germany (11th century). Construction industry also appears twice in the case of Japan through Kongo Gumi (oldest company in the world) and Nakamura Shaji. A possible explanation is the link of the products made (regardless being goods of services) with the country's culture. For example, beer has been recognized as part of the German culture for centuries. This is reflected nowadays in the Oktoberfest, a celebration where beer turns out to be the center. What is more, a specific type of beer that follows a crafting procedure stipulated by a rule dating back to 1516, promulgated by William IV and known as Reinheitsgebot, is defended by 85% of Germans as a guarantee and distinctive seal of quality (Lederman, 2016). Indeed, this rule has only suffered little modifications ever since.

It is also interesting the case of Japanese hotels, as 3 of the top 5 companies sorted by age are classified like this. For example, Nishiyama Onsen Keiunkan, the oldest hotel in the world (Guiness World Records, 2022) states in its corporate website that "no matter how much time has passed, Keiunkan embodies the unchanging hospitality fueled by the spirit of Japanese harmony towards our guests" (Koshu Nishiyama Hot Spring, 2022), a taste of the respect attitude towards the culture of the environment the hotel is embedded in. Hoshi Ryokan is also a hotel with hot spring baths (very popular in the Japanese culture), and keep a similar philosophy regarding the respect for traditions: the sentence "Houshi has been loved by many generations, and continues to maintain precious tradition in modern times" appears in their webpage where the business is described (Awazu onsen Houshi ryokan, 2017). However, this is not exclusive of Japanese firms. For example, the Château de Goulaine turns out to be linked to its history and, more specifically, with the history of France, as its founder (Jean de Goulaine) was Captain of the city of Nantes for the Duke of Brittany (Château de Goulaine, 2022).

The link of these companies with tradition is not only reflected by the statements they make as their actions also offer examples in this direction. Tanaka-Iga and Shumiya-Shinbutsuguten make Buddhist religious goods (Tanaka-Iga, 2022). The same happens for Pontificia Fonderia Marinelli, a casting bell factory which name already reveals the recognition for Catholicism, something that they even state in their website, where they declare that Pope Pio XI granted them the use of the Papal Arm Coast in the production process (Pontificia Fonderia Marinelli, 2022).

Despite the abovementioned, sometimes the company is not just embedded in the environment, it becomes an active part of it. Guerras Martín & Navas López (2016) state that every company is part of the environment. However, some companies go a step further and are related in such a way to it that there is almost no distinction between both. This phenomenon is reflected in the cases of Monnaie de Paris and The Royal Mint, responsible for coin manufacturing for France and the United Kingdom, respectively. In this sense, both companies have the exclusive right for this task (Monnaie de Paris, 2022; The Royal Mint, 2022). In the case of Monnaie de Paris, it is intended as a public service company that has even survived to the French Revolution, while The Royal Mint is owned by His Majesty's Treasury, a department depending on the Government of the United Kingdom.

The prior analysis shows that embeddedness in the environment may generate certain behaviors that enhance the odds of survival. It is, the fit of the company allows it to grow at the same pace of the environment that surrounds it, so mutual benefits are reached: on the one hand, the company enhances its survival probability; on the other hand, the environment benefits from the value created by the company.

The Companies From the Inside

In addition to the external analysis, further conclusions can be extracted from the companies themselves. In this sense, a possible way to assess them is by developing an analysis of the set of resources and capabilities they have. Resources can be defined as the set of assets the company disposes of and controls, while capabilities are the skills a company has in order to develop a specific task (Martín & López, 2016). In this sense, resources belong to the company, while capabilities are the way the company explodes those resources. In this regard, the following questions arises: do the oldest firms in the world have common assets and capabilities? Where do their advantages come from?

The abovementioned questions can be answered by doing an analysis of the resources and capabilities those companies have and how they use them. To do so, the analysis of these elements is developed in two steps: both are individually enumerated, classified and, from the results extracted by putting in common the evaluation from the companies whose information is available, conclusions are finally obtained.

Resource Tenure by the Oldest Firms in the World

Resources can be divided into two main groups: tangibles and intangibles. At the same time, those groups can be split into more specific parts. According to Guerras Martín and Navas López (2016), resources are classified as follows:

- Tangibles: resources with physical presence that, in consequence, are easy to evaluate.
    - Material: facilities, machinery, raw materials, etc.
    - Financial: liquidity, bonds and stocks, debt capacity, etc.
- Intangibles: resources based on information and knowledge.
    - Human: knowledge, abilities and aptitudes brought by those who work in the company.
    - Non-human: intangible resources that belong to the company itself, regardless of human resources.
        - Technological: knowledge that allows to create goods and services by the use of different techniques.
        - Organizational: those that create value for the company by being associated to it (brand, reputation, client portfolio, etc.).

In this sense, the resource-based view theory in which the resource and capabilities analysis is built depends on two premises (Barney, 1991):

- Heterogeneity or difference in the set of resources and capabilities among firms.
- Imperfect mobility or asymmetries in the availability of resources and capabilities.

In this sense, the more resources and capabilities a company attains, the more likely they are to survive. Regarding tangible assets, there are many differences among the firms considered in order to locate their competitive advantage there. For example, Kongo Gumi is a construction company that has Takamatsu Construction Work as mother firm (Calvo, 2022), which has a net income of almost 20 billion dollars per year. Monnaie de Paris and The Royal Mint, by the activity carried, also dispose of considerable tangent assets, mainly in the form of facilities and machinery. On the other hand, Sean's Bar, The Bingley Arms, Nishiyama Onsen Keiunkan and Hoshi Ryokan, among others, are classified as small and medium enterprises (SMEs), with lesser tangible resources than the previous ones.

If the features that allow to business longevity do not come from tangible resources, the next step to analyze are intangibles. In this stream, one of the potential, differentiating resources is the culture within the organization. These companies have demonstrated to have a deep culture, strongly linked to their roots. For example, Kongo Gumi kept for centuries the precepts of internal competition, teamwork, meritocracy, and internal promotion of the managers (Sone, 2013). Pontificia Fonderia Marinelli (2022) show their history as part of the reason for their success by facing prosper and tough moments (embeddedness of the history in culture). The same applies to Château de Goulaine (2022), whose differential value comes from the history that surrounds the business. By their side, Weihenstephan Brewery were awarded as having the best Kristallweißbier in the world (Weihenstephan, 2022), which results in an increase of the brand's value by possessing the technological resources and knowledge to apply the best techniques.

Following a similar logic, Tanaka-Iga and Shumiya-Shinbutsuguten are supposed to have a strong culture related to Buddhism, both for the tradition of their economic activity and the fact of being strongly related to a religion. Owners of Ichimonjiya Wasuke, a confectionery shop in Kyoto, have always prioritized tradition and stability over profit and growth (Dooley & Ueno, 2020), it is, culture over finance.

The mentioned examples prove the oldest companies in the world share a common feature: their unique intangible resources allow them to differentiate from their competitors. As these intangibles come from centuries of experience, they are barely imitable, and are recognized by customers as distinguishing attributes. The fact of having survived and having these assets is not just coincidence. As it is stated above, tangible resources do not seem to influence the odds of survival for such long periods of time (despite many researchers defend the opposite, the samples are limited in terms of time frame and do not account for these extreme cases, so their conclusions may not be applicable to these firms). On the other hand, human resources usually do not allow to appropriate the rents from the competitive advantage that they may generate (Guerras Martín & Navas López, 2016). Thus, the difference (in terms of resources) seems to come partially from technological and, to a greater extent, organizational resources.

However, this resource tenure does not come from nowhere. In order to create this kind of intangibles, several actions must be carried out. It is, the companies must have the ability to get, create and retain those resources or, at least, their value. That is the role of organizational capabilities.

Capabilities and Oldest Firms in the World: The Ability to Make History

Resource tenure is not enough in order to create, sustain and appropriate the benefits of a competitive advantage as they do not create value for themselves (Martín & López, 2016). In order to do so, resources must be used together in a coordinated way. The more efficient the use of the resources, the better the results, as two possible situations may take place:

- An optimization of resources leads to an increase in the outcome.
- If the outcome value is fixed, an optimization of resources allows to relocate idle ones in different activities.

It is expected that the most long-lasting organizations in the world are able to do a rational, efficient use of the resources they have gathered over their life, it is, to exploit them by the use of their capabilities.

For example, all the companies must have the capability of resilience, it is, the ability to resist the changes and ambiguity in the environment. The time frame that comprises the years of establishment for these firms goes from 578 to 1,068. It means that all of them have suffered historical events, both in their countries and worldwide. Table 2 summarizes some of the most important events all these firms had to face to. Among events exposed economic crisis, national and international wars and technological disruptions are included.

All of them have imposed changes in the paradigm the whole society has to face and companies, therefore. For example, Kongo Gumi took part in rebuilding Shitennoji Temple after it burned down in World War II (Sone, 2013). A good proof of resilience is given by Pontificia Fonderia Marinelli, as their facilities were destroyed in 1950, but they could recover in another location (Pontificia Fonderia Marinelli, 2022).

Another capability that emerges by using a similar argument is adaptability. Pontificia Fonderia Marinelli (2022) recovered relatively fast from World War II. Château de Goulaine (2022) escaped from the French Revolution, being later recovered by the family that owned it when Patrice de Goulaine rebought it. Moreover, Kongo Gumi is the more extreme in terms of power rotation: 40 generations of the Kongo family have held the reins of the business, being some of them not part of the biological lineage of the family (Sone, 2013). Despite all internal and external changes, Kongo Gumi has always been able to overcome those dynamics and stay in the market. The same applies to the rest of companies.

Table 2. Some historical events that threatened business survival. Source: own elaboration

Start Year	Event
1492	Colonization of the Americas
1760	1st Industrial Revolution
1776	United States Declaration of Independence
1792	French Revolution
1804	Napoleon Bonaparte declared himself Emperor
1870	2nd Industrial Revolution
1914	World War I
1929	Great Depression
1939	World War II
1973	Oil crisis
1979	
1991	General release of the World Wide Web
2008	Financial crisis
2020	COVID-19 crisis

Kongo Gumi also serves as an example for exposing another capability: learning. According to Sone (2013), even the veteran supervisors recognized the importance of operating computers, so they made an effort to overcome the barriers they found for the company's sake. This is a specific example, but in overall terms, all companies had to learn many different things through the several dimensions that affect their businesses. In the technological field, many changes have arisen: industrialization and digitalization are the main ones. In social terms, companies have been required to develop sustainable business in recent years. Globalization has opened markets and, thus, has forced companies to two possible solutions: focusing in a specific market (in geographical terms) or expanding to another countries. Most of the companies considered in this work have decided to use the first one, in part because a considerable amount of their value depends on their linkage to their roots. However, some companies (not the ones considered) failed in their attempt for internationalization. In this sense, some of the oldest companies just did not want to expand, while others may have noticed the risks related to that strategy.

The capabilities exposed above are the so-called dynamic capabilities, it is, the ones that allow a company to face changes in the environment. It is not by chance that the oldest firms in the world are able to rebuild and maintain their set of assets and capabilities despite the hostility, dynamicity and uncertainty of the environment: strategic adjustment (compatibility between business strategy and the environment) and organizational adjustment (compatibility between business strategy and structure) are a must for survival (Guerras Martín & Navas López, 2016). A fact that may be confirmed by companies like the ones assessed.

CONCLUSION AND DISCUSSION

Most of the companies tend to disappear in a matter of years since their creation. For example, 43% of the Spanish firms do not make it to 10 years (Crédito y Caución, 2020). This pattern is similar around the globe, as a cleaning effect seems to exist in the different economic fabrics regardless of the country they belong to. However, among these firms some organizations are found to have obtained outstanding results in terms of longevity: while some cannot exceed 10 years of existence, others have existed for more than 10 centuries. In this set of firms, both goods and service businesses are found, as well as SMEs and large companies. It is, according to the brief, explanatory review carried out, no patterns emerged in terms of tangible resources tenure. However, the fact of having access to valuable resources and capabilities (in particular, dynamic capabilities) seems to play a key role in the ability of those firms to have outperformed others in age, being able to resist the threats imposed by the environment.

More concretely, all firms have demonstrated the ability to cope with the environment, get adapted and learn, many times through contributing to it. For example, Kongo Gumi has taken care of the Shitennoji Temple since its creation (Sone, 2013), contributing to its restoration after World War II. Ichimonjiya Wasuke prioritizes tradition over profit, and all the companies assessed recognize the importance culture from their native society has, so they have kept it as a valuable source. For example, the respect German breweries have for Reinheitsgebot has allowed to keep traditional recipes that are linked to the Bavarian history. Tradition seems to play a key role in the resilience of these companies, as they tie themselves to their origins. The only way to be able to resist for so many centuries is not only by respecting the environment (recognizing its importance), but also by developing real actions in terms of contributing to its preservation, a cornerstone of corporate sustainability. None of these companies have seen themselves involved in scandals. They have recognized the importance of the environment and the work that previous workers did by valuing their history.

In this sense, a clear conclusion arises: in order to remain alive, companies must develop real corporate sustainability practices that transcend press releases. Recognition for this kind of actions is important, but it is crucial to implement them with the real aim of contributing to the environment, as those actions allow the companies to become adapted to the environment and, thus, improve their survival odds. To do so, long-term actions must be done. The set of resources and capabilities these companies possess and the contribution they make to the environment is not achieved in a matter of years: it can only be developed by constant interaction and mutual collaboration with the environment, by living times of prosperity and decadency, and by recognizing the value of the past work, actively participating in present developments that are part of our society and protecting the future generations at the same time. All that can be only done by existing for centuries and keeping it as a treasure.

LIMITATIONS AND FUTURE RESEARCH

Despite the contributions that have been achieved, some limitations are also present in this work. First of all, the qualitative nature of the analysis does not allow to determine whether the issue has been sufficiently dissected. In this sense, there is no guarantee that important variables may have been missed, as the information from these companies, despite addressing all their history, has been developed in recent years, not existing coeval documents from the early years accessible to the authors.

Another limitation may be that the text is not completely focused on CSR. The latter has been purposely intentional, as one of the goals pursued is to demonstrate that CSR practices are reachable for any firm, as the tools needed are available for all those with a real aim for getting them: resources and capabilities. However, this approach has also allowed the authors to demonstrate that the use of resources and capabilities for making businesses can contribute to the environment at the same time with little effort.

Sample size is also another limitation: only 20 companies have been initially considered in this study, and some of them do not offer enough information to be properly analyzed. Despite so, by focusing on a few companies, more information can be extracted from them and, as a consequence, some particular conclusions are extracted that may compliment future works, even quantitative, by uncovering possible elements that may influence the odds of survival.

Finally, the use of just qualitative data does not allow to confirm the abovementioned statements, so a quantitative analysis that statistically validates them is needed. However, this exploratory work can be considered as the first step of future works, as it arises possible elements that should be analyzed together with more common variables used in survival models like firm age, size, innovation or agglomeration. More specifically, the work shows the need for research based on primary data, as some variables that may influence business survival and are not commonly considered in most research works because they are not available in most databases due to the intangible elements that they represent. As a solution to this, a possible future development is the creation of a model that considers both primary data that captures the uniqueness of these companies' intangibles and secondary data with more standard variables.

REFERENCES

Antheaume, N., Robic, P., & Barbelivien, D. (2013). French family business and longevity: Have they been conducting sustainable development policies before it became a fashion? *Business History*, *55*(6), 942–962. doi:10.1080/00076791.2012.744583

Awazu onsen Houshi ryokan. (2017). *Welcome*. Awazu onsen Houshi ryokan. https://www.ho-shi.co.jp/en/

Banbury, C. M., & Mitchell, W. (1995). The effect of introducing important incremental innovations on market share and business survival. *Strategic Management Journal*, *16*(S1), 161–182. doi:10.1002mj.4250160922

Barney, J. (1991). Firm resources and sustained competitive advantage. *Journal of Management*, *17*(1), 99–120. doi:10.1177/014920639101700108

Calvo, J. (2022). Kongo Gumi, la empresa en activo más antigua del mundo [Kongo Gumi, the oldest active company in the world]. *Eleconomista*. https://www.eleconomista.es/podcasts/noticias/12002183/10/22/Kongo-Gumi-la-empresa-en-activo-mas-antigua-del-mundo.html

Caves, R. E. (1998). Industrial organization and new findings on the turnover and mobility of firms. *Journal of Economic Literature*, *36*(4), 1947–1982.

Cefis, E., Bettinelli, C., Coad, A., & Marsili, O. (2021). Understanding firm exit: A systematic literature review. *Small Business Economics*. doi:10.100711187-021-00530-4

Cefis, E., & Marsili, O. (2006). Survivor: The role of innovation in firms' survival. *Research Policy, 35*(5), 626–641. doi:10.1016/j.respol.2006.02.006

Château de Goulaine. (2022). *The history.* Château de Goulaine. http://www.chateaudegoulaine.fr/english-informations/opening-hours-admission-prices/the-history

Clark, D. (2022a). Estimated number of companies worldwide from 2000 to 2021. *Statista.* https://www.statista.com/statistics/1260686/global-companies/#:~:text=There%20were%20estimated%20to%20be,were%20around%20328%20million%20companies.%20

Clark, D. (2022b). Oldest 20 companies still operating worldwide in 2021. *Statista.* https://www.statista.com/statistics/1259761/oldest-companies-worldwide/

Colli, A., Howorth, C., & Rose, M. (2013). Long-term perspectives on family business. *Business History, 55*(6), 841–854. doi:10.1080/00076791.2012.744589

Crédito y Caución. (2020). *La pandemia incrementa la mortalidad entre las empresas con tres años de vida. [The pandemic increases mortality among companies with three years of life].* Iberinform. https://www.iberinform.es/noticias/detalle/La-pandemia-incrementa-la-mortalidad-entre-las-empresas-con-tres-anos-de-vida

Dimara, E., Skuras, D., Tsekouras, K., & Tzelepis, D. (2008). Productive efficiency and firm exit in the food sector. *Food Policy, 33*(2), 185–196. doi:10.1016/j.foodpol.2007.08.003

Dooley, B., & Ueno, H. (2020). This Japanese shop is 1,020 years old. It knows a bit about surviving crises. *The New York Times.* https://www.nytimes.com/2020/12/02/business/japan-old-companies.html

Fontana, R., & Nesta, L. (2009). Product innovation and survival in a high-tech industry. *Review of Industrial Organization, 34*(4), 287–306. doi:10.100711151-009-9210-7

Geroski, P. A. (1995). What do we know about entry? *International Journal of Industrial Organization, 13*(4), 421–440. doi:10.1016/0167-7187(95)00498-X

Guerras Martín, L. Á., & Navas López, J. E. (2016). *La dirección estratégica de la empresa: Teoría y aplicaciones [The strategic direction of the company: theory and applications]* (5th ed.). Thomson Reuters Civitas.

Guiness World Records. (2022). *Oldest hotel.* https://www.guinnessworldrecords.com/world-records/oldest-hotel

Hofstede, G. (1984). *Culture's consequences: International differences in work-related values.* Sage.

Hofstede, G. (2001). *Culture's consequences: Comparing values, behaviors, institutions and organizations across nations.* Sage publications.

Hofstede Insights. (2022). *Compare Countries.* https://www.hofstede-insights.com/fi/product/compare-countries/

Koshu Nishiyama Hot Spring. (2022). *The world's longest-standing hot spring inn.* Keiunkan. https://www.keiunkan.co.jp/en/

Lederman, N. (2016). How pure is the beer in Germany? *BBC*. https://www.bbc.com/travel/article/20161027-how-pure-is-the-beer-in-germany

Millan-Tudela, L. A., Marco-Lajara, B., Martínez-Falcó, J., & Poveda-Pareja, E. (2022). *Longevidad empresarial: revisión bibliométrica sobre la supervivencia y caída de las compañías [Buisness longevity: bibliometric review on the survival and fall of companies].* Paper presented at the XXXVI AEDEM Annual Congress, Madrid, Spain.

Millan-Tudela, L. A., Marco-Lajara, B., Poveda-Pareja, E., & Martínez-Falcó, J. (2022). Is business longevity a way of management success? Recepty na sukces w zarzadzaniu [Recipes for success in management] (pp. 308-311).

Monnaie de Paris. (2022). *La Monnaie de Paris.* Monnaie de Paris. https://www.monnaiedeparis.fr/fr/presentation-institution

Pontificia Fonderia Marinelli. (2022). *Campane Marinelli.* Campane Marinelli http://campanemarinelli.com/en/

Sone, H. (2013). Tradition and Innovation in Japanese Long-Established Companies: Focus on E-Business. Paper presented at the *2013 Seventh International Conference on Innovative Mobile and Internet Services in Ubiquitous Computing*, (pp. 739-742). IEEE. 10.1109/IMIS.2013.156

Talay, M. B., Calantone, R. J., & Voorhees, C. M. (2014). Coevolutionary dynamics of automotive competition: Product innovation, change, and marketplace survival. *Journal of Product Innovation Management*, *31*(1), 61–78. doi:10.1111/jpim.12080

Tanaka-Iga. (2022). 納入実績 *[Delivery Record].* Tanaka-Iga. http://www.tanakaiga.com/works/

The Royal Mint. (2022). *The history of the Royal Mint.* The Royal Mint. https://www.royalmint.com/brand/our-story/

The World Bank. (2022). *Population, total.* The World Bank. https://data.worldbank.org/indicator/SP.POP.TOTL?end=2021&start=2012

Ugur, M., & Vivarelli, M. (2021). Innovation, firm survival and productivity: The state of the art. *Economics of Innovation and New Technology*, *30*(5), 433–467. doi:10.1080/10438599.2020.1828509

United Nations. (1987). *Report of the World Commission on Environment and Development: Our Common Future*. UN. http://www.un-documents.net/our-common-future.pdf

Weihenstephan. (2022). *The World's Best Kristallweißbier is brewed in Weihenstephan!* Weihenstephan. https://www.weihenstephaner.de/en/news/the-world-s-best-kristallweissbier-is-brewed-in-weihenstephan

ENDNOTE

1 This definition can be found in Hofstede's work. In order to allow readers to find the concept in the original work, the name "masculinity" has been kept in this research. However, the authors want to state that no discrimination is intended by the use of this term, and its use is done just to homogenize with previous literature.

Chapter 3
Corporate Sustainability as a Tool for Improving Economic, Social, and Environmental Performance:
The Effects of Work Stress and the Work Environment on Employee Commitment Through Job Satisfaction

Mohammed Saud Mira
Alfaisal University, Saudi Arabia

ABSTRACT

Saudi government pays high attention to the public sectors, such as Saudi Port Authority, in order to gain high level of competition in the global market. Saudi ports, which are considered as one of the busiest ports in the world, and the largest in the Middle East area. However, it has recently faced a severe problem of overstock of commodities. Although, the ports have significant contribution to the local economy, but, improper work environments and the heavy duty of the work has resulted in dissatisfaction and a low level of employees comments among cargo employees, which results in overstock of commodities at Saudi Ports Authority. Questionnaires were distributed to 365 government workers in the cargo sector, 285 were filled up. The outcomes of the study imply that work stress and working conditions may positively affect employee commitment, and that job happiness is an essential factor that workers can embrace in reaching their goals. On the other hand, workplace stress and working conditions might enhance commitment indirectly by giving job satisfaction.

DOI: 10.4018/978-1-6684-7422-8.ch003

INTRODUCTION

Employees play a significant function in the company as a stimulant, allowing them to complete the job commitment. Commitment is a necessary reaction to an individual's responsibility to finish a job with limited resources and time restrictions (Vance, 2006). Employee commitment is defined as conduct that is important to the organization's goals is measurable, observable, and develops over time (Rameshkumar, 2020). Problems that have established a trend in companies, particularly in the government personnel environment, demonstrate that employees' dedication needs to match organizational objectives. The issues with Employee satisfaction, unhappiness with work, unsupportive working environment, and work stress difficulties contribute to the failure to enhance employee commitment to the business (Schermerhorn et al.,2020). This is because the job done does not correspond to the employee's wishes, so the work cannot offer satisfaction to the employee with the work done. Employment contentment concerns a person's overall attitude toward his or her work; a man with a high degree of job satisfaction has a good attitude toward his or her work, whereas a guy who is dissatisfied with the job has a negative attitude toward his or her work (Alzalabani, 2017). According to Kattuah (2013), Saudi ports are one of the world's busiest ports; however, due to work stress in the form of extra work and heavy burdens in an unsafe work environment, workers in the cargo section have a low level of satisfaction and commitment, which result in cargo overstock (Elentably, 2015; Buchari & Basri, 2015). The Kingdom of Saudi Arabia is the world's largest oil exporter. It boasts the most extensive and diverse economy in the Middle East, with internationally focused manufacturing exports. As a result, the Kingdom must have efficient, properly equipped ports to execute the work as it should be done. Employee happiness has remained a topic of discussion in companies as a matter of enjoying and disliking when at work Job satisfaction is a personal experience.

; every person has a distinct amount of this job satisfaction depending on their wants and value systems (Amin, 2021), as well as up to which their work happiness satisfies their requirements (Jayaweera, 2015). The greater the degree of satisfaction, the more the particular employee enjoys their work (Kurniawaty et al., 2019). Employee happiness is influenced by not only the work but also the workload of employees, which is not in line with reality, causing stress. According to McShane and Glinow (2017), behavioral, bodily, and psychological reactions might give a product, such as stress or stress. Because work-related stress has a significant influence on employee contentment with their employment (Greer, 2021), Kurniawaty et al. (2019); Jehangir et al. (2011). The study of Venkataraman and Ganapathi (2013) demonstrates that stress in the work process has fallen, even if the outcomes are obtained. This is similar to the findings of Riaz et al. (2016) and Essiam et al. (2015), who found that a high workload reduces employee commitment, and This demonstrates that workplace stress has a direct influence on employees., resulting in lower work results and lower expected job satisfaction (Greer, 2021). However, challenges in organizations, particularly in dealing with and managing employees, can be recognized by proposing numerous study questions, such as:

- What is the impact of Work Stress on employees' job satisfaction?
- What is the impact of Work Environment on employees' commitment?
- What is the impact of Job Satisfaction on employees' commitment?
- What is the impact of Job satisfaction as mediating element between the work stress, work environment and commitment?

LITERATURE REVIEW

Work Stress and Employees' Commitment

Stress is a negative feeling at the workplace due to the heavy-duty or more tasks that exceed the responsibility regarding the job description. In addition, the challenges or requirements of a potential position could be considered a part of stress (Greenberg, 2010). Although stress could be positive such as contact or communication with others to gain skills etc. However, the main point of stress leads the workers to decrease their commitment (Drucker, 2012). Based on the literature, the propose hypothesis is as under:

H1: Work stress significantly relates to employees' commitment

Work Environment and Employees' Commitment

The work environment is the situation that the workers face at the workplace; the workplace is considered an excellent environment for the workers once they receive support, knowledge etc. On the other hand, discrimination and lack of communication present an unpleasant work environment, which results in low commitment (Nitisemito, 2015). Based on the literature, the proposed hypothesis is as under:

H2: work environment significantly relates to employees' commitment

Job Satisfaction and Employees' Commitment

Job satisfaction is a crucial part of each firm; it is related to the work environment, job description, and decision makers at the workplace. The organization should pay close attention to these factors to increase satisfaction. On the other hand, low satisfaction levels could result from stress or discrimination (Gibson et al., 2011). Ismail and Razak (2016) indicate that a high level of satisfaction will increase commitment.

H3: job satisfaction significantly relates to employees' commitment

Job Satisfaction as Mediating Element Between the Work Stress, Work Environment and Commitment

Job satisfaction is defined as an emotional attitude, which is considered a unique emotion among workers regarding the work environment (Veithzal & Sagala, 2004). Job satisfaction could be affected by security, motivation, and job fitting (As'ad, 2004). Thus, once these factors are correctly applied, the number of satisfied workers will be increased (Drucker, 2012).

H4: job satisfaction significantly mediates between job stress, work environment and employees' commitment

RESEARCH METHODS

The cross-sectional research approach is employed to explain essential methods in gathering data on the sample required in research and the research problems that must be answered (McNeill, 2006). The positivist paradigm is the research paradigm used in this study. The positivist approach is more scientific and can be extended to the social world on the assumption that the social world can be examined in the same manner as the natural world. Secondly, there is a value-free technique for researching the social world; thirdly, there are causal explanations. Since it seeks to test hypotheses to explain the origins of the connection between variables, this study employs an explanatory technique (Walliman, 2010). Given this study's scope and significant goal, the positivist paradigm is the most appropriate choice. This is due to the positivist paradigm's ability to evaluate suggested hypothetical relationships based on current theories' assumptions. This method is also relevant when the researcher does not engage with the individuals under observation (Eriksson & Kovalainen, 2008).

In contrast, the Kenji and Morgan table was used to select a sample of 367 government personnel in the Field cargo section regarding the population (8000). Sampling was done according to convenience. According to Simply Psychology, a questionnaire based on a five-Likert scale was adopted from previous studies (Brayfield & Rothe, 1951; Riaz et al., 2016; Razak al., 2016). As per Simply Psychology, a five Likert scale can make the data gathered easy to interpret due to the numbering assigned to each option. Since observations might vary from one to five or low to high, it provides more flexibility than a conventional yes/no asking approach. Responses are straightforward to code, and total scores are simple to calculate to get an overall result for survey participants. The route analysis model is utilized to demonstrate the phenomena of independent factors directly or indirectly influencing the dependent variable (Dane, 1990). Out of the 367, (285) two hundred and were completed.

Table 1. Determining sample size of a known population

N	S	N	S	N	S	N	S	N	S
10	10	100	80	280	162	800	260	2800	338
15	14	110	86	290	165	850	265	3000	341
20	19	120	92	300	169	900	269	3500	346
25	24	130	97	320	175	950	274	4000	351
30	28	140	103	340	181	1000	278	4500	354
35	32	150	108	360	186	1100	285	5000	357
40	36	160	113	380	191	1200	291	6000	361
45	40	170	118	400	196	1300	297	7000	364
50	44	180	123	420	201	1400	302	8000	367
55	48	190	127	440	205	1500	306	9000	368
60	52	200	132	460	210	1600	310	10000	370
65	56	210	136	480	214	1700	313	15000	375
70	59	220	140	500	217	1800	317	20000	377
75	63	230	144	550	226	1900	320	30000	379
80	66	240	148	600	234	2000	322	40000	380
85	70	250	152	650	242	2200	327	50000	381
90	73	260	155	700	248	2400	331	75000	382
95	76	270	159	750	254	2600	335	1000000	384

Note: N is Population Size; S is Sample Size *Source: Krejcie & Morgan, 1970*

RESULTS AND DISCUSSION

If the Corrected Item-Total Correlation > 0.30, data analysis of each variable indicator item can be completed., the validity and reliability of measurement items can be accepted once it achieved >0.60 (Hair et al., 2010; Brzoska & Razum, 2010). As shown in Table 1.

Figure 1. Conceptual framework model

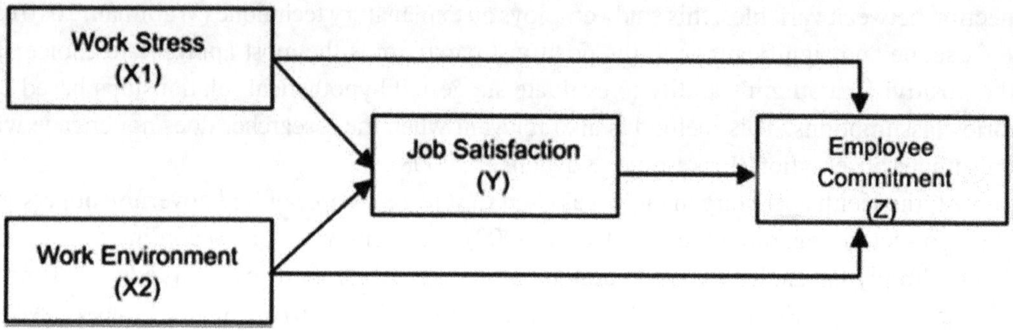

According to Table 1, the six job stress indicators studied each had an item-total correlation (corrected) coefficient of 0.692; 0.856; 0.451; 0.691; 0.891; 0893 > critical value 0.30. Employees may overcome all of the indicators built into generating work stress so that the issues they confront do not cause excessive work stress and the outcomes are legitimate. The adjusted item-total correlation coefficient values for the seven work environment indicator items are 0.643; 0.815; 0.604; 0.641, 0.832, 0.842, 0.606 > critical value of 0.30. Employees can build each and every one of the indication elements in establishing a pleasant working atmosphere to help perform job tasks, ensuring that they do not arise during work activities and that the results are legitimate. There is a coefficient value for job satisfaction. Adjusted item-total correlation of 0.655; 0.401; 0.664; 0.670; 0.651 > critical value 0.30 for the five indicator items. All indicator items produced in satisfying job satisfaction have been effectively enabled by the organization's leadership so that workers feel happy and comfortable while carrying out work tasks, and the results are legitimate. The adjusted item-total correlation coefficient values for the four-government employee commitment indicator items are 0.808; 0.408; 0.462; 0.831 > critical value 0.30. Those are all indicators that can help create high-quality work and fulfill their obligations in accordance with organizational objectives, whether generated with quality, quantity, timeliness, or independence, so the outcomes can be deemed genuine. Result presented at Table 2.

Table 2. Instrument analysis on indicator items and reliable.

Variable	Item	Corrected Item-Total Correlation					
		X1	X2	Y	Z	Description	Cronbach's Alpha
Work Stress	1	0.692				Valid	0.906
	2	0.856				Valid	
	3	0.451				Valid	
	4	0.691				Valid	
	5	0.891				Valid	
	6	0.893				Valid	
Work Environment	1		0.643			Valid	0.903
	2		0.815			Valid	
	3		0.604			Valid	
	4		0.641			Valid	
	5		0.832			Valid	
	6		0.842			Valid	
	7		0.606			Valid	
Job Satisfaction	1			0.651		Valid	0.815
	2			0.401		Valid	
	3			0.661		Valid	
	4			0.670		Valid	
	5			0.651		Valid	
Employees Commitment	1				0.808	Valid	0.802
	2				0.408	Valid	
	3				0.462	Valid	
	4				0.831	Valid	
Critical Value α = 0.05						>0.30	>0.60

The corrected overall correlation value for all variable markers of labor stress, working environment, employee satisfaction, and commitment of government professionals in the field of the cargo section, which is evaluated as a measurement, yields a Cronbach's Alpha coefficient value 90.6 > 0.06. Work stress has a Cronbach's Alpha value of 0.906 > 0.60, the work environment has a Cronbach's Alpha value of 0.903 > 0.06, job satisfaction has a Cronbach's Alpha value of 0.815 > 0.06, and employee commitment has a Cronbach's Alpha value of 0.802 > 0.06. As shown in Figure 2, the route model analysis results are consistent with the variable connection model based on the conceptual framework model that describes the effects of work stress and the work environment on job satisfaction and employee commitment. Using the overt and covert substructure models impacts among variables given in the model of the connection among factors for the effects of job stress and the workplace environment on employees' commitment via job satisfaction can be examined similarly according to Table 2, the standardized coefficients beta on the factors of job stress among government employees are 0.538, and their influence is demonstrated on the value of t = 5.889 with a critical threshold of 0.05. Work stress has a positive and large and direct impact on job satisfaction, according to the findings of this study. However, the results of this study support the findings of (Ćulibrk et al.,2018; Wang et al.,2020; Ahmed al., 2019), that work stress employees face is not a burden but that the work performed during the company furnishes job satisfaction as per worker wishes, and that the discoveries of Mansoor et al. (2011) and Dehghan et al (2016), which uncovered that job pressure negatively affects job satisfaction since workers have not felt that they have gotten job satisfaction true to form. The effect is also demonstrated on the value of t = 2.088 with a significant level of 0.05, as evidenced by standardized coefficients beta on the environment variable employee with a significant level of 0.191, and the impact is also shown on the value of t = 2.088 with a significant scale of 0.05. According to the findings of this study, the work environment of government employees has a favorable and considerable straight impact on job satisfaction. The results of this particular research are consistent with Reisel et al. (2010) and Davidescu et al (2020). The standardized beta coefficients on job stress variables of government employees of 0.381 are given in Table 2, and their influence is also demonstrated by the value of t = 4.032 and having a significant threshold of 0.05. According to this study, job stress has a good and sizeable direct influence on employee commitment. This study's results are supported by those of Ates (2016) and Wang (2020) that job stress from a heavy workload does not detract from his desire to finish his task. However, research by Ekienabor (2016) and Ruzungunde et al. (2016) does not support this study because job stress has an impact that is not in line with increased dedication; rather it is progressively creating reduced outcomes.

Similarly, beta standardized coefficients on the variable environment government workers of 0.400 its impact were revealed, as well as on the basis of the value t = 4.235 and a significance level of 0. 05. According to the findings of this study, workers' work environments have a direct positive and substantial influence on their dedication. Environmental factors that might boost employee job activities are influenced by a good working environment for cargo personnel. Leaders' interactions with their followers have the potential to generate positive and important outcomes. The findings of this study hold up the Ahmed et al's (2019) findings that a peaceful, pleasant, or uninterrupted work environment might favorably affect employees' dedication to their job, and vice versa. Due to the working environment which is thought to be capable of producing ease and quiet with no disruption is not favorably received, the commitment results do not demonstrate good outcomes, this study's conclusions do not reinforce the notion of Zehra et al (2017).

Table 3 shows the effect of the beta standardized coefficients on the variable work satisfaction of 0.564, as well as the value that is t = 6.140 with a significance level of 0.05.

According to the findings of this study, work satisfaction has a favorable and considerable direct impact on government employees' commitment. The results corroborate Suma and Lesha (2013) and Hedayat et al. (2018). Table 2 shows that job stress has a direct and positive and substantial impact on government employees' commitment by work satisfaction, with a standardized coefficient beta of 0.305. This beneficial effect of work stress contributes to organizational performance by instilling passion for work, providing guidance and direction, and resulting in strong dedication, which can lead to reasonable job satisfaction in sustaining the company. The results are consistent in this research with the research of Wang et al (2020). Work stress is a job load to achieve organizational goals, yet it can generate commitment as an organization's leaders must be sufficiently satisfied, and as employees anticipate it, they do not feel anxious, disappointed, mentally or physically tired of the burdensome task. Alternatively, the results of this study contradict the findings of Bhatti et al., (2016) and Ruzungunde et al., (2016), because the work stress that employees experience as a result of their workload is not aligned with organizational goals, resulting in low job satisfaction and a lack of employee commitment. Table 2 shows that the working environment has a substantial and beneficial impact on government employees' commitment via job satisfaction, with a standardized beta value of 0.108.

Workers are more enthusiastic to work as a consequence of the beneficial impact of this work environment, as sought by employees after achieving job satisfaction that leads to high commitment. Comfort, tranquility, and freedom from the sensation of being disturbed are all factors that contribute to employees' dedication. Due to a pleasant work atmosphere is bolstered by how satisfied employee is with the work performed in accordance with organizational objectives. The findings of this study are consistent with research by Ardakani et al. (2012), Almanae (2013), Widodo (2014), Tjio and Anggela (2017), which found that a pleasant working environment and a sense of peace at work can completely change how the employee behaves, allowing them to be more passionate, centered on work, and avoid boredom with the work given to them, even if it is considered burdensome, resulting in increased in the job satisfaction.

Figure 2. Model analysis of the relationship path between variables.

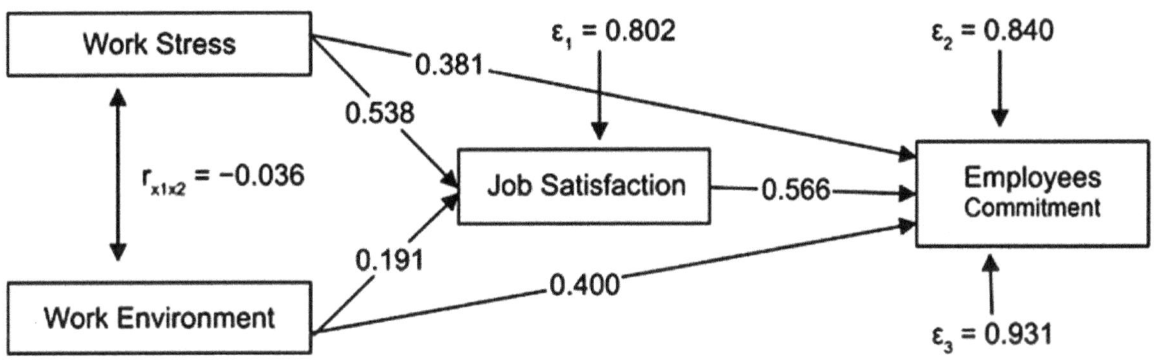

Table 3. An evaluation of the relationship between work stress and the work environment and employee commitment as measured by job satisfaction.

Variable Effect	Causality Effect			Test Result	Description	R	R Square
	Direct	Inderect	Total				
X1 on Y	0.538	-	0.538	Ho rejected	Significant	0.592	0.354
X2 on Y	0.191	-	0.191	Ho rejected	Significant		
X1 on Z	0.381	-	0.381	Ho rejected	Significant	0.541	0.294
X2 on Z	0.400	-	0.400	Ho rejected	Significant		
Y on Z	0.566	-	0.566	Ho rejected	Significant	0.562	0.320
X1 on Z	0.538	0.305	0.597	Ho rejected	Significant		0.112
X2 on Z	0.191	0.108	0.626	Ho rejected	Significant		

CONCLUSION

The government considers work stress and work environment as essential workplace issues, especially in the public sector. In practice, the cargo department has significantly contributed to adjustments and improvements in employee engagement. This process involved a connection between variables and staff workload, resulting in positive commitment since the cargo section's services can be handled correctly and efficiently. This is owing to the leadership's proximity to its members and the duty of monitoring, leading, and supporting their views. The more the management engages with its people, the more attention and interaction of the employees (members) have with everyone in the company, ensuring that the job stress load is not considerably increased. Employees, alternatively, are very comfortable with the circumstances they are working in, peer collaboration, and the task itself, resulting in higher job satisfaction and the ability to enhance the outcomes of their commitment. No barriers are identified in the working environment, which is the primary necessity for workers in carrying out job tasks.

Employees feel comfortable and peaceful, and disruptions surrounding the office are enjoyable. The working environment is more pleasant, the accessibility of work-related amenities is adequate to fulfill employees' feelings of self-worth, and work happiness boosts employee passion and pleasure. Once the organization pays excellent attention to employee satisfaction, the level of satisfaction will increase, and the dissatisfaction level will be decreased. As a result, the beneficial impact of stress caused by work and the working environment on employee commitment to the integrity of various products cannot be detached from the happiness of employees doing their tasks.

RECOMMENDATIONS

Following the findings and Research Discussion, intended that the organization's headship would have a better understanding of the obstacles that employees encounter due to their employment. Employees also should avoid work-driven stress and seek refuge in relief. It requires concentration and support from those who can always engage and give items to help employees improve their dedication to the task they accomplish. Furthermore, the company must promote calmer, more pleasant working circumstances without leading employees to worry, as well as offer facilities for even more comfortable working conditions to devote more focus to work happiness for employees. Employees may create better commitment on their own.

RESEARCH LIMITATIONS

This study was carried out to gain better understand of the workers at cargo section in term of commitment. As a consequence, the researcher picked this area because it offer vital role to the success of Saudi Ports Authority among other ports in the world

ACKNOWLEDGMENT

The author states that he has no conflicts of interest with relation to the publishing of this paper.

REFERENCES

Abdulkhaliq, S. S., & Mohammadali, Z. M. (2019). The Impact of Job Satisfaction on Employees' Performance: A Case Study of Al Hayat Company-Pepsi Employees in Erbil, Kurdistan Region-Iraq. *Management and Economics Review*, *4*(2), 163–176. doi:10.24818/mer/2019.12-07

Ahmed, N., Ashraf, M., & Mangi, R. A. (2019). Relationship of working environment, employee empowerment, training & development and organizational commitment. *Pakistan Business Review*, *21*(3), 113–125.

Alzalabani, A. H. (2017). Antecedents of job satisfaction in Saudi Arabia: Impact of industrial sector. *International Journal of Business and Management*, *12*(11), 61–72. doi:10.5539/ijbm.v12n11p61

Amin, F. A. B. M. (2021). A Review Of The Job Satisfaction Theory For Special Education Perspective. [TURCOMAT]. *Turkish Journal of Computer and Mathematics Education*, *12*(11), 5224–5228.

As'Ad, M. (2004). *Seri ilmu sumber daya manusia: Psikologi rganiza. Edisi Keempat. Cetakan Kesembilan [Human resource science series: Organiza psychology, fourth ed., ninth printing]*. Liberty.

Ates, Ö. T., & Ihtiyaroglu, N. (2019). Analysis of the Relationship between Stress and Organizational Commitment in Employees: A Meta-Analysis Study. *Journal of Education and Training Studies*, *7*(1), 94–106. doi:10.11114/jets.v7i1.3702

Bhatti, M. H., Bhatti, M. H., Akram, M. U., Hashim, M., & Akram, Z. (2016). Relationship between job stress and organizational commitment: An empirical study of banking sector. *Journal of Business Management and Economics*, *7*(1), 29–37.

Brayfield, A. H., & Rothe, H. F. (1951). An index of job satisfaction. *The Journal of Applied Psychology*, *35*(5), 307–311. doi:10.1037/h0055617

Brzoska, P., & Razum, O. (2010). *Validity issues in quantitative migrant health research: The example of illness perceptions* (Vol. 58). Peter Lang.

Buchari, E., & Basri, H. (2015). The importance of human resources development and its impact in increasing of national port productivity. *Procedia Engineering*, *125*, 519–525. doi:10.1016/j.proeng.2015.11.049

Ćulibrk, J., Delić, M., Mitrović, S., & Ćulibrk, D. (2018). Job satisfaction, organizational commitment and job involvement: The mediating role of job involvement. *Frontiers in Psychology*, *9*, 132. doi:10.3389/fpsyg.2018.00132 PMID:29503623

Dane, F. C. (1990). *Research methods*. Thomson Brooks/Cole Publishing Co.

Davidescu, A. A., Apostu, S. A., Paul, A., & Casuneanu, I. (2020). Work flexibility, job satisfaction, and job performance among Romanian employees—Implications for sustainable human resource management. *Sustainability*, *12*(15), 6086. doi:10.3390u12156086

Dehghan, H., Mobinyzadeh, V., & Habibi, P. (2016). The effects of heat stress on job satisfaction, job performance and occupational stress in casting workers. *Jundishapur Journal of Health Sciences, 8*(3).

Drucker, P. (2012). *Management*. Routledge. doi:10.4324/9780080939063

Ekienabor, E. E. (2016). Impact of job stress on employees' productivity and commitment. *International journal for research in business, management, and accounting, 2*(5), 124-133.

Elentably, A. (2015). Strategic and Operational Plan Implementation of Seaports (Utilization Jeddah Port). TransNav. *International Journal on Marine Navigation and Safety of Sea Transportation, 9*(4).

Eriksson, P., & Kovalainen, A. (2015). Qualitative methods in business research: A practical guide to social research. *Sage (Atlanta, Ga.)*.

Essiam, J. O., Mensah, M. E., Kudu, L. K., & Gyamfi, G. D. (2015). Influence of job stress on job satisfaction among university staff: Analytical evidence from a public university in Ghana. International Journal of Economics. *Commerce and Management*, *3*(2), 1–15.

Gibson, J., Ivancevich, J., & Konopaske, R. (2011). *Organizations: Behavior, structure, processes*. McGraw-Hill Higher Education.

Greenberg, J. (2010). Organizational injustice as an occupational health risk. *The Academy of Management Annals*, *4*(1), 205–243. doi:10.5465/19416520.2010.481174

Greer, C. R. (2021). *Strategic human resource management*. Pearson Custom Publishing.

Hair, J. F., Anderson, R. E., Babin, B. J., & Black, W. C. (2010). *Multivariate data analysis: A global perspective* (*Vol. 7*). Pearson.

Hedayat, A., Sogolitappeh, F. N., Shakeri, R., Abasifard, M., & Khaledian, M. (2018). Relationship between Organizational Commitment and Job Satisfaction. *International Letters of Social and Humanistic Sciences, 81*.

Ismail, A., & Razak, M. R. A. (2016). Effect of job satisfaction on organizational commitment. *Management & Marketing Journal, 14*(1).

Jayaweera, T. (2015). Impact of work environmental factors on job performance, mediating role of work motivation: A study of hotel sector in England. *International Journal of Business and Management, 10*(3), 271. doi:10.5539/ijbm.v10n3p271

Jehangir, M., Kareem, N., Khan, A., Jan, M. T., & Soherwardi, S. (2011). Effects of job stress on job performance & job satisfaction. *Interdisciplinary Journal of Contemporary Research in Business, 3*(7), 453–465.

Kattuah, S. E. (2013). *Workforce training for increased productivity in Saudi Arabia* [Doctoral dissertation, Victoria University].

Krejcie, R. V., & Morgan, D. W. (1970). Determining sample size for research activities. *Educational and Psychological Measurement, 30*(3), 607–610. doi:10.1177/001316447003000308

Kurniawaty, K., Ramly, M., & Ramlawati, R. (2019). The effect of work environment, stress, and job satisfaction on employee turnover intention. *Management Science Letters, 9*(6), 877–886. doi:10.5267/j.msl.2019.3.001

Mansoor, M., Fida, S., Nasir, S., & Ahmad, Z. (2011). The impact of job stress on employee job satisfaction a study on telecommunication sector of Pakistan. *Journal of Business Studies Quarterly, 2*(3), 50.

McNeill, P. (2006). *Research methods*. Routledge. doi:10.4324/9780203133729

McShane, S., & Glinow, M. A. V. (2017). *Organizational behavior*. McGraw-Hill Education.

Nitisemito, A. S. (2015). *Manajemen Personalia, Cetakan kedelapan [Personal Management, eighth edition]*. Ghalia Indonesia.

Rameshkumar, M. (2020). Employee engagement as an antecedent of organizational commitment–A study on Indian seafaring officers. *The Asian Journal of Shipping and Logistics, 36*(3), 105–112. doi:10.1016/j.ajsl.2019.11.003

Razak, N. A., Ma'amor, H., & Hassan, N. (2016). Measuring reliability and validity instruments of work environment towards quality work life. *Procedia Economics and Finance, 37*, 520–528. doi:10.1016/S2212-5671(16)30160-5

Riaz, M., Ahmad, N., Riaz, M., Murtaza, G., Khan, T., & Firdous, H. (2016). Impact of job stress on employee job satisfaction. *International Review of Management and Business Research, 5*(4), 1370.

Robbins, S. P., & Coulter, M. A. (2012). *Management*. Pearson Education.

Robbins, S. P., & Judge, T. A. (2008). *Organizational behavior* (15th ed.). Prentice Hall.

Robbins, S. P., & Judge, T. A. (2018). *Organizational Behavior* (18th ed.). Pearson Education.

Ruzungunde, V. S., Murugan, C., & Hlatywayo, C. K. (2016). The influence of job stress on the components of organisational commitment of health care personnel in the Eastern Cape province South Africa. [IBER]. *International Business & Economics Research Journal, 15*(5), 219–226. doi:10.19030/iber.v15i5.9780

Schermerhorn, J. R. Jr, Bachrach, D. G., & Wright, B. (2020). *Management*. John Wiley & Sons.

Suma, S., & Lesha, J. (2013). Job satisfaction and organizational commitment: The case of Shkodra municipality. *European Scientific Journal, 9*(17).

Vance, R. J. (2006). *Employee engagement and commitment*, 1-53. SHRM foundation.

Veithzal, R., & Sagala, E. J. (2004). *Manajemen sumber daya manusia untuk perusahaan [Human resource management for companies]*. PT Raja Grafindo Persada.

Venkataraman, P., & Ganapathi, R. (2013). A Study of Job Stress on Job Satisfaction among the Employees of Small Scale Industries. *IOSR Journal of Business and Management, 13*(3), 18–22. doi:10.9790/487X-1331822

Walliman, N. (2010). *Research methods: The basics*. Routledge. doi:10.4324/9780203836071

Wang, P., Chu, P., Wang, J., Pan, R., Sun, Y., Yan, M., Jiao, L., Zhan, X., & Zhang, D. (2020). Association between job stress and organizational commitment in three types of Chinese university teachers: Mediating effects of job burnout and job satisfaction. *Frontiers in Psychology, 11*, 11. doi:10.3389/fpsyg.2020.576768 PMID:33132985

Zehra, S. Z., Ather, M., & Zehra, B. (2017). A correlation between workplace stress and organizational commitment: Doctors response from public and private hospitals in Karachi, Pakistan. MPRA.

APPENDIX

Table 4.

		Strongly Agree	Agree	Neutral	Disagree	Strongly Disagree
Work Stress	I feel comfortable to work with latest technologies.					
	I work for long hours, on overtime and even on holidays.					
	I experience excessive work pressure.					
	I feel great stress on my job.					
	My relationship with colleagues and peers is smooth and friendly.					
	I am able to get the necessary information to perform my job effectively.					
Work Environment	There_are some conditions concerning my job that could be improved.					
	My job is like a hobby to me.					
	My job is usually interesting enough to keep me from getting bored.					
	It seems that my friends are more interested in their jobs.					
	I consider my job rather unpleasant.					
	I enjoy: my work more than my leisure time.					
	I find real enjoyment in my work					

Continued on following page

Table 4. Continued

		Strongly Agree	Agree	Neutral	Disagree	Strongly Disagree
Employees' commitment	I tell my friends this is a good rganization to work for.					
	I feel very little loyalty to this organization					
	I would accept almost any type of job assignment in order to keep working for this organization					
	I find that my values and the organisationís values are very similar.					
	I understand how my job contributes to the organisationís goals and objectives					
Job Satisfaction	I enjoy my work most days.					
	I do interesting and challenging work.					
	I am satisfied with my job.					
	I am noticed when I do a good job					
	I get full credit for the work I do					

Chapter 4
Development of New Energy Vehicles in Entrepreneurial Ecosystem Under the Carbon Neutrality Policy in China

Poshan Yu
https://orcid.org/0000-0003-1069-3675
Soochow University, China & Australian Studies Centre, Shanghai University, China

Xiaochang Chang
Independent Researcher, China

Kudzai Mandizvidza
Independent Researcher, Canada

ABSTRACT

This chapter aims to study how the New Energy Vehicle (NEV) industry is developing in the entrepreneurial ecosystem, under the Carbon Neutrality policy in China. This chapter explores the role of the Chinese Government, post the 14th Five-year plan period, in promoting sustainable development of new energy vehicles. This work also sheds more light on China's policies and how these institutions promote the development of environmental awareness in various industries. The overall effect on the environment of these developments, as well as the impact of China's environmental research and institutional changes of enterprises under the sustainable aims of carbon neutrality, will be discussed. This chapter also collates statistical information mainly on the carbon neutrality, carbon trading market, development of new energy vehicles and ESG investment. Cases from China are presented for deeper and funneled insights. The chapter also provides suggestions for the development of new energy vehicles and investment under China's environment-based ecosystems.

DOI: 10.4018/978-1-6684-7422-8.ch004

INTRODUCTION

The ecological environment is the foundation of human survival and development, and it refers to the sum of human society and the various natural factors that surround it (Wang & Zhao, 2016). China's economy has experienced great development since its reformation and opening to international markets. For instance, since 1978, China's economy has witnessed significant growth and its gross domestic product (GDP) now ranks second in the world (Bamisile et al., 2020; Zhang & Hao, 2020). Overall, China's GDP trajectory shows some rapid growth from about 364.5 billion Yuan in 1978 to about 14700 billion Yuan as of 2020. The country's contribution to the global GDP over the same period, also shows remarkable growth, with an increase from about 1.75% in 1978 to about 17.4% in 2020 (NBS, 2020). These and other indicators qualify China as the largest exporter and 33rd most complex economy in the world (Bamisile et al., 2020).

However, such economic growth does not come on a silver platter; with energy consumption in China's economy expecting to increase by 28% - 29% from 2017 to 2040 (Bamisile et al., 2020; Kennedy et al., 2020), many environmental problems are inevitable. Some obvious impacts of such growth and industrialisation, include severe environmental pollution, excessive resources waste and deterioration of ecological environment (Yang, 2013; Fan et al., 2019). On the other hand, environmental hazards increase great concerns due to the ripple effects of the resultant problems caused by economic development, such as air pollution (PM2.5), higher carbon emission (CO2 emission) (Chien et al., 2021a; Chien et al., 2021b; Li et al., 2021b), and greenhouse gas (GHG) (Bamisile et al., 2020; Malla & Brewin, 2020). As part of the country's mitigation strategies, the 18th National Congress of the Communist Party of China attached great importance to ecological construction (Wu et al., 2020a; Wu et al., 2020b), which meant a turning point in the process of China's ecological protection and the stricter ecological supervision systems.

China's economic growth continues to gain velocity, despite the influence of the outbreak of Covid-19. In 2020 for instance, China was the only country to achieve economic growth globally (Statistical Analysis Division, 2021). There is general consensus among the world economy, on the other hand, to achieve green economic recovery (International Environmental Protection Organization, 2021), thus China alike is faced with an increased priority to boost its green initiatives. In this process, the Chinese President Xi Jinping pledged at the UN General Assembly that China will reach their "carbon peak" in 2030, as well as achieve the goal of "carbon neutralization" by 2060. Such commitment sent a clear signal to other countries that China alike, would contribute to coping with climate problems and promoting economic "green recovery". The proposal of the goal of carbon neutralization will raise China's green development strategy to a new level and clarify the tone of China's development in the coming decades (Yu, Jiao & Sampat, 2022). Under the goal of "double carbon", China should establish a green, low-carbon and circular economic system, and establish a clean, low-carbon, efficient and safe modern energy production and consumption system.

China's 14th Five Year Plan is the top-level policy guiding the development of the 14th Five Year Plan. Based on the five-year plan at the national level, energy, ecological civilization, industry, transportation, construction, social development and other fields will also formulate their own five-year plans. Provinces and cities will also formulate local five-year plans based on their own positioning, current situation, and development objectives. During the 14th Five Year Plan period, the main task of China's economic development is to change the mode of economic development, vigorously develop green economy and low-carbon economy, reduce energy consumption per unit of GDP by 13.5% and carbon emissions by 18%, and achieve carbon peak as soon as possible. Carbon neutralization lays a good foundation (China

Environmental Protection Industry Research Institute, 2020). With the flourishing of remote sensing technology, the methods of ecological-environment assessment increasingly improve (Foody, 2007; Zhang et al., 2017), which makes it easier for Chinese government to regulate and monitor whether developments of the enterprises at least meet the minimal ecological requirements.

In the context of carbon peak and carbon neutralization, the demand for clean and low-carbon new energy is rampant, to replace traditional fossil-based energy. All new source fields in China are expected to receive a new round of policy support and enjoy the dividends brought by a new round of energy reform. In this situation, there are good investment opportunities in green energy and related supporting facilities such as photovoltaic, wind power and nuclear power (Yu, Tang, Ahuja & Chang, 2022). As technological development become critical in achieving carbon neutrality (Chien et al., 2021a; Chien et al., 2021b; Chien et al., 2021c; Ji et al., 2021; Li et al., 2021a; Umar et al., 2021), transportation mode continually updates itself to meet the requirements of environmental improvement. This manifests through increasing popularity of greener transportation technology such as subways and also the development of new energy vehicles (NEVs), which become among others, national key projects of environmental protection in China.

Regulations also play an important part when it comes to development of NEVs (Yu, Xu, Cheng & Sampat, 2023). Meanwhile, environmental, social and governance (ESG) investment under the background of carbon neutralization has gradually attracted the attention of investors (Yu, Jiang, Mandizvidza & Chen, 2022). ESG provides a consensus information disclosure and clarifies the framework for carbon neutralization, in unison with providing investment tools for market investors, which is conducive to building a sustainable financial investment ecology. At the same time, ESG's investment in new energy has also attracted extensive attention in various industries. NEVs are an important part of new energy investment. The implementation and deployment of carbon peak and carbon neutralization strategies provide important opportunities for China's ESG investment and development (Yu, Weng & Ahuja, 2022).

CARBON NEUTRALITY

Carbon neutralization, originated in Samso Island, Denmark in 1997, which involves the use of methods of carbon capturing, storage and conversion, to offset the generated carbon dioxide (CO2) within a certain period of time, to realize "zero emission" of greenhouse gases goals (Wuet al., 2022). To better realize the Paris Agreement (PA) as adopted in the Paris Climate Change Conference on December 12, 2015, which aimed to control the rise of the global average temperature within 2 degrees Celsius compared with the level before industrialization, and strive to control the temperature rise within 1.5 degrees Celsius (Salvia et al., 2021), on September 22, 2020, the Chinese government proposed directly at the 75th United Nations General Assembly that China will strive to reach the peak of carbon dioxide emissions by 2030 and strive to achieve carbon neutrality by 2060.

Figure 1. Proportion of China's greenhouse gas emissions
Source: https://iea.uoregon.edu, 2019

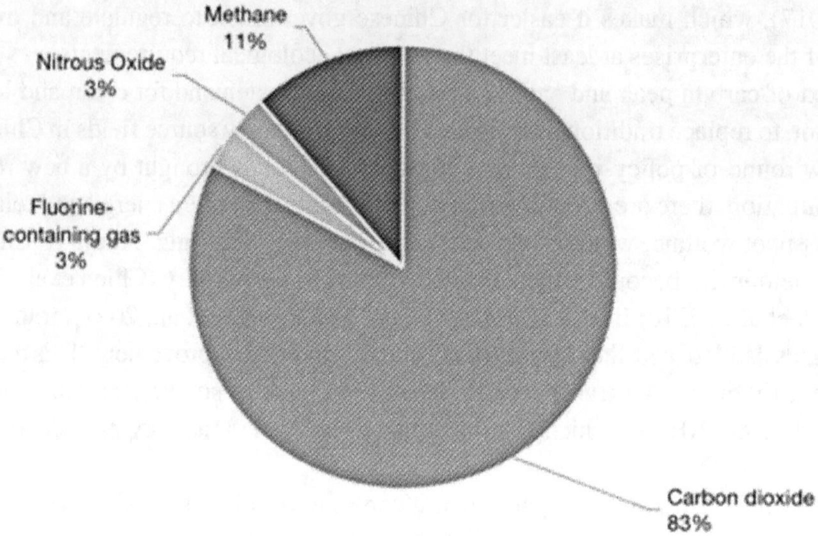

According to data from the Netherlands Evaluation Agency, carbon dioxide accounted for 82.6% of my country's greenhouse gas emissions in 2019. About 10 percentage points higher than the global average. In addition to carbon dioxide, 11.6% of carbon emissions come from methane, and about 3.0% and 2.8% come from nitrous oxide and fluorinated gases as shown in Figure 1. Figure 2 analyses carbon dioxide emission sources in China as of 2018 according to the International Energy Agency.

Figure 2. Analysis of carbon emission sources in China
Source: International Energy Agency, 2018

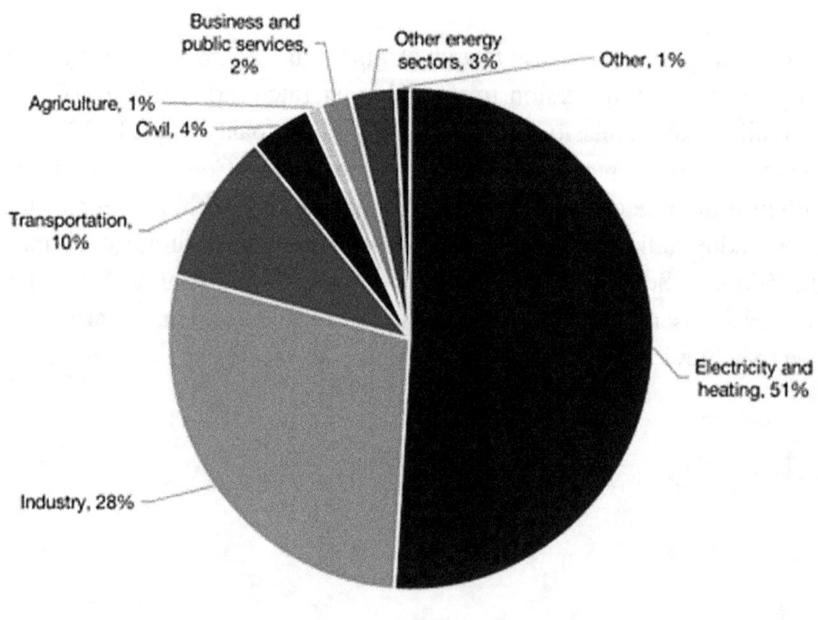

According to International Energy Agency (IEA) data: In 2018, China's carbon emissions from electricity and heating accounted for about 51%, industry accounted for 28%, followed by transportation, civil, other energy sectors, business and public services, agriculture, etc., accounting for 10%, respectively. 4%, 3%, 2%, 1% as displayed in Figure 2. Figure 3 summarises the research on China's 2030 energy and power development plan and outlook for 2060, which helps us understand the country's energy structure as of 2020. According to Figure 3, coal dominates China's energy source, followed by hydropower, wind energy, solar energy, natural gas, bioenergy and others, nuclear power and hydrogen energy. Efforts are aimed at reducing reliance on fossil fuels and shifting towards greener alternatives as shown in Figures 4 and 5. As China strives to reach the peak of carbon dioxide emissions by 2030, Figure 4 shows that reliance on solar shall have more or less the same magnitude as coal in the country's energy mix. The joint contribution of cleaner energy such as solar, wind and hydropower is expected to surpass the use of coal by the time China reaches the peak of carbon dioxide emissions. As China aims to achieve carbon neutrality by 2060, Figure 5 shows that solar shall be the most dominant source of energy contributing about 47% of the country's energy mix. Wind shall also increase in importance as an energy source, followed by hydropower and others. Figure 5 shows that no coal shall be used for energy beyond the carbon neutrality mark.

In a nutshell, with the continuous advancement of supply side structural reform and the rapid development of new energy in recent years, the proportion of coal in China's energy structure has decreased, though it still maintains the dominant position. At the same time, although China follows the international mainstream trend of replacing coal with natural gas and comprehensively promotes the heating reform of "coal to gas", China's low content of natural gas and high external dependence lead to the low proportion of natural gas in China's energy structure, which has caused some obstacles to the energy reform of "coal to gas".

Figure 3. 2020 China's energy structure
Source: Research on China's energy and power development plan in 2030 and outlook for 2060, 2021

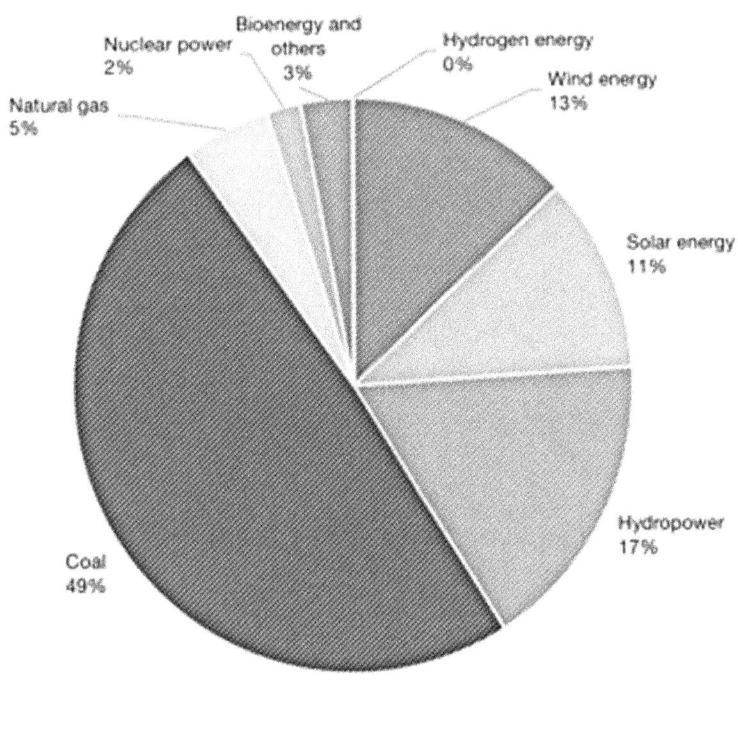

Figure 4. 2030 China's energy structure (Carbon Peak)
Source: Research on China's energy and power development plan in 2030 and outlook for 2060, 2021

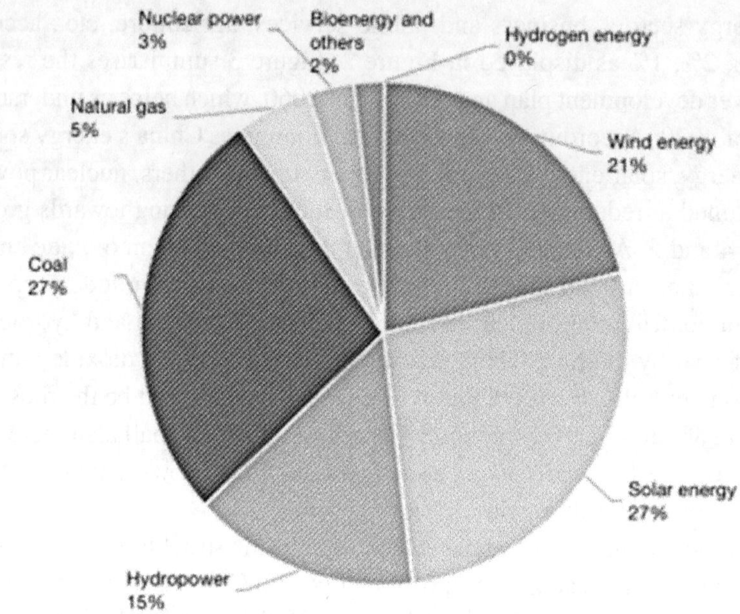

Figure 5. 2060 China's energy structure (Carbon Neutrality)
Source: Research on China's energy and power development plan in 2030 and outlook for 2060, 2021

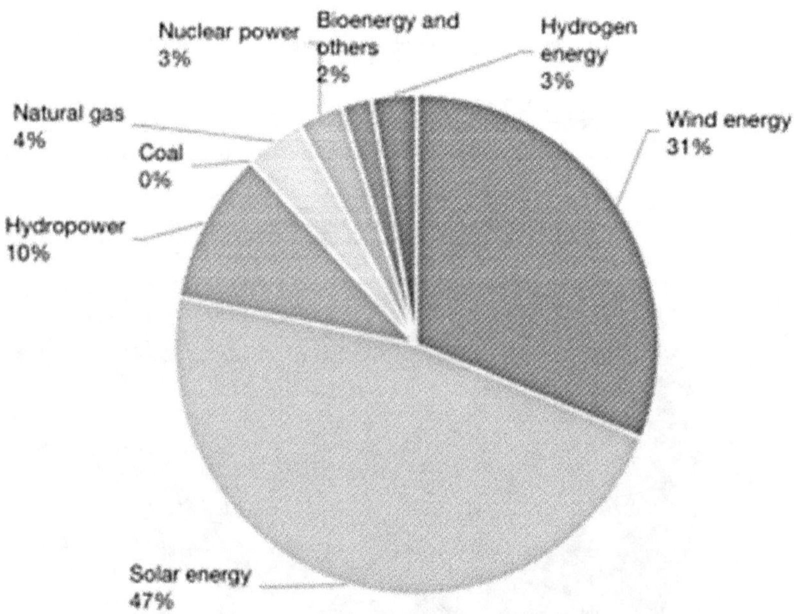

On March 18, 2021, the Global Energy Internet Development Cooperation Organization held the China Carbon Peak Carbon Neutrality Achievement Release and Seminar. According to the plan, China needs to promote the development of clean energy and its consumption. The use of electricity is the leading factor, and part of the main agenda is the decoupling of energy and power development from carbon, as well as the decoupling of economic and social development from carbon emissions. It is estimated that by 2060, under the state of carbon neutrality, coal energy in China's energy structure will completely withdraw. Solar energy (light energy) will account for 47% and wind energy shall contribute 31%, occupying the top two positions in China's energy structure as illustrated in Figures 3, 4 and 5.

All these data draw us to the conclusions that if industries would want to maintain sustainability in China during the next three to four decades, they should pay more attention to energy innovation and optimize their corporate facilities and endeavors towards reducing carbon emissions. Meanwhile, increasing the innovative use of solar energy, wind energy, biomass, hydrogen energy and other energy sources are also essential (Yu, Liu, Mahendran & Lu, 2022). These will fundamentally adapt to China's basic environmental policies in the next three to four decades. Development of NEVs in China is not an exception either, henceforth the need for them to meet the basic requirements of China's carbon neutralization policy.

CARBON TRADING MARKET ANALYSIS

The National Carbon Emissions Trading Market (National Carbon Market) is a major institutional innovation for the country to control greenhouse gas emissions through market mechanisms and promote green and low-carbon development. Beijing Green Exchange is the first batch of China's voluntary emission reduction trading institutions recorded by the National Development and Reform Commission. On November 28, 2013, Beijing Carbon Emission Rights Market was officially opened for trading. On July 16, 2021, the National Unified Carbon Emission Trading Market was officially launched in Shanghai Environment and Energy Exchange, and the world's largest carbon trading market was born.

As of December 10, 2021 the total turnover of the national carbon market's carbon emission allowance (CEA) was 7.521219 million tons, with a total turnover of 308.6 million yuan, a new high since the opening of the National Carbon Emission Trading Market on July 16, 2021. The trading activity of the national carbon market continue to rise with energy industry welcoming the "golden period" of rapid growth. With the implementation of carbon peak schemes in key industries and the continuous expansion of the national carbon market, there may be greater structural opportunities for new energy industrial chains such as NEVs.

Carbon peak and carbon neutralization involve the grid connection needs of industry, transportation, energy, agriculture, construction, consumption, and other industries. There are many ways to realize this, including energy substitution, source reduction, recycling, energy conservation and efficiency improvement, process transformation, carbon capture, etc. The realization of carbon neutralization involves many industries and covers three major links:

Carbon Sources

China will reform the energy structure and replace traditional fossil energy with low-carbon energy and zero carbon energy. With the declining demand for traditional energy such as oil and natural gas, the concentration of traditional energy industry may increase rapidly, and leading enterprises in coal, oil and natural gas industries may show obvious advantages. To achieve carbon neutrality, China's energy structure will undergo major changes; the demand for traditional energy will continue to decline, and the inefficient and backward production capacity will be gradually eliminated. With the continuous improvement of industry concentration, industry giants with multiple advantages such as capital and technology will achieve better development. Specifically, the carbon emissions of diesel, gasoline, natural gas and liquefied petroleum gas account for a relatively large proportion of the total carbon emissions, and the concentration of these industries may take the lead in improving the situation.

Carbon Application

The application of carbon source in the production process after energy conversion requires continuous energy conversion. At this stage, the focus of carbon emission reduction should be on improving energy efficiency and saving energy. Specifically, it is to promote the transformation and upgrading of manufacturing industry, and the product design is energy-saving oriented.

Carbon Emissions

It is common knowledge that most of traditional production processes produce carbon emissions, which may be in gaseous, solid, or liquid form. Fossil fuels used in industry and electricity are the main source of carbon emissions. The main measure of this sustained discharge is to purify the waste gas and waste. Carbon emissions trading has a significant impact on energy production and consumption (Dutta, 2017). The industrial sector needs to balance energy use costs and carbon emissions to maximize profits (Henriques, 2008).

DEVELOPMENT OF NEW ENERGY VEHICLE

New Energy Vehicle Market

In 2020, the global automobile sales volume reached 77.97 million, and the decline expanded to 13.8% after reaching the peak of 95.66 million in 2017. In 2020, China's automobile market remained stable on the whole, with sales of 25.31 million vehicles, a year-on-year decrease of 1.9%, a decrease of 6.3 percentage points compared with 2019, and the proportion of global automobile sales increased to 32.5%, ranking first in the world for 12 consecutive years. In recent years, the domestic market share of Chinese brand cars has stabilized at about 40%. Many countries around the world regard the development of NEVs as an important strategic measure to deal with climate change and optimize the energy structure. The global NEV market has entered a period of rapid growth, and the market scale has increased year by year. It exceeded 1 million vehicles for the first time in 2017 and 2 million vehicles in 2018. In 2020, against the background of the sharp decline in the global automobile market, the NEV market has a strong development momentum, with a year-on-year increase of 41.6% to 3.07 million vehicles, and the penetration rate increased to 4.0%, 1.6 percentage points higher than that in 2019. NEVs inject new impetus into the development of the world economy as can be seen in Figure 6.

Figure 6. Global new energy vehicle sales and permeability
Source: Ministry of Industry and Information Technology, 2021

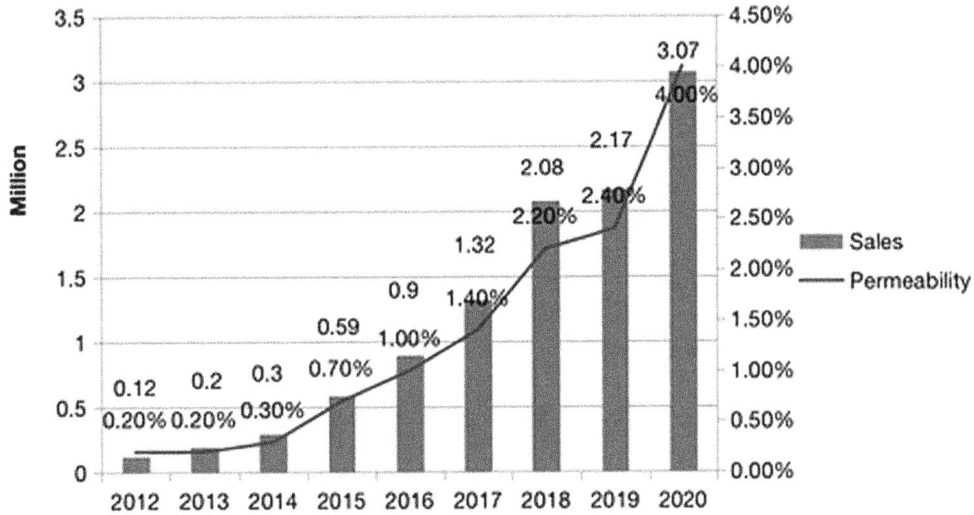

Figure 6 shows an interesting trend in the global NEV sales and permeability where both have grown remarkably over the period under study (2012- 2020). This position development is expected to continue owing to the increased demand and need for cleaner transportation. There is a direct correlation between global and the Chinese NEV sales and permeability. From Figure 7, similarities in data behavior can picked from the two markets (China and the globe).

Figure 7. Chinese new energy vehicle sales and permeability
Source: Ministry of Industry and Information Technology, 2021

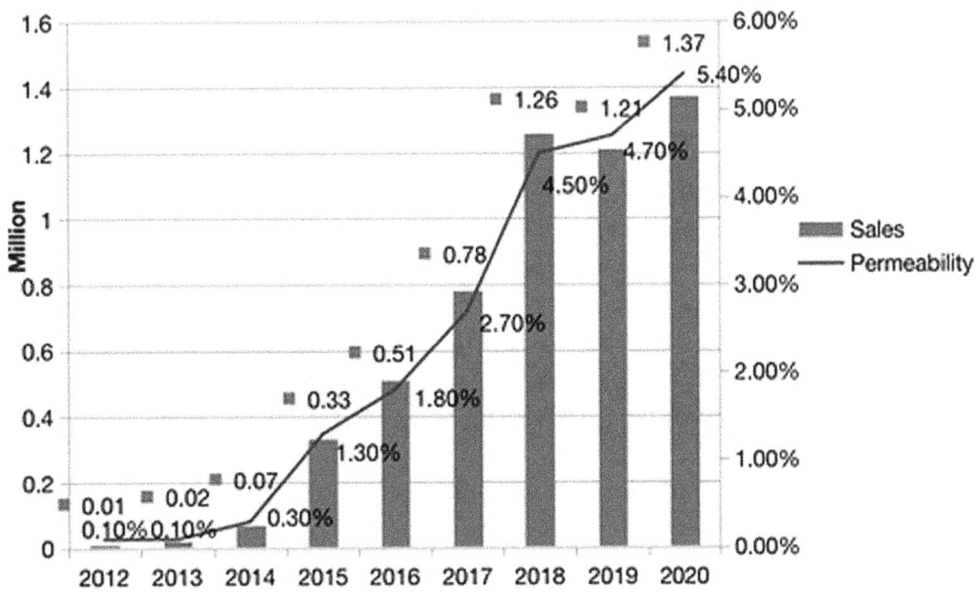

In 2020, the sales volume of NEVs in China was 1.367 million, with a year-on-year increase of 10.9% and the penetration rate also increased to 5.4%. By the end of 2020, the number of NEVs in China had reached 4.92 million, accounting for 1.75% of the total number of vehicles. With the total number of pure electric vehicles standing at 4 million, accounting for 81.32% of the total number of NEVs. The sales volume of NEVs exceeded 1 million for three consecutive years, which shows a sustained and rapid growth trend, thus ranking China first in the world for six consecutive years. China has and shall continue to be the hub of electric transformation of the global automobile industry as evidenced by Figure 7. Figure 8 focuses on China's proportion of sales volume of NEVs in different product categories such

Figure 8. Proportion of sales volume of new energy vehicles in different product categories
Source: Ministry of Industry and Information Technology, 2021

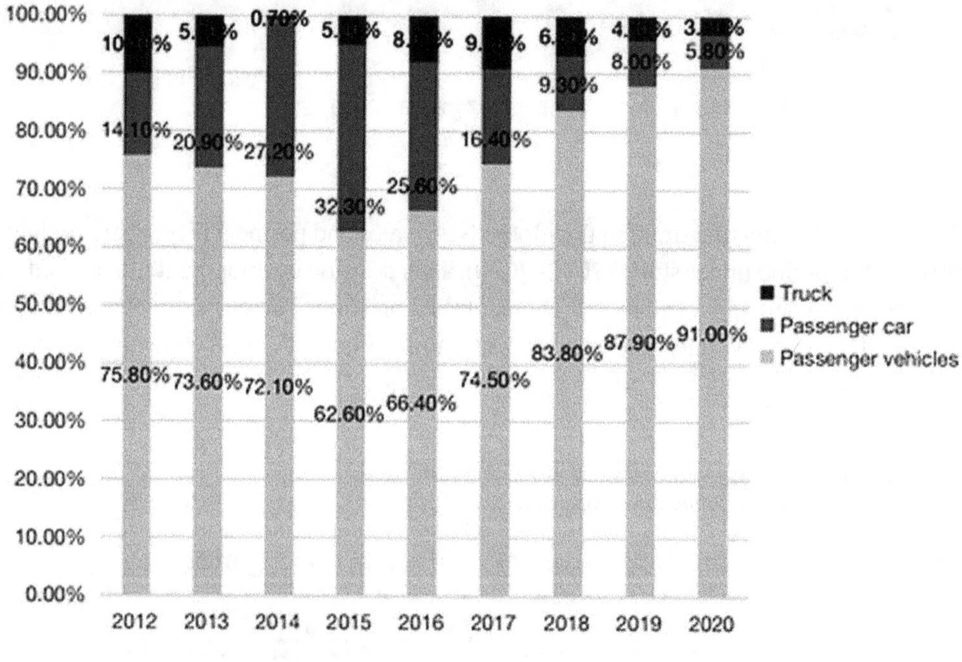

as truck, private passenger cars and public passenger vehicles.

In 2020, the sales volume of NEVs in China was about 1.37 million, and Figure 7 helps us understand that new energy passenger vehicles accounted for about 91.1% of the sales volume of NEVs. The sales volume reached 1.246 million, a year-on-year increase of 14.6%. Meanwhile, in recent years, the process of bus electrification has been promoted rapidly, and the market penetration of new energy buses is high. The sales volume in 2020 was 79000, a year-on-year decrease of 18.4%. The sales volume of new energy trucks was 42000, a year-on-year decrease of 13.9%. Figure 8 attempts to summarise these dynamics between 2012 and 2020.

The promotion and application of NEVs are concentrated in Guangdong, Shanghai, Beijing, Zhejiang and other regions. The consumer of new energy passenger vehicles has gradually changed from the public sphere to private purchase, and the proportion of private consumption has increased significantly by about 70%. The main consumption areas have changed from restricted cities to non-restricted cities.

Private consumption accounts for 60% in non-restricted cities. Non-restricted cities have increased their contribution to the NEV market (China Banking and Insurance Regulatory Commission, 2020).

Technological Development

Green innovation is a technological innovation activity that follows the requirements of ecological and economic development and it realizes resource conservation and environmental protection (Eiadat, 2008). Globally, China's energy production and consumption rank first in the world, and the new total of carbon emissions ranks first in the world. In addition, China has the world's largest clean energy market (State Council, 2020), and its clean energy output ranks first. Therefore, China occupies the core position in the new round of global energy revolution, and China's energy structure is gradually changing towards low-carbon and clean development.

China's clean energy development already has global leadership. In the field of renewable energy, the investment ranks first in the world, and this achievement has been maintained for five years (National Energy Administration, 2021). According to the data released by the Ministry of Ecological Environment, China invests US $100 billion in the field of renewable energy every year, twice that of the United States and the sum of Europe and the United States. As early as 2017, the scale of wind power and photovoltaic power generation in China has ranked first in the world, forming a highly competitive industrial chain. In the semiconductor lighting industry, China has also become the world's largest product research and development (R&D), production base and application market. At the same time, Chinese enterprises are playing a higher and higher role in the global renewable energy value chain. China's investment in overseas renewable energy is also among the highest in the world. In the renewable energy value chain, the advantages of Chinese enterprises are becoming more and more obvious. For example, in the field of solar panel production, Chinese enterprises have low production costs. In the field of wind turbines, with major breakthroughs in related technologies, Chinese enterprises have gradually overtaken American enterprises and they have occupied a leading position in the global market.

NEVs mainly include pure electric vehicles, plug-in hybrid vehicles and fuel cell vehicles. Among them, the development trend of NEV technology includes hybrid electric vehicle technology, pure electric vehicle technology, limited hydrogen fuel vehicle technology, biofuel vehicle technology and solar energy vehicle technology. Figure 9 attempts to visualize the carrying rate of energy-saving technology for gasoline passenger vehicles in China.

Figure 9. Carrying rate of energy-saving technology for gasoline passenger vehicles
Source: Annual report on the development of China's automobile industry, 2021

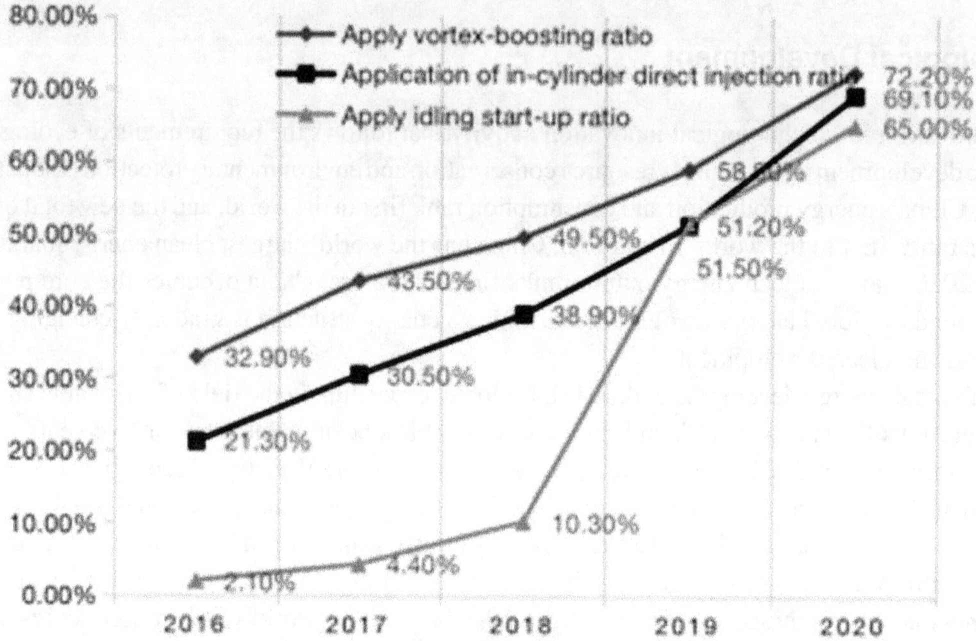

In order to cope with the increasingly severe energy and environmental pressure, the automotive industry has continuously improved the R&D and application capacity of traditional power, hybrid power and vehicle energy-saving technologies, and practiced green and low-carbon development. In terms of traditional power technology, the gradual improvement of engine thermal efficiency drives the improvement of fuel saving level. The main path is to continuously improve the compression ratio, optimize the combustion process, electrification of accessories and low friction technology. The maximum thermal efficiency of gasoline engine and diesel engine mass-produced products independently developed in China has reached 40% and 50% respectively. Turbocharging, in cylinder direct injection, idle start stop and other technologies have been widely used in gasoline engines. According to Figure 9, in 2020, the carrying rates of turbocharging, in cylinder direct injection and idle start stop of gasoline passenger vehicles will be 65.0%, 69.1% and 72.2% respectively (National Energy Information Platform, 2020).

Figure 10. Average driving range of pure electric passenger vehicles and buses
Source: Equipment industry development center of the Ministry of Industry and Information Technology, 2021

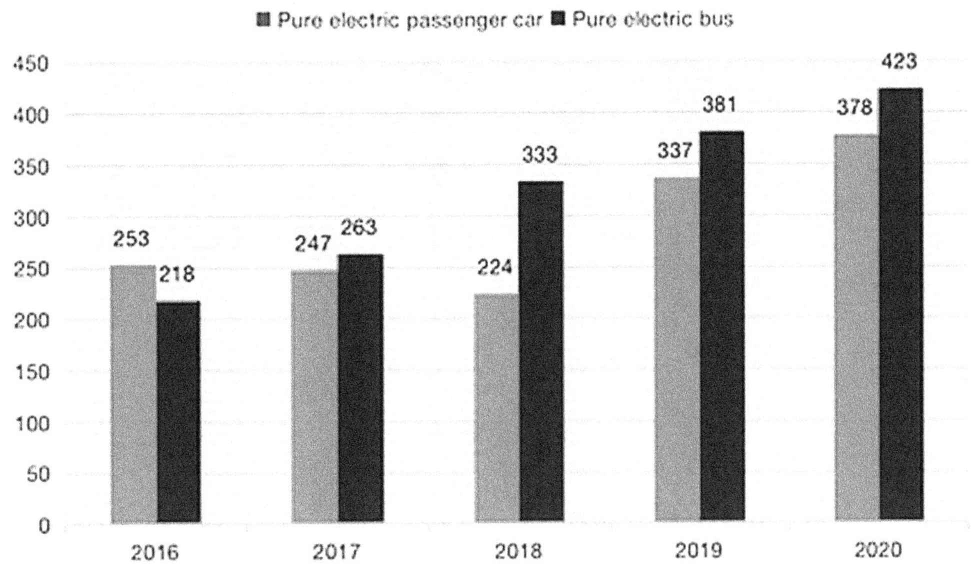

The average driving ranges of the Chinese pure electric passenger vehicles and buses are summarized in Figure 10. Figure 10 generally shows that the driving range of pure electric vehicles in China has increased year by year. According to the model data of the announcement, the average driving range of pure electric passenger vehicles has increased from 253km in 2016 to 378km in 2020, with an increase rate of 49.4%, and that of pure electric buses has increased from 218km in 2016 to 423km in 2020, with an increase rate of 94.0%. The increase of driving range of NEVs is mainly due to the increase of vehicle power and the reduction of power consumption. However, pure electric vehicles still have the problem of reducing driving range in low temperature environment. It is necessary to further develop low-temperature battery and high-efficiency thermal management technology.

Another focus area of the Chinese automobile industry has been to reduce the power consumption of vehicles and Figure 11 shows the average power consumption per 100 km of pure electric passenger vehicles.

Figure 11. Average power consumption per 100 km of pure electric passenger vehicles
Source: Equipment industry development center of the Ministry of Industry and Information Technology, 2021

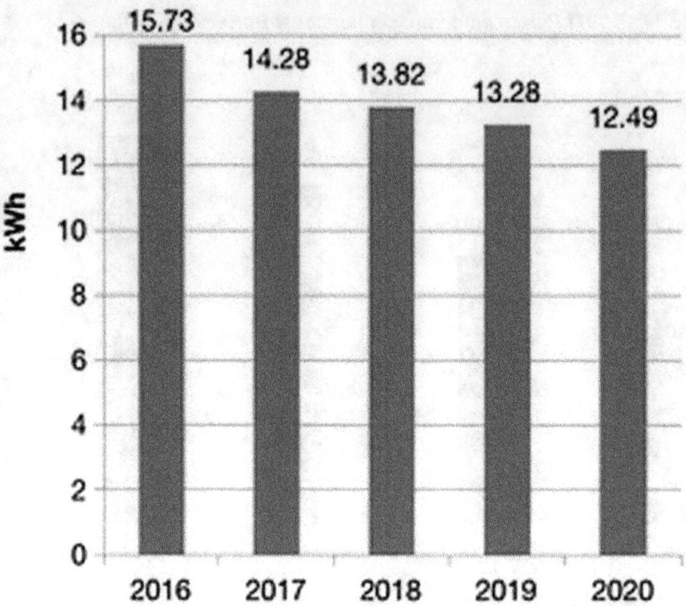

The power consumption of the whole vehicle is reduced by means of pure electric platform and integrated designs, vehicle lightweight and low wind resistance designing, improvement of battery energy density and thermal management technology, optimization of electric drive efficiency and so on. Figure 11 shows that in 2020, the average power consumption of new vehicles under NEDC working conditions was 12.49kwh/100km, a decrease of 20.6% compared with 2016 (Annual report on the development of China's automobile industry, 2021)

Patents

The number of patent applications in the field of NEVs has generally been increasing. Figure 12 shows the relationship between these patent applications in China against global figures.

Figure 12. Number of patent applications in the field of new energy vehicles: The contribution of China to global figures.
Source: CCID think tank, 2021

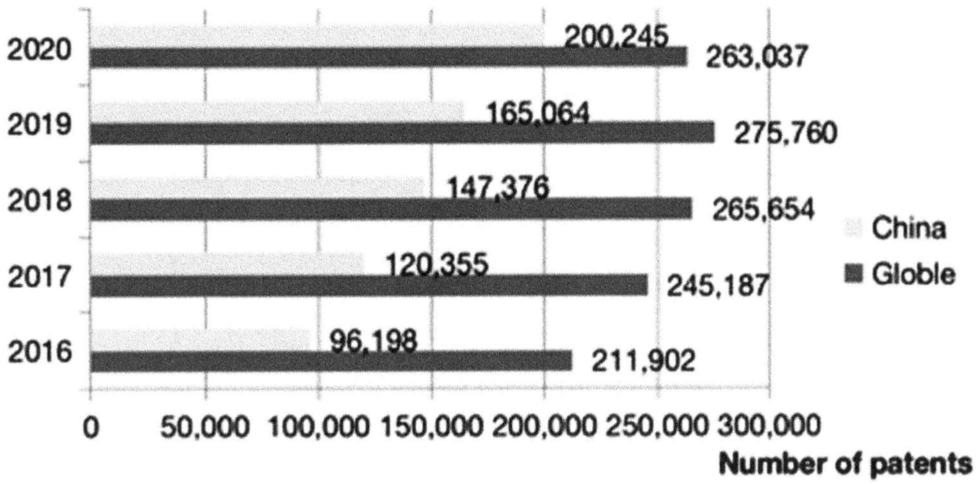

As of 2021, there were about 4.683 million patents in the field of NEVs worldwide, of which 1.197 million were applied by Chinese enterprises. In the past 20 years, patent applications in the field of NEVs have increased year by year, showing a rapid development trend as shown in Figure 12 (CCID think tank, 2021).

With the innovation quality of automobile patents continuing to improve, and the technological innovation ability of automobile enterprises gradually strengthening, Figure 13 compares the automobile patent disclosure and invention authorization, as well as dissects the patents by type.

Figure 13. Automobile patent disclosure and invention authorization
Source: Global automobile patent database service platform, 2020

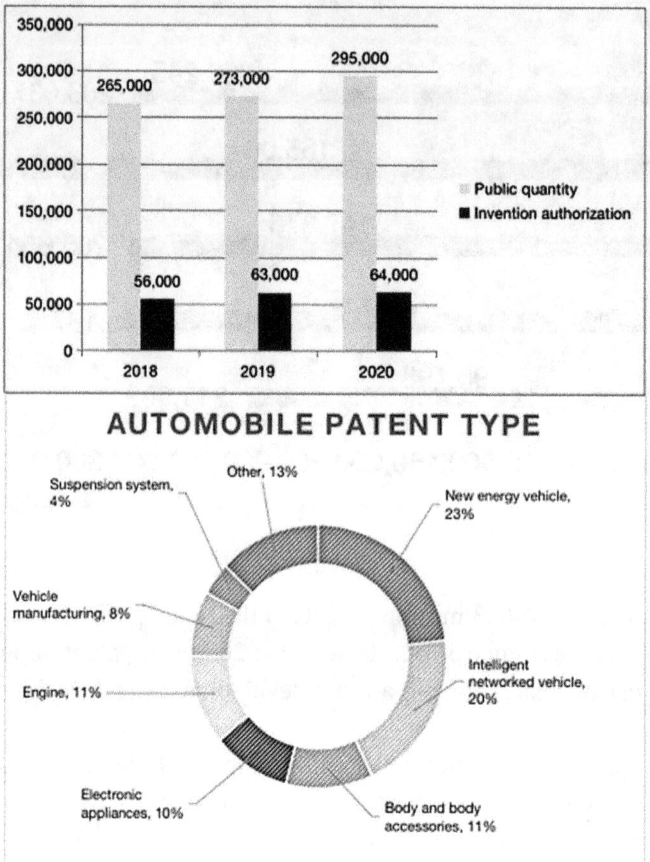

In 2020, the number of automobile patents in China was 295000, with a year-on-year increase of 8.0%, and continued to maintain a steady growth trend. The number of invention patents authorized was 64000, with a year-on-year increase of 2.6%. The patents of NEVs and intelligent networked vehicles accounted for 43%, of which the patent disclosure of NEVs and intelligent networked vehicles increased by 16% and 18% year-on-year. Figure 13 shows a growing number of innovation over time where a relatively stable rate of authorisations remain much less than the total public quantity. The majority of automobile patent applications is dominated by NEV and intelligent networked vehicle categories.

Double Points Policy Support

NEVs have been regarded as an ideal substitute for vehicle exhaust emissions and reducing direct oil demand in the road transportation sector (Wang and Dong, 2016; Choi et al., 2020).

In the context of carbon neutrality, new energy in the transportation industry, including NEVs, new energy batteries and charging piles, has attracted extensive attention, and there are huge investment opportunities in relevant industrial chains. For the transportation industry, replacing fuel vehicles with NEVs is an important measure of carbon emission reduction and an inevitable trend. In recent years,

China's NEV credit policy has been tightened continuously, and this trend will continue for a long time to promote the popularization and application of NEVs.

The new energy automobile industry development plan for 2021-2035, clearly states that "new energy automobile is the only way for China to move from a large automobile country to a powerful automobile country, and it is a strategic measure to deal with climate change and promote green development". The rapid development of NEVs will have a huge demand for upstream batteries, electronic components, and related equipment. At the same time, it will also actively promote the construction of infrastructure such as charging piles. These fields will show good investment opportunities.

In September 2017, the Ministry of industry and information technology, the Ministry of Finance, the Ministry of Commerce, the General Administration of Customs and the General Administration of Market Supervision jointly issued "the measures for the parallel management of average fuel consumption and NEV points of passenger vehicle enterprises". The NEV point system, which has played a positive role in guiding the progress of energy-saving technology in the automotive industry, has also promoted the development of NEVs industry. To adapt to the new situation of industrial development, further optimize the management mechanism and better promote the high-quality development of energy-saving and NEV industry, the NEV points system was revised in 2020 and Figure 14 shows the development of the NEV points.

Figure 14. Proportion of new energy vehicle points
Source: China Daily, 2020

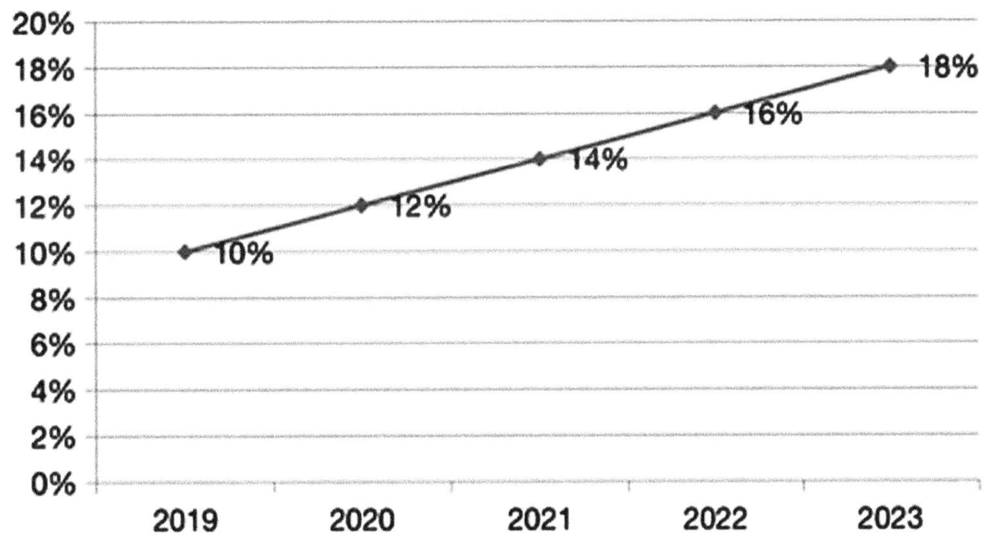

This revision proposed NEVs and 2021-2023's integral ratio requirements increased to 14%, 16% and 18% respectively as shown in Figure 14. The core of this policy is the average fuel consumption points and NEV points, hence the name, the double points policy. The double score policy is an assessment system. The assessment indicators are the average fuel consumption score and the score of NEVs. The purpose is to promote enterprises to develop NEVs, so as to improve the energy-saving level of passenger vehicles and alleviate the pressure on energy and the environment. Enterprises should strive to achieve zero or even positive points for average fuel consumption and NEVs, otherwise they will be punished.

The punishment includes the suspension of the declaration of high fuel consumption products and the production of high fuel consumption products. According to the relevant regulations, the car enterprises should clear the negative points by buying points from the positive points car enterprises within 90 days after the announcement of the double points of the previous year. If the negative points are not returned to zero in time, the production of high fuel consumption vehicles must be taken as the punishment.

There are two ways in which car companies with negative points can avoid punishment. Firstly, they can obtain new energy points through the production of NEVs and use the new energy points to bridge the negative fuel consumption points. Secondly, car companies with negative points can go to the carbon emission trading market to find car companies with surplus points then buy some corresponding points, so as to balance out their negative fuel consumption points.

The purpose of the double credit policy is very clear, which is to promote the development of new energy industry, thus enabling car enterprises to strengthen their R&D in NEVs at the expense of their traditional fuel-based counterparts. China issued the double points policy as early as September 2017 and officially implemented it in April 2018. The original intention of the state's dual credit policy has been to improve vehicle efficiency and promote the development of NEVs. The double score policy does not only enable traditional fuel vehicle enterprises to reduce the fuel consumption of vehicles but it also promotes improvement of their fuel consumption scores. It is envisaged that car manufacturers will in response, produce more cost-effective NEVs as much as possible to improve their energy score, thus helping encourage environmental protection.

Since 2020, Tesla's revenue of "carbon emission credit line" alone has exceeded US $4 billion (about 26 billion yuan), and international auto giants such as Volkswagen, Honda, and General Motors have traded with it. Figure 15 shows the top 10 automobile companies ranked according to their number of positive points as of 2020.

Figure 15. Top 10 positive points automobile companies in 2020
Source: Auto online review, 2021

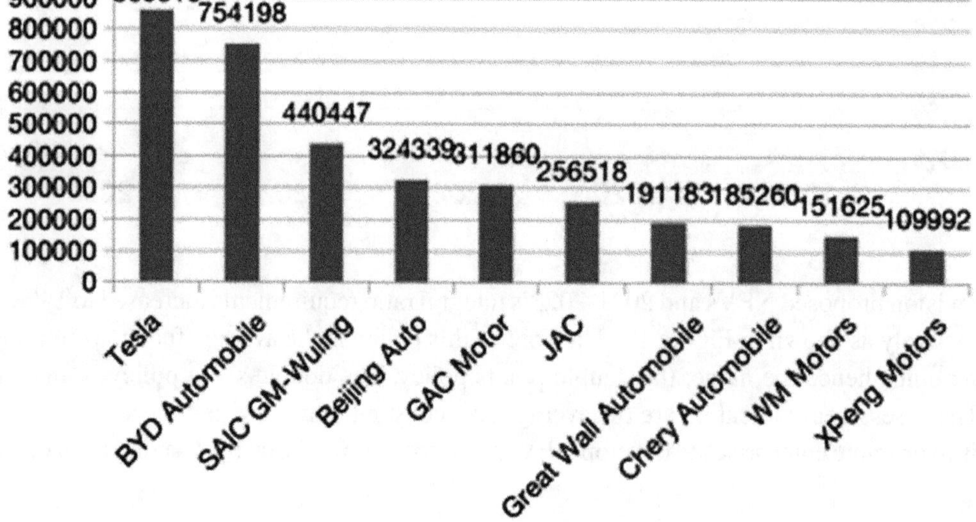

In 2020, Tesla, BYD and SAIC GM-Wuling ranked among the top three in terms of NEV points, with their NEV points reaching 860000, 754000 and 443000 respectively as shown in Figure 15. Figure 16 shows the top 10 automobile companies ranked according to their number of negative points as of 2020. According to Figure 16, a number of companies still had mammoth work, as of 2020, in as far as improving their NEV credit scores is concerned.

Figure 16. Top 10 negatives points automobile companies in 2020
Source: Auto online review, 2021

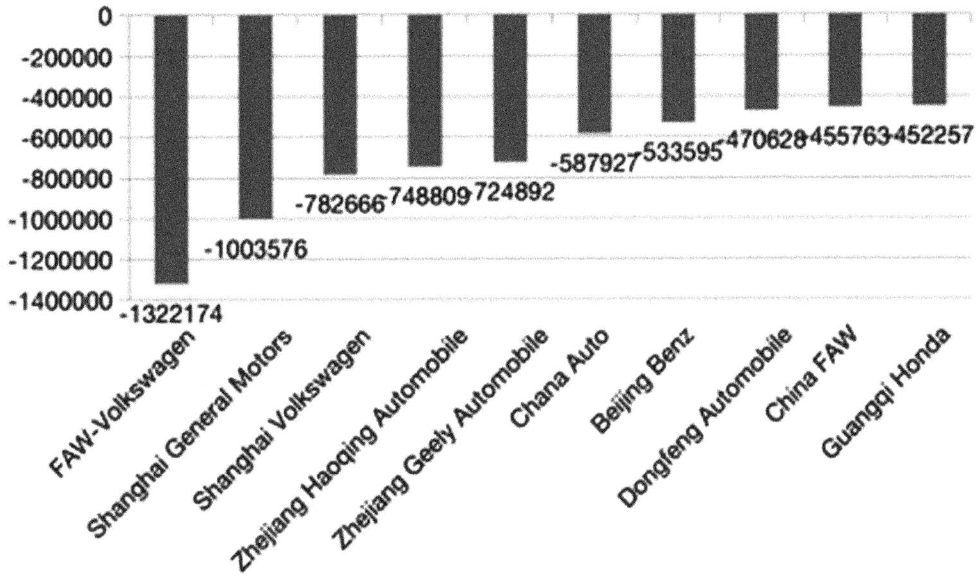

Under the dual credit policy, the prospect of meeting these two credit standards is not optimistic for most Chinese carmakers. A report by the Ministry of Industry and Information Technology (MIIT) of China shows that according to the historical sales data from 2017 to 2019, all Chinese automobile manufacturers could be divided into two categories: one had NEV credit deficit and the other had NEV credit surplus. The former included Green Wall, Changan, Ford, Dongfeng, FAW Toyota and GAC Fiat. They were strictly facing NEV credit shortage with a deficit of more than 100000, while BYD, BAIC, Geely, SAIC, Zotye, JAC and Chery belonged to the latter, and the upper limit of NEV credit surplus of BYD and BAIC exceeding 200000 (ICET, 2020).

REGULATIONS ANALYSIS UNDER INSTITUTIONAL SETTINGS

The following are the policies on promoting the development of NEVs issued by the Ministry of Industry and Information Technology, the Ministry of Transport, the National Development and Reform Commission, the Ministry of Science and Technology, the Ministry of Finance and the State Council in 2020. The main contents include government policy subsidies to support the development of new energy industry in the fields of technological innovation, system design and infrastructure construction as shown in Table 1.

Table 1. Some important regulations related to the development of NEVs in China in 2020

Release Time	Release Unit	File Name	Primary Coverage
2020.04.23	Ministry of Industry and Information Technology	Notice On Improving The Financial Subsidy Policy For The Promotion And Application Of New Energy Vehicles	The implementation period of the financial subsidy policy for the promotion and application of new energy vehicles will be extended to the end of 2022. Among them, the subsidy standard will not decline in 2020, and the subsidy standard will decline by 10% and 20% respectively from 2021 to 2022. In principle, the annual subsidy scale is limited to about 2 million vehicles.
2020.06.15	Ministry of Industry and Information Technology	Decision On Amending The Measures For The Parallel Management Of Average Fuel Consumption And New Energy Vehicle Points Of Passenger Vehicle Enterprises	The requirements for the integral proportion of new energy vehicles in 2021 to 2023 are defined as follows: 14%, 16% and 18%, respectively, giving accounting preference to models with the advantages of energy conservation and emission reduction, and modifying the calculation method of points for new energy vehicles.
2020.07.15	Ministry of Industry and Information Technology	Notice On Launching New Energy Activities In The Countryside	From July to December 2020, new energy vehicles will go to the countryside in China. There are 16 models participating in the activity, with a minimum price of less than 30000 yuan. The enterprise also promised to give certain profits based on deducting the national purchase subsidies.
2020.07.30	Ministry of Industry and Information Technology	Regulations On Amending The Management Of New Energy Vehicle Production Enterprises And Product Access	The deleting of the requirements of "design and development capacity", related to the application for the admission of new energy vehicle manufacturers. Adjusting the time when new energy vehicle manufacturers stop production from 12 months to 24 months. Deleting the interim period for new energy vehicle manufacturers to apply for admission.
2020.08.06	Ministry of Transport	Guidance On Promoting The Construction Of New Infrastructure In The Field Of Transportation	Guiding the construction of ultra-fast charging and high-power electric vehicle charging facilities in key expressway service areas such as urban agglomeration.
2020.09.11	National Development and Reform Commission	Guidance On Expanding Investment In Strategic Emerging Industries, Cultivating And Expanding New Growth Points And Growth Poles	Accelerating the construction of charging and replacement power stations for new energy vehicles, and improving the coverage of rapid charging and replacement power stations in expressway service areas and public parking spaces.

Continued on following page

Table 1. Continued

Release Time	Release Unit	File Name	Primary Coverage
2020.09.21	Ministry of Finance	Application Notice On The Development Of Fuel Cell Vehicle Demonstration Applications	The subsidy policy for the purchase of fuel cell vehicles will be adjusted to support the policy for the demonstration and application of fuel cell vehicles, and the qualified urban agglomerations will be rewarded for the industrialization of key core technologies and demonstration and application of fuel cell vehicles.
2020.09.23	National Development and Reform Commission	Guidance On Expanding Investment In Strategic, Emerging Industries, Cultivating And Expanding New Growth Points And Growth Poles	Accelerating the leapfrog development of new energy industry and the research & development of core technology components. Accelerating the construction of new energy vehicle charging / replacement power stations and improving the coverage of fast charging / replacement power stations in expressway service areas and public parking spaces.
2020.10.09	The State Council	New Energy Vehicle Industry Development Plan	Supporting the new energy vehicle industry to accelerate its development in the fields of technological innovation, system designing, infrastructure and so on. The plan specifies that by 2025, the sales volume of new energy vehicles in China will account for about 25%.
2020.10.10	Ministry of Industry and Information Technology	Management Measures For Echelon Utilization Of Power Batteries Of New Energy Vehicles	Encouraging enterprises to develop and produce echelon products suitable for the fields of base station power backup, energy storage, charging and replacement. Drum exploration adopts the business model of renting goods and large-scale utilization, which is convenient for echelon utilization and product recycling.
2020.10.23	National Development and Reform Commission and the Ministry of Science and Technology	Implementation Opinions On Supporting Private Enterprises To Accelerate Reform, Development, Transformation And Upgrading	The newly added capacity of new energy vehicles, commercial vehicles and other industries shall be fairly qualified on the condition that they meet the requirements of market access. For certification and approval, no additional preconditions shall be set.

Source:China business intelligence network, 2021

INTELLIGENT NETWORK CONNECTING ENERGY VEHICLES UNDER THE DUAL CARBON STRATEGY

Intelligent networked vehicle refers to the vehicle equipped with advanced on-board sensors, controllers, actuators, and other devices, and integrating modern communication and network technology to realize the intelligent information exchange and sharing between vehicles and people, vehicles, roads and clouds. It has the functions of complex environment perception, intelligent decision-making, and collaborative control, and can realize the form of "safety, efficiency, comfort and energy saving", finally realizing a new generation of cars that self-operate. It is a typical application of multi-disciplinary and multi technology in-depth integration of automobile, information, communication, and other disciplines. Intelligent networked vehicles, is the strategic direction of intelligent vehicle development. Networked collaboration is the future trend of intelligent driving, energy conservation and emission reduction, and the future development trend of digitalization and networking of NEVs (China information and Communication Research Institute, 2021).

At present, a new round of global scientific and technological revolution and industrial reform are booming. A variety of transformative technologies such as internet, big data and artificial intelligence have penetrated the automotive industry, giving birth to historic changes in the automotive industry. Electrification and smart networking have become an irreversible development trend of the automotive industry. The ecological chain of the automotive industry is being reconstructed, resulting in emerging value growth points. Structural changes are taking place in the automotive industry. Emerging technologies are rapidly integrated into the automotive industry chain and continue to grow iteratively, laying a technical foundation for the development of intelligent electric vehicles.

Mobile internet has changed people's way of life. People are no longer satisfied with taking cars solely as a means of transportation, but also hope to move the application of mobile internet to automotive products. With the rapidly developing technology and increasing needs of users, there is plenty room to integrate computing, vehicle power supply and some intelligent software engineering, thus giving rise to more intelligent passenger electric vehicles in the future. Under the industrial transformation, intelligent electric vehicles are gradually replacing the traditional vehicle transportation tools and becoming an important partner in people's travel process.

China's development of intelligent, networked, NEVs, has important strategic significance. On one hand, the development of intelligent, networked, NEVs will help better implement the goals of carbon peaking and carbon neutralization. On the other hand, China needs to accelerate the process of energy transformation to realize the development of green transportation.

China has formed a global first mover and leading advantage in the field of new energy, so it is of great significance to accelerate the development of NEVs. Electrification, networking, and artificial intelligence have become the development trend of the automobile industry, with electrification being the technical basis of the three modernizations. With its core advantages of multiple energy sources, high energy efficiency and zero emission, electric vehicles have become an irreversible international trend. The major automobile countries in the world have formulated a timetable for banning the sale of traditional fuel vehicles. In the wave of automobile electrification, artificial intelligence and networking are developing, and are expected to bring a safer, efficient, comfortable, and convenient driving experience (Future Automotive Ecology Conference, 2021).

NEVs are the best carriers for the application of intelligent networking technology. Benefiting from its own electrical and electronic architecture, most parts of NEVs can be driven by chips to achieve linear control, which provides the basic conditions for the internet of things. Therefore, electric vehicles have become the best platform for informatization and intelligence (Vehicle observation, 2021). With the rapid development of China's networked energy industry, China's intelligent vehicle industry is also actively evolving. Based on China's national conditions, relevant departments have formulated and issued a series of policy documents and preliminarily established a system of policies, regulations, and technical standards to support industrial development. In line with the development trend of intelligent internet connection, China's major automobile enterprises have successively released the development plan of intelligent internet connection as summarized in Table 2.

Table 2. Some important regulations related to the development of intelligent connected NEVs in China (2017 – 2021)

Release Time	Policy Name	Release Unit
2017.12	National Car Networking Industry Standard System Construction Guide (Intelligent Cars)	Ministry of Industry and Information Technology, National Standards Commission
2018.06	National Car Networking Industry Standard System Construction Guide (General Requirements)	Ministry of Industry and Information Technology, National Standards Commission
2018.06	National Car Networking Industry Standard System Construction Guide (Information and Communication)	Ministry of Industry and Information Technology, National Standards Commission
2018.06	National Car Networking Industry Standard System Construction Guide (Electronic Products and Services)	Ministry of Industry and Information Technology, National Standards Commission
2018.12	The Car Networking (Intelligent Cars) Industry Development Plan of Action	Ministry of Industry and Information Technology
2019.09	Outline of Building a Transport Power	The State Council
2020.02	Innovation and Development Strategy of Intelligent Vehicles	National Development and Reform Commission
2020.04	Guidelines for The Construction of The National Standard System for The Internet of Vehicles Industry (Intelligent Vehicle Management)	Ministry of Industry and Information Technology, Ministry of Public Security, National Standards Commission
2020.04	Measures for the Evaluation of The Application of New Technologies, New Processes and New Materials for The Admission of Road Motor Vehicle Products (Draft)	Ministry of Industry and Information Technology
2020.11	New Energy Vehicle Industry Development Plan (2021-2035)	The State Council
2020.12	Guidance on Promoting the Development and Application of Road Traffic Automatic Driving Technology	Ministry of Transport
2021.02	Outline of National Comprehensive Three - dimensional Transportation Network Planning Outline	CPC Central Committee, State Council
2021.03	National Standard System Construction Guide for Internet of Vehicles Industry (Related to Intelligent Transportation)	Ministry of Industry and Information Technology, Ministry of Transport, National Standards Commission
2021.04	Guide for Access Management of Intelligent Connected Vehicle Manufacturers and Products (Draft)	Ministry of Industry and Information Technology
2021.06	Guidelines for the Construction of Internet of Vehicles (Intelligent Connected Vehicles) Network Security Standard System (Draft)	Ministry of Industry and Information Technology
2021.06	Management Code for Road Test and Demonstration Application of Intelligent And Connected Vehicles (Draft)	Ministry of Industry and Information Technology,

Source: Ministry of Industry and Information Technology, National Standards Committee, Ministry of Public Security, State Council, n.d.

SOCIAL IMPACT ANALYSIS: GREEN INVESTMENT

At present, the principle of carbon neutrality and sustainable development has been highly valued by the global financial and investment circles. In response to the Paris Agreement on global solutions to climate change, more than 275 large-scale asset management institutions in 16 countries have established the Institutional Investors Group on Climate Change (IIGCC, 2021). A plan consistent with the Paris Agreement the Net Zero Carbon Emission Investment Framework, has been put in place, and it may be upgraded in the future. The plan has already reached $35 trillion in assets under the management of institutions participating in this organization (IIGCC, 2021).

China's own carbon neutrality commitment will also accelerate the formulation and implementation of codes of conduct for carbon neutrality and sustainable development in all walks of life, including the financial and investment community. Under the new climate goals, the 14th five-year plan and the longer-term policy framework are expected to introduce new goals and measures for China to achieve green development. China's consumption scale is expanding rapidly, so the transformation period of consumption upgrading is a window of opportunity to cultivate green consumption and lifestyle. Green consumption has penetrated all aspects of residents' lifestyle such as clothing, food, general usage, housing, and transportation, among others. With the continuous improvement of per capita disposable income of Chinese residents and the transformation of consumption mode and enhanced living standards, the demand for environment-friendly and resource-saving goods and services is soaring.

In 2017, the Research Report on Sustainable Consumption in China released by the United Nations Environment Programme and other agencies showed that more than 70% of Chinese consumers have a certain awareness of sustainable consumption, and about 50% of consumers are willing to pay a premium of about 10% for sustainable development products. In the 2019 survey and research report on the current situation of Chinese public green consumption, the concept of green consumption is becoming more and more popular in the public's daily consumption concept, and 83% of the respondents expressed support for green consumption behavior. According to the research report on family low-carbon life and low-carbon consumption behavior released in 2020, 54% of the respondents will consider energy conservation, low use cost and low-carbon environmental protection when purchasing household appliances. The public's concept of energy conservation and low-carbon consumption is increasing, and more and more people have become practitioners of green and simple lifestyle. Therefore, in the future, China will advocate a green, low-carbon, simple and moderate lifestyle, promote residents' green consumption and advocate residents' green investment through relevant policies.

SOCIAL IMPACT ANALYSIS: ESG INVESTMENT

The rapid development of China's economy has brought serious environmental problems. Therefore, green innovation has become the key driving force of green development (Razzaq, 2021). Green innovation entails large investments, high risks, and long return periods.

As the global weather becomes more extreme, institutional investors tend to integrate environmental, social and governance into their investments in environmental sustainability or climate risk hedging. Green innovation requires a lot of investment and long-term returns (Río, 2010). The expansion and enrichment of the concepts of ESG and socially responsible investment (SRI) are important measures for the sustainable development of enterprises (Michelson, 2004; Nekhili, 2021).

According to the 2015 ESG rating of SynTao Green Financial Institution and the data of Chinese A-share listed companies from 2010 to 2018, this paper reveals the quasi natural experiment of how ESG rating affects enterprise green innovation. The results show that ESG rating significantly improves the quantity and quality of green innovation, and mediates by alleviating financial constraints and improving managers' environmental awareness.

Wide array of empirical evidence shows that incorporating non-financial environmental, social and governance factors into traditional investment decisions can bring excess returns and reduce downside risks (Beasley et al., 2003; Li and Bao, 2014; Xu et al., 2018; Kaucic et al., 2020; Cesarone et al., 2019).

In global market, sustainable investment has become popular. The scale of global ESG investment assets in 2020 has reached 45 trillion, and the scale of global ESG fund management has exceeded 1 trillion by the end of 2020. According to the Global Sustainable Investment Annual Report 2020 issued by the Global Sustainable Investment Alliance (GSIA), in the five major markets it surveyed (Europe, the United States, Canada, Australia and Japan), the overall scale of sustainable investment reached $35.3 trillion, which has increased by as much as 55% from 2016 to 2020. ESG is becoming the mainstream of global investment. Although China's ESG investment started late, it is developing rapidly.

Moreover, 90% of more than 2,000 foreign-invested overseas companies are confident about the investment opportunities that Chinese companies may generate in the ESG field in the future (HSBC, 2020), which include the new energy automobile industry. With the goal of carbon neutrality putting higher demands on the industry, the importance of financial support for the zero-carbon transformation has become increasingly prominent. As China's annual investment in carbon emissions reduction requiring 2.2 trillion yuan before 2030, 3.9 trillion yuan from 2030 to 2060 being invested annually (Central Bank, 2020), more social capital will be guided and be encouraged to participate in investing low carbon industry in the future. At the same time, the rapid growth of green investment has also created new development space for the new energy automobile industry.

As the global weather becomes more extreme, institutional investors tend to integrate environmental, social and governance into their investments in environmental sustainability or climate risk hedging. Empirical evidence shows that incorporating non-financial environmental, social and governance factors into traditional investment decisions can bring excess returns and reduce downside risks (Bollen, 2007; Friede et al., 2015; Van Duuren et al., 2016; Nagy et al., 2017).

CONCLUSION AND RECOMMENDATIONS

In previous industrial revolutions, automobile is an important application carrier of scientific and technological innovation and technological progress. As an important pillar industry of the national economy, the automobile industry drives the rapid development of upstream and downstream related industries, which is of great significance in stabilizing industrial development, promoting residents' consumption, ensuring taxes and employment, and promoting scientific and technological innovation.

At present, science and technology and industrial life represented by the new generation of information and communication, cloud computing, big data, artificial intelligence, and other technologies are developing rapidly. Emerging technologies such as artificial intelligence, 5G, cloud computing and biometrics are rapidly penetrating the whole automobile industry chain, causing profound changes in the global automobile industry. As a landmark product of scientific and technological innovation and industrial upgrading and a key node of cross-border integration, NEVs continue to promote major technological application innovation and pay attention to protecting the ecological environment while realizing scientific and technological progress.

Under the goal of carbon neutrality, through the analysis of carbon trading market, the development of China's NEVs is in line with environmental policies and has investment potential. The government formulates laws and regulations to ensure the development of enterprises in an entrepreneurial ecosystem, and in line with environmental protection. The global industry can seize the opportunity to make better green investment and join China's NEV market.

ACKNOWLEDGMENT

The authors extend sincere gratitude to:

- Our colleagues from Soochow University, The Australian Studies Centre of Shanghai University, The European Business University of Luxembourg and Krirk University as well as the independent research colleagues who provided insight and expertise that greatly assisted the research, although they may not agree with all of the interpretations/conclusions of this chapter.
- China Knowledge for supporting our research.
- The Editor and the International Editorial Advisory Board (IEAB) of this book who initially desk reviewed, arranged a rigorous double/triple blind review process and conducted a thorough, minute and critical final review before accepting the chapter for publication.
- All anonymous reviewers who provided very constructive feedbacks for thorough revision, improvement and fine tuning of the chapter.

REFERENCES

Bamisile, O., Obiora, S., Huang, Q., Okonkwo, E. C., Olagoke, O., Shokanbi, A., & Kumar, R. (2020). Towards a Sustainable and Cleaner Environment in China: Dynamic Analysis of Vehicle-To-Grid, Batteries and Hydro Storage for Optimal Re Integration. *Sustainable Energy Technologies and Assessments*, *42*, 100872. doi:10.1016/j.seta.2020.100872

Beasley, J. E., Meade, N., & Chang, T. J. (2003). An Evolutionary Heuristic for the Index Tracking Problem. *European Journal of Operational Research*, *148*(3), 621–643. doi:10.1016/S0377-2217(02)00425-3

Bollen, N. P. (2007). Mutual Fund Attributes and Investor Behavior. *Journal of Financial and Quantitative Analysis*, *42*(3), 683–708. https://www.jstor.org/stable/27647316. doi:10.1017/S0022109000004142

Bruni, R., Cesarone, F., Scozzari, A., & Tardella, F. (2015). A Linear Risk-Return Model for Enhanced Indexation in Portfolio Optimization. *Spectrum (Lexington, Ky.)*, *37*(3), 735–759. doi:10.100700291-014-0383-6

Canakgoz, N. A., & Beasley, J. E. (2009). Mixed-integer Programming Approaches for Index Tracking and Enhanced Indexation. *European Journal of Operational Research*, *196*(1), 384–399. doi:10.1016/j.ejor.2008.03.015

Chien, F., Ajaz, T., Andlib, Z., Chau, K. Y., Ahmad, P., & Sharif, A. (2021). The Role of Technology Innovation, Renewable Energy and Globalization in Reducing Environmental Degradation in Pakistan: A Step Towards Sustainable Environment. *Renewable Energy*, *177*, 308–317. doi:10.1016/j.renene.2021.05.101

Chien, F., Anwar, A., Hsu, C. C., Sharif, A., Razzaq, A., & Sinha, A. (2021). The Role of Information and Communication Technology in Encountering Environmental Degradation: Proposing an SDG Framework for the BRICS Countries. *Technology in Society*, *65*, 101–115. doi:10.1016/j.techsoc.2021.101587

Chien, F., Chau, K. Y., Ady, S. U., Zhang, Y., Tran, Q. H., & Aldeehani, T. M. (2021). Does the Combining Effects of Energy and Consideration of Financial Development Lead to Environmental Burden: Social Perspective of Energy Finance?, pp. 1-14. Environmental Science and Pollution Research. doi:10.100711356-021-13423-6

China Environmental Protection Industry Research Institute. (2020). *Policy Suggestions on Promoting the Formation of Green Consumption and Lifestyle in the 14th Five Year Plan*. CEPIRI. http://www.zghbcyyjy.cn/?p=21564

China Information and Communication Research Institute. (2021). *White Paper on Vehicle Networking*. CEPIRI. https://my.mbd.baidu.com/r/CIiYSYgucw?f=cp&u=c98d9d27995e162d

Choi, W., Yoo, E., Seol, E., Kim, M., & Song, H. (2020). Greenhouse Gas Emissions of Conventional and Alternative Vehicles: Predictions Based on Energy Policy Analysis in South Korea. *Applied Energy*, *265*, 114754. doi:10.1016/j.apenergy.2020.114754

del Río, P., Carrillo-Hermosilla, J., & Könnölä, T. (2010). Policy Strategies to Promote Eco-Innovation: An Integrated Framework. *Journal of Industrial Ecology*, *14*(4), 541–557. doi:10.1111/j.1530-9290.2010.00259.x

Dutta, A. (2017). Modeling and Forecasting the Volatility of Carbon Emission Market: The Role of Outliers, Time-Varying Jumps and Oil Price Risk. *Journal of Cleaner Production,* doi:10.1016/j.jclepro.2017.11.135

Eiadat, Y., Kelly, A., Roche, F., & Eyadat, H. (2008). Green and Competitive? An Empirical Test of the Mediating Role of Environmental Innovation Strategy. *Journal of World Business*, *43*(2), 131–145. doi:10.1016/j.jwb.2007.11.012

Fan, Y., Fang, C., & Zhang, Q. (2019). Coupling Coordinated Development between Social Economy and Ecological Environment in Chinese Provincial Capital Cities-Assessment and Policy Implications. *Journal of Cleaner Production*, *229*, 289–298. doi:10.1016/j.jclepro.2019.05.027

Filippi, C., Guastaroba, G., & Speranza, M. (2016). A Heuristic Framework for the Bi-Objective Enhanced Index Tracking Problem. *Omega*, *65*, 122–137. doi:10.1016/j.omega.2016.01.004

Foody, G. M. (2007). Editorial: Ecological Applications of Remote Sensing and GIS. *Ecological Informatics*, *2*(2), 71–72. doi:10.1016/j.ecoinf.2007.06.001

Friede, G., Busch, T., & Bassen, A. (2015). ESG and Financial Performance: Aggregated Evidence From More Than 2000 Empirical Studies. *Journal of Sustainable Finance & Investment*, *5*(4), 210–233. doi:10.1080/20430795.2015.1118917

Gnägi, M., & Strub, O. (2020). Tracking and Outperforming Large Stock-Market Indices. *Omega*, *90*, 101999. doi:10.1016/j.omega.2018.11.008

Guastaroba, G., & Speranza, M. G. (2012). Kernel Search: An Application to the Index Tracking Problem. *European Journal of Operational Research*, *217*(1), 54–68. doi:10.1016/j.ejor.2011.09.004

Henriques, I., & Sadorsky, P. (2008). Oil Prices and the Stock Prices of Alternative Energy Companies. *Energy Economics*, *30*(3), 998–1010. doi:10.1016/j.eneco.2007.11.001

ICET. (2019). *Research Report on Dual Credits of China's Passenger Vehicles in 2018*. ICET. http://www.icet.org.cn/english/admin/upload/news/202003/977824.html

IIGCC. (2021). *The Institution Investors Group on Climate Change*. https://www.iigcc.org /about-us/our-members/

Ji, X., Zhang, Y., Mirza, N., Umar, M., & Rizvi, S. K. A. (2021). The Impact of Carbon Neutrality on the Investment Performance: Evidence from the Equity Mutual Funds in BRICS. *Journal of Environmental Management*, *297*, 113228. doi:10.1016/j.jenvman.2021.113228 PMID:34273643

Lejeune, M. A. (2012). Game Theoretical Approach for Reliable Enhanced Indexation. *Decision Analysis*, *9*(2), 146–155. https://pubsonline.informs.org/doi/abs/10.1287/deca.1120.0239. doi:10.1287/deca.1120.0239

Li, W., Chien, F., Hsu, C. C., Zhang, Y., Nawaz, M. A., Iqbal, S., & Mohsin, M. (2021). Nexus between Energy Poverty and Energy Efficiency: Estimating the Long-Run Dynamics. *Resources Policy*, *72*, 102063. doi:10.1016/j.resourpol.2021.102063

Li, W., Chien, F., Kamran, H. W., Aldeehani, T. M., Sadiq, M., Nguyen, V. C., & Taghizadeh-Hesary, F. (2021). The Nexus between COVID-19 Fear and Stock Market Volatility. *Econ. Ekonomska Istraživanja. Economic Research Journal*, 1–22.

Malla, D. G. B. (2020). An Economic Account of Innovation Policy in Canada: A Comparison of Canola, Wheat, and Pulses. *AgBioForum*, *22*(1), 25–36. https://hdl.handle.net/10355/86604

Michelson, G., Wailes, N., Van Der Laan, S., & Frost, G. (2004). Ethical Investment Processes and Outcomes. *Journal of Business Ethics*, *52*(1), 1–10. doi:10.1023/B:BUSI.0000033103.12560.be

Nagy, Z., Kassam, A., & Lee. L. E. (2017). Can ESG Add Alpha? An Analysis of ESG Tilt and Momentum Strategies. *The Journal of Investing*, *43* (2APP), 28-32. doi:10.3905/joi.2016.25.2.113

National Energy Administration. (2021). *Renewable Energy in China*. NEA. https://mi.mbd.baidu.com/r/CI0SrVaZQk?f=cp&u=f3673e088bb6486d

Nekhili, A., Boukadhaba, A., Nagati, H., & Chtioui, T. (2021). ESG Performance and Market Value: The Moderating Role of Employee Board Representation. *International Journal of Human Resource Management*, *32*(14), 3061–3087. doi:10.1080/09585192.2019.1629989

Razzaq, A., Wang, Y., Chupradit, S., Suksatan, W., & Shahzad, F. (2021). Asymmetric Inter-Linkages between Green Technology Innovation and Consumption-Based Carbon Emissions in BRICS Countries Using Quantile-On-Quantile Framework. *Technology in Society*, *66*, 101656. doi:10.1016/j.techsoc.2021.101656

Salvia, M., Reckien, D., Pietrapertosa, F., Eckersley, P., Spyridaki, N. A., Krook-Riekkola, A., Olazabal, M., De Gregorio Hurtado, S., Simoes, S. G., Geneletti, D., Viguié, V., Fokaides, P. A., Ioannou, B. I., Flamos, A., Csete, M. S., Buzasi, A., Orru, H., de Boer, C., Foley, A., & Heidrich, O. (2021). Will Climate Mitigation Ambitions Lead to Carbon Neutrality? An Analysis of the Local-Level Plans of 327 Cities in the EU. *Renewable & Sustainable Energy Reviews*, *135*, 110253. doi:10.1016/j.rser.2020.110253

State Council. (2020). *China's Energy Development in the New Era*. State Council. http://www.scio.gov.cn/zfbps/32832/Document/1695117/1695117.htm

Umar, M., Ji, X., Mirza, N., & Naqvi, B. (2021). Carbon Neutrality, Bank Lending, and Credit Risk: Evidence from the Eurozone. *Journal of Environmental Management*, *296*, 113156. doi:10.1016/j.jenvman.2021.113156 PMID:34225048

UNFCCC. (2015). *Paris Agreement Report of the Conference of the Parties on Its Twenty-First Session*. UNFCCC. https://unfccc.int/sites/default/files/paris_agreement.pdf

United Nations Environment Programme. (2007). *The United Nations Environment Programme (UNEP) Developed a Guidance Document on Desalination*. UN. https://www.unep.org/resources/report/guidance-chemicals-con trol-contributing-national-progress-and-safety

VanDuuren, E., Plantinga, A., & Scholtens, B. (2016). ESG Integration and the Investment Management Process: Fundamental Investing Reinvented. *Journal of Business Ethics*, *138*(3), 525–533. doi:10.100710551-015-2610-8

Wang, C., & Zhao, H. (2016). The Assessment of Urban Ecological Environment in Watershed Scale. *Procedia Environmental Sciences*, *36*, 169–175. doi:10.1016/j.proenv.2016.09.028

Wang, Z., & Dong, X. (2016). Determinants and Policy Implications of Residents' New Energy Vehicle Purchases: The Evidence from China. *Natural Hazards*, *82*(1), 155–173. doi:10.100711069-016-2185-4

Wu, M., Liu, Y., Xu, Z., Yan, G., Ma, M., Zhou, S., & Qian, Y. (2020). Spatio-temporal Dynamics of China's Ecological Civilization Progress after Implementing National Conservation Strategy. *Journal of Cleaner Production*, *285*, 124886. doi:10.1016/j.jclepro.2020.124886

Wu, W., Wu, J. J., Wang, X., Zhong, B., & Yang, A. X. (2020). Ecological Environment Assessment for Greater Mekong Sub-Region Based on Pressure-State-Response Framework by Remote Sensing. *Ecological Indicators*, *117*, 106521. doi:10.1016/j.ecolind.2020.106521

Yang, X. J. (2013). China's Rapid Urbanization. *Science*, *342*(6156), 310. doi:10.1126cience.342.6156.310-a PMID:24136949

Yiwei, L. (2022). *Series Research on Patent Situation of Strategic Emerging Industries New Energy Vehicles*. Sadie Think Tank. https://mp.weixin.qq.com/s/1I47qihqITCFbmkipXdt6A

Yu, P., Jiang, Z., Mandizvidza, K., & Chen, Z. (2022). Impact Investing and the Roles of Family Offices: Sustainable and Responsible Investment Strategies. In R. Sharma & K. Mehta (Eds.), *Handbook of Research on Stock Market Investment Practices and Portfolio Management* (pp. 244–268). IGI Global. doi:10.4018/978-1-6684-5528-9.ch013

Yu, P., Jiao, A., & Sampat, M. (2022). The Effect of Chinese Green Transformation on Competitiveness and the Environment. In P. Ordóñez de Pablos, X. Zhang, & M. Almunawar (Eds.), *Handbook of Research on Green, Circular, and Digital Economies as Tools for Recovery and Sustainability* (pp. 257–279). IGI Global. doi:10.4018/978-1-7998-9664-7.ch014

Yu, P., Liu, X., Mahendran, R., & Lu, S. (2022). Analysis and Comparison of Business Models of Leading Enterprises in the Chinese Hydrogen Energy Industry. In R. Felseghi, N. Cobîrzan, & M. Raboaca (Eds.), *Clean Technologies and Sustainable Development in Civil Engineering* (pp. 179–216). IGI Global. doi:10.4018/978-1-7998-9810-8.ch008

Yu, P., Tang, S., Ahuja, A., & Chang, X. (2022). Active Equity Investing: Post-COVID-19 Investment Strategies and Portfolio Construction Under the Unique Institutional Settings of China. In R. Sharma & K. Mehta (Eds.), *Handbook of Research on Stock Market Investment Practices and Portfolio Management* (pp. 301–328). IGI Global. doi:10.4018/978-1-6684-5528-9.ch016

Yu, P., Weng, Y., & Ahuja, A. (2022). Carbon Financing and the Sustainable Development Mechanism: The Case of China. In A. Rafay (Ed.), *Handbook of Research on Energy and Environmental Finance 4.0* (pp. 301–332). IGI Global. doi:10.4018/978-1-7998-8210-7.ch012

Yu, P., Xu, S., Cheng, Z., & Sampat, M. (2023). Does the Development of New Energy Vehicles Promote Carbon Neutralization?: Case Studies in China. In A. Pego (Ed.), *Climate Change, World Consequences, and the Sustainable Development Goals for 2030* (pp. 109–131). IGI Global. doi:10.4018/978-1-6684-4829-8.ch006

Zhang, T., Wang, L., Wang, H., Peng, L., & Luo, C. (2017). Assessment of Soil Salinization Ecological Environment Change in the Manas River Basin Using Remote Sensing Technology. *Acta Ecologica Sinica, 37*(9), 3009–3018. doi:10.5846txb201601310225

Zhang, Y., Luo, H., & Wang, C. (2021). Progress and Trends of Global Carbon Neutrality Pledges. *Climate Change Research, 17*, 88–97. doi:10.12006/j.issn.1673-1719.2020.241

Zhang, Y. X., & Hao, Y. (2020). Rethinking China's Environmental Target Responsibility System: Province-Level Convergence Analysis of Pollutant Emission Intensities in China. *Journal of Cleaner Production, 242*, 118472. doi:10.1016/j.jclepro.2019.118472

Chapter 5
Drift in Research in Women Empowerment and NGOs:
A Bibliometric Analysis of Scopus-Indexed Publications (1993-2022)

Pallavi Bhardwaj
Gurukula Kangri (Deemed), India

Pankaj Madan
https://orcid.org/0000-0002-4648-9863
Gurukula Kangri (Deemed), India

ABSTRACT

The purpose of this study is to demonstrate women empowerment through social entrepreneurship and to show the scope of social entrepreneurship and NGOs that analysts are presently unaware of, and to inspire those who have not yet studied this field and wish to conduct research on women empowerment through NGOs. In this study, the authors chose a quantitative strategy and used the Scopus database to identify the research areas with the most significant research results; the beginning of the research in the field of women empowerment and NGOs, the source of the research, and the subject area. The focus of this research is on 130 documents published in the field of women empowerment in context with NGOs. The study showed that the bibliometric research on women participation in social entrepreneurship can be systematically carried, and fresh scopes of social entrepreneurship research can be set.

1. INTRODUCTION

Women contribute to almost half of the world's population. Empowerment of women is an urge need in developing countries like India. Nowadays, women's empowerment is a buzzword on which everyone talks, debate and discuss. The best method to strengthen the family—a micro-unit of the national economy—and its economic, nutritional, and health conditions is through educating and empowering women. In this context, it may be claimed that women's low levels of education may constitute a barrier

DOI: 10.4018/978-1-6684-7422-8.ch005

to the nation's economic growth. Women in India are educated significantly less than males. According to the Census data from 2001, 54.16 percent of women and 65.38 percent of males are literate. According to the results of the 2011 Census, literacy levels are rising nationwide. The country's literacy rate is 74.04%, with 82.14 percent of men and 65.46 percent of women.

Actions to raise women's position via education, awareness, literacy, and training are considered empowerment. Women's empowerment is about encouraging women to overcome a variety of social difficulties and make decisions that will change their lives. The process of empowering women is known as women empowerment. When we talk about women's empowerment, however, we mean embracing and permitting women who are not already involved in decision-making to join in the process. In ancient times, women were not allowed to take the decision or to participate in any such decision-making activity either in the house or outside the house. Women have remained in house like a prisoner in four walls. Then the word women empowerment came, which made society realise that women are equally important as men and, therefore, women's opinion is also as important as the opinion of men. It made them aware of their rights and the importance of their existence in society. However, there is a long way to go to make our country in which a woman has equal rights, equal powers and equal authority to participate in the decision-making process and step out of the house to gain self-respect and confidence.

There are quite a few gender-related social norms in India that prohibit and limit women's participation in many normal activities in their communities and in the general economy. For example, women have social obligations as daughters, mothers, and caregivers. These obligations and associated societal expectations result in women being left behind, both socially and economically.

NGOs are today acknowledged as major players in the third sector in the fields of development, human rights, humanitarian aid, environmental protection, and many other areas of public engagement. NGOs have existed in various forms for centuries, but in the 1980s and 1990s, they gained significant significance in international development and sharply surged in number. Due to the lack of thorough or trustworthy information, it is challenging to determine the exact number of NGOs. If official and informal groups are included, some estimates place the number at a million, but the number of registered NGOs receiving international funding is likely closer to "a few hundred thousand" (Lewis 2010). Social entrepreneurship has the effect of alleviating social constraints by empowering marginalized women to make choices and transforming that choice into desired outcomes (Sinkovics et al., 2015). This result is consistent with the World Bank's definition of empowerment as women's empowerment through social enterprise interventions. However, as some scholars have pointed out, business acceptance of women in developing countries has yet to be tested (Maria 2017). Most research has focused on female entrepreneurship in advanced economies (Yadav & Unni 2016). Women are often employed in the informal sector, such as "petty-trading and street vending (of vegetables, poultry, processed food, or handcrafts), paid domestic work, casual employment in unregulated small enterprises, and on construction sites and agricultural schemes" adapt to their availability and family and social responsibilities by choice or coercion (Mitra 2002). There is very little academic and research coverage on the impact of social entrepreneurship on women in India, whereas there has been some recent media coverage from government and other international initiatives. Several studies have focused on female entrepreneurship in India, with particular attention to social issues such as the caste system (Mahajan 2011) and the intersectionality of gender and domestic violence (Dey and Orton). Intersectionality is a concept based on the hierarchical nature of inequality and dominance in women's social life (Bilge 2010). A good example of intersectionality is domestic violence, which has an indirect impact on women's participation in social entrepreneurship. Since freedom and power are intrinsically linked to the self, starting from the premise that empowerment and its processes originate from inside each of us as people and "how we relate to ourselves and others" may hold the key to achieving change through corporate sustainability (Crane et al., 2008, p. 315). When we assume what women need to be freed from or how this might be accomplished, "liberating" women through corporate sustainability empowerment programmes from poverty or inequality may become problematic. Research and practice should aim to promote introspection, conversation space, and women's and men's personal interests in the workplace (McCarthy, 2017).

This research paper adds to the body of knowledge by answering the following questions:

- RQ1. What are the annual trends of publications in the field of women empowerment and NGOs?
- RQ2. Which sources contribute the most to the research in this field?
- RQ3. Which countries contribute the most to the research in this field?
- RQ4. What are the subjects in which research related to this field is taken into consideration?
- RQ5. What are the most important documents and authors in the field of women empowerment and NGOs?

2. LITERATURE REVIEW

Researchers and development groups are interested in the topic of women's empowerment, and the United Nations designated it as the fifth of its 17 Sustainable Development Goals in 2015. (United Nations General Assembly, 2015). A new corporate governance paradigm is described by the term "corporate sustainability". The more general phrase "environmental and social governance" also applies to ESG. Corporate Sustainability focuses on achieving expansion and profitability through planned business operations in three societal domains. The goal is to create long-term benefits for stakeholders without sacrificing people, the environment, or the economy. However, academics have major difficulties in evaluating women's empowerment (Mason 1986; Kabeer 1999; Kishor 2005). Poor measurement impedes efforts to identify the causes and effects of poor empowerment and to evaluate the effectiveness of social policies aimed at enhancing empowerment (Malhotra & Schuler, 2005). (Alsop & Heinsohn 2005). There are several ways to define women's empowerment (Batliwala 1994; Kabeer 1999; Alsop & Heinsohn 2005; Mosedale 2005;). The concept offered by Kabeer (1999), who characterises it as the process by which women enhance their capacity to make life decisions, maybe the most significant.

According to (Van Eck, N. J., & Waltman, L., 2010), "separated from bibliometric indicators, these inquiries about incorporating science mapping: the VOS viewer software". This software is widely used in bibliometric research, using bibliometric graphs to show the structure and systems of researchers, journals, universities or countries. In this case, we examine the co-occurrence of author keywords (words appearing below theoretical keywords) (Cancino, 2017) authorship (number of co-authors in primary beneficial sources) and citations against authors and citations document. This method takes after the foremost pertinent considerations within bibliometric writing. As per the discussion done by (Bakker et al., 2005), a "bibliometric analysis comprises of incorporating factual strategies to decide qualitative and quantitative changes in a given logical research subject, set up the profile of publications on the subject, and identify propensities inside an area." In expansion, this sort of analysis gives valuable information for specialists looking to assess logical action (Oliva et al., 2006; Pandey & Joshi, 2021) since a bibliometric analysis gives a direction to the researchers and academicians who want to pursue research into the social business enterprise. This ponders employing the Scopus online database, which houses logical records of overall disciplines. Since Scopus provides information about performance, dispersion, collaboration, and effectiveness, the fact that Scopus provides logical query information about performance enhances bibliometric analysis.

3. RESEARCH METHODOLOGY

Since Pritchard (1969) coined the term bibliometrics to understand the impact and impact of these publications, bibliometrics, information scientists, and research scientists have a particular subject, journal, or research. To look up a collection of literature (Chellappandi & Vijayakumar, 2018). Bibliometric studies are conducted in an interdisciplinary manner to assess "author patterns", "levels of collaboration", "cited journal rankings", "productive author rankings," and "national productivity rankings". An assessment of the characteristics of "citations and citations" examines articles", "Impact Factors and Immediacy Indexes for Specific Journals" and measures many other aspects of academic research publications (Samanta, Rautary, & Swain, 2021).

The VOS viewer program was utilised in this study to perform bibliometric analysis. Data from the Scopus core database were retrieved in July 2022 to get information relevant to this study. The authors examined the Scopus database for women empowerment and NGOs and found 148 items ranging from 1993 to July 2022. The author then searched for the keywords 'women empowerment', 'NGOs,' 'women NGOs' and 'female NGOs' and added some additional filters, limiting the data to the final stage of publishing, source type of journals, books, and conference proceedings, and language of just English. The authors discovered 130 documents relevant to the research after filtering the data to these filters. Figure 1 shows the data retrieval process.

Figure 1. Data retrieval process
Source: *"The authors' creation."*

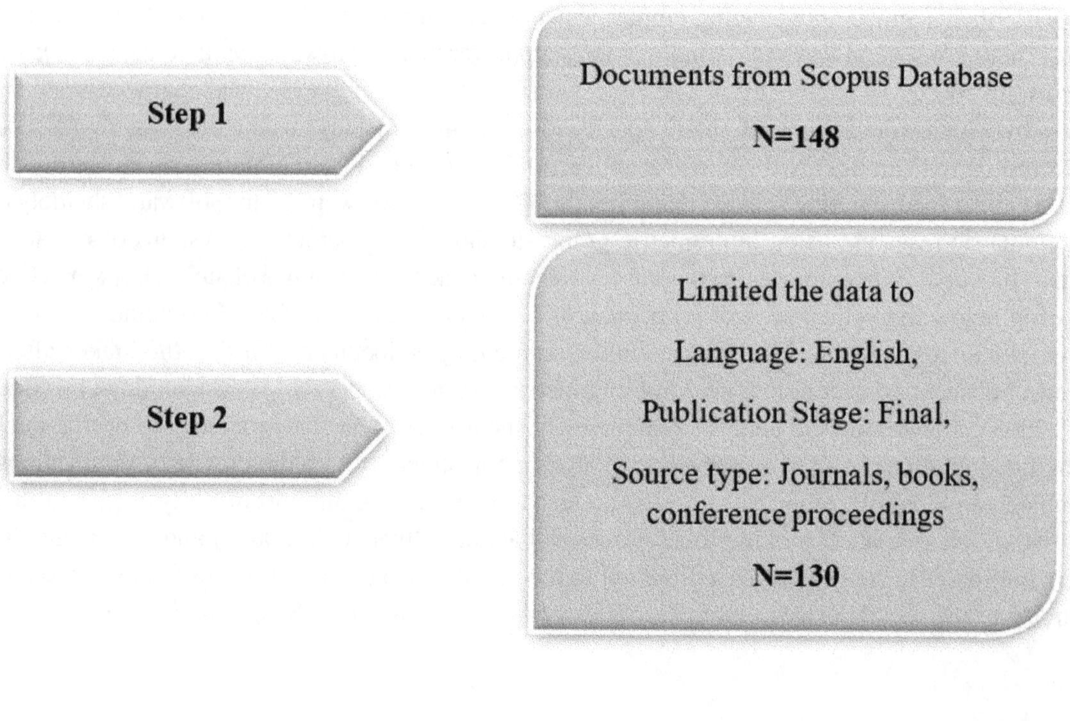

4. RESULTS AND DISCUSSION

The data in this study will be analyzed in two ways: descriptive analysis and visual analysis. In the descriptive part researcher will study the annual trends of publication, analysis of source titles, and countries focusing on this field are published. In the visual analysis part, the researcher will be showcasing the co-occurrence analysis and co-authorship analysis.

4.1. Annual Trends of Publication

In this study, the data has been fetched from the Scopus database. In this data, we can see in figure 2 also that the study started from the year 1993 with only 1 paper. In the year 1994, total 5 articles were published, which were indexed in Scopus. The figure remained same in the year 2005 as well, followed up with in the year 2010 and 2011. In the year 2020, the researchers hyped their studies and gave 12 articles published under Scopus. Till the date, the data was retrieved, there were 5 new articles published under Scopus-indexed journals in the field of women empowerment through NGOs.

Figure 2. Trend line showing publications as per year based on Scopus database
Source: *"Compiled by authors based on the database of Scopus"*

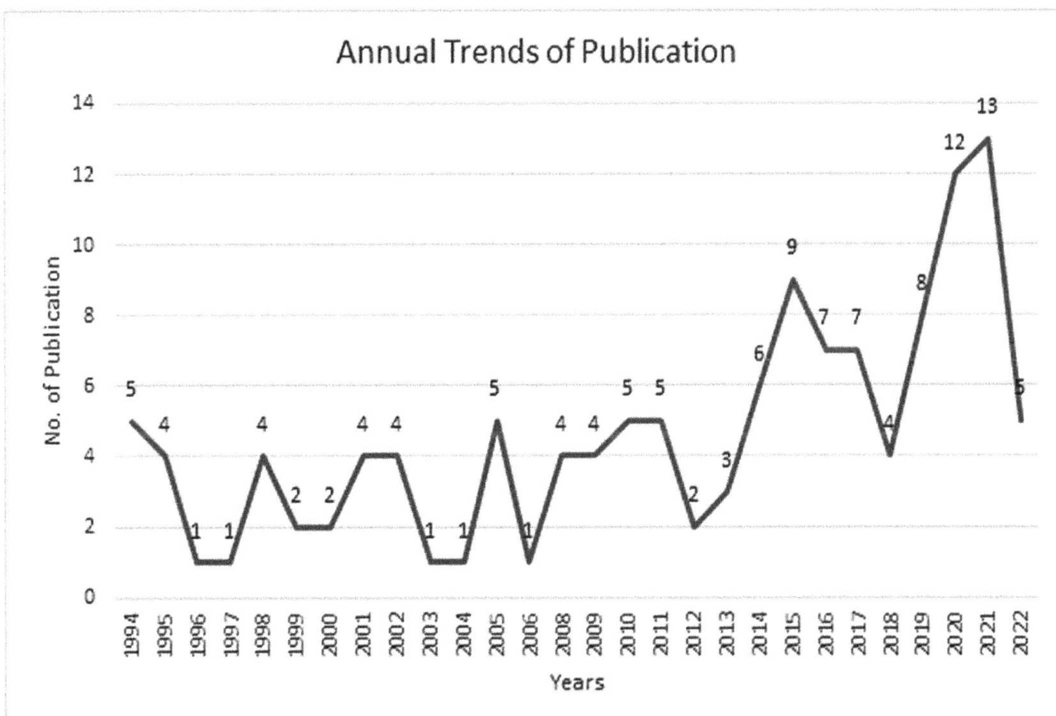

4.2. Analysis of Source Titles

Source Titles here means Journals in which the articles are published related to women empowerment and NGOs from 1993 to July 2022. From the data retrieved from the Scopus database, researchers found that the journal "Gender and Development" has the highest number of articles published i.e., 4. And the journal "ACM International Conference Proceeding Series" and "AIDS Care Psychological and Socio Medical Aspects of AIDS HIV" has the least number of articles published i.e., 1.

Table I and Figure 3 show the data for better understanding.

Table 1. Top 15 journals that have published the highest numbers of documents from 1993 to 2022

Rank	Source Titles	No. of Articles Published
1.	"Gender And Development"	4
2.	"Joicfp News"	4
3.	"Development In Practice"	3
4.	"Journal Of Rural Development"	3
5.	"World Development"	3
6.	"Administrative Sciences"	2
7.	"Cedpa Network Online"	2
8.	"Development"	2
9.	"Geographical Journal"	2
10.	"Journal Of International Women S Studies"	2
11.	"Social Change"	2
12.	"Studies In Comparative International Development"	2
13.	"Sustainability Switzerland"	2
14.	"ACM International Conference Proceeding Series"	1
15.	"AIDS Care Psychological and Socio Medical Aspects of AIDS HIV"	1

Source: "Compiled by authors based on the database of Scopus"

Figure 3. Bar chart showing publications in different sources based on Scopus database
Source: *"Compiled by authors based on the database of Scopus"*

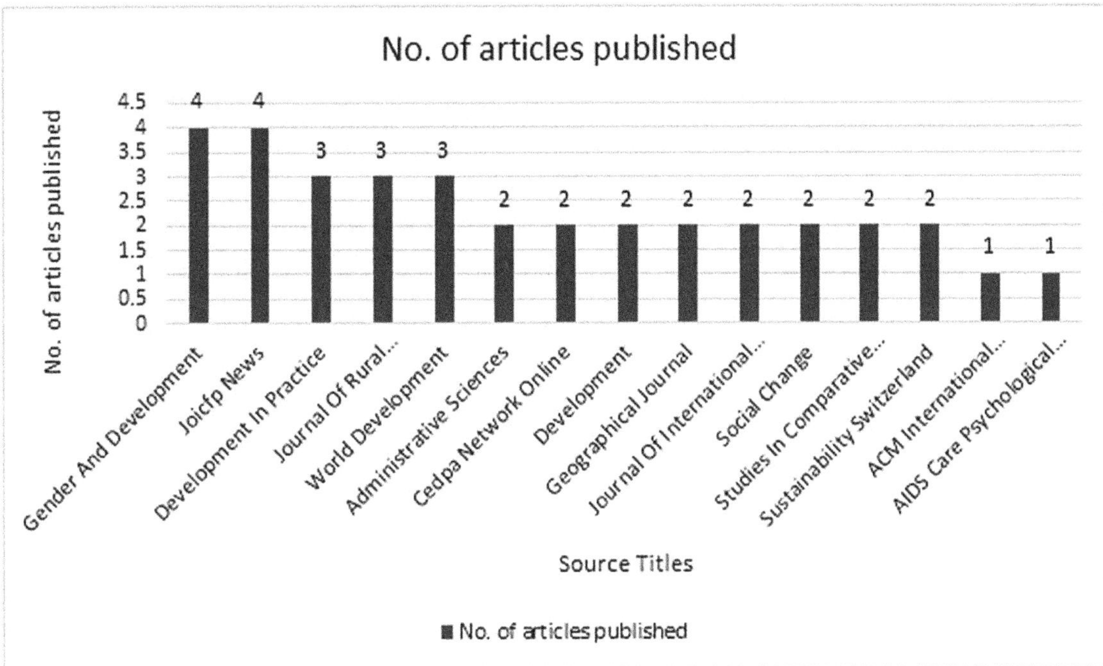

4.3. Countries

In this section, the researcher studied the Scopus data and analysed the top 15 countries which are listed according to their number of publications. After analysing the results of Scopus database, the researcher found that United States is at the rank I for the highest publication in this field of women empowerment and NGOs i.e., 28 followed up with India which is at second position in publishing the articles. India has published 20 articles in this field till date. Malaysia and Mexico are at the second last and last position respectively with 2 articles published in Scopus-indexed journals. Table II and Figure 4 shows the data for better understanding.

Table 2. Top 15 countries that have released the most documents between 1993 and 2022

Rank	Country/Territory	No. of Publications
1.	United States	28
2.	India	20
3.	United Kingdom	9
4.	Australia	8
5.	Canada	8
6.	Indonesia	6
7.	Bangladesh	5
8.	Germany	3
9.	Lebanon	3
10.	South Africa	3
11.	Belgium	2
12.	Ghana	2
13.	Japan	2
14.	Malaysia	2
15.	Mexico	2

Source: "Compiled by authors based on the database of Scopus"

Figure 4. Graph showing publications as per countries based on Scopus database
Source: *"Compiled by authors based on the database of Scopus"*

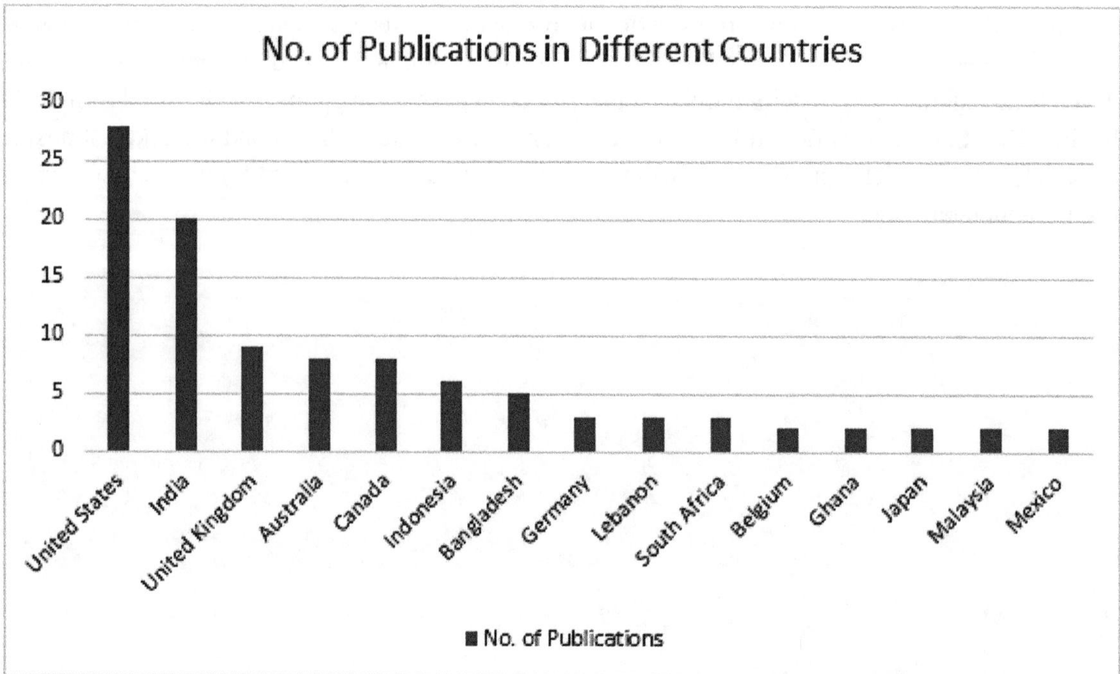

4.4. Subjects

In this section, the researcher studied the Scopus data and analysed the top 15 subjects in which the articles were published related to women empowerment and NGOs. After analysing the results of Scopus database, the researcher found that the subject of Social Sciences is at the rank I for the highest publication in this field of women empowerment and NGOs i.e., 92 documents followed up with Business, Management and Accounting which is at second position with 19 documents. Decision Sciences and Energy has 2 documents published till date. Table III and Figure 5 shows the data for better understanding.

Table 3. Top 15 subjects that have released the most documents between 1993 and 2022

Rank	Subject Area	No. of Articles Published
1.	"Social Sciences"	92
2.	"Business, Management and Accounting"	19
3.	"Medicine"	19
4.	"Environmental Science"	15
5.	"Arts and Humanities"	12
6.	"Economics, Econometrics and Finance"	12
7.	"Earth and Planetary Sciences"	5
8.	"Computer Science"	4
9.	"Psychology"	4
10.	"Agricultural and Biological Sciences"	3
11.	"Engineering"	3
12.	"Biochemistry, Genetics and Molecular Biology"	2
13.	"Decision Sciences"	2
14.	"Energy"	2
15.	"Undefined"	1

Source: "Compiled by authors based on the database of Scopus"

Figure 5. Graph showing publications as per subjects based on Scopus database
Source: *"Compiled by authors based on the database of Scopus"*

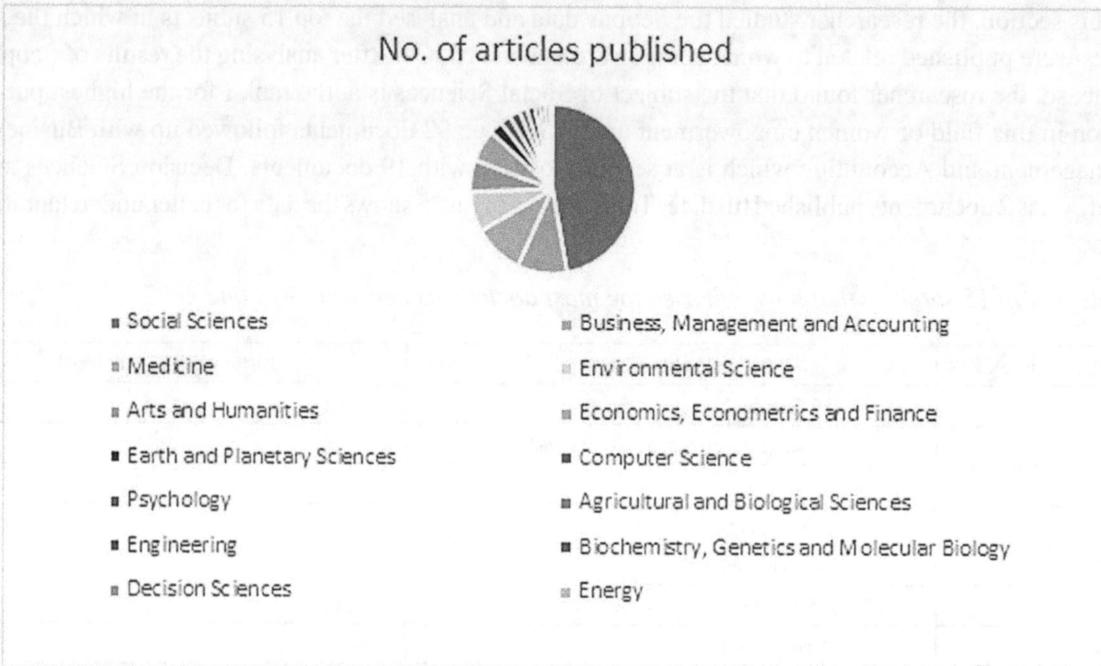

4.5. Co-occurrence Analysis

4.5.1. Keyword Analysis

In this study, the authors used Vos Viewer Software to evaluate co-occurrences networking. Through this keyword co-occurrence analysis, the researcher visualises the number and the frequencies of the keywords and the keywords which occur frequently. The authors picked co-occurrences in the kind of analysis column, all keywords in the unit of analysis column, and 10 as the minimum number of keywords. After combining the effects, the authors discovered that there was a total of 679 keywords, of which 18 met the criteria. The overall strength of co-occurrence links with other keywords will be determined for each of the 18 keywords. The keywords with the most overall link strength are chosen. Top 10 keywords' occurrence with their total link strength is shown in table IV below. The "empowerment" is the keyword that has the highest link strength with 34 times of occurrences. The keyword "article" has second highest link strength with 17 times of occurrences followed by the keyword "nongovernment organisations" with 26 times of occurrences.

Table 4. Top 10 keywords' occurrence with their total link strength

S.No.	Keywords	Occurrence	Total Link Strength
1.	Empowerment	34	97
2.	Article	17	76
3.	Nongovernment organisations	26	74
4.	Women status	24	71
5.	Developing Countries	13	66
6.	Asia	13	63
7.	Developing country	13	60
8.	organisations	11	53
9.	women	17	49
10.	Family planning	10	47

Source: "Compiled by authors based on the Vos viewer software"

There has been a total of two clusters produced. Figure 6 shows the map of co-occurrences of keywords. First cluster consisted of 9 items which are in red colour and second cluster also contained 9 items in total which are in green colour. Table V showcase the detailed description of clusters formed through Vos Viewer software.

Table 5. Detailed description of keywords in different clusters

Clusters	Cluster 1	Cluster 2
Keywords	Article	Empowerment
	Asia	Gender
	Bangladesh	India
	Developing countries	NGOs
	Developing country	Nongovernment organisations
	Family planning	women
	organization	Women empowerment
	Organizations	Women status
	Women's empowerment	Women's empowerment

Source: "Compiled by authors based on the Vos viewer software"

Figure 6. Map of Co-occurrences of keywords
Source: *"Framed by authors using VOS viewer Software"*

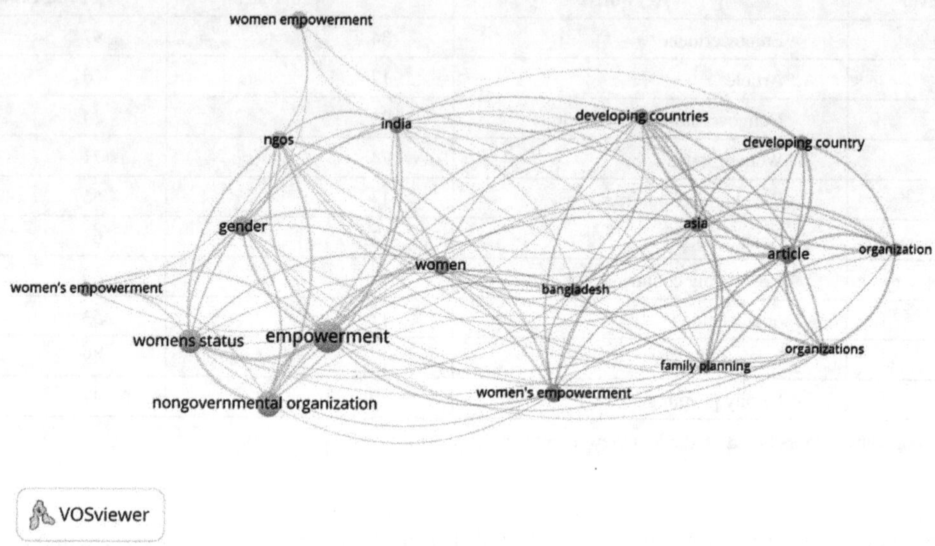

From this analysis, the authors found that the most searched keywords for "women empowerment" are "empowerment", "women status" and "nongovernmental organisations."

4.6. Co-Authorship Analysis

4.6.1. Co-authorship Analysis as Authors' Network

The authors in this study have used Vos Viewer Software to analyse co-authorship networking. The authors have selected co-authorship in the type of analysis column and selected authors in the unit of analysis column. The minimum number of documents of an author was chosen as 01 and the minimum number of citations of an author was chosen as 05. After incorporating the effects, the researchers found out that from 245 authors, 115 met the verges and for each of 115 authors, the total strength of the co-authorship links with other authors was calculated. The authors with the greatest total link strength were selected. Some of the 115 items in the network are not connected. The largest set of connected items consisted of 9 items only which is been shown in figure 6. Only 1 cluster has been drawn through Vos viewer software which contains 9 items. Table VI and figure 7 shows the list of the items in the cluster.

Table 6. Detailed description of Co-authorship among authors

Clusters	Cluster 1
Authors	Ayagirwe r.b.b.
	Azine p.c.
	Bindelle j.
	Chiuri w.l.
	Kampemba f.m.
	Maass b.l.
	Metre t.k.
	Mugisho a.b.
	Tsongo f.

Source: Compiled by authors based on the Vos viewer software

Figure 7. Network mapping of Co-authorship among different authors
Source: *"Framed by authors using VOS viewer Software"*

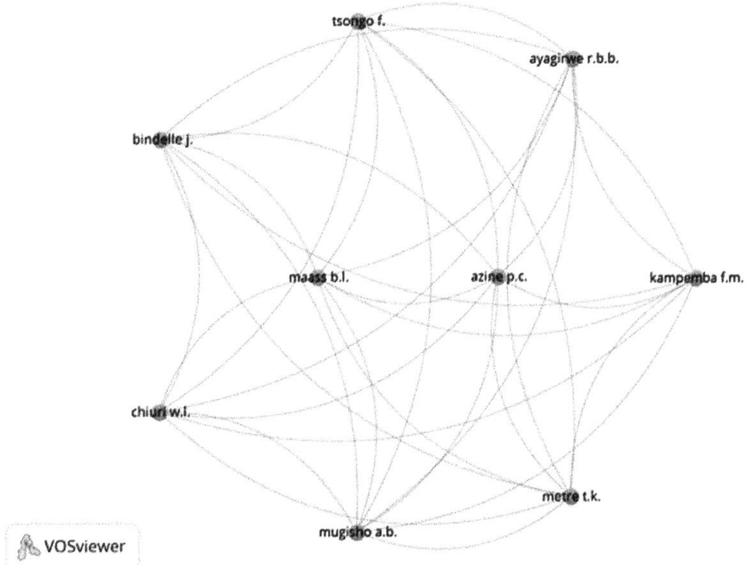

In this analysis, the authors found that there are so many authors who worked on women empowerment and NGOs, but among them only 9 authors collectively have done the remarkable publications with a minimum of 5 citations.

CONCLUSION

In India, there is a lot of gender discrimination and violence against women. A National Health and Family Survey study states that one in three Indian women, beginning at the age of 15, had experienced some type of domestic or sexual abuse. According to the same poll, domestic violence is viewed as usual by 54.4 percent of rural women and 46.8 percent of urban women. Women are taught from an early age that they are less than males. They are instructed to rely on the male role models in their lives. Because of how deeply ingrained these patriarchal and misogynistic attitudes are, women stop caring about the assault. Numerous women have been forced to suffer in silence due to a lack of knowledge, lack of awareness, and fear of societal shame. Only 14% of women who reported being assaulted actively sought assistance, according to NHFS-4. Some pro-woman NGOs assist women in obtaining justice through the legal system and motivate them to take control of their own lives.

There is an urge need to start spreading awareness through the field and in academic field as well so that researchers can do more studies and can help finding solutions to several issues faced by women in India and around the globe. With this viewpoint, the authors in this study provided a summary for the researchers who wants to work in the field of women empowerment and NGOs for women. The study showcases the most prolific authors, the prominent journals which are publishing the articles related to this theme, the most search keywords for the same and the trend of this topic.

LIMITATIONS AND FUTURE DIRECTION

Researchers can do a bibliometric evaluation on additional databases such as WOS (Web of Science), Publons, and Google Scholar, as well as other research prospects on the subject women empowerment, according to this study. Additionally, researchers can use various filters in the data like all publication stages of the articles, and different languages of the articles in addition to English. The researcher can conduct a bibliometric review of the different journal databases related to women empowerment.

REFERENCES

Alsop, R., & Heinsohn, N. (2012). *Measuring empowerment in practice: Structuring analysis and framing indicators* (Vol. 3510). World Bank Publications.

Bilge, S. (2010). Recent feminist outlooks on intersectionality. *Diogenes*, *57*(1), 58–72. doi:10.1177/0392192110374245

Cancino, C., Merigó, J. M., Coronado, F., Dessouky, Y., & Dessouky, M. (2017). Forty years of Computers & Industrial Engineering: A bibliometric analysis. *Computers & Industrial Engineering*, *113*, 614–629. doi:10.1016/j.cie.2017.08.033

Chellappandi, P., & Vijayakumar, C. S. (2018). Bibliometrics, Scientometrics, Webometrics/Cybermetrics, Informetrics and Altmetrics—An Emerging Field in Library and Information Science Research. *Shanlax International Journal of Education*, *7*(1), 5–8.

Das, L. (2015). Work participation of women in agriculture in Odisha. *IOSR Journal of Humanities and Social Science (IOSR-JHSS), 20*(7), 66-78.

De Bakker, F. G., Groenewegen, P., & Den Hond, F. (2005). A bibliometric analysis of 30 years of research and theory on corporate social responsibility and corporate social performance. *Business & Society*, *44*(3), 283–317. doi:10.1177/0007650305278086

Dey, A., & Orton, B. (2016). Gender and caste intersectionality in India: An analysis of the Nirbhaya case, 16 December 2012. In gender and race matter: Global perspectives on being a woman. Emerald Group Publishing Limited.

Eck, N. J. V., & Waltman, L. (2014). Visualising bibliometric networks. In *Measuring scholarly impact* (pp. 285–320). Springer.

Figueroa-Armijos, M. (2017). Women's Entrepreneurship in Global and Local Contexts, Growth and Change, 48(3), 487-489.

Kabeer, N. (1999). Resources, agency, achievements: Reflections on the measurement of women's empowerment. *Development and Change*, *30*(3), 435–464. doi:10.1111/1467-7660.00125

Legovini, A. (2005). *Measuring women's empowerment and the impact of Ethiopia's women's development initiatives project.* The World Bank.

Lewis, D. (2010). Nongovernmental organisations, definition and history. *International encyclopedia of civil society, 41*(6), 1056-1062.

Mahajan, S. (2011). Entrepreneurship among marginalised groups in India: an empirical study of scheduled castes with special reference to Maharashtra. Entrepreneurship and New Venture Creation: International Models and Benchmarks, Bangalore.

Malhotra, A., & Schuler, S. R. (2005). Women's empowerment as a variable in international development. *Measuring empowerment: Cross-disciplinary perspectives, 1*(1), 71-88.

McCarthy, L. (2017). Empowering women through corporate social responsibility: A feminist Foucauldian critique. *Business Ethics Quarterly*, *27*(4), 603–631. doi:10.1017/beq.2017.28

Mishra, N. (2015). Empowering Women through Self Help Groups (SHGs) In Odisha–An Empirical Analysis. *International Journal of Novel Research in Humanity and Social Sciences*, *2*(3), 85–91.

Mitra, J. (2002). Consider Velasquez: Reflections on the development of entrepreneurship programmes. *Industry and Higher Education*, *16*(3), 191–202. doi:10.5367/000000002101296289

Mohanty, S. R., Das, B., & Mohanty, T. (2013). Empowerment of Women in Rural Odisha through Micro Enterprises. *IOSR Journal of Humanities and Social Sciences*, *12*(1), 1–8. doi:10.9790/0837-1210108

Pritchard, A. (1969). Statistical bibliography or bibliometrics. *The Journal of Documentation*, *25*(4), 348–349.

Sinkovics, N., Sinkovics, R. R., & Yamin, M. (2014). The role of social value creation in business model formulation at the bottom of the pyramid–implications for MNEs? *International Business Review*, *23*(4), 692–707. doi:10.1016/j.ibusrev.2013.12.004

Torri, M. C., & Martinez, A. (2014). Women's empowerment and micro-entrepreneurship in India: Constructing a new development paradigm? *Progress in Development Studies*, *14*(1), 31–48. doi:10.1177/1464993413504347

Yadav, V., & Unni, J. (2016). Women entrepreneurship: Research review and future directions. *Journal of Global Entrepreneurship Research*, *6*(1), 1–18. doi:10.118640497-016-0055-x

KEY TERMS AND DEFINITIONS

Bibliometric Analysis: By examining all publications related to a particular topic or field, bibliometric analysis is a computer-aided scientific review method that identifies significant authors or studies, and the relationships among them.

Corporate Sustainability: Corporate sustainability is a way to creating long-term stakeholder value via the implementation of a corporate plan that focuses on the environmental, ethical, cultural, social, and economic components of conducting business.

Economic Growth: Economic growth is defined as a rise in the economy's capacity to create more products and services than it did the previous year.

NGO: It is an acronym for non-governmental organisations. NGOs rely heavily on volunteers and others to pay their employees. The term "NGO" is often used to denote largely non-profit, private entities that operate independently of the government.

Social Entrepreneurship: The process by which people, companies and entrepreneurs create and develop innovations aimed at reducing societal challenges is known as social entrepreneurship. A social entrepreneur is therefore someone who seeks out business opportunities that benefit their community, society or the planet as a whole.

Social Issues: A social problem is a problem or problem that affects a large number of people. They usually reflect current events, but can also symbolize long-standing difficulties or unresolved disputes.

Women Empowerment: Empowering women entails ensuring that they have access to all economic, social, and educational rights. It aims to eliminate gender inequity for women in the workplace to provide them equal rights in the workplace, family, society, and community.

Chapter 6
Environmental Management in the Wine Industry: A Multiple Case Study

Javier Martínez Falcó
https://orcid.org/0000-0001-9004-5816
University of Alicante, Spain & Stellenbosch University, South Africa

Bartolomé Marco-Lajara
https://orcid.org/0000-0001-8811-9118
University of Alicante, Spain

Eduardo Sánchez-García
https://orcid.org/0000-0002-8524-4906
University of Alicante, Spain

Luis A. Millan-Tudela
https://orcid.org/0000-0003-3669-9960
University of Alicante, Spain

Joaquín Martínez-Falcó
University of Alicante, Spain

ABSTRACT

To overcome the adverse effects of climate change, wineries can develop environmental management programs to save and reutilize the resources they use. This represents a change of business paradigm in the wine sector that can be extremely beneficial, given that, on the one hand, wineries that develop their environmental management can save costs and protect the environment, favoring the preservation of the environment to ensure the permanence of the sector in the territory; and, on the other hand, such management can serve as a differentiating element in the market, allowing the winery to generate a competitive advantage. The objective of this study is to know precisely what practices can be developed to ensure a correct environmental management. To this end, through a multiple case study, a decalogue of practices is identified that every winery can develop to favor the preservation of the environment in which it operates.

DOI: 10.4018/978-1-6684-7422-8.ch006

INTRODUCTION

There is now a certain scientific consensus that the way we produce and consume energy is causing global climate change, which in turn is having serious impacts on both land and socioeconomic systems (Tziperman, 2022). The impact of this climate change is enormous, with predictions of lack of drinking water, major changes in conditions for food production and an increase in mortality rates due to floods, storms, droughts and heat waves. In short, climate change is not only an environmental phenomenon but a factor with profound economic and social consequences (Herndon & Whiteside, 2019).

Climate and its variability affect many areas, but the agricultural sector, in general, and the wine sector, in particular, are more vulnerable to climate change (Venios et al., 2020). Wine needs certain environmental conditions, so it is not difficult to deduce that an increase in temperature or a decrease in rainfall can have consequences for vineyards. Wine is an alcoholic beverage that is the product of total or partial fermentation of fresh grapes or their must. Complex biological and biochemical interactions take place between grapes and different microorganisms, mainly yeasts and lactic acid bacteria (Fleet, 2003). Cooler than normal temperatures result in incomplete ripening with high acid content, low sugar content and immature flavors; while warmer than normal temperatures create overripe fruit with low acid content and high sugar and alcohol content (Holland & Smit, 2010). The ability of the vine to adapt to these changes will depend on many factors, some intrinsic, such as the grape variety, and others extrinsic, such as the preventive measures applied during the growing process, as well as the production methods used for winemaking (Scrimgeour et al., 2015).

Although it may seem that vine cultivation is an environmentally harmless process, the reality is quite different. Hence, the wine industry must make changes in its processes, both in terms of cultivation and winemaking, to reduce its greenhouse gas emissions and thus contribute to improving the environment. Faced with the serious threat of climate change, wine producers and winery managers must in the short term consider a wide range of climate change adaptation and mitigation measures to preserve the quality, identity and profitability of wines (Merloni et al., 2018). Therefore, wine-producing countries must promote the environmental management of their wineries to mitigate the adverse effects of climate change. In this sense, Spain one of the main players, being the third largest producer of wine worldwide with 3,930 million liters produced in 2016, representing 14.70% of the wine produced in the world, only behind France and Italy with 4,556 and 5092 million liters respectively. The average global wine consumption, calculated between 2010 and 2016, stands at 3.4 liters per person per year (Anderson et al., 2017).

The industrialization of the agri-food system following the green revolution of the mid-20th century has led to increased productivity and made the agri-food industry one of the most energy- and resource-demanding. As a result, it is one of the activities that contributes most to global environmental problems (Zanin et al., 2019). In this context, consumers have become increasingly aware in recent years of the environmental impacts of food production. Thus, society has been pressuring government agencies to implement various measures to reduce the harmful effects of human activity on the environment.

The aim of this work is to identify the best practices developed by wineries in environmental management to proactively mitigate the adverse effects of global warming. This work aims to serve as a guide of best practices for all those wineries that are becoming aware of the importance of protecting the environment in which they operate, so that, based on individual contributions, the sector as a whole becomes more sustainable and a scalable effect is achieved. This is not always easy, due, on the one hand, to the lack of awareness and willingness to act and, on the other hand, to the existing barriers, ranging from the lack of knowledge of the techniques to be applied and their reliability, to the high economic costs involved in implementing some of them. Thus, the research contributes to previous academic literature on the importance of environmental management in the wine industry (Marco-Lara et al., 2022a; Marco-Lara et al., 2022b; Marco-Lara et al., 2022c; Marco-Lara et al., 2022d; Marco-Lara et al., 2022e; Marco-Lara et al., 2022f; Marco-Lara et al., 2022g; Marco-Lara et al., 2022h; Marco-Lara et al., 2022i; Marco-Lara et al., 2022j; Marco-Lara et al., 2022k; Marco-Lara et al., 2022l; Marco-Lajara et al., 2022m; Marco-Lajara et al., 2022n; Marco-Lajara et al., 2022o; Marco-Lajara et al., 2022p; Marco-Lajara et al., 2023a; Martínez-Falcó et al, 2023a; Marco-Lajara et al., 2023b; Marco-Lajara et al., 2023c; Marco-Lajara et al., 2023d; Martínez-Falcó et al., 2023b) Martínez-Falcó et al., 2023c; Martínez-Falcó et al., 2023d; Martínez-Falcó et al., 2023e; Martínez-Falcó et al., 2023f; Martínez-Falcó et al., 2023g; Martínez-Falcó et al., 2023h; Martínez-Falcó et al., 2023i; Martínez-Falcó et al., 2023j; Martínez-Falcó et al., 2023k; Millan-Tudela et al., 2022; Fuentes-Fernández et al., 2022; Sánchez-García et al., 2022; Seva-Larrosa et al., 2022).

To achieve this research objective, after this brief introduction, section 2 presents the methodology followed in the study, section 3 shows the research results, section 4 presents the main conclusions derived from the study and, finally, section 5 presents the limitations and future lines of research.

METHODOLOGY

The case method is used for this study. This qualitative approach is usually used and suggested in conditions where it is necessary to study exhaustively several elements and multiple dimensions of a subject (Benbasat et al., 1987, Eisenhardt, 1989, Yin, 2002). In this research study, different environmental practices developed by wineries should be studied and analyzed in order to protect the environment and thus ensure the survival of the wine industry. Yin (2002) defines the case study method as an empirical inquiry that investigates a contemporary phenomenon within its real context, especially when the boundaries between the phenomenon and the context are not clearly evident.

A case study can be based on a single, unique case or involve more than one unit of analysis. In the first case, it is a single case study and is appropriate for investigating the particularity of a specific case. It can be used for descriptive purposes, to illustrate, test or confirm a theory or to investigate revealing cases (Bassey, 2003). The second typology corresponds to the multiple case study, which allows exploring more than one unit of analysis providing the basis for generalization (Rule & John, 2015). Investigating more than one case provides criteria of internal and external validity and reliability to the data, allowing to better deal with the problems associated with scientific rigor. Some authors, such as Ragin & Schneider (2011) consider the multiple case study as a comparative method, because its strategy allows examining similar and differential patterns among a moderate number of cases, being a fundamental characteristic of comparative methods, its interest in diversity. Therefore, it focuses its attention on the correspondence that exists between the different parts of each case. This is the main difference compared to those who consider multiple case studies as a variant of case studies (Yin, 2011), since these focus on finding common aspects that allow them to consider multiple cases as manifestations of the same thing.

Given the benefits of the multiple case study, this type of case study was selected through a non-probabilistic convenience sampling. Thus, five Spanish wineries considered as environmental references in the Iberian country were selected, since the research units should be selected based on characteristics or attributes that are important for the evaluation (Schoch, 2020). In particular, the following were selected: Bodegas Matarromera (located in Valladolid), Bodega Campo Viejo (located in Logroño), Beronia Rioja (located in Ollauri), Bodegas Juan Gil (located in Jumilla) and Bodegas Borsao (located in Borja).

Secondary data sources were used for data collection through information available on the wineries' corporate websites, promotional videos, press releases and articles written about the environmental management of the selected wineries. The data collection period lasted two months, from September 1, 2022 to October 31 of the same year, so the environmental practices identified were prior to that period. Table 1 shows the different secondary sources used to identify the best environmental practices in the wineries under study.

Table 1. Data collection through secondary data sources

	Bodegas Matarromera	Bodega Campo Viejo	Beronia	Bodegas Juan Gil	Bodegas Borsao
You Tube Channel	Bodegas Familiares Matarromera [https://www.youtube.com/c/VinosMatarromera]	Carrefour España [https://www.youtube.com/watch?v=rowRP-BldX8]	Bodegas Beronia [https://www.youtube.com/watch?v=5gCQom7J32M]	Vinos de Jumilla [https://www.youtube.com/watch?v=sp9TKHCYoAM]	Bodegas Borsao [https://www.youtube.com/watch?v=ViuxNYXVAko]
Corporate Web Page	https://matarromera.es/	https://www.campoviejo.com/es/	https://www.beronia.com/es-es/validate	https://gilfamily.es/bodegas_juan_gil	https://bodegasborsao.com/es/
Press releases	Corresponsables (2022)	Redondo (2019)	Indisa (2022)	Corresponsables (2022)	EnjoyZaragoza (2021)
	Vinetur (2018)	Financial Food (2019)	García-Rodríguez (2019)	Cañete (2022)	IgastroAragon (2021)

Source: Own elaboration

RESULTS

Bodegas Matarromera

The trajectory of the winery group from Valladolid went unnoticed by the Spanish Association for Standardization and Certification (AENOR), which, on the occasion of its 25th anniversary, certified the Matarromera Group's CO_2 balance of three of its wines at all stages: from the vineyard, to the production and winemaking process, transport, distribution, consumption and its own recycling. This certificate determined that its Emina Verdejo emits 829 grams of CO_2 into the atmosphere. This data, called carbon footprint, made the Castilian and Leonese Group the first Spanish company to know this calculation for its wines. On the other hand, Matarromera Group embodies in its Emina Wine Interpretation Center, the first integral project of Sustainable Development of the wine industry in Spain. Sustainability has been from the beginning a hallmark of the winery promoted by its founder, Carlos Moro, a commitment that is carried out in all areas of the company by his conviction and principles, in addition to his training as an agronomist engineer. In fact, the location of the winery is no coincidence, nor is its building half-buried in the traditional way, covered with earth on the sides and at the back. In this way, the temperature is kept stable inside with hardly any need for energy consumption.

The process of putting the environmental commitment into practice has been progressive and is embodied in a strategic plan called "Matarromera Sostenible en Planeta Tierr"', which includes a set of priority measures such as reducing energy dependence and emissions, organic production or the spherical economy. In the Matarromera Esencia project, sustainability has been one of the fundamental axes. The main objective was to improve the winery's energy management in order to reduce its energy consumption and become more efficient. This has also made it possible to introduce the winery into Industry 4.0

by analyzing multiple data related to production. It symbolizes its commitment to the environment and has, as stated on its label, the Wineries for Climate Protection certificate, which ensures that it has been treated in an environmentally sustainable winery. This certification has been developed by the Spanish Wine Federation and is based on four points: reduction of greenhouse gas emissions, water management, waste reduction and energy efficiency and renewable energy. Bodega Matarromera is committed to sustainability and the environment in the fight against climate change.

Bodega Matarromera is clearly committed to renewable energies through an extensive system of photovoltaic solar panels. In this sense, it is worth mentioning the bifacial panels on the roof of its parking lot, which more than satisfies the energy needs of the winery during the day. Their efficiency is superior to conventional ones. They incorporate the latest technology applied by means of Bifacial Photovoltaic Modules, generating energy through direct sun radiation and also by reflecting it on the ground at the front. In the winery, there are also two double charging points for electric cars and places for people with disabilities. In this way, Matarromera promotes sustainable wine tourism. Taking advantage of the visit to the winery, users can charge their cars in approximately one hour. This reaffirms a hallmark of all Matarromera Group wineries: being a pioneer in the installation of these charging points, which also provide added value to the rural areas where they are located. The Matarromera Esencia project, on the other hand, will involve the expansion of the existing wastewater treatment plant through the construction of two biological reactors and an ultrafiltration system. The design includes the removal of organic matter, nitrogen and phosphorus from the wastewater. The treated water will be used to irrigate the complex's 20 hectares of vineyards and gardens. In fact, Matarromera winery has the most advanced technology in energy efficiency, such as the system known as the Energy Hub (from Austria), through which the thermal energy generated is stored.

Bodega Campo Viejo

Campo Viejo is a winery located on a high plateau 100 meters above the Ebro Valley, in the vicinity of Logroño. It is semi-buried and integrated into the landscape, to minimize the environmental impact, not having to use air conditioning thanks to the constant interior temperature all year round and to achieve natural ventilation. Its main feature is the harmony between architecture and engineering, which makes it a functional, efficient, sustainable and environmentally friendly facility. In fact, the winery has won several awards for its sustainable design. In 2003 it received the Best of Architecture award. And in 2011 the Sustainable Wine Tourism Practices award given by The World Network of Capitals and Great Vineyards. The Campo Viejo winery has achieved the Spanish Wineries for Emission Reduction seal of the Wineries for Climate Protection certification, a certificate held by the winery since 2017, which requires a greater commitment to reducing greenhouse gas emissions. This certification developed by the Spanish Wine Federation, is the first and only certification in the field of sustainability specific to the wine sector. It began in 2011 as a sectoral movement in the fight against climate change and was officially presented as certified in 2015 with the backing of the Ministry of Agriculture. According to the company, its daily activity is based on respect for the environment, since the very original conception of the winery more than 20 years ago, sustainability is the driving force.

Recently, Campo Viejo has installed 1,071 solar panels in its facilities with a power of 487 kWp that generate enough solar energy to cover up to 20% of the winery's consumption. In addition, the winery already has geothermal energy that provides electricity to its social area. The new infrastructure has a photovoltaic generation area of 2,380 square meters. In the facility, 100% of the electricity consumption comes from renewable energy sources. There are no fossil fuel boilers, the heat pumps use gas and the air conditioning of the social area is achieved with a geothermal system from 11 boreholes drilled in the vineyards. The installation has been carried out considering the visual impact on the landscape, so the angle of inclination of the panels has been reduced to 10º to achieve a good integration with the winery. However, Campo Viejo, as a winery belonging to the Pernod Ricard Winemakers Group, has an even more ambitious goal for 2030: to reduce its emissions by 50% through various projects that will help to achieve this goal: sustainable packaging, renewable energy, environmental awareness and agreements with suppliers.

One of Campo Viejo's latest environmental initiatives has been the biodiversity study of the entire vineyard area surrounding the winery. A commitment that has resulted in the installation throughout the estate of "a biodiversity trail" with 16 points of interest with elements such as nests for birds, along with feeders for the cold months. Visitors can learn about the company's sustainability practices along this route and see the "hotels" and stone walls that house lizards, toads and other insects, as well as water ponds or stone animal guards that prevent insects harmful to the vine, thus controlling their population in a natural and sustainable way, maintaining the balance of the vineyard without using pesticides.

Beronia

Fellowship, hard work and passion for wine have marked the day to day life of Beronia, a winery founded by a group of friends in 1973. Their friendship led them to build the first Beronia winery in 1977 and today, nearly half a century later, they see another episode of their history written. It stars the Beronia winery of great Reserva and terroir wines in Rioja, the first in the world to achieve LEED V4 BD+C:NC (Leadership in Energy Efficiency and Sustainable Design) and LEED Gold sustainable building certification. Awarded by the US Green Building Council, this seal recognizes and distinguishes buildings with sustainable construction and low environmental impact.

The design of this unique winery, fully integrated into the Rioja landscape; the revolutionary system of using geothermal energy to heat the facilities and achieve lower energy consumption; the use of three other renewable energies (aerothermal, photovoltaic and solar thermal), together with the technological innovations it boasts, such as the "Cleanwood" system, make it one of the most efficient and sustainable wineries in the world. In addition, thanks to its design and operation, it ensures indoor environmental quality and well-being for its occupants and visitors in terms of thermal comfort, lighting and air quality with intelligent CO_2 detection systems, as well as the use of healthy and environmentally responsible products and materials.

These characteristics come together in the Beronia winery, whose winemaking management has been guided by Matías Calleja, winemaker and manager of the winery; its architectural work has corresponded to IDOM, with architects Gonzalo Tello and Borja Gómez at the head, and its landscaping, to Isaac Escalante Camus. Patrizia Laplana, of Asla Green Solutions, managed the Leed certification. Civil and industrial engineers, architects, ecologists, hydrogeologists, experts in indoor environmental quality and physicists, among others, have participated in this project that represents a holistic approach in the creation of a winery, where all the elements that compose it affect the evolution of the wines that are produced. Machinery, fermentation tanks and barrels, as well as the building itself, with its location and layout on the ground, its materials and the systems that integrate it converge towards a single objective: the production of unique wines that faithfully express the essence of this wine region and provide moments of enjoyment among friends.

"Climate change in this area has been somehow benefiting us until now, but that is no longer the case," says Matías Calleja, winemaker and manager of Beronia. That is why it became increasingly necessary to have a winery that respects the grapes from the highest technology. A sustainable and self-sufficient winery, prepared for what is to come. "It is clear that climate change is already happening, and we are part of that change. Starting from the field. For us, the farmer is part of the winery," he adds.

In the new Beronia winery, every visit is an experience. In addition to housing a Wine Bar overlooking the vineyard and a Txoko as a tribute to its four founding friends, the facilities have different spaces for tastings and multiple activities that aim to bring the wine world closer to visitors in an original way. Wine tourism follows the same line of sustainability and low environmental impact. Thanks to the crescent shape of the winery, its southeast orientation and various protective elements to reduce direct sunlight, you can be in the winemaking area while you can see the vineyard and enjoy natural light, as all the main spaces are interconnected by a work corridor. The barrel cellar, dug into the ground and without exterior facades, has a constant temperature throughout the year, which translates into significant energy savings.

Bodegas Juan Gil

At Bodegas Juan Gil they have certified the calculation of the organization's carbon footprint to work on its reduction so that since 2018 the waste ratios generated have been reduced by 22%. The enhancement of this work and awareness is reflected in obtaining the Wineries for Climate Protection certification, a specific industry standard that requires a commitment to reduce all areas of the winery's environmental impact. The Jumilla winery group not only wants to maintain its commitment, which began more than a decade ago, but also wants to be demanding of itself, and this certification is proof of this. Miguel and Ángel Gil, managers and co-owners of Bodegas Juan Gil, are proud to point out that their plant in Jumilla self-produces 20% of the energy it consumes. In addition, all the energy needed by Viñas Familia Gil is green and four of its work centers are disconnected from the grid and work with solar energy. But undoubtedly, the project that currently shows that once again Juan Gil is leading the way is the development of an R+D+i project that will reduce by 28% the weight of several of the glass bottles used in some of its brands. This reduction is applied in the new vintage to a quarter of its wines, which will reduce its carbon footprint by the indicated percentage in the coming months. The wines of Bodegas Juan Gil are made with Monastrell grapes, a native variety of great personality, from very old goblet-trained vineyards at high altitude. They are grown using environmentally friendly processes in the Jumilla Denomination of Origin, in the southeast of Spain, at an altitude of over 700 meters above sea level in the area known as Término de Arriba. The climate, dry and harsh, and the stony and limestone soils transmit all their virtues to the wine. With this value that the land gives us, Juan Gil is convinced that "it is our responsibility to take care of it". In Viñas Familia Gil they have been winemakers for more than 100 years and if there is something they love, it is the land. This passion leads them to work tirelessly to produce the best wines with the best possible quality/price ratio, and to take them to the five continents. Today it is a group of eleven wineries spread over 10 appellations of origin throughout Spain, all domiciled in Murcia, making clear their commitment to the land where they were born.

On the other hand, they maintain their firm commitment to sustainability, in addition to the care of the vineyard without herbicides or phytosanitary products, where they have been focusing their efforts for years on the implementation of facilities to combat climate change. Thus, they have built in Jumilla the largest energetically sustainable winery in Europe in which they valorize all the waste and waste generated in the same, transforming them into their own worm humus or vermicompost, thus obtaining a fertile fertilizer, magnificent natural and ecological food that returns to the earth to care for the same Monastrell plants from which they come mostly, thus closing a circular process that eliminates a large part of the bio-economic and environmental cost so necessary today to fight global warming.

Respect for the land bears fruit, and not only as a slogan or slogan. The Spanish Association of Wine Journalists and Writers, chose Juan Gil Etiqueta Plata 2018 as Best Red Wine of Spain in the XII edition of the contest they organize. The members of the AEPEV had to decide among the 700 brands proposed in the first phase of the competition, from which a total of 146 wines and vermouths and 61 spirits passed to the final in the 15 chapters for which they were competing. Miguel and Ángel Gil, managers and co-owners of the winery group, indicate that Juan Gil Etiqueta Plata, the flagship of the winery that gives it its name, is made masterfully and consistently vintage after vintage by winemaker Bartolomé Abellán, and although its vineyards have always been cared for sustainably, since the 2018 vintage it has been certified as an organic wine, giving shape to our commitment to the land and its people.

Wineries that want to voluntarily access this category, in addition to meeting the requirements of the Wineries for Climate Protection scheme, must verify additional conditions and the indexes to be met are very strict. Bodegas Juan Gil has more than met these standards. These successes are no coincidence. Being generous, sharing and knowing how to manage resources are intrinsic values to the fact of being a large family and have been part of the winery's DNA since its beginnings. This is demonstrated by the new construction of the Juan Gil winery, which began in 2000 in Jumilla and was born with the idea of building a winery that would be integrated into its environment and would be sustainable in terms of energy. A winery that is proposed with a construction system that is capable of assuming a thermal difference of 15 degrees without energy expenditure, which is essential in an area of strong thermal contrasts such as Jumilla.

Bodegas Juan Gil is currently the only winery in Murcia with certification for waste management. Currently its vermicompost project allows them to transform organic waste from winemaking into more than 300,000 kilos of humus. On the other hand, the implementation of a solar park allows them to generate 1.4 MW, which represents much more energy than what is consumed by all the wineries of the Viñas Familia Gil group. The group already has three wineries and a logistics base that are energy self-sufficient. These processes implemented by Bodegas Juan Gil are a demonstration and another example that profitability and sustainability are compatible. And they have also been recognized at the European level. At the end of 2018 the winery was selected as one of the most relevant projects with the greatest impact in Spain by the European Agricultural Guarantee Fund line of Funds and received a visit from a delegation of the European Commission, representatives of the Ministry of Agriculture and the Region of Murcia.

Bodegas Borsao

Bodegas Borsao is much more than a modern space of 16,500 square meters, it is a commitment to the future as well as a look at the tradition and history of the best quality grapes in the area. Equipped with state-of-the-art technology, the winery's facilities are characterized by their functionality. Thus, it has 132 stainless steel tanks -with a capacity of more than 9 million liters-, a wine aging room for more than 2.5 million bottles and a bottling line with a capacity of up to 10,000 bottles per hour. In the choice of the materials used, respect for the environment and proximity, such as the wooden structure and the local rustic face brick, as well as resistance, low maintenance cost and maximum thermal inertia, have been the main considerations. All materials are fireproof or have undergone fire-resistant treatment and the finishes of the interior linings are coated with food-grade epoxy resins.

Sustainable wine production at the new Borsao winery goes from grape to bottle, demonstrating a capacity for continuous improvement in processes, the minimization of polluting emissions thanks to highly efficient machinery and the increase of renewable resources towards a circular and socially responsible economy. Thanks to its commitment to sustainability, Borsao has established actions to reduce its environmental impact by 10% by September 2022 and, among the short-term objectives, are the reduction of greenhouse gas emissions and inorganic fertilizers during the 2021 and 2022 harvests. The new facilities have also been equipped with a purification system in an aerobic reactor, as well as a steam and hot water boiler with an output of 1,500 liters per hour for cleaning the equipment. The facility also has LED lighting and an 80-kilowatt photovoltaic installation, which reduces the contracted power and saves energy and costs. Bodegas Borsao has been committed to the territory since 1958, when the Borja cooperative took its first steps in the wine market. In 2001, the Tabuenca, Pozuelo and Borja cooperatives joined forces with the financial institutions Ibercaja, CAI and Caja Rural de Aragón, thus forming the Bodegas Borsao Group, a benchmark for Garnacha wines. With 375 professional wine-growers and 2,200 hectares of vineyards, it represents 36% of the surface area of the Campo de Borja Denomination of Origin.

In order to satisfy an increasingly demanding market, which demands ethical wines, and in response to the needs of the planet, Bodegas Borsao aims to be an example of sustainability. Corporate social responsibility plays an important role in this area, to which the winery attaches great importance. In fact, every year the winery presents a Corporate Social Responsibility (CSR) report, where all the actions carried out during the year are reflected. These include the hiring of personnel linked to the area and financial support for local and regional entities that work with the disabled, the elderly and other vulnerable groups. In addition, Bodegas Borsao promotes leisure, cultural and sports activities held in the region and sponsors gastronomic and musical events.

Bodegas Borsao holds the IFS and BRC international certifications, quality standards aimed at consumer protection that guarantee food safety and quality control and have become an indispensable requirement for the commercialization of wine worldwide. It also holds the Eco-Prowine environmental sustainability certification, approved by the European Union, which provides information to consumers so that they can recognize wine produced in a more sustainable manner, from an environmental, social and economic point of view, as well as constituting a seal of distinction for the wineries that have it. Borsao also registers its carbon footprint, a voluntary measurement that reflects the company's efforts to calculate, reduce and offset the Greenhouse Gas (GHG) emissions generated by its activity. It thus contributes to the fight against climate change, to controlling and reducing GHG emissions, as well as reducing costs by improving energy efficiency. Table 2 summarizes the environmental practices developed by the wineries under study.

Table 2. Sustainable practices of the analyzed wineries

Bodega Matarromera	Bodega Campo Viejo	Beronia	Bodegas Juan Gil	Bodegas Borsao
Carbon footprint quantification	Eco-efficient facilities	Fight against climate change	Measuring the carbon footprint of the organization	Energy savings
Integrated sustainable development project	Wineries for Climate Protection Certification	Betting on aerothermal, photovoltaic, and solar thermal energy	Wineries for Climate Protection Certification	Valorization of by-products
Sustainability as a sign of identity	Sustainability as an identifying element	Use of geothermal energy for air-conditioning of facilities	Sustainability as a hallmark	Eco-efficient facilities
Eco-efficient facilities	Photovoltaic panels system	Eco-efficient installations	Installation of eco-efficient panels	CSR program
Matarromera Sustainable Matarromera Strategic Plan in Planet Earth	Geothermal energy to provide light to its social area	Promotes sustainable wine tourism	R&D&I project to reduce the weight of glass bottles	Economic and social support to the area where the winery is located
Matarromera Esencia Project	Long-term objectives linked to the improvement of the winery's sustainability	Sustainability as an element of identity	Valorization of by-products	Eco-Prowine, IFS and BRC certifications
Wineries for Climate Protection Certification	Biodiversity study	Commitment to organic vineyards	Fight against climate change	Carbon footprint calculation
Commitment against climate change	Commitment to organic vineyards	-	Commitment to organic vineyards	Commitment to organic vineyards
Extensive system of photovoltaic solar panels	Fight against climate change	-	-	-
Double charging points for electric cars	Eco-efficient facilities	-	-	-
Expansion of the wastewater treatment plant.	-	-	-	-
Introduction of domotics for lighting sectorization and intensity variability.	-	-	-	-

Source: Own elaboration

CONCLUSION

This research identifies the main sustainable practices developed by wineries through a multiple case study, so the study can be very useful both for academics who are analyzing the link between the wine industry and sustainability and for winemakers who want to identify potential sustainable practices to develop in their wineries.

In particular, the study identifies a decalogue of practices that are repeatedly identified in the wineries analyzed and which represent a high commitment to society and the environment in which they operate. The wineries studied have eco-efficient buildings that make the most of natural sunlight and are integrated into the environment and landscape. They also have energy self-management systems through the panels they have installed, as well as through the biomass boiler to heat the building and the water treatment plant, which allows the water to be reused to irrigate the wineries' surroundings. These wineries, pioneers in environmental management, measure the carbon footprint of both their wines and their own organization and work to reduce it. They promote employment in rural areas, involve their workers in caring for the environment, and extend the knowledge and experience acquired to the entire sector through their participation in different sustainability forums. Likewise, they have charging stations for electric vehicles, are committed to the rural environment and its people, and value the by-products generated in the wine production process. All these environmental management actions are certified through different labels, among which Wineries for Climate Protection stands out as the main label in Spain to accredit the winery's social and environmental commitment.

Therefore, a series of theoretical and practical contributions can be extracted from the study. On the one hand, with regard to the theoretical contributions of the research, the study advances our knowledge of the sustainable practices that wineries can develop to improve social and environmental wellbeing. Thus, it contributes to improve the knowledge of the practices that wineries can develop to improve their environmental management, complementing recent research on the subject such as those of Carrillo-Higueras et al. (2018), Bandinelli et al. (2020), Galbreath and Tisch (2020) and Ouvrard et al. (2020). On the other hand, in terms of practical contributions, the study can serve as a guide for winemakers and environmental managers who are considering which sustainable practices to implement, what are the latest trends in sustainability in the industry, which certificates are the most commonly used to accredit the sustainable practices carried out by the winery and which wineries are considered as benchmarks in the field of sustainability.

FUTURE RESEARCH DIRECTIONS

Despite the important contributions derived from the study, it should be noted that the research also suffers from certain limitations. The fundamental limitation is related to the nature of the data, given that only secondary sources were used to carry out the multiple case study. To overcome this deficiency, as a future line of research we intend to complement the secondary information gathered in this study with primary information through personal interviews with the winemakers, winemakers and environmental managers of the selected wineries.

REFERENCES

Anderson, K., Nelgen, S., & Pinilla, V. (2017). *Global wine markets, 1860 to 2016: A statistical compendium*. University of Adelaide Press. doi:10.20851/global-wine-markets

Bandinelli, R., Acuti, D., Fani, V., Bindi, B., & Aiello, G. (2020). Environmental practices in the wine industry: An overview of the Italian market. *British Food Journal*, *122*(5), 1625–1646. doi:10.1108/BFJ-08-2019-0653

Bassey, M. (2003). Case study research. In J. Swann & J. Pratt (Eds.), Educational research in practice: Making sense of methodology (pp. 111 123). Continuum.

Benbasat, I., Goldstein, D., & Mead, M. (1987). The case research strategy in studies of information systems. *Management Information Systems Quarterly*, *11*(3), 369–386. doi:10.2307/248684

Cañete. (2022). *Bodegas Juan Gil apuesta por el respeto al medio ambiente y la calidad sostenible* [Bodegas Juan Gil is committed to respect for the environment and sustainable quality]. Laverdad. https://www.laverdad.es/economia-region-murcia/empresa/bodegas-juan-apuesta-20220409001917-ntvo.html?ref=https%3A%2F%2Fwww.google.com%2F

Carrillo-Higueras, F., Prajogo, D., & Smith, L. (2018). Environmental commitment and its drivers in the Australian wine industry: A behavioural approach. *Australasian Journal of Environmental Management*, *25*(4), 439–458. doi:10.1080/14486563.2018.1460630

Corresponsables. (2022). *Debemos romper con la visión errónea de que el medio ambiente lo soporta todo* [We must break with the erroneous view that the environment supports everything]. Corresponsables. https://www.corresponsables.com/entrevistas/matarromera-romper-vision-erronea-medio-ambiente

Corresponsables (2022). Somos una de las bodegas más grandes de Europa energéticamente sostenibles [We are one of the largest energy-sustainable wineries in Europe]. Corresponsables. https://www.corresponsables.com/entrevistas/juan-gil-bodegas-grandes-europa-energeticamente-sostenibles

Eisenhardt, K. M. (1989). Building theories from case study research. *Academy of Management Review*, *14*(4), 532–550. doi:10.2307/258557

EnjoyZaragoza. (2021). *Bodegas Borsao, un referente europeo de sostenibilidad* [Bodegas Borsao, a European benchmark in sustainability]. EnjoyZaragoza. https://www.enjoyzaragoza.es/instalaciones-borsao/

Financial Food. (2019). *Bodegas Campo Viejo avanza en sostenibilidad* [Bodegas Campo Viejo advances in sustainability]. Financial Food. https://financialfood.es/bodegas-campo-viejo-avanza-en-sostenibilidad/

Fleet, G. (2003). Yeast interactions and wine flavour. *International Journal of Food Microbiology*, *86*(1-2), 11–22. doi:10.1016/S0168-1605(03)00245-9 PMID:12892919

Fuentes-Fernández, R., Martínez-Falcó, J., Sánchez-García, E., & Marco-Lajara, B. (2022). Does Ecological Agriculture Moderate the Relationship between Wine Tourism and Economic Performance? A Structural Equation Analysis Applied to the Ribera del Duero Wine Context. *Agriculture*, *12*(12), 2143.

Galbreath, J., & Tisch, D. (2020). The effects of women in different roles on environmentally sustainable practices: Empirical evidence from the Australian wine industry. *Australasian Journal of Environmental Management*, *27*(4), 434–451. doi:10.1080/14486563.2020.1838351

García-Rodríguez, J. (2019). Beronia es premiada por su apuesta enoturística basada en la sostenibilidad [Beronia receives award for its commitment to wine tourism based on sustainability]. *La Gaceta del Vino*. https://lagacetadelvino.com/nuestras-firmas/reconocimiento-a-beronia-rioja-por-sus-buenas-practicas-medioambientales/

Herndon, J. M., & Whiteside, M. (2019). Geophysical consequences of tropospheric particulate heating: Further evidence that anthropogenic global warming is principally caused by particulate pollution. *Journal of Geography. Environment and Earth Science International, 22*(4), 1–23. doi:10.9734/jgeesi/2019/v22i430157

Holland, T., & Smit, B. (2010). Climate change and the wine industry: Current research themes and new directions. *Journal of Wine Research, 21*(2-3), 125–136. doi:10.1080/09571264.2010.530095

IgastroAragon. (2021). *Bodegas Borsao invierte 16,5 millones de euros en sus nuevas instalaciones, referente europeo en sostenibilidad* [Bodegas Borsao invests 16.5 million euros in new facilities, a European benchmark in sustainability]. IgastroAragon. https://www.igastroaragon.com/2021/10/bodegas-borsao-inviert e-165-millones-de-euros-en-sus-nuevas-instalaciones-referent e-europeo-en-sostenibilidad.html

Indisa (2022). *Beronia es premiada por su apuesta enoturística basada en la sostenibilidad* [Beronia receives award for its commitment to wine tourism based on sustainability]. Indisa. https://www.indisa.es/al-dia/beronia-premiada-apuesta-enotur istica-basada-sostenibilidad

Marco-Lajara, B., Falcó, J. M., Fernández, L. R., & Larrosa, P. S. (2022a). Evolución del pensamiento en la disciplina de dirección estratégica: la visión de la empresa basada en las capacidades dinámicas y en el conocimiento. [Evolution of thinking in the discipline of strategic management: the Dynamic capabilities and knowledge-based view of the enterprise] In Investigación y transferencia de las ciencias sociales frente a un mundo en crisis [Social science research and transfer in the face of a world in crisis], (pp. 1801–1826). Dykinson.

Marco-Lajara, B., Martínez-Falcó, J., Sánchez-García, E., & Millan-Tudela, L. A. (2023a). Wine Tourism, Designations of Origin and Business Performance: An Analysis Applied to the Valencian Community Wine Industry. *Businesses, 3*(1), 70–82. doi:10.3390/businesses3010006

Marco-Lajara, B., Zaragoza-Sáez, P., Martínez-Falcó, J., & Millan-Tudela, L. A. (2023b). The Export Intensity of Spain's Autonomous Communities in Terms of the Marketing of Wine and Their Geographical Destinations. In *The Transformation of Global Trade in a New World* (pp. 1–21). IGI Global.

Marco-Lajara, B., Zaragoza-Sáez, P., Martínez-Falcó, J., & Sánchez-García, E. (2023b). The Internationalization of the Spanish Wine Industry: An Analysis of Trade Flows and Their Degree of Concentration. In *The Transformation of Global Trade in a New World* (pp. 22–46). IGI Global.

Marco-Lajara, B., Martínez-Falcó, J., Millán-Tudela, L. A., & Sánchez-García, E. (2023d). Analysis of the structure of scientific knowledge on wine tourism: A bibliometric analysis. *Heliyon (London), 9*, e13363.

Marco-Lajara, B., Sáez, P. D. C. Z., Falcó, J. M., & García, E. S. (2022b). El capital intelectual verde como hoja de ruta para la sostenibilidad: El caso de bodegas Luzón [Green intellectual capital as a roadmap for sustainability: the case of bodegas Luzón]. *GeoGraphos, 13*(147), 137–146.

Marco-Lajara, B., Sáez, P. D. C. Z., Falcó, J. M., & García, E. S. (2022c). Las rutas del vino de España: el impacto económico derivado de las visitas a bodegas y museos. [Spain's wine routes: the economic impact of visits to wineries and museums] In Investigación y transferencia de las ciencias sociales frente a un mundo en crisis [Social science research and transfer in the face of a world in crisis]. (pp. 1774–1800). Dykinson.

Marco-Lajara, B., Seva-Larrosa, P., Martínez-Falcó, J., & García-Lillo, F. (2022d). Wine clusters and Protected Designations of Origin (PDOs) in Spain: An exploratory analysis. *Journal of Wine Research*, *33*(3), 146–167. doi:10.1080/09571264.2022.2110051

Marco-Lajara, B., Seva-Larrosa, P., Martínez-Falcó, J., & Sánchez-García, E. (2021b). *How Has CO-VID- 19 Affected The Spanish Wine Industry? An Exploratory Analysis*. NVEO-Natural Volatiles & Essential Oils Journal.

Marco-Lajara, B., Seva-Larrosa, P., Ruiz-Fernández, L., & Martínez-Falcó, J. (2021a). The Effect of COVID-19 on the Spanish Wine Industry. In *Impact of Global Issues on International Trade* (pp. 211–232). IGI Global., doi:10.4018/978-1-7998-8314-2.ch012

Marco-Lajara, B., Zaragoza-Saez, P., Falcó, J. M., & Millan-Tudela, L. A. (2022h). Analysing the Relationship Between Green Intellectual Capital and the Achievement of the Sustainable Development Goals. In *Handbook of Research on Building Inclusive Global Knowledge Societies for Sustainable Development* (pp. 111–129). IGI Global. doi:10.4018/978-1-6684-5109-0.ch005

Marco-Lajara, B., Zaragoza-Sáez, P., Falcó, J. M., & Millan-Tudela, L. A. (2022i). Corporate Social Responsibility: A Narrative Literature Review. In Frameworks for Sustainable Development Goals to Manage Economic, Social, and Environmental Shocks and Disasters (pp. 16-34). IGI GLOBAL. doi:10.4018/978-1-6684-6750-3.ch002

Marco-Lajara, B., Zaragoza-Saez, P., Falcó, J. M., & Sánchez-García, E. (2022j). COVID-19 and Wine Tourism: A Story of Heartbreak. In Handbook of Research on SDGs for Economic Development, Social Development, and Environmental Protection (pp. 90-112). IGI Global.

Marco-Lajara, B., Zaragoza-Saez, P., & Martínez-Falcó, J. (2022g). Green Innovation: Balancing Economic Efficiency With Environmental Protection. In Frameworks for Sustainable Development Goals to Manage Economic, Social, and Environmental Shocks and Disasters (pp. 239-254). IGI Global.

Marco-Lajara, B., Zaragoza-Sáez, P., Martínez-Falcó, J., & Ruiz-Fernández, L. (2022l). The effect of green intellectual capital on green performance in the Spanish wine industry: A structural equation modeling approach. *Complexity*, *2022*, 2022. doi:10.1155/2022/6024077

Marco-Lajara, B., Zaragoza-Sáez, P. C., Martínez-Falcó, J., & Sánchez-García, E. (2022k). Does green intellectual capital affect green innovation performance? Evidence from the Spanish wine industry. British Food Journal.

Marco-Lajara, B., Zaragoza Sáez, P., & Martínez-Falcó, J. (2022m). Does Green Intellectual Capital Affect Green Performance? The Mediation of Green Innovation. *Telematique*, *21*(1), 4594–4602.

Marco-Lajara, B., Zaragoza-Saez, P., & Martínez-Falcó, J. (2022n). Green Innovation: Balancing Economic Efficiency With Environmental Protection. In Frameworks for Sustainable Development Goals to Manage Economic, Social, and Environmental Shocks and Disasters (pp. 239-254). IGI Global.

Marco-Lajara, B., Sánchez-García, E., Martínez-Falcó, J., & Poveda-Pareja, E. (2022o). Regional Specialization, Competitive Pressure, and Cooperation: The Cocktail for Innovation. *Energies*, *15*(15), 5346.

Marco-Lajara, B., Zaragoza-Sáez, P., Martínez-Falcó, J., & Sánchez-García, E. (2022p). Las rutas del vino de España: el impacto económico derivado de las visitas a bodegas y museos. [Spain's wine routes: the economic impact of visits to wineries and museums] In *Investigación y transferencia de las ciencias sociales frente a un mundo en crisis* (pp. 1774–1800). Dykinson.

Martínez-Falcó, J., Marco-Lajara, B., Zaragoza-Sáez, P., & Sánchez-García, E. (2023a). Vino, Turismo y COVID-19: El impacto de la COVID-19 en las Rutas del Vino de España. *PASOS Revista de Turismo y Patrimonio Cultural*, *21*(1), 83–97. doi:10.25145/j.pasos.2023.21.006

Martínez-Falcó, J., Marco-Lajara, B., Zaragoza Sáez, P., & Sánchez-García, E. (2023b). Wine tourism in Spain: The economic impact derived from visits to wineries and museums on wine routes. *Investigaciones Turísticas*, *25*(25), 168–195. doi:10.14198/INTURI.21219

Martínez-Falcó, J., Marco-Lajara, B., Zaragoza-Sáez, P., & Sánchez-García, E. (2023c). Vino, Turismo y COVID-19: El impacto de la COVID-19 en las Rutas del Vino de España [Wine, Tourism and COVID-19: The Impact of COVID-19 on the Wine Routes of Spain]. *PASOS Revista de Turismo y Patrimonio Cultural*, *21*(1), 83–97.

Martínez-Falcó, J., Sánchez-García, E., Millan-Tudela, L. A., & Marco-Lajara, B. (2023d). The Role of Green Agriculture and Green Supply Chain Management in the Green Intellectual Capital–Sustainable Performance Relationship: A Structural Equation Modeling Analysis Applied to the Spanish Wine Industry. *Agriculture*, *13*(2), 425.

Martínez-Falcó, J., Marco-Lajara, B., Zaragoza Sáez, P. D. C., & Sánchez-García, E. (2023e). Wine tourism in Spain: The economic impact derived from visits to wineries and museums on wine routes. *Investigaciones Turísticas*, *25*, 168–195.

Martínez-Falcó, J., Lajara, B. M., & Zaragoza-Sáez, P. (2023f). Sustainable Intellectual Capital: A Comprehensive Construct for Understanding the Economic, Social, and Environmental Intangibles. In Intellectual Capital as a Precursor to Sustainable Corporate Social Responsibility (pp. 214-236). IGI Global.

Martínez-Falcó, J. M., Lajara, B. M., & Zaragoza-Sáez, P. (2023g). Analyzing the Evolution From Intellectual Capital to Green Intellectual Capital: A Literature Review. Intellectual Capital as a Precursor to Sustainable Corporate Social Responsibility, 72-90.

Martínez-Falcó, J., Marco-Lajara, B. M., Zaragoza-Sáez, P., & Ruiz-Fernández, L. (2023h). Green Intellectual Capital as a Catalyst for the Sustainable Development Goals: Evidence From the Spanish Wine Industry. In Climate Change, World Consequences, and the Sustainable Development Goals for 2030 (pp. 163-182). IGI Global.

Martínez-Falcó, J., Marco-Lajara, B., & Zaragoza-Sáez, P. (2023i). Corporate Social Responsibility: A Comprehensive Analysis. In Positive and Constructive Contributions for Sustainable Development Goals (pp. 131-160). IGI Global.

Martínez-Falcó, J., Marco-Lajara, B., & Zaragoza-Saez, P. (2023j). Corporate Social Responsibility vs. Corporate Sustainability: Different Concepts for a Common Goal. In Positive and Constructive Contributions for Sustainable Development Goals (pp. 76-87). IGI Global.

Martínez-Falcó, J., Marco-Lajara, B., & Zaragoza-Saez, P. (2023k). Theoretical Perspectives on Corporate Social Responsibility: A Narrative Review. Positive and Constructive Contributions for Sustainable Development Goals, 96-113.

Merloni, E., Camanzi, L., Mulazzani, L., & Malorgio, G. (2018). Adaptive capacity to climate change in the wine industry: A Bayesian Network approach. *Wine Economics and Policy*, *7*(2), 165–177. doi:10.1016/j.wep.2018.11.002

Millan-Tudela, L. A., Marco-Lajara, B., Martínez-Falcó, J., & Sánchez-García, E. (2022). Pursuing Business Longevity: Ways to Enhance Sustainable Development. In Frameworks for Sustainable Development Goals to Manage Economic, Social, and Environmental Shocks and Disasters (pp. 79-95). IGI Global.

Ouvrard, S., Jasimuddin, S. M., & Spiga, A. (2020). Does sustainability push to reshape business models? Evidence from the European wine industry. *Sustainability*, *12*(6), 2561. doi:10.3390u12062561

Ragin, C., & Schneider, G. (2011). Case-oriented Theory Building and Theory Testing. In M. Williams & W. Vogt (Eds.), *The Sage Handbook of Innovation in Social Research Methods* (pp. 150–166). Sage. doi:10.4135/9781446268261.n11

Redondo, M. (2019). Campo Viejo, viticultura integrada en el medio ambiente [Campo Viejo, viticulture integrated with the environment]. *Cinco Dias*. https://cincodias.elpais.com/cincodias/2019/11/27/companias/1574875847_496710.html

Rule, P., & John, V. M. (2015). A necessary dialogue: Theory in case study research. *International Journal of Qualitative Methods*, *14*(4), 1609406915611575. doi:10.1177/1609406915611575

Sánchez-García, E., Marco-Lajara, B., Seva-Larrosa, P., & Martínez-Falcó, J. (2022). Driving Innovation by Managing Entrepreneurial Orientation, Cooperation and Learning for the Sustainability of Companies in the Energy Sector. *Sustainability*, *14*(24), 16978.

Schoch, K. (2020). Case study research. *Research design and methods: An applied guide for the scholar-practitioner*, 245-258.

Scrimgeour, N., Nordestgaard, S., Lloyd, N. D. R., & Wilkes, E. N. (2015). Exploring the effect of elevated storage temperature on wine composition. *Australian Journal of Grape and Wine Research*, *21*, 713–722. doi:10.1111/ajgw.12196

Seva-Larrosa, P., Martínez-Falcó, J., & Ruiz-Fernández, L. (2022). Analizando las principales variables empresariales en los clusters vinícolas españoles teniendo en cuenta la localización de las empresas y su pertenencia a una marca colectiva. [Analysing the main business variables in Spanish wine clusters taking into account the location of the companies and their membership of a collective brand.] In *Miradas sobre el emprendimiento ante la crisis del coronavirus* (pp. 629–634). Dykinson.

Tziperman, E. (2022). *Global Warming Science: A Quantitative Introduction to Climate Change and Its Consequences*. Princeton University Press.

Venios, X., Korkas, E., Nisiotou, A., & Banilas, G. (2020). Grapevine responses to heat stress and global warming. *Plants, 9*(12), 1754. doi:10.3390/plants9121754 PMID:33322341

Vinetur (2018). *La apuesta sostenible de Matarromera obtiene cuatro certificados de AENOR [Matarromera's commitment to sustainability obtains four AENOR certificates]*. Vinetur. https://www.vinetur.com/2018101748520/la-apuesta-sostenible-de-matarromera-obtiene-cuatro-certificados-de-aenor.html

Yin, R. (2002). *Case study research: Design and methods*. SAGE Publications.

Yin, R. (2011). *Applications of case study research*. SAGE Publications.

Zanin, A., Dal Magro, C. B., Mazzioni, S., & Afonso, P. (2019, July). Triple Bottom Line Analysis in an Agribusiness Supply Chain. In *International Joint Conference on Industrial Engineering and Operations Management* (pp. 264-273). Springer.

ADDITIONAL READING

Bandinelli, R., Acuti, D., Fani, V., Bindi, B., & Aiello, G. (2020). Environmental practices in the wine industry: An overview of the Italian market. *British Food Journal, 122*(5), 1625–1646. doi:10.1108/BFJ-08-2019-0653

Cordano, M., Marshall, R. S., & Silverman, M. (2010). How do small and medium enterprises go "green"? A study of environmental management programs in the US wine industry. *Journal of Business Ethics, 92*(3), 463–478. doi:10.100710551-009-0168-z

Hughey, K. F., Tait, S. V., & O'Connell, M. J. (2005). Qualitative evaluation of three 'environmental management systems' in the New Zealand wine industry. *Journal of Cleaner Production, 13*(12), 1175–1187. doi:10.1016/j.jclepro.2004.07.002

Marshall, R. S., Akoorie, M. E., Hamann, R., & Sinha, P. (2010). Environmental practices in the wine industry: An empirical application of the theory of reasoned action and stakeholder theory in the United States and New Zealand. *Journal of World Business, 45*(4), 405–414. doi:10.1016/j.jwb.2009.08.009

Marshall, R. S., Cordano, M., & Silverman, M. (2005). Exploring individual and institutional drivers of proactive environmentalism in the US wine industry. *Business Strategy and the Environment, 14*(2), 92–109. doi:10.1002/bse.433

Silverman, M., Marshall, R. S., & Cordano, M. (2005). The greening of the California wine industry: Implications for regulators and industry associations. *Journal of Wine Research*, *16*(2), 151–169. doi:10.1080/09571260500331574

Tee, E., Boland, A. M., & Medhurst, A. (2007). Voluntary adoption of Environmental Management Systems in the Australian wine and grape industry depends on understanding stakeholder objectives and drivers. *Australian Journal of Experimental Agriculture*, *47*(3), 273–283. doi:10.1071/EA06024

Walsdorff, A., Van Kraayenburg, M., & Barnardt, C. A. (2004). A multi-site approach towards integrating environmental management in the wine production industry. *Water S.A.*, *30*(5), 82–87.

KEY TERMS AND DEFINITIONS

Carbon Footprint: Carbon footprint is an environmental indicator that aims to reflect the total greenhouse gases emitted by direct or indirect effect of an individual, organization, event or product.

Environmental Management: Environmental management is the name given to the set of actions that lead to the integral management of the environmental system. In other words, and including the concept of sustainable development, it is the strategy through which human activities that affect the environment are organized in order to achieve an adequate quality of life, preventing or mitigating potential or current environmental problems.

Sustainability: Sustainability consists of meeting the needs of current generations without compromising the needs of future generations, while ensuring a balance between economic growth, respect for the environment and social welfare.

Wineries for Climate Protection: Wineries for Climate Protection is the first and only specific certification for the wine sector in terms of environmental sustainability and its objective is to position itself as an international benchmark in the wine and environmental field, seeking solutions and best practices for wineries.

Chapter 7
Socio-Economic Sustainability in the Post-Pandemic Era:
An Organizational Structural Framework for Reliability, Safety, and Deployment

José G. Vargas-Hernandez
Instituto Tecnológico Mario Molina, Mexico

Omar C. Vargas-González
https://orcid.org/0000-0002-6089-956X
Tecnológico Nacional de México, Ciudad Guzmán, Mexico

ABSTRACT

This paper has the purpose to analyze the socio-economic sustainability in the post-pandemic era based on an organizational structural construct based on a framework for elements for reliability, safety, and deployment of organizational resources. It is assumed that theoretical and empirical studies in organizational resilience have limited contributions on the concepts of high-reliability organization applied to a diversity of entities and with a variety of characteristics. The method employed is the analytical reflective of the theoretical and empirical literature review. This study concludes that the emerging concept of organizational resilience confirms that the creation and development of an organizational resilience framework for structural construct can be supported by elements based on flexibility of organizational culture, organizational safety, and reliability, the promotion elements, and the deployment of organizational resources.

INTRODUCTION

Organizations seek to improve resilience of structure and functions, assets and infrastructure against disruption, degradation, and destruction. Organizational resilience can be evaluated on its facilities, infrastructure, and supply chains (Kohno et al. 2012). Organizational resilience is considered as a second-order construct but manifests at the first-order level constructs identified by Richtnér and Löfsten

DOI: 10.4018/978-1-6684-7422-8.ch007

(2014) as cognitive, structural and emotional resources linked to organizational creativity. Resilience is also the considered as the ability to absorb, stabilize the system structure, achieve function and identity in the cope of shocks.

A methodology to develop organizational resilience is based on structures and processes aimed to enhance the ability to respond to disruptions and create opportunities (Denyer, 2017, 20). Organizational resilience can be defined in terms of its outcome or what does, as *"the maintenance of positive adjustment under challenging conditions such that the organization emerges from those conditions strengthened and more resourceful"* (Sutcliffe & Vogus, 2003; Vogus & Sutcliffe, 2007).

Enhancing organizational resilience has a variety of concepts, principles, approaches, guidelines, and elements which combined enable to design a framework to be implemented at different organizational levels combined with varied factors at each level, creating and developing a theoretical model to influence organizational resilience. The concept of organizational resilience can be a single at the organizational level or multi-level concept (Linnenluecke, 2017) constructed and achieved at different organizational collective levels. Organizational resilience from the perspective of individual level is based on the inference that the organization is resilience as its individuals (Coutu, 2002; Horne, 1997; Horne & Orr, 1998; Mallak, 1998; Shin et al., 2012).

The concept of organizational resilience emerges from cognitive and engineering sciences among others to create and develop a framework for structural construct of organizational resilience supported on elements based on flexibility of organizational culture, organizational safety and reliability, the promotion elements, and the deployment of organizational resources. The analysis of data and information emerged from the research within the theoretical framework of adaptive socio-economic systems based on socio-ecology and sustainability after the COVID-19 pandemics and the co-management and resilience needed.

SOCIO-ECONOMIC SUSTAINABILITY IN THE POST-PANDEMIC ERA

Crises and perturbations push the entire socio-economic sustainability and ecological system into chaos and escalating risks of ecological damages, financial crashes, resources depletion, climate change, etc., before settling into an alternative stable state (Scheffer et al., 2012; Homer-Dixon et al., 2015). The socio-economic and ecological disruption caused by COVID-19 pandemic has triggered impacts on economic, social, political, ecological and health systemic changes leading to crises and opportunities for technological innovations leading to convergence and transition. COVID-19 pandemics was the perfect storm for the intersection of epidemiological and socio-ecological changes and economic growth, financial, and geopolitical instability. The COVID-19 pandemic extended the health problems to medicine, economic, financial, socio-ecological, and geopolitical.

Socio-economic variables are important for sustainability in the post-pandemic era and for the vulnerability to climate change such as economic growth, and social development that are seen as age, gender, race, and socio-economic status (Lundgren & Jonsson, 2012). Socio-economic growth and development are limited and eroding the socio-ecological regime and social innovation change leading to widespread economic, social, and political collapse. This dynamic has sustainable socio-economic development problems, health effects, mental distress, loss of food security, etc. (Whitmee et al., 2015; Butler, 2016).

The implications of short supply chains weakening the global knowledge flows and connectivity due to the COVID-19 pandemic are leading to the regimen transition of socio-ecological alternatives to capitalism, aimed to leverage opportunities for prosocial forms of production, distribution and consumption of goods and services. This socio-ecological alternative is a different proposal of the mainstream of green economics and politics.

The drivers converging transitions to ecological socio-economic sustainability promoted by local governance and resilience strategies with the support of the intersection of mutual trust, common vision of actors supported by technological and socio-ecological innovations to cover the fault-lines of the socio-economic and ecological global system. COVID-19 pandemic contributes to the global socio-ecological regime departing from the modernity concept of economic growth away from the health and wellbeing depending upon the collective capacity to contribute to the wellbeing of the community.

A socio-economic transition to sustainable development after the COVID-19 pandemics requires of formulation and implementation of strategies aimed to the facilitation of socio-ecological changes. for rent-seeking. Green socio-economic sustainable development differentiated strategies must be formulated and implemented based on factors of resources endowment, institutional quality support and socio-economic strength.

Socio-economic growth and development toward more sustainable environmental relations after COVID-19 pandemic between the natural and renewable resources in the market system with science and technology innovations, must be promoted to accelerate the transition towards more sustainable forms of production, distribution, and consumption patterns. This transition must aim to achieve sustainable goals at higher levels of health standards, economic growth, social justice, equity, diversity and inclusion and sustainable socio-ecological environmental systems.

FRAMEWORK OF ORGANIZATIONAL RESILIENCE

The concept of resilience is very promising theory and empirical research in organizational studies, despite that the conceptual and operational issues are considered of being fuzzy and the urgent need to develop taxonomies and construct frameworks (Clement & Rivera, 2017; DesJardine et al. 2017; Limnios et al. 2014; Linnenluecke, 2017; Williams et al. 2017). The constituent elements of the concept of organizational resilience are not clear under any specific discipline encompassing a set of diverse organizational disciplines and challenging the validity of unconnected concepts in a theoretical paradigm (Hirsch & Levin 1999).

There is a lack of a process framework for individual elements in different resilience phases. There is not an exhaustive list of elements and practices that constitutes organizational resilience which is contextualized in various settings. The definition of organizational resilience includes common elements and context-specific aspects. Definitions of resilience lack some common constituent elements (Aleksić et al. 2013). Organizations that experience collapse are more specific in benefits rather than a general organizational resilience frame (Hamel & Välikangas, 2003). The collapse of an organizations can be reframed as a process of resilience.

A comprehensive and integrated model that draws on various frameworks and approaches combines elements (Pasteur, 2011). Several factors improve organizational resilience which can be enhanced by the elements of people, core business systems and facilities (Foster and Dye 2005). An institutional, legal, organizational and procurement aspects of societal resilience are used as a framework to retrieve indicators and patterns able to identify critical issues (Becker, Abrahamsson, & Tehler, 2014; Herrera, Pasquini, Ragosta, Vennesland, 2014; Van Der Beek, Schraagen 2015). The components of the organizational resilience framework may change depending on the cumulative or individual weather extremes. The multi-disciplinary perspective of organizational resilience inquires the contribution of organization science and developing more robust framework with reification of assumptions to benefit from adverse and disturbing events and conditions.

A rigid quantitative framework for assessing organizational resilience allow to compare the levels of resilience between organizations and improve their engagement. Indicators for social resilience developed by Cuthill et al. (2008) adopted the SMARTT framework referring to indicators being specific, measurable, achievable, reviewable, time-lined, and talking. Indicators of resilience may represent what is considered healthy and successful.

Organizations use a resilience framework mindset to reinvent and reintegrate beyond former homeostasis. Key resilience practices are not always considered in many companies that might be reluctant towards establishing comprehensive and integrated resilience frameworks. The organizational resilience framework must be based on international best standards and practices.

STRUCTURAL CONSTRUCT OF ORGANIZATIONAL RESILIENCE

From the systemic perspective Tierney (2003) organizational resilience is a structural construct with the dimensions of robustness, resourcefulness, redundancy, and rapidity. A three-dimension construct of organizational resilience based on robustness, agility and integrity was developed by Kantur and Iseri Say (2015). To evaluate resilience, Tompkins (2007) proposes robustness, responsiveness, resourcefulness, rapidity, and redundancy. The ways to increasing organizational resilience are the redundancy, flexibility, and cultural change, which intends to address the resilience of future known and unknown events. Resilience is the ability to recover from disruption and improve by building redundancy and flexibility (Sheffi & Rice 2005).

Potential threat scenarios provide specific organizational resilience, but not general resilience which can be supported through the organizational structure that encourages collaboration shared mission and enhance robustness. The organizational resilience of hazardous industries depends on reliability and robustness which determines their ability to avoid degradation, failure, and errors. Structural resilience includes factors such as physical strength and robustness.

Organizational resilience is the ability to maintain positive adjustment, which emerge from conditions strengthened and more resourceful under challenging conditions (Sutcliffe & Vogus, 2003). Mindset and engagement in resourcefulness and nature of social resources facilitate resilience (Williams and Shepherd 2016). Some leadership aspects are related to resilience such as integrity, accountability, resourcefulness, effective communications, etc. (Helwig, 2013).

The advantage of redundancy is the ability to increase organizational resilience in the face of failures. A resilience building approach after resource depletion in a post shock implies efficiency, supported by redundancy and overlap. Inter-organizational relationships in supply chain resilience enhances organizational resilience draw from the design principles of redundancy and flexibility (Linnenluecke, 2017; Pettit et al. 2010; Sheffi & Rice 2005; Zsidisin & Wagner 2010; Ponomarov & Holcomb 2009).

A characterization of factors leading to impact resistance and rapidity elaborated by McDaniels et al. (2008) included several indicators ex-ante decisions and ex post adjustments of organizational resilience in the context of future climate variabilities and weather extremes.

Resilience can be fragile, antifragile, and robust. Resilience relates to the concepts of fragility, antifragility, and robustness. Fragility is a broken system damaged by variations (Taleb, 2012; Taleb & Douady, 2013). Resilience is critical to organizational success during times of high disruption relying more on policies, procedures, enforcement, and accountability and moving towards agility and analytics. Antifragility is the property of a system to face challenges, failures, and volatility (Taleb, 2012).

Resilience is the capacity of a system, organization, or person to maintain the core purpose and integrity in the face of dramatic changes of circumstances (Zolli & Healy, 2012). Responsibility lines in organizations fosters accountability and low tolerance for failure in potential conflict between specific and general resilience (Tetlock, 1985).

Collective leadership has a relevant role in organizational resilience and social responsibility. The motivation of employees may raise the level of organizational resilience to be able to behave responsively when facing unexpected situations (Dawson, 2010). Technological knowledge of systems supports specific resilience against known and unanticipated operations which can be balanced distribution of responsibilities and personnel programs in the organization.

Organizational resilience splits between defensive, progressive, consistent, and flexible behaviors forming a framework termed as the tension quadrant. However, a fifth strand termed fitness for purposes has emerged. An inflexible organization becomes unproductive as well as the excessive cost cutting impedes resilience. Resilience is a mental restoration ability characterized as the internal individual ability to flexibly cope with and recover from temporary mental illness because of unexpected contingency (Oshio, Nakatani, Kaneko, & Nagamine, 2002).

Resilience is the physical ability to return and recover the original state, flexibility, and stability. Resilience is the ability of recovery flexibility minimizing the damages in coping with an unexpected event and recover from the negative effects. Technological resources are used by organizations to achieve flexibility as required by the organizational resilience under the technology-in-practice framework.

A flexible heuristics orientation may increase organizational resilience in adverse situations more than the efficient orientation of routines. In building strong and flexible processes, Fuzzy Resilience Grade is distinct that fuzzy Resilience Early Warning Grade (Omidvar et al., 2017). In the micro-foundations of resilience, the organizational information systems may have risk and enabling factors. Organizations require a balance between the two processes Disembodying the system optimizes control of operations, but resilience decreases du to inflexibility, while embedding increases resilience but damage the organization (Ignatiadis & Nandhakumar, 2007)

FLEXIBILITY OF ORGANIZATIONAL CULTURE

The hurdle to organizational resilience is the inflexibility of organizational culture (Wilkinson et al., 2003). The principle of organizational resilience encompasses the ethos, values, behaviors, and cultural change of the organization. Organizational resilience can be increased by the support of features such as organizational culture, social capital, leadership, communication (Castleden et al., 2011; Lewis, Donaldson-Feilder, & Pangallo, 2011). Resilience is the result of a combination of attitude, culture, process, and framework (Hiles, 2011; Daskon, 2010)

The objectives of organizational resilience related to maturity levels in which the higher the level, the more organizational resilience. These levels are decline, survive, bounce back, and bounce forward within an integrated framework and the establishment of resilience culture. An organizational culture of resilience sets the foundations for recovery and socio-economic sustainability (Alesi, 2008; Coles and Buckle, 2004). Cultures are dynamic and can influenced resilience levels in organizations. Culture has an influence on various model frameworks for measuring organizational resilience and societal resilience. Organizational resilience supports the equal involvement and participation of both women and men, subject to cultural influences.

Resilience focuses more on the cultural change to facilitate problems (Sutcliffe & Vogus, 2003). Resilience is an on-going process that relates the individual with the organizational cultures that have the potential to self-correct after traumatic experiences (Paton et al. 2000). Cultural factors influence organizational resilience based on knowledge that enable to implement and operate correctly. Cultural factors influence resilience at organizational level and introduce appropriate action plans and solutions required to reduce the negative impact. Active resilience motivates and inspires others with a manifesting compounding effect on the organization that provides a framework strengthen by culture and values to make decisions in tricky situations and required to survive, thrive, and stabilize.

Organizational resilience is optimized by developing and maintaining a resilience culture, (Valastro 2011, Hiles, 2011, Pasteur, 2011, Daskon, 2010; Somers, 2009). The promotion of organizational resilience features has been already identified such as organizational culture, leadership, communication, resources, etc. (Crichton, Ramsay, & Kelly, 2009; Lengnick-Hall, Beck, & Lengnick-Hall, 2011; McManus et al.; Norris, Stevens, Pfefferbaum, Wyche, & Pfefferbaum, 2008; Stephenson, 2010).

Fostering organizational culture change to build commitment towards resilience. The organizational cultural change perspective that promotes the involvement of anybody in the needed concerns and issues without any barriers can enhance the organizational resilience. The individual resilience characteristics can be applied to organizational resilience which are essential to create a growing organizational culture of resilience.

Development of an organizational resilience approach is underpinned by organizational cultural change and branding built on sharing experiences and interactions with others. Organizational resilience requires training based on leadership, culture of trust, empathy, and acceptance. Organizations can build their own resilience leading to reduce stress in change Culture of organizational resilience building should be supported by the served individuals. Some new cultural identified trends need further investigation and can stimulate more in-depth research.

ORGANIZATIONAL SAFETY AND RELIABILITY

Organizational resilience is organizing for safety and reliability. The safety and reliability perspective of organizational resilience is a response to operate chaos without equilibria. Reliability and robustness determine organizational resilience when degradation, failure and error are no tolerated (Roberts, 1990). The system´s safety and reliability affect the dimensions of service aiming towards resilience.

Resilience is defined as the ability in tricky situations to stay safe and avoid accidents (Hale, 2006: 40). A framework for assessing resilience of systems and its components in a relationship of multiple risks to current operating parameters and the boundary of its safe operations is and indicator of resilience. Organizational resilience enact safety by handling exceptional events (Antunes 2011). Beyond the trade-offs between safety and production, and the link between the failure to balance production with safety risks and accidents, there are more to be studied and learnt about the enhancement of organizational resilience (Woods, 2003).

Create safety is inherent to resilience engineering perspective (Dekker et al., 2008). Employee enactment of safety to handle and deal unexpected events enhances organizational resilience (Antunes 2011; Borges & Menegon, 2012; Carvalho et al., 2012) supported by information technology (Chewning et al., 2013; Gimenez et al., 2017).

More efficient and reliable organizations are also more committed to resiliency mindset to recognize and identify events that go wrong and resolve with the minimum of harm. The organizational resilience research links the reactions to unexpected events focusing on responses and organizational reliability dealing with mindfulness for the presence of unexpected events (Weick & Sutcliffe, 2007).

Organizational resilience is a positive perspective focusing on the enhancement of safety and reliability and the salotungenetic understanding of coping (Sutcliffe & Vogus, 2003). The essential elements of organizational resilience in functional domains are the combination of the of people behavior, process reliability and product excellence to provide experience, trust, and reputation aimed to achieve information, supply, and operational resilience. Resilience can be integrated with operating reliability across a range of conditions. The organizational structures and procedures ensure reliability and facilitate organizational resilience.

Resilience has been analyzed in the context of high-reliability organizations (Weick & Sutcliffe, 2001) and in the context of responses to weather extremes events (Linnenluecke & Griffiths, 2012). Some assumptions of empirical studies in organizational resilience limit their contributions such as the concept of high-reliability organization applied to a diversity of entities with a variety of characteristics (La Porte & Consolini, 1998; Bigley & Roberts, 2001; La Porte & Thomas, 1995). A high reliable organization can learn from errors rather than rigidity (Weick & Sutcliffe, 2007) enabling to analyze the conditions of resilience in an interactionist perspective questioning the notion of organizational resilience. A high reliable organization exhibits resilience in unanticipated occurrences (Kendra & Wachtendorf, 2003: 14).

Organizations are more organizational resilience reliability-seeking then reliability-achieving (Linnenluecke, 2017). The interdependent relationship between organizational and community reliability is basic for the resilience between the organization and community (Lee, Vargo, & Seville, 2013; McManus et al., 2008).

PROMOTION ELEMENTS FOR ORGANIZATIONAL RESILIENCE

Resilience promotes the mitigation and preparedness relying on the quantitative conception of determining the real probability risk of adverse events and the severity of their consequences (Gephart, Van Maanen, & Oberlechner, 2009). Some factors promoting organizational resiliencies can be identified and assessed through different approaches. Some of the practices that are effective in enabling and fostering organizational resilience are to provide training and development of resiliency (Coutu, 2002).

Organizational resilience may be promoted by decentralization, redundancy, diversity, deployment of organizational resources and structures (Bruneau et al., 2003; Wildavsky, 1988; Vogus & Sutcliffe, 2007). From the same perspective, Akgün, & Keskin, (2014) there are several elements that integrate organizational resilience, among others, competence orientation, behavioral preparedness, social capital, original and unscripted agility, practical habits, and resource networks.

The resilience framework accommodates a qualitative capacity to absorb shocks and unexpected events maintaining the functions of recognition, recombination and renewal of organizational structures and processes. Networks are relational resources and protective factors that facilitate organizational resilience (Gittell et al., 2006; Kahn et al., 2013; Vogus & Sutcliffe, 2007). The range of a personal network relationships is an antecedent of resilience that have influence in the availability of resources to recover from crises. The framework is the contextual resilience are characterized by the social capital and the resource network.

The communication systems using network theory are relevant to evaluate organizational resilience (Ruiz-Martin et al. 2017, Ruiz-Martin et al. 2015). Using a personal narrative helps credibility that fosters organizational resilience. Experience and expertise are the power that foster organizational resilience (Lengnick-Hall et al. 2011; Sutcliffe & Vogus 2003; Weick et al. 1999) in organic structures than contribute to improve resilience more than hierarchical and mechanistic management structures (Jaaron & Backhouse, 2014). The hierarchy composition principle determines the importance of the elements of organizational resilience.

The resilience processes considered as the ability of the system to absorb and recover from disruptions and shocks, transforming structures and means for functioning in the face of stresses (Van der Vegt et al., 2015: 972; Williams and Shepherd 2016). Organizational resilience support structural and contextual ambidexterity (Eltantawy, 2016). A viable system model can be used to assess resilience and structural arrangements (Chan 2011). Tests on a structural model may provide empirical evidence of a set of exogenous variables to determine endogenous variables can be used to determine the antecedent and positive outcomes of organizational resilience.

An approach of organizational resilience from the internal structural and workflow articulation between occupational groups characterized by symbolic and identity values. Social network analysis (Borgatti et al., 2009; Borgatti et al., 2018) is a tool to analyze the structure of interactions in organizational resilience. The diverse types of structures, actors and contents of networks may affect the organizational resilience.

Some of the distinct attributes used to define organizational resilience are closely related to structure. Organizational resilience is the ability to maintain a structural configuration (McCarthy et al. 2017), surviving and retaining the structure and functions (Lampel et al. 2014; Salwan & Gada 2018), business functions (Antunes, 2011; Clement and Rivera, 2017) above-average returns (de Oliveira Teixeira and Werther 2013). A loss of resilience of organizational structures and processes may have consequences with direct and indirect impacts for organizations (Wilbanks et al. 2007; O'Brien et al. 2004). Organizational interruption impacts determine losses from actual events with limited insights on predictive elements of future organizational resilience. Behavior has an impact on vulnerability from structural change impact of resilience (Gallopín, 2006).

Organizational resilience requires more distributed control with central coordination and not centralized control with distributed implementation. Functional decentralization as being simultaneously bureaucratic and decentralized facilitates organizational resilience in such a way that authority patterns shift to functional skills (Clarke 1993; La Porte & Consolini, 1991).

Diversity is the variability of features impacted by threat and unexpected events attacking species, physical attributes. Diversity provides increased resilience. Organizational diversity and variation are initiative-taking in nature to ensure resilience. Some characteristics that can be used as indicators of resilience can be diversity, skills, physical substance, etc. Resilience rather than stability is supported by diversity (Brock et al., 2002, p. 272). Organizational resilience has indicators such as level of knowledge, adequacy of resources, diversity, information sharing, etc.

DEPLOYMENT OF ORGANIZATIONAL RESOURCES

Organizational resilience is multilevel related to resources, processes, and routines. The multi-level conception of organizational resilience across the organization, groups and individual interactions is related to the effective use of resources, processes, and routines dependent. Literature on organizational resilience is more based on normative and prescriptive methodology focusing on attributes, behaviors and resources (Boin & van Eeten, 2013; Duit, 2016; Sutcliffe & Vogus, 2003). Synergy between organizational resilience theory development and the ambiguous and resource constrained operating decision contexts may result in cyclical processes.

Contextual resilience integrates the resources and connections to provide the setting for using the behavioral and cognitive resilience. Collective sensemaking is a relevant element of cognitive resilience (Lengnick-Hall & Beck, 2009; Lengnick-Hall et al. 2011; Linnenluecke et al. 2012; Maitlis, 2005; Patriotta, 2003; Maitlis and Christianson, 2014). Conceptualization of organizational resilience focus on typologies of specific behaviors (Coutu, 2002; Hamel and Välikangas, 2003; Horne and Orr, 1998; Ishak and Williams, 2018), to integrate resilient resources and behaviors (Lengnick-Hall and Beck, 2005; Sutcliffe and Vogus 2003; Vogus and Sutcliffe 2007).

The organizational resilience approach is likely where there are resources constraints. Organizations that must deal with unexpected events, identify resources, develop practices and processes to facilitate organizational bricolage leading to organizational resilience (Bechky & Okhuysen, 2011).

The slack resources are a concept that is an antecedent to organizational resilience contributing to the problem solving of the organization (Acquaah et al. 2011; Gittell et al. 2006; Lengnick-Hall & Beck, 2005; Linnenluecke & Griffiths, 2012). In adverse events the resources are brought from external sources, regional and state level to support the organizational resilience in order that organizations can be able to bounce back (Carpenter et al. 2001). Organizational resources losses and the conditions of failure and tough times require organizational resilience leading to renewal and constant change.

Accessible financial, human and time resources are the foundation for adequate reactions under challenging situations (Hamel & Vaelikangas, 2003; Lengnick-Hall & Beck, 2009; Vogus & Sutcliffe, 2007). Human capital, social and financial resources are influencing factors that facilitate organizational resilience (Danes et al. 2009). The financial growth is an element of organizational resilience. Social resources such as social capital are a source of organizational resilience (Gittell et al. 2006; Powley, 2009; Sutcliffe & Vogus, 2003) in time of crisis and offer contextual benefits (Lengnick-Hall & Beck, 2009, Leana & van Buren, 1999; Faraj & Sproull, 2000; Gittell et al. 2006; McGuinness & Johnson, 2014).

Organizations foster resiliency by increasing the psychological resources and motivation through task autonomy and discretion of employees to build competences, self-efficacy, and confidence to respond during challenging situations (Sutcliffe & Vogus, 2003; Masten & Reed, 2002). Employees play relevant the role in resilience to deal with unexpected events and access to resources. Efficacy as an outcome of organizational resilience that enhances the ability to process feedback, rearrange and transfer resources and knowledge (Sutcliffe & Vogus, 2003). A low level of organizational resilience is present during the phase of release characterized by the rapid disbanding of the resources accumulated in the system. During the phase of reorganization, the organizational resilience increase characterized by the reassembly of resources and components of the system.

The ability of building organizational resilience against unanticipated and unexpected threats by organizations can increase their resilience with limited resources. Building and enhancing organizational resilience against unanticipated threats requires an ability to act outside of the response plans by investing some resources in risk-assessment and testing in the individual and system critical elements. Organizational work resilience empowers the human resources, the business model, and interactions (Foster & Dye 2005). Recovery operations may improve organizational resilience from testing and assuring availability of skilled human resources. Team and individual resilience can be developed and improved by training and human resources development (Lengnick-Hall et al. 2011).

Organizational resources make different contributions to resilience. Resource allocation decisions are made to support organizational resilience in anticipation of adverse conditions. The element of anticipation of organizational resilience emphasize to maintain effectiveness and avoiding degradation. Organizational resilience decisions on the use of resources requires a lot of sensitivity to continue consequences. Sensing process helps the organizational resilience orientation to perceive threats and opportunities from emerging resource factors and options, partnerships, business models, etc. Organizational resilience requires a buffer to maximize the potential to regenerate allowing more time for the emergence of a better option to enhance resilience and maximize resources.

Resources and practices of organizational bricolage is relevant to resilience characterized by mindfulness (Bechky & Okhuysen, 2011). The use of *salutogenic* lens, organizational resources, and assets as indicators for organizational resilience contribute to the evaluation and engagement of organizational contingency planning.

Entrepreneurial resilience is distinguished from organizational resilience in both theorizations and in practices in terms of resources, experiences, and slacks (Manfield & Newey, 2017). Resilience in family organizations is evaluated by the role clarity, decision authority ownership equality, fairness of compensation, failure to resolve conflicts, unfair workloads, and competition for resources (Danes et al. 2009). SMEs vulnerability and resilience are associated to resources, experiences, mindset, and risk taking (Kish-Gephart & Campbell 2015; Doern, 2016).

CONCLUSION

Socio-economic sustainability development and socio-ecological equilibrium after the COVID-19 pandemic is a path dependence process, temporary and provisional produced by dynamic evolution and generative endogenous transformation processes in transition towards new systemic equilibriums. While these processes are taking place, significant tradeoffs shift from global connectivity toward localized resilience approaches.

The reflective analysis of the concept of organizational resilience emerging from cognitive, ecology and engineering sciences, among others, confirms that the creation and development of an organizational resilience framework for structural construct can be supported by elements based on flexibility of organizational culture, organizational safety and reliability, the promotion elements, and the deployment of organizational resources.

The concept of organizational resilience is linked to the differing backgrounds of respondents despite their similarities, it is related as the ability to cope with risks and disturbances, planning and organizational structures. The structural arrangements of the working groups to cope with unexpected events question the boundaries to enhance the organizational resilience. Organizational resilience is dependent on the specific situation.

Resilience can be developed, practiced, and enhanced at large scale state-wide and international level frameworks. Organizational resilience requires commitment of all involved to transform and build upon characteristics of values and behaviors achieved through interactions and ongoing relationships that focus on the protection of resources and assets from the external threats.

REFERENCES

Acquaah, M., Amoako-Gyampah, K., & Jayaram, J. (2011). Resilience in family and nonfamily firms: An examination of the relationships between manufacturing strategy, competitive strategy, and firm performance. *International Journal of Production Research, 49*(18), 5527–5544. doi:10.1080/00207543.2011.563834

Akgün & Halit Keskin. (2014). Organizational resilience capacity and firm product innovativeness and performance. *International Journal of Production Research, 52*(23), 6918–6937.

Aleksić, A., Stefanović, M., Arsovski, S., & Tadić, D. (2013). An assessment of organizational resilience potential in SMEs of the process industry, a fuzzy approach. *J Loss Prevent Proc, 26*, 1238–1245. doi:10.1016/j.jlp.2013.06.004

Alesi, P. (2008). Building enterprise-wide resilience by integrating business continuity capability into day-to-day business culture and technology. *Journal of Business Continuity & Emergency Planning, 2*(3), 214–220.

Antunes, P. (2011). BPM and exception handling: Focus on organizational resilience. *IEEE Transactions on Systems, Man, and Cybernetics, 41*, 383–392. doi:10.1109/TSMCC. 2010.20625 04

Bechky, B. A., & Okhuysen, G. A. (2011). Expecting the unexpected? How SWAT officers and film. *Academy of Management Journal, 54*(2), 239–261.

Becker, P., Abrahamsson, M., & Tehler, H. (2014). An emergent means to assurgent ends: societal resilience for safety and sustainability C.P. Nemeth, E. Hollnagel (Eds.), Becom. Resilient, pp. 1-12. Ashgate Publishing, Ltd.

Boin, A., & van Eeten, M. J. B. (2013). The Resilient Organization—A critical appraisal. *Public Management Review, 15*, 429–445.

Borgatti, S. P., Everett, M. G., & Johnson, J. C. (2018). Analyzing social networks. *Sage (Atlanta, Ga.).*

Borgatti, S. P., Mehra, A., Brass, D. J., & Labianca, G. (2009). Network analysis in the social sciences. *Science, 323*(5916), 892–895. doi:10.1126cience.1165821

Borges, F. M., & Menegon, N. L. (2012). Different roles in the quest for system resilience. *Work (Reading, Mass.), 41*, 3238–3245.

Brock, W. A., Mäler, K. G., & Perrings, C. (2002). Resilience and Sustainability: The Economic Analysis of Nonlinear Dynamic Systems. In L. H. Gunderson & C. S. Holling (Eds.), *Panarchy: Understanding Transformations in Human and Natural Systems* (pp. 261–289). Island Press.

Bruneau, M., Chang, S. E., Eguchi, R. T., Lee, G. C., O'Rourke, T. D., Reinhorn, A. M., Shinozuka, M., Tierney, K., Wallace, W. A., & von Winterfeldt, D. (2003). A framework to quantitatively assess and enhance the seismic resilience of communities. *Earthquake Spectra*, *19*(4), 733–752. doi:10.1193/1.1623497

Butler, C. D. (2016). Sounding the Alarm: Health in the Anthropocene. *International Journal of Environmental Research and Public Health*, *13*, 665.

Carpenter, S., Walker, B., Anderies, J. M., & Abel, N. (2001). From metaphor to measurement: Resilience of what to what? *Ecosystems (New York, N.Y.)*, *4*, 765–781.

Carvalho, F. A., Koren, O., & Goodrich, J. K. (2012). Transient Inability to Manage Proteobacteria Promotes Chronic Gut Inflammation in TLR5-Deficient Mice. *Cell Host & Microbe*, *12*(2), 139–152. https://www.sciencedirect.com/science/article/pii/S1931312812002272. doi:10.1016/j.chom.2012.07.004

Castleden, M., McKee, M., Murray, V., & Leonardi, G. (2011, September). Resilience thinking in health protection. *Journal of Public Health*, *33*(3), 369–377. doi:10.1093/pubmed/fdr027

Chan, J. K. (2011). Enhancing Organisational Resilience: Application of Viable System Model and MCDA in a Small Hong Kong Company. *International Journal of Production Research*, *49*(18), 5545–5563. doi:10.1080/00207543.2011.563829

Chewning, L. V., Lai, C.-H., & Doerfel, M. L. (2013). Organizational resilience and using information and communication technologies to rebuild communication structures. *Management Communication Quarterly*, *27*, 237–263. doi:10.1177/08933 18912 46581 5

Clarke, K. R. (1993). Non-parametric multivariate analyses of changes in community structure. *Austral Ecology*, *18*(1), 117–143. doi:10.1111/j.1442-9993.1993.tb00438.x

Clement, V., & Rivera, J. (2017). From adaptation to transformation: An extended research agenda for organizational resilience to adversity in the natural environment. *Organization & Environment*, *30*, 346–365. doi:10.1177/10860 26616 65833 3

Coles, E., & Buckle, P. (2004). Developing community resilience as a foundation for effective disaster recovery. *Australian Journal of Emergency Management*, *19*(4), 6–15.

Coutu, D. L. (2002). How resilience works. *Harvard Business Review*, *80*(5), 46–55.

Crichton, M. T., Ramsay, C. G., & Kelly, T. (2009). Enhancing organizational resilience through emergency planning: Learnings from cross-sectorial lessons. *Journal of Contingencies and Crisis Management*, *17*, 24–37.

Cuthill, M., Ross, H., Maclean, K., Owens, K., & Witt, B. (2008). Reporting Social Outcomes of Development: An Analysis of Diverse Approaches. *The International Journal of Interdisciplinary Social Sciences: Annual Review*, *3*, 145–158.

Danes, S. M., Lee, J., Amarapurkar, S., Stafford, K., Haynes, G., & Brewton, K. E. (2009). Determinants of family business resilience after a natural disaster by gender of business owner. *Journal of Developmental Entrepreneurship*, *14*(4), 333–354. doi:10.1142/S1084946709001351

Daskon, C. (2010). Cultural resilience – the roles of cultural traditions in sustaining rural livelihoods: A case study from rural kandyan villages in central Sri Lanka. *Sustainability*, *2*(4), 1080–1100.

Dawson, C. S. (2010). *Leading culture change: what every CEO needs to know*. Stanford University Press.

de Oliveira Teixeira E, Werther WB (2013) Resilience: continuous renewal of competitive advantages. *Bus Horiz 56*, 333–342. https://doi.org/ r.2013.01.009 doi:10.1016/j.busho

Dekker, J. M., Funahashi, T., & Nijpels, G. (2008, April 1). Prognostic Value of Adiponectin for Cardiovascular Disease and Mortality. *The Journal of Clinical Endocrinology and Metabolism*, *93*(4), 1489–1496. doi:10.1210/jc.2007-1436

Denyer, D. (2017). *Organizational Resilience: A summary of academic evidence, business insights and new thinking*. BSI and Cranfield School of Management.

DesJardine, M., Bansal, P., & Yang, Y. (2017). Bouncing back: Building resilience through social and environmental practices in the context of the 2008 global fiscal crisis. *Journal of Management*, *26*, 014920631770885. doi:10.1177/01492 06317 70885 4

Doern, R. (2016). Entrepreneurship and Crisis Management: The Experiences of Small Business during the London 2011 Riots. *International Small Business Journal*, *34*(3), 276–302. doi:10.1177/0266242614553863

Duit, A. (2016). Resilience thinking: Lessons for Public Administration. *Public Administration*, *94*, 364–380.

Eltantawy, R. A. (2016). The role of supply management resilience in attaining ambidexterity: A dynamic capabilities approach. *Journal of Business and Industrial Marketing*, *31*(1), 123–134. doi:10.1108/JBIM-05-2014-0091

Faraj, S., & Sproull, L. (2000). Coordinating expertise in software development teams. *Management Science*, *46*, 1554–1568.

Foster, S., & Dye, K. (2005). Building continuity into strategy. *Journal of Corporate Real Estate*, *7*(2), 105–119.

Gallopín, G. C. (2006). Linkages between Vulnerability, Resilience and Adaptive Capacity. *Global Environmental Change*, *16*(3), 293–303.

Gephart, R. P., Van Maanen, J., & Oberlechner, T. (2009). Organizations and risk in late modernity. *Organization Studies*, *30*(2–3), 141–155.https://doi.org/ doi:10.1177/0170840608101474

Gimenez, R., Hernantes, J., Labaka, L., Hiltz, S. R., & Turoff, M. (2017). Improving the resilience of disaster management organizations through virtual communities of practice: A Delphi study. *Journal of Contingencies and Crisis Management*, *25*, 160–170. doi:10.1111/1468-5973.12181

Gittell, J. H., Cameron, K., Lim, S., & Rivas, V. (2006). Relationships, layoffs, and organizational resilience: Airline industry responses to September 11. *The Journal of Applied Behavioral Science*, *42*, 300–329.

Hale, A., & Heijer, T. (2006). Defining Resilience. In E. Hollnagel, D. D. Woods, & N. Leveson (Eds.), *Resilience Engineering: Concepts and Precepts* (pp. 35–40). Ashgate.

Hamel, G. and Välikangas, L. (2003). The quest for resilience. *Harvard Business Review, 81*(9), 52–63. 5.

Helwig, K. R. (2013). Resilience: A responsibility that can't be delegated. *Frontiers of Health Services Management, 30*(2), 31–35. https://www.ache.org/pubs/Frontiers/frontiers_index.cfm

Herrera, I. A., Pasquini, A., Ragosta, M., & Vennesland, A. (2014). The SCALES framework for identifying and extracting resilience related indicators: preliminary findings of a go-around case study. *SIDs 2014-Proc. SESAR Innov. Days*. EUROCONTROL.

Hiles, A. (2011). *The Definitive Handbook of Business Continuity Management*. Wiley.

Hirsch, P. M., & Levin, D. Z. (1999). Umbrella advocates versus validity police: A life-cycle model. *Organization Science, 10*, 199–212.

Homer-Dixon, T., Walker, B., Biggs, R., Crépin, A.-S., Folke, C., Lambin, E., Peterson, G., Rockström, J., Scheffer, M., & Steffen, W. (2015). Synchronous failure: The emerging causal architecture of global crisis. *Ecology and Society*, 20.

Horne, J. F. (1997). The coming of age of organizational resilience. *Business Forum, 22*, 24–28.

Horne, J. F., & Orr, J. E. (1998). Assessing Behaviors that Create Resilient Organizations. *Employment Relations Today, 24*, 29–39.

Ignatiadis, I. and Nandhakumar, J. (2007). The Impact of Enterprise Systems on Organizational Control and Drift: A Human-Machine Agency Perspective, *International Journal of Enterprise Information Systems (IJEIS), 3*(3), 36-51. IGI Global. doi:10.1057/palgrave.jit.2000087

Ishak, A. W., & Williams, E. A. (2018). A dynamic model of organizational resilience: Adaptive and anchored approaches. *Corporate Communications, 23*, 180–196.

Jaaron, A. A. M., & Backhouse, C. J. (2014). Service organisations resilience through the application of the vanguard method of systems thinking: A case study approach. *International Journal of Production Research, 52*, 2026–2041.

Kahn, W. A., Barton, M. A., & Fellows, S. (2013). Organizational crises and the disturbance of relational systems. *Academy of Management Review, 38*, 377–396. doi:10.5465/amr.2011.0363

Kantur, D., & İşeri -Say. (2015). Measuring organizational resilience: A scale development. *Journal of Business. Economics & Finance, 4*(3), 456–472.

Kendra, J. M., & Wachtendorf, T. (2003). Elements of Resilience after the World Trade Center Disaster: Reconstituting New York City's Emergency Operations Center. *Disasters, 27*(1), 37–53.

Kish-Gephart, J. J., & Campbell, J. T. (2015). You Don't Forget Your Roots: The Influence of CEO Social Class Background on Strategic Risk Taking. *Academy of Management Journal, 58*(6), 1614–1636. doi:10.5465/amj.2013.1204

Kohno, Y., Masuda, Y., Nagahashi, H., Tanaka, K., & Tashiro, K. (2012). Form development for self-rating an organization's vulnerability and resilience to disruption. *Journal of Disaster Research, 7*(4), 392–407. doi:10.20965/jdr.2012.p0392

La Porte, T. R., & Consolini, P. M. (1991). Working in practice but not in theory: Theoretical challenges of "high-reliability organizations". *Journal of Public Administration Research and Theory. J-PART, 1*(1), 19–48.

La Porte, T. R., & Consolini, P. M. (1998). Theoretical and operational challenges of "high-reliability organizations": Air-traffic control and aircraft carriers. *International Journal of Public Administration, 21*(6–8), 847–852. doi:10.1080/01900699808525320

La Porte, T. R., & Thomas, C. W. (1995). Regulatory compliance and the ethos of quality enhancement: Surprises in nuclear power plant operations. *Journal of Public Administration Research and Theory. J-PART, 5*(1), 109–137.

Lampel, J., Bhalla, A., & Jha, P. P. (2014). Does governance confer organisational resilience? Evidence from UK employee-owned businesses. *European Management Journal, 32*, 66–72.

Leana, C. R., & van Buren, H. J. III. (1999). Organizational social capital and employment practices. *Academy of Management Review, 24*, 538–555.

Lee, A. V., Vargo, J., & Seville, E. (2013). Developing a Tool to Measure and Compare Organizations' Resilience. *Natural Hazards Review, 14*, 29–41. doi:10.1061/(ASCE)NH.1527-6996.0000075

Lengnick-Hall, C. A., & Beck, T. E. (2005). Adaptive fit versus robust transformation: How organizations respond to environmental change. *Journal of Management, 31*, 738–757.

Lengnick-Hall, C. A., & Beck, T. E. (2009). Resilience capacity and strategic agility: Prerequisites for thriving in a dynamic environment. In Christopher P. Nemeth, Erik Hollnagel, and Sidney Dekker (eds.) Resilience engineering perspectives, Volume 2. Preparation and restoration, 39–70. Aldershot: Ashgate Publishing.

Lengnick-Hall, C. A., Beck, T. E., & Lengnick-Hall, M. L. (2011). Developing a capacity for organizational resilience through strategic human resource management. *Human Resource Management Review, 21*, 243–255.

Lewis, R., Donaldson-Feilder, E., & Pangallo, A. (2011). *Developing resilience*. Affinity Health at Work. https://www.cipd.co.uk/

Limnios, A. M., Mazzarol, T., Ghadouani, A., & Schilizzi, S. G. M. (2014). The Resilience Architecture Framework: Four Organizational Archetypes. *European Management Journal, 32*(1), 104–116.

Linnenluecke, M. K. (2017). Resilience in business and management research: A review of influential publications and a research agenda. *International Journal of Management Reviews, 19*(1), 4–30.

Linnenluecke, M. K., & Griffiths, A. (2012). Assessing organizational resilience to climate and weather extremes: Complexities and methodological pathways. *Climatic Change, 113*, 933–947.

Lundgren, L., & Jonsson, A. (2012). *Assessment of social vulnerability: A literature review of vulnerability related to climate change and natural hazards (CSPR briefing 9)*. Linköping University Centre for Climate Science and Policy Research.

Maitlis, S. (2005). The social processes of organizational sensemaking. *Academy of Management Journal, 48*, 21–49.

Maitlis, S., & Christianson, M. (2014). Sense making in organizations: Taking stock and moving forward. *The Academy of Management Annals, 8*, 57–125. doi:10.1080/19416520.2014.873177

Mallak, L. A. (1998). Measuring resilience in health care provider organizations. *Health Manpower Management, 24*(4), 148–152. doi:10.1108/09552069810215755

Manfield, R. C., & Newey, L. R. (2017). Resilience as an Entrepreneurial Capability: Integrating Insights from a Cross-Disciplinary Comparison. *International Journal of Entrepreneurial Behaviour & Research*. doi:10.1108/IJEBR-11-2016-0368

Masten, A. S., & Reed, M. J. (2002). Resilience in development. In C. R. Snyder and S. Lopez (Eds.). Handbook of positive psychology (pp. 74-88). Oxford Uk. Oxford. Oxford University Press.

McCarthy IP, Collard M, Johnson M (2017) Adaptive organizational resilience: an evolutionary perspective. *Curr Opin Environ Sustain, 28*, 33–40. https://doi.org/ t.2017.07.005 doi:10.1016/j.cosus

McDaniels, T., Chang, S., Cole, D., Mikawoz, J., & Longstaff, H. (2008). Fostering resilience to extreme events within infrastructure systems: Characterizing decision contexts for mitigation and adaptation. *Global Environmental Change, 18*, 310–318.

McGuinness, M., & Johnson, N. (2014). Exploiting social capital and path-dependent resources for organisational resilience: Preliminary findings from a study on flooding. *Procedia Economics and Finance, 18*, 447–455.

McManus, S., Seville, E., Vargo, J., & Brunsdon, D. (2008). Facilitated process for improving organizational resilience. *Natural Hazards Review, 9*, 81–90. doi:10.1061/(ASCE)1527-6988(2008)9:2(81)

McManus, S., Seville, E., Vargo, J., & Brunsdon, D. (2008). Facilitated process for improving organizational resilience. *Natural Hazards Review, 9*(2), 81–90. doi:10.1061/_ASCE_1527-6988_2008_9:2_81

O'Brien, K., Sygna, L., & Haugen, J. E. (2004). Vulnerable or resilient? A multi-scale assessment of climate impacts and vulnerability in Norway. *Climatic Change, 64*, 193–225.

Omidvar, M., Mazloumi, A., Mohammad Fam, I., & Nirumand, F. (2017). Development of a framework for resilience measurement: Suggestion of fuzzy resilience grade (RG) and fuzzy resilience early warning grade (REWG). *WOR, 56*, 463–474. doi:10.3233/WOR-17251 2

Oshio, S., Nakatani, M., Kaneko, M., & Nagamine, K. (2002). Negative na dekigoto karanotatchinaoriwomichibikushinritekitokusei; seishintekikaihukuryokusyakudo nosakusei. [The psychological properties that promote bounce back from negative states]. *Japanese Journal of Counseling Science, 35*, 57–65.

Pasteur, K. (2011). *From Vulnerability to Resilience: A Framework for Analysis and Action to Build Community Resilience*. Practical Action Publishing.

Paton, D., Smith, L., & Violanti, J. (2000). Disaster response: Risk, vulnerability, and resilience. *Disaster Prevention and Management, 9*(3), 173–179.

Patriotta, G. (2003). Sensemaking on the shop floor: Narratives of knowledge in organizations. *Journal of Management Studies*, *40*, 349–375.

Pettit, T. J., Fiksel, J., & Croxton, K. L. (2010). Ensuring supply chain resilience: Development of a conceptual framework. *Journal of Business Logistics*, *31*(1), 1–21.

Powley, E. H. (2009). Reclaiming resilience and safety: Resilience activation in the critical period of crisis. *Human Relations*, *62*(9), 1289–1326.

Richtnér, A., & Löfsten, H. (2014). Managing in turbulence: How the capacity for resilience influences creativity. *R & D Management*, *44*, 137–151.

Roberts, K. H. (1990). Some Characteristics of One Type of High Reliability Organization. *Organization Science*, *1*(2), 160.

Ruiz-Martin, C., López-Paredes, A., & Wainer, G. (2015). Applying complex network theory to the assessment of organizational resilience. *IFAC-PapersOnLine*, *48*(3), 1224–1229. doi:10.1016/j.ifacol.2015.06.251

Ruiz-Martin, C., Pérez Ríos, J., Wainer, G., Pajares, J., Hernández, C., & López-Paredes, A. (2017). The Application of the Viable System Model to Enhance Organizational Resilience. In Advances in Management Engineering (pp. 88–100). https://doi.org/ doi:10.1007/978-3-319-55889-9_5

Salwan, P., & Gada, V. P. (2018). Antecedents of resilience: An investigation into bharat forge. *Indian Journal of Industrial Relations*, *53*, 449–461.

Scheffer, M., Carpenter, S. R., Lenton, T. M., Bascompte, J., Brock, W., Dakos, V., Koppel, J. d., Leemput, I. A. d., Levin, S. A., & Nes, E. H. (2012). Anticipating Critical Transitions. *Science*, *2012*(338), 344–348.

Sheffi, Y., & Rice, J. B. (2005). A supply chain view of the resilient enterprise. *MIT Sloan Management Review*, *47*, 41–48.

Shin, J., Taylor, M. S., & Seo, M.-G. (2012). Resources for change: The relationships of organizational inducements and psychological resilience to employees' attitudes and behaviors toward organizational change. *Academy of Management Journal*, *55*, 727–748.

Somers, S. (2009). Measuring resilience potential: An adaptive strategy for organizational crisis planning. *Journal of Contingencies and Crisis Management*, *17*(1), 12–23.

Sutcliffe, K. M., & Vogus, T. (2003). Organizing for resilience. In K. S. Cameron, J. E. Dutton, & R. E. Quinn (Eds.), *Positive organizational scholarship* (pp. 94–110). Berrett-Koehler.

Taleb, N. N. (2012). *Antifragile: Things that Gain from Disorder* (Vol. 3). Random House.

Taleb, N. N., & Douady, R. (2013). Mathematical definition, mapping, and detection of (anti)fragility. *Quantitative Finance*, *13*(11), 1677–1689. doi:10.1080/14697688.2013.800219

Tetlock, P. E. (1985, September). Accountability: A Social Check on the Fundamental Attribution Error. *Social Psychology Quarterly*, *48*(3), 227–236.

Tierney, K. J. (2003). Conceptualizing and measuring organizational and community resilience: lessons from the emergency response following the September 11, 2001, attack on the World Trade Center. Univ. of Delaware, Newark, DE.

Tompkins, J. A. (2007). 4 Steps to business resilience. *Industrial Management (Norcross, Georgia), 49*(4), 14–18.

Valastro, J. (2011), Organisational resilience: a position paper for critical infrastructure, pp. 1-41. Commonwealth of Australia.

Van Der Beek, D., & Schraagen, J. M. (2015). ADAPTER: Analysing and developing adaptability and performance in teams to enhance resilience. *Reliability Engineering & System Safety*, 141.

van der Vegt, G. S., Essens, P., Wahlstrom, M., & George, G. (2015). Managing risk and resilience. *Academy of Management Journal, 58*, 971–980.

Vogus, T. J., & Sutcliffe, K. M. (2007). Organizational resilience: Towardsa theory and research agenda. Paper presented at *the Systems, Manand Cybernetics, ISIC*. IEEE.

Weick, K. E., & Sutcliffe, K. M. (2001). *Managing the unexpected: Assuring high performance in an age of complexity*. Jossey-Bass.

Weick, K. E., & Sutcliffe, K. M. (2007). Managing the unexpected: Resilient performance in an age of uncertainty (2. ed.). San Francisco, CA: Jossey-Bass.

Weick, K. E., Sutcliffe, K. M., & Obstfeld, D. (1999). Organizing for High Reliability: Processes of Collective Mindfulness. In R. S. Sutton & B. M. Staw (Eds.), *Research in Organizational Behavior* (Vol. 1, pp. 81–123). Jai Press.

Whitmee, S., Haines, A., Beyrer, C., Boltz, F., Capon, A. G., Dias, B. F. S., Ezeh, A., Frumkin, H., Gong, P., & Head, P. (2015). *Safeguarding human health in the Anthropocene epoch*: Report of The Rockefeller Foundation–Lancet Commission on planetary health. *Lancet, 386*, 1973–2028.

Wilbanks, T. J., & Romero Lankao, P. BaoMet al (2007) Industry, settlement, and society. In: Parry ML, Canziani OF, Palutikof JP, van der Linden PJ, Hanson CE (eds) Climate change 2007: impacts, adaptation, and vulnerability: contribution of Working Group II to the Fourth Assessment Report of the Intergovernmental Panel on Climate Change. Cambridge University Press, Cambridge.

Wildavsky, A. B. (1988). Searching for safety (3rd ed.) 2004. New Bruns-wick, London: Transaction Publishers.

Wilkinson, A., Elahi, S., & Eidinow, E. (2003). Section 2. Background and dynamics of the scenarios. *Journal of Risk Research, 6*, 365–401.

Williams, T., & Shepherd, D. (2016). Building resilience or providing sustenance: Different paths of emergent ventures in the aftermath of the haiti earthquake. *Academy of Management Journal*. doi:10.5465/amj.2015.0682

Williams, T. A., Gruber, D. A., Sutcliffe, K. M., Shepherd, D. A., & Zhao, E. Y. (2017). Organizational response to adversity: Fusing crisis management and resilience research streams. *The Academy of Management Annals*, *11*, 733–769.

Woods, D. (2003). Creating Foresight: How Resilience Engineering Can Transform NASA' s Approach to Risky Decision Making. Testimony on the future of NASA for Committee of Commerce, Science and Transportation.

Zolli, A., & Healy, A. M. (2012). *Resilience: Why Things Bounce Back*. Simon and Schuster, Inc.

Chapter 8
On Sustainable Entrepreneurship:
Can Resource Efficiency Be an Economic Opportunity for Small and Medium Enterprises?

Joana Moniz Monteiro
University of Aveiro, Portugal

Nicole Agostinha dos Muchangos
University of Aveiro, Portugal

Nina Szczygiel
https://orcid.org/0000-0001-5026-1629
University of Aveiro, Portugal

ABSTRACT

The aim of this chapter is to analyze the extent to which resource efficiency can be considered an economic opportunity to businesses, and to discuss the benefits and limitations of resource efficiency as perceived by companies. Based on established methodology, the authors performed literature review on benefits and limitations of improving resource efficiency, and opportunities resource efficiency could bring to businesses, and carried out interviews with six SMEs entrepreneurs. Results suggest the need to innovate in production and consumption and call for a more rigorous, science-based approach in decision making, especially when it comes to natural resources. International cooperation is seen as a means to making a transformation to resource-efficient future. The interviews also show that components most appreciated in promoting the efficient use of resources are (actual) financial aid and tax benefits, as well as education for sustainability and resource efficiency.

DOI: 10.4018/978-1-6684-7422-8.ch008

INTRODUCTION

Technological advances have shrunken the world to a system in which everything and everyone is interconnected. Nowadays, it is within seconds that one can get the latest news from the other side of the globe and learn about a specific subject even if in a geographically distant location. This is how people now know they share and are drawn, together, by the serious problems they face: a widening gulf between rich and poor, food insecurity (Eurostat, 2022), infectious diseases, military conflicts, climate change (European Commission [EC], 2018; United Nations Environment Programme [UNEP], 2020; European Commission, 2011; European Commission, 2010), (un)sustainability, and several other pressing issues that are increasingly threatening global security and stability (EC, 2018).

Among these subjects, extraction of resources and progressive environmental degradation have become of particular interest over the past century. Currently, it is generally acknowledged that the access to natural resources is already in jeopardy what creates genuine concerns about the world's future economy, society and environment (EC, 2011).

When discussing the access to and the use of resources, one of the biggest issues under debate is the pace at which renewable resources are being exploited, not giving the planet enough time to regenerate (EC, 2005). For instance, as reported by the European Union [EU] (2011), each person living in the EU territory consumes 16 tons of materials every year but ends up wasting 6 of a total of 16. In total, people in the EU throw away 2.7 billion tons of waste, 98 million tons of which is hazardous. On average, only 40% of solid waste is re-used or recycled (EC, 2011). Even if Europe is dependent on resources coming from outside, the negative impact of resource scarcity is being experienced around the world, with economies such as Brazil using their natural resources very quickly (EC, 2005).

It seems consensual that the environmental degradation is mainly caused by human activity what implies that people urgently need to change the traditional patterns of decision making and behavior (Chatzistamoulou & Tyllianakis, 2022; EC, 2018; Garrido-Prada et al., 2021) to adjust this tendency. If the society continues to follow the regular pattern of consumption, it is estimated that the global usage of resources will quadruple within the next two decades (EC, 2005). On the bright side, the analysis of material and waste streams in the EU suggests that even if the total consumption per capita remains the same, economy has grown by 50% over the last 20 years, which means that Europe has managed to enhance material efficiency over time (EC, 2005).

In response to the challenges of responsible and sustainable resource use, new concepts of business venturing have been proposed and tested. It is argued that balancing business goals with sustainably oriented management can provide the necessary means to minimize negative impacts of human activity on the environment without compromising business objectives. As resources and ecosystems are finite, the involved stakeholders need to be on the same page when it comes to values and decisions. It becomes essential to understand how environmental concerns impact business strategies and how they affect primary and support activities, and supply chain activities in particular.

The aim of this chapter is to examine and discuss if and how resource efficiency (RE) could be an economic opportunity for business, more specifically, for small and medium enterprises (SMEs). For this purpose, the authors first present the basic concepts used in the chapter, and then conduct six semi-structured interviews with SMEs entrepreneurs, followed by the discussion of the results and conclusions. The focus on SMEs in this chapter can be explained by the role they play in most economies given their share in businesses and their contribution to the national GDP (European Investment Bank [EIB], 2022).

BACKGROUND

Sustainability

Sustainability became widely discussed in the late 1980's by the Brundtland Commission (World Commission on Environment and Development [WCED], 1987). The report defined sustainable development as the ability to meet the needs of the present generation without compromising the ability of future generations to meet their own needs. It regarded sustainable development as a critical component of international development. It reflected the need to examine, and better understand, the impact of human activity on the environment. This report marked a path for upcoming years. With the goal to balance human development, prosperity and environmental risks, sustainability has been (gradually) placed at the heart of the transformation of societies and economies (Bocken et al., 2018; Chatzistamoulou & Tyllianakis, 2022; EC, 2018, 2020; Geissdoerfer et al., 2018; Organization for Economic Co-operation and Development [OECD], 2018; UNEP, 2020). Over time, organizations, including companies, have started to integrate sustainability through the entire value chain (Abrahamsson, 2007; Anderson, 1998; Cohen et al., 2008; Gast et al., 2017; Schlange, 2006).

Resource Efficiency

Longstanding unresponsible use of resources has been generating widespread environmental degradation, climate change and critical scarcities, all of which have and will likely continue to have great consequences on the planet and well-being of the populations. Resource efficiency allows to "create more with less, delivering greater value with less input, using resources in a sustainable way and minimizing their impacts on the environment" (EC, 2011). It is capable of increasing competitiveness (EC, 2011, 2018, 2020; Eurostat, 2022), creating new opportunities for growth and producing new jobs (EC, 2011; Eurostat, 2013). For instance, "green jobs" represent a total of 4 million jobs in the European Union (EC, 2018). Not just enterprises, but also consumers, can reduce costs with the adoption of resource efficiency. In the case of consumers, they need to avoid waste, buy products with longer life cycles, or that can be easily repaired and recycled (EC, 2010).

Promoting and improving resource efficiency by reducing materials, water, energy, carbon emissions and waste used to the production of one unit of economic product is just a part of the solution as it seems to not be enough for achieving sustainability (UNEP, 2020). There are four important conditions for ecological sustainability to be successfully implemented depending on the sustainable initiatives that are to take place, namely (Gast et al., 2017):

- regulations,
- public concern,
- top management commitment and,
- expected competitive advantage

The first two are framed within a macro setting: general policy making and macro-level orientations regarding the economy, society, and environment, as well as a society as a whole and its awareness and perception about importance of environmentally oriented decisions and practices. The other two are related to the organizational setting with specific strategies, visions and policies.

One approach to resource efficiency is that of the UNEP (2018), in whose understanding people and the economy all depend on natural resources and, thus, need to recognize and account for challenges that lie ahead. This specific work of the UNEP has shed some light on growing environmental challenges related to natural resources, their socio-economic implications and potential new pathways towards their sustainable management and it provided assessment of concrete economic opportunities and their implications in a form of science-based policy options on how to decouple economic growth from environmental degradation while enhancing people's well-being. In this regard, the European Commission (2013) has supported the position of the UNEP and holds that sustainable resource use is essential to human prosperity, and, therefore, resource efficiency is a crucial concept to be adopted by businesses. The macro setting has also been used as a framework for Ma et al. (2022), who have proposed that there is a strong exponential relationship between the country's economic complexity index and resource efficiency. They have found that the relationship between the two variables appears stronger for countries with stable institutions and primary material importers and that countries that rely on imports of primary resources experience stronger and a more positive impact of economic complexity on resource efficiency than those whose economic development is resource and export driven (Ma et al., 2022). In order to study resource efficiency and its implications, the International Resource Panel [IRP] (UNEP, 2016) has employed several assessments, reports and talks with policy makers, civil society and industry leaders to produce its vision of current status and future trends. The IRP suggests that resource efficiency yields both, short and long-term benefits that might lead to improving overall economic and environmental resilience. They suggest that articulating technological and economic aspects of resource efficiency yields a particularly high potential of improving and investing in resources efficiency.

At organizational level, implementing sustainable strategies and policies seem to depend on the top management commitment and the expected competitive advantage (Gast et al., 2017). When studying sustainable businesses, variables in analysis should suitably reflect its multi-faceted nature and account for both, financial performance and measures of social wealth that consider economic, social, and environmental impacts of new ventures (referred as 'the triple bottom line': People, Planet and Profit) (Cohen & Winn, 2007). Environmental, social and governance (ESG) frameworks are important to sustainable investing due to the fact that can help individuals and organizations to determine whether another organization is aligned with their values. Thus, any business strategy that results on either environmental, social, cultural, or economic impact or a combination of the above during the decision-making process is sustainability-enhancing (Chatzistamoulou & Tyllianakis, 2022).

Sustainable Entrepreneurship

Entrepreneurship has traditionally been seen as a tool capable of generating positive economic outcomes. The call for sustainability as a pressing factor that is affecting the systems globally has allowed to recognize entrepreneurial activities beyond the economic perspective and has led to the idea of sustainable entrepreneurship. Cohen and Winn (2007) have argued that entrepreneurs are likely to be a critical force in enabling the world to change its path and to offer future generations a sustainable future, supporting the idea that today's business practices are not exclusively associated to profit generation (Tilley & Young, 2009). In this understanding, sustainable entrepreneurship combines the traditional view on entrepreneurial behavior driven by economic benefits with sustainable gains. These gains are broadly construed to include economic and non-economic gains to individuals, the economy, and the society (Chatzistamoulou & Tyllianakis, 2022; EC, 2011, 2020; Kuckertz & Wagner, 2010; Shepherd

& Patzelt, 2011; UNEP, 2020) relevant to both, internal and external stakeholders (De Palma & Dobes, 2010). Simply put, sustainable entrepreneurship envisions a business logic that preserves the future of the planet. This vision has been regarded differently by different authors. For instance, Abrahamsson (2007) has proposed to use the term "sustainopreneurship" and Choi and Gray (2008) have suggested to approach it as "values-oriented entrepreneurship". Independently on the taxonomy, entrepreneurship has been seen as means to advance sustainable initiatives (Cohen et al., 2008; Schlange, 2006) and is a key element when attaining a green economy.

Entrepreneurship, Sustainability and Resource Efficiency

Alvarez and Barney (2007) have suggested a separation between two entrepreneurial action theories: discovery and creation. In an original way, they have compared the two theories to "mountain climbing" (the former) and "mountain building" (the latter). Both are used as examples of teleological theories of human action and can be used as a tool to explain human behavior, more precisely, the impact of that behavior on the ability of individuals to achieve their goals. In entrepreneurship, the first to find and exploit an opportunity will likely end up experiencing more success than those who come after. Following this logic and the traits of the 'first' and the others', two separate theories come into play, discovery and creation. Discovery (innovation) is risky, but opportunities do exist and even if these opportunities are yet to be perceived, one cannot deny they really exist. Additionally, decision makers must collect enough information (of good quality) to anticipate possible positive or negative outcomes. Creation, on the other hand, is uncertain since opportunities are believed to not exist. As there is no searching, entrepreneurs must act, they must "build the mountains" themselves (Alvarez & Barney, 2007).

When translated into entrepreneurship venturing, these theories may result in different professional approaches. Discovery entrepreneurs need to spend time and effort developing a business plan, having in mind its direction and duration, as well as to be prepared for the essence of their search work. They are also more likely to obtain financing from external sources and will often be able to make changes in marketing mix. Creation entrepreneurs believe that business plans can only be written after an opportunity has been created and argue that planning too early in the business cycle can result in waste of resources and deceptive information to everyone involved. According to this second perspective, entrepreneurship needs to be iterative, inductive, and incremental to support creating and decision making. Charismatic leaders are more likely to be successful when cooperation is needed to exploit a creation opportunity and it will be almost impossible to anticipate what kind of skills to look for in human capital (Alvarez & Barney, 2007). Shepherd and Patzelt (2011) argue that the key is the analysis of intentional behavior that results in entrepreneurial action. For instance, creative people tend to be more flexible and to adapt better to changes in their business environment people who pay attention to the environment are inclined to protect and respect it (Shepherd & Patzelt, 2011).

Whether entrepreneurship and entrepreneurs can generate sustainable economies it is still to be confirmed. For this question to be answered it is necessary to first get comprehensive answers on a number of others, such as those regarding the conditions associated into entrepreneurial ventures, the conditions created by public policies expected to positively impact sustainable entrepreneurship initiatives, the conditions expected to be in place when entrepreneurs pursue sustainable ventures, and the conditions in which entrepreneurship can simultaneously contribute to economic growth and to the advancement of social and environmental matters (Hall et al., 2010). In this discussion, it is important to distinguish between social, environmental and sustainable faces of entrepreneurship as only sustainable entrepreneurship is regarded as the one that combines economic, social and environmental perspectives and concentrates on ensuring the well-being of future generations (Anderson, 1998).

Small and Medium-Sized Enterprises (SMEs)

The legal definition of SMEs differs between countries and takes into account the number of employees, and/or annual sales, and/or asset value (revenue), and/or net income (balance sheet). The definition in place in the European Union regards an SME as "an enterprise with fewer than 250 employees, with a turnover of less than €50 million or a balance sheet total not exceeding €43 million" (OECD, 2018).

SMEs constitute approximately 99% of all businesses and represent 66% of the total EU workforce (Chatzistamoulou & Tyllianakis, 2022; OECD, 2018). Interestingly, SMEs are also responsible for 60–70% of all industrial pollution in Europe (Chatzistamoulou & Tyllianakis, 2022; OECD, 2018) but represent a great potential of developing green practices and contribute to developing greener economies (OECD, 2018). The OECD (2018) has defined the following principal drivers for SMEs to adopt green practices:

- The rising prices of commodities and a key raw material.
- Potential cost savings and competitive advantage.
- Market pressure from consumers.
- Misperception that protecting the environment comes with burdens, costs, and technical complexity.
- Uncertainty of the payback period.

Several business associations in the OECD countries have urged governments to provide support to SMEs in the transition process to a greener economy what has resulted in some recent policy initiatives such as the Green Action Plan for SMEs aimed to develop resource efficiency in European SMEs (OECD, 2018). However, success of such initiatives depends on overcoming several barriers such as diversity of activities, lack of information, scarcity of time and expertise, and the number of operators. It is also important to refer that SMEs entrepreneurs are more risk-averse and tend to suffer more from task pressure due to the size of their enterprises what can be explained by capital limitations and a smaller market presence (Garrido-Prada et al., 2021).

METHODOLOGY

In order to answer the main research question and to better understand whether, and if so, how resource efficiency can be perceived as an opportunity to business, in particular, to SMEs, the authors conducted a literature review and carried out a series of semi-structured interviews with Portuguese entrepreneurs (E) involved in small and medium business venturing.

The interview guide included questions about the profile of the company and its current approach to sustainability, awareness of resource efficiency, willingness to invest in resource efficiency, perceived challenges concerning investment and/or running a business in a country like Portugal, and personal opinions about possible solutions to problems regarding sustainable entrepreneurship and resource efficiency.

The interviews were carried out between October and December 2021 using communication technologies, more specifically, videoconferencing software. One interview was conducted over the phone because of technical difficulties. The interviews were transcribed and analyzed, using cross-case analysis and case-by-case analysis approach.

RESULTS

The participants considered doing business in Portugal as generally challenging. The factors that had more impact on their experiences in business venturing were support from the government, taxes and interest rates, funding, and human factors. The latter was explained as a potential challenge because "people are difficult to manage and deal with" (E1). For instance, Entrepreneur 3 (E3) shared that he could not recall a single moment where there were no financial problems. E6 recalled that his company had needed a (public) loan to launch the business and had been struggling since the due interests started arriving (30% of the total). E4 confessed having initially a lot of dreams and wanting to create jobs and expanding the company but, because of the lack of formal aid from the government, he ended up losing the motivation to do so.

Those participants who had move forward with investing in resource efficiency admitted have sought more specific information in the matter first (E4) as they believed that it would help their business in the long run (E1). In this regard, E5 admitted being afraid investing in something that would take years to create return on investment. E6 would consider such investment as long as the government started to ease the financial pressures against entrepreneurs and their businesses. On the other hand, E3 would not follow that path as he believed this would be the "beginning of the end".

Still, the entrepreneurs had all taken actions toward sustainability. E5 invested in partnerships with sustainable SMEs, E4 aimed to change their construction methods slowly and applied measures to use less energy and E3 organized and supported trainings, so that the employees made more responsible and sustainable decisions. E6 also concentrated on the employees and took steps toward sustainability, more specifically, applied to transportation. Three participants referred to recycling and repairing: reusing resources and materials to create energy (E1), recycling and repairing wood to be reused (E2), "as much as possible" (E5).

DISCUSSION

The aim of this chapter was to examine the extent to which resource efficiency could be perceived as economic opportunity for small and medium businesses. Most of the interviewed SMEs entrepreneurs were aware of resource efficiency and had already considered investing in it. As possible solutions to challenges faced by sustainable entrepreneurship and resource efficiency, the interviewees' suggestions were threefold: financial aid, public support, and education. More specifically, E1, E2, E5 and E6 seemed all to agree on the importance of financial support to companies. E1 came up with the idea that sustainable enterprises could be offered financial support at zero cost. E3 advocated to soothe the current high taxes so that SMEs can prosper. In addition, E6 proposed that the government started asking for just 5 to 10% of interest rate and the other 20% could be used to invest in the company. Therefore, the government's role was perceived fundamental in the process. Finally, E5 pointed out that education in changing human perception and behaviour was the key to success. He advocated the creation of programs and initiatives aimed to educate entrepreneurs about the advantages and profits of sustainability. In Table

1, the authors have summarized the benefits and limitations of initiatives aimed to promote resource efficiency identified in the literature. It is possible to see that the analysed documents share similar opinions on increasing the reuse, reparation and recycling activities. On the other hand, it seems that resource efficiency represents a somewhat optimistic view about the environment-economy relationship. More specifically, implementation of the measures in companies is lacking and businesses are likely to cherry pick those measures they believe to serve them best.

Table 1. Benefits and limitations of resource efficiency approaches

Benefits	Limitations
• Higher economic growth and employment. • Entrepreneurship and innovative opportunities in many areas due to the lack of inefficiency. • Macroeconomic benefits.	• Barriers can be overcome through changes of the rate and direction of innovation and technical change, and some combination of intelligent and targeted regulation. • Appropriate investment in enabling infrastructure, environmental tax reform and strategic use of fiscal policy. • Economies with an increasing share of services and imported manufactured goods increase their material productivity, resulting in their economic structure. • *Rebound effect:* Stimulation of economic growth that will increase resource use and environmental impacts. • Modelling of technical progress leading to cost reductions in the use of resources.
• Increase of industrial production concerns over environmental pressures associated with the resource use. • Resource efficiency is seen as a way to reconcile economic objectives, such as competitiveness, employment and growth, and environmental responsibility. • Can reduce input costs for firms and increase profitability or market share. • Material losses can be prevented.	• Technological shifts are bound to increase the demand for certain material resources. • Unable or unwilling to invest on resource efficiency measures. • Economy-wide effects may be smaller than expected. • Mobilization of capital both from public and private sector.
• Keeping resources in use for longer, and reducing the environmental impacts associated with the whole life cycle of resources. • Reduces the speed at which natural resources are depleted. • Reduces waste flows and emissions and reduces costs for producers and consumers. • Creation of new industries and further economic competitiveness. • Limits the environmental impacts of resource extraction in agriculture, forestry, fishing, mining, and quarrying. • Resource efficiency leads to a 7% higher GDP in the G20 countries as compared to existing trends.	• Achieving economic and environmental outcomes simultaneously is possible but requires concerted policy effort and carefully selected and designed policies. • Material footprint is unequally distributed across G20 countries. • Inequality in sharing the benefits of material use has not been reduced.
• Benefits will reoccur annually and give rise to a long-term stream of benefits. • The existing environment for business includes incentives for resource efficiency, increasing commodity prices, to which companies already respond without the need for intervention.	• Businesses will be concerned to understand the level of investment required to realize economic opportunities and the range of time over which such investment may be allocated. • Estimates are highly influenced by the assumptions made on resource prices, material flows in the economy, the net effect of the measures and where businesses are starting from in respect of resource efficiency. • The quantification of the opportunity is based on implementation of all measures available to businesses to improve resource efficiency.

The International Resource Panel argues that the economic opportunity of increased resource efficiency can be expressed in three ways. First, organizations can always find another way to increase resource efficiency that would provide more net cost savings. Second, cost reductions originating from increased resource efficiency not only have positive organizational repercussions, but also result in positive macroeconomic implications, such as increased employment and economic outputs. Third, inefficient use of resources brings the negative environmental effects and substantial external costs (UNEP, 2018).

In the EU, sustainable transition means reaching the "Net-Zero Targets" by 2050. For this objective to be achieved, awareness and knowledge about sustainability among individuals and organizations, including SMEs, are important (Garrido-Prada et al., 2021). The transition is considered "socially-fair" and "cost-efficient" and goes well beyond jobs and technology: it involves people and their quality of life (EC, 2018). Geissdoerfer et al.'s (2018) research, that has aimed to contribute to the understanding of how organizations transition to sustainable business models, argues that the way organizations apply new business models and the role and applicability of sustainable business models and their innovation are uncharted territories. They have pointed out the design-implementation gap in sustainable business model innovation and the challenges of running sustainable business model innovation, that are threefold: (a) ideas from meetings and workshops do not have a follow-up; (b) well-developed concepts are not implemented; and (c) most start-ups with business models fail. Thus, while moving toward a new sustainable business model represents an opportunity for businesses, research suggests it is not an easy task (Geissdoerfer et al., 2018).

What remains clear in literature is that innovation is seen as a foundation to a successful transition (EC, 2011). In this regard, three categories have been distinguished (EC, 2010):

- Smart growth ("developing an economy based on knowledge and innovation"),
- Sustainable growth ("promoting a more resource efficient, greener and more competitive economy"),
- Inclusive growth ("high-employment economy delivering social and territorial cohesion").

Traditional business rationale has no longer place in this new reality. Experimentation in business provides means to innovate processes and structures with reasonably limited risks and resources (Bocken et al., 2018). For example, simulations in product development can translate into a better use of materials, and simulations in production and simulations in logistics can lead to less waste in the material flows (Brüggemann et al., 2020). The use of sensor technology (with low-cost sensors already available on the market) and artificial intelligence could be of particular interest when seeking comprehensive examination of material movements and energy consumption. In other words, they could result in greater awareness regarding material and energy savings and reflect in future decision-making processes (Brüggemann et al., 2020). When accompanied by collective learning, it offers a chance of involving all stakeholders to finding ways of maximizing the value of products and services without compromising natural resources, society, and the environment (Bocken et al., 2018).

In particular, business model innovation is important because it can create a more sustained way of doing business (Bocken et al., 2018). A truly sustainable business model incorporates a triple bottom line approach and takes every stakeholder's needs into account as equally important as those of the environment. Bocken et al. (2018) point out that, to date, there are hardly any active fully sustainable businesses and emphasize that transitional business models could have a positive impact in the environment and society. Whalen (2019) has denominated one business model archetype previously identified by Bocken et al. (2016) as Extending Product Value (EPV). The EPV model is a generic type of business models assumed to contribute to resource efficiency in two ways, one, because it prevents a product's end-of-life, and second, because it prevents production of newly manufactured products. It is believed that there are two types of value propositions with a positive impact on product placement. On one hand, the company is the end costumer, on the other, the costumer is also the supplier. It is expected that the first one results in reduction of primary production and the second one results in high product displacement rates since suppliers do not replace obsolete products with new ones (Whalen, 2019). These two types of value propositions are associated to what Whalen (2019) has identified as further EPV archetypes: Facilitators, Redistributors, and Doers. More specifically, he has argued that the two value propositions are associated to Redistributors and Doers suggesting that these companies would contribute more to resource efficiency. In this logic, Redistributors and Doers can impact the product's lifespan and can expand the existing products' resource efficiency. But value propositions may also contribute little to reducing overall environmental impacts. For example, when customers aim to save money by buying lower-priced products or when financial gains are pursued at any cost, even that involving potential environmental rebound effects. Moreover, product type and company interaction may influence environmental impacts. This is important because while Redistributors do exert some direct influence over products, they can apply strategies that will allow products to stop being used after they reach their optimal lifespan, the third EPV archetype, Facilitators, do not have any direct interaction with products, and, as a result, some products, such as electronic equipment, can continue to be used past optimal lifespan, even if they are responsible for greater emissions than more recent models. Additionally, companies' physical facilities, such as offices and warehouses, contribute to the overall consumption of resources. The same can be said about transportation-related activities which have, indirect, environment-associated costs. This is, as argued, because Facilitators and many of Redistributors and Doers do not transport goods themselves and rely on partners (Whalen, 2019).

SMEs are believed to be important players in achieving the combination of sustainable growth and net-zero goals (Chatzistamoulou & Tyllianakis, 2022). When studying resource efficiency in SMEs, literature review shows that other authors have explored topics such as reducing energy use, minimizing waste and the re-using raw materials (Chatzistamoulou & Tyllianakis, 2022; Cunha et al., 2020; Garrido-Prada et al., 2021). In one study, Özbuğday et al. (2020) have examined resource efficiency investments and company performance and focused specifically on SMEs that operate in European energy-intensive sectors. They argue that enhancing resource efficiency can lead to very specific positive outcomes, such as productivity improvements and costs minimization (at the intra-organization level), can provide further business and collaboration opportunities in the circular value chain (at the inter-organization level), and move the country forward into a more resource-efficient, low-carbon economy (macro level). Özbugday et al. (2020) conclude by suggesting that 1% annual turnover investment on resource efficiency can increase by 13 to 18% the likelihood of sales growth performance and decrease by 13 to 18% the likelihood to experience a decrease in its turnover when compared to another small or medium enterprise with similar specifications but which has not invested in resource efficiency as much. Focused on European SMEs, the study of Bodas-Freitas and Corrocher (2019) has aimed to examine the use of external support and the perceive benefits of the adoption of resource efficiency practices. The authors conducted a survey in which they asked companies to specify the type of support used in the process of adoption of resource efficiency practices and to evaluate the effect of adoption of resource efficiency practices on their production costs. Furthermore, they asked companies if they had adopted the following resource efficiency practices: water saving, energy saving, using renewable energy (including own energy produced from solar panels), materials saving, waste minimizing (related to process reengineering) and recycling and selling scrap material to other companies (related to waste management). Some of these practices would represent a change to the production process to save resources, while others would not implicate the change in the process (for instance, reuse and recycling waste). In their sample, 63% of participating companies reported a reduction in production costs, 15% reported no impact on the costs and 21% reported an increase in production costs. Companies that used indirect external support (in a form of consultancy or advice) were more likely to adopt a high number of process reengineering practices. In other words, the extent of adoption of resource efficiency practices increased with the use of external advice. In adoption of waste management practices, its extension seemed to be directly and positively related to direct external support (funding) and indirect external support (advice and consultancy) related to best practices and new technologies. Bodas-Freitas and Corrocher (2019) conclude that the use of external funding provided more benefits to the companies when they decided to adopt resource efficiency measures, mainly in terms of reduced production costs and that these benefits were related to re-adaptation and process reengineering. In their work, Dobbs et al. (2011) have cited the most frequent cost estimations of increasing resource efficiency and suggested that from the perspective of a private investor, the savings in 2030 arising from implementing all the considered technologies would reach USD 2.9 trillion per year. In 70% of cases, the required resource-efficient investment would offer a rate of return greater than 10% per year. The total USD 900 billion investment required "could potentially create 9 million to 25 million jobs" (Dobbs et al., 2011). To support small and medium enterprises in identifying and selecting industrial resource efficiency projects, a guidebook developed by Choi et al. (2019) was established on an idea that resource efficiency, from a circular economy viewpoint, can generate more savings than traditional energy procedures. In fact, Choi and colleagues (2019) have identified more than a million USD of potential savings per year, with an average payback of six months providing a valuable contribution to SMEs in identifying manufacturing practices from a resource efficiency perspective. Their work shows that resource efficiency practices can achieve both, economic and environmental benefits through indirect and induced benefits. It is believed that frameworks such as this can help involved stakeholders make the most impactful decisions regarding resource efficiency and the environment and promote the interest in the EU programs and initiatives related to resource efficiency (EC, 2010).

CONCLUSION

The capacity of Earth to continue providing resources for people around the globe in the immediate and more distant future has reached critical level. In order to avoid depleting that capacity, it is vital that individuals, organizations and societies use Earth's resources more efficiently. In this regard, international and national programs and initiatives have been proposed with the aim to increase awareness and foster the adoption of environmentally oriented, sustainable practices. At organizational level, interest in resource efficiency and sustainable management of natural resources has been growing and has given rise to new perspectives for doing business, in which the business approach to creating long-term customer value is combined with taking into consideration how the organization operates in the economy, society and environment. Sustainable business models foster innovation while addressing environmental impacts and prioritizing sustainability, and represent a shift toward resource efficiency and sustainable development goals. However, the link between innovation, business venturing and sustainability comes with a lot of uncertainty and resource efficiency still represents a somehow optimistic vision of the environment-economy relationship.

Small and medium enterprises are the backbone of the European economy and can provide a substantial contribution to the indicators of resource and material use methods, waste streams or emissions. Given the role SMEs play, it becomes essential to understand how environmental concerns impact business strategies and until which extent can resource efficiency be considered an opportunity to them. This chapter has aimed to provide a contribution to this topic and used a qualitative methodology to examine SMEs entrepreneurs' perceptions about the importance, awareness and willingness to invest in resource efficiency in Portugal. The participants recognized the importance of resource efficiency and sustainability in business but referred to several challenges an entrepreneur meets on their way. Most of the participants had already advanced toward implementing measures promoting sustainability in their companies and would consider investing more in resource efficiency if the government eased the financial pressures they experienced on a daily basis.

REFERENCES

Abrahamsson, A. (2007). Sustainopreneurship - business with a cause. Conceptualizing entrepreneurship for sustainability [Master's thesis, Växjö University, School of Management and Economics]. https://www.diva-portal.org/smash/get/diva2:205051/FULLTEXT01.pdf

Alvarez, S. A., & Barney, J. B. (2007). Discovery and creation: Alternative theories of entrepreneurial action. *Strategic Entrepreneurship Journal*, *1*(1-2), 11–26. doi:10.1002ej.4

Anderson, A. R. (1998). Cultivating the garden of Eden: Environmental entrepreneuring. *Journal of Organizational Change Management*, *11*(2), 135–144. doi:10.1108/09534819810212124

Bocken, N. M., de Pauw, I., Bakker, C., & van der Grinten, B. (2016). Product design and business model strategies for a circular economy. *Journal of Industrial and Production Engineering*, *33*(5), 308–320. doi:10.1080/21681015.2016.1172124

Bocken, N. M., Schuit, C. S., & Kraaijenhagen, C. (2018). Experimenting with a circular business model: Lessons from eight cases. *Environmental Innovation and Societal Transitions*, *28*, 79–95. doi:10.1016/j.eist.2018.02.001

Bodas-Freitas, I. M., & Corrocher, N. (2019). The use of external support and the benefits of the adoption of resource efficiency practices: An empirical analysis of European SMEs. *Energy Policy*, *132*, 75–82. doi:10.1016/j.enpol.2019.05.019

Brüggemann, H., Stempin, S., & Meier, J. M. (2020). Consideration of digitalization for the purpose of resource efficiency in a learning factory. *Procedia Manufacturing*, *45*, 140–145. doi:10.1016/j.promfg.2020.04.085

Chatzistamoulou, N., & Tyllianakis, E. (2022). Commitment of European SMEs to resource efficiency actions to achieve sustainability transition: A feasible reality or an elusive goal. *Journal of Environmental Management*, *321*, 115937. doi:10.1016/j.jenvman.2022.115937 PMID:35988398

Choi, D. I., & Gray, E. R. (2008). The venture development processes of sustainable entrepreneurs. *Management Research News*, *31*(8), 558–569. doi:10.1108/01409170810892127

Choi, J. K., Thangamani, D., & Kissock, K. (2019). A systematic methodology for improving resource efficiency in small and medium-sized enterprises. *Resources, Conservation and Recycling*, *147*, 19–27. doi:10.1016/j.resconrec.2019.04.015

Cohen, B., Smith, B., & Mitchell, R. (2008). Toward a sustainable conceptualization of dependent variables in entrepreneurship research. *Business Strategy and the Environment*, *17*(2), 107–119. doi:10.1002/bse.505

Cohen, B., & Winn, M. I. (2007). Market imperfections, opportunity and sustainable entrepreneurship. *Journal of Business Venturing*, *22*(1), 29–49. doi:10.1016/j.jbusvent.2004.12.001

Cunha, P., Neves, S. A., Marques, A. C., & Serrasqueiro, Z. (2020). Adoption of energy efficiency measures in the buildings of micro-, small- and medium-sized Portuguese enterprises. *Energy Policy*, *146*, 4215. doi:10.1016/j.enpol.2020.111776

Dobbs, R., Oppenheim, J., Thompson, F., Brinkman, M., & Zornes, M. (2011). *Resource revolution: meeting the world's energy, materials, food, and water needs*. McKinsey Global Institute.

European Commission. (2005). *Thematic strategy on the sustainable use of natural resources*. EC. https://ec.europa.eu/environment/archives/natres/index.htm

European Commission. (2010). *Europe 2020: A strategy for smart, sustainable and inclusive growth*. EC. https://eur-lex.europa.eu/LexUriServ/LexUriServ.do?uri=COM:2010:2020:FIN:EN:PDF

European Commission. (2011). *Roadmap to a resource efficient Europe*. EC. https://eur-lex.europa.eu/legal-content/EN/TXT/?uri=CELEX:52011DC0571

European Commission. (2013). *The opportunities of business of improving resource efficiency - final report*. EC. https://ec.europa.eu/environment/enveco/resource_efficiency/pdf/report_opportunities.pdf

European Commission. (2018). *A clean planet for all: A European strategic long-term vision for a prosperous, modern, competitive and climate neutral economy*. EC. https://eur-lex.europa.eu/legal-content/EN/TXT/?uri=CELEX%3A52018DC0773

European Investment Bank. (2022). *Small and medium enterprises: overview*. EIB. https://www.eib.org/attachments/lucalli/smes_overview_2022_en.pdf

Eurostat. (2013). *Resource Efficiency Scoreboard: Thirty indicators to measure resource efficiency in the EU*. Eurostat. https://ec.europa.eu/environment/resource_efficiency/news/up-to-date_news/11122013_en.htm

Eurostat. (2022). *Sustainable development in the European Union - 2022 edition*. Eurostat. https://ec.europa.eu/eurostat/web/products-flagship-publications/-/ks-09-22-019

Garrido-Prada, P., Lenihan, H., Doran, J., Rammer, C., & Perez-Alaniz, M. (2021). Driving the circular economy through public environmental and energy R&D: Evidence from SMEs in the European Union. *Ecological Economics*, *182*, 106884. doi:10.1016/j.ecolecon.2020.106884

Gast, J., Gundolf, K., & Cesinger, B. (2017). Doing business in a green way: A systematic review of the ecological sustainability entrepreneurship literature and future research directions. *Journal of Cleaner Production, 147*, 44–56. doi:10.1016/j.jclepro.2017.01.065

Geissdoerfer, M., Vladimirova, D., & Evans, S. (2018). Sustainable business model innovation: A review. *Journal of Cleaner Production, 198*, 401–416. doi:10.1016/j.jclepro.2018.06.240

Hall, J. K., Daneke, G. A., & Lenox, M. J. (2010). Sustainable development and entrepreneurship: Past contributions and future directions. *Journal of Business Venturing, 25*(5), 439–448. doi:10.1016/j.jbusvent.2010.01.002

Kuckertz, A., & Wagner, M. (2010). The influence of sustainability orientation on entrepreneurial intentions. Investigating the role of business experience. *Journal of Business Venturing, 25*(5), 524–539. doi:10.1016/j.jbusvent.2009.09.001

Ma, F., Wang, H., Schandl, H., Fishman, T., Tan, X., Li, Y., Shi, L., Wang, P., & Chen, W. Q. (2022). Exploring the relationship between economic complexity and resource efficiency. *Resources, Conservation and Recycling, 186*, 106530. doi:10.1016/j.resconrec.2022.106530

OECD (2018). *Environmental policy toolkit for SME greening in EU Eastern partnership countries.* OECD Publishing. . doi:10.1787/9789264293199-4-en

Özbuğday, F. C., Fındık, D., Özcan, K. M., & Başçı, S. (2020). Resource efficiency investments and firm performance: Evidence from European SMEs. *Journal of Cleaner Production, 252*, 119824. doi:10.1016/j.jclepro.2019.119824

Schlange, L. E. (2006). What drives sustainable entrepreneurs? *Indian Journal of Economics and Business*, (Special Issue), 35–45.

Shepherd, D. A., & Patzelt, H. (2011). The new field of sustainable entrepreneurship: Studying entrepreneurial action linking "what is to be sustained" with "what is to be developed". *Entrepreneurship Theory and Practice, 35*(1), 137–163. doi:10.1111/j.1540-6520.2010.00426.x

Tilley, F., & Young, W. (2009). Sustainability entrepreneurs: could they be the true wealth generators of the future? *Green Management International, 55*, 79-92. https://www.jstor.org/stable/greemanainte.55.79

United Nations Environment Programme. (2016). *Resource efficiency: Potential and economic implications. A report of the International Resource Panel.* UN. file:///C:/Users/ninas/Downloads/resource_efficiency_summary_report_english.pdf

United Nations Environment Programme. (2018). *Resource efficiency for sustainable development. Key messages for the group of 20.* UN. https://www.resourcepanel.org/resource-efficiency-sustainable-development-key-messages-group-20

United Nations Environment Programme. (2020). *Resource efficiency and climate change: Material efficiency strategies for a low-carbon future, A report of the International Resource Panel.* UN. https://www.unep.org/resources/report/resource-efficiency-and-climate-change-material-efficiency-strategies-low-carbon

Whalen, K. A. (2019). Three circular business models that extend product value and their contribution to resource efficiency. *Journal of Cleaner Production*, *226*, 1128–1137. doi:10.1016/j.jclepro.2019.03.128

World Commission on Environment and Development. (1987). *Report of the World Commission on Environment and Development: Our common future*. United Nations. https://sustainabledevelopment.un.org/content/documents/5987our-common-future.pdf

ADDITIONAL READING

Bliesner, A., Liedtke, C., & Rohn, H. (2014). Resource efficiency and culture—Workplace training for small and medium-sized enterprises. *The Science of the Total Environment*, *481*, 645–648. doi:10.1016/j.scitotenv.2013.11.053 PMID:24364995

Cainelli, G., D'Amato, A., & Mazzanti, M. (2020). Resource efficient eco-innovations for a circular economy: Evidence from EU firms. *Research Policy*, *49*(1), 103827. doi:10.1016/j.respol.2019.103827

Dobes, V. (2016). An integrated diagnostic tool for identifying and quantifying the opportunities for sustainable consumption and production in industry. *Journal of Cleaner Production*, *135*, 567–576. doi:10.1016/j.jclepro.2016.06.140

Fadly, D. (2020). Greening industry in Vietnam: Environmental management standards and resource efficiency in SMEs. *Sustainability*, *12*(18), 7455. doi:10.3390u12187455

Hoogendoorn, B., Guerra, D., & van der Zwan, P. (2015). What drives environmental practices of SMEs? *Small Business Economics*, *44*(4), 759–781. doi:10.100711187-014-9618-9

Lopez, F. J. D., Bastein, T., & Tukker, A. (2019). Business model innovation for resource-efficiency, circularity and cleaner production: What 143 cases tell us. *Ecological Economics*, *155*, 20–35. doi:10.1016/j.ecolecon.2018.03.009

Rentschler, J., Bleischwitz, R., & Flachenecker, F. (2018). On imperfect competition and market distortions: The causes of corporate under-investment in energy and material efficiency. *International Economics and Economic Policy*, *15*(1), 159–183. doi:10.100710368-016-0370-2

Schulte, U. G. (2013). New business models for a radical change in resource efficiency. *Environmental Innovation and Societal Transitions*, *9*, 43–47. doi:10.1016/j.eist.2013.09.006

KEY TERMS AND DEFINITIONS

Competitive Advantage: An attribute or a set of factors that allow an organization to outperform its competitors.

Efficiency: Ability to achieve the desired result in an optimal way, without wasting resources.

Entrepreneur: A person who takes on financial risks in the hope of profit. In some definitions, also refers to a person who sets up a business/company.

Renewable Resources: resources that can replenish themselves over an extended period of time as they are used.

Stakeholder: An individual, a group or an organization that is impacted by the outcome of the business activity.

Strategy: A general direction of an organization that determines the actions and the use of resources to achieve the goals.

Sustainability: Ability to fulfil one's generation needs without compromising this ability in future generations.

Chapter 9
Organizational Management Variables Enhancing Organizational Citizenship Behaviors

José G. Vargas-Hernandez
Tecnológico Superior de Jalisco, Mexico

Omar C. Vargas-González
https://orcid.org/0000-0002-6089-956X
Tecnológico Nacional de México, Ciudad Guzmán, Mexico

ABSTRACT

This study analyses the implications of organizational management variables in the enhancement of organizational citizenship behaviors. It departs from the assumption that management, motivation, commitment, leadership styles, innovation, and other relevant ideas have effects on the organizational citizenship behaviors. The method employed links the analysis, description, and reflection base on the theoretical and empirical literature review. It is concluded that organizational management variables enhance the self-efficacy of organizational members and the effectiveness of the organization involved in organizational citizenship behaviors.

INTRODUCTION

Some variables enhance organizational citizenship behaviors in organizations. Organizations in the scope of globalization face a lot of challenges in areas such as transformational leadership, organizational citizenship behaviors, motivation and working environment (Cichorzewska & Rakowska, 2017). Organizational citizenship behaviors increase the average level of organizational effectiveness by the enhancement and evaluation of their inducements for the organizational members.

DOI: 10.4018/978-1-6684-7422-8.ch009

Generalizability of research findings is a concern in that gender, males, and females, might have a significant difference in cognition about leadership (Hyde, 1981). Research focus on behaviors as sequentially mediating mechanisms, roles, strengths, and job crafting that link humble leadership to organizational citizenship behavior. These underlying mechanisms of humility leadership that represent social interpersonal characteristics (Owens & Hekman, 2012). Humble leadership is positively related to organizational citizenship behavior. Leadership is relevant in the models of organizational citizenship behaviors with the relationships between leadership and subordinates that provide valuable sources of organizational citizenship behaviors leading to competitive advantage to the organization and to the people. This situation is crucial in organizational environments.

Social exchange theory is limited to explain the affective, cognitive, and unconscious processes underlying the dynamic nature of organizational citizenship behavior. The leader-member exchange theory addresses the social relationship between leaders and their followers. When the power distance is low having a positive effect on organizational citizenship behavior (Dansereau et al. 1975; Anand et al. 2018; Zhang et al. 2020). Leader-followers exchange relationships and organizational citizenship has a mutual sense of respect, treatment, and obligation to reciprocate discretionary behaviors (Wayne and Green 1993).

Relationships among the variables of ethical leadership, leader-member exchange, prosocial motivation are relevant to organizational citizenship behavior. Prosocial motivation is positively associated to organizational citizenship behavior (Miao, 2011; Kaplan, Ö ˇgüt, Karayel, & Ilhan, 2013). Motivation at the work environment takes consideration of concerns and problems of communication aimed to improve organizational citizenship behavior (Luu, 2017). Work environment and personal predisposition are crucial elements for influencing organizational citizenship behaviors (Paillé et al. 2013). Organizational support on organization citizenship behavior for environment, health and safety is mediated by perceived self-efficacy. Attitudes influence the adoption of organizational citizenship behavior environment health and safety Fugas et al. (2013).

Organizational management support is a predictor to organizational citizenship behavior. Supportive management theoretically improves the organizational commitment and organizational citizenship behavior of workers. The permanent interaction between workers and management is related to supportive behaviors that fosters organizational citizenship. Fatigue from organizational citizenship behavior depends on the perceived organizational support and team-members exchanges (Bolino et al. 2015). When an organizational member perceives and experiences a positive influence, he or she returns the favor.

The analysis departs from the hypothesis that management, motivation, commitment, leadership styles, innovation and other relevant have effects on the organizational citizenship behaviors. This study has the purpose to analyze the implications of organizational management variables in the enhancement of organizational citizenship behaviors.

MANAGERIAL VARIABLES IN THE ORGANIZATIONAL CITIZENSHIP BEHAVIOR

The instances and contexts of OCB as an ingratiation form of impression management practices of good actors (Bolino, 1999). Organizations providing services to customers with the quality of relationships between the workers and customers and other factors leading to organizational citizenship behaviors that become the main expressions in organizations because the contributions and challenges that ensures the improvement of management (Ruizalba et al. 2014). These behaviors can be explained by organizational, task and motivational characteristics.

Self-interest motives involves self-concern and impression management. Beliefs based on management and coworker display other forms of OCB but cautioning OCB models of moderated and mediated causal structures (Masterson 2011, Yaffee & Kark 2011). Perceived organizational support and social norms are considered as predictors influenced by contextual factors. Organizational support and social norms have a mediation effect on organization citizenship behavior for the environment and health and safety.

Personal attitudes have a mediation effect between social norms and organizational citizenship behaviors related to environmental and health and safety issues. Practitioners require useful information on the factors determining organizational citizenship behavior to facilitate discussion perspectives in relation to health, safety and environmental issues occurring at most organizations. Organizational citizenship behaviors for health, safety and the environment are related to general issues, climate change, regulations, role of governments.

The antecedents and drivers of organizational citizenship behaviors for the environment, health, and safety (OCBHS) provide organizational management with knowledge and skills to support initiatives related to health, safety, and environment issues. Health, safe and environment attitudes, and personal self-efficacy are related organizational citizenship behaviors for health, environment, and safety (OCB-HES). Environmental awareness entails knowledge to protect natural environment with performing activities (Madsen & Ulhøi, 2001).

Perception of supportive management by the workers leading to demonstrate organizational commitment and organizational citizenship behaviors and organizational commitment. Perception of workers from organizational supportive management lead to demonstrate a response in terms of organizational citizenship behavior and organizational commitment. Organizational citizenship behaviors are mediated by work commitment (Salanova et al. 2011).

Prosocial motivation is related to organization citizenship behavior. Organizational citizenship behaviors are established through prosocial motivations (Zhang et al. 2016). Organizational citizenship behaviors and prosocial motivation include behaviors displayed by organizational members that are not recognized by any award system with the objective to depose self-motivations and support others. Organizational members pro socially motivated are engaged in organizational citizenship behavior. Prosocial motivation behavior has a positive relationship with the organizational citizenship behavior. Prosocial motivated has a positive correlation with employee citizenship behavior, and the relationship is mediated by an ethical leadership by a low impact.

Prosocial motivation is driven by persons that are emphatic with the needs of others which promotes the discretionary culture (Grant et al. 2014). Prosocial motivation has an impact on the organizational citizenship behaviors and organizational commitment. The relationship between prosocial motivation and organizational citizenship behavior is supportive. Organizational citizenship behavior is related to prosocial motivation. Prosocial motivation is concerned with the contributions of organizational members to others of preferred resources (Hu & Liden, 2015; Grant, 2008a, 2008b). The evidence supports the relationship between prosocial motivation and organizational citizenship behavior.

Organizational citizenship behavior is an adaptive process and goal-oriented influenced by motivation and governance (Bowler et al. 2010; Mossholder et al. 2011). Prosocial motivation has a positive effect on citizenship behavior and organizational commitment.

There is a strong negative correlation between public service motivation and untheatrical behavior (Gans-Morse et al. 2020; Olsen et al. 2019). There is no direct significant relationship between prosocial motivation and the dependent variable organizational citizenship behavior. Organizational citizenship behavior in public administration attempts at determining factors improving efficiency of organizational members (Podsakoff & et al. 2000; Jepsen & Rodwell, 2006).

Prosocial motivation has a positive relation to organizational citizenship behavior Between prosocial motivation and the dependent variable organizational citizenship behavior, there is not direct significant relationship despite the indirect impact evident through the construct. There is a relationship between prosocial motivation and organizational citizenship behavior. Association of prosocial motivation and organizational citizenship behaviors is positively related (Miao, 2011; Kaplan, Ö˘güt, Karayel & ˙Ilhan, 2013).

THE LEADERSHIP STYLES

Leadership has a crucial role in facilitating proactive behaviors such as organizational citizenship behavior (Grant, 2000). The different leadership styles are related to organizational citizenship behaviors such as attributional charismatic leadership (Deluga, 1995) transformational leadership (Jiao et al., 2011), shared leadership (Khasawneh, 2011), and developmental leadership (Yan & Chen, 2013). Transformational leadership behavior is related to organization citizenship behaviors (AlKindy et al., 2016).

The acceptance of leadership exhibits positive organizational behaviors and encourages (Brown, Treviño & Harrison, 2005; Şenyurt & Dinc, 2015). Organizational support theory explains the mediation effect of perceived organizational support (POS) on the relationship between ethical leadership and organizational citizenship behavior, and the moderating effect of ethical dissimilarity (Tan, Yap, Choong, Choe, Rungruang, & Li, 2019).

The nature of ethical leaders plays as role in muddling effectiveness, reinforcing organizational citizenship behaviors and promote ethical behaviors (Quenson, 2013). The notion of organizational citizenship behavior is traces back to Katz (1964) who considered to be a set of discretionary behaviors essential for organizational effectiveness (Katz, 1964; Organ, 1988). Organizational citizenship behavior of members is in relationship with organizational effectiveness in the workplace. Organizational citizenship behavior has an effective function in the working place where employees perform beyond the claim of duty.

Perceived self-efficacy partially mediates organizational support on organizational citizenship behavior for the environment and health and safety. The perceived self-efficacy has a positive relationship with the adoption of organizational citizenship behaviors for the environment, health, and safety. Organizational members helping colleagues beyond the accepted levels of punctuality and personal attendance aimed to attend higher levels efficiency, productivity, customer satisfaction, etc. The organizational citizenship behavior facilitates employees in the tourism and hospitality industry to behave beyond the ethical role, encouraging the workers to become serious citizens and behave effectively in the organization.

Perceived organizational support is an antecedent of organizational citizenship behavior that have an impact related to environment, health and safety and mediated by the perceived self-efficacy. Firms leverage this factor by selecting and hiring the right people with conscious attitudes towards specific object and self-efficacy. Organizational citizenship behavior has some predictors in relation to health, safety, and environmental issues in the organizational complexity of multinational enterprises and related to perceived organizational support, self-efficacy, attitudes, and social norms.

Perception of organizational support on organizational citizenship behavior is related to social exchange relationship and determined by the effect of perception of organizational support on self-efficacy. Citizen behaviors are influenced by a social exchange relationship development between the organizational members (Konovsky & Pugh, 1994).

Problems, opportunities, and challenges confronted by the organizational members in which organizational citizenship behavior is a predictor of organizational effectiveness. Research on organizational citizenship behavior has effects on organizational effectiveness through the lubrication of social machinery to increase resilience and flexibility through unforeseen contingencies (Smith, Organ, & Near, 1983, p. 654). A process-oriented behavioral model focusing on the generative mechanisms and organizational contingencies was proposed by (Argote & Greve 2007) that lies at the core of the behavioral perspective.

The reputation of participants in experimental settings is a control variable and a core mechanisms making effective gossip in influencing the behaviors of targets (Feinberg et al., 2012; Wu et al., 2016a, 2016b). Negative gossip relates to low organizational citizenship behavior targets damaging their organizational identification (Ye, et al., 2019). There is a causal relationship between negative gossip and social and organizational inclusion for targets. Social organizational inclusion is the process of explaining the behavioral intentions of gossip targets.

People accepts negative gossip as part of everyday life and overhear it about themselves (Dunbar et al., 1997). Negative gossip is associated to social organizational inclusion and considered to have a causal related to lower social inclusion of targets. Low feelings of social organizational inclusion are related to the target of negative gossip becoming less supportive toward members. Damaging social inclusion for targets, negative gossip disrupts the reciprocity loops tended by people with the groups they are part.

Ethical leadership is the appropriate behavior for interpersonal relationships and actions leading to equitable conduct through communications and decision making (Brown and Treviño 2006; Moore et al. 2019). Equity sensitivity partially mediates relationships between honesty-humility and conscientiou-subjective normess with organizational citizenship behavior and counterproductive working behavior (Bourdage et al. 2018a). Older employees at high levels in the organizational hierarchy become the role models for the employees at lower levels engaging in more organizational citizenship behavior and less counterproductive working behaviors.

The leadership style has a mediating role of the relationship between prosocial motivation and organizational citizenship. Prosocial motivation of organizational members cast ethical leadership to moral agents, assist them in execution of tasks and influence leadership (Yam et al. 2019).

The prosocial motivation variable affects the relation leader-member exchange connected to impersonal citizenship behavior. Pro socially motivated leaders and employees get strong discretionary behavior to care for each other. Organizational citizenship and prosocial motivation behavior interlink a leader-member exchange relationship. Organizational leadership, leader-member exchange and ethical leadership and pro-social motivation are interrelated variables.

Moral agents are a causative force to practice moral laden conducts considering the ethical leadership to benefit moral patients of ethical conducts (Gray et al. 2007). Ethical leadership and leader-member exchange has mediating roles. Some of the characteristics of ethical leadership are integrity, honesty, care, balanced judgment, trustworthiness. The relationship of ethical leadership and ethical climate, have a relationship with organizational citizenship behavior. Ethical leadership improves the organizational climate and have effect on organizational citizenship behavior.

Ethical leadership influences the formation of citizenship behavior. Organizational citizenship behaviors can predict ethical leadership and ethical climate. Some conditions are needed to achieve organizational efficiency. Self-efficacy and self-determination may be mediating in the relationship between leadership and organizational citizenship behavior. Ethical leadership requires targeting interventions for developing organizational citizenship behavior and ethical climate through training and promotion of the leadership style workshops and counseling. There is a significant correlation between ethical leadership, ethical climate, and organizational citizenship behaviors. The correlation coefficients of ethical leadership, ethical climate, and organizational citizenship behavior.

Empirical research has shown evidence of existing a significant correlation between ethical leadership, organizational citizenship behavior and ethical climate. Using regression analysis, the result confirms the relationships between the variables, ethical leadership and ethical climate are predictors of organizational citizenship behavior. There is a significant correlation between ethical climate and organizational citizenship behavior. Ethical leadership is correlated with organizational citizenship behaviors and ethical climate (Wu, et al. 2018a) Ethical leadership and ethical climate is related to organizational citizenship behavior (Podsakoff, MacKenzie, Moorman, & Fetter, 1990).

Social cognitive theory (SCT) is atheoretical approach to analyze the relationships between ethical leadership, ethical climate, and organizational citizenship behavior. The leadership style such as ethical leaderships is an antecedent of ethical climate leading to outcomes of organizational citizenship behaviors (Newman, Round, Bhattacharya, & Roy 2017). Ethical leadership has positive attitudes such as organizational commitment and occupational satisfaction that increase the organizational citizenship behaviors (Baharlo, Beshlideh, Naami, & Hashemi sheikh Sabaani, 2015).

The leader-member exchange is a mediator between the relationships between prosocial motivation and organizational citizenship behavior. Leadership – member exchange tends to mitigate and reverse the decline and organizational citizenship behaviors (Cerne et al. 2015).

The exchange relationships of the leader-member are associated with the citizenship behavior (Kahya & Şahin, 2018). Ethical leadership and leader-member exchange supports the relationship between the prosocial motivation and organizational citizenship behavior. The ethical leadership and leader-member exchange mediate the relationship between prosocial motivation and organizational citizenship behaviors. Prosocial motivation has an impact and mediating roles of ethical leadership and leader-member exchange between prosocial motivation and organizational citizenship behaviors.

Ethical leadership is a mediator of the relationship between organizational citizenship behaviors and prosocial motivations. Ethical leadership encourages organizational citizenship behaviors considering prosocial motivated people appreciated the attitudes of organizational members engaged in citizenship behavior. Organizational citizenship behavior is influenced by prosocial motivation. The ethical leadership motivates and respects subordinates to achieve desired goals (Işik, 2020). Ethical leadership influences the behaviors and attitudes of organizational members (Mo et al. 2012). Ethical leadership is positively related to organizational citizenship behavior influencing the motivational orientation to achieve the organizational orientation (Neubert et al. 2013).

The ethical leadership is a mediator of the relationship between organizational citizenship behavior and prosocial motivation. Leader-member exchange and ethical leadership is a mediator of the relationship between organizational citizenship behavior and prosocial motivation. Leader-member exchange is a mediator between the prosocial motivation and organizational citizenship behavior. Prosocial motivation and organizational citizenship behavior are sequential mediators on the relationships between ethical leadership and the leader-member exchange. There is empirical evidence that ethical leadership and leader-member exchange are mediators of the relationship between organizational citizenship behavior and prosocial motivation.

Ethical practices in ethical leadership of organizational members are leading to become more motivated and obliged to practice discretionary behavior aimed to achieve outcomes at the workplaces (Mayer et al. 2009; Newman et al. 2014). Ethical leadership has effects on the subordinate prosocial motivation to benefit others and the organization (Zhang et al. 2016).

Empirical research evidence that ethical leadership, ethical climate, and organizational citizenship behavior have positive multiple correlation. The dependent variable organizational citizenship behavior can be predicted by the independent variables, ethical leadership, and ethical climate. A positive behavior drives to ponder relationships between citizens to preserve the leadership services such as the maintenance of attitudes required to implement organizational goals. However, in contrast to these findings, the improvement of organizational climate has not effects on organizational citizenship behaviors (Sabzipoor et al., 2012).

Transformational, servant and humble leadership styles are a critical contextual factor (Podsakoff et al., 1990; Walumbwa et al., 2010) related to organizational citizenship behaviors, although the relationship between humble and organizational citizenship behavior has not been fully explored. There is a positive correlation between organizational citizenship behavior and transformational leadership behavior. Humble leadership has a positive correlation with organizational citizenship behavior. Humble leadership is related to proactive behaviors (Chen et al., 2018). The relationship between humble leadership and organizational citizenship behaviors has implications.

Humble leadership is the willingness to view oneself accurately, and to appreciate the strengths and contributions of others (Owens et al., 2013). Organizational citizenship behavior and humble leadership are related because followers experience self-efficacy and self-determination as significant predictors (Wang et al., 2018, Chen et al., 2018, Schlechter & Maharaj, 2007; Yan & Chen, 2013; Kao, 2017). Humble leadership is characterized by the strengths of followers that may be leveraged at work and result in enhanced organizational citizenship behavior (Owens & Hekman, 2012, Govindji & Linley, 2007, Van Woerkom & Meyers, 2015).

Prediction of subordinate experiencing humble leadership respond to organizational citizenship behavior (He, Enhai, Xixi, Yanbin, & Kashif, 2020). Humble leadership is related to strengths use and affect organizational citizenship behavior by the strengths use. Strength's use has not significant mediation on the relationship between humble leadership and organizational citizenship behavior (He, Enhai, Xixi, Yanbin, & Kashif, 2020). Humble leadership appreciate the strengths of subordinates who enhance their perceptions of self-worth and self-efficacy that has a close relationship with organizational citizenship behavior (Wang et al. 2018, Owens & Hekman, 2012, Dussault, 2006; Kao, 2017). Humble leadership is related to organizational citizenship behavior.

The strengths use and deficit correction is evaluated by a questionnaire developed by Van Woerkom et al. (2016a). Strength's use is a mediator of the relationship between humble leadership and organizational citizenship behavior. Humble leadership has a positive behavior that has a positive correlation with organizational citizenship behaviors and improves it. Humble leadership is positively related to organizational citizenship behavior.

Humble leadership acknowledge its deficits and is open to new ideas to provide opportunities for the self-determination of subordinates leading to organizational citizenship behaviors (Chen et al., 2018, Yan & Chen, 2013). Humble leadership is linked with organizational citizenship behavior.

Spiritual leadership influences the organizational discretionary environmental behaviors (Afsar, Badir & Kiani, 2016). Spiritual leadership has a significant positive relationship with organizational citizenship behavior for the environment. Spiritual leadership has a positive direct association relationship with the organizational citizenship behavior contingent upon the harmonious passion for the environment in such a way that a strong relationship corresponds with high harmonious environmental passion (Anser, Shafique, Usman, Akhtar, & Ali, 2021).

Research on the link between spiritual leadership and organizational citizenship behavior for the environment should explore the mechanisms used to explain and enhance the knowledge of the linkages. Spiritual leadership has an indirect influence in pro-environmental behaviors (Afsar, Badir, & Kiani, 2016) which leads to have an impact on the potential for the enhancement of organizational citizenship behaviors for the environment. There is a significant positive direct association between spiritual leadership and organizational citizenship behavior for the environment.

The role of leadership styles should be studied in the future regarding the enhancement of organizational citizenship behavior for the environment (Robertson & Barling, 2017; Khan et al. 2019).

ORGANIZATIONAL INNOVATION

Among other organizational-level variables that increases organizational innovation and organizational citizenship behavior is the cooperative culture while organizational management support decreases them. Cooperative organizational culture is associated with innovative behavior and organizational citizenship behavior. The association of helping behavior at the workplace and organizational citizenship behaviors influence innovative behavior (Danaei & Iranbakhsh, 2016). The innovative work of innovative behavior contributes to knowledge as part of organizational citizenship behavior (Tajeddini & Trueman, 2008; 2014; Tajeddini et al., 2006; Tajeddini, 2010; Tajeddini & Truemanc, 2012).

Organizational citizenship behavior is a predictor that can influence the organization to become innovative and provides a lot of benefits to employees in the hospitality industry (Organ, 1988). Organizational support is associated with innovative behavior and organizational citizenship behavior. Organizational factors support innovative behavior and organizational citizenship behaviors only explained by the perceived organizational behavior (POS) theory. Positive factors such as organizational support increase the innovative behavior and the organizational citizenship behaviors.

Organizational support is a moderator of autonomy, role conflict, and positive supportive management effects on organizational citizenship behavior and innovative behavior. Support of organizational autonomy provided to organizational members to improve their strengths use (Kong & Ho, 2016). Self-efficacy and other personal resources mediate the relationships between autonomy and organizational citizenship behaviors. Studies on innovative behavior and organizational citizenship behavior have been conducted in the public and private sectors dealing with research subjects and topics (Al-Hawari et al., 2019; Aryee et al., 2012; Yuan & Woodman, 2010). There is a positive influence of autonomy and supportive management in organizational citizenship behavior and innovative behavior.

Innovative behavior and organizational citizenship behavior is linked to entrepreneurial and rule-bending activities broadening the managerial vision to facilitate innovation behavior. Cooperative organizational culture facilitates the emergence of organizational citizenship behaviors and innovation behaviors which are influences by the capacity of change management. Change management capacity is associated with innovative behavior and organizational citizenship behavior.

Public service motivation is associated to organizational citizenship behavior and innovative behaviors. The effect of public service motivation increases with the lack or organizational support. The public service motivation has a weaken effects on innovate behaviors and organizational citizenship behaviors when there is lack of organizational support. Public service motivation increases innovative behavior and organizational citizenship behaviors. Circular purchasing is an innovative process that requires regulations, and facilitated by engagements in pro-active and risk-taking behaviors, organizational support, and resources

The support perceived by workers from organizational management leads to respond in terms of organizational citizenship behaviors and organizational commitment. Workers tend to perceive from organizational supportive management and respond in terms of organizational citizenship behaviors and organizational citizenship. The support perceived by workers from organizational management leads to respond in terms of organizational citizenship behaviors and organizational commitment. Workers perceive the organizational management support leading to a response on organizational citizenship behavior and organizational commitment.

Supportive management mediates relationships between prosocial motivation and organizational citizenship behaviors. Prosocial motivation has a positive relationship with organizational citizenship behavior mediated by the managerial support. There is a positive relationship between prosocial motivation and organizational citizenship behavior mediated by a supportive management. Prosocial motivation behavior has an impact on organizational citizenship behavior and organizational commitment coordinated with supportive management.

Prosocial motivation has an impact on organizational citizenship behavior and organizational commitment with a mediating role of managerial support. A relationship between prosocial motivation is positively related to organizational citizenship behavior mediated by the management support (Miao, 2011; Kaplan, Ö ˇgüt, Karayel, & Ilhan, 2013. Management support has a mediated role on the relationship between the prosocial motivation and organizational citizenship behavior. There is no direct relationship between prosocial motivation and the dependent variable organizational citizenship behavior as evidenced by the construct managerial support. Prosocial motivation has an impact on organizational citizenship behaviors and organizational commitment of workers mediating the managerial support.

Workers involved in citizenship behavior respond to supportive organizational management. Workers supported from their management are motivated and payback demonstrating organizational commitment and organizational citizenship behaviors. Involvement of workers in organizational citizenship behavior respond to organizational managerial support. The involvement of employees must be achieved through formal roles and the development of organizational citizenship behavior (Chandani et al., 2016). The workers getting support from management are motivated and payback demonstrating organizational citizenship behaviors and organizational commitment.

Workers involved in citizenship behaviors responded to supportive organizational management to predict positively the organizational citizenship behaviors. Workers supported by management are motivated to pay back by demonstrated organizational citizenship behaviors and organizational commitment. Workers involved in citizenship behavior respond to a supportive management.

Management support is a predictor of the organizational citizenship behavior. Management support motivates the workers who payback the organization with organizational citizenship behaviors and organizational commitment. Involved workers responding to managerial support positively with predicted organizational citizenship behaviors. Organizational support management encourages prosocial motivation spurring the organizational citizenship behavior. Managerial support is a mediator of the association between prosocial motivation and organizational citizenship behaviors. Prosocial motivation is associated to supportive behaviors by managerial and Organizational Citizenship Behavior. Managerial support is a mediator of the relationship between prosocial motivation and organizational citizenship behavior.

Prosocial Motivation is associated to supportive managerial behaviors and organizational citizenship (Van der Voet, Steijn, Kuipers, 2017). There is a relationship between managerial support and organizational citizenship behavior. Managerial support and organization citizenship behavior are variables related to organizational commitment. Managerial support is mediating the significant relationship between prosocial motivation and organizational citizenship behavior. Supportive management mediates the relationship between prosocial motivation and organizational citizenship behavior. The relationship between prosocial motivation is not directly significant with the independent variable organizational citizenship behavior, although this indirect impact of prosocial motivation is evidence through the managerial support construct.

The indirect impact of prosocial motivation is checked through the construct of supportive management (Miao, 2011; Kaplan, Ö ˘güt, Karayel, & Ilhan, 2013). There is no direct relationship between prosocial motivation and the dependent variable organizational citizenship behavior, although the indirect impact of prosocial motivation is conducted through the construct supportive management.

Non-explicit motives are responsible for demonstrating citizenship behavior through social values, organizational concerns, impression management (Rioux & Penner 2001). Managerial support mediates the relationship between prosocial motivation and the organizational commitment and citizenship behavior. Supportive management mediates the association between prosocial motivation and organizational citizenship behaviors. Supportive management and prosocial motivation lead to organizational behaviors. Prosocial motivation exerts a positive influence on citizenship behavior at working environments.

Studies in the public management on organizational innovation and organizational citizenship behavior are frequent less than on the private sector (Hansen & Pihl-Thingvad, 2019). Public service motivation in cross-level effect with lack of organizational support change management capacity do not have a significant effect on organizational citizenship and innovation management but may have indirect effects with other factors.

Task characteristics and the level of motivation explain innovative behavior and organizational citizenship behaviors (Chen & Kao, 2011; Giebels et al., 2016; Pandey et al., 2008; Todd & Kent, 2006).

MEASUREMENT

The organizational citizenship behavior is measured with a scale (Smith et al. 1983). Smith et al. (1983) developed a measure on organizational citizenship behavior (OCB) to include the factor of altruism pertaining to support and the factor of compliance with interpersonal dimensions, such as work time, punctuality, adherence to regulations, etc. Podsakoff (2000) has developed a scale to measure organizational citizenship behavior based on dimensions of civic virtue, courtesy, sportsmanship, conscientiousubjective normess, and altruism.

Cross-sectional research on measurement of organizational citizenship behavior should be longitudinal rather than a at given point of time with a short time fluctuations, to include other relevant variables of time to model change (Ployhart & Vandenberg, 2010). Results of research of two measurement waves in organizational citizenship behavior is marginally better that the cross-sectional studies (Ployhart & Vandenberg, 2010; Singer & Willett, 2003).

Personality measures predicts CP which has much in common with OCB. Emotional stability, openness and extraversion have incremental validity (Chiaburu et al. 2011). Emotional experiences result in increasing organizational citizenship behaviors and decreasing counterproductive working behaviors

(Carstensen, 1992; Spector & Fox, 2002). Measurement of humble leadership is based on dimensions' self accurately, appreciation strengths and contributions and teachability (Owens et al. 2013). Different methodologies partially biased the substantial variability to be considered more than measurement error (Dalal et al., 2014). Humble leadership leads to increased organizational citizenship behavior (Chen et al., 2018, Bavik et al., 2017).

The time-intervals of measurement reveal the dynamic relationship between organizational citizenship behavior and psychological construct fulfillment. The control variables influence the average level of organizational citizenship behavior. The measurement of organizational citizenship behavior has limitations in which attrition is an extensive threat in longitudinal research (Bliese & Ployhart, 2002).

CONCLUSION

The research contributions to the literature of organizational citizenship behavior must evaluated considering the study limitations. A cooperative organizational culture nurtured and supported by workers is an imitative positively evaluated to improve the institutional support and extrinsic motivation towards innovative behavior and organizational citizenship behavior. Workers supported by organizational management are motivated to payback in terms of organizational citizenship behavior and organizational commitment. Workers can exhibit organizational citizenship behavior if they have appropriate motivational incentives. There is a strong positive correlation between organizational citizenship behavior and incentives.

Psychological ownership is closed linked to organizational citizenship behavior that cannot be separated. Psychological ownership as the state of mind that develop the feelings of belonging toward the object of the target, positively sharing, and endeavoring for successful achievement (Avey et al., 2009). The sense of psychological ownership to an organization leads to organizational psychological attachment as the roots of the organizational citizenship behavior. There is a positive correlation between organizational citizenship behavior and organizational psychological ownership. The psychological ownership influences organizational citizenship behavior among the workers.

A positive relationship between prosocial motivation and organizational citizenship behavior is mediated by a supportive management. Prosocial motivation has an impact on the organizational citizenship behaviors and organizational commitment. The relationship between prosocial motivation and organizational citizenship behavior is supported. The relationship between prosocial motivation and organizational citizenship behavior is mediated by supportive management. Prosocial motivation is associated positively to organizational citizenship behavior. Prosocial motivation has an impact on the workers' organizational citizenship behavior.

Management support has a mediating role between organizational citizenship behaviors and organizational commitment. Supportive management mediates the relationship between prosocial motivation and organizational citizenship behavior. Supportive management of operations enhance organizational commitment and organizational citizenship behavior.

The role of leadership styles should be studied in the future regarding the enhancement of organizational citizenship behavior for the environment. Cooperation between leadership and followers is critical for the achievement of organizational goals. The leader-member exchange with employee citizenship behavior. Prosocial behavior is a mechanism through which ethical leadership and leader-member exchange has its effects on organizational citizenship behavior. Voluntary practices of an engaged leadership in organizational citizenship behaviors have implications with values, actions, and behaviors of workers.

A complex process mechanism underlies a relationship between organizational citizenship behaviors and humble leadership. Humble leadership style characteristics in promoting organizational citizenship behavior has practical implications in learning more knowledge from training projects. More knowledge is needed between the boundaries of the relationship between humble leadership and organizational citizenship behavior. The complex process mechanisms underlie the relationship between humble leadership and organizational citizenship behaviors.

Organizational ethics and standards result in practice of organizational citizenship behavior. Ethical leadership and leader-member exchange are sequentially mediators of associations among organizational citizenship behavior and prosocial behavior. Organizations giving support to the members if the form of leadership and coworker support, they respond reciprocally to the supervisors and coworkers. Organizational members involved in citizenship behaviors are ethically grateful to reciprocate and give back to the organization the quality leadership.

Future research on the mechanisms related to perceived organizational discretionary environmental behaviors in the relationship between the spiritual leadership and organizational citizenship behavior for the environment. Future organizational environments may change the innovative behaviors and organizational citizenship behaviors as extra role behaviors.

REFERENCES

Afsar, B., Badir, Y., & Kiani, U. S. (2016). Linking Spiritual Leadership and Employee Pro-Environmental Behavior: The Influence of Workplace Spirituality, Intrinsic Motivation, and Environmental Passion. *Journal of Environmental Psychology*, *45*, 79–88. doi:10.1016/j.jenvp.2015.11.011

Al-Hawari, M. A., Bani-Melhem, S., & Shamsudin, F. M. (2019). Determinants of frontline employee service innovative behavior: The moderating role of co-worker socializing and service climate. *Management Research Review*, *42*(9), 1076–1094. doi:10.1108/MRR-07-2018-0266

AlKindy, A. M., Shah, I. M., & Jusoh, A. (2016). The impact of transformational leadership behaviors on work performance of omani civil service agencies. *Asian Social Science*, *12*(3), 152. doi:10.5539/ass.v12n3p152

Anand, S., Vidyarthi, P., & Rolnicki, S. (2018). Leader-member exchange and organizational citizenship behaviors: Contextual effects of leader power distance and group task interdependence. *The Leadership Quarterly*, *29*(4), 489–500. doi:10.1016/j.leaqua.2017.11.002

Anser, M. K., Shafique, S., Usman, M., Akhtar, N., & Ali, M. (2021). Spiritual leadership and organizational citizenship behavior for the environment: An intervening and interactional analysis. *Journal of Environmental Planning and Management*, *64*(8), 1496–1514. doi:10.1080/09640568.2020.1832446

Argote, L., & Greve, H. R. (2007). A behavioral theory of the firm: 40 years and counting: Introduction and impact. *Organization Science*, *18*(3), 337–349. doi:10.1287/orsc.1070.0280

Aryee, S., Walumbwa, F. O., Zhou, Q., & Hartnell, C. A. (2012). Transformational leadership, innovative behavior, and task performance: Test of mediation and moderation processes. *Human Performance*, *25*(1), 1–25. doi:10.1080/08959285.2011.631648

Avey, J. B., Avolio, B. J., Crossley, C. D., & Luthans, F. (2009). Psychological ownership: Theoretical extensions, measurement, and relation to work outcomes. *J. Org. Behav. Int. J. Indus. Occup. Org. Psychol. Behav*, *30*(2), 173–191. doi:10.1002/job.583

Baharlo, M., Beshlideh, K., & Naami, A., & Hashemi Sheikh Sabaani S.E. (2015). Analysis of the relationship between ethical leadership and organizational citizenship behavior. *Ethics Sci Technol*, *10*, 19–27.

Bavik, A., Bavik, Y. L., & Tang, P. M. (2017). Servant leadership, employee job crafting, and citizenship behaviors: A cross-level investigation. *Cornell Hospitality Quarterly*, *58*(4), 364–373. doi:10.1177/1938965517719282

Bliese, P. D., & Ployhart, R. E. (2002). Growth modeling using random coefficient models: Model building, testing, and illustrations. *Organizational Research Methods*, *5*(4), 362–387. doi:10.1177/109442802237116

Bolino, M. C. (1999). Citizenship and impression management: Good soldiers or good actors? *Academy of Management Review*, *24*(1), 82–98. doi:10.2307/259038

Bolino, M. C., Hsing, H.-H., Harvey, J., & LePine, A. (2015). "Well, I'm tired of tryin'." Organizational citizenship behavior. *The Journal of Applied Psychology*, *100*(1), 56–74. doi:10.1037/a0037583 PMID:25111252

Bourdage, J. S., Goupal, A., Neilson, T., Lukacik, E. R. E.-R., & Lee, N. (2018). Personality, equity sensitivity, and discretionary workplace behavior. *Personality and Individual Differences*, *120*, 144–150. doi:10.1016/j.paid.2017.08.018

Bowler, W. M., Halbesleben, J. R. B., & Paul, J. R. B. (2010). If you're close with the leader, you must be a brownnose: The role of leader–member relationships in follower, leader, and coworker attributions of organizational citizenship behavior motives. *Human Resource Management Review*, *20*(4), 309–316. doi:10.1016/j.hrmr.2010.04.001

Brown, M. E., & Treviño, L. K. (2006). Ethical leadership: A review and future directions. *The Leadership Quarterly*, *17*(6), 595–616. doi:10.1016/j.leaqua.2006.10.004

Brown, M. E., Treviño, L. K., & Harrison, D. A. (2005). Ethical leadership: A social learning perspective for construct development and testing. *Organizational Behavior and Human Decision Processes*, *97*(2), 117–134. doi:10.1016/j.obhdp.2005.03.002

Carstensen, L. L. (1992). Social and emotional patterns in adulthood: Support for socioemotional selectivity theory. *Psychology and Aging*, *7*(3), 331–338. doi:10.1037/0882-7974.7.3.331 PMID:1388852

Cerne, M., Babic, K., Connelly, C. E., & Skerlavaj, M. (2015). Team—Level knowledge hiding, social leader-member exchange, and PM. In Academy of management proceedings. (Vol. 1, p. 16302). Academy of Management, Briarclif Manor.

Chandani, A., Mehta, M., Mall, A., & Khokhar, V. (2016). Employee engagement: A review paper on factors affecting employee engagement. *Indian Journal of Science and Technology*, *9*(15), 1–7. doi:10.17485/ijst/2016/v9i15/92145

Chen, C.-H. V., & Kao, R.-H. (2011). A multilevel study on the relationships between work characteristics, self-efficacy, collective efficacy, and organizational citizenship behavior: The case of Taiwanese Police Duty-Executing Organizations. *The Journal of Psychology*, *145*(4), 361–390. doi:10.1080/00223980.2011.574168 PMID:21834327

Chen, S.-L., Shih, C.-T., & Chi, N.-W. (2018). A multilevel job demands–resources model of work engagement: Antecedents, consequences, and boundary conditions. *Human Performance*, *31*(5), 282–304. doi:10.1080/08959285.2018.1531867

Chen, S.-L., Shih, C.-T., & Chi, N.-W. (2018). A multilevel job demands–resources model of work engagement: Antecedents, consequences, and boundary conditions. *Human Performance*, *31*(5), 282–304. doi:10.1080/08959285.2018.1531867

Chiaburu, D. S., Oh, I.-S., Berry, C. M., Li, N., & Gardner, R. G. (2011). The five-factor model of personality traits and organizational citizenship behaviors: A meta. *J.L. Pletzer Personality and Individual Differences, 173* (2021), 110550

Cichorzewska, M., & Rakowska, A. (2017). Organizational citizenship behavior of Polish and Ukrainian civil servants – a comparative study. In *Management Challenges in a Network Economy: Proceedings of the MakeLearn and TIIM International Conference* (pp. 393–394). ToKnowPress.

Dalal, R. S., Bhave, D. P., & Fiset, J. (2014). Within-person variability in job performance a theoretical review and research agenda. *Journal of Management*, *40*(5), 1396–1436. doi:10.1177/0149206314532691

Danaei, A., & Iranbakhsh, F. (2016). Key drivers of innovative behavior in hotel industry: evidence from a developing country. Iran. J. Manage. Stud., 9(3): 599-625.

Dansereau, F. Jr, Graen, G., & Haga, W. J. (1975). A vertical dyad linkage approach to leadership within formal organizations: A longitudinal investigation of the role making process. *Organizational Behavior and Human Performance*, *13*(1), 46–78. doi:10.1016/0030-5073(75)90005-7

Deluga, R. J. (1995). The relationship between attributional charismatic leadership and organizational citizenship behavior. *J. Appl. Soc. Psychol. 25*, 1652–1669. doi:. 1995.tb02638.x doi:10.1111/j.1559-1816

Dunbar, R. I. M., Marriott, A., & Duncan, N. D. C. (1997). Human conversational behavior. *Human Nature (Hawthorne, N.Y.)*, *8*(3), 231–246. doi:10.1007/BF02912493 PMID:26196965

Dussault, M. (2006). Teachers' self-efficacy and organizational citizenship behaviors. *Psychological Reports*, *98*(2), 427–432. doi:10.2466/pr0.98.2.427-432 PMID:16796098

Feinberg, M., Willer, R., & Schultz, M. (2014). Gossip and ostracism promote cooperation in groups. *Psychological Science*, *25*(3), 656–664. doi:10.1177/0956797613510184 PMID:24463551

Fugas, C. S., Silva, S. A., & Meliá, J. L. (2013). Profiling safety behaviors: Exploration of the socio-cognitive variables that best discriminate between different behavioral patterns. *Risk Analysis*, *33*(5), 838–850. doi:10.1111/j.1539-6924.2012.01913.x PMID:23078368

Gans-Morse, J., Kalgin, A. S., Klimenko, A. V., Vorobyev, D., & Yakovlev, A. A. (2020). Public service motivation and sectoral employment in Russia: New perspectives on the attraction vs. socialization debate. [Paper presentation]. *Higher School of Economics Research Paper No. WP BRP, 26.*

Giebels, E., de Reuver, R. S. M., Rispens, S., & Ufkes, E. G. (2016). The critical roles of task conflict and job autonomy in the relationship between proactive personalities and innovative employee behavior. *The Journal of Applied Behavioral Science, 52*(3), 320–341. doi:10.1177/0021886316648774 PMID:27536008

Govindji, R., & Linley, P. A. (2007). Strength's use, self-concordance and well-being implications for strengths coaching and coaching psychologists. Int. Coach. *Psychological Review, 2*, 143–153.

Grant, A. M. (2008a). Does intrinsic motivation fuel the prosocial free? Motivational synergy in predicting persistence, performance, and productivity. *The Journal of Applied Psychology, 93*(1), 48–58. doi:10.1037/0021-9010.93.1.48 PMID:18211134

Grant, A. M. (2008b). The significance of task significance: Job performance effects, relational mechanisms, and boundary conditions. *The Journal of Applied Psychology, 93*(1), 108–124. doi:10.1037/0021-9010.93.1.108 PMID:18211139

Grant, D. E. (2000). *The impact of mentoring and gender -specific role models on women college band directors at four different career* [Dissertation, University of Minnesota]. ProQuest Dissertations Publishing, 9966225.

Grant, L. (2014). Hearts and minds: Aspects of empathy and wellbeing in social work students. *Social Work Education, 33*(3), 338–352. doi:10.1080/02615479.2013.805191

Gray, H. M., Gray, K., & Wegner, D. M. (2007). Dimensions of mind perception. *Science, 315*(5812), 619–619. doi:10.1126cience.1134475 PMID:17272713

Hansen, J. A., & Pihl-Thingvad, S. (2019). Managing employee innovative behavior through transformational and transactional leadership styles. *Public Management Review, 21*(6), 918–944. doi:10.1080/14719037.2018.1544272

He, D., Enhai, Y., Xixi, Ch., Yanbin, L., & Kashif, A. (2020). Humble Leadership Affects Organizational Citizenship Behavior: The Sequential Mediating Effect of Strengths Use and Job Crafting *Journal Frontiers in Psychology, 11.* YEAR=2020URL=https://www.frontiersin.org/article/10.3389/fpsyg.2020.00065 DOI=10.3389/fpsyg.2020.00065

Hu, J., & Liden, R. C. (2015). Making a difference in the teamwork: Linking team PM to team processes and effectiveness. *Academy of Management Journal, 58*(4), 1102–1127. doi:10.5465/amj.2012.1142

Hyde, J. S. (1981). How large are cognitive gender differences? A meta-analysis using w2 and d. *The American Psychologist, 36*(8), 892–901. doi:10.1037/0003-066X.36.8.892

Işik, A. N. (2020). Ethical leadership and school effectiveness: The mediating roles of affective commitment and job satisfaction. *Int J Educ Leadersh Manag, 8*(1), 60–87. doi:10.17583/ijelm.2020.4114

Jepsen, D. M., & Rodwell, J. J. (2006). A side by side comparison of two OCB models and their measures: expanding the construct domain's scope, *Proceedings of the 11th Annual Conference of Asia Pacific Decision Sciences Institute*, (pp. 670-674). Macquarie University.

Jiao, C., Richards, D. A., & Zhang, K. (2011). Leadership and organizational citizenship behavior: OCB-specific meanings as mediators. *Journal of Business and Psychology, 26*(1), 11–25. doi:10.100710869-010-9168-3

Kahya, M., & Şahin, F. (2018). The effect of leader personality on follower behavior: The mediating role of leader–member exchange. *Leadership and Organization Development Journal, 39*(1), 14–33. doi:10.1108/LODJ-08-2016-0206

Kao, R. H. (2017). Task-oriented work characteristics, self-efficacy, and service-oriented organizational citizenship behavior. *Personnel Review, 46*(4), 718–739. doi:10.1108/PR-08-2015-0234

Kaplan, M.; Ö ˇgüt, A.; Karayel, S. & Ilhan, ˙I. (2013). *The effects of ethical climate types on job satisfaction: The case of tourism industry.* Hacet. Üniversitesi ˙Iktisadi ˙Idari Bilimler Fakültesi Derg, *31*, 117–133.

Katz, D. (1964). The motivational basis of organizational behavior. *Behavioral Science, 9*(2), 131–146. doi:10.1002/bs.3830090206 PMID:5888769

Khasawneh, S. (2011). Shared leadership and organizational citizenship behaviour in jordanian public universities: Developing a global workforce for the 21st century. *Educational Management Administration & Leadership, 39*(5), 621–634. doi:10.1177/1741143211408447

Kong, D. T., & Ho, V. T. (2016). A self-determination perspective of strengths use at work: Examining its determinant and performance implications. *The Journal of Positive Psychology, 11*(1), 15–25. doi: 10.1080/17439760.2015.1004555

Konovsky, M. A., & Pugh, S. D. (1994). Citizenship behavior and social exchange. *Academy of Management Journal, 37*(3), 656–669. doi:10.2307/256704 PMID:10134637

Luu, T. T. (2017). CSR and organizational citizenship behavior for the environment in hotel industry: The moderating roles of corporate entrepreneurship and employee attachment style. *International Journal of Contemporary Hospitality Management, 29*(11), 2867–2900. doi:10.1108/IJCHM-02-2016-0080

Madsen, H., & Ulhøi, J. P. (2001). Greening of Human Resources: Environmental Awareness and Training Interests within the Workforce. *Industrial Management & Data Systems, 101*(2), 57–65. doi:10.1108/02635570110384320

Masterson, S. S. (2011). A trickle-down model of organizational justice: Relating employees' and customers' perceptions of and reactions to fairness. *The Journal of Applied Psychology, 86*(4), 594–604. doi:10.1037/0021-9010.86.4.594 PMID:11519644

Mayer, D. M., Kuenzi, M., Greenbaum, R., Bardes, M., & Salvador, R. B. (2009). How low does ethical leadership fow? Test of a trickle-down model. *Organizational Behavior and Human Decision Processes, 108*(1), 1–13. doi:10.1016/j.obhdp.2008.04.002

Miao, R. T. (2011). Perceived organizational support, job satisfaction, task performance and organizational citizenship behavior in China. *Journal of Behavioral and Applied Management, 2011*(12), 105. doi:10.21818/001c.17632

Mo, S., Wang, Z., Akrivou, K., & Booth, S. A. (2012). Look up, look around: Is there anything different about team-level OCB in China? *Journal of Management & Organization, 18*(6), 818–832. doi:10.5172/jmo.2012.18.6.818

Moore, C., Mayer, D. M., Chiang, F. F., Crossley, C., Karlesky, M. J., & Birtch, T. A. (2019a). Leaders matter morally: The role of ethical leadership in shaping employee moral cognition and misconduct. *The Journal of Applied Psychology, 104*(1), 123–145. doi:10.1037/apl0000341 PMID:30221953

Neubert, M. J., Wu, C., & Roberts, J. A. (2013). The influence of ethical leadership and regulatory focus on employee outcomes. *Business Ethics Quarterly, 23*(2), 269–296. doi:10.5840/beq201323217

Newman, A., Kiazad, K., Miao, Q., & Cooper, B. (2014). Examining the cognitive and effective trust-based mechanisms underlying the relationship between ethical leadership and organizational citizenship: A case of the head leading the heart? *Journal of Business Ethics, 123*(1), 113–123. doi:10.100710551-013-1803-2

Olsen, A. L., Hjorth, F., Harmon, N., & Barfort, S. (2019). Behavioral dishonesty in the public sector. *Journal of Public Administration: Research and Theory, 29*(4), 572–590. doi:10.1093/jopart/muy058

Organ, D. W. (1988). *Organizational citizenship behavior: The good soldier syndrome*. Lexington Books.

Owens, B. P., & Hekman, D. R. (2012). Modeling how to grow: An inductive examination of humble leader behaviors, contingencies, and outcomes. *Academy of Management Journal, 55*(4), 787–818. doi:10.5465/amj.2010.0441

Owens, B. P., Johnson, M. D., & Mitchell, T. R. (2013). Expressed humility in organizations: Implications for performance, teams, and leadership. *Organization Science, 24*(5), 1517–1538. doi:10.1287/orsc.1120.0795

Owens, B. P., Johnson, M. D., & Mitchell, T. R. (2013). Expressed humility in organizations: Implications for performance, teams, and leadership. *Organization Science, 24*(5), 1517–1538. doi:10.1287/orsc.1120.0795

Paillé, P., Boiral, O., & Chen, Y. (2013). Linking environmental management practices and organizational citizenship behavior for the environment: A social exchange perspective. *International Journal of Human Resource Management, 24*(18), 3552–3575. doi:10.1080/09585192.2013.777934

Pandey, S. K., Wright, B. E., & Moynihan, D. P. (2008). Public service motivation and interpersonal citizenship behavior in public organizations: Testing a preliminary model. *International Public Management Journal, 11*(1), 89–108. doi:10.1080/10967490801887947

Ployhart, R. E., & Vandenberg, R. J. (2010). Longitudinal research: The theory, design, and analysis of change. *Journal of Management, 36*(1), 94–120. doi:10.1177/0149206309352110

Podsakoff, P. M., MacKenzie, S. B., Moorman, R. H., & Fetter, R. (1990). Transformational leader behaviors and their effects on followers' trust in leader, satisfaction, and organizational citizenship behaviors. *The Leadership Quarterly, 1*(2), 107–142. doi:10.1016/1048-9843(90)90009-7

Podsakoff, P. M., Paine, J. B., & Bachrach, D. C. (2000). Organizational citizenship behaviors: A critical review of the theoretical and empirical literature and suggestions for future research. *Journal of Management, 26*(3), 513–563. doi:10.1177/014920630002600307

Quenson, Y. (2013). *The relationship between ethical leadership and individual directed organizational citizenship behavior: the moderating effect of leader-member-exchange.* Baptist University.

Rioux, S. M., & Penner, L. A. (2001). The causes of organizational citizenship behavior: A motivational analysis. *The Journal of Applied Psychology, 86*(6), 1306–1314. doi:10.1037/0021-9010.86.6.1306 PMID:11768072

Ruizalba, J. L.; Guillermo, B.G.; Miguel, A. R.-M.; Blanca, M. J., (2014). Internal market orientation: empirical research in hotel sector. *Int. J. Hospit. Manage., 38*, 11-19.

Sabzipoor, M., Ahmadizad, A., & Ismaeel-Givi, M. (2012). Analysis of the relationship of organizational atmosphere with attitude variables and meta-role behaviors in the personnel of public libraries. [in Persian]. *Res Inf Sci Public Libr, 17*, 581–602.

Salanova, M., Lorente, L., Chambel, M. J., & Martínez, I. M. (2011). Linking transformational leadership to nurses' extra-role performance: The mediating role of self-efficacy and work engagement. *Journal of Advanced Nursing, 67*(10), 2256–2266. doi:10.1111/j.1365-2648.2011.05652.x PMID:21535088

Schlechter, A. F., & Maharaj, I. (2007). Meaning in life and meaning of work: Relationships with organizational citizenship behavior, commitment, and job satisfaction. *Manag. Dyn., 26*, 24–4.

Şenyurt, H., & Dinc, M. S. (2015). The Relationship among Ethical Leadership and Organizational Citizenship Behavior: a study of private primary and high school teachers in Bosubjective normia and Herzegovina. In: *International Conference on Economic and Social Studies - ICESoS'15,* (p. 138–44). International Burch University..

Singer, J. D., & Willett, J. B. (2003). *Applied longitudinal data analysis: Modeling change and event occurrence.* Oxford university press. doi:10.1093/acprof:oso/9780195152968.001.0001

Smith, C. A., Organ, D. W., & Near, J. P. (1983). Organizational citizenship behavior: Its nature and antecedents. *The Journal of Applied Psychology, 68*(4), 653–663. doi:10.1037/0021-9010.68.4.653

Spector, P. E., & Fox, S. (2002). An emotion-centered model of voluntary work behavior: Some parallels between counterproductive work behavior and organizational citizenship behavior. *Human Resource Management Review, 12*(2), 1–24. doi:10.1016/S1053-4822(02)00049-9

Tajeddini, K. (2010). Effect of customer orientation and entrepreneurial orientation on innovativeness: Evidence from the hotel industry in Switzerland. Tourism Manage., 31(2), 221-231.

Tajeddini, K., & Trueman, M. (2008). The potential for innovativeness: a tale of the Swiss watch industry. J. Market. Manage., 24(1-2), 169-184.

Tajeddini, K., & Trueman, M. (2012). Managing Swiss Hospitality: How cultural antecedents of innovation and customer-oriented value systems can influence performance in the hotel industry. Int. J. Hospital. Manage., 31(4): 1119-1129.

Tajeddini, K., & Trueman, M. (2014). Perceptions of innovativeness among Iranian hotel managers. J. Hospital. Tourism Technol., 5(1): 62-77. doi:10.1108/JHTT-12-2012-0036

Tajeddini, K., Trueman, M., & Larsen, G. (2006). Examining the effect of market orientation on innovativeness. J. Market. Manage., 22(5-6): 529-551. doi:10.1362/026725706777978640

Tan, L. P., Yap, C. S., Choong, Y. O., Choe, K. L., Rungruang, P., & Li, Z. (2019). Ethical leadership, perceived organizational support and citizenship behaviors: The moderating role of ethnic dissimilarity. *Leadership and Organization Development Journal*, *40*(8), 877–897. doi:10.1108/LODJ-04-2019-0160

Todd, S. Y., & Kent, A. (2006). Direct and indirect effects of task characteristics on organizational citizenship behavior. *North American Journal of Psychology*, *8*(2), 253–268.

Van der Voet, J., Steijn, B., & Kuipers, B. S. (2017). What's in it for others? The relationship between prosocial motivation and commitment to change among youth care professionals. *Public Management Review*, *2017*(19), 443–462. doi:10.1080/14719037.2016.1183699

Van Woerkom, M., & Meyers, M. C. (2015). My strengths count! effects of a strengths-based psychological climate on positive affect and job performance. *Hum. Resour. Manag. 54*, 81–103. doi:. 21623 doi:10.1002/hrm

Van Woerkom, M., Mostert, K., Els, C., Bakker, A. B., de Beer, L., & Rothmann, S. Jr. (2016a). Strengths use and deficit correction in organizations: Development and validation of a questionnaire. *European Journal of Work and Organizational Psychology*, *25*(6), 960–975. doi:10.1080/1359432X.2016.1193010

Walumbwa, F. O., Wang, P., Wang, H., Schaubroeck, J., & Avolio, B. J. (2010). Psychological processes linking authentic leadership to follower behaviors. *The Leadership Quarterly*, *21*(5), 901–914. doi:10.1016/j.leaqua.2010.07.015

Wang, Y., Liu, J., & Zhu, Y. (2018). How does humble leadership promote follower creativity? the roles of psychological capital and growth need strength. *Leadership and Organization Development Journal*, *39*(4), 507–521. doi:10.1108/LODJ-03-2017-0069

Wayne, S. J., & Green, S. A. (1993). The effects of leader-member exchange on employee citizenship and impression management behavior. *Human Relations*, *46*(12), 1431–1440. doi:10.1177/001872679304601204

Wu, J., Balliet, D., & Van Lange, P. A. M. (2016a). Gossip versus punishment: The efficiency of reputation to promote and maintain cooperation. *Scientific Reports*, *6*(1), 23919. doi:10.1038rep23919 PMID:27039896

Wu, J., Balliet, D., & Van Lange, P. A. M. (2016b). Reputation, gossip, and human cooperation. *Social and Personality Psychology Compass*, *10*(6), 350–364. doi:10.1111pc3.12255

Wu, L.-Z., Birtch, T. A., Chiang, F. F. T., & Zhang, H. (2018a). Perceptions of negative workplace gossip: A self-consistency theory framework. *Journal of Management*, *44*(5), 1873–1898. doi:10.1177/0149206316632057

Yam, K. C., Fehr, R., Burch, T. C., Zhang, Y., & Gray, K. (2019). Would I really make a diference? Moral typecasting theory and its implications for helping ethical leaders. *Journal of Business Ethics*, *160*(3), 675–692. doi:10.100710551-018-3940-0

Yan, Z., & Chen, C. C. (2013). Developmental leadership and organizational citizenship behavior: Mediating effects of self-determination, supervisor identification, and organizational identification. *The Leadership Quarterly*, *24*(4), 534–543. doi:10.1016/j.leaqua.2013.03.007

Ye, Y., Zhu, H., Deng, X., & Mu, Z. (2019). Negative workplace gossip and service outcomes: An explanation from social identity theory. *International Journal of Hospitality Management*, *82*, 159–168. doi:10.1016/j.ijhm.2019.04.020

Yuan, F., & Woodman, R. W. (2010). Innovative behavior in the workplace: The role of performance and image outcome expectations. *Academy of Management Journal*, *53*(2), 323–342. doi:10.5465/amj.2010.49388995

Zhang, J., Chen, Y., & Liu, J. (2016). *Ethical leadership and OCBE: The influence of prosocial motivation and self-accountability.* Paper presented at the Academy of Management Proceedings, Briarcliff Manor, NY. 10.5465/ambpp.2016.15588abstract

Zhang, L., Jiang, H., & Jin, T. (2020). Leader-member exchange and organisational citizenship behavior: The mediating and moderating effects of role ambiguity. *Journal of Psychology in Africa*, *30*(1), 17–22. doi:10.1080/14330237.2020.1721948

Chapter 10
Scaling Up "Sustainability Development":
Analyzing the Intricacies and Application of Blockchain Technology vis-à-vis Financial Markets

Ridhi Rani
https://orcid.org/0000-0001-8820-171X
Symbiosis International University (Deemed), India

Ved Srinivas
Thiagarajar School of Management, India

Anita Sable
Symbiosis International University (Deemed), India

ABSTRACT

Blockchains are currently recognized as a new area of digitization with difficulties in attaining sustainability. The research has not yet produced a unified framework for understanding the characteristics of blockchains that allow the development of financial trading markets over the long term. The topic of how blockchains support the growth of sustainable financial trading platforms and services still exists. A qualitative and iterative investigation was done to compile the basic concepts found in the literature to provide a conceptual framework with four sustainability themes and eleven types of affordances. The results are significant because they show how closely related these categories are, leading to conflicts between various sustainability-related concepts.

DOI: 10.4018/978-1-6684-7422-8.ch010

INTRODUCTION

The definition of digitalization is the expansion of technology networking and connectivity to enhance individual services, communications, and transactions (Evangelista et al., 2014). Unique opportunities to enhance social and environmental well-being are presented by the rapid growth and maturation of the digital world, where an increasing number of private and public actions are being recorded, digitized, and analyzed for future technological improvement (Croo, 2015). The amount of software and data people utilize is exploding (Sivarajah et al., 2017). The productivity of local and global economies will benefit from the trend's rapid growth, but it will also potentially lead to sustainability problems like the carbon footprint associated with rising electricity demand, cybersecurity vulnerabilities, and social inequalities caused by the widening gap in access to information and communication technologies (Irfan, 2017). The Brundtland Report, "Our Common Future," on the other hand, defines "sustainability" as "development that satisfies the requirements of the present without compromising the ability of future generations to satisfy their own needs."(Brinck, 1992)

Blockchain technology, a revolutionary development based on the information and computational improvements, is still expanding quickly (Bai et al., 2020). Applications for blockchain technology have grown across several industries, including financial. These rapid improvements for numerous industries present numerous opportunities, but these businesses face several social, ethical, and technological issues in addition to the implementation costs (Bai et al., 2020). The research (Noble & Patil, 2021) sheds light on the current status of blockchain in stock markets and highlights the need to address this technology's dangers and negative societal effects. Additionally, blockchains are one of three newly developing domains of digitalization that are currently thought to be facing long-term difficulties (Linkov et al., 2018). Financial institutions struggle with sustainability, especially when one institution fails and impacts all the other network players (Al-Shaibani et al., 2020). According to Mishra & Kaushik, (2021), a sustainable financial sector is a crucial component of economic progress. Frameworks for sustainability have been developed while taking IT and digitalization into account generally. The most encouraging piece of research by Linkov et al., (2018) discusses three adaptive governance solutions that nations can use to address challenges to digital sustainability by using the Triple Bottom Line (TBL) dimensions. Ten requirements are listed in research by Stuermer et al., (2017) for ensuring sustainability in digital artifacts. The academic study on blockchain technology and its uses in various fields are gradually growing. The sustainable use of blockchain in supply chain management is a hot topic that raises various issues, advantages, difficulties, and limitations. Blockchain technology's level of development and commercial viability have both been questioned. Business Wang et al., (2018), academics Montecchi et al., (2019), and government all have distinct perspectives on the Blockchain (Jeanbart et al., 2020). A conceptual framework that describes the sustainability of blockchains with a holistic approach while considering social, environmental, economic, and technical elements in Financial Trading Markets (*hereinafter* FT markets) is not yet established by the existing research.

BACKGROUND

Describing a relatively recent phenomenon, blockchain technology supports the mechanism underlying cryptocurrencies and is currently the subject of intense discussion in the media, with governments and businesses worldwide. People pushed for safer and more decentralized currency governance due to the 2008 financial crisis. As a response to the financial crisis and unquestionably the most important development in the field of digitalization, Satoshi Nakamoto first saw blockchain in the form of Bitcoin in 2009 (Dallyn, 2017). Following the global financial crisis of 2008, the world has focused on improving the financial market sector's infrastructure while ensuring long-term stability from various angles. Blockchain is a game-changing technology that is altering the way that financial institutions carry out many of their operations. Blockchain will transform the financial markets and their function by giving consumers far more control and transparency over their data and offering a foundation for point-to-point connectivity in a highly scalable, sustainable manner. Blockchain lowers risk, cost, and time for these transactions and complex workflows by addressing new value chain elements from primary issues and services to settlement (Nguyen, 2016). Using blockchain technology, users can precisely manage who sees their information, orders, prices, inventories, and holdings and when and how it appears.

Furthermore, the advantages of blockchain technology to all market participants are enormous. Numerous research has been done to develop FT platforms that get around the drawbacks of conventional FT platforms, like single points of failure, settlement delays, and the lack of transparency offered to stakeholders (Al-Shaibani et al., 2020). Blockchain is, without a doubt, the structure of the future of financial markets. Businesses are eager to use blockchain technology to promote the long-term growth of FT markets. Additionally, a working group was established by the London Stock Exchange (LSE) in 2015 to look into the potential use of blockchain technology for reporting and trade clearance in the European market (Popescu, 2020). Like many other industries, financial markets are seeing significant changes due to blockchain technology. To produce execution that is fundamentally better and more sustainable over time, practitioners must start this change. Using this breakthrough technology, authorities can strategically plan for long-term success by implementing financial systems. As a result, this study aims to compile and analyze data focusing on blockchain's roles in the long-term technological, social, economic, and environmental sustainability of FT markets.

MAIN FOCUS OF THE CHAPTER

The need for in-depth research on this technology in FT markets is demonstrated by numerous academic efforts, the innovative SSEI program from the UN, and the blockchain-driven revolution that market heavyweights in the financial industry have observed. An extensive review of the body of literature pointed out that there is a considerable research gap when it comes to considering blockchains for the implementation of sustainable FT markets using a comprehensive framework. The general goal of this study is to provide a conceptual framework by reviewing the literature to comprehensively summarize the affordances of blockchain technology from the viewpoints of the environment, society, economy, and technology in the domain of FT markets. Through an iterative process of revising and evaluating the initial conceptual framework taken from the literature, this study subsequently highlights the fundamental elements of blockchain technology that contribute to forming a sustainable FT market. Throughout this research, current research findings from previous studies were considered and examined to establish the original conceptual framework of affordances. Much of the offered current knowledge is dispersed and disordered. The early stages of blockchain sustainability studies in FT markets should become clearer and more consistent due to exploring and understanding these discrepancies. In particular, at this early stage, it would be helpful to identify standard criteria that serve as a systematic guide for future research.: This study was conducted to answer the following question, "Which features of blockchains are key enablers of affordances that allow for developing sustainable financial trading markets?"

Blockchains for a Sustainable Change

Development and use of Cryptocurrencies such as BitCoin are the most popular and notable application of blockchain (Parmentola et al., 2022). Beyond its usage in financial services, blockchain has been the subject of numerous research in areas like taxation, international trade, corporate operations, and governance (Kimani et al., 2020; Pólvora et al., 2020). A recent review of blockchain studies, (Centobelli et al., (2021) demonstrate how academics have taken advantage of the advantages of blockchain information technologies in several fields, including supply chain management. Blockchain technology can increase transaction efficiency, share transparent data, and lower operational expenses(Francisco & Swanson, 2018). The integration of numerous IT systems and databases in supply chains is hampered by the variety of organizational data formats, which prevents seamless data exchange solutions (Galvez et al., 2018; Wang et al., 2018). The United Nations Conference (2021) report, "Harnessing blockchain for sustainable development: prospects and challenges," lists several examples of blockchain implementations to get around this problem and enhance data traceability to use blockchain for sustainable development. In addition to its many other advantages, blockchain can assist with several environmental sustainability challenges, with three key elements relating to resource rights, product origins, and behavioral incentives for environmental sustainability (Hughes et al., 2019). Blockchains may make it easier to implement new green industrial techniques. As a result, it will be simpler to implement, as well as to monitor and store data-related activities that contribute to pollution and environmental degradation, real-time collection, and analysis of green or low-carbon data for timely decision-making, and to support the development of a green supply chain (C. Bai & Sarkis, 2017). It is currently exceedingly challenging to physically verify carbon credits with emission rights. Following a recent review of 30 papers that connected supply chains and blockchains, Varriale et al., (2020) concluded that by keeping track of and lowering CO2 emissions throughout supply chain activities, blockchains could support the development of environmentally sustainable supply chains. This also makes it possible to keep an eye on the exchange of hazardous waste, develop a system of incentives that encourage recycling, advance the use of the circular economy, and monitor the use of natural resources, notably in the agri-food sector. To create a governance framework for the UN-SDGs, Kim & Huh, (2020) used blockchain to verify the rights to carbon emissions and the other 17 UN-SDGs duties.

This innovation appears to be a promising driver for achieving the world's sustainable development goals, according to (Parmentola et al., 2022). Smart cities could be established, for instance, by establishing shared financial services using blockchain technology (Sun et al., 2016). Security considerations must be considered while implementing trust-free sharing services in a smart city, along with other issues like confidentiality, availability, and integrity. A distributed ledger is the foundation of a particular technology known as blockchain technology. As data availability is not dependent on other parties, copies of files are maintained, and modifications are approved by consensus, meeting the standards for a secure smart city, information is kept private. According to energy calculations by Malone & O'Dwyer, (2014), the entire Bitcoin mining network uses the same amount of electricity as Ireland. According to Dimitriou & Karame, (2013), this is not entirely true because the network's performance affects the financial and technological costs of obtaining a coin. Consequently, it would seem that the assertion that bitcoin "trades and consumes a large quantity of energy" is untrue (Malone & O'Dwyer,

2014). Governments, as well as academics, have taken note of blockchain's potential to advance SDGs, as shown (Glavanits, 2020). The Share & Charge project, which was first launched in the UK and then expanded to the EU and promotes the use of blockchain to monitor electric car charging systems, is also mentioned by the author about environmental SDGs. California is also using blockchain to monitor and manage Sacramento's groundwater.

Blockchains for the Financial Sector and Financial Trading Markets

The four main advantages of implementing blockchains in the financial sector are: faster transaction processing; preservation of sustainability for financial and banking activities; increased privacy and security of financial data; and finally, automation of financial contracts (Jaoude & Saade, 2019). Financial institutions worry about sustainability, especially when a single institution files for bankruptcy and impacts all other eco-system stakeholders (Al-Shaibani et al., 2020). The adoption of Blockchain Rouhani & Deters, (2019) can aid in financial industry stabilization, particularly when local or national financial regulations do not constrain the decentralized money database. Utilizing blockchains in conjunction with timely development would boost the predicted economic growth even more. Most problems encountered in the conventional FT market can be resolved decentralized thanks to Blockchain technology Mishra & Kaushik, (2021). To provide fair trade for the stakeholders, smart contracts eliminate the need for third-party intermediaries and run transactions following an established set of rules (Tsai et al., 2016). With the help of real-time validation, auditing, and reconsolidation of transactions, post-trade processes like clearing and settlement are more effective (Mishra & Kaushik, 2021). Businesses may create streamlined processes and effective financial transactions thanks to the blockchain's data, which is visible, traceable, and resistant to fraudsters and hackers (Mori, 2016).

Although many tangible items can be transferred in exchange, the actual transfers, the associated paperwork, and legal agreements are demanding. The introduction of digital assets through tokenization is a remedy for this flaw. Although real-world physical stocks must be bought in bulk, it is now possible to buy a fraction of a digital stock through your digital wallet, much like buying a bitcoin (Mishra & Kaushik, 2021). Numerous academics have tried to replicate distributed market infrastructures to better address the centralized market's flaws (Al-Shaibani et al., 2020). Created a novel, fully decentralized stock market using a private Ethereum blockchain where traditional market participants from centralized markets are designated validation nodes in this network consortium. According to the statistics gathered, the throughput is more than sufficient to meet the needs of major stock exchanges, including the Singapore Stock Exchange. Similar efforts are made in a study by Pop et al., (2018) to build an Ethereum-based Bucharest Stock Exchange. The trials' results show that when a decentralized solution is adopted in place of a centralized one, the decentralized solution can provide cheaper transaction costs by replacing the commission owed to brokers with a mining fee, which is used to compensate miners for their mining efforts (Tsai et al., 2016). Creating a blockchain-based clearing and settlement system for a genuine Chinese clearinghouse is another trading-related usage of blockchains. Over 3 billion real transactions from an exchange have been processed in a clearinghouse where the system has been implemented and tested for more than two months. The results indicate that the proposed design has addressed a realistic trade clearing and settlement system's scalability, privacy, and performance issues.

THEORETICAL FRAMEWORKS

Affordance Theory

James J. Gibson first proposed the idea of "Affordance" in 1979. A person with a goal observes an object of interest in an environment by comprehending how it can be used rather than simply characterizing the object by its qualities, according to Gibbs' explanation of the affordance theory (*hereinafter* AT) (Gibson, 2014: 127-137). In 2017, Volkoff & Diane M. Strong, (2017) introduced an improved version of AT that offered instructions on effectively using the theory in IS research. A socio-technical paradigm known as AT enables users to express their technology usage explicitly while simultaneously considering social and contextual considerations. Given that AT is based on domain-specific users and technologies, IS researchers can develop a variety of mid-level social-technical theories using it (Volkoff & Diane M. Strong, 2017). A mid-level conceptual framework was developed as the solution to the study's research question to pinpoint the key blockchain characteristics that make FT markets and services sustainable. People or organizations must act goal-oriented to take advantage of a particular technology's benefits. There is currently a very small corpus of literature devoted to comprehending blockchain's capabilities, whether concealed, apparent, or actual (Ostern et al., 2020). AT can assist with brainstorming and developing user-centered blockchain services (Gaver, 1991). A good theory must explain problems in the real world, identify basic concepts, and explain how they relate to one another (Tsoukas, 1989). As a result, AT was used since this study uses an iterative strategy to summarize the affordances and important characteristics of blockchains given in the literature and assess them in light of expert judgments.

Triple Bottom Line

Business, as usual, is being driven more and more by corporate social responsibility, forcing organizations to streamline their processes from the inside out. To keep stakeholder trust, businesses must recover control over their operations, ensuring they follow the rules and are far more transparent than before. As a result, entities struggle to use current reporting procedures to communicate their performance's good and bad aspects. Traditional methods are criticized for not accurately reflecting a company's social and financial performance. The term "Triple Bottom Line" (*from now on* TBL) was initially coined in 1994 by John Elkington, regarded as the foremost authority on sustainability, to evaluate how well American businesses performed. This concept contends that businesses can be managed to increase their financial, societal, and environmental benefits (Elkington, 1999). The TBL's derivative, ESG disclosure, and sustainability have recently become hot subjects in the financial markets. ESG is a strong idea that seeks to establish uniform standards for businesses to report on their environmental and social responsibilities.

Blockchains are known as the "trust machine" that flourishes in financial markets, a social setting with numerous stakeholders and competing requirements, and also has the potential to play a significant role in trustworthy ESG reporting. To harness sustainable financing utilizing digital technologies, numerous people and nonprofit organizations, like the UN and Green Finance Digital Alliance, do a lot of research and studies. At the same time, Giungato et al., (2017) attempt to fill the gap in defining the sustainability of a bitcoin by evaluating environmental impacts, social issues, and economic aspects; the three themes of the TBL Bendell, (2017) attempted to understand bitcoins from various perspectives, including social, economic, and environmental (Giungato et al., 2017). Studies and efforts highlight the need to change financial institutions and markets to meet sustainable development criteria better.

In addition, the UN Secretary-General announced the Sustainable Stock Exchanges project in 2009 to promote sustainable trade and investment growth to achieve sustainable development goals. When the SSE initiative released its Model Recommendations for Exchanges in September 2015, it was noted that less than 10% of stock exchanges worldwide gave guidance on ESG data for their market. Due to the lack of guidance for ESG reporting, there is insufficient corporate data, making it challenging for investors to fully understand a company's key problems.

METHODOLOGY

As this study deals with conceptual testing of the framework and managing qualitative data received from various data collection methods, a multi-method qualitative approach was chosen as the research methodology. According to Tashakkori et al., (2003), multiple techniques are efficient because they enable you to assess the research findings and conclusions more thoroughly in a way that can be relied upon, presenting better solutions to research problems. To improve the framework's usefulness, it is crucial to note that using a mixed methodology that analyzes both qualitative and quantitative data would be the best methodological decision. This also implies that, given the period, individual research is unrealistic.

DATA ANALYSIS

A thorough analysis of the available literature on sustainable financial markets and the function of blockchains revealed several fundamental ideas that provided a comprehensive method to address the study's research issue. The condensed theories, which include 11 categories of affordances overall, are divided into four themes: technological, societal, environmental, and economical. The three sustainability features of the TBL are considered motivating factors for the three dimensions: societal, environmental, and economical. The researcher primarily uses the fourth dimension, the technological component, to discuss the technological efficiency blockchains have brought to the subject.

Technological

Software Quality and Security of Financial Trading Markets

The developers' choice of technology and the underlying code are the only factors that affect a software application's quality and security. The underlying principles of blockchain technology are presented in research Iansiti & Lakhani, (2017), along with the main distinctions between blockchain technology and conventional database systems. They have distributed technology, direct node-to-node communication, immutability, network accessibility, and computational logic. As a result, disintermediation, automation, and non-repudiation were listed as three benefits in the book "Blockchain Basics: A Non-Technical Introduction in 25 Steps" (Drescher, 2017). These intrinsic qualities and advantages enable various potential blockchain applications, including secure digital payments, cryptocurrencies, and more, which improve the technical sustainability and efficiency of FT markets and services. For the conventional market structure, centralization has a variety of drawbacks, such as a single point of failure, a potential performance bottleneck, or vulnerability to attacks, in addition to being time-consuming (Bhandarkar et al., 2019).

The ability of blockchain technology to construct a distributed ledger with smart contracts between parties for the transfer of financial assets has the potential to alter old processes while also raising the level of the market as a whole. By automating payments when certain criteria are met, smart contracts eliminate the need for intermediaries in reconciliation, asset exchange, and settlement. Additionally, independent individuals and groups will use an automated process to carry out the transactions' intermediary functions in auditing, inspections, data authentication, and data transmission (Al-Shaibani et al., 2020). Effective and high-quality communication on channels creates a psychological connection between the parties, creating a cycle of trust that grows over time (Hurley, 2011). Communication with trading partners in the financial markets has been made more difficult by the error-prone and time-consuming exchange of paper documents. Blockchain technology can boost partners' confidence while increasing communication effectiveness and quality. A strong argument in favor of FT markets appears to be the idea of immutable contracts between the parties involved in a trading platform, where all transaction data is secure, disintermediation and non-repudiation are crucial, and trust and integrity are fundamental intrinsic components of the architecture (Hughes et al., 2019).

Cost and Scalability of Transactions

Higher operating expenses in managing financial transactions, such as fees for brokers and other intermediaries, back-office and post-trade services, and payment and settlement systems, harm their net profitability (Mishra & Kaushik, 2021). The literature claims that by reducing the cost of manual labor, employing blockchain technology to streamline transactions and settlement procedures will increase economic benefits. Swan's study from 2017 focuses on the financial gains made possible by blockchain technology in digital payments and asset management. Additionally, verifying the particular characteristics of traded assets is less expensive. Blockchain technology is being used as a consensus method to reduce the overall cost that financial institutions connected to the trading market must endure because verifying assets and individuals is a time-consuming process that costs a lot of money (Tapscott & Tapscott, 2016). An approach like this for decentralized consensus will result in lower operational costs for physical verification, computation, and storage costs (Zhao et al., 2016). However, developing such a platform will necessitate a wider agreement among financial institutions, which may impact the trading platform's overall scalability (Tsai et al., 2016). Due to technical difficulties, financial institutions are losing crucial clients. Blockchain will speed up payment, clearance, and settlement compared to current techniques and stabilize trading markets and real-time transaction capabilities (Tsai et al., 2016). According to various studies, the immutable nature of blockchain means that any changes to the smart contracts or blocks, no matter how small, are likely to be computationally expensive and require a new block in the chain, which will affect everyone's costs and turnaround times (Hughes et al., 2019).

Societal

Data Security and Privacy of Participants

Blockchain technology can help trading markets expedite processes while ensuring secure financial transactions because it is transparent and impervious to hackers and fraudsters. Thieves and con artists use modern technology worldwide to commit financial crimes without physical contact with the systems. Blockchain technology can stop such crimes, especially in the case of private blockchains, because every transaction from the start to the end in the chain of blocks is immutable (Mori, 2016). Similarly, Rechtman, (2017) said that users are drawn to the system because of the independent record that blockchain maintains to protect against fraud and errors, as well as the technology's ability to reduce the likelihood of asset-related data being lost greatly. It is crucial to emphasize that varying data security and privacy levels come from the different levels of user access to information between public and private blockchains. Therefore, financial institutions are more interested in establishing private blockchains because doing so enables them to keep information more discreetly and maintain the anonymity of both individuals and transactions (Buterin, 2015). Therefore, data availability is ensured even if some nodes are compromised or fail (Kowalski et al., 2021). On the other hand, safeguarding these keys necessitates that each user store and handle them carefully, which might be scary for individuals who are unfamiliar with the technology. According to Gan et al., (2021), the drawback is that financial sector users believe security and privacy issues to be the most common user-related obstacles. Users worry about various security difficulties in the financial sector, such as identity theft, hackers, and money laundering (Ante et al., 2018). As a result, this worry calls for developing a blockchain eco-system that eliminates the danger of incorrect privacy management (Mavilia & Pisani, 2020).

Building Trust and Reliability

Blockchain technology is a game changer because it can address trust issues in transactions and offer a more affordable, secure, and effective option for data exchanges (Van Wersch, 2019). Financial institutions were among the first to adopt blockchain technology as they recognized its potential to enhance securities settlement (Swa, 2015). The elimination of intermediaries in a transaction was made possible by the trust-establishing capabilities of blockchain technology and dependable peer-to-peer connections. Blockchain technology's "trustless trust" and "trust-by-computation" features have the potential to transform economic transactions that previously relied on mutual trust between human agents and reputable third-party institutions (Ducuing, 2019). According to Sadhya et al., (2018), blockchain technology can address interpersonal and technological trust issues. The degree of trust between the parties involved is called "interpersonal trust" (Löbbecke et al., 2018). When one knows and trusts one's trading partners, believes in their goodwill, and shares common norms, interpersonal trust develops in trade, leading to an expectation that every stakeholder will behave responsibly in trade Ostrom & Eggertsson, (1990) Ostrom, (1990). On the other hand, interpersonal trust building is typically confined to a small scale and becomes harder to maintain as the number of participants in the trade increases (Loebbecke, et al., 2018). Once a new block is created, a distributed consensus algorithm must approve it (Zheng et al., 2017). Although the blockchain has a trust-based architecture, adoption of the technology won't happen unless consumers have faith in it (Hawlitschek et al., 2018).

Easy Access to Trading Services and Their Usability

The technology allows projects and efforts to crowdsource funding from many different investors rather than just a few big ones since it can efficiently manage complex financial settings and accommodate various stakeholders (Herweijer et al., 2018). Financial inclusion provides financial services to people or low-income companies at fair and sustainable costs (Gan et al., 2021). The possibility for a new method of project finance with efficiency, cost savings, and speed of execution exists with blockchain-enabled

ICOs. Depending on the type of rights granted to ICO tokens, companies can access risk capital without sharing ownership, eliminating one of the main obstacles to employing public equity funding (Nassr, 2019).

Environmental

Energy Consumption

Researchers have highlighted the advantages and disadvantages of employing blockchain technology for environmental purposes. For instance, technical implementation issues, particularly in large-scale permissionless blockchain implementations, and the energy needed for crucial algorithms, processing, and computations within the blockchain are of concern (Saberi et al., 2019). Additionally, having huge servers necessitates huge buildings, which can harm the area they are built on and hurt the environment (Parmentola et al., 2022). Private networks don't need a robust consensus procedure like proof-of-work because transactions can be changed as long as all primary members concur. Although the network's security is decreased, efficiency and latency are increased. Therefore energy usage is barely a concern Vranken, (2017). The level of security offered by these alternative consensuses to public blockchains is still questioned, even though they will significantly reduce energy usage compared to proof-of-work (Gan et al., 2021; Vranken, 2017). One example of a public blockchain is a cryptocurrency, which has grown significantly in popularity among investors for trading and investing and whose market capitalization has surpassed $2 trillion in 2021 (Mazer, 2021). Energy use is soaring, and it's estimated that bitcoin uses more electricity annually than Ireland (Belt & Kok, 2018).

Green Financing

Blockchain can facilitate a shift from shareholder to stakeholder value on a bigger scale and broaden traditional financial capital accounting to account for social and environmental capital. These changes could raise the trillions of dollars needed to finance the switch to low-carbon, ecologically sustainable economies if implemented at once (Wang et al., 2018). Blockchain benefits all kinds of bonds, but new technological developments have given green bonds even more choices, positioning green bonds to be at the forefront of the change. Along with the Internet of Things (IoT) and artificial intelligence (AI), blockchain is also developing (Chen & Volz, 2022).

Economic

Interoperability With Cross-Country Markets

A nation's financial growth is directly and favorably impacted by the health and performance of its financial market (Al-Shaibani et al., 2020). Both the 2011 TMX-London Stock Exchange merger proposal and the recent announcement by Deutsche Boerse AG of its acquisition of NYSE Euronext continue the trend of cross-border exchange mergers that are creating chances for the integration of the world's financial markets (Mohindra, 2011). It is possible to keep many open, shared distributed ledgers for foreign exchanges. This suggests that a trader can trade any asset from any financial market or nation as long as they are connected to the Blockchain (Belt & Kok, 2018). Another problem preventing this movement is the absence of a uniform architecture across international financial markets. To address these issues, financial institutions are currently assessing the viability of strategies using decentralized finance, such as Hyperledger (Hughes et al., 2019).

Sustainable Investments

Environmentally sustainable investment is a critical enabler for a more resilient, greener recovery, according to the G20 Infrastructure Working Group (IMF, 2021), as it creates jobs, accelerates economic growth, combats climate change, and improves people's quality of life. Additionally, it may spur much-needed private sector investment in environmentally friendly and resilient initiatives (IMF, 2021). The financial markets have embraced sustainability-themed investments at a rapid rate during the past five years, including sustainable assets that include ESG components (UNCTAD, 2021). According to polls, while choosing investments, investors are increasingly taking social impact and sustainability into account (Jeanbart et al., 2020). It creates a consistent procedure for registering and certifying assets in the blockchain network by utilizing the many aspects of blockchain technology, including timestamps and public and private key methods. Additionally, by mobilizing data on the use of money raised, the development of green initiatives, the execution of the project and its environmental and social implications, metering, billing, and income streams, blockchain may be utilized for data life cycle management (Chen & Volz, 2022). Additionally, digital platforms have increased access to a global market, making it more desirable for asset owners to make their assets investable (Jeanbart et al., 2020).

Market Risk Management

Numerous market failures might affect the established financial markets. The market's structural weaknesses cause many problems, including systemic risk and investor control over their assets (Paech, 2017). Blockchain networks preserve a record of the traders' assets. These resources are a component of a sizable, intricate risk management procedure that continuously involves all participants in the financial industry (Avgouleas & Kiayias, 2019). When all transactions and activities are traceable on the blockchain, and the risk associated with the settlement is greatly reduced, if not eliminated, blockchain can be utilized as a risk management tool (Avgouleas & Kiayias, 2019). The clearinghouse can also receive relatively comprehensive instructions on permitted trades from market authorities, enabling it to control efficiently and lower market risks, aiding the government and investors in protecting their investments, and boosting investor trust (Tsai et al., 2016). This is typically caused by the same behavioral patterns of the decision makers, ideally the investors, or, in the event of investment or risk management decisions left up to machines and the use of algorithms, identical results are produced in both cases (Bundesbank, 2016). The independent and unstoppable execution of transactions with smart contracts in blockchain financial networks may worsen this problem. When the human aspect is eliminated, the elasticity in the behaviors of the financial market's stakeholders is also gone. Eliminating elasticity may improve market efficiency in prosperous times, but it may exacerbate inefficiencies in difficult times (Wright & De Filippi, 2015).

Automated Auditing and Reporting for Governance

The Securities and Exchange Commission (SEC) is in charge of policing the investing industry and ensuring it doesn't hurt a nation's economy. Blockchain technology might help government agencies in their work. The SEC needs assistance from interested parties to stay on top of the changing financial markets. Furthermore, there are several bottlenecks while performing KYC and Anti Money Laundering (AML) checks due to the current use of numerous internal and outside technologies. During the on-boarding traders and investors, more time is spent validating and repeating information between parties. Once everyone using the blockchain maintains the same version of reality, this should be gone. Since every entry is recorded on the ledger, it would be nearly hard to falsify such a record to hide activity. A blockchain seems especially relevant in light of the moral hazard problems brought on by inaccurate reporting in legacy systems (Jessel & DiCaprio, 2018). Transactions may be audited automatically since they are automated, reducing most human labor and the time and expense associated with them. Each block in the blockchain has a reference to the block before it, making it possible to create a thorough audit trail and complete history of all transactions (Bendell, 2017).

RESULTS FROM THE THEMATIC ANALYSIS

See Table 1.

Table 1. Results from thematic analysis

Category	Feature	Affordances
		Technological
Software quality and security of financial trading markets	• Automation • Decentralization • Immutability • Traceability • Transparency • Tokenization	• Allows automation of trade activities. • Improves quality and security of transactions. • New space to create new types of assets. • Reduce frauds. • It does not require the reconciliation of transactions. • Faster transactions. • Disintermediation of intermediaries.
Cost and scalability of transactions	• Decentralization • Cryptography • Transparent • Consensus mechanism	• Negative effects on scalability and validation costs in public blockchains. • Increase efficiency of the transactions. • Reduces delay.
		Societal
Data Security and privacy of participants	• Anonymity • Immutable • Transparent	• Sensitive information about a person is secured. • It gives a digital identity. • Enables a seamless 'Know Your Customer process. • Easy access to asset information. • Activities of digital identities are openly available. • GDPR concerns are raised.
Building trust and reliability	• Validation • Disintermediation • Transparency	• Enables zero-knowledge proof. • Builds trust in a trustless network. • Gets rid of untrusted counterparties. • Full transparency of the users in the network.
Easy Access to trading services and their usability	• Complexity • Tokenization • Validation • Automation	• Demands higher proficiency. • Provides easy access to funds. • Seamless processes when onboarding members. • Integration of digital wallets. • Accommodates the usage of smart contracts.
	Economic	
Interoperability with cross-country markets	• Digital currency • Disintermediation • Common ledger • Automation	• The increased popularity of stable coins or central bank digital currencies. • Increased interoperability. • New concerns for legal and administrative regulations. • Increased efficiency. • Doubtful of a possible significant economic growth. • The division between countries leads to the concentration of trading in one part of the world.
Sustainable Investments	• Transparency • Tokenization • Disintermediation	• Builds trust in the network. • Quicker Investment opportunities. • A higher number of participants. • New asset types. • Doubtful of a possible significant economic growth.
Market Risk Management	• Traceability • Transparency	• Cannot predict market failures. • Easy to perform audit trails. • Improved monitoring of the market • The improved decision-making process for regulators of the market. • Improved quality of information.
Automated auditing and reporting for governance	• Traceability	• Improved surveillance of trade activities.

DISCUSSION AND CONTRIBUTION

Blockchain Affordances: Key Features to Develop Sustainable FT Markets

The blockchain literature has advanced in various ways because of this study. The study, which has four main themes—technological, sociological, environmental, and economic—expands our understanding of the opportunities presented by blockchain technology to create sustainable financial markets and related services. The sustainability of blockchains has been the subject of various studies in the literature (Giungato et al., 2017; Mishra & Kaushik, 2021; Nguyen, 2016; Rossi et al., 2019), and the use of blockchains to develop FT markets (Al-Shaibani et al., 2020; Bhandarkar et al., 2019; Tsai et al., 2016). But a gap in the literature must be filled because there is a lack of an integrated strategy to synthesize the affordances made possible by the technology to create sustainable FT markets. Second, our study addressed the literature's call for investigating important blockchain elements that support these affordances to create sustainable FT markets and preliminary testing these ideas. The framework's analysis and the fine-tuning process revealed implications for the major 11 types of affordances and their relationships that could be either complementary or incompatible with sustainability's overall outcome. According to the research, blockchains' main advantages are enhanced FT market software quality and security, data protection and privacy, stakeholder trust and dependability, green financing, sustainable investments, lower transaction costs, and energy use. The main characteristics of blockchains that made these kinds of affordances possible are immutability, anonymity, automation, transparency and traceability, decentralization and disintermediation, and tokenization. Utilizing Gibson, (1979) Affordance Theory and the Triple Bottom Line, the eleven categories of affordances were comprehended and summarized (Elkington, 1999). By comprehending how technology may be applied in a specific social environment, affordability theory enables academics to examine IT installations' technical and social elements. Because Blockchain's IT artifacts are complex and challenging, it is important to consider this relational component while using blockchain technology (Du et al., 2019). Due to blockchain's rising popularity, a detailed grasp of its capabilities would help leverage the technology's ability to innovate in establishing sustainable models, as this study aimed to do (Shin et al., 2020).

Blockchain Affordances: They Are Interconnected

The second theoretical contribution is that the framework's development and testing revealed a strong interconnection between the major blockchain elements that facilitate the development of a sustainable FT market. Cost savings are implemented by decentralization, automation of pre-and post-trade processes, and removing counterparties from markets, enhancing technical and economic sustainability (Hughes et al., 2019; Rechtman, 2017). Disintermediation of intermediaries, however, functions as an accelerator for the development of unbalanced societies since it results in the loss of jobs, which increases tensions along the continuum of societal sustainability. Similarly, automatic trade fulfillment and settlement increase market inefficiencies by placing the risk on trading a certain asset type (Wright & De Filippi, 2015). This implies the human element's importance in maintaining the stability of the entire market infrastructure and adding flexibility in a highly regulated environment. Because of encryption (Rechtman, 2017), anonymity (Buterin, 2015), and the use of consensus methods for validation, blockchains enhance the security of traditional trading marketplaces (Tapscott & Tapscott, 2016). This increases societal sustainability by enhancing data security and privacy (zero-knowledge proof). However, it is impossible to ignore the fact that these new consensus processes are less safe than the popular proof of work (PoW) mechanism, which might have a detrimental impact on data security and privacy and have a cascading effect on social sustainability (Gan et al., 2021; Vranken, 2017). A revolutionary development that has created new asset classes for trade and enabled fractionalized funding and investing is the tokenization of assets (Bhandarkar et al., 2019). This lowers the entrance hurdles that small-scale green initiatives and investors face in the traditional markets, enhancing both societal and economic sustainability.

CONCLUSION AND FUTURE RESEARCH

By examining the fundamental theories of blockchain affordances discovered in the literature, this research intended to identify critical characteristics of blockchains for developing sustainable financial markets. In particular, the research attempted to validate these derived affordances in the light of industry experts, organize and analyze them into four sustainability themes (technological, economic, environmental, and societal), and present them as a whole with the aid of a conceptual framework. Thus, the research question was: "Which characteristics of blockchains are essential enablers of affordances that allow for creating sustainable financial trading markets?"

Literature research was initially carried out to summarize and map the current use cases of Blockchain in FT markets with the four sustainability themes to accomplish the study's purpose and provide a solution to the abovementioned topic. A conceptual framework comprising 11 distinct kinds of affordances that fall under four different sustainability-related topics served as a summary of the review's findings. The data analysis showed that each sustainability issue is intricately interwoven, and that comprehension of many tradeoffs is essential. Transparency and traceability, decentralization and disintermediation, immutability, anonymity, automation, and tokenization are some of the basic capabilities of blockchain technology that can be used to drive the transformations required to create sustainable infrastructure. The review showed that two areas for improvement in the traditional market were the existence of various counterparties and the rise in cost inefficiencies. The remedy to this issue has been determined to be process efficiency through automation, decentralization, and disintermediation; although this can harm the equilibrium of society and the market—the attributes of traceability and transparency foster confidence among the stakeholders. A value chain with an integrated network to monitor and manage green assets can be created if there is open access to accurate information about assets. This environment allows investors to make well-informed judgments. However, users of the system lack confidence and trust in it, as blockchain technology is still in its infancy. On the other hand, accurate analysis of traceable and available market data can provide clues about a person's potential future behavior, which could result in major GDPR compliance problems and impair societal sustainability.

Immutability was persuaded to be another crucial aspect of the technology since it gives an additional layer of security to market data with blockchains. By eliminating human transaction validation through the consensus mechanism, regulators' data reconciliation becomes automatic and frictionless. The significant adverse environmental impact of this has attracted a lot of attention. It is necessary to switch over to more ESG-friendly consensus processes, such as Point of Stake (PoS), which has a lower carbon footprint, from using cost-inefficient consensus procedures like PoW. Asset tokenization enables the simple exchange of fungible and non-fungible assets over a trusted ledger without intermediaries. The owners and investors of small to medium-sized green projects were encouraged to use fractionalized fundraising and investing, but they were also required to be tech-savvy. Finally, the outcomes dramatically highlighted the need for extensive legal and administrative reforms to long-term support this shift. Given the temporal constraints, the researcher contends that it is unacceptable to hypothesize only the categories of affordances in the conceptual framework that have been confirmed. Since further investigation of the unverified categories of affordances seemed to be valuable in the future, it was decided to keep all of the categories of affordances as part of this initial edition of the framework. This research aims to comprehend the fundamental characteristics of blockchains that enable the affordances necessary for the development of blockchain-based FT markets and services. Qualitative mixed methods were used to confirm most of the affordances evaluated using the framework. Further incorporating quantitative methodologies is necessary to deliver a fully improved and functionally validated architecture. Although the framework could pinpoint important sustainability-related aspects, particularly the societal and economic impact dimensions, they also highlighted consequences of sustainability that were more difficult to understand.

REFERENCES

Al-Shaibani, H., Lasla, N., & Abdallah, M. (2020). Consortium Blockchain-Based Decentralized Stock Exchange Platform. *IEEE Access: Practical Innovations, Open Solutions*, *8*, 123711–123725. doi:10.1109/ACCESS.2020.3005663

Avgouleas, E., & Kiayias, A. (2019). The Promise of Blockchain Technology for Global Securities and Derivatives Markets: The New Financial Ecosystem and the 'Holy Grail' of Systemic Risk Containment. *European Business Organization Law Review*, *20*(1), 81–110. doi:10.100740804-019-00133-3

Bai, C., & Sarkis, J. (2017). Improving green flexibility through advanced manufacturing technology investment: Modeling the decision process. *International Journal of Production Economics*, *188*(C), 86–104. https://ideas.repec.org//a/eee/proeco/v188y2017icp86-104.html. doi:10.1016/j.ijpe.2017.03.013

Bai, C. A., Cordeiro, J., & Sarkis, J. (2020). Blockchain technology: Business, strategy, the environment, and sustainability. *Business Strategy and the Environment*, *29*(1), 321–322. https://ideas.repec.org//a/bla/bstrat/v29y2020i1p321-322.html. doi:10.1002/bse.2431

Belt, A., & Kok, S. (2018). *A Reality Check for Blockchain in Commodity Trading*. Boston Consulting Group.

Bendell, J. (2017). Currency Innovation for Sustainable Financing of SMEs: Context, Case Study and Scalability. *Journal of Corporate Citizenship*, *67*(67), 39–62. https://www.jstor.org/stable/26629178. doi:10.9774/TandF.4700.2017.se.00005

Bhandarkar, V. V., Bhandarkar, A. A., & Shiva, A. (2019). Digital stocks using blockchain technology the possible future of stocks? *International Journal of Management*, *10*(3). doi:10.34218/IJM.10.3.2019/005

Brinck, P. (1992). Our Common Future and Beyond: Interpretations of Sustainable Development. In U. Svedin & B. H. Aniansson (Eds.), *Society and the Environment: A Swedish Research Perspective* (pp. 3–12). Springer Netherlands., doi:10.1007/978-94-011-2799-8_1

Buterin, V. (2015, August 7). *On Public and Private Blockchains*. Ethereum Foundation Blog. https://blog.ethereum.org/2015/08/07/on-public-and-private-blockchains

Centobelli, P., Cerchione, R., Esposito, E., & Oropallo, E. (2021). Surfing blockchain wave, or drowning? Shaping the future of distributed ledgers and decentralized technologies. *Technological Forecasting and Social Change*, *165*, 120463. doi:10.1016/j.techfore.2020.120463

Chen, Y., & Volz, U. (2022). Scaling up sustainable investment through blockchain-based project bonds. *Development Policy Review*, *40*(3), e12582. doi:10.1111/dpr.12582

Croo, A. D. (2015, March 20). *Why digital is key to sustainable growth*. World Economic Forum. https://www.weforum.org/agenda/2015/03/why-digital-is-key-to-sustainable-growth/

Dallyn, S. (2017). Cryptocurrencies as market singularities: The strange case of Bitcoin. *Journal of Cultural Economics*, *10*(5), 462–473. doi:10.1080/17530350.2017.1315541

Dimitriou, T., & Karame, G. (2013). Privacy-friendly tasking and trading of energy in smart grids. *Proceedings of the 28th Annual ACM Symposium on Applied Computing*, (pp. 652–659). ACM. 10.1145/2480362.2480488

Drescher, D. (2017). *Blockchain Basics: A Non-Technical Introduction in 25 Steps*. Springer. https://link.springer.com/book/10.1007/978-1-4842-2604-9

Du, W., Pan, S. L., Leidner, D. E., & Ying, W. (2019). Affordances, experimentation and actualization of FinTech: A blockchain implementation study. *The Journal of Strategic Information Systems*, *28*(1), 50–65. doi:10.1016/j.jsis.2018.10.002

Ducuing, C. (2019). How to Make Sure My Cryptokitties Are Here Forever? The Complementary Roles of Blockchain and the Law to Bring Trust. *European Journal of Risk Regulation*, *10*(2), 315–329. doi:10.1017/err.2019.39

Elkington, J. (1999). *Cannibals with Forks: The Triple Bottom Line of 21st Century Business*. Capstone.

Evangelista, R., Guerrieri, P., & Meliciani, V. (2014). The economic impact of digital technologies in Europe. *Economics of Innovation and New Technology*, *23*(8), 802–824. doi:10.1080/10438599.2014.918438

Francisco, K., & Swanson, D. (2018). The Supply Chain Has No Clothes: Technology Adoption of Blockchain for Supply Chain Transparency. *Logistics*, *2*(1), 1. doi:10.3390/logistics2010002

Galvez, J. F., Mejuto, J. C., & Simal-Gandara, J. (2018). Future challenges on the use of blockchain for food traceability analysis. *Trends in Analytical Chemistry*. https:// doi:10.1016/j.trac.2018.08.011

Gan, Q., Lau, R. Y. K., & Hong, J. (2021). A critical review of blockchain applications to banking and finance: A qualitative thematic analysis approach. *Technology Analysis and Strategic Management*, *0*(0), 1–17. doi:10.1080/09537325.2021.1979509

Gaver, W. W. (1991). Technology affordances. *Proceedings of the SIGCHI Conference on Human Factors in Computing Systems Reaching through Technology - CHI '91*, (pp. 79–84). ACM. 10.1145/108844.108856

Gibson, J. J. (1979). *The Ecological Approach to Visual Perception*. Psychology Press. doi:10.4324/9781315740218

Giungato, P., Rana, R., Tarabella, A., & Tricase, C. (2017). Current Trends in Sustainability of Bitcoins and Related Blockchain Technology. *Sustainability*, *9*(12), 12. doi:10.3390u9122214

Glavanits, J. (2020). Sustainable Public Spending Through Blockchain. *European Journal of Sustainable Development*, *9*(4), 4. doi:10.14207/ejsd.2020.v9n4p317

Hawlitschek, F., Notheisen, B., & Teubner, T. (2018). The limits of trust-free systems: A literature review on blockchain technology and trust in the sharing economy. *Electronic Commerce Research and Applications*, *29*, 50–63. doi:10.1016/j.elerap.2018.03.005

Herweijer, C., Waughray, D., & Warren, S. (2018). *Building Block(chain)s for a Better Planet*. World Economic Forum. https://www.weforum.org/reports/building-block-chain-for-a-better-planet/

Hughes, L., Dwivedi, Y. K., Misra, S. K., Rana, N. P., Raghavan, V., & Akella, V. (2019). *Blockchain research, practice and policy: Applications, benefits, limitations, emerging research themes and research agenda*. Brad Scholars. https://bradscholars.brad.ac.uk/handle/10454/17473

Hurley, R. F. (2011). *The Decision to Trust: How Leaders Create High-Trust Organizations* (1st ed.). Jossey-Bass.

Iansiti, M., & Lakhani, K. R. (2017, January 1). The Truth About Blockchain. *Harvard Business Review*. https://hbr.org/2017/01/the-truth-about-blockchain

IMF. (2021). *G20 Note On Environmentally Sustainable Investment For The Recovery*. IMF. https://www.imf.org/en/Publications/Policy-Papers/Issues/2021/04/29/G20-Note-On-Environmentally-Sustainable-Investment-For-The-Recovery-460112

Irfan, U. (2017, December 2). *Bitcoin's price spike is driving an extraordinary surge in energy use*. Vox. https://www.vox.com/energy-and-environment/2017/12/2/16724786/bitcoin-mining-energy-electricity

Jaoude, J., & Saade, R. (2019). Blockchain Applications – Usage in Different Domains. IEEE Access, (pp. 45360–45381). IEEE. doi:10.1109/ACCESS.2019.2902501

Jeanbart, R., & Dahinden, D. Roitinger, A., & Kalberer, G. A. (2020). *Data, the Future of Financial Information* [A SIX White Paper.]. https://www.six-group.com/dam/download/company/report/whitepapers/six-whitepaper-future-of-financial-information-full-version-en.pdf

Jessel, B., & DiCaprio, A. (2018). Can blockchain make trade finance more inclusive? *Journal of Financial Transformation*, *47*, 35–50. https://ideas.repec.org//a/ris/jofitr/1608.html

Kim, S.-K., & Huh, J.-H. (2020). Blockchain of Carbon Trading for UN Sustainable Development Goals. *Sustainability, 12*(10), 4021. doi:10.3390u12104021

Kimani, D., Adams, K., Attah-Boakye, D., Ullah, S., Frecknall-Hughes, J., & Kim, J. R. (2020). Blockchain, business and the fourth industrial revolution: Whence, whither, wherefore and how? *Technological Forecasting and Social Change, 161*, 120254. doi:10.1016/j.techfore.2020.120254

Kowalski, M., Lee, Z. W. Y., & Chan, T. K. H. (2021). Blockchain technology and trust relationships in trade finance. *Technological Forecasting and Social Change, 166*(C), 120641. https://ideas.repec.org//a/eee/tefoso/v166y2021ics0040162521000731.html. doi:10.1016/j.techfore.2021.120641

Linkov, I., Trump, B. D., Poinsatte-Jones, K., & Florin, M.-V. (2018). Governance Strategies for a Sustainable Digital World. *Sustainability, 10*(2), 2. doi:10.3390u10020440

Löbbecke, C., Lueneborg, L., & Niederle, D. (2018). *Blockchain Technology Impacting the Role of Trust in Transactions: Reflections in the Case of Trading Diamonds*. European Conference on Information Systems. https://www.semanticscholar.org/paper/Blockchain-Technology-Impacting-the-Role-of-Trust-L%C3%B6bbecke-Lueneborg/74037353be4d9f0e3312a1833b731b50ac29ccbe

Malone, D., & O'Dwyer, K. J. (2014). *Bitcoin Mining and its Energy Footprint*, 280–285. IET. doi:10.1049/cp.2014.0699

Mavilia, R., & Pisani, R. (2020). Blockchain and catching-up in developing countries: The case of financial inclusion in Africa. *African Journal of Science, Technology, Innovation and Development, 12*(2), 151–163. doi:10.1080/20421338.2019.1624009

Mazer, J. (2021). *Demystifying Cryptocurrencies, Blockchain, and ICOs*. Toptal Finance Blog. https://www.toptal.com/finance/market-research-analysts/cryptocurrency-market

Mishra, L., & Kaushik, V. (2021). Application of blockchain in dealing with sustainability issues and challenges of financial sector. *Journal of Sustainable Finance & Investment, 0*(0), 1–16. doi:10.1080/20430795.2021.1940805

Mohindra, N. (2011, February 16). *Transparent exchanges; As stock exchanges merge, regulators should remove the barriers to entry that stifle competition - Appeared in the Financial Post: Op-ed*. Fraser Institute. https://www.fraserinstitute.org/article/transparent-exchanges-stock-exchanges-merge-regulators-should-remove-barriers-entry-stifle

Montecchi, M., Plangger, K., & Etter, M. (2019). It's real, trust me! Establishing supply chain provenance using blockchain. *Business Horizons, 62*(3), 283–293. https://ideas.repec.org//a/eee/bushor/v62y2019i3p283-293.html. doi:10.1016/j.bushor.2019.01.008

Mori, T. (2016). Financial technology: Blockchain and securities settlement. *Journal of Securities Operations & Custody, 8*(3), 208–227.

Nassr, I. (2019). *Initial Coin Offerings (ICOs) for SME Financing*. OECD.

Nguyen, Q. K. (2016). Blockchain—A Financial Technology for Future Sustainable Development. *2016 3rd International Conference on Green Technology and Sustainable Development (GTSD)*, (pp. 51–54). IEEE. 10.1109/GTSD.2016.22

Noble, D., & Patil, K. (2021). Blockchain in Stock Market Transformation: A Systematic Literature Review. *Revista Gestão Inovação e Tecnologias, 11*(4), 5088–5111. doi:10.47059/revistageintec.v11i4.2551

Ostern, N., Rosemann, M., & Moormann, J. (2020, December 14). *Determining the Idiosyncrasy of Blockchain: An Affordances Perspective*. Research Gate.

Ostrom, E., & Eggertsson, T. (1990). *Governing the Commons: The Evolution of Institutions for Collective Action*. Cambridge University Press. doi:10.1017/CBO9780511807763

Paech, P. (2017). The Governance of Blockchain Financial Networks. *The Modern Law Review, 80*(6), 1073–1110. doi:10.1111/1468-2230.12303

Parmentola, A., Petrillo, A., Tutore, I., & Felice, F. D. (2022). Is blockchain able to enhance environmental sustainability? A systematic review and research agenda from the perspective of Sustainable Development Goals (SDGs). *Business Strategy and the Environment, 31*(1), 194–217. https://ideas.repec.org//a/bla/bstrat/v31y2022i1p194-217.html. doi:10.1002/bse.2882

Pólvora, A., Nascimento, S., Lourenço, J. S., & Scapolo, F. (2020). Blockchain for industrial transformations: A forward-looking approach with multi-stakeholder engagement for policy advice. *Technological Forecasting and Social Change, 157*(C), 120091. https://ideas.repec.org//a/eee/tefoso/v157y2020ics0040162520309173.html. doi:10.1016/j.techfore.2020.120091

Pop, C., Pop, C., Marcel, A., Vesa, A., Petrican, T., Cioara, T., Anghel, I., & Salomie, I. (2018). Decentralizing the Stock Exchange using Blockchain An Ethereum-based implementation of the Bucharest Stock Exchange. *2018 IEEE 14th International Conference on Intelligent Computer Communication and Processing (ICCP)*. IEEE. https://www.academia.edu/40383802/Decentralizing_the_Stock_Exchange_using_Blockchain_An_Ethereum_based_implementation_of_the_Bucharest_Stock_Exchange

Popescu, A.-D. (2020). Transforming Capital Markets by means of Financial Digital Assets. *Emulations - Revue de Sciences Sociales, 68*, 109–119.

Rechtman, Y. (2017). Blockchain: The Making of a Simple, Secure Recording Concept. *The CPA Journal, 87*(6), 15–17. https://www.proquest.com/docview/2213055088

Rossi, M., Mueller-Bloch, C., Thatcher, J., & Beck, R. (2019). Blockchain Research in Information Systems: Current Trends and an Inclusive Future Research Agenda. *Journal of the Association for Information Systems, 20*, 1388–1403. doi:10.17705/1jais.00571

Saberi, S., Kouhizadeh, M., Sarkis, J., & Shen, L. (2019). Blockchain technology and its relationships to sustainable supply chain management. *International Journal of Production Research, 57*(7), 2117–2135. doi:10.1080/00207543.2018.1533261

Sadhya, V., Sadhya, H., Hirschheim, R., & Watson, E. (2018). *Exploring Technology Trust in Bitcoin: The Blockchain Exemplar*. European Conference on Information Systems. https://www.semanticscholar.org/paper/Exploring-Technology-Trust-in-Bitcoin%3A-the-Exemplar-Sadhya-Sadhya/df10f099c7cecb30d1dfa89dbe431f81ee868f27

Shin, D., Zhong, B., & Biocca, F. A. (2020). Beyond user experience: What constitutes algorithmic experiences? *International Journal of Information Management*, *52*, 102061. doi:10.1016/j.ijinfomgt.2019.102061

Sivarajah, U., Kamal, M. M., Irani, Z., & Weerakkody, V. (2017). Critical analysis of Big Data challenges and analytical methods. *Journal of Business Research*, *70*, 263–286. doi:10.1016/j.jbusres.2016.08.001

Stuermer, M., Abu-Tayeh, G., & Myrach, T. (2017). Digital sustainability: Basic conditions for sustainable digital artifacts and their ecosystems. *Sustainability Science*, *12*(2), 247–262. doi:10.100711625-016-0412-2 PMID:30174752

Sun, J., Yan, J., & Zhang, K. Z. K. (2016). Blockchain-based sharing services: What blockchain technology can contribute to smart cities. *Financial Innovation*, *2*(1), 26. doi:10.118640854-016-0040-y

Swa, M. (2015). *Blockchain: Blueprint for a New Economy*. O¢Reilly.

Tapscott, D., & Tapscott, A. (2016). *Blockchain Revolution: How the Technology Behind Bitcoin and Other Cryptocurrencies is Changing the World*. Portfolio Penguin.

Tashakkori, A., Teddlie, C., & Teddlie, C. B. (2003). *Handbook of Mixed Methods in Social & Behavioral Research*. SAGE.

Tsai, S.-B., Chen, K.-Y., Zhao, H., Wei, Y.-M., Wang, C.-K., Zheng, Y., Chang, L.-C., & Wang, J. (2016). Using a Mixed Model to Explore Evaluation Criteria for Bank Supervision: A Banking Supervision Law Perspective. *PLoS One*, *11*(12), e0167710. doi:10.1371/journal.pone.0167710 PMID:27992449

Tsoukas, H. (1989). The Validity of Idiographic Research Explanations. *Academy of Management Review*, *14*(4), 551–561. doi:10.2307/258558

UNCTAD. (2021). *Chapter 5—Capital Markets and Sustainable Finance*. World Investment Report. https://worldinvestmentreport.unctad.org/world-investment-report-2021/ch5-capital-markets-and-sustainable-finance/

Varriale, V., Cammarano, A., Michelino, F., & Caputo, M. (2020). The Unknown Potential of Blockchain for Sustainable Supply Chains. *Sustainability*, *12*(22), 22. doi:10.3390u12229400

Volkoff, O., & Diane, M. Strong. (2017). Affordance theory and how to use it in IS research. In The Routledge Companion to Management Information Systems (pp. 232–245). Routledge. doi:10.4324/9781315619361-18

Vranken, H. (2017). Sustainability of bitcoin and blockchains. *Current Opinion in Environmental Sustainability*, *28*, 1–9. doi:10.1016/j.cosust.2017.04.011

Wang, Y., Singgih, M., Wang, J., & Rit, M. (2018, February 19). *Making sense of blockchain technology: How will it transform supply chains?* Wright, A., & De Filippi, P. (2015). Decentralized Blockchain Technology and the Rise of Lex Cryptographia. SSRN *Electronic Journal.* doi:10.2139/ssrn.2580664

Zhao, J. L., Fan, S., & Yan, J. (2016). Overview of business innovations and research opportunities in blockchain and introduction to the special issue. *Financial Innovation*, *2*(1), 28. doi:10.118640854-016-0049-2

Zheng, Z., Xie, S., Dai, H.-N., Chen, X., & Wang, H. (2017, June 25). *An Overview of Blockchain Technology: Architecture, Consensus, and Future Trends*. IEEE. doi:10.1109/BigDataCongress.2017.85

ADDITIONAL READING

Arnone, G. (2022). Blockchain And Cryptocurrency Innovation For A Sustainable Financial System. *International Journal of Information Management*, *15*(1), 1–16. doi:10.15282/ijim.15.1.2022.8994

Chen, N.-P., Shen, K.-Y., & Liang, C.-J. (2021). Hybrid Decision Model for Evaluating Blockchain Business Strategy: A Bank's Perspective. *Sustainability*, *13*(11), 11. doi:10.3390u13115809

Chen, Y., & Volz, U. (2022). Scaling up sustainable investment through blockchain-based project bonds. *Development Policy Review*, *40*(3), e12582. doi:10.1111/dpr.12582

Evans, O. (2019). Blockchain Technology and the Financial Market: An Empirical Analysis. *Actual Problems of Economics*, 82–101.

Javaid, M., Haleem, A., Singh, R. P., Suman, R., & Khan, S. (2022). A review of Blockchain Technology applications for financial services. *BenchCouncil Transactions on Benchmarks. Standards and Evaluations*, *2*(3), 100073. doi:10.1016/j.tbench.2022.100073

Kumar, S., Sharma, D., Rao, S., Lim, W. M., & Mangla, S. K. (2022). Past, present, and future of sustainable finance: Insights from big data analytics through machine learning of scholarly research. *Annals of Operations Research*. doi:10.100710479-021-04410-8 PMID:35002001

Schulz, K., & Feist, M. (2021). Leveraging blockchain technology for innovative climate finance under the Green Climate Fund. *Earth System Governance*, *7*, 100084. doi:10.1016/j.esg.2020.100084

Smajgl, A., & Schweik, C. M. (2022). Advancing sustainability with blockchain-based incentives and institutions. *Frontiers in Blockchain, 5*. https://www.frontiersin.org/articles/10.3389/fbloc.2022.963766

Wu, B., & Duan, T. (2019). The Application of Blockchain Technology in Financial markets. *Journal of Physics: Conference Series*, *1176*(4), 042094. doi:10.1088/1742-6596/1176/4/042094

Xu, M., Chen, X., & Kou, G. (2019). A systematic review of blockchain. *Financial Innovation*, *5*(1), 27. doi:10.118640854-019-0147-z

KEY TERMS AND DEFINITIONS

Blended Finance: This phrase describes the strategic use of development finance to raise additional funds for the long-term development of developing countries. Through blended finance, commercial money is drawn to projects supporting long-term growth while rewarding investors financially.

Central Bank Coins: Digital currencies, akin to bitcoin, can be issued by a company's central bank. They are correlated with the value of the nation's fiat currency.

Equity Financing: To raise money, a business will sell shares to investors.

Green Bonds: A green bond is a fixed-income security created primarily to collect money for environmental and climate change initiatives. These bonds typically have an asset attached to them and are supported by the financial records of the issuing company.

Hyperledger: A trustworthy set of frameworks for permission, enterprise-grade blockchain deployments is the goal of the open-source Hyperledger project. The Linux Foundation hosts this international cooperation, with participants from the financial, banking, Internet of Things, supply chains, manufacturing, and technology sectors. Among the sub-projects are Cello, Sawtooth, Composer, and Hyperledger Fabric.

Market Capitalization: Also known as "market cap," this term refers to the full market value of an organization. Since it represents the "market" worth of the company, it is determined using the firm's current market price (CMP) and the total number of outstanding shares.

Stablecoin: A stablecoin is a sort of cryptocurrency that strives to maintain price stability and is backed by a reserve asset. Since they attempt to combine the greatest aspects of both worlds—the quick processing, security, and anonymity of cryptocurrency payments, as well as the stable and unchanging pricing of fiat currencies—stablecoins have grown in popularity.

Tokenization: The process by which an issuer creates digital tokens representing real or virtual assets on a distributed ledger or blockchain is known as asset tokenization.

Chapter 11
Strategic Transformational Transition of Green Economy, Green Growth, and Sustainable Development:
An Institutional Approach

José G. Vargas-Hernandez
Instituto Tecnológico Mario Molina, Mexico

Carlos Rodriguez-Maillard
https://orcid.org/0000-0003-2406-196X
Universidad Cristobal Colòn, Mexico

Omar C. Vargas-Gonzàlez
https://orcid.org/0000-0002-6089-956X
Tecnològico Nacional de Mèxico, Ciudad Guzmàn, Mexico

ABSTRACT

This paper aims to analyze a strategic transformational transition of green economy, green growth, and sustainable development from the institutional perspective. The analysis begins questioning the implications of the concepts and principles of green economy, green growth, and sustainable development from different perspectives in the transformational transition considering the investment, trade, and capacity building though the design and implementation of strategies and policies, as well as measures from an institutional analysis. The methodology followed was the analytical review of the literature to derive inferences, challenges, proposals, and conclusions. It is concluded that the green economy concept addresses current challenges delivering economic development opportunities and multiple benefits for the welfare of all human beings.

DOI: 10.4018/978-1-6684-7422-8.ch011

INTRODUCTION

The green economy has been criticized by being wonderful slogan which does not always lead to wonderful actions (Schmalensee, 2012). Emergence of greener development pathways may have critical effects on the reduction of emissions and the use of natural resources. The framework of green economy and practices are relevant to the ongoing debates in economic growth, social justice and environmental sustainability reorganization. The green economy is an imperative framework for all economic activities that affects sustainable development supported by coordinated action of government, private sector and civil society.

The green economy is a means and enabler of delivering sustainable development between the intrinsic links between economy and environment. From this perspective, green economy improves well-being, lessens social and economic inequality, and reduces environmental risks and ecological scarcities. Green economy is environmentally friendly, sensitive to preserve natural resources, produce more ecosystems services and products and reduce emissions and pollutants that create environmental crisis.

The transition to green economy has environmental priorities to restore, preserve and enhance ecosystems and promote natural resources efficiency supporting the shift towards a low-carbon and climate resilience. The development of green economy depends on the capacity to design sustainable ecosystem service programs. Ecosystem services scheme may promote stakeholder's acceptance and participation in a green economy.

The green economy provides the instruments required to transform economic activity in more growing and inclusive economies with more social justice and healthier and environments. The green economy relaunches the global economy with higher rates of economic growth than the current model.

This paper has the aim to analyze a strategic transformational transition of green economy, green growth, and sustainable development from the institutional perspective. It begins analyzing the evolution of concepts and definitions of green economy, green growth and sustainable development, to continue with the principles that support the transformation transition towards a greener economy. It continues analyzing some requirements in terms of investment, trade and capacity building for the strategic and policy formulation and implementation of a green economic development plan, from the institutional approach. It also takes into consideration some specific challenges before some concluding remarks.

EVOLUTION OF THE CONCEPT OF GREEN ECONOMY

The concept of green economy has emerged in the last decade as a policy framework for sustainable development and poverty eradication. The concept of green economy was coined and used in 1989 in the report Blueprint for a green economy (Pearce, Markandya, & Barbier, 1989) commissioned to advice on the applications, projects, policies and measures of sustainable development.

On the middle of the economic crisis in 2008, green economy was presented as a means to reduce the growing social inequality and achieving sustainable development. The concept of green economy rises in the aftermath of 2008 global financial crisis challenging a radical transformation of development practices (Davies 2013, 1285). The concept of green economy was initially a response to the financial crisis (Bina & La Camera, 2011), and an operational policy for growth based on sustainable development at the environment– economy nexus (Schmalensee, 2012).

After the financial crisis of 2008, green stimulus programs were launched as an incentive for investments in green energy sources and technologies. The global recession has led to design green energy sources. The United Nations Environmental Program (UNEP) launched the green economy initiative in climate change mitigation. Green economy aims to improve human well-being and social equity while significantly reducing environmental risks and ecological scarcity according to the concept of The United Nations Environmental Program (UNEP).

In 2009 was proposed the Global Green New Deal as a strategy to revive the global economy, mitigate climate change and environmental degradation and reduce poverty. The objective UNEP's GE Initiative (GEI) was to provide policy support for investing in greening sectors and environment. Green economy delivers transformations for more egalitarian and inclusive societies and shared economic prosperity.

In 2011, The UNEP published the Green Economy Report "Towards Green Economy - Pathways to Sustainable Development and Poverty Eradication" stated the conceptual basis for policy action of green economy as one which is resource efficient, low carbon and socially inclusive aimed to capture the environmental, economic and social dimensions of sustainable development. Green economy is defined as the "improved human well-being and social equity, while significantly reducing environmental risks and ecological scarcities" (United Nations Environment Program, UNEP, 2011).

The report of the United Nations Conference on Sustainable Development (UNCSD) that took place in Rio de Janeiro in 2012 had intended to promote green economy and sustainable development policies to reduce poverty. The Rio +20 declaration focused on green economy and sustainable development as relevant tools aiming to poverty eradication. The Rio +20 Conference articulated the elements needed for a green growth policy framework more oriented towards developing countries and framed and promoted the green economy as tool for sustainable development, driving economic growth, creating employment, and poverty eradication, while maintaining the healthy functioning of the bio ecosystems.

The United Nations Conference on Sustainable Development (UNCSD, or Rio +20) in 2012 emphasized a green and inclusive economy but missed the opportunity and vision (Clark, 2013, 19; Clémençon, 2012; Halle, 2012; Powers, 2012; Barbier, 2013; Bernstein, 2013). The Green Growth Knowledge Platform (GGKP) was stablished in 2012 by major international institutions to spread and share strategies, policies, tools, data and practices developing technical and human capabilities to support governments in the transition to green economy.

The concept of green economy is broad including the definition of economic measurement. Green economy, green growth, green companies, or green jobs are imprecise terms that some countries do not yet recognize them. The concepts of green economy and sustainable development have contextual interpretations depending of the priority of economic efficiency, social equity, environmental issues and community ownership, as well as the international agreements and standards.

The Green Economy concept emphasizes the finite environmental limits. The concept of green economy recognizes that economic development and environmental policies are interrelated (Barbier, 2013). The green economy is "an economy in which economic growth and environmental sustainability work together in a mutually reinforcing fashion while supporting progress on social development" (International Chamber of Commerce Green Economy Task Force). The concept of green economy is considered to be at the intersection between environment and economy by some authors while for others is green economy is a subsystem to society and thus, to the environment.

The concept of green economy is being promoted by international organizations, non-governmental organizations, academic and research institutions, and partnerships. The concept of green economy policy has been analyzed and discussed in the international arena on the context of negotiations and issues involving the fields of ecological and environmental economics. The concept of green economy relies on future technologies to generate action in industrial policy and not in the Brundtland sustainability criteria (Lorek and Spangenberg 2014). The green economy should reflect the different economic, social, cultural and environmental contexts.

Green economy concept responds to significant national differences and priorities on environmental and social challenges (Death, 2015; Morrow, 2012; AfDB, 2014; Gupta & Wong, 2014; Republic of Rwanda, 2011; Sonnenschein & Mundaca, 2015). The green economy concept is related to an economic model in transition towards green growth and low-carbon development as the foundations for the benefits of a sustainable environment, social equity, and economic efficiency.

The concepts of green growth and green economy are left deliberately imprecise in unresolved transitional tensions. The concepts green growth and green economy are ambiguous and contested discourses among different organizations that have led to post-growth and transformational concepts (Ferguson 2014). Green economy practices conflict with the assertion that green economy is not part of the economy at large because the whole economy needs to be green to maximize value and growth (HM Government 2011, 4).

A SWOT analysis of the Green Economy concept has been elaborated by Fosse, Petrick et al., (2016), which is being reproduced literally considering it is well developed:

Some strengths of the green economy concept are:

- Broadly popular concept at international level
- Positive impact on environmental, economic, and social transformation
- Cross-cutting approach thus promoting cross sectoral integration
- Uses local/regional practices and knowledge
- Promotes stakeholder engagement and empowerment of local communities

Some weaknesses of the green economy concept are:

- No global definition of green economy
- Situational concept and characteristics vary according to the area under consideration
- Lack of full understanding of the financial gains of transitioning to a green economy
- Unknown damages to conventional business models, "brown" jobs, and incumbent economic actors.

Some opportunities of the green economy concept are:

- Addresses climate change and sustainability issues
- Creates qualified, stable, and fair jobs
- Revitalizes economies and opens new business opportunities
- Contributes to energy independency as well as water and food security
- Reduces poverty, promotes equitable distribution of wealth and social equity
- Increases societal resilience to internal and external shocks

Some threats of the green economy concept are:

- Lack of public and private funding
- Challenges to changes in consumption and production patterns and life styles
- Resentment to change by those who feel that their interests may be compromised or threatened.

There have been published numerous reports on the concept of green economy providing working definitions and guiding benefits. Green economy concepts and initiatives have the capacity to bring benefits to citizens (Caprotti and Bailey 2014,199). It has also been criticized that the current concept of green economy is based on the trickled down principle of traditional economic growth theory.

DEFINITION OF GREEN ECONOMY

Green economy has not been well defined, and depending of the context is poorly understood. The definition of green economy is in tension and still in development between competing discourses focusing more on transformational green economy given the sustainable development goals, but defaulting its measurement in the interactions between economy, society and environment. Green economy, society and the natural environment are interrelated and inter dependent.

Green economy has been defined by different authors and organizations according to their purposes which can be cleaner economic grow, reducing carbon emissions, climate change economy; resource efficiency, social equity and justice. One of the most accepted definitions of green economy is the "one that results in improved human wellbeing and social equity, while significantly reducing environmental risks and ecological scarcities. It is low carbon resource efficient, and socially inclusive" (UNEP, 2011; UNEP, Green Economy Reports: A Preview, 2010, p. 4-5).

Another well accepted definition is "Green growth means fostering economic growth and development while ensuring that natural assets continue to provide the resources and environmental services on which our well-being relies." (Organization for Economic Cooperation and Development (OECD), Towards Green Growth, 2011, p. 9). The UN Environment Management Group in 2011 identified and clarified the use of the term green economy in the publication working towards a balanced and inclusive green economy.

The International Chamber of Commerce Chamber of Commerce (2012, 2011) defines green economy as the one in which economic growth work together with environmental responsibility mutually reinforcing each other to support social development. The Green Economy Coalition has defined green economy as the resilient economy providing better quality of life for all within the ecological limits. "An economy that provides better quality of life for all within the ecological limits of the planet" (Green Economy Coalition).

THE CONCEPT OF GREEN GROWTH

Green economy and green growth are emerging concepts used to foster low-carbon, natural resource efficiency, social inclusive and environmentally sustainable development associated with other multidimensional benefits. Green growth and green economy are similar concepts that have been promoted in recent years. The crisis represented an opportunity for green growth as being more attractive than brown growth alternative to economic recovery (van der Ploeg & Withagen, 2013), although it came with re-legitimization of statist and intervention (Death 2015) evolving into a policy framework. Green growth emphasizes economic and market oriented instruments and metrics, rather than on changing and greening the whole economic model. Green growth depends more upon the creation of enabling conditions for grassroots green innovation and local developed technology.

Green growth pursues the economic growth for environmentally sustainable development mitigating the collateral damages and ensuring that natural resources provide the environmental services needed for the human well-being. The aim of an inclusive green growth is to bring the creation of green jobs to benefit the living standards of the poorest in terms of clean water supply, less pollution, healthy soils, under the assumption that trickle-down economics and not necessarily addressing the equity issues. Green Growth aims at sustainable production and consumption and resource efficiency but not necessarily guided by ecological principles. The efforts to pursuit sustained green growth are concerned with delivering higher incomes, social benefits, reduce environmental degradation and vulnerability to climate change.

The institutional green economy approach is not detached from conventional economic growth (Ferguson, 2014). The concept of green economy is related to the concept of green growth in the international context of sustainable development. However, Ferguson (2014) identifies some tensions in the green economy concept and concludes that the concept of green growth is different from green economy and should be separate discussions. Green growth relies on harnessing the green economy. For green growth policies, inclusive green growth to be environmentally sustainable over the long term must consider local development contexts (World Bank, 2012). However, there is criticism and skepticism about these concepts of green economy and green growth (Brockington, 2012; Brown et al., 2014; McAfee, 2016).

Green growth is more incremental than radical development policy concerned with poverty reduction and socio-economic development. However, the economic growth approach does not integrate local communities and societal stakeholders into the policy analysis and formulation processes.

GREEN ECONOMY, GREEN GROWTH AND SUSTAINABLE DEVELOPMENT

The green economy concept is called the next oxymoron after sustainable development because they overlap each other (Brand, 2012). Conference on Sustainable Development (Rio+20) in 2012 agreed that in the context of sustainable development, the concept of green economy should be promoted. The transition to a green economy has economic and social justifications for public and private actors to contribute offering opportunities for investments and green procurement by providing new market-based incentives and mechanisms.

Environmental sustainability and economic growth are compatible. Green economy prioritizes well-being for the present and for future generations and not necessarily is sufficient the efficiency of improved technology. A green economy is essential to sustainable development, improving social equity, human well-being, reducing ecological scarcities and environmental risks. The Global Green New Deal report based on green economy proposed policy actions to stimulate a sustainable economic development. Identification and eradication of unsustainable activities in different economic sectors to enhance an enabling environment, are necessary actions of the green economy.

Green economy supports sustainable development aimed to replace the social and environmental costs of the current economic model that is reaching limits in terms of greenhouse gas emissions, use of natural resources, water, land, forests, etc. Green economy transformation and inclusive greener growth strategy initiatives are needed to pursue the economic and social benefits of sustainable development while reducing negative environmental, inequality and poverty impacts, sustainable management of natural resources, reduce greenhouse gas emissions, climate change, resilience to natural disasters, improve public services, etc. Green economy and sustainable development strategies strengthen the resilience of communities and regions.

Green growth responds to critical emerging issues by facing the global challenge of environmental sustainability. However, the elements of the green economy concept are already integrated in strategic documents focused on achieving sustainable green growth, rather than merely achieving a green economy. Green growth is based upon the sustainable development strategies used to support the transition to green economy defined as the process of improving the economic, social, and cultural and environmental well-being of future generations.

Green growth fosters economic growth and development, ensures natural assets providing the resources and environmental services to the benefit of humanity well-being focusing on the synergies and tradeoffs between the environmental and economic sustainable development. The interactions between society and the environment drive forces for change and transformation for the green economy as an opportunity to achieve sustainable development and human well-being. Green economy is worth to pursuit as an opportunity to prioritize well-being and sustainable development for the present and for future generations.

Green economy is one of tools used to achieve sustainable development goals (SDG) of end poverty, hunger and food security, good health and well-being, education, gender equality and women´s empowerment, water and sanitation, energy, economic growth, infrastructure, industrialization, inequality, cities, sustainable consumption and production, climate change, oceans, biodiversity, partnerships, etc. The socio-ecological and SDGs' indicators of the green economy outlined moves beyond the GDP as the transformational concept to measure the wellbeing (Ferguson 2014; Fioramonti 2014; Stiglitz et al. 2009). Green economy visions are relevant for the legitimacy and global green economy under the SDGs.

The post-2015 development agenda and The Sustainable Development Goals (SDGs) overcome inherent conflicts emerging from the implementation of the green economy concept at different spatial levels and created the imperative for the implementation of the green economy beginning to deliver changes. The SDGs is a platform to reintegrate the green economy into the sustainable development agenda. Green economy framework has universal goals flexible to be adapted for different contexts and aligned on monitoring green growth (Kamp-Roelands, 2013; OECD, 2011; UNEP, 2012a 2012b 2014b).

Green sectors and industries have the potential to become engines of green growth by reducing the use of fossil fuels as climate-resilient development. Some of the most relevant sectors to green economy are agriculture, energy, water management, tourism, waste, etc. Green growth policies promote economic growth and environmental development ensuring that natural resources provide environmental services to human well-being.

Green economy is acritical component of sustainable development which implies a greening change in the social construct of all the economy sectors. Details about the scale of the greening of specific sectors of the green economy development and implementation are required to be explicitly for absolute decoupling. Rural and urban development programs are a vehicle for enabling the transition from traditional rural and urban economy to a rural and urban green economy. Locally led development programs and group actions can often respond more effectively to local needs in the transition to the green economy. Urban green brands are already developing focusing more on green growth and low carbon economy which may be stronger and attract greater interest.

Green economy approaches offer economic opportunities of low carbon transitions under the framework of an agreement of a collective carbon finance goal (United Nations, 2015). Resource and energy efficiency supports green products, services, and low-carbon green economy as part of the transition to deliver economic, social and environmental benefits. Low carbon actions are part of a transition towards green economies can make the most of the resources available. The transition towards a green economy by investing and preserving the natural capital to generate growth, create jobs and eradicate poverty. A green job is defined as one that works with information, data, technologies, and materials, and requires specialized knowledge, training, skills, and experience for activities that minimize environmental impact.

The green economy concept is mutually complementary between different dimensions of sustainable development and poverty eradication to enhance convergence through different approaches, among systemic economic structure, reconciling social goals, policies and objectives and the macroeconomic framework of development strategy (UNDESA, 2010).

The design of green economy to contribute to sustainable development is away from the dysfunctionalities of traditional mainstream economy and results in human well-being and equitable access to opportunities safeguarding economic and environmental economic integrity. Green economy contributes to sustainable development with different forms of implementation for different countries. Resource efficiency is a green economy process that is supported by environmental awareness and technological green innovation, although the increase in consumption may occur when efficiency gains are lost leading to the so-called Jevons paradox, which may be addressed by specific policies on fiscal mechanisms and education.

GREEN ECONOMY PRINCIPLES

Guiding principles of a Green Economy helping practitioners in the application of the green economy concept are sustaining that it is a means for sustainable development, is equitable, just and fair, creating green jobs, protects biodiversity and ecosystem services, provide green resources and efficient green energy within the ecological limits, delivers well-being, access to essential services, poverty reduction, livelihoods, social protection. The principles of a green economy that according to GEC deliver a sustainable, inclusive and participative green economy are: sustainability, justice, dignity, healthy planet, inclusion, good governance and accountability, resilience, efficiency and sufficiency and generations.

The sustainable development and green economy strategies and policies is a model based on the core principles of economic efficiency, equity, social inclusion, environmental sufficiency, and accountability which requires dialogue among all the involved stakeholders and participative policy design.

Also, these principles consider the measurement of green economy using appropriate metrics and indicators, improves governance and the rule of law being democratic, participatory, inclusive, transparent, and accountable and more other principles. A good indicator of the relevance of green growth and economy for a specific society is to identify the number or share of population involved in any form, as employee, consumer, etc.

Equitable green economy is linked to sustainable development supported by principles and informed by policy and market decisions. Green economy principles must be integrated in sustainable development programs and initiatives such as in pollution prevention and sustainable production and consumption. Green economy principles aimed to develop a fair and inclusive economy to provide a better quality of life are the sustainability, justice, dignity, healthy planet, inclusion, good governance and accountability, resilience, efficiency and sufficiency and generations principles (Green Economy Coalition, 2012).

Green economy principles can be applied to urban sustainable development by coordinating some deliverables with other organizations and donors relating to methodologies, platforms, best practices, and tools that contribute to poverty eradication (UNCSD, 2012). Green economy principles must be developed after engaging in discussion with the different stakeholders to meet the vision, priorities and needs of each sector. A set of green economy principles emerging from dialogue can serve as guidelines for making decisions which can be applied across sectors and institutions to operationalize a green economy. Social equity, ecological limits and community ownership are core principles for green economy.

TRANSFORMATIONAL TRANSITION OF GREEN ECONOMY

The transition towards green economy can solve the interconnected economic, social, and environmental crises. Green economy and transformation as enabling approaches are related to potentially create dynamic change (Pelling & Manuel Navarrete, 2011; Pelling et al., 2014). Green economies integrate economic, social and environmental activities. The concept of green economy represents a transition for more environmentally friendly and resource-efficiency technologies to tackle environmental degradation by reducing carbon emissions and mitigating the effects of climate change (Jänicke, 2012).

Transition to green economies require that green activities and investments in the interlinkages between rural-urban areas can contribute to green economic growth. Public and private funding of green economy has to be scaled up at all institutional levels and sectors supporting sustainable and responsible green investments in green business and companies, clean technology, green investments, etc. A green company is defined as a company that produces goods and services designed to reduce their environmental impact.

Green technologies should be developed with government financial support and subject to wider dissemination. Private investment flows in green technology should ensure that achieve full potential in spin-off benefits. Any percentage of global GDP invested to green economy sectors increase the growth, employment and reduce water, energy, etc. Public and private investments in green economy, promote revenue growth and employment from a rational use of natural and financial resources and energy efficiency that reduce carbon emissions and pollution and prevent loss of biodiversity and environmental services.

Development programs structured according to priorities supports transition to the green economy in practice although the term may not be explicitly used, planning authorities may use different approaches and measures. Design and implementation of rural and urban development programs support the transition of business activities to the green economy and the environmental performance. Development programs can provide financial support to assist the transition towards a green economy with impact in long-term business opportunities. Business can foster practices that contribute to the green economy transition.

Equitable green economy is a transformation process in constant dynamic progression, although it has been questioned if green economy is equitable. One of the four green economy typologies is green transformation of economic growth through political interventions (Death, 2015, 2216). Building on Ferguson's typologies based on weak/strong green economy, the UNEP's concept is more transformational providing enabling conditions for green economy transitions (UNEP, 2011). Transformational green economy renders strong green economy and growth concepts deployed as organizing principles for climate change (Pelling et al., 2014).

The term green economy comprises the application of some economic instruments which requires social, institutional, and political contexts to harness economic activities in support of sustainable development goals. Design of development plans can contribute to the transition to the green economy activities such as:

- Mitigation of climate warming
- Sustainable water and waste management
- Sustainable infrastructure
- Ecosystems services and buildings
- Investment in natural resources and capital
- Renewable energy feedstocks and energy efficiency
- Green research, green tourism, and eco-innovation
- Agricultural and forest land management
- Forestry and fisheries (bio economics)
- Green manufacturing and supply chain green public procurement, etc.

The transition to the green economy makes sure that agriculture and forestry are both economically and environmentally sustainable activities for the long-term. For example, the use of procurement policies for the greening of business. Green agriculture requires natural and physical capital assets, knowledge and financial investments and enhance the capacity building in efficient and sustainable management of soil fertility, water use, farm mechanization, crop and livestock diversification; etc. the analysis of investments measures benefits and costs of green economy and green energy policies taking into account capacity building, management, operation, research and development, expenditures in infrastructure, incentives, etc.

Measures for business and farm diversification can support transition activities to green economy. The sectors considered to have green potential are energy renewable, water, waste/recycling, sustainable farming and forestry, fisheries, public transport, green buildings, tourism, health care, education and training, green finances, etc.

Greening the fishery sector requires strengthening the fisheries management and financing fishing activities to maintain sustainable stocks within biological limits limit the environmental impact. Assessment of the impact on the dynamics of the fishing and marine ecosystem and biodiversity using quantitative indicators for socio-economic factors is required for a more effective exploitation of fisheries.

Greening the sector of forestry must be focused on reducing deforestation and increasing reforestation in accordance with economic and market mechanisms including payments for ecosystem services, certified benefit sharing and other schemes, community-based partnerships, sustainable forest management instruments aimed to carbon reduction, enhance protection of forests against fires and pollution, biodiversity and forest ecosystems, provision of environmental services, etc.

Greening the industry and manufacturing sector implies design to extend the useful life of goods and recycling them to support the use of by-products and alternatives for substitution to achieve a circular economy with a close-loop manufacturing in eco-industrial parks.

Greening the building sector requires a policy framework with instruments for development of sustainable building capacities and standards, cost-efficiency and incentives. Greening building requires investment and incentives for energy supply and renewable performance for sustainability of new and renovated buildings.

Greening transport policies intend to integrate land use and transportation planning for more environmentally efficient modes shifting to non-motorized transport and improving vehicle and fuel technology, avoiding or reducing trips and using water and rail transport for freight. All these policies are aimed to reduce the negative environmental and social effects. A greening transport policy framework to enhance sustainability though greener and efficient roads includes a strategy focused on the cost of transport in terms of environmental damage to society and reducing noise pollution.

Greening the tourism sector can be done by increasing the involvement of the local community in the tourism value chain and the interplay between internal factors and structural conditions.

Greening the waste management sector requires decoupling waste from economic growth and addressing the challenges of increasing the recycle rate of electrical and electronic equipment or e-waste, turning biomass waste into recovered energy and other valuable resources, reducing food waste in the food chain, etc. The treatment of waste in the whole cycle from waste generation to waste disposal, should emphasize recovery for reuse and recycling of waste materials. Strategy for the prevention of industrial waste are based on industrial symbiosis resulting of collaboration to facilitate the exchange of by-products, water, energy and other materials.

Greening the water sector requires water management based on quality standards, to increase investments with better financial arrangements, to achieve a more efficient water supply, to improve the institutional arrangements and allocation systems, entitlements and use pf payments for ecosystem services.

Green economy transition is relevant to all economic sectors and requires a change in their economic activities perspective. Green economic transformation should be supported by new institutional forms for organization and decision making supported by participation and collaboration structures between public, private and community agents and actors for sharing resources and knowledge in green economic activities.

INVESTMENT, TRADE AND CAPACITY BUILDING

The term green economy was used as a green public packages-policy response of the financial crisis of 2008 to identify opportunity areas for large scale public investment. Investments in green economy growth can improve resource efficiency, generate employment and income, reduce carbon emissions and loss of biodiversity. Global green economy was considered an international response launched as a transformational tool for economic recovery of multiple crisis.

Green economy focuses on the creation of green employment in fields resulting on building resilience to climate change and adapting the effects of mitigating carbon emissions. Green economy relies on an ecosystem approach to the use of technology, management practices and capacity building to improve biodiversity conservation, efficient renewable energies, carbon sequestration, better land uses in agro-ecological practices, to avoid soil erosion, air and soil pollution, water contamination, etc. Capacity building on green economy and related research activities are a major institutional concerns at all levels of government to develop a robust socio-economic model. Voluntary agreements as a tool of green economy involving different stakeholders is an alternative to regulations and rules and more inclusive solution.

The Green Economy Initiative supported a policy for investment in greening resources and investments. A green economy creates incentives for economic activities to ensure environmental sustainability and social inclusion. Private actors can take investment opportunities from the green economic policies. UNESCO (2011) has identified some priority areas for the transition from traditional economy to green economy, among which are: education, science, culture, information, oceans and the water systems in a new green economy. The blue economy is vital for the provision of food, water and energy coming from seas and oceans to people living in and near coastal areas and islands.

Public and private flows and finance institutions, regulations and policies are all relevant in attracting and mobilizing investments into green economy. However, the investments flows on green finance flows are difficult to estimation due to their complexity of aggregated data.

The UNEP´s model of investment in green economy transition to influence economic transformation is supported by heterogeneous economic thinking for funding projects, responding to different challenges of context. However, the model is criticized by Victor and Jackson (2011) because the model assigns more funding to the green economy on the assumption that growth faster.

Trade and investment policy and the position that trading partners have in pursuing green economy are two factors that contribute to green economy. Trade and investment policies are drivers in the green economy and green growth with low carbon activities, considering the need to reduce the contentions nature of the process and covering some essential economic measures. Green protectionism concerns about socio-economic changes to correct market dislocations.

The new green protectionism is an option in the interplay between trade, investments and green economy policies conformed with green regulations and standards, avoiding the asymmetric relationships between takers and makers. Natural resources should focus more on greener activities and away from brown activities through instruments such as local content, financing, carbon taxes, tariffs, subsidies, etc. The measures of green protectionism should promote the transition to greener economy and reduce the eventual emerging trade tensions.

New green protectionism has been propelled by commercial tensions and dispute settlements in import-restricting measures and export restrictions. Export restraints justified as green environmental protection is a form of green protectionism amidst the requirements for some materials fueled and the deployment of green energy technologies. Transition towards inclusive, an equitable and development-led green economy require to be practical to prevent new forms of green protectionism and comprehensive to support the participation of developing countries.

Green technologies licensing and patented green innovation knowledge protection require also more flexibility aimed to facilitate the dissemination subject to the different domestic environments and access to finances. Drivers of green innovation and profits are creating green growth and are having market opportunities using technologies more suited to the needs of emerging economies more than the notions of corporate social responsibility policies. Green innovations are accessible for a large share of the consumer market.

R&D efforts must focus on fostering green innovation and absorbing green technology to local needs, are key policies to sustaining economic growth. Green technology transfers benefits from international collaboration on research and development and these transfers require more flexibility in the regime of global intellectual and industrial property.

STRATEGIC AND POLICY IMPLEMENTATION: AN INSTITUTIONAL APPROACH

Green economy exists at a microeconomic and macroeconomic levels. At microeconomic level, green economy concerns with emissions trading, externalities, taxes, subsidies, etc. The revenue raised from taxes can be used to promote green economy activities and tax incentives / exemptions can provide preferential support for new market, technology and practices development in a larger framework evaluated in terms of equity and social justice. Green tax system requires phasing out government policies and regulations supporting for environmentally harmful products, services and activities, which perpetuate wasteful production and consumption patterns that are costly to society. At macroeconomic level, some issues are relevant in environmental effects, intergenerational welfare, supply and demand protection policies, structural change, etc.

The foundations of the green economy in strategic orientations are found with different levels of commitment across the strategic and sectoral policy frameworks. Sustainable development policies and green economy strategies have been designed at the different local, national and global levels and supported by civil society organizations, governments and business and implemented through communities' and stakeholders' engagement.

The green economy concept becomes more supportive for economic transformations towards a more sustainable development and its implications for institutional arrangements and socioeconomic and environmental impacts on policy related to specific issues such as renewable energy and climate change strategies. Local and sectorial green economy and sustainable development strategies must be supported and endorsed by stakeholder consultations undertaken during the analysis, design and implementation processes. National local governments, businesses and civil society organizations are the main promoters and drivers of sustainable development and green economy strategies, policies and initiatives.

The green economy coexists at different levels with sustainable development concepts at global, national, regional and local contexts, which it is relevant to differentiate priorities and visions of institutional structures in the implementation of strategic plans. Sustainable urban planning institutions are instrumental in mainstreaming green policies in development strategies and policies. Green economy strategies have to be robust and involving a wide range of owned stakeholders developing green entrepreneurship aimed to generate environmental, social and economic co-benefits in high-tech sectors like water, solar and wind energy renewable.

The design and implementation of sustainable development and green economy strategies, policies and initiatives frameworks not only requires the commitment of all stakeholders involved but also financial instruments and support for investment, technological, organizational and political capacities, and good communication tactics on the issue from the public authorities to all the stakeholders involved. Development of green technology serving sustainable development and greening of the economy should be supported by the appropriate policies and strategies. Green economy policies and green innovation enable local communities to generate more value, while maintaining the natural bio diversity and ecosystems that sustain it.

Green economy approaches should be supported by stakeholder's mechanisms for developing green policies, partnering in agreements of collaboration and cooperation through political process mechanisms and processes such as the use for planning platforms, inclusive dialogues, etc. to legitimate green economy strategies. Participatory processes of green policy formulation and implementation outcomes have to be transformed to be feasible and meaningful to public (Resnick & Birner, 2010). An integral part of green economy policies is the engagement, participation and cooperation of stakeholders and the forging of public, private and community partnerships.

The policy making framework used for the concept of green economy considers it is a new tool for transition of development in the logic of sustained growth to solve the environmental crisis supported in the existing power and market structures and mechanisms. Sustainable development and green economy strategies, policies and initiatives they need not only being in place but actually implemented and extended into assessing and evaluating the impact. The proposed methodology to assess the strategies, policies and initiatives on green economy and sustainability begins with the identification, description and assessment of the issues through literature research and conducting a survey to get feedback. Green economy policies responding to national contexts where appear to be transformational but are of economic growth make some governments skeptical.

Green economy policy formulation, implementation, assessment and evaluation requires the analysis of potential trends of the specific economic sectors related to the natural environment, analyzing the underlying causes and impacts on the well-being of the population, advantages and disadvantages, etc. An incremental approach to green economy policies takes into consideration the constraints and limitations over the issue-driven analysis, design and implementation of green economy strategies. Designing effective green economy policies requires a framework to support the services and tools required to cover the needs in a contextual approach and specific cases, as well as the cross-sectoral impacts of green policy interventions.

Green economy transition has as priorities the strategic support for natural resource efficiency, reducing climate change and promoting greener economic activities. Encouragement of investments for sustainable management of natural resources in all scales of the economic sectors should contribute to green economic growth in resource efficiency and low-carbon and creating jobs. Public and private investments in the green economy reduce carbon emissions and pollution, enhance natural resources and energy efficiency, ecosystem services and biodiversity, and drive growth in income and employment.

Developing economies required not only technical but financial support in terms of environmental development investments. An inclusive green economy in developing and emerging economies may use the social economy as a tool. Some emerging economies have implemented green growth policies and taken actions in the process of developing infra-structure and manufacturing systems towards greener solutions.

Developing economies should make trade analyses on institutional regulations and policies identify their own comparative advantages for the production, distribution and export of green goods and services of their own green sectors. The impact of global trade on the transitions toward green economy has uncertain positive and negative effects in terms of increasing emissions to the environment and natural biodiversity from production to consumption of natural resources. Some opportunities that trade offers for a green economy transition are the increasing of efficiency, reduction of costs, waste and in general negative environmental impacts.

Green economy strategies aligned with sustainable development refocusing on global environmental challenges is supported by sustainable urbanism and natural capital valuation. Natural capital is a critical economic asset that requires rebuilding policies calling for investments and measures to be enhanced by the formulation and implementation of biodiversity and ecosystem services strategies. Green economy implementation phases out brown incentives, subsidies, and initiatives to enhance economic, social, and environmental sustainability, taking care of the natural and financial resources.

The implementation of green economy policies to drive growth resource-constrained is based on 10 conditions: Economic, social, and environmental green innovation and collaboration between government, business and civil society sectors, integrated coordination of governance, economic growth, social equity and environmental protection, short and long-term strategies to reconcile shared values and profits and multilateral approaches (International Chamber of Commerce, 2012). The relation between green economy, society and the environment gives the foundation to governance. Green economic governance, policy and practice is experimenting an evolution process based on the supporting demands of stakeholders connected and in communication directly to people in a green economy agenda to gain the political support.

Institutions for sustainable development play a relevant role in governance opportunities and challenges of green economy (Pardee Centre, 2011). The institutional frameworks and means are required with clearly defined roles within the context of equitable green economy as well as the responsibilities and accountability of empowered actors and stakeholders, contributors and beneficiaries of green economy (The Danish 92 Group Forum for Sustainable Development, 2012). The green economy connects global and multi stakeholder actions at government, finance business and civil society levels to transform economies in the benefit of all human beings and the planet (Green Economy Coalition, 2012)

To meet the sustainable development and green economy visions and goals require higher levels of commitment and dedication of public authorities, business and financial sector, civil organizations and the community at large. The green economy vision can be conceived and implemented through the stakeholders and communities' involvement and engagement. Local governments must promote funding to green economy sectors aimed to provide green economic recovery stimulus, poverty eradication, reducing carbon emissions and ecosystems degradation, among other goals and actions. Green fiscal stimulus provides the foundations for sustainable growth (Bowen et al., 2009).

Governments pursue green policies in the production and consumption of new green goods and services. Low carbon development strategies are forward-looking national economic development plans and strategies that encompass low-emission and/or climate resilient economic growth (OECD).

Green economy can also contribute to poverty eradication involving interested stakeholders in the formulation and implementation of innovative policies and practices. Several existing platforms and initiatives based on green economy knowledge propose goals, structural governance arrangements, best practices, promotion of networks and partnerships connecting knowledge providers and seekers, sectoral issues, etc. (Allen, 2012).

The core elements of the green economy concept must be integrated into its own strategic and policy-making framework to be implemented in different sectors. The use of indicators as a tool for implementing green economy policies helps to identify issues, analyze them, formulate, and assess policy options, implement, and evaluate their performance in a specific geographical, economic, social, and cultural context. A critical element of green economy policies is the access to information, the improvement of data availability and quality.

MEASUREMENT OF GREEN ECONOMIC TRANSFORMATIONS

A policy framework in place must provide a basis for measurement of transition to green economy aiming to make more sustainable sectors such as agriculture, fisheries, forestry, water, energy supply, industry, building, tourism, transport, waste management, etc. Measuring green economy transformations requires better and improved economic, society and environmental measurement interactions. The relationships between natural and social capital (Nellis & Parker, 2004), and the green economy to measure the transformation in terms of income and wealth. Green economy requires new methods to measure wealth to encompass what needs to achieve in terms of human well-being and environmental sustainability.

Measurement of green economy transformations requires better measures of development, green economic transformations, interactions economy-society-environment interactions, data sources and methodologies to analyze the composition, growth, and quality (OECD 2011). Measures in rural and urban economic development can be used as an instrument to promote a transition to green economy with economic, environmental, and social benefits. Measurement of the greening of the agriculture sector includes the promotion of Agri-environmentally sustainable rural development and farming practices.

Green economy management concepts should advance the transformational green economy supported by measurement of indicators between the economy, society and environment interactions. Green economy is much more than the environment which is not possible to equate with spending. The use of macroeconomic and sectoral sustainability indicators is a supporting tool for the green economy and the integration of environmental matters on some specific policy areas such as biodiversity, agriculture, fisheries, forestry, industry, building, transport, tourism, natural resource efficiency, water, renewal energy efficiency, waste management, climate change, cohesion policy, etc. The Environmental Performance Index (EPI), focuses on the development of the environmental green economy towards greening and efficiency sectors and social implications.

Indicators of green economy measurement must measure the economic opportunities and challenges for policy adoption and implementation. Measuring green economy transitions should capture the potential for creating and restructuring economic activities. Some output indicators for green economy must estimate and measure the feasibility of each policy making option. The area or percentage of green zones and surfaces such as organic and agro-ecological agriculture and the number of farmers cultivating are good indicators.

Current economic measurement approaches of green economy visions to assess the economic impact and practices may limit their transformative potential by extending the data collection to traditional environmental sectors. Transactional data may contribute to economic measurement of green economy transformations. Data constraints and capacities of green economic measurement does not necessarily measure green economy transformations but entrenches weak visions of the green economy. Green economy data from official sources causes some concerns by entrenching path dependency towards different weak green economy visions.

The EGSS methodology measures the green economy performance of a country with national statistics that may not capture all the green uses from biodiversity and ecosystems limiting the indicators of green economy measurement. EGSS, green R&D, environmental innovation and green patents are measures of the OECD framework (OECD, 2014). Technological research, innovations and patents are relevant indicators to green economy and growth. EGSS may be a green economy opportunity related to System of environmental economic accounting (SEEA), although some analysis concludes that the EGSS neither accurately reflect the scale of green economy opportunities nor the green economy transitions. Innovations in green economy and environmentally related practical uses and applications have a high impact on development.

The measurement of the transformational green economy contribution is limited and it is not possible to identify and capture due to the complexity of using standard statistical classifications (Eurostat 2009, 71) which may lead to distortions (Hood, 2012). Measuring the transformational green economy does not necessarily is aligned with measuring the environmental sector and ecosystem services. The economic greenness of industrial sectors, regions and countries can be compared by measuring green economy transformations using different scales for different priorities and contexts. Local governments and businesses are playing increasingly roles to implement greener growth actions and developing a green city index despite the lack of data and reporting availability on indicators related to green economy.

Transformational green economy is a policy proposal to ensure inclusive measurement of economic growth, social justice and environmental sustainability. Indicators may measure transitions but not tradeoffs of decision-making processes for green economy transformations of socioeconomic systems. Green economy indicators to measure the natural capital can be incorporated into environmental policy-making for sustainable development to assess trends in use of natural resources, emissions to the environment, economic activities for environmental purposes, etc. Measurement of growth and composition of green economic activity is relevant for decision-making.

Measurement of green economy policy outcomes should measure the opportunities and effects of the environmental and the economy interactions. International comparison of policy performance can contribute to green economy transformations either through a weak approach of economic growth or addressing the structural issues of the greening economy. However, policy performance measurement linked to the environment not necessarily leads to green economy transformational effects.

The green economy framework for actions might be complemented by a measurement framework including policies and indicators (Vossenaar, 2013) such as The Green Growth Knowledge Platform (GGKP) used to measure green growth and environmental policies and opportunities (GGKP 2013). The indicators must measure the green economy concepts and goals to determine the levels of effort support more than the GDP growth of the greening economies (Schmalensee, 2012). Some green growth indicators are identified in environmental life and resource productivity, natural resources, economic opportunities and policy responses. A narrow measurement approach to environment and economy interactions favors the green economy concepts. Green economy was estimated in 2011 by United Sates institutions using narrow measures (US Department of Commerce, 2010a, Barbier, 2014).

Measurement of transformational green economy actions requires a strong approach and data availability towards a vision (Barnett, 2015; Bevan & Hood, 2006; Heal, 2012; Hood, 2012). Data collection may limit the support of inclusivity in green economy transformations such as the forum adoption and climate change to emphasize the connection between businesses and communities. The green economy definitions of the UNEP, the Organization for Economic Co-operation and Development (OECD) and the World Bank are aligned to current systems using oversimplified models and absent measurements of green economic activities (Borel-Saladin & Turok, 2013).

Measuring the economic scale of green economy activities can measure the opportunities of green economy transformations. Policy monitoring and evaluation aims to measure the impacts and effects of policy implementation in relation to the environmental development and ecological system. The Earth Observation (EO) approach has potential for cost-effective monitoring in green economy measurement. The short term costs associated to green economy transformation makes it not always considered a viable objective. EO has a role in measuring green economy transformations.

EO supports the green economy and SDG measurement in traditional earth system and social applications such as forest cover (Da Ponte et al., 2015), disaster risk management (Briggs & Ward 2012) wetlands (Jones et al., 2009), sustainable urban development planning (Musakwa & Van Niekerk 2014), public health (Weng et al., 2013). Green economy measurement using the same SDG between nations may causes the greenness to improve interactions between the environment and the economic activities.

Green economy outcomes can be measured by any of the proposed approaches as the green growth framework, indicators for policymaking, the WAVES Partnership and the international environmental economy accounting. The national accounting for green economy using measurement frameworks for different contexts has serious limitations. Using metric indicators beyond the GDP will have an impact on delivering green economy transformations. Alternative measurement approaches of green economy have the indicators to measure the transformation of the economic growth-based green economy approach. Unavailability of indicators is problematic for the measurement of transformational green economy, and the framework permits not to measure transformational issues such as inequality and environment–economy interactions.

Finance evaluation of green economy focuses mainly on climate finance and renewable energy, which are useful for other green economy sectors. International financial flows are also relevant to green economy and growth. Green subsidy regulations and support schemes for renewable energy have a relevant effect on the promotion green economy. Agricultural subsidies are an economic tool that should be considered to implement for progress toward a green economy. Triple bottom line (TBL) of green economy assessment of performance standards in economic investments are based on economic, social and environmental benefits.

Measures to promote the environmental concern of green economy is in tension with protection from competition in the context of the WTO framework and outside to achieve an agreement on acceptable trade green economy policies. The applicability of the WTO rules to green economy for environmental protection focusing on non-discrimination is at stake.

Efforts toward the measurement of green economy transformations may be obstructed by other visions and deliver unintended consequences. Different measurements of green economy obstruct its vision and interactions with the bureaucratic and political contexts (Hood, 2012). Recording and reporting green economy activities is important to keep track of development.

PRACTICAL IMPLICATIONS AND CHALLENGES

Green economy has a lot of practical implications. Logistical operations of poor people lacking green practices and activities have a significant positive relationship with environmental degradation. Reduction of environmental degradation in poor communities should encourage green practices in logistical operations supported by the use of renewable energies, which have policy implications (Khan, 2019). According to Khan, S.A.R and Zhang Yu (2019) and Khan, S.A.R (2018), green economy is expanding with innovative techniques aimed to protect environmental sustainability, such as ecological design, sustainable or green purchasing and supply chain management, green material sourcing, green transportation and reverse logistics, green manufacturing, recycling and remanufacturing, recycling and remanufacturing, green and renewable energy and biofuels, green waste management, green marketing, green distribution and warehousing, green management and corporate social responsibility, among other innovations.

The panel study integrated by Khan, Sharif, Golpira, Kumar (2019) found that logistics operations, particularly efficiency of customs clearance processes, quality of logistics services and trade and transport-related infrastructure have a significant positive correlation with manufacturing value added, trade openness and per capita income. They found also that logistics operations are negatively associated with carbon emissions, climate change, global warming, and poisoning atmosphere. These findings have practical and policy implications in favor of green economy practices. An empirical study conducted in manufacturing firms of Pakistan found that green supply chain practices measured through the independent variables of green manufacturing, green purchasing, green information systems, eco-design and cooperation with customers have impacts on organizational performance except green purchasing (Khan, and Dong 2017). The authors recommend that in order to increase the organizational performance, manufacturing firms should implement eco-design and implement green information systems.

Also, Khan, Dong, Zhang, and Khan (2017) have analyzed the impact that green economy has on the enterprise performance using the Green Supply Chain Management (GSCM) to resolve issues of economic development, green environment, and society to enhance the economic performance and environmental responsibility of manufacturing enterprises in Guangzhou and Shenzhen provinces of China. An ABC analysis on order-filling process based on a case study identify current practices used to propose a redesigning plan of the warehouse layout, hopefully applied some principles of green economy (Khan, Dong, & Zhang, 2017).

The green economy concept addresses current challenges delivering economic development opportunities and multiple benefits for all human beings. The green economy concept in the context of sustainable development, poverty eradication and equity challenges. Identification of challenges and opportunities for greening economies can include sectors using low carbon profile, renewable energies, waste management, ecotourism activities, agriculture and farming, forestry, sustainable urban spaces, etc., through the implementation of green policies and incentive mechanisms. Climate change is social, community and business risk and the response is a low-carbon, socially inclusive and resource efficient implemented in a green economic growth that cannot be separated from social, community and business well-being.

Some identified barriers and challenges to transitioning toward a green economy are the political disincentives, inadequate legal and regulatory frameworks, declining human resources, weak bottom-up demand. Green trade can be boosted trade barriers on environmental goods and services. The relationship between international trade and the green economy is a complex interaction involving challenges and opportunities for the transition.

To become effective and transformative, green economy initiatives and activities should be promoted as a form of active citizenship alongside accountability (Mohan, 2007). Addressing the green economy challenge for most of the sectors of an economy implies to take into account the recommendations in strategy and policymaking framework for a successful transition.

Green growth policy framework is a real challenge that should be supported by learning, participation, consultation and consensus of all the involved stakeholders. Stakeholders have the challenge to exploit the opportunities and strengths while reduce the threats and weaknesses, in order to maximize the contribution on well-being and sustainable development that makes to the transition toward a greener economy.

Emerging economies have a lot of concerns on the conceptual green growth agenda and the related global and international cooperation. Emerging economies have a lot of concerns on the conceptual green growth agenda and the related global and international cooperation. Transitioning toward a green economy enhance international cooperation and accelerate sectorial changes creating jobs by increasing taxes on pollution rather than on labor, which anticipate skills gaps. Also international cooperation to promote trade on green economy products and services require further agreements on trans-border adjustments, public and private labels, subsidy rules.

Green innovative approaches to a green economy should promote intergovernmental transitional policy frameworks practical in essence and relevant to international cooperation on research and development, technology transfer, greening agriculture, manufacturing, services, finance, etc., in support of the transition towards green economy.

An international cooperation forum, as an institutional space on trade-related green economy issues and challenges is required to create with the objective of building capacity of issues related to green economy and trade, generate new trade approaches, and develop practical rules. International cooperation in bottom-up policy approaches is required to promote the green economy on relevant global environmental issues such as the climate change.

CONCLUSION

The objective of turning to a smart green economy, sustainable and inclusive, must be committed to absolute decoupling, with sector-specific strategies and policies aimed to deliver high levels of social cohesion, productivity and employment. The green economy is in line with the green growth strategy, where the economic growth is an imperative that has resulted in further liberal economies aiming more to improve production efficiency rather than sufficiency of consumption. Green growth strategy provides measurement tools and recommendations to achieve economic growth and development while ensuring that natural resources provide ecosystem services. Support should be aligned and consistent with the existing rules and the objectives of the green economy.

Green economy transition strategy is centered on transformative actions responding to economic, social and environmental challenges. A shift from more traditional economy to a more resilient and green economic development for long term prosperity requires more effective natural and ecological resources management, democratic foundations and equitable distribution of benefits. Transformation towards green economy must provide green growth strategy initiatives which should be economically viable and socially inclusive and other benefits.

Some measures are needed to promote both green jobs and green energy, but may be prohibited such as the subsidies under the WTO Agreement on Subsidies and Countervailing Measures (ASCM) and by some regional trading agreements. Trade policies must be improved to support the green economy initiatives in specific issues such as trade barriers, subsidies, investment measures, export restrictions, government procurements, etc.

The core elements of the green economy concept should be formulated into strategies and policy orientations for the different sectors. The biodiversity strategy and policy addressed to specific sectors must aim to implement elements of green economy such as the efficient use of natural resources decoupled from value creation and growth within the limits of environmental thresholds. In fact, green economy inclusive approaches have limited impact due to the green economic framework has not clear inclusive green objectives. More countries have no current sources of data and information regarding the characteristics of green sectors operating on green economy.

REFERENCES

AfDB. (2014) *Green growth Sierra Leone: investing in environmentally sound economic growth.* African Development Bank, Tunis (www.afdb.org/fileadmin/ uploads/afdb/Documents/Project-and-Operations/Sierra_

Allen, C. (2012). *A green economy knowledge sharing platform: Exploring options.* UNCSD Secretariat.

Barbier, E. B. (2013). The green economy postRio+20. *Science, 33*, 887–888.

Barbier, E. B. (2014). *Whither the green economy?* Triple Crisis. (http:// triplecrisis.com/whither-the-green-economy/)

Barnett P (2015) If what gets measured gets managed, measuring the wrong thing matters *Corporate Finance Review.*

Bernstein, S. (2013). Rio+20: Sustainable development in a time of multilateral decline. *Global Environmental Politics, 13*(4), 1312–1321. doi:10.1162/GLEP_e_00195

Bevan, G., & Hood, C. (2006). What's measured is what matters: Targets and gaming in the English public health care system. *Public Administration, 84*(3), 517–538. doi:10.1111/j.1467-9299.2006.00600.x

Bina, O., & La Camera, F. (2011). Promise and shortcomings of a green turn in recent policy responses to the 'double crisis'. *Ecological Economics, 70*(12), 2308–2316. doi:10.1016/j.ecolecon.2011.06.021

Borel-Saladin, J. M., & Turok, I. N. (2013). The green economy: Incremental change or transformation? *Environmental Policy and Governance, 23*(4), 209–220. doi:10.1002/eet.1614

Bowen, A., Fankhauser, S., Stern, N., & Zenghelis, D. (2009) *An outline of the case for a 'green' stimulus Grantham Research Institute on Climate Change and the Environment*, London E-Prints. (http://eprints.lse.ac.uk/24345/1/An_outline_of_the_case_for_a_green_stimulus.pdf)

Brand U (2012) Green economy – the next oxymoron? No lessons learned from failures of implementing sustainable development GAIA - *Ecological Perspectives for Science and Society, 21*, 28–32

Briggs, S. A., & Ward, S. (2012). Earth observation from satellites: Supporting the outcomes of UNCSD (Rio+20*). Environmental Policy and Law, 42*, 357–364.

Brockington, D. (2012). A radically conservative vision? The challenge of UNEP's towards a green economy. *Development and Change, 43*(1), 409–422. doi:10.1111/j.1467-7660.2011.01750.x

Brown, E., Cloke, J., Gent, D., Johnson, P. H., & Hill, C. (2014). Green growth or ecological commodification: Debating the green economy in the global South. *Geografiska Annaler. Series B, Human Geography, 96*(3), 245–259. doi:10.1111/geob.12049

Caprotti, F., & Bailey, I. (2014). Making sense of the green economy. *Geografiska Annaler. Series B, Human Geography, 96*(3), 195–200. doi:10.1111/geob.12045

Clark, H. (2013). What does Rio+20 mean for sustainable development? *Development, 56*(1), 16–23. doi:10.1057/dev.2013.13

Clémençon, R. (2012). Welcome to the Anthropocene: Rio+20 and the meaning of sustainable development. *Journal of Environment & Development, 21*(3), 311–338. doi:10.1177/1070496512457289

Da Ponte, E., Fleckenstein, M., Leinenkugel, P., Parker, A., Oppelt, N., & Kuenzer, C. (2015). Tropical forest cover dynamics for Latin America using Earth observation data: A review covering the continental, regional, and local scale. *International Journal of Remote Sensing, 36*(12), 3196–3242. doi:10.1080/01431161.2015.1058539

Davies, A. R. (2013). Cleantech clusters: Transformational assemblages for a just, green economy or just business as usual? *Global Environmental Change, 23*(5), 1285–1295. doi:10.1016/j.gloenvcha.2013.07.010

Death, C. (2015). Four discourses of the green economy in the global South. *Third World Quarterly, 36*(12), 2207–2224. doi:10.1080/01436597.2015.1068110

Eurostat (2009). *The environmental goods and services sector: a data collection handbook*. Eurostat, Luxembourg.

Ferguson, P. (2014). The green economy agenda: Business as usual or transformational discourse? *Environmental Politics*, *24*(1), 17–37. doi:10.1080/09644016.2014.919748

Fioramonti, L. (2014). The world's most powerful number: An assessment of 80 years of GDP ideology. *Anthropology Today*, *30*(2), 16–19. doi:10.1111/1467-8322.12098

Fosse, J., & Petrick, K.. (2016). *Towards a Green Economy in the Mediterranean - Assessment of National Green Economy and Sustainable Development Strategies in Mediterranean Countries. eco-union, MIO-ECSDE*. GEC.

Government, H. M. (2011). *Enabling the transition to a green economy: government and business working together*. HM Government.

Green Economy Coalition (2012). *Principles for a green, fair and inclusive economy.* .

Green Economy Coalition (2012). *The Green Economy Pocketbook – The case for action*. Green Economy Coalition.

Green Growth Knowledge Platform (GGKP). (2013). Moving towards a common approach on green growth indicators: Green Growth Knowledge Platform scoping paper. Green Growth Knowledge Platform, Geneva.

Halle, M. (2012) *Life after Rio: a commentary by Mark Halle*, IISD (https://www.iisd.org/sites/default/files/publications/com_li fe_ after_rio.pdf)

Heal, G. (2012). Reflections–defining and measuring sustainability. *Review of Environmental Economics and Policy*, 6147–6163.

Hood, C. (2012). Public management by numbers as a performance-enhanced drug: Two hypotheses. *Public Administration Review*, *71*, S85–S92.

International Chamber of Commerce (2011) *Ten conditions for a transition toward a* "Green Economy", ICC.

International Chamber of Commerce. (2012). *Green Economy Roadmap*. ICC.

Jänicke, M. (2012). Green growth: From a growing eco-industry to economic sustainability. *Energy Policy*, *48*, 13–21. doi:10.1016/j.enpol.2012.04.045

Jones, K., Lanthier, Y., van der Voet, P., van Valkengoed, E., Taylor, D., & Fernández-Prieto, D. (2009). Monitoring and assessment of wetlands using Earth Observation: The GlobWetland project. *Journal of Environmental Management*, *90*(7), 2154–2169. doi:10.1016/j.jenvman.2007.07.037 PMID:18640766

Kamp-Roelands, N. (2013). *Private sector initiatives on measuring and reporting on green growth*. OECD Publishing.

Khan, S. A. R and Zhang Yu (March 25th 2019). *Introductory Chapter: Purchasing and Supply Management [Online First]*. IntechOpen, . https://www.intechopen.com/online-first/introductory-chapter-purchasing-and-supply-management doi:10.5772/intechopen.85380

Khan, S. A. R. (November 5th 2018). *Introductory Chapter: Introduction of Green Supply Chain Management [Online First]*. IntechOpen, . https://www.intechopen.com/online-first/introductory-chapter-introduction-of-green-supply-chain-management doi:10.5772/intechopen.81088

Khan, S. A. R. (2019). The nexus between carbon emissions, poverty, economic growth, and logistics operations-empirical evidence from Southeast Asian countries. *Environmental Science and Pollution Research International*, *26*(13), 13210–13220. doi:10.100711356-019-04829-4 PMID:30903475

Khan, S. A. R., & Dong, Q. (2017). Impact of green supply chain management practices on firms' performance: An empirical study from the perspective of Pakistan. *Environmental Science and Pollution Research International*, *24*(20), 16829–16844. doi:10.100711356-017-9172-5 PMID:28573559

Khan, S. A. R., Dong, Q., & Zhang, Y. (2017). Role of ABC Analysis in the process of efficient order fulfillment: Case study. *Advanced Engineering Forum*, *23*(7), 114-121.

Khan, S. A. R., Dong, Q., Zhang, Y., & Khan, S. S. (2017). The impact of green supply chain on enterprise performance: In the perspective of China. *Journal of Advanced Manufacturing Systems*, *16*(3), 263–273. doi:10.1142/S0219686717500160

Khan, S. A. R., Sharif, A., Golpira, H., & Kumar, A. (2019). A green ideology in Asian emerging economies: From environmental policy and sustainable development. *Sustainable Development*, *27*(2), 1063–1075. doi:10.1002d.1958

Lorek, S., & Spangenberg, J. H. (2014). Sustainable consumption within a sustainable economy – beyond green growth and green economies. *Journal of Cleaner Production*, *63*, 33–44. doi:10.1016/j.jclepro.2013.08.045

McAfee, K. (2016). Green economy and carbon markets for conservation and development: A critical view. *International Environmental Agreement: Politics, Law and Economics*, *16*(3), 333–353. doi:10.100710784-015-9295-4

Mohan, G. (2007). Participatory development: From epistemological reversals to active citizenship. *Geography Compass*, *1*(4), 779–796. doi:10.1111/j.1749-8198.2007.00038.x

Morrow, K. (2012). Rio+20, the green economy and reorienting sustainable development. *Environmental Law Review*, *14*, 279–297.

Musakwa Wand Van Niekerk, A. (2014). Monitoring sustainable urban development using built-up area indicators: A case study of Stellenbosch, *South Africa Environment. Development and Sustainability*, *17*(3), 547–566. doi:10.100710668-014-9560-7

Nellis, J. G., & Parker, D. (2004). *Principles of macroeconomics*. Pearson.

OECD. (2011). *Towards green growth: monitoring progress: OECD indicators Organisation for Economic Co-operation & Development OECD Publishing, Paris Pardee Centre. Beyond Rio+20: Governance for a Green Economy*. Boston University.

OECD. (2014) OECD green growth studies: green growth indicators 2014. Organisation for Economic Co-operation & Development OECD Publishing, Paris

Pearce, D. W., Markandya, A., & Barbier, E. B. (1989). *Blueprint for a green economy Earthscan.*

Pelling, M., & Manuel-Navarrete, D. (2011). From resilience to transformation: The adaptive cycle in two Mexican urban centers. *Ecology and Society*, *16*(2), 1–11. doi:10.5751/ES-04038-160211

Pelling, M., O'Brien, K., & Matyas, D. (2014). Adaptation and transformation. *Climatic Change*, *133*(1), 113–127. doi:10.100710584-014-1303-0

Powers A. (2012) The Rio+20 process: forward movement for the environment? *Transnational Environmental Law,* 1403–12.

Republic of Rwanda. (2011) Green growth and climate resilience: national strategy for climate change and low carbon development. Republic of Rwanda, Kigali.

Resnick, D., & Birner, R. (2010). Agricultural Strategy Development in West Africa: The False Promise of Participation. *Development Policy Review*, *28*(1), 97–115. doi:10.1111/j.1467-7679.2010.00476.x

Schmalensee, R. (2012). From 'green growth' to sound policies: An overview. *Energy Economics*, *34*, S2–S6. doi:10.1016/j.eneco.2012.08.041

Sonnenschein J and Mundaca L (2015). Decarbonization under green growth strategies? The case of South Korea. *Journal of Cleaner Production. 123.* 180–93

Stiglitz, J. E., Sen, A., & Fitoussi, J.-P. (2009). *Report by the Commission on the Measurement of Economic Performance and Social Progress*. Commission on the Measurement of Economic Performance and Social Progress.

The Danish 92 Group Forum for Sustainable Development. (2012). *Building an Equitable Green Economy.* Danish 92 Group.

UNCSD. (2012). *The Future we want, outcome of the United Nations Conference on Sustainable Development (Rio+20)*. UNCSD.

UNDESA. (2010). Progress to date and remaining gaps in the implementation of the outcoms of the major summits in the area of sustainable development, as well as an analysis of the themes of the Conference. Preparatory Committee for the UNCSD.

UNEP. (2012a). *Indicators: a UNEP green economy briefing paper*. United Nations Environment Programme.

UNEP. (2012b) *Measuring progress towards a green economy: draft working paper* United Nations Environment Programme, Nairobi.

UNEP. (2014b). *Using indicators for green economy policymaking United Nations Environment Programme*.

UNEP (United Nations Environment Programme). (2011). *Towards a green economy: Pathways to Sustainable Development and Poverty Eradication*. United Nations Environment Programme.

UNESCO. (2011). *From Green Economies to Green Societies.* UNESCO.

United Nations (2015) *Adoption of the Paris Agreement: FCCC/CP/2015/L.9/Rev.1.* UN.

US Department of Commerce. (2010a). *Measuring the green economy United States Department of Commerce.* Washington DC US Department of Commerce.

Van der Ploeg, R., & Withagen, C. (2013). Green growth, green paradox and the global economic crisis. *Environmental Innovation and Societal Transitions, 6,* 116–119. doi:10.1016/j.eist.2012.11.003

Victor, P., & Jackson, T. (2011). Doing the maths on the green economy. *Nature, 472*(7343), 295. doi:10.1038/472295a PMID:21512560

Vossenaar, R. (2013). *The APEC list of environmental goods: an analysis of the outcome & expected impact.* International Centre for Trade and Sustainable Development.

Weng Q, Xu B, Hu X and Liu H (2013) Use of earth observation data for applications in public health *Geocarto International, 29,* 33–16–16

KEY TERMS AND DEFINITIONS

Capacity Building: A process through which people, organizations and societies obtain, strengthen and maintain the necessary skills to establish and achieve their own development goals over time.

Green Economy:That which leads to the improvement of human well-being and social equality: while environmental risks and ecological scarcity are significantly reduced.

Green Growth: The one that promote economic growth and development while ensuring that natural assets continue to provide the environmental resources and services on which our well-being depends

Institutional Approach: Analysis of the economic relations that need a regulatory framework that allows them to interact in the market, is where the institutions take action by establishing certain limits - whether formal and informal - that regulate economic negotiations, in an imperfect market.

Strategic Plan: It is a document integrated in the business plan that includes the planning at the economic-financial, strategic and organizational level with which a company or organization has to address its objectives and achieve its future mission.

Sustainable Development: It is development that meets the needs of the present without compromising the ability of future generations to meet their own needs

Transformation: The result of a process of change of form. It happens when one thing: fact or idea is converted into another.

Transition: A change from one form or type to another, or the process by which this happens.

Chapter 12
Promoting Responsible Research and Innovation in China's Hi-Tech Zones:
Based on Case Studies of Zizhu Hi-Tech Zone, East Lake Hi-Tech Zone, and Guangzhou Hi-Tech Zone

Poshan Yu
https://orcid.org/0000-0003-1069-3675
Soochow University, China & Australian Studies Centre, Shanghai University, China

Xiyan Shen
Independent Researcher, China

Emanuela Hanes
Independent Researcher, Austria

ABSTRACT

The establishment of high-tech zones (HTZs) is an important strategic arrangement for the development of high-tech industries in China. As knowledge-intensive areas, HTZs aim to enhance networking as well as innovative and economic performances of firms and regions. There are extensive studies on the factors affecting the economic development of HTZs. But some regulatory gaps remain on the topic of responsible research and innovation (RRI) of HTZs. This chapter expounds the development status of China's HTZs. Case studies will be used for discussion. This chapter finds that the flexibility of RRI practice in China's industrial zones is related to the regional institutional setting, and the existing policy setting will help to strengthen the RRI practice in high-tech industrial zones. Finally, some suggestions are put forward for the development of HTZs in China, hoping to perfect the regulatory framework and promote the research and innovation of China's HTZs.

DOI: 10.4018/978-1-6684-7422-8.ch012

INTRODUCTION

Responsible research and innovation (RRI) is a process that involves the public and all stakeholders in innovation research and takes into account social expectations and potential impacts, and can be effective in alleviating concerns about technological safety. In the 2011 European Commission report Horizon 2020, the concept of 'responsible innovation' was included for the first time as an important element of the EU's development strategy and became one of the EU's visions. In the report "Addressing ethical and regulatory challenges in research policy at the global level", European Commission (2012) pointed out that the basic elements of responsible innovation include social interest, moral and ethical acceptability and risk management. Currently, many countries have adopted responsible research and innovation as a fundamental concept in their policy development and are actively pursuing it in the process of innovation practice to speed up technological development and promote regional economic growth (Yang and Lee, 2021). For example, workshops on responsible research and innovation were held in Brussels and London in May 2011, and practical activities such as the construction of the Rotterdam port extension in the Netherlands and SPICE project management in the UK have been implemented.

However, research on responsible innovation in China is still in its infancy, and is currently focused on reviewing and summarising the research results of foreign scholars, with the scope of research mainly covering the concept, model, indicator evaluation design and implementation of responsible innovation. The lack of holistic assessment and institutional-level research on the implementation of responsible research and innovation has left many high-tech institutions in China unaware of the importance of responsible research and innovation (Fan and Dan, 2018). Therefore, this paper will focus on the application of responsible research and innovation practices in high-tech zones (HTZs), which are industrial clusters formed by the agglomeration of high-tech enterprises. The synergistic effect of individual firms' responsible research and innovation practices on other firms in the industrial zone.

This chapter examines, from the perspective of different stakeholders:

1. Does the current system in HTZs help them practice RRI?
2. How do HTZs promote RRI?
3. Has the application of RRI produced synergy in the HTZ, or intensified the competition among enterprises in the zone?

LITERATURE REVIEW

With the release of China's 13th Five-Year Plan for Science and Technology Development in 2016, HTZs have become increasingly prevalent, developing into new forms of high-tech industrial cluster (Zhuang and Ye, 2020). What's more, Sergio et al. (2020) reported that HTZs were important mediators of knowledge flows between universities and new technology-based firms. Nicoletta et al. (2019) also suggested that HTZs play a positive role in stimulating open innovation initiatives in firms. There is a great deal of research on the factors that promote the development of HTZs. For example, Wei et al. (2019) pointed out that the scope and intensity of university links were essential for the growth of HTZs (i.e. job, revenue of tenants), while Zheng and Li (2020) believed that the determining factor for its growth was the pilot policy of the central government. Moreover, Bai et al. (2015) employed the Dynamic Network Slack-based Measurement to evaluate the performance of national HTZs in China after the financial crisis and found that technical efficiency improvement impacted both production sectors and R&D sectors in HTZs. All in all, there is strong evidence that the factors above have exerted a profound influence on HTZs.

In recent years, Chinese scholars have also conducted research on the topic, advocating responsible research and innovation for the first time. Liu (2015), based on a combination of many foreign scholars' studies, argues that responsible innovation is the understanding and practice of innovation in which the innovation community takes respect for human rights and the promotion of social well-being as its value ascriptions and actively assumes full responsibility as its methodological characteristics. Based on the research results of Stigoe et al. (2013), on responsible innovation and the technological innovation situation in China, Mei et al. (2014) constructed a theoretical framework of responsible innovation consisting of "subject, activity and norm", "prediction, self-reflection, inclusiveness and responsiveness". The framework is composed of "subject, activity and norm", "predictability, introspection, inclusiveness and responsiveness", which are the basic elements of responsible innovation and form a spiral dynamic evolution to achieve the development of responsible innovation. Yu et al. (2016) constructed a corporate responsibility innovation evaluation index system including corporate product design concepts, product production processes, and evaluation supervision to evaluate China's Dalian HTZ.

DEVELOPMENT OF HIGH-TECH ZONES

Innovation Level

HTZ is a kind of special geographical location that gathers a number of enterprises in an area with the goal of promoting certain industrial development (Shen et al., 2018). It is an important spatial combination form of regional economic development and industrial transformation and upgrading (Lu et al., 2020). HTZs can gather resources and deepen industrial connections, which is of great significance for cultivating emerging industries and promoting urbanization development. In recent years, HTZs have been developing rapidly in China, and the GDP of HTZs has maintained steady growth. By the end of 2019, the number of national HTZs has reached 169, and the GDP of the national HTZs was 12.14 trillion yuan, accounting for 12.3 percent of China's GDP. In addition, the total innovation capability index of the national HTZs in 2019 increased to 326.4 points, with an average annual increase of 25.2 points from 2010 to 2019. In 2019, the innovation and entrepreneurship environment index was the highest contributing factor to the growth of the total index, reaching 56.4% (National Innovation Capability Evaluation Report of High-tech Zones, 2019), indicating that the innovation and entrepreneurship environment of HTZs has been rapidly and continuously improved.

Figure 1. GDP of China's high-tech zones
Data source: China National High-tech Zone Development Report, 2019

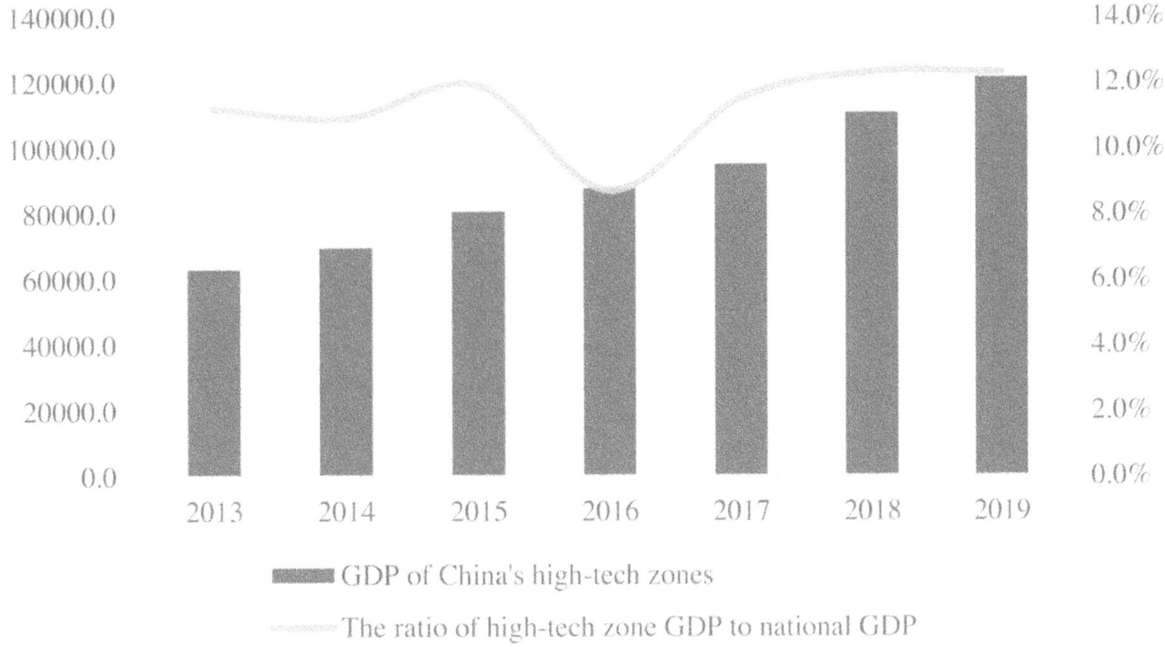

Figure 2. Overall Index of Innovation Capacity of National High-tech Zones from 2010 to 2019
Data source: National Innovation Capability Evaluation Report of High-tech Zones, 2019

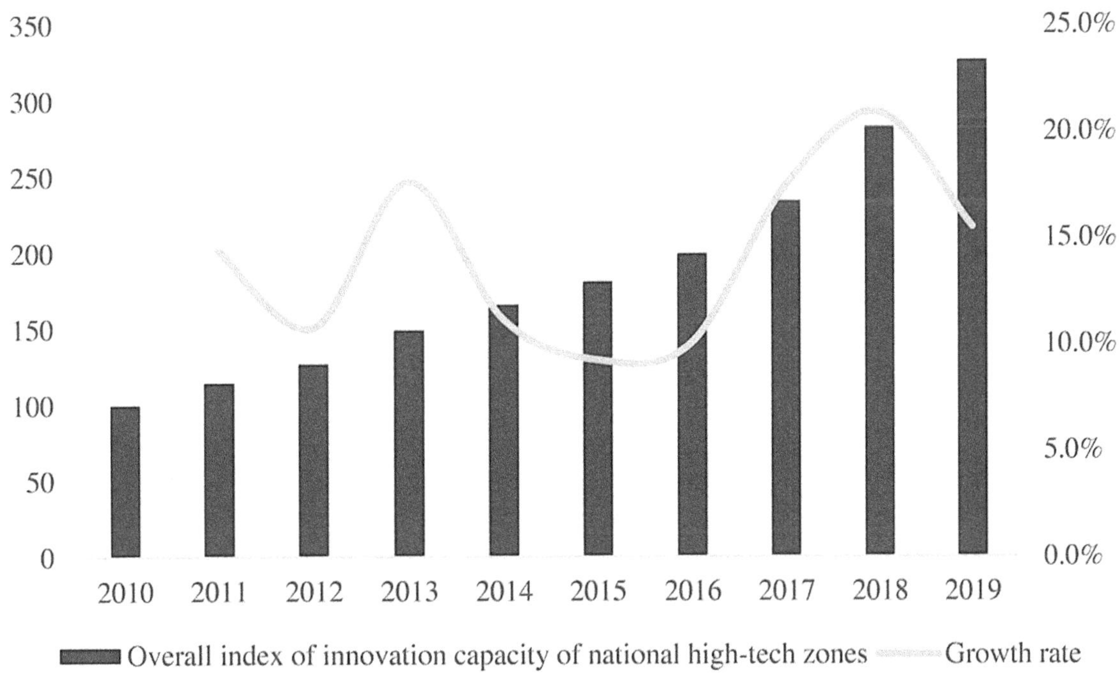

Figure 3. Five Sub-indexes of Innovation Ability of National High-tech Zones from 2010 to 2019
Data source: National Innovation Capability Evaluation Report of High-tech Zones, 2019

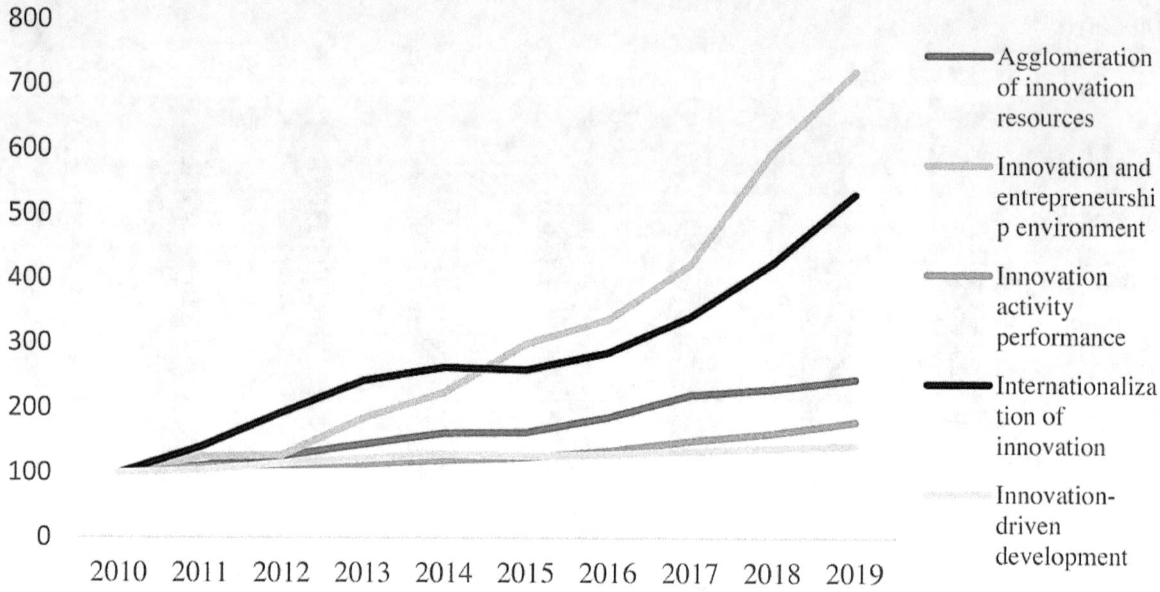

In 2019, the labor productivity of enterprises in HTZs was 363,000 yuan/person, which was 2.8 times of the national total labor productivity (128,000 yuan/person). The profit rate of enterprises was 6.8%, 0.9 percentage points higher than the operating profit rate of industrial enterprises with main business income of above 20 million yuan in China. Among them, the average salary of employees in enterprises was 151,000 yuan, an increase of 10.2% in comparison to the year before and 2.1 times the average salary of employees in urban units nationwide.

Figure 4. Average Salary of Employees in Enterprises from 2011 to 2019
Data source: National Innovation Capability Evaluation Report of High-tech Zones, 2019

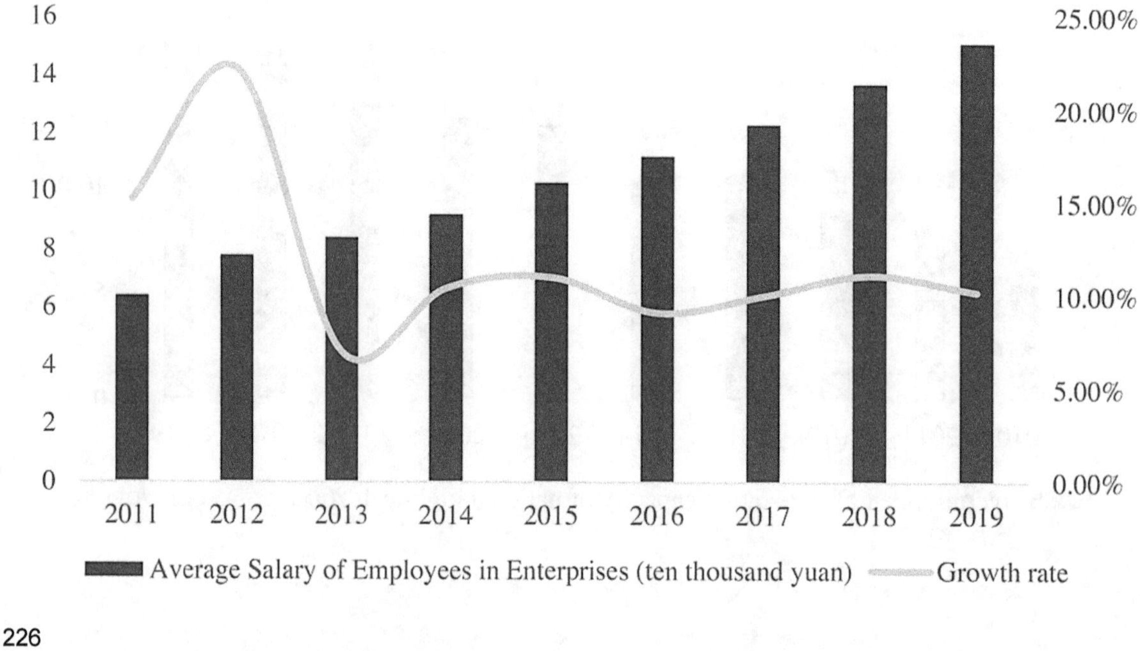

Current Problems

However, there are also a series of problems in China's HTZs, such as unbalanced regional development, inadequate ecological construction, and ethical and moral disputes. Some regional governments in Western China regard HTZs as "development engines" rather than "innovation engines", and the main purpose of establishing HTZs is to increase income and promote employment, since regional economic growth is the primary focus (Wang et al., 2021). Therefore, this reduces the potential of HTZs in innovation.

Meanwhile, since the 21st century, under the leadership of the government, China's HTZs have paid more and more attention to ecological construction, which has not only deepened the understanding of local enterprises on the concept of green production, but also played an important demonstration role in the construction of ecology in China (Xiong and Luo, 2021). However, as the construction of HTZs gradually matures, the marginal effect of environmental protection measures within HTZs begins to decline, and HTZs in China are in urgent need of improvement in both innovation and environmental aspects.

In addition, the transfer of international industrial layout has also brought new opportunities and challenges to China's HTZs. After the 2008 financial crisis, the international industrial layout started to change, and China, as the main export country, mainly presents the characteristics of two-way transfer. On the one hand, high-end industrial value chains move back to developed countries in Europe and the United States; On the other hand, the lower end of the value chain is moving to lower-cost countries in Southeast Asia. This trend puts forward higher requirements for industrial upgrading and industrial adjustment in China, so it poses new challenges to the support and governance of industrial parks. At present, the yet unsolved park management problems, such as repetitive construction, industrial similarity, and low intensity, all need to be improved urgently.

Future Trend: Informatization and Green Transformation

With the integrated development of manufacturing and the new generation of information technology, the current HTZs are transforming into smart zones. In 2019, the scale of China's industrial park informatization market was about 313.6 billion yuan, an increase of 16%. By 2019, HTZ at or above the provincial level were approved by the Ministry of Intelligent Manufacturing and the new HTZ with more than 100 Projects account for 21.4% of HTZs. There were 41 approved Industrial Internet Pilot Demonstration Projects, accounting for 27% or the total projects, plus 80 Manufacturing and Internet fusion development pilot demonstration projects, accounting for 24% of all HTZs. In addition, with the continuous progress of "ecological civilization" construction, green and low-carbon development has become the only way for the transformation and development of HTZs. In recent years, HTZs have continued to promote technological transformation, recycling transformation and environmental optimization transformation, and made certain progress and achievements. However, according to statistics from the Ministry of Environmental Protection, as of 2019, only 51 HTZs in China have passed the examination and were accepted as national eco-industrial demonstration parks, and only 42 have been approved for construction, which is far from meeting the needs of the green development of industrial sectors. Thus, the green development of HTZs still has a long way to go. (Evaluation report on innovation capacity of National High-tech Zones, 2019)

DEVELOPMENT OF RRI

Analysis of Current RRI Research Focus Using CiteSpace

This section uses the subject terms in the Web of Science Core Collection database to search the global literature on RRI-related topics. In this section, we searched for papers with the subject term "responsible research and innovation " from 2010 to 2022. Based on these criteria, 1000 records were retrieved in CiteSpace. We removed duplicates from the text. In order to compare RRI cases in China with those in other countries, we classified the selected literature by country, and again used CiteSpace to check the main directions of global RRI research in recent years. This part of the study found that the research cases on RRI are mainly concentrated in the US (163 articles), the UK (139 articles) and the Netherlands (128 articles), while there are fewer relevant studies in China (75 articles), which confirms the previous statement that RRI research in China is still in its infancy. In the keyword analysis, this paper finds that the most frequent keywords are science (107), technology (73), framework (71) and management (60), and there are no keywords related to the HTZ. Therefore, this chapter believes that there is a lack of global research using the RRI framework to analyze HTZ. The actual case of RRI in reviewing China's HTZ is also insufficient. Therefore, this chapter will study the role of RRI theory in the HTZ case of first-tier and second-tier cities in China, which can be applied to third-tier and fourth-tier cities in China and other developing countries.

Figure 5. Country classification of RRI studies

Figure 6. Key terms of RRI studies

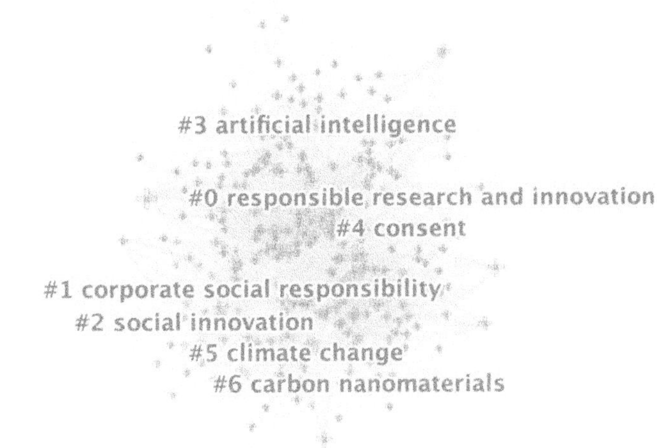

Pillars of Responsible Research and Innovation

The theory of RRI was first proposed by Hellstrom (2003). It has been widely recognized by the international academic community and included into the 'Horizon 2020' strategy of the European Union. It mainly discusses how to preventively solve the ethical and moral problems that may be encountered in research and innovation processes (Wang and Gao, 2019).The most commonly accepted definition of RRI is from von Schonberg, who defined RRI as "a transparent, interactive process by which societal actors and innovators become mutually responsive to each other with a view on the (ethical) acceptability, sustainability and societal desirability of the innovation process and its marketable products (in order to allow a proper embedding of scientific and technological advances in our society)" (Ellen et al., 2021). To better implement RRI into research, the Engineering and Physical Sciences Research Council (EPSRC) recommends the APREA-4P framework approach, which focuses on anticipating the effects of a research of an innovation, reflecting on these effects, engaging with the public and acting accordingly (Paulo and Cristina, 2019). Besides, the EU vision of RRI focuses on six aspects: public engagement, gender equality, science education, ethics, open access and governance (European Union, 2012). More broadly, the following elements can also be included, namely, sustainability, inclusion and social justice. In this chapter, the four pillars of "sustainability, governance, public engagement and open access" defined below will be mainly used for our case studies.

Table 1. Four Pillars in RRI measurement

Pillar	Definition	Common Applications	Influence
Sustainability	Enterprises should consider both the needs of current development and the needs of future development.	● Innovate sustainable development strategy ● Cultural sustainable development strategy ● Strategy for sustainable development of the system ● Sustainable development strategy of core competitiveness ● Sustainable development strategy of factors	● It can promote the extension of the overall life of the enterprises ● It is the guarantee for enterprises to obtain long-term benefits
Governance	Guide research and innovation via internal policies and tools	● Ethics review panel ● Green policies ● Long-term risk assessment process	● Make certain resistance to research activities that may cause harm or have moral uncertainty or unpredictability ● The formulation of CSR policies and actions will impose a cost burden on enterprises
Open access	● Use online technology to make academic research more accessible and free to read ● More general use of concepts such as open data and open science	Share data and results	● Potential benefits for research and innovation ● May harm company's interests and arise intellectual property disputes
Public engagement	Incorporate the views, opinions and concerns of stakeholders into the research process to ensure that research and innovation are in the interest of society.	● Public consultation system and public decision-making system ● Interviews, surveys and focus groups ● Using social media to reach end users	● Help ensure R&D are in the public interest ● Direct the integration of public resources ● Companies have concerns about the ability of non-experts to guide the development of new technologies

Data source: Wei et al. (2019) and Yang (2021)

RESPONSIBLE RESEARCH AND INNOVATION IN CHINA

In recent years, RRI has been gradually introduced into China, but some of its guiding principles are in conflict with the current Chinese system, especially in the fields of science and technology innovation.

First, China's current system emphasizes developmentalism and scientism. China regards economic growth as the prerequisite and primary goal of social development and considers the natural sciences as the leading force determining social development and the only effective guiding ideology for regulating and improving social relations. This is the mainstream ideology after the Reform and Opening Up (Li and Liao, 2021). Developmentalism and scientism have promoted the development of scientific and technological innovation in China, but at the same time they have neglected the emphasis on social responsibility and ethics (Fan and Zhang, 2018). Second, China's top-down management and decision-making system also is in conflict with RRI, which is very obvious in the scientific and technological system. For example, scientific and technological innovation resources are highly concentrated in the government departments. At the same time, in the process of decision-making, the public participation channel, to some extent, should also be much broader. Therefore, this paper will provide recommendations to those challenges encountered in the RRI practices in China.

Moreover, there is no unified standard for responsible research and innovation practices in China. Compared to European countries that have started practising them earlier, responsible research and innovation practices in China's HTZs are still in their infancy, and some first- and second-tier cities with good economic development have already carried out pilot projects, mainly in the form of collaborative development between industry, education and research. In the future, more high-tech industrial zones in third and fourth tier cities in China will have to be popularised for responsible research and innovation practices.

STUDY DESIGN AND INFORMATION SOURCES

Method Selection: Multiple Case Studies

The method of case study in this paper is mainly based on the following considerations: There have been relevant studies on the factors promoting the development of HTZs, but there is a lack of in-depth discussions on how RRI can support HTZs. Siggelkow (2007) believes that the study method should be determined by the purpose of the case analysis. In order to put forward theoretical suggestions, the approach is to start from the case and then focus on theoretical analysis. This study will first use the RRI pillars to classify the highlights of the cases, then summarize the experiences of the cases, and then come up with more practical suggestions for the development of Chinese HTZs. This also follows the theoretical construction paradigm advocated in current case studies. In deciding the number of cases analyzed, due to the differences in Chinese HTZs' development environment and path, it's hard to deduct a general law from one single case study, so choosing the multi-cases study method helps to better understand the current situation of Chinese HTZs and form a more complete theory while improving the validity of the study. Sanders (1982) believes that the optimal number of multiple case studies is 3 to 6. Following this principle, three cases are selected for study.

Case Selection and Information Collection

The selection of specific cases should be based on the cases' extraordinary inspiration, or extreme examples, or a rare research opportunity. Shanghai Zizhu HTZ, Wuhan East Lake HTZ, Guangzhou HTZ, Suzhou HTZ and Chengdu HTZ are five important national HTZs with special positioning and demonstration significance. Shanghai Zizhu HTZ is the only HTZ in China that operates mainly with private economy. Wuhan East Lake HTZ is the second national independent innovation demonstration zone after Beijing Zhongguancun, with a long history and rich experience. Guangzhou HTZ is an important bearing area of the Guangdong-Hong Kong-Macao Greater Bay Area's comprehensive National Science Centre. In order to ensure the accuracy and validity of the case data, two strategies are adopted in the selection of public data. One is to pay attention to the source of information. This includes selecting information of academic value, including literature from core journals, selecting information with legal effect, such as the announcement and annual report of listed companies in Zizhu HTZ, selecting authoritative information released by the authorities, such as Regulations of East Lake National Independent Innovation Demonstration Zone, etc. The second strategy is to pay attention to the cross-verification of information by collecting data from a variety of sources, including literature, corporate websites, public media, etc. Additionally, the analysis compares multiple sources to ensure the authenticity of data as much as possible.

CASE STUDY OF RESPONSIBLE INNOVATION IN HTZS IN CHINA

Shanghai Zizhu HTZ

The Road of Zizhu -- Coordinated Development of Industry, Education and Research

In 2002, the Shanghai Zizhu HTZ was approved to be established with a planned area of 130,000 square kilometers, including the campuses of Shanghai Jiaotong University and East China Normal University, Zizhu Basic Education Park, and Zizhu Peninsula International Living Community (Luo, 2019). With a reputation for science and engineering, the Shanghai Jiao Tong University was included into the Zizhu HTZ as well as the East China Normal University, whose Humanities Department form a powerful 'think tank' (Luo, 2020). At the same time, the Zizhu Business Incubator is built to support innovation and entrepreneurship. The new development model of a science park integrating production, learning and research is an important support for the sustainable development of Zizhu HTZ. By 2020, Zizhu HTZ has accumulated more than 1,000 intellectual property rights of various kinds, among which invention patents account for more than 50%. There are 12 state-level industrial service promotion institutions and 194 enterprises under incubation. Intellectual property trusteeship rate of incubated enterprises reached 100% (Shanghai Zizhu High-tech District Government Network, 2020).

Figure 7. The overall framework of Zizhu HTZ
Source: Authors' own Visualization

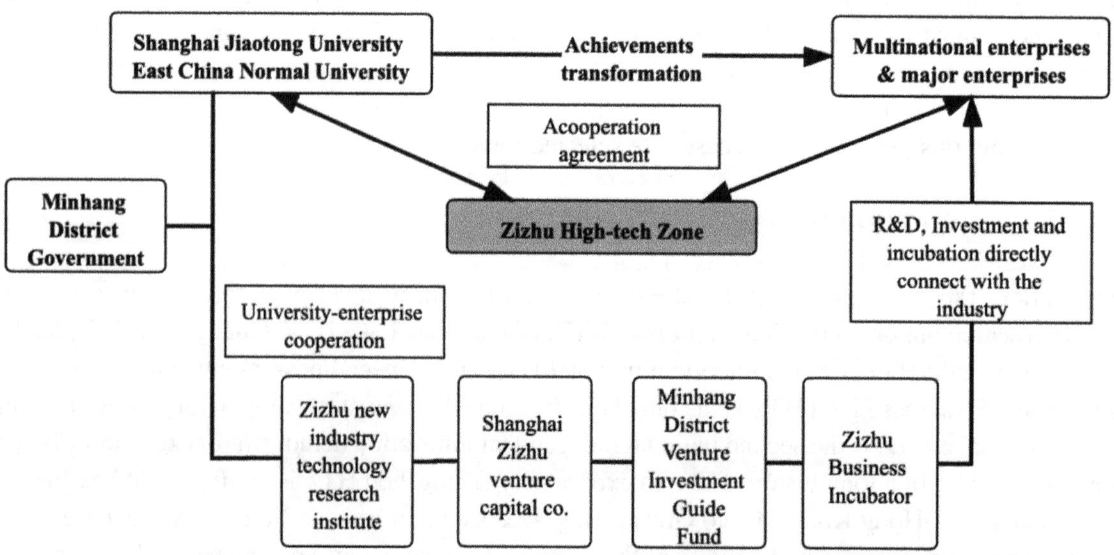

Figure 8. Total financial revenue of Zizhu High-tech Zone
Source: Zizhu High-tech Zone Official website

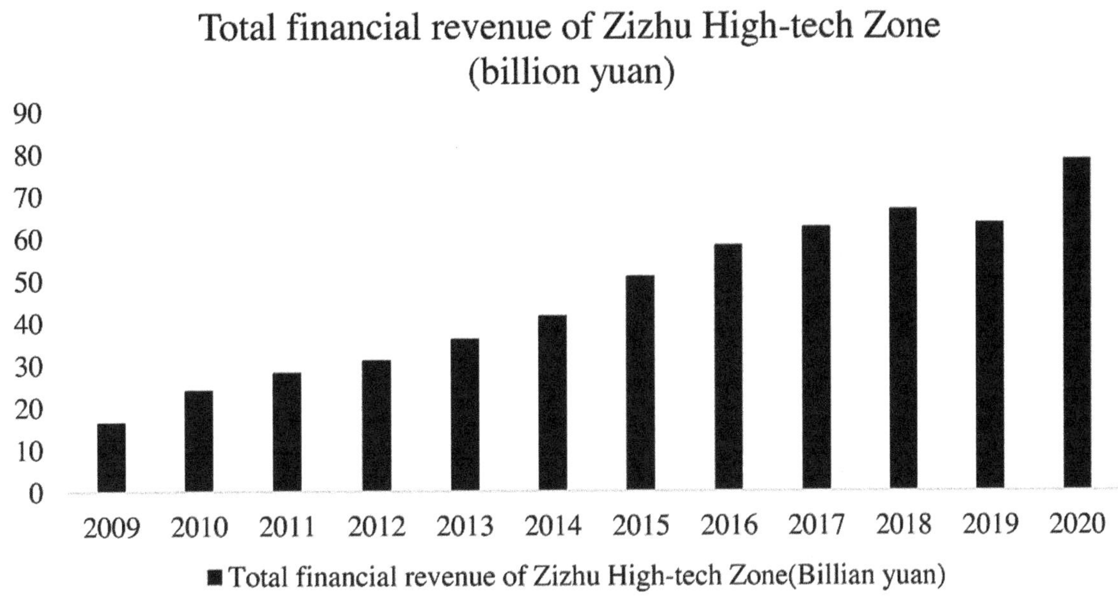

The Road of Zizhu -- Sustainable Development

The Shanghai Zizhu HTZ embeds RRI in the whole process of innovation and integrates the theme of sustainable development into its daily operations. The Zizhu Social Responsibility Alliance is China's first alliance with the theme of corporate social responsibility (CSR). Since the establishment of the Zizhu Chamber of Commerce in 2006, the Zizhu Youth Association in 2010, the Zijiang Charity Foundation in 2015, and the Zizhu HTZ CSR Alliance in 2016, the Zizhu HTZ has gradually established a social responsibility management organizational structure with high execution and high responsiveness (Sun, 2019). In 2019, the Zizhu National HTZ Social Responsibility Work Manual and Social Responsibility Triennial Strategic Plan (2019-2021) was released, which interpreted the future development direction of Zizhu HTZ and gave an overview of corporate social responsibility work. It has provided six classes of Zizhu high-tech leading industries (information software, digital audio-visual, life science, intelligent manufacturing, aerospace electronics, new energy and new material) with constructive implementation plans, including strategic positioning, overall target and multi-stakeholder involvement (Luo, 2020). This is the first of China's national HTZs to carry out the work of CSR and sustainable development. It is of landmark significance and provides authoritative and systematic guidance for enterprises in the HTZs to build up a social responsibility system. In addition, the Zizhu HTZ has absorbed a large number of multinational technology companies with sustainable development thinking and experience, such as Microsoft, Intel, Coca Cola, Anji Avionics, etc., which have provided advanced experience for the sustainable development governance of enterprises in the zone. For example, in 2018, the CSR Alliance of Zizhu HTZ launched the TEDxZizhuPark annual conference with the theme of 'For Good' where Microsoft was invited to share how to apply artificial intelligence technology to the development of social undertakings and Entron Technology shared cutting-edge mixed reality technology and introduced how to balance technological innovation and ethics.

Through the exploration of CSR and sustainable development schemes, the high-tech enterprises in Zizhu HTZ have taken humanistic concern and moral rules into consideration while researching and innovating. 'Xindongyuan Happy Home', led by Zizhu HTZ, is the first smart new model community for elderly care in Shanghai which owns more than 50 design and user-friendly service facilities for the Ageing population. At the same time, there are supporting enterprises in the park dedicated to early disease screening, life science, safety evaluation and other basic technology research, aiming to serve the people and improve the life quality of vulnerable groups (Sun, 2019). In addition, the Zizhu HTZ responds to the national strategy to promote industrial transformation and upgrading, such as supporting the research and development of new energy vehicles, providing copyright monitoring services for cultural and creative industries and improving the digital capabilities of the aviation industry in order to realize the social function of new technologies while driving the development of science and technology.

Wuhan East Lake HTZ

Founded in 1991, the Wuhan East Lake HTZ is one of the first state-level high-tech industrial development zones in China. In 2000, the Hubei Provincial Government announced that the Wuhan HTZ would be extended to become the "Wuhan China Optical Valley". In 2020, the GDP of East Lake HTZ increased by 5.1%, taking the lead in Wuhan city to reach 200 billion yuan. Among them, total GDP and growth, total industrial investment and growth, total investment investment and other 7 indicators all ranked first in the city (Official website of Wuhan East Lake HTZ)

East Lake Experience -- Coordinated Development of Industry, Education, and Research

In 2001, the East Lake HTZ united a number of universities to build university science and technology parks with the mode of 'one-zone and multiple-parks' (Zhang and Huang, 2015). At present, successive Wuhan East Lake University parks are being built: the Great Wall Innovation Park, the Science Park of Wuhan University, Huazhong Technology University and Central China Normal University etc. This project has realized the industrialization of research by surrounding campuses with incubation facilities, and developed a relatively mature production-study-research cooperation chain. Since 2009, the government has made many joint investments with universities and enterprises to set up eleven industrial technology research institutes with a modern enterprise system, such as the Optoelectronic Industrial Technology Research Institute, the Wuhan Institute of Biological Technology and so on. Also, it formed a sharing platform for new batches of high-level research institutions and international resources, encouraging schools and enterprises to build industry-university-research associations and communities of shared interests.

The East Lake Experience--Open Access to the IP Navigation Industry

The Wuhan East Lake HTZ guides enterprises to conduct responsible research and innovation, emphasizing open access to technological resources. East Lake HTZ is one of the first batch of patent navigation pilot zones approved by the Chinese government. Based on the analysis and utilization of patent resources, patent navigation applies patents to industrial technology innovation, product innovation, organizational innovation and business model innovation, so as to improve the patent application ability of enterprises.

The HTZ provides a series of supporting infrastructure for the patent navigation industry. It promotes the construction of the Central Center of National Technology Transfer, the Yangtze River Economic Belt Intellectual Property Operation Platform for Universities and other service platforms. It also supports a number of universities to set up intellectual property transformation operation centers (Wang and Chen, 2019). At the same time, it has extensively expanded the commercialization of intellectual property, focusing on promoting patent pledge financing. For example, it has built a comprehensive service platform for patent investment and financing with Wuhan Optics Valley Joint Property Exchange and handled 159 patent pledge loans with the financing amount of more than 1 billion yuan. On the basis of improving the patent layout, the East Lake HTZ guides enterprises to undertake personalized intellectual property evaluation, analysis and early warning according to the senior situation, so as to provide technical support for enterprises with weak innovation ability and help enterprises to carry out the work of patent mining and patent use related to product technology.

Figure 9. IP navigation industry in East Lake
Source: Hua (2021)

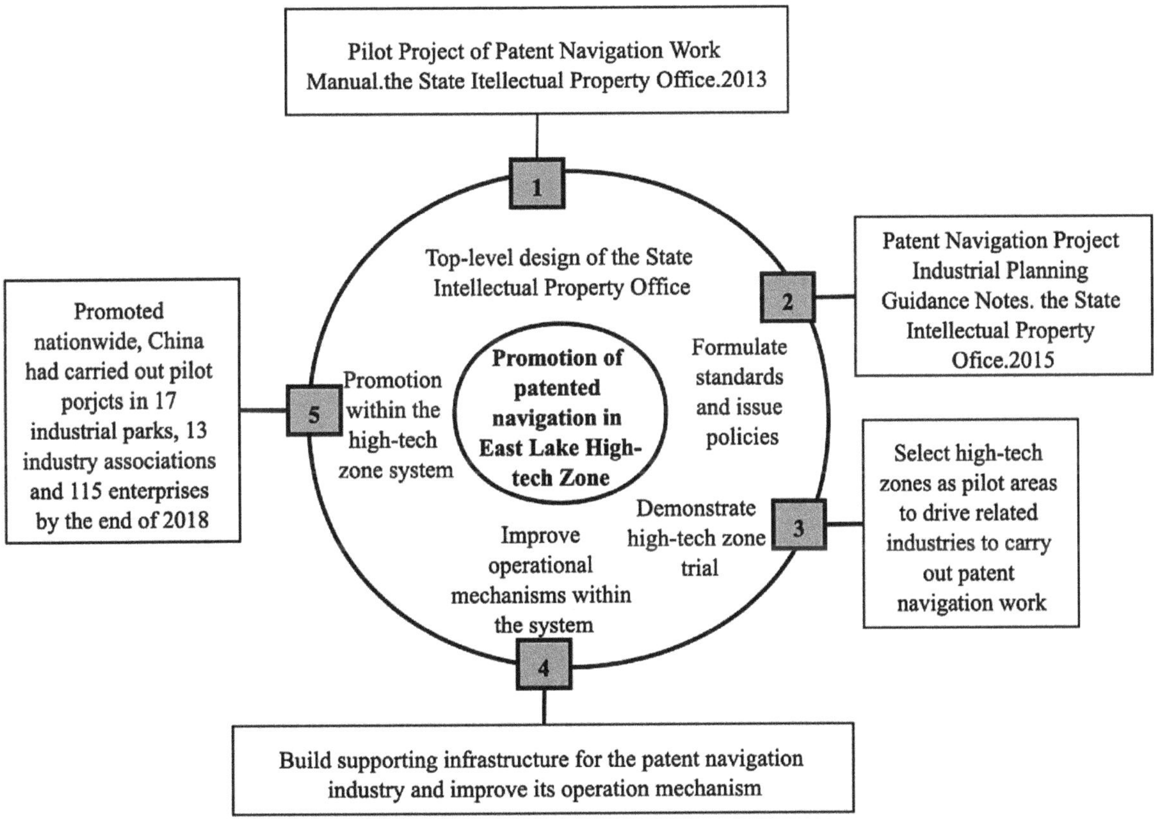

The East Lake Experience -- Top-Down Public Engagement

While guiding enterprises to make efficient use of technological resources, the Wuhan East Lake HTZ also emphasizes public participation in the process of research and innovation. In the process of industrial policy innovation, HTZs will solve most of the problems through democratic decision-making. For example, before the decision is made, a symposium will be held to know different enterprises' needs in relation to the current policy and suggestions for improvement. At the same time, relevant institutions will be consulted to optimize the current plan. These links like solicitation of opinions, participation of stakeholders, and publicity in the East Lake HTZ have greatly enhanced the public participation in research and innovation. In addition, in terms of resource integration, Wuhan East Lake HTZ also brings together major stakeholders from top to bottom. In the first step, the pilot work consultation mechanism between the National Development and Reform Commission and Hubei Province has been established, and the work information notification system has been established to enable the solving of key problems in the construction of the policies. As a second step, a three-parties demonstration and guidance group for entrepreneurship and innovation between Hubei Province, Wuhan City and East Lake HTZ was set up to mobilize forces at all levels to provide support for the HTZ. The third step was to establish an expert decision-making mechanism. This expert consultation committee is composed of domestic and foreign industry experts, scholars, entrepreneurs, and entrepreneurship mentors and regularly advises entrepreneurship and innovation activities in the HTZ (Li, 2017). Through the establishment of top-down stakeholder participation process, the Wuhan HTZ has improved the public governance ability of the zone and effectively integrated resources, thus providing a good social environment for research and innovation in the zone.

Guangzhou HTZ

Established in March 1991 with the approval of the State Council, Guangzhou HTZ is one of the first state-level high-tech industrial development zones, and ranks 6th in the comprehensive evaluation of national HTZs (Torch High-tech Industry Development Center of Ministry of Science and Technology, 2020). On February 18, 2019, the CPC Central Committee and The State Council published the Outline of the Development Plan for the Guangdong-Hong Kong-Macao Greater Bay Area and issued a notice, requiring all regions and departments to earnestly implement the plan in light of actual conditions. In the future, the Guangzhou HTZ will fully connect with the construction of Guangzhou-Shenzhen-Hong Kong-Macao Science and Technology Innovation Corridor, promoting science and technology cooperation and exchanges with Hong Kong and Macao regions, and strive to build a core innovation center hub in the Greater Bay Area.

Experience From the Guangzhou HTZ -- Coordinated Development of Industry, Education and Research

In 2019, to better serve the development of the Guangdong-Hong Kong-Macao Greater Bay Area as an international science and technology innovation center, the Guangdong-Hong Kong-Macao Greater Bay Area Collaborative Innovation Institute was established in the Guangzhou HTZ by the Guangdong Provincial Department of Science and Technology, the Guangzhou Municipal People's Government, the Guangzhou HTZ, the South China University of Technology, the Southern University of Science and Technology, the University of Hong Kong, the Hong Kong University of Science and Technology, the University of Macau and the Beijing Collaborative Innovation Institute. In 2020, there were more than 1,000 scientific research institutions in the region, and eight high-level innovation research institutes recognized by Guangdong Province will be established in the Guangzhou HTZ, accounting for two-thirds of the province, as well as three new national enterprise technology centers, accounting for 40% of the province. Four new National Science Progress Awards were awarded, including three first prizes and one second prize. At present, Guangzhou HTZ has built the largest science and technology incubator cluster in south China. There are 3,599 national high-tech enterprises in the zone, 15 of which are listed in the list of Guangzhou high-tech enterprises.

Experience From the Guangzhou HTZ -- Green Industrialization

The Guangzhou HTZ adheres to the closed circuit circulation system of waste plastic which is called "waste production, raw material production, waste recycling and reproduction". Taking Guangzhou Wanluda Group Co., the leading enterprise of resource recycling in the zone, as an example, it collects waste plastic, iron and steel in the zone for processing and utilization. The waste plastic particles are supplied to Jinfa Technology Co. for modification and processing. Modified plastics are used by Guangzhou Echom Company. The leftover materials and waste plastics produced in the production process of Yichang technology are recycled by Wanluda or Jinfa technology according to different types of the waste materials (Ye and Fan, 2021). For a long period, the Guangzhou HTZ has greatly improved the utilization rate of plastics through this circulation system, which not only saves the cost but also promotes the sustainable development of plastics industry.

Figure 10. The closed-circuit circulation system of waste plastic in the Guangzhou HTZ
Source: Authors' Visualization

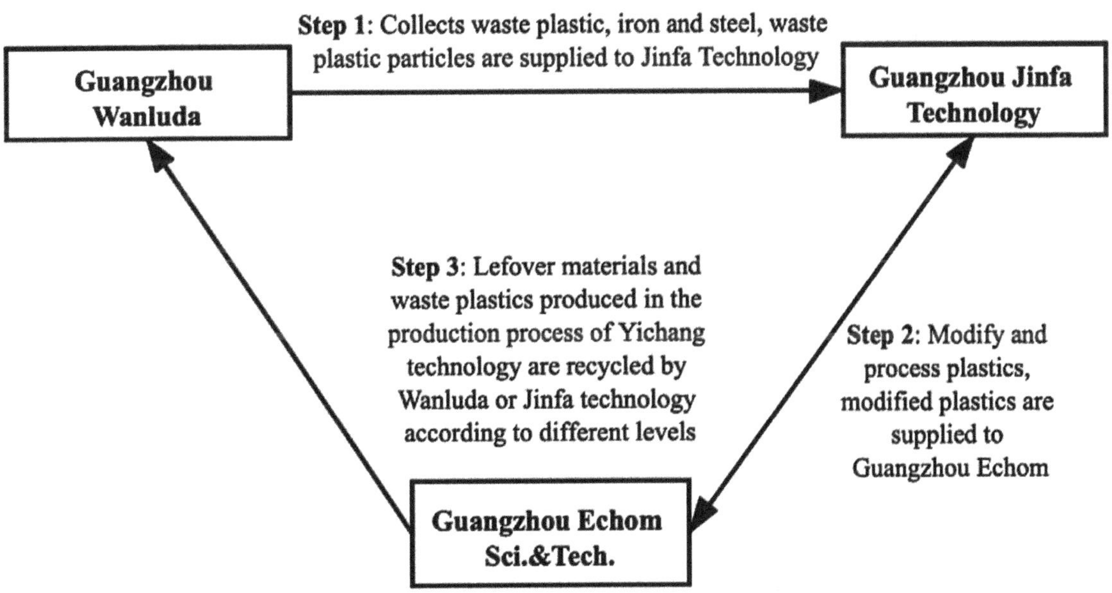

In addition, the Guangzhou HTZ also sets a "green threshold" in the process of attracting investment. Since 2016, the HTZ's government has taken the energy consumption per unit of output value as one of the core indicators of project access evaluation and implemented the one-vote veto system for environmental protection for enterprises. It has also issued policies to promote enterprises to increase investment in green technology innovation, cultivating a number of green industry leading enterprises, segmentation field leading enterprises, and realize the development and growth of green industry. Until the end of 2020, there were more than 200 large-scale enterprises in green industry in the region, with an output value of more than 230 billion yuan, among which there are more than 25 leading enterprises with an annual output value of more than 1 billion yuan (Chen, 2021).

At the same time, beyond the green industrialization, the management of the HTZ has also established a set of green technology platforms, and jointly promoted the transformation of green technology achievements with domestic and foreign universities and institutes. Since 2019, most of these are in the field of green industry. In the next step, the management of the zone plans to organize breakthroughs in key technology research and development by adopting the list-opening system, in order to realize chain-link innovation and promotion of technologies and products. By 2025, the total scale of green industry will exceed 250 billion yuan, and Guangzhou HTZ will be built into a pilot zone for clean energy industry development in the Guangdong-Hong Kong-Macao Greater Bay Area (Ye and Fan, 2021).

Moreover, in 2020, the Guangzhou HTZ also published the biggest regional green financial policy in China--the "Green Finance 10" (Guangzhou government, 2017) and issued the first batch of carbon neutral bonds in the Greater Bay Area. Also, in 2020, the green credit balance and green insurance premium of the Guangzhou HTZ both ranked among the best in Guangzhou. The "Green Finance 10" is the most powerful local green finance policy in China since the State Council approved the five Green Finance Reform and Innovation Pilot Zones in June 2017, and a number of measures in the "Green Finance 10" are national initiatives. In the next stage, Guangzhou HTZ will take the "double carbon[1]" goal as the focus of financial work, explore the effective path of green financial support in industrial parks, promote green financial product innovation (Yu, Weng & Ahuja, 2022; Yu, Jiao & Sampat, 2022), and develop new energy for green economic development (Yu, Xu, Cheng & Sampat, 2023; Yu, Liu, Mahendran & Lu, 2022).

Experience From the Guangzhou HTZ -- Take on Social Responsibility Against COVID

In the battle against COVID in 2020, as the "key town" of the national biomedical industry, the Guangzhou HTZ was one of the first regions in China to organize strong scientific research forces. The Guangzhou HTZ has implemented the requirements of Chinese President Xi Jinping on "taking biosafety as an important part of overall national security, and strengthening the system and capability of disease prevention and control and public health research" (Chen, 2021). In the first step, the Guangdong Provincial Laboratory of Regenerative Medicine and Health, Guangzhou Institute of Biomedical and Health, and The Greater Bay Area Research Institute of Nanoscience Center jointly established two platforms, the Guangzhou Biosafety Innovation Institute and the Nanobiosafety Center, to take the lead in building the National Biosafety Management Pilot Area. About 200 scientific research institutions and enterprises in the district speed up the research on clinical treatments and drugs, vaccine detection technologies and products. The area has thus become the main force of the provincial science and technology supporting COVID control, integrating all-round prevention, screening and treatment of COVID facilities. In terms of clinical treatment and drugs, the first novel coronavirus strain from a locally infected case was isolated by the Guangdong Provincial Laboratory of Regenerative medicine and health, and the new application plan of chloroquine and other already existing drugs was put forward and clinically researched with good results. Dabo, Birnbaum, Sharp, and other eight technology companies became the absolute main driving force of COVID vaccine research and production in Guangdong. Dabo's project of vaccine development and production is listed as a major provincial science and technology projects. Birnbaum's new coronavirus antigen vaccine has an optimized design and has already passed the immune experimentation phase with monkeys. But the zone also boosts testing technology and product development. 47 enterprises in the HTZ account for more than 90% of the province's testing capacity. The daily production of COVID diagnostic testing reagents can reach 2.5 million people, accounting for a quarter of the country's total. In the aspect of animal model construction, the Provincial Laboratory Animal Monitoring Institute and Guangzhou Health Center jointly worked on key problems, established the humanized ACE mouse model by using gene knock-in technology, accelerated the preclinical experiments of COVID vaccine and targeted drugs, and promoted the early clinical application of relevant vaccines and drugs (Official website of Guangzhou HTZ).

FINDINGS: CROSS-CASE ANALYSIS

The Common Experience

This study found that the RRI process in Shanghai Zizhu HTZ, Wuhan East Lake HTZ and Guangdong HTZ is based on collaborative innovation between industry, academia and research institutes. The collaborative innovation in HTZs is mainly based on the sharing of resources among enterprises, universities and research institutes, following the criteria of capital integration, joint public relations, result sharing, benefit distribution and risk sharing, which are jointly accomplished through a contract of division of labour and cooperation (Liang et al., 2019). In this form, enterprises are the technology demanders and universities and research institutes are the technology suppliers. Through the facilities and practice sites provided by the HTZ, enterprises solve key technological problems, break down innovation barriers and maximise the use of innovation factors such as talent, capital and technology (Acs and Szerb, 2007). For example, the Shanghai Zizhu HTZ facilitated the joint construction of the Zizhu Science and Technology Park by Shanghai Jiaotong University and East China Normal University. It has also provided innovation and venture capital to build the Zizhu Business Incubator, which has constructed an integrated research and innovation platform. However, Wuhan East Lake HTZ and Guangdong HTZ have played an irreplaceable role in accelerating regional economic development by adopting the "one zone, multiple parks" model, adopting integrated innovation between industry, university and research, establishing research institutes in multiple universities, breaking the limitations of space and geographical location, expanding the scale of high-tech industries, and improving high-tech research and innovation capabilities. The three HTZs differ in the specific layout of collaborative innovation between industry, university and research, but this is an important strategic support for all HTZs in the RRI process. Therefore, this chapter argues that the current system of collaborative innovation between industry, academia and research in HTZs in first and second-tier cities in China is conducive to promoting the practice of RRI. The differences in specific systems are due to the geographical location and resource layout of the industrial park. The more developed the industrial ecosystem of the park is, the smoother the implementation of RRI will be. Moreover, if the enterprises in the park have successfully carried out the practice of RRI, they can have a synergistic effect on the surrounding enterprises.

Specialized Experience

Setting up HTZs to develop technology while creating employment opportunities is an important national strategy widely used by countries around the world. HTZs are particularly important for developing countries whose R&D resources are relatively limited. China's current HTZ are characterized with different geographical location and market development degree. This complicates drawing specific development experiences and policy suggestions with general applicability. Therefore, this paper will summarize their respective experiences for HTZs under different development modes according to the different characteristics of the three cases.

The implementation of RRI in the Shanghai Zizhu HTZ is mainly embodied in the governance of the park that emphasizes sustainable development, and the RRI of the Wuhan East Lake HTZ is mainly embodied in improving public participation and integrating stakeholder resources, while the Guangzhou HTZ practices RRI through developing green industrialization.

The Zizhu HTZ is an innovative experimental area with sufficient marketization. RRI is not only reflected in promoting innovation itself, but also in the sustainable development of the whole scientific and technological innovation chain, which starts with the initial scientific experiment to the project incubation and the final industrialization. For example, the social problems brought by the transformation of scientific research achievements, the balance of rights, responsibilities and interests and other specific issues are all related to RRI. This feature is also reflected in the special operation mechanism of the Zizhu HTZ: 'government-led, enterprise-dominated, university-involved, market-oriented operation'. Under this mechanism, enterprises in Zizhu need to be responsible for their own profits and losses. The initial investment of these enterprises is mainly supported by the government. The HTZ makes profits by providing office space, corporate finance, real estate and other supporting services for enterprises. In the later stage, enterprises gradually grow larger and realize independent production after scale effect is generated, creating brand effect for the industrial park and playing a role in attracting investment. The company's survival and development are closely tied to the Zizhu HTZ. In this mechanism, the government 'takes a back seat' and transforms the traditional leading role into serving and managing the society and adjusting the market as its main function. This fundamentally changed the government's excessive interference in social economy and internal affairs of enterprises, so that the government can better participate in macro management and industrial ecosystem planning. Enterprises' investment and service efficiency is higher with market-oriented means of development and operation, whose system is more flexible, but also more favored by enterprises (Gao and Zhang, 2020). Therefore, the operation mechanism of the Zizhu HTZ provides a good policy basis for RRI's practice in the zone, and also enables enterprises to change from being motivated to accept the concept of sustainable development to taking the initiative to undertake corporate social responsibility. The government performance of the Zizhu HTZ provides a good model for other HTZs which are relatively more marketized, and the operation mechanism of 'government leading, enterprise dominating, university participating and market-oriented operation" is worthy of reference for other HTZs in China (Gao and Zhang, 2020).

However, the entrepreneurial pattern of Wuhan East Lake HTZ is large but relatively scattered, and its comprehensive supporting service capacity is high. How to effectively integrate RRI into community construction and create a good entrepreneurial culture and atmosphere is the focus of promoting the current RRI. As the Wuhan East Lake HTZ is located in Wuhan city, which belongs to the key demonstration city of the 'rise of central China strategy' (Li, 2017), the East Lake HTZ has a geographical advantage. It not only relies on central government to provide innovative entrepreneurial activity, but also it can rely on dividend policy supported by the government of Hubei province and the preferential policies provided by the Wuhan municipal government, such as actual policy biases or subsidies for the construction of the park. The introduction of the 'Regulations on The East Lake National Independent Innovation Demonstration Zone' (Standing Committee of Hubei Provincial People's Congress, 2015) shows that the three levels of government of 'East Lake District-Wuhan city-Hubei Province' firmly support the national policies and vigorously promote the development and growth of the HTZ. In addition, the government of the HTZ also actively promotes the simplification and standardization of the examination and approval procedures, in order to achieve the optimal integration of resources in the HTZ and remove obstacles for the application of RRI in the HTZ. Therefore, the implementation of RRI in large HTZs whose marketization degree needs to be improved cannot be separated from the support of the superior government. The government's policy inclination gives confidence to enterprises in HTZs, so as to promote enterprises to take up their social responsibilities while enjoying the favorable policies.

The Guangzhou HTZ, on the other hand, carries out RRI layout through green industrialization, constructs green technology platforms and green financial systems, and relies on the advantageous geographical location and policy bias of The Hong Kong-Zhuhai-Macao Greater Bay Area to build the green leading industrial pattern, and can doubly harvest the green environmental protection as well as the economic benefits. As early as 2017, Guangzhou HTZ took the lead in the development of hydrogen industry and took the development of hydrogen industry as an important starting point for cultivating strategic emerging industry, improving the energy structure and realizing the goal of carbon peak and carbon neutrality. The 'Measures for Promoting the Development of Hydrogen Energy Industry' 2.0 version (Guangzhou government, 2021), which have the highest comprehensive strength in China, have been issued successively to implement the whole-chain support for the hydrogen energy industry, and have accumulated more than 100 million yuan of various financial support funds. Therefore, when RRI is practiced in HTZs with mature industrial layout, attention should be paid to making use of existing industrial layout to create green industries and realize clean production (Official website of Guangzhou HTZ).

CONCLUSION

This chapter critically discusses the development of Chinese HTZs. While maintaining a good economic growth rate and innovation transformation rate, enterprises in Chinese HTZs are faced with moral challenges that lack social roles and are difficult to maintain sustainable development. In order to solve these problems, this paper introduces the RRI theory which is popular in Europe and the United States. Although we have never seen a "one size fits all" approach, the experience of developed countries will help China to develop its own RRI standards. Besides, our case study demonstrates that China's RRI practice in HTZs is often based on the coordinated development model of industry-university-research, which provides important innovation factors such as technology, talent and capital, and provides a good industrial ecosystem for RRI. The more complete the industrial ecosystem of the HTZ, the more conducive to the implementation of RRI. For highly market-oriented high-tech development zones, although the focus is on innovation itself, RRI emphasizes the contribution of innovation to the sustainable development of the whole region. At the same time, the RRI practice of companies in the HTZ can have synergy effects on other companies. However, this article does have its limitations. Due to the limited information available to HTZ in China, it is difficult to obtain sufficient data and analyze the potential impact of RRI in a more quantitative way. Future research in this field will focus on how to quantify the impact of RRI on HTZs.

ACKNOWLEDGMENT

The authors extend sincere gratitude to:

- Our colleagues from Soochow University, The Australian Studies Centre of Shanghai University, The European Business University of Luxembourg and Krirk University as well as the independent research colleagues who provided insight and expertise that greatly assisted the research, although they may not agree with all of the interpretations/conclusions of this chapter.
- China Knowledge for supporting our research.
- The Editor and the International Editorial Advisory Board (IEAB) of this book who initially desk reviewed, arranged a rigorous double/triple blind review process and conducted a thorough, minute and critical final review before accepting the chapter for publication.
- All anonymous reviewers who provided very constructive feedbacks for thorough revision, improvement and fine tuning of the chapter.

REFERENCES

Acs, Z. J., & Szerb, L. (2007). Entrepreneurship, Economic Growth and Public Policy. *Small Business Economics*, *28*(2-3), 109–122. doi:10.100711187-006-9012-3

Bai, X. J., Yan, W. K., & Chiu, Y. H. (2015). Performance Evaluation Of China's Hi-Tech Zones In The Post Financial Crisis Era— Analysis Based On The Dynamic Network SBM Model. *China Economic Review*, *34*, 122–134. doi:10.1016/j.chieco.2015.04.001

Chen, J. C. (2017). Innovative Practice and Thinking on the Construction of Zizhu Innovation and Entrepreneurship Corridor. *China Journal of Commerce*, 6.

Chen, L. (2021). Guangzhou High-tech Zone: Strive to Build an Important Engine for High-Quality Development of the Guangdong-Hong Kong-Macao Greater Bay Area. *Guangdong Science and Technology.*

Corrocher, N., Lamperti, F., & Mavilia, R. (2019). Technological Forecasting and Social Change Do Science Parks Sustain or Trigger Innovation? Empirical Evidence from Italy. *Technological Forecasting and Social Change*, *147*, 140–151. doi:10.1016/j.techfore.2019.07.005

European Commission. (2012). *Ethical and Regulatory Challenges to Science and Research Policy at the Globle Level.* European Commission.

Fan, Y. Y., & Zhang, D. (2018). Review of Research on Responsible Innovation and Its Enlightenment to Innovation Management. *Science-Technology and Management,* 20.

Forsberg, E. M., Thorstensen, E., Casagrande, F. D., Holthe, T., Halvorsrud, L., Lund, A., & Zouganelic, E. (2021). Is RRI a New R&I Logic? A Reflection from an Integrated RRI Project. *Journal of Responsible Technology,* 5.

Gao, H. W., & Zhang, Y. L. (2020). Research on Ways to Improve Innovation Ability of High-Tech Zones. *Economic Research,* 5.

Guangzhou Government. (2017). *Policies and Measures for Promoting Green Finance Development in Huangpu District and Guangzhou High-tech Zone.* Author.

Guangzhou Government. (2021). *Measures for Promoting hydrogen Industry development of Guangzhou Development Zone and Guangzhou Huangpu District, 202107.* Author.

Hanson, A. (2019). Ecological Civilization in the People's Republic of China: Values, Action, and Future Needs. Asian Development Bank.

Hellstrom, T. (2003). Systemic Innovation and Risk: Technology Assessment and the Challenge of Responsible Innovation. *Technology in Society*, *25*(3), 369–384. doi:10.1016/S0160-791X(03)00041-1

Hua, Z. L. (2021). Exploration and Practice of Patent Navigation Theory in Universities -- A Case Study of North China Electric Power University. *Science and Technology in Chinese Universities, 3.*

Jia, H. R., Liu, Z. X., & Xia, B. H. (2014). Research on Responsible Innovation in China Wireless Valley. *Natural Dialectics Research*, *33*(9), 55.

Li, P., & Liao, M. (2021). Rethinking the Reflexivity of Responsible Innovation. *Journal of Dialectics of Nature,* 43.

Li, Z. G. (2017). Construction Experience and Enlightment to the Western Region of Wuhan East lake Hi- Tech Development Area Mass Entrepreneurship and Innovation Demonstration Base. Chongqing Academy of Science and Technology, 3, 629-635.

Liang, B. B., Chen, Y., Xie, K. F. & Liang, D. (2019). Analysis on the Influence Mechanism of Cooperative Innovation in High-tech Zone: A Case Study of East Lake National Innovation Demonstration Zone. *Science and Technology Management Research,* 15.

Liu, Z. X. (2015). A Review of Responsible Innovation Research: Background, Status and Trends. *Science and Technology Progress and Countermeasures*, *32*(11), 155.

Loureiro, P. M., & Conceição, C. P. (2019). Emerging Patterns in the Academic Literature on Responsible Research and Innovation. *Technology in Society*, *58*, 58. doi:10.1016/j.techsoc.2019.101148

Lu, X. H., Chen, D. L., Kuang, B., Zhang, C. Z., & Cheng, C. (2020). Is High-Tech Zone a Policy Trap or a Growth Drive? Insights from the Perspective of Urban Land Use Efficiency. *Land Use Policy*, *95*, 95. doi:10.1016/j.landusepol.2020.104583

Luo, S. H. (2020). Zizhu High-Tech Park Promotes Sustainable Development Through Scientific And Technological Innovation. *China Sustainability Tribune,* 11.

Luo, S. Y. (2019). Industry and City Integration under the Requirement of High-quality Development Implementation Path Study. *East China Science & Technology,* 9.

Mei, L., Chen, J., & Sheng, W. Z. (2014). Responsible Innovation-An Emerging Paradigm for Research and Innovation. *Natural Dialectics Research*, *30*(10), 83.

Official website of Guangzhou HTZ. (2020). http://www.gddidg.com

Official website of Wuhan East Lake HTZ. (2020). http://www.wehdz.gov.cn

Official website of Zizhu High-Tech Zone. (2020). http://www.zizhupark.com

Sergio, E. S., Ana, V. J., Joaquim, R. S., & Carlos, A. G. (2020). Technological Forecasting and Social Change Open Innovation in Science Parks: The Role of Public Policies. *Technological Forecasting and Social Change*, 151.

Shen, Z. P., Jian, X. B., & Zhao, J. (2018). Study on the Construction Modes of China's Overseas Co-operation Industrial Parks along the Belt and Road. *International Urban Planning,* 33.

Siggelkow, N. (2007). Persuasion with Case Study. *Academy of Management Journal*, 50.

Standing Committee of Hubei Provincial People's Congress. (2015). *Regulations on East Lake National Independent Innovation Demonstration Zone.* Author.

Stigoe, J., Oven, R., & Machaghten, P. (2013). Developing a Framework for Responsible Innovation. *Research Policy*, *42*(9), 1568–1580. doi:10.1016/j.respol.2013.05.008

Sun, J. (2019). Path Identification of Government Promotion of Business Incubation: Multiple Case Studies in Zhangjiang, Zizhu and Wujiaochang. *Shanghai Economy,* 1.

Sun, Y. J. (2019). Research on the Path of Establishing Science and Technology Service System in Industrial Park - Take Zizhu High-Tech Park as an Example. *Science & Technology Vision,* 8.

Wang, D., & Chen, R. S. (2019). Exploration and Practice of Patent Navigation Industry Development Model - Taking Wuhan East Lake High Technology Development Zone as an Example. *China Invention & Patent,* 16.

Wang, L. C., Liu, L., & Wu, C. S. (2021). Research on Evaluation of High-quality Development of National High-tech Zones in the New Economic Environment: Empirical Research on 10 National High-tech Zones. *Science and Technology Management Research*, *3*, 33–39.

Wang, Q., & Gao, X. (2019). Is It Possible To Build An Innovation Responsibility Community? The Necessity and Reality of the Western Theory of Responsible Innovation. *Journal of Nantong University,* 35.

Wei, K. B., Rianne, A. M., Myriam, C., & Theo, A. (2019). Towards a Segmentation of Science Parks: A Typology Study on Science Parks in Europe. *Research Policy*, *48*(3), 719–732. doi:10.1016/j.respol.2018.11.004

Xie, K. F., Song, Y., Zhang, W. Y., Hao, J. H., Liu, Z. M., & Chen, Y. (2018). Technological Entrepreneurship in Science Parks: A Case Study of Wuhan East Lake High-Tech Zone. *Technological Forecasting and Social Change*, *135*, 156–168. doi:10.1016/j.techfore.2018.01.021

Xiong, B. G., & Luo, Y. D. (2021). Promote the Innovative Development of My Country's Eco-Industrial Parks with "Responsible Innovation". *Ecological Economics*, *37*, 68–73.

Yang, C. H., & Lee, W. H. (2021). Establishing Science Parks Everywhere? Misallocation in R&D and its Determinants of Science Parks in China. *China Economic Review*, *67*, 6. doi:10.1016/j.chieco.2021.101605

Ye, Q., & Fan, M. L. (2021). Take the Lead in Layout to Support Guangzhou High-Tech Zone to Green Industry to Economic Benefits. *Science and Technology Daily, 7*.

Yu, J., Liu, S. B., & Wang, Q. (2016). Research on the Innovation Evaluation Index System of Enterprise Leaders in Dalian High-Tech Zone. *Science and Technology Management Research, 20*, 37.

Yu, P., Jiao, A., & Sampat, M. (2022). The Effect of Chinese Green Transformation on Competitiveness and the Environment. In P. Ordóñez de Pablos, X. Zhang, & M. Almunawar (Eds.), *Handbook of Research on Green, Circular, and Digital Economies as Tools for Recovery and Sustainability* (pp. 257–279). IGI Global. doi:10.4018/978-1-7998-9664-7.ch014

Yu, P., Liu, X., Mahendran, R., & Lu, S. (2022). Analysis and Comparison of Business Models of Leading Enterprises in the Chinese Hydrogen Energy Industry. In R. Felseghi, N. Cobîrzan, & M. Raboaca (Eds.), *Clean Technologies and Sustainable Development in Civil Engineering* (pp. 179–216). IGI Global. doi:10.4018/978-1-7998-9810-8.ch008

Yu, P., Weng, Y., & Ahuja, A. (2022). Carbon Financing and the Sustainable Development Mechanism: The Case of China. In A. Rafay (Ed.), *Handbook of Research on Energy and Environmental Finance 4.0* (pp. 301–332). IGI Global. doi:10.4018/978-1-7998-8210-7.ch012

Yu, P., Xu, S., Cheng, Z., & Sampat, M. (2023). Does the Development of New Energy Vehicles Promote Carbon Neutralization?: Case Studies in China. In A. Pego (Ed.), *Climate Change, World Consequences, and the Sustainable Development Goals for 2030* (pp. 109–131). IGI Global. doi:10.4018/978-1-6684-4829-8.ch006

Zhang, L., & Huang, G. Q. (2015). Research on Collaborative Innovation Mechanism of In-Depth Integration of Industry, Education and Research in 'One-Zone, Multiple-parks' of East Lake National Independent Innovation Demonstration Zone. *Science Technology and Industry, 15*.

Zheng, S. L., & Li, Z. C. (2020). Pilot Governance and the Rise of China's Innovation. *China Economic Review, 63*, 63. doi:10.1016/j.chieco.2020.101521

Zhuang, L., & Ye, C. (2020). Changing Imbalance: Spatial Production of National High-Tech Industrial Development Zones in China. *Land Use Policy*, 94.

ENDNOTE

1 China plans to reach peak carbon use by 2030 and become carbon neutral by 2060.

Chapter 13
Research on Cross-Industry Digital Transformation Under the New Normal:
A Case Study of China

Poshan Yu
https://orcid.org/0000-0003-1069-3675
Soochow University, China & Australian Studies Centre, Shanghai University, China

Yanjuan Zhang
Independent Researcher, China

Michael Sampat
Independent Researcher, Canada

Yijun Chen
Independent Researcher, China

ABSTRACT

This chapter aims to study the implications of digital transformation across businesses in China. This chapter will attempt to explore whether and how social capital can become a major driving force in designing a whole new digitally competent social fabric under the new normal in China. By analyzing the institutional impacts driven by the Chinese government, this chapter will explore how these impacts will achieve to generate any synergic effects when conducting digital transformation in business sectors. This chapter will use bibliometric analysis to perform statistical and correlation analysis on the cross-industry digital transformation. Cases from China will be used for comparison. This chapter will provide suggestions for the sustainable development of digital transformation-based business ecosystems in emerging economies.

DOI: 10.4018/978-1-6684-7422-8.ch013

INTRODUCTION

Since the beginning of the 21st century, especially after the international financial crisis in 2008, the proportion of the digital economy in the composition of the world economy has continued to rise and has become an important driving force for the reform of the world mode of production (Wang, 2018). Although China has entered a mature period of digital economy development after 2013, there has been little progress in its digital transformation (Hu, 2018). It was not until 2020, when the COVID-19 epidemic significantly accelerated the digitization of the global economy and trade (China Academy of Information and Communication Technology (CAICT), 2021), that China began to produce many policy documents on digital transformation. In the outline of the 14th Five-year Plan of the People's Republic of China for National Economic and Social Development and the long-term goals of 2035 issued in March 2021, China for the first time made a systematic layout of digital development and proposed to welcome the digital age. The overall change in the mode of production, lifestyle and governance driven by the digital transformation (Zhongguancun Alliance for the Integration and Development of Information Technology and Real Economy (AIITRE) & China Enterprise Federation, 2021) has indeed made it clear that the digital transformation will be one of the main tasks of the country in the future.

China has only begun to make major moves related to digital transformation in the past two years, and there are few complete articles and periodicals related to this topic, and the content of this chapter can be used as a supplement. Considering the characteristics of China's national conditions, this chapter focuses on the synergy of Chinese policy, government role, government, and enterprises. This paper combs the Chinese policy in recent years to facilitate readers to have a general understanding of the process of digital transformation in China. Considering the essential difference between Chinese state-owned enterprises (SOEs) and western enterprises, it is reflected in that SOEs have to take into account many goals and tasks, cannot make a large number of innovative attempts, and choose a limited range of social venture capital (China Central State owned Companies Digital Development Academy, 2021), this chapter introduces the performance of Chinese SOEs in the process of digital transformation, and provides some reference value for western countries. Returning to the essence of digital transformation, digital technology occupies an important position. As Accenture argues, the role of digital technology is rapidly shifting from improving marginal efficiency to promoting fundamental innovation and subversion. Combined with the case of China, this chapter introduces the innovation brought about by the integration of digital technology and business in China. Finally, an overview of the characteristics of China's digital transformation, the article puts forward some suggestions for China.

BACKGROUND

With the rapid development of cloud computing, big data, artificial intelligence, 5G and other digital technology, the digital wave characterized by digital networking, information and intelligence has swept the world (Cloud Computing and big data Research Institute of China Academy of Information and Communications, 2021). In addition, the COVID-19 epidemic has also accelerated the process of digital transformation. Opinion papers (Fletcher & Griffiths, 2020), reports of advisory and opinion-makers (UN opinion Governors 2020 McKinsey Digital, 2020), and statements of respected personalities from the worlds of science and business (Martin-Barbero, 2020) have confirmed that the COVID-19 pandemic has undoubtedly led to organizational change, forced a redefinition of business strategy, and acted as a catalyst for digital transformation in many areas of the economy, health care, and education (Renata, 2020). By 2020, the global digital economy has accounted for more than 40% of GDP (Figure 1). The digital economy has become an important power source of world economic growth and the trend of digitization has been irresistible.

Figure 1. The internal structure of global GDP in 2020

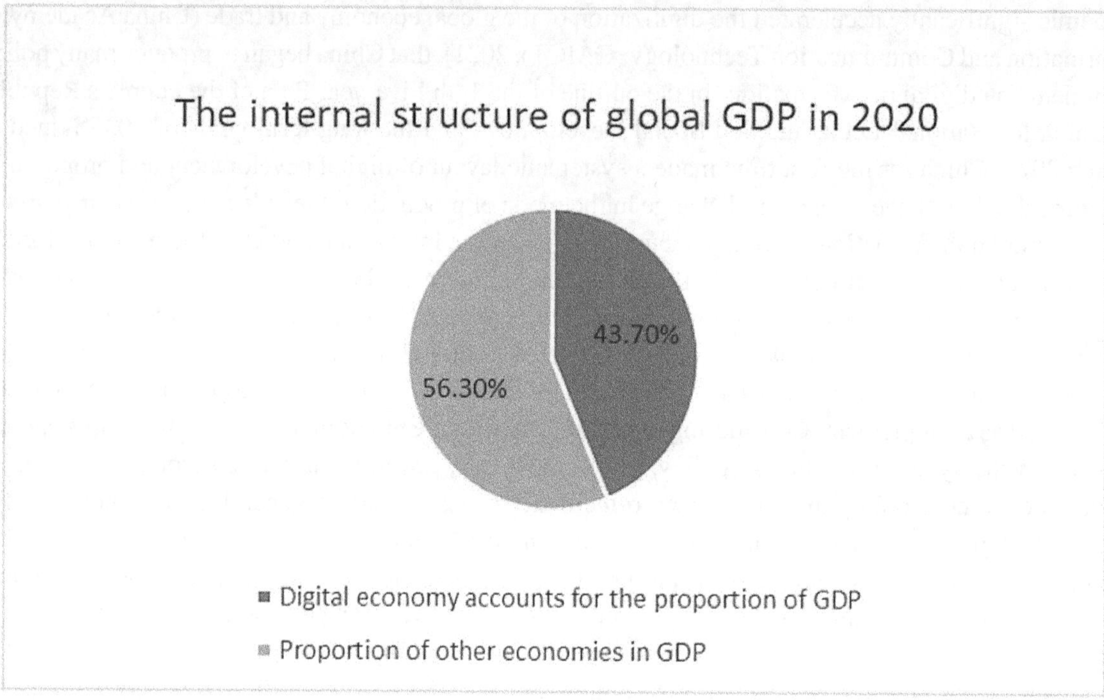

Source: CAICT

CHINA'S DIGITALIZATION MOTIVES

COVID-19 Accelerates Digital Transformation

The "Black Swan" incident of the epidemic in 2020 has brought great challenges to China's economic and social activities. However, historical experience has repeatedly shown that every major public crisis will prompt new growth opportunities (Wang & Wen, 2020). During the epidemic, all kinds of offline behaviors were transferred to online due to travel restrictions. Various offline activities in the past, from catering (Yu, He & Sampat, 2022), shopping and entertainment (Yu, Wang & Hanes, 2022; Yu, Tang, Tang & Hanes, 2022) to office, education (Yu, Kwok & Jiang, 2022; Yu, Gu, Sampat, Lin & Chen, 2022; Yu, Lu, Hanes & Gu, 2022), medical care (Yu, Xue & Mahendran, 2022), finance (Yu, Lu, Hanes & Chen, 2022), and conferences, have been largely online, reshaping people's concepts of use and consumption. People's consumption behavior has shifted online, digital education business digital medical care, digital entertainment, digital finance, digital office, and other digital services have also been revolutionized, forming a new model of a new business type (Cloud Computing and big data Research Institute of China Academy of Information and Communications, 2021).

For enterprises with different fields and different degrees of digital transformation, the outbreak of the COVID has tested the achievements of digital transformation in recent years (Yu, Kwok & Jiang, 2023; Yu, Liu & Hanes, 2022; Yu, Liu, Hanes & Mumtaz, 2022; Yu, Chen, Sampat & Misuko, 2022). The online digital system fully supports and ensures the production and management of enterprises during the epidemic, highlighting the value of enterprises in promoting digital transformation in response to the crisis (Institute for Global Industry & Tsinghua University, 2020). According to Ma et al. (2020), although the economic impact of the epidemic is mainly negative, there are also some industries and enterprises with the help of online sales, telecommuting and other digital means to alleviate the economic losses during the epidemic as much as possible, and some even achieve reverse growth. One example is the empirical test of Chang and Meyerhoefer (2020) based on the data of Taiwan's largest agricultural and non-staple food e-commerce platform. They found that for each additional confirmed case of COVID-19, sales of the platform increased by 5.7 percent and the number of customers increased by 4.9 percent, with demand for grains, fresh fruits, vegetables, and frozen foods growing the fastest. Also, according to the statistics of the Mob Research Institute, during the Spring Festival epidemic prevention period, the sales of the "JD.com[1] to Home" platform increased by 470% compared with the same period last year (Wu et al., 2020).

To sum up, the value of digitization has been fully reflected in the process of fighting the epidemic of COVID-19. In the "Research Report and Cases of Management Accounting Industry" issued by the Accounting Department of the Ministry of Finance of China (2020), almost all the enterprises interviewed expressed their intention to attach importance to the development of digital transformation and invest in digital projects. Facts have shown that industries with a high degree of automation, a high degree of digital origin, and wide popularity generally suffered less damage during the epidemic period. According to the data of the China Association of Small and Medium-Sized Commercial Enterprises, the proportion of enterprises returning to normal business operation and management within three months under the impact of the epidemic, and the recovery rate of enterprises with high digital maturity can reach 60%, while that of enterprises with relatively low digital maturity is only 48% (Figure 2). Driven by the epidemic, China is speeding up its digital transformation on the one hand to resist the impact of the epidemic on the economy and society, and on the other hand to adapt to the new opportunities brought about by the COVID-19 epidemic for the development of the digital economy (Yu, Chen & Ahuja, 2022; Yu, Ge, Mandizvidza & Mulli, 2023).

Figure 2. Recovery of enterprises within 3 months under the impact of the epidemic

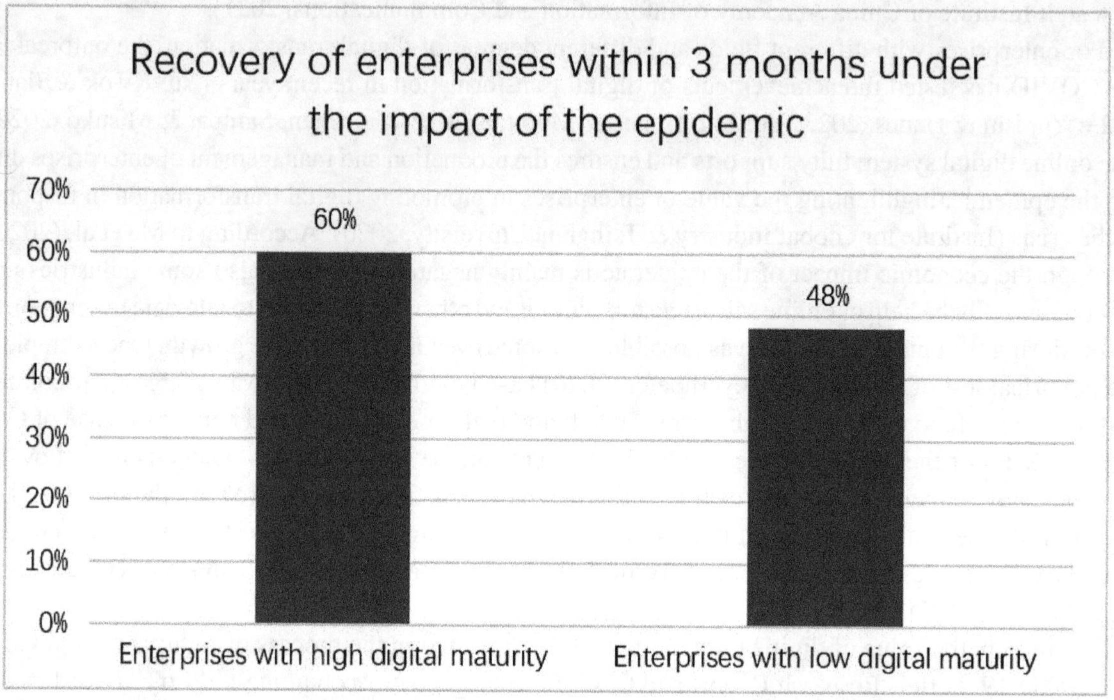

Source: China Association of Small and Medium-sized Commercial Enterprises

Requirements Under the New Economic Situation

The global economy is accelerating its transformation from an industrial economy to a digital economy. With the new generation of information technology as the core, a new round of scientific and technological revolution and industrial reform is on the rise, showing five trend characteristics of "reform bureau, high technology, strong industry, excellent policy and new economy" as a whole (AIITRE & China Enterprise Federation, 2021). The reform accelerates the transition from an industrial economy to a digital economy, from the development mode of scale economy with specialization as the core to the development mode of scope economy with diversification and innovation as the core (AIITRE & China Enterprise Federation, 2021). China's digital transformation is not only a new opportunity for the development of its economy but also a necessary measure to ensure its competitiveness.

On the one hand, China's economic development has entered the stage of changing from high-speed growth to medium-to-high-speed growth, and from a resource economy to a scientific and technological innovation economy. Under the guidance of the idea of sustainable development, China's economy is developing in the direction of high quality with a more complex division of labor and a more reasonable structure, and the growth model has also changed from scale and speed growth to quality and efficiency intensive growth. At the same time, the rapid change of Internet technology has injected new vitality into the traditional business model, and the traditional industry has been able to cooperate with the Internet to carry out Internet marketing with lower cost and more transparent information on the Internet platform (Zhao, 2020). From a macro point of view, the integration of informatization and industrialization in

China has gradually deepened and entered a new stage with digital transformation as the core. Therefore, in this process, the digital economy has developed rapidly, the efficiency of resource allocation has been improved, and the structure of economic development has been optimized, which conforms to the needs of China's economic development (Zhang, 2020).

On the other hand, the pattern of competition and cooperation in the world has evolved deeply. The balance of international power has been profoundly adjusted, the status of emerging countries has risen steadily, and the world competition situation has intensified. Economic globalization has encountered countercurrent, and the stability of the supply chain is also facing severe challenges (AIITRE & China Enterprise Federation, 2021). In this situation, any country should actively take measures to ensure its international competitiveness, and China is no exception. What's more, the real economy with manufacturing as the main body is still the core of national competition, and digital transformation plays a more important role in improving the efficiency of the traditional real economy. Digitalization is the development trend of the future, and the development of traditional agriculture, industry, and service industries with the integration of digital technology will help to achieve substantial improvement in production efficiency (Ma et al., 2020). Under the pressure of the world situation, it is inevitable for China to actively carry out digital transformation.

What's more, with the escalation of trade frictions between China and the United States and the rapid development of China's technological strength, as well as the problem of mutual trust between China and the United States caused by the recent epidemic, it is expected that the technological decoupling between China and the United States will be further accelerated. The technological restrictions imposed by the United States on China are also gradually increasing. In this case, the situation of Chinese enterprises using locally customized solutions to replace the original Western enterprise packages in the digital transformation is gradually increasing (Strategy &, 2020; Yu, Yu & Sampat, 2022).

In 2020, China's digital economy reached 39.2 trillion yuan, accounting for 38.6% of GDP, maintaining a high growth rate of 9.7% (China Internet Network Information Development Association (CNNIA), 2021).

VISUAL ANALYSIS OF THE RESEARCH HOTSPOT OF DIGITAL TRANSFORMATION

Time Series Distribution of Literature

From the point of view of the time distribution of the number of posts, the research on digital transformation began gradually in 2017, as shown in Figure 3. This may be because around 2017, countries around the world begin to transform their layout digitally, and the policies they have issued can confirm this.

For example, in 2016, the U.S. released the Federal Big Data R&D Strategic Plan, the National Artificial Intelligence R&D Strategic Plan, preparing for the Future of Artificial Intelligence, and the U.S. National Machine Intelligence Strategy to build a policy system based on open innovation, aiming to promote the transformation of traditional industries and effectively drive the development process of digital transformation (Advanced Manufacturing, 2021). The UK government released the UK Digital Strategy in 2017, proposing to build a first-class digital infrastructure, carry out advanced skills training and effective regulation to build the UK's digital competitive advantage (Department for Digital, Culture, Media & Sport, 2017). The European Commission formally introduced the European Industrial Digitalization Strategy in 2016, aiming to integrate the industrial digitalization strategies of EU member states and accelerate the process of industrial digitalization in Europe (Wang et al., 2019). In 2017, the Russian government released the Strategy for the Development of the Information Society of the Russian Federation 2017-2030 and the Digital Economy Plan of the Russian Federation (Advanced Manufacturing, 2021).

Obviously, in 2020 and 2021, the research heat on digital transformation has doubled. This is undoubtedly closely related to the previously mentioned COVID-19's acceleration of the digital transformation of the world. It can be expected that the topic of digital transformation will still attract people's attention in the future.

Figure 3. Time series distribution of literature on digital transformation

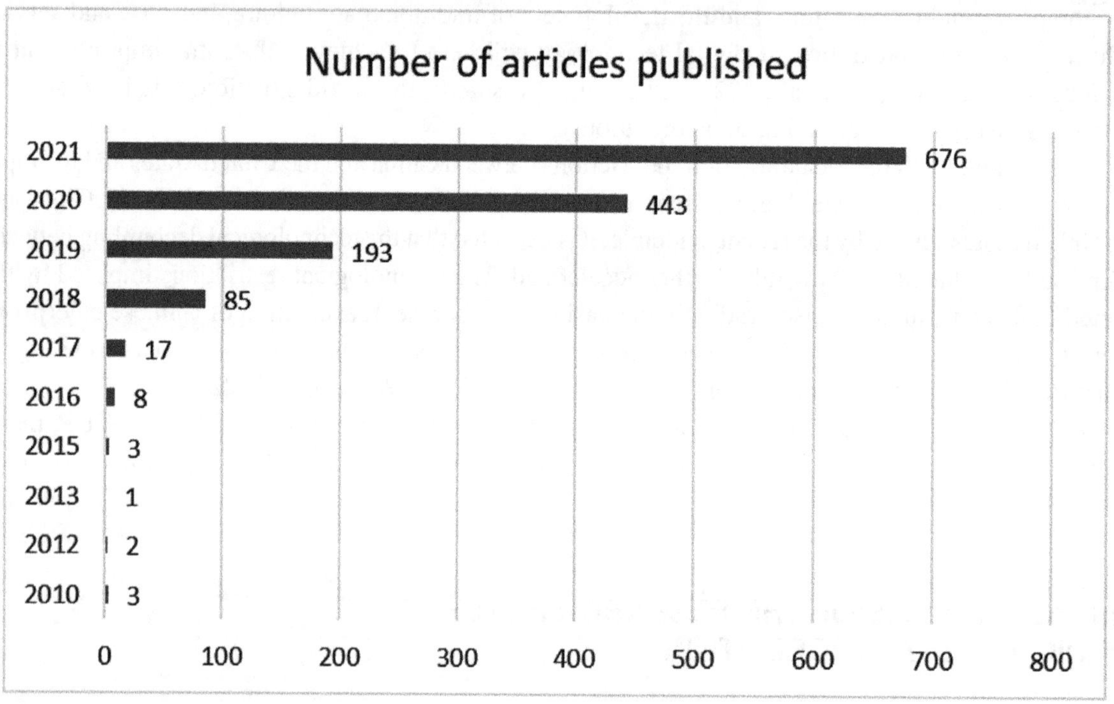

Source: Web of Science, 2021

Countries and Institutions That Conduct Research

The distribution of research in different countries and institutions can be identified through the network map of national and institutional cooperation generated by CiteSpace. Set the network nodes as institutions and countries, and the resulting national and institutional cooperation network map is shown in Figure 4.

Figure 4. Countries and institutions that conduct research

Source: Web of Science, 2021

A total of 384 nodes and 1441 connections are generated in the figure. The larger the nodes in the picture, the more documents the countries or institutions send, and the thicker the connections between the nodes, the closer the links between countries or institutions, and the greater the intensity of cooperation. As can be seen in Figure 4, Germany, the United States, Italy, and the United Kingdom are at the forefront and are the main forces in the research of digital transformation, while China ranks sixth.

From the distribution of institutions, we can see that colleges and universities are the main force in the research of management accounting, in which Univ Queensland, Politecn Milan, Copenhagen Business Sch, UCL and so on are at the forefront.

Keyword Analysis

Keywords are the core words that summarize the main points and research contents of the paper. Through the statistical analysis of the keywords in the literature by CiteSpace software, we can find the key nodes, that is, the hot spots in the research. The frequency of keyword occurrence is directly proportional to the research heat, and the higher the keyword frequency is, the stronger the research heat is. According to statistics, from 2010 to 2021, the words that appeared more than 100 times were “innovation”, “technology", "industry 4.0", "management", "performance", "system" and "big data" (Figure 5). To some extent, these high-frequency keywords reflect the focus and research tendency of scholars.

Cluster analysis of keywords, the results are shown in the figure. The digital transformation and business model innovation, COVID-19's influence on the digital transformation, the innovation of the digital transformation and so on are hot research topics.

Figure 5. Key words of research on digital transformation

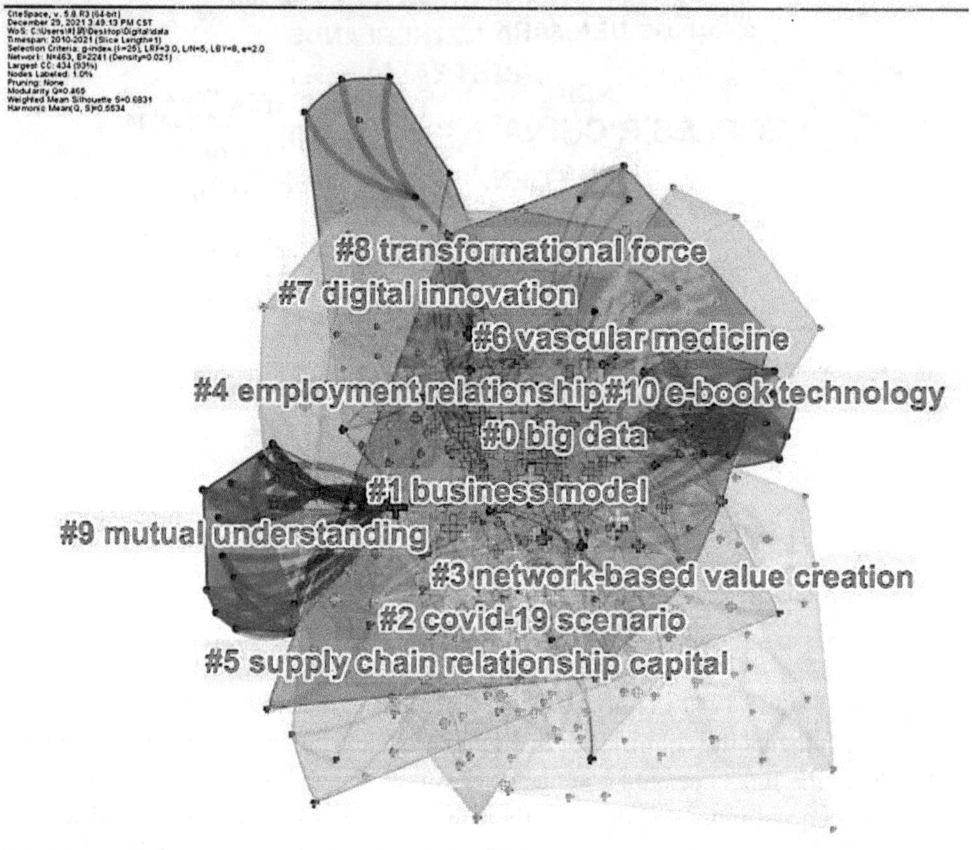

Source: Web of Science, 2021

POLICIES ANALYSIS RELATED TO CHINA'S DIGITAL TRANSFORMATION

Review of Policies

In China, the development of policies related to the digital economy has roughly experienced three stages of evolution (Hu, 2018).

The first stage is the initial stage of information construction. At the beginning of the entry of the Internet into China, the relevant policies mainly focused on information construction, including the construction and support of information infrastructure, services, and industries, such as mobile communication networks, spatial information infrastructure, software industry, and so on. For example, in July 2001, The General Office of the State Council forwarded the Notice of Opinions on Promoting the Construction and Application of China's National Spatial Information Infrastructure issued by the State Planning Commission and other departments, aiming to strengthen the construction of spatial information infrastructure.

The second stage is the in-depth stage of e-commerce development and information construction. The release of "Some Opinions of the State Council on Accelerating the Development of Electronic Commerce" in 2005 indicates that the development of the digital economy represented by electronic commerce has become an important part of the national strategy. With the vigorous development of the Internet industry, information construction has entered a new stage. Based on the in-depth improvement of infrastructure, the state has made important plans for the sharing of information resources and the disclosure of government information (Yu, Gu, Zhao & Ahuja, 2022).

The third stage is a new stage in the development of the digital economy (so far). Since the first important discussion on the development of the world digital economy in 2015, the digital economy has gradually risen to the national strategic level, and the policy content of this stage is mainly based on industrial planning and guidance. And formed a relatively clear industrial development direction and development goals. As mentioned earlier, the outbreak of the COVID-19 epidemic in 2020 has greatly promoted the process of China's digital transformation. The number and content of policies in recent years can also reflect this. As the policy of the third stage is of more research significance, the author combs some of the digitization-related policies issued by China during this stage, as shown in Table 1.

In the years after 2015, China's policies focused on the construction of basic digital facilities such as big data and artificial intelligence. In 2020, China clarifies the digital transformation development plan for enterprises. From 2021, China mapped out a further practical path, emphasizing a cross-industry development path, while improving relevant regulatory policies.

Table 1. An overview of some important policies in the new stage of digital economy development

Release Time	Policy Document	The Main Content
July 2015	Guidance on actively promoting the "Internet +" Action	"Internet +" collaborative manufacturing.
September 2015	Platform for Action to promote the Development of big data	Promote the application of big data in all aspects of industrial R & D, manufacturing, product life cycle and the whole process of the industrial chain.
January 2017	Big data Industrial Development Plan 2016-2020	Big data industrial development plan.
July 2017	Development Planning of New Generation Artificial Intelligence	China will speed up the upgrading of industrial intelligence and promote artificial intelligence to secure the major needs of manufacturing powers.
March 2020	Special Action Plan for Digital Empowerment of Small and Medium-sized Enterprises	Cultivate and promote many digital platforms, system solutions, products and services that meet the needs of small and medium-sized enterprises.
April 2020	On the implementation Plan for promoting the Action of "Shangyun Yongshu Fuzhi" to cultivate New Economic Development	Vigorously cultivate the digital economy new business type, further promote the digital transformation of enterprises, build a data supply chain, and lead the upstream and downstream of the industrial chain and the digital ecosystem of cross-industry integration with data flow.
September 2020	Circular on accelerating the Digital Transformation of State-owned Enterprises	China will promote digital product innovation, intelligent production and operation, agile user service, and an ecological industrial system.
January 2021	Action Plan for the Innovation and Development of Industrial Internet (2021 - 2023)	Put forward five aspects, 11 key actions and 10 key projects, strive to solve the deep-seated and difficult problems in the development of the industrial Internet and promote industrial digitization.
February 2021	Antitrust Guide in the Field of the Platform Economy	Further, clarify the principles of anti-monopoly law enforcement in the field of the platform economy, refine the analysis ideas pertinently, provide clearer guidance for operators in the field of platform economy to operate by the law, enhance the pertinence of law enforcement, and enhance the scientific nature of supervision.
March 2021	Outline of the 14th Five-Year Plan (Chapter on "Accelerating Digital Development and Building Digital China" chapter)	To meet the digital age, activate the potential of data elements, promote the construction of a strong network, and drive the overall transformation of production, lifestyle, and governance with digital transformation.
September 2021	Law of the People's Republic of China on data Security	China's first law on data security marks that China has laws to follow in the field of data security, providing a regulatory basis for data security in various industries.
November 2021	Big data Industrial Development Plan during the 14th Five-year Plan	Strengthen the application of big data in all aspects of the manufacturing industry; take the digital transformation of the manufacturing industry as the guide to cultivate professional and scene big data solutions.
December 2021	The National Informatization Plan of the 14th Five-year Plan	The plan specifies the development goals and main directions of the 14th Five-Year National Informatization, deploys 10 major tasks, and specifies 17 key projects such as the 5G innovation and application project as important grasps for implementing the tasks, and identifies 10 priority actions.

Source: according to the official websites of the State Council, Ministries and Commissions; Yu, Gong & Sampat (2022)

Under the wave of digitization, the local level is also constantly strengthening the strategic guidance of the digital economy, and local authorities have issued their own digital policies. However, due to the different levels of economic development in different places, the focus of planning often varies. Take Beijing, Guangzhou, and Shenzhen as examples.

As the capital of science and technology, Beijing enjoys the advantages of national policy and financial support and talent gathering. Beijing's policy focuses on "concentrating superior resources to break through a number of key core technologies in niche areas" (Zhou, 2021), making an example to address the shortcomings of high-tech.

Among Beijing, Shanghai, Guangzhou and Shenzhen, the urbanization rate is the lowest in Guangzhou. In the local 14th Five-year Plan, Guangzhou mentioned "urban and rural areas" 58 times, paying more attention to speeding up the digital construction of urban and rural areas and bridging the digital gap.

Shenzhen, as a talent gathering place with a strong Internet atmosphere, especially mentioned in the digital policy that it is necessary to "vigorously develop the network security industry, form a number of internationally competitive network security backbone enterprises, and create a network security industry gathering area" (Wang, 2022).

New Infrastructure

In terms of investment, new infrastructure construction will be a hot spot for China's investment in the next few years. On the one hand, investment is needed to promote economic growth; on the other hand, new infrastructure fits the demand for digital transformation and gives social capital more room for investment.

New infrastructure, including information infrastructure, convergence infrastructure and innovation infrastructure, includes seven specific directions: 5G, big data, artificial intelligence, industrial Internet, ultra-high voltage, new energy vehicle charging pile, high-speed rail transit (Xia et al., 2020). Starting from 2020, provinces and cities began to deploy new infrastructure intensively, issued new infrastructure construction roadmaps one after another, and promised to invest hundreds of billions of yuan or even trillions of yuan. For example, Chengdu and Zhejiang Province plan to complete new infrastructure investments of 1.13 trillion yuan and 1 trillion yuan respectively during the three years from 2020 to 2022 (Sun, 2022). According to China Center for Information Industry Development (CCID) (2020), by 2025, direct investment in the seven major areas of new infrastructure will reach about 10 trillion yuan, driving investment to accumulate or exceed 17 trillion yuan. It is worth noting that in May 2021, four national departments jointly issued the "Implementation Plan for the Arithmetic Hub of the National Integrated Big Data Center Collaborative Innovation System", which aims to balance the mismatch between demand and supply in the east and west and reduce the average cost of arithmetic. The related "East Data and West Computing" project was officially launched in February 2022, which greatly promoted the development of new infrastructure (Yu, Gu, Zhao & Ahuja, 2022).

Among the seven major areas of investment, 5G, high-speed rail transit, extra-high voltage, and new energy vehicle (Yu, Xu, Cheng & Sampat, 2023) charging piles have received the most attention, and investment in these areas has been massively rolled out (Huang, 2022). Taking 5G as an example, by the end of 2021, China had built and opened a total of 1.425 million 5G base stations, accounting for more than 60% of the world (Operation Monitoring Coordination Bureau, 2022). Beijing, Shanghai, Guangzhou and Shanghai have been in the leading position. In December 2021, these four cities were selected as the first "Gigabit Cities" in China. According to data released by the Communications Administration, by the end of September 2021, Beijing had built 47,000 5G base stations, ranking first in the country (Wu, 2021). Shenzhen achieved full coverage of the city's 5G independent group network in August 2020 (Shi, 2020). By the end of November 2021, Shanghai had built more than 52,000 5G outdoor base stations and 120,000 indoor small stations (Yu, 2021). The China Academy of Information and Communications predicts that the cumulative investment in 5G network construction in China will reach 1.2 trillion yuan by 2025, which will lead to a cumulative investment of more than 3.5 trillion yuan (China Business Network (CBN), 2022).

In the context of new infrastructure, the main beneficiary sectors are Internet Data Center, 5G, IoT, and F5G (the fifth generation of the fixed network). China also does reflect its international competitiveness in these sectors.

In terms of the scale of the Internet data center (IDC) market, the world continues to thrive, and China is growing rapidly. The global IDC market in 2021 is USD 67.93 billion, and the CAGR[2] from 2017 to 2021 is 9.9%. In 2021, China's IDC market is 301.27-billion-yuan, accounting for 33% of the world, and the CAGR from 2017 to 2021 is 33.6%, which is higher than the average global IDC growth rate (Huang, 2022). It is expected that CAGR will remain at around 24.8% from 2022 to 2024. The 5G era is the turning point of global technological power, while China's deep TDD[3] technology in 3G and 4G has become the global 5G core standard. Huawei and ZTE represent the acceleration of the rise of technology. The global 5G patent share ranking in 2022 is shown in Table 2. In the F5G segment, according to the "Top 10 Most Competitive Companies in Global/China Optical Communication in 2020" published by the Optical Communication Committee of the China Communications Society, four of China's companies have entered the list, as shown in Table 3. The number of global and Chinese IoT connections is exploding. According to the GMSA forecast, the global IoT industry will reach $1.1 trillion in 2025, with IDC forecasting that China's IoT spending is expected to reach 26.7% of the global share, ranking first (Huang, 2022).

Table 2. 2022 Global 5G patent share ranking (company)

Ranking	Company	Patent Share (%)
1	Huawei (China)	14.61
2	Samsung	12.98
3	ZTE Corporation (China)	11.89
4	LG Electronics	10.68
5	Nokia	9.98
6	Ericsson	6.94
7	Qualcomm	6.00
8	Intel	4.04
9	Sharp	3.47
10	NTT Docomo	3.35
11	Oppo (China)	3.00
12	China CATT (China)	2.65

Source: IPlytics & Research Department of CITIC Securities

Table 3. Global fiber optic cable industry 2018-2020 market share distribution

Company	Domestic Ranking	Global Ranking	Market Share (%)
Yangtze Optical Fibre and Cable (YOFC)	1	3	9
Hengtong Optic-electric	2	4	8
Fortis	3	7	7
Fiberhome	4	9	6

Source: Optical Communication Committee of China Communications Society & Foresight Industry Research Institute

THE ROLES OF GOVERNMENT IN DIGITALIZING BUSINESS AND INDUSTRIAL ECOSYSTEMS

Facilitators

First of all, the policies issued by the Chinese central government play a clear guiding and leading role in the innovation and construction of digital business and industrial ecosystems. For example, in April 2020, the General Office of the Ministry of Industry and Information Technology issued a "Special Action Plan for the Digital Empowerment of Small and Medium-sized Enterprises". This policy puts forward the action plan of enterprise digitization for the first time, which defines the direction for the digital transformation of small and medium-sized enterprises (SMEs). In September 2020, SASAC issued the "Circular on Accelerating the Digital Transformation of State-owned Enterprises", further clarifying the path and direction for SOEs with the background of SOEs, such as central enterprises and local SOEs, to implement digital transformation. After the release of the central document, it soon received feedback from the local government. After the local government interprets the central policy, it issues the local policy according to the local situation. Central enterprises and local state-owned assets also actively respond to the policy and release the company's relevant measures and achievements. For example, China Merchants Group issued "Digital Building New Competitiveness to Promote the Construction of World-class Enterprises" (Miu, 2021), and SAIC issued "Seeking Results in New Changes to Promote SAIC's High-Quality Development through Digital Transformation" (Chen, 2021) and so on. China's top-down government governance model makes the whole process respond quickly, for the relatively blank areas, the leading effect of government policy is obvious. On the other hand, for regions with a medium or higher level of development, companies benefit by establishing political connections with the government, which is mainly reflected in the fact that political connections can bring access, taxation, financing, subsidies, mergers and acquisitions, and other policy facilities for companies (Yao & Ye, 2021). In this way, government policies can stimulate and promote the development of digital business and industrial ecosystems.

In 2016, the Government work report released by the State Council formally put forward the "Internet + government service". In October 2017, the 19th National Congress of the Communist Party of China proposed for the first time the construction of a digital government. Since then, China has attached great importance to the work of "Internet + government service", and the special study has issued a series of policy documents around the construction, development and management of "Internet + government service" (Yu, 2021). It mainly includes: "Guidance of the State Council on Accelerating the Work of "Internet + Government Services", "Several Provisions of the State Council on Online Government

Services" and so on. Digital government is an important part and core hub of digital China. Through the digital transformation of national governance means and governance mode, digital government leads and drives the all-around coordinated development of digital economy, digital society, digital ecology, and digital culture (Wang, 2022).

Participants

First, the government itself participates in the digital transformation. According to Wang and Tang, the government occupies a leading position in the process of government governance, mainly following the top-down hierarchical management model under the traditional government governance model, and the fragmentation is obvious, especially since the reform and opening up. There is an obvious boundary between the government, the market and the society, resulting in a blank field of governance (as cited in Wei & Guo, 2021). The rapid penetration and wide application of digital technology provides a good opportunity for the reform of government governance. In the era of the digital economy, the digital transformation of the government is the only way for the reform of governance. Digital technology innovation provides an important technological driving force for the digital transformation of the government and promotes the innovation of the means, technology, institutional structure, and values of government governance (Wei & Guo, 2021). Moreover, as a member of a key role ("social partner") that benefits society, once society faces the challenges posed by the new industrial revolution, it needs to enhance its digital knowledge and capacity to address the new situation of the digital economy (Mas & Gómez, 2021).

Second, in the process of developing digital government, the government is not only a provider of digital platforms but also a consumer of digital government-related products. For example, Internet companies such as Tencent and Alibaba have deeply participated in the practice of digital government construction using technological empowerment (Yao & Ye, 2021). So, for the government, through the rethinking and reengineering of the existing process, the introduction of digital technology to build a one-stop, integrated online government service platform, through "data running instead of human running", to meet the convenience needs of the public. For enterprises, in all aspects of product design, production, promotion and service, the digital platform can quickly gather users' needs, reduce intermediate consumption, optimize resource allocation in a more flexible and broader range of time and space, and improve production and management efficiency (Zhai et al., 2021). From the perspective of inter-organizational relations, cross-border between organizations continue to produce (Li et al., 2020), and inter-organizational cooperation is also more frequent, constantly developing towards a win-win direction.

Third, as we know, the laissez-faire approach does not apply to the digital economy. That is to say, when the market cannot allocate resources within a reasonable range or is plagued by externalities and information gaps, the government must intervene in the name of fairness and equity as well as social, political and social cohesion (Spence, 2021). So, of course, this confirms once again that the Government must be a participant. In digital business activities, data provides convenience, but it also brings new problems, such as personal privacy and national security issues. From the perspective of privacy economics, Acquisti et al. (2016) believed that the sharing and protection of personal data can have a positive and negative impact at the individual and social levels. The sharing of these data can reduce market friction and promote transactions, but on the other hand, its private value may be reduced. What the government needs to do is to grasp the yardstick of data sharing and try to avoid doing more harm than good. In terms of national security, it is a race to promote innovation and timely regulation. To address this problem, Chinese regulators effectively allow innovation to happen and regulate when things get messy. The delayed listing of Ant Financial Services Group in 2020 has changed the model, and Chinese regulators are setting capital requirements for financial technology entities to deal with the regulatory gaps caused by excessive innovation (RMB Trading and Research, 2020). In addition, the transnational cooperation of sovereign governments can reduce trade barriers and facilitate the development of the digital economy market (Spence, 2021).

Regulators

As a trusted institution, the Chinese government has the right to manage data directly or to monitor and access data when needed, and the Chinese government's intervention in the digital economy has created favorable conditions (Spence, 2021). The government, as a regulator, controls market access conditions, supervises intra-market platforms, and limits its abuse of power by relying on data advantage. As suggested by Tenet and Polonetsky (2012), policymakers should regulate some of the most basic concepts of privacy law, including the definition of "personally identifiable information", the role of consent and the principle of purpose limitation and data minimization, to strike a balance between the useful use of data and protect personal privacy (as cited in Spence, 2021). In November 2021, the Personal Information Protection Law of the People's Republic of China was formally implemented, which laid the legal foundation of China's network society and digital economy.

CORPORATE REACTIONS TO DIGITALIZATION

Background of Enterprise Digital Transformation

In 2017, the 19th National Congress of the Communist Party of China put forward the goal of a new round of state-owned enterprise reform, that is, to cultivate world-class enterprises with global competitiveness. Central enterprises are the focus of the reform and should be built as a model. In June 2020, the State-owned Assets Supervision and Administration Commission of the State Council issued the "Circular on carrying out World-class Management Promotion Action for Standardization". It is pointed out that central enterprises need to target world-class enterprises from eight aspects, such as strategic management, organizational management, operation management, risk management and so on. In August 2020, the State-owned Assets Supervision and Administration Commission issued the "Circular on Accelerating the Digital Transformation of State-owned Enterprises", which clearly put forward the basis, direction, focus and measures for the digital transformation of SOEs, guided SOEs to accelerate the transformation and upgrading of traditional drivers, and cultivated new drivers of development in the era of digital economy (China Software Research Institute, 2022). The outline of the 14th Five-year Plan for National Economic and Social Development of the People's Republic of China and the long-term goals of 2035 make a systematic layout of digital development for the first time and propose to use digital transformation to drive changes in the mode of production, way of life, and the way of governance.

In addition to the domestic policy and environmental incentives for developing the digital transformation process, there are also emerging technological development needs, industry competition, digital advantages of enterprise development and other factors, which the author will not repeat here.

The Process of Enterprise Digital Transformation

In September 2021, Shanghai issued "Several Policies and Measures for Promoting Urban Digital Transformation in Shanghai", formally launched the data capitalization of pilot SOEs, and strived to double the revenue of the core industries of the digital economy in five years, and more than 80% of SOEs initially realized digital transformation (Zhang, 2021). In the same month, Beijing SASAC issued "The Implementation Opinions on Accelerating the Digital Transformation of Municipal Management Enterprises", promoting the deep integration of the digital economy and the state-owned economy, and comprehensively enhancing the industrial basic capacity and the modernization level of the industrial chain (State Capital Jingjing, 2021). While the local level is constantly increasing, the promotion at the ministerial level is also increasing. In October 2021, SASAC of the State Council and the Ministry of Industry and Information Technology signed the Agreement on Strategic Cooperation on accelerating the Integration and Digital Transformation of Central Enterprises to jointly accelerate the digital reform of SOEs. Various phenomena demonstrate that the pace of digital transformation of SOEs is accelerating.

As an important pillar of China's national economy, SOEs are changing from leaders in the industrial age to leaders in the digital age. This is not only the responsibility of SOEs, but also meets their needs, and they have a better foundation and advantages than other enterprises. "To a certain extent, the digital transformation of enterprises is equivalent to starting a second business, and the degree of difficulty and complexity can be imagined." In an interview with Outlook Newsweek, Lu Feng, deputy director of the Electronic Information Research Institute of the Saadi Research Institute of the Ministry of Industry and Information Technology, said. McKinsey reported that in their previous survey, the success rate of corporate digital transformation was only 20% in 2016. In this context, it is not the responsibility of SOEs to set an example for Chinese enterprises to carry out digital transformation. On the other hand, the larger enterprises, the more collaborative problems, the more resources can be shared, and the greater the benefits brought by digital transformation. Therefore, as PricewaterhouseCoopers (PwC) said (2019), in the general situation of state-owned enterprise reform, capacity optimization and changes in the international situation, the demand for digital change in SOEs has been stronger than in other enterprises. In recent years, SOEs have actively promoted the innovative application of a new generation of information and communication technology (ICT), accelerated the digitization of production and operation, and made great efforts to cultivate a new digital model, new business type, which has laid a relatively solid foundation for digital transformation. Finally, according to Yang Jidong, "the cycle of digital transformation is long, the cost is high, and more sustainable resources are needed." SOEs have relatively richer internal resources, including capital investment, facilities and equipment investment, and so on." "If the previous digital transformation is dominated by private enterprises, then SOEs will become another main battlefield of digital transformation in the future." Pan Helin, executive dean of the Institute of Digital Economics, Central South University of Economics and Law, said (Shang, 2022).

By 2021, the index of digital transformation of SOEs has been 40.83%, 8.58% higher than the national average. Most SOEs are in the transition from deepening scene application to comprehensive integration, flexible collaboration and integrated operation in enterprise-level main business areas (AIITRE & China Enterprise Federation, 2021). Based on the results of the digital transformation of SOEs, to summarize the experiences and practices of digital transformation of SOEs and play an exemplary and leading role in SOEs, the Science and Technology Innovation Bureau of SASAC issued a "Typical Case of Digital Transformation of State-owned Enterprises In 2020" in March 2021. There are 100 typical cases in 8 categories, including product and service innovation, intelligent production and operation, digital marketing services, digital ecology, new generation information technology, industrial control security, integrated management system, etc., including 30 excellent cases and 70 typical cases (Science and Innovation Bureau of SASAC, 2021).

In these officially recognized cases, we can see that some Chinese companies have slowly found the path of transformation and have achieved good results. For example, China Three Gorges Corporation has significantly improved its operational efficiency by building a cloud platform for the management of a cross-basin cluster of giant power plants. The achievement is an integrated application of cloud computing, big data, Internet of things, mobile Internet, and artificial intelligence as the representative of a new generation of information technology, which has saved 325 hours of overhaul time, 36 million yuan of inventory, 30 million yuan of controllable management costs, more than 700 million yuan of financial costs, and 95.66% of inventory material guarantee rate in the year after it was put into use in 2020 (Industrial Internet Theory, 2021). Sinochem Energy High-Tech Co., Ltd. has successfully realized digital transformation by building the “66 Cloud Chain” platform. The platform has built China’s first digital infrastructure for the energy-chemical supply chain covering “vehicle-ship-warehouse closed-loop logistics”. It empowers credible warehouses with blockchain, IoT and other credible technologies, and at the same time derives “blockchain digital warehouse receipt” tools. By the end of February 2022, 66 Cloud Chain has successfully implemented a digital warehouse receipt pledge lending business with 6 banks, with the accumulated lending amount exceeding 420 million yuan, effectively solving the pain points of financing difficulties and expensive financing for energized SMEs, and effectively helping the development of real economy (10000link, 2022).

However, these cases are not exhaustive, and Chinese SOEs still face many difficulties in the early stages of digital transformation. According to the research feedback, Chinese SOEs lack a deep understanding of digital transformation, there are large differences in understanding within the enterprise, the inability to find the entry point for the integration of digital technology and business scenarios, and the difficulty of internal organizational collaboration and breaking the existing departmental boundaries and interest barriers, which are the main obstacles to digital transformation within the enterprise (Niu et al., 2021b). Moreover, the transformation of Chinese enterprises is more like figuring out the road, and it is hard to find mature cases as references for the digital transformation of SOEs. Even the typical cases released by officials can hardly cover the digital transformation needs of different enterprises in various scenarios (Niu et al., 2021a).

COLLABORATIVE DIGITAL DEVELOPMENT IN GUANGDONG-HONG KONG-MACAO GREATER BAY AREA

Many urban scholars believe that with the advance of globalization, megalopolises around the world are forming (Hall, 2009; Wu & Zhang, 2007; Xu & Yeh, 2010) (cited by Hui et al., 2020). In China, a new, trans-regional metropolitan area called Guangdong-Hong Kong-Macau Greater Bay Area (GBA) is developing. The GBA is a new metropolitan area and one of the most important growth poles for Chinese economic growth and technological innovation. It consists of nine cities in the Pearl River Delta (PRD) and two special administrative regions of Hong Kong and Macao. “One country, two systems, three customs zones” is its motto (Lin, 2017), and it will become the largest and most influential metropolitan area in the world (Zhao & Su, 2020).

This part will introduce the case of collaborative digital development of the GBA in China and study how the development of a business ecosystem based on digital transformation can help improve the whole economy.

Policy Background

As we know, China has a centralized government system and a strong state intervention in urban decision-making. China's urban governance system is characterized by strong leadership (Wu, 2000; Xu & Yeh, 2005), involving multi-level governance (e.g. national, provincial and municipal). Therefore, it is necessary to understand the policy background of GBA development.

The construction of the GBA is a major national strategy. It was formally proposed in 2017, but the official launch came in 2019, marked by the release of the "Outline of the Development Plan for the Greater Bay Area of Guangdong, Hong Kong and Macao" by the Central Committee of the Communist Party of China and the State Council. This is a programmatic document to guide the cooperation and development of the GBA, from spatial layout, building an international center of science and technology innovation, accelerating infrastructure interconnection and interoperability, building a modern industrial system with international competitiveness, promoting ecological civilization, building a quality living area that is pleasant to live, work and travel, cooperating closely to participate in the "Belt and Road" construction and building a platform for development cooperation among Guangdong, Hong Kong and Macao (Deloitte, 2021).

As mentioned earlier, China's consistent style of governance exhibition is that the central government plans the development pattern and all levels of government issue updated policies to ensure the implementation of the plan on the ground. This is the synergy between the central and local levels. According to the analysis of public data on government websites, since the outline of the plan in 2019, as of April 2021, Chinese governments at all levels have issued 231 policy documents related to the GBA (Figure 6). Among the 231 documents, the top three areas of concern are employment and entrepreneurship, financial and taxation support, and science and technology innovation, accounting for 23%, 13%, and 11% respectively. The 66 policy documents issued at the provincial level focused on science and technology innovation, employment and entrepreneurship, and modern industry (Wang & Han, 2021).

Under layers of policies, the digital transformation of the GBA is hotly underway. According to Tu et al. (2021), by 2020, nearly 80% of the traditional industries in the GBA will have gradually digitized their industries. In April 2022, Guangdong Province issued the "Guangdong Province Digital Economy Promotion Regulations", which upgrades the relatively mature policy measures related to the digital economy into a more normative legal system to provide legal protection for the development of the digital economy. This also reflects that the digital development of the GBA is already on the right track.

Figure 6. Number of policy documents issued by governments at all levels

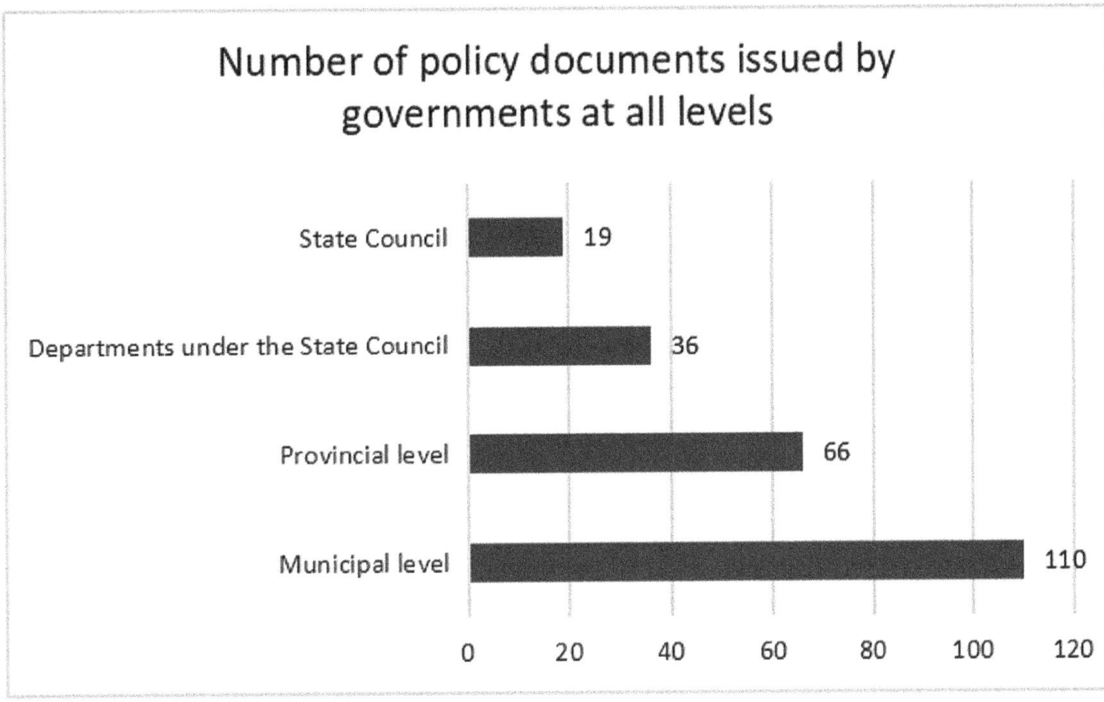

Source: China Government Website

How Digital Transformation Enhances the Economy

'The Strong Ones Help Create Other Strong Ones' Brings Industrial Transformation

The GBA's "the strong ones help create other strong ones" model applies to both city and enterprise development. Between cities, it manifests itself in the direct industrial upgrading of first-tier cities through industrial spillover to other cities and in the win-win situation brought by urban industrial cooperation. As Hong Kong and Macao have already realized the industrial upgrading of the modern service industry, when it turns to the transformation of the manufacturing industry, we talk more about the PRD city cluster. From the perspective of urban spatial patterns, the PRD city cluster presents a twin-city structure with Shenzhen and Guangzhou as the core. Under the twin-city structure, second-tier cities are often linked to the nearest economic growth pole (Guo et al., 2020). Foshan and Dongguan, as second-tier cities in the PRD city cluster, directly benefit from the spillover effects of the leading cities and become the third and fourth cities in Guangdong with GDPs over a trillion (CBRE, 2022). In the case of Shenzhen and East Ivana, for example, Shenzhen has significant industrial spillover effects due to land area constraints. East Ivana was able to introduce many powerful Shenzhen enterprises, such as Huawei, ZTE, OPPO, and so on, which undertook the manufacturing of a large number of technological R&D achievements and directly realized the transformation from foundry to smart manufacturing (Poly Investment Consultancy Research Institute et al., 2019).

Concerning urban cooperation, Chinese state institutions have extensively mobilized different discourses of intercity cooperation to seek spatial resources for development, such as the Twin Cities

Strategy (Shen, 2014) and the Cities Helping Cities Program (Zhang & Sun, 2019). In the case of the Pearl River Delta, the risk of joint construction of cross-border industrial parks by local countries lies in the potential industrial complementarity between cities (Zhang et al., 2020). That is, the fundamental reason for cities to engage in industrial cooperation comes from the fact that industrial clusters bring great benefits, including lower investment costs, facilitating access to specialized labor, knowledge, and technology, resulting in access to common suppliers, developing a specialized workforce, generating technology and knowledge spillovers, and improving competitiveness (Amin & Thrift, 1995; Bell et al., 2009; Casanueva et al., 2013; Connell & Voola, 2013; Gertler, 2003; Tallman et al., 2004). Indeed, the complete industrial chain has become a resounding signature of GBA. Taking Xinbao Electric as an example, 260 components are needed to produce a high-end coffee machine, of which 40% of the components are procured locally in Shunde, 50% of the components are procured without leaving Foshan City, and 80% of the components are procured without leaving Guangdong Province. The advantages of a small procurement radius and low cost make the enterprises in the industrial cluster more competitive in the market (Guangdong Guangdong-Hong Kong-Macau Hong Kong-Macau Greater Bay Area Research Institute, 2022). On this basis, the GBA has also created several core strategic platforms in regions with a good innovation base, and the "Guangzhou-Shenzhen-Hong Kong" and "Guangzhou-Zhuhai-Macau" science and technology innovation corridors provide the impetus for science and technology innovation in the GBA (CRIC in Shenzhen, 2022). Patents represent technological change and development and are important indicators of innovation activities (Enzmann & Moesli, 2022). We may visualize the urban cooperation in the GBA through patent cooperation, as shown in Table 4. Digital information transmission, wireless communication networks and data processing are popular research areas for GBA. In October 2021, the Chief Executive's Policy Address 2021 proposed the construction of a northern metropolitan area and a spatial pattern of Hong Kong-Shenzhen "twin cities and three circles" (Xu & Sun, 2021), which implies a further deepening of the cooperation between Shenzhen and Hong Kong in the future.

Table 4. Cross-city patent cooperation

Cities Involved	Patent Cooperation Rate (‰)	Main Directions of Cooperation
Guangzhou & Dongguan	6.8	Data processing systems and methods, measurement tests, electrical digital and data processing, circuit devices, cable and wire installation, conductive connections, etc.
Guangzhou & Foshan	7.7	Measurement tests, calculations, data processing systems and methods, circuit devices, electro-digital data processing, medical preparations, medical pharmaceuticals, heating or ventilation system applications, etc.
Shenzhen & Dongguan	3.71	Lighting devices, wireless communication networks, electro-digital data processing, etc.
Shenzhen & Hong Kong	54.06	Electro-digital data processing, data processing systems and methods, digital information transmission, data recognition, image communication, biomaterials, etc.
Macau & Zhuhai	15.45	Electro-digital data processing, digital information transmission, data recognition, polymer compound combination, image data processing and generation, electrical component manufacturing, etc.

Source: Clarivate Analytics Patent Database (2016 - 2020) & GDI Think Tank

The development pattern of "the strong ones help create other strong ones" among enterprises is mainly reflected in the helping role of the leading enterprise. GBA's road to science and technology creation can't be separated from the leadership of Huawei, Tencent, Guangzhou Automobile, Gree and other fields, which play a key role in accelerating the formation of the science and technology innovation ecology of "scientific research peak + technology transformation", the industrial ecology of "giant engine + hardware innovation" and the digital ecology of "platform drive + business incubation" (China Development Institute (CDI), 2022). On the one hand, according to Shenzhen's experience, the professional and technical service industry is a bridge between two major areas of the digital economy (Tang & Dai, 2021), and many SMEs can find nodes in the huge industrial chain of leading enterprises, thus achieving huge innovation across many disciplines (Fan, 2022). On the other hand, leading digital enterprises provide information technology conditions for manufacturing enterprises, creating momentum for industrial digital transformation. In 2019, the Department of Industry and Information Technology of Guangdong Province and Alibaba Cloud Computing Co., Ltd. jointly announced the launch of the "Guangdong Industrial Cluster Digital Transformation and Upgrading Plan". By March 2020, Ali cloud service users will exceed 250,000 and industrial enterprises will reach 60,000, injecting new momentum for the digital transformation of manufacturing industries in the GBA from scratch, from zero to scale and clustering (Ali Research Institute & 21st Century Institute of Economics, 2020).

The GBA's urban synergy has clearly been successful, especially in advanced manufacturing. In 2020, the GBA showed strong economic resilience in the face of the pressure of the epidemic (Deloitte, 2021). All nine cities in the GBA achieved positive growth, except for Hong Kong Macau, which had negative GDP growth due to the high impact on the service sector, as shown in Figure 7.

Figure 7. GDP growth rate in different regions of the GBA in 2020

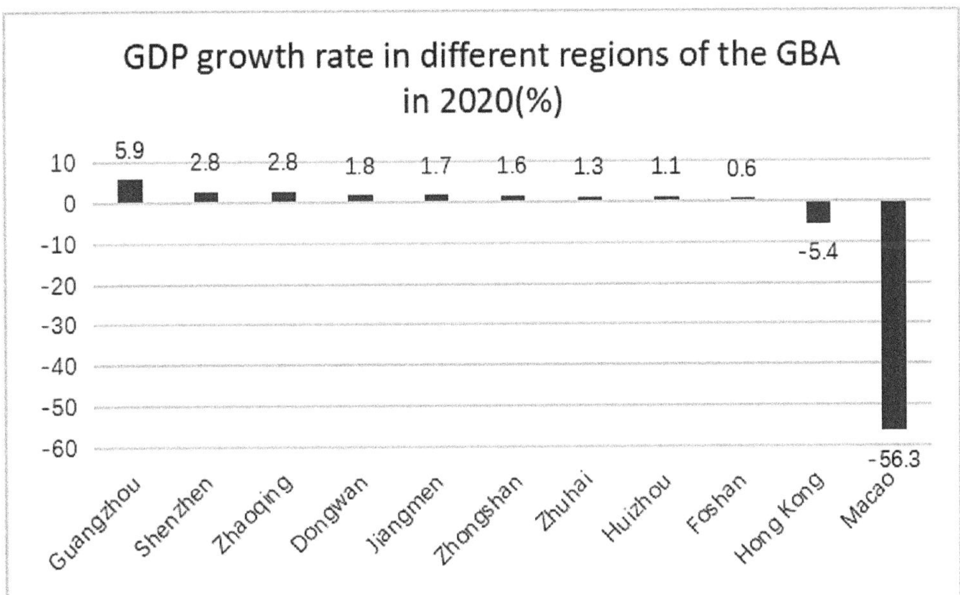

Source: National Bureau of Statistics of China, Statistics Department of the Government of the Hong Kong Special Administrative Region, Governo da Região Administrativa Especial de Macau Direcção dos Serviços de Estatística e Censos & IMF

New Industry Hotspots Under the Trend of Industry Clusters and Digitalization

There is no doubt that digital transformation is bringing new demands to various industries, resulting in new markets. Combined with the strong cluster development characteristics of GBA, this section gives examples of two industrial hotspots.

There is a coupling relationship between urban economic growth and transportation infrastructure development (Guo et al., 2020). In the GBA, the need for a dense and efficient integrated transportation system is more prominent, as it is not only a new way to promote regional connectivity, integration and cooperation but also helps the GBA to compete in the global market (Hui et al., 2020). While the transportation system continues to improve, it is accompanied by the problem of increasing traffic pressure (Ping An Securities, 2019). In addition, the smart city boom and 5G Internet technology have likewise added to the development of intelligent transportation. With the support of Chinese policies, the future of intelligent transportation development is bright.

Currently, enterprises in the GBA prioritize the transformation of manufacturing mode among the six transformation directions, accounting for about 56% (Tu et al., 2021). The real estate industry, as the largest manufacturing industry in China, is the front-runner in digital transformation and upgrading. On the one hand, in 2021, under the main tone of "Housing, Housing without Speculation and City-Based Policies", the real estate market in the GBA cools down and the downward pressure intensifies (CRIC in Shenzhen, 2022). On the other hand, the technological penetration of emerging technologies such as cloud computing, big data, IoT, artificial intelligence, 5G, BIM and other technologies in the real estate industry has expanded the data acquisition sources and application scenarios in the real estate industry, bringing opportunities for industry transformation and upgrading (Zhang et al., 2020). According to TMT Post (2021), China's top real estate companies have started digital transformation to maintain sustainable and healthy corporate development, transforming from development and construction-oriented to a service-operating enterprise, and achieving an organic combination of standardization and refinement. The fast-growing GBA attracts a large influx of people and a large demand for the operation and management of industrial parks and office buildings, which provides potential for the real estate market.

CONCLUSION AND RECOMMENDATION

This chapter focuses on the implications of digital transformation across businesses in China. By analyzing the institutional impacts driven by the Chinese government, this chapter discusses how these impacts achieve to generate synergic effects when the business sector undergoes digital transformation. This chapter also uses bibliometric analysis to perform statistical and correlation analysis on the cross-industry digital transformation. Based on our study, China's digital transformation is still in its infancy, so its traditional industry digital transformation level belongs to the bottom echelon of the industry. For example, the digital transformation index of the power generation industry, construction industry and extractive industry is lower than the average level of SOEs (China Central State-Owned Companies Digital Development Academy, 2021). As above-mentioned, in China's digital transformation process, the government and SOEs are in an important position. In this regard, the author puts forward some suggestions to the Chinese government and enterprises. On the one hand, enterprises should attach importance to their own digital transformation and better realize the four core capabilities of service, process, decision-making and data sharing. On the other hand, the government should strengthen policy guidance, create a more business-friendly digital economy ecosystem, and help industries better apply ICT in terms of capital, talent and incentives. In order to achieve the goal of digital transformation of Chinese enterprises, stakeholders must coordinate various interests to produce synergy based on technical feasibility, economic rationality and social acceptability.

ACKNOWLEDGMENT

The authors extend sincere gratitude to:

- Our colleagues from Soochow University, The Australian Studies Centre of Shanghai University, The European Business University of Luxembourg and Krirk University as well as the independent research colleagues who provided insight and expertise that greatly assisted the research, although they may not agree with all of the interpretations/conclusions of this chapter.
- China Knowledge for supporting our research.
- The Editor and the International Editorial Advisory Board (IEAB) of this book who initially desk reviewed, arranged a rigorous double/triple blind review process and conducted a thorough, minute and critical final review before accepting the chapter for publication.
- All anonymous reviewers who provided very constructive feedbacks for thorough revision, improvement and fine tuning of the chapter.

REFERENCES

Acquisti, A., Taylor, C., & Wagman, L. (2016). The Economics of Privacy. *Journal of Economic Literature, 54*(2), 442–492. doi:10.1257/jel.54.2.442

Advanced Manufacturing. (2021). *Global digital transformation in major countries.* https://mp.weixin.qq.com/s/bCm-x0h5XHuwbsm2yzrnjA

Ali Research Institute & 21st Century Institute of Economics. (2020). *Guangdong-Hong Kong-Macau Greater Bay Area Digital Integration Innovation Report.* https://yuegangao.cn/news/3672.html

Amin, A., & Thrift, N. (1995). Institutional issues for the European regions: From markets and plans to socioeconomics and powers of association. *Economy and Society, 24*(1), 41–66. doi:10.1080/03085149500000002

Bell, S. J., Tracey, P., Jan, B., & Heide, J. B. (2009). The organization of regional clusters. *Academy of Management Review, 34*(4), 623–642.

Casanueva, C., Castro, I., & Galán, J. L. (2013). Informational networks and innovation in mature industrial clusters. *Journal of Business Research, 66*(5), 603–613. doi:10.1016/j.jbusres.2012.02.043

CBRE. (2022). *Guangdong-Hong Kong-Macau Greater Bay Area: China's pioneer urban agglomeration, the first bay in the world in the future.* http://www.199it.com/archives/774509.html

Chang, H., & Meyerhoefer, C. (2020). COVID-19 and the Demand for Online Food Shopping Services: Empirical Evidence from Taiwan. *American Journal of Agricultural Economics, 103*(2), 448–465. doi:10.1111/ajae.12170

Chen, H. (2021). *SAIC Group: seeking results in the process of change to promote SAIC's high-quality development through digital transformation.* http://www.sasac.gov.cn/n4470048/n13461446/n15927611/n15927638/n16135043/c16574872/content.html

China Academy of Information and Communication Technology (CAICT). (2021). *White Paper on Global Digital Governance.* http://www.caict.ac.cn/kxyj/qwfb/bps/202012/P020201215465405492157.pdf

China Business Network (CBN). (2022). *China's 5G network deployment for three years, the scale of application into a critical period.* https://www.sohu.com/a/554771719_114986

China Center for Information Industry Development (CCID). (2020). *White Paper on the Development of New Infrastructure.* https://v1.cecdn.yun300.cn/site_1801180113/%E2%80%9C%E6%96%B0%E5%9F%BA%E5%BB%BA%E2%80%9D%E5%8F%91%E5%B1%95%E7%99%BD%E7%9A%AE%E4%B9%A6.pdf

China Central State-Owned Companies Digital Development Academy. (2021). *White Paper on Development Index and method path of Digital Transformation of State-owned Enterprises.* http://www.clii.com.cn/lhrh/hyxx/202112/P020211215020914.pdf

China Development Institute. (2022). *Shared Innovation-accelerating towards the Global Top Science and Technology Bay area.* Author.

China Internet Network Information Development Association (CNNIA). (2021). *China Internet Development report (2021).* https://mp.weixin.qq.com/s/H-Zl9avqjJp_zYBcwwuvEQ

China Software Research Institute. (2022). *White Paper on the Integration of Operation and Management of Central Enterprises in the Digital era (2022).* http://www.199it.com/archives/1365318.html

Connell, J., & Voola, R. (2013). Knowledge integration and competitiveness: A longitudinal study of an industry cluster. *Journal of Knowledge Management, 17*(2), 208–225. doi:10.1108/13673271311315178

CRIC in Shenzhen. (2022). *White Paper on Guangdong-Hong Kong-Macau Greater Bay Area's Investment in 2022.* https://mp.weixin.qq.com/s/uc1ZozjFzD9ph1uRSdHjww

Deloitte. (2021). *The Great Bay area under the New Development pattern-- the focal Point of Guangdong-Hong Kong-Macau Greater Bay Area's Development during the 14th five-year Plan period.* https://www2.deloitte.com/cn/zh/pages/about-deloitte/articles/gba-new-develop-with-dtt.html

Department for Digital Culture, Media & Sport. (2017). *UK Digital Strategy 2017.* https://www.gov.uk/government/publications/uk-digital-strategy/uk-digital-strategy

Enzmann, P., & Moesli, M. (2022). Seizing opportunities: ASEAN country cluster readiness in light of the fourth industrial revolution. *Asia and the Global Economy,* 2(1), Article 100021. doi:10.1016/j.aglobe.2021.100021

Fan, G. (2022). *Sharing Innovation.* In Science and Innovation Bay Area Seminar.

Fletcher, G., & Griffiths, M. (2020). Digital transformation during a lockdown. *International Journal of Information Management*. doi:10.1016/j.ijinfomgt.2020.102185

Gabryelczyk, R. (2020). Has COVID-19 Accelerated Digital Transformation? Initial Lessons Learned for Public Administrations. *Information Systems Management*, *37*(4), 303–309.

Gertler, M. S. (2003). Tacit knowledge and the economic geography of context, or the undefinable tacitness of being (there). *Journal of Economic Geography*, *3*(1), 75–99.

Guangdong Guangdong-Hong Kong-Macau Greater Bay Area Research Institute. (2022). *Guangdong-Hong Kong-Macau Greater Bay Area's digital "accelerated run": speed up the construction of a new digital infrastructure "base", cluster transformation and reshape industrial advantages.* https://mp.weixin.qq.com/s/QAXrsKRXC2ZphPoGRzMZWQ

Guo, Y., Li, B., & Han, Y. (2020). Dynamic network coupling between high-speed rail development and urban growth in emerging economies: Evidence from China. *Cities*, *105*. doi:10.1016/j.cities.2020.102845

Hu, W. (2018). Review and Prospect of the Development of Digital economy in China. *Civil-Military Integration on Cyberspace*, *013*(06), 18–22.

Huang, W. (2021). *Investment outlook for the new infrastructure of the digital economy*. https://www.baogaoting.com/info/143751

Hui, C., Li, X., Chen, T., & Lang, W. (2020). Deciphering the spatial structure of China's megacity region: A new bay area—The Guangdong-Hong Kong-Macao Greater Bay Area in the making. *Cities*, *105*. doi:10.1016/j.cities.2018.10.011

Industrial Internet Theory. (2021). *61 cases! SASAC release! Summary of digital transformation cases of state-owned enterprises!* https://mp.weixin.qq.com/s/ZEHsgdYBASl3Mlm_qgQGHQ

Institute for Global Industry & Tsinghua University. (2020). *Research report on Digital Transformation of Chinese Enterprises*. http://www.clii.com.cn/lhrh/hyxx/202101/t20210113_3947977.html

Li, Q., Cao, S., & Wu, W. (2020). A systematic interpretation of the Digital Transformation of Governance in China: patterns and paths. *Chinese Public Administration*, (10), 44-51. doi:10.19735/j.issn.1006-0863.2020.10.06

Lin, G. C. S. (2017). Planning for the development of the city-regions in the Guangdong-Hong Kong-Macao Greater Bay Area: What can and cannot be done. *Tropical Geography*, *37*(6), 755–756.

link. (2022). *Exclusive! 2022 Supply Chain Finance White Paper Case -- 66Cloud Chain: Reconstructing Business Credit in the Commodity Industry with Trusted Warehouse Receipts.* https://mp.weixin.qq.com/s/8v82-0Ci1hR_65c67uapcA

Lu, Y. (2020). Fresh e-commerce demand surged Dada said vegetable sales during the Spring Festival increased fivefold compared with the same period last year. *The Beijing News*. https://baijiahao.baidu.com/s?id=1657402183597469100&wfr=spider&for=pc

Ma, Y., Cai, Y., & Chen, N. (2020). The influence and effect of Enterprise Digitalization Construction on COVID-19 's response to epidemic situation. *Review of International Economics*, *2020*(05), 80–94.

Martin-Barbero, S. (2020). COVID-19 has accelerated the digital transformation of higher education. *World Economic Forum*. https://www.weforum.org/agenda/2020/07/covid-19-digital-transformation-higher-education

Mas, J. M., & Gómez, A. (2021). Social partners in the digital ecosystem: Will business organizations, trade unions and government organizations survive the digital revolution? *Technological Forecasting and Social Change*, *162*. doi:10.1016/j.techfore.2020.120349

Ministry of Finance of the People's Republic of China. (2020). *Research report and case of Management Accounting Industry, Accounting Department of the Ministry of Finance of China*. http://kjs.mof.gov.cn

Miu, J. (2021). *China Merchants Group: using digitalization to create new competitiveness to promote the construction of world-class enterprises*. http://www.sasac.gov.cn/n4470048/n13461446/n15927611/n15927638/n16135038/index.html

Niu, F., Chen, W., & Chen, X. (2021b). *Current process, challenges and ideas of digital transformation of SOEs*. https://mp.weixin.qq.com/s/AlzwYU1Cj7MExdtL68YyGw

Niu, F., Chen, W., & Wang, X. (2021a). *The core idea of digital transformation of SOEs: small mouth cut, open integration, rapid iteration*. https://mp.weixin.qq.com/s/HR1Iz4YXQfPRCxwC9zZqkg

Operation Monitoring Coordination Bureau. (2022). *Interpretation of the statistical bulletin of the communications industry in 2021*. https://wap.miit.gov.cn/gxsj/tjfx/txy/art/2022/art_e2c784268cc74ba0bb19d9d7eeb398bc.html

Ping An Securities. (2019). *Guangdong-Hong Kong-Macao Greater Bay Area Special Report-Speed up the construction of "rail + intelligent transportation" to create an integrated transportation network in the Greater Bay Area*. https://www.hibor.com.cn/docdetail_2556657.html

Poly Investment Consultancy Research Institute, Jinghui Think Tank, Hexun, & 58 Anjuke Research Institute. (2019). *Guangdong-Hong Kong-Macau Greater Bay Area's Blue Book on Economic Development (2019)*. http://www.199it.com/archives/978652.html

PwC. (2019). *The Core position of data Governance in the Digital Transformation of State-owned Enterprises*. https://www.pwccn.com/zh/blog/state-owned-enterprise-soe/core-position-data-governance-digital-transformation-soe.html

RMB Trading and Research. (2020). *The central bank responded to the interview with Ant Group: to return to the origin of the payment to establish a financial control company in accordance with the law to ensure adequate capital*. https://mp.weixin.qq.com/s/zcV2GntTCyyMQ684XTQOrw

Science and Innovation Bureau of SASAC. (2021). *Notice on the Release of Typical Cases of Digital Transformation of State-owned Enterprises in 2020*. http://www.sasac.gov.cn/n4470048/n13461446/n15927611/n15963955/c17505367/content.html

Shang, Q. (2022). Why should State-owned Enterprises accelerate the Digital Transformation? *Lookout*, 6-7. http://lw.news.cn/2022-02/14/c_1310468941.htm

Shen, J. (2014). Not quite a twin city: Cross-boundary integration in Hong Kong and Shenzhen. *Habitat International*, *42*, 138–146. https://doi.org/10.1016/j.habitatint.2013.12.003

Shi, N. (2020). *Shenzhen takes the lead in achieving full coverage of 5G independent group network, many placesacceleratethesprinttothe5Gera.* https://company.cnstock.com/company/scp_gsxw/202008/4579088.htm

Spence, M. (2021). Government and economics in the digital economy. *Journal of Government and Economics*, *3*. doi:10.1016/j.jge.2021.100020

State Capital Jingjing. (2021). *Beijing Municipal State-owned Assets Supervision and Administration Commission Releases Implementation Opinions on Accelerating Digital Transformation of Municipal Enterprises.* https://mp.weixin.qq.com/s/Ld2UNKcR9CHkQ4E_8jUsRQ

Strategy. (2020). *Under the new situation, how do enterprises carry out digital transformation.* Strategy& Part of the PwC network. https://www.strategyand.pwc.com

Sun, Y. (2022). *10 trillion huge investments, where will the money for new infrastructure come from?* https://mp.weixin.qq.com/s/laRv5KsuswEMybmg3B6iNw

Tallman, S., Jenkins, M., Henry, N., & Pinch, S. (2004). Knowledge, clusters and competitive advantage. *Academy of Management Review*, *29*, 258–271.

Tang, J., & Dai, X. (2021). Innovation Linkages in Digital Economy Industries - Evidence from Innovative Companies in Shenzhen. *Zhongshan Daxue Xuebao. Zhexue Shehui Kexue Ban*, *61*(06), 165–176. https://doi.org/10.13471/j.cnki.jsysusse.2021.06.017

TMT Post. (2021). *White Paper on Digital Capability Watch for Chinese Real Estate Companies in 2021.* https://www.tmtpost.com/base/report/5630989

Tu, C., Tian, F., Li, L., Tan, W., Wang, X., & Liang, S. (2021). *Report of reform and innovation of Guangdong-Hong Kong-Macau Greater Bay Area in China (2021).* https://www.pishu.com.cn/skwx_ps/bookdetail?SiteID=14&ID=12719944

UN E-Government. (2020). *Digital government in the decade of action for sustainable development. With addendum on COVID-19 Response. United Nations E-Government Survey.* https://publicadministration.un.org/egovkb/en-us/Reports/UN-E-Government-Survey-2020

Wang, H., & Wen, K. (2020). The opportunity in danger of COVID-19 's epidemic situation-accelerating the Digital Transformation of our country. *Studies in Science of Science*, *38*(03), 393–395.

Wang, J. (2022). *Digital policy involution: Beijing, Shanghai, Guangzhou and Shenzhen, who is the leader?* https://mp.weixin.qq.com/s/aQlx4fUkBjlmJp-RzG98HQ

Wang, Q. (2022). Comprehensively build a digital government and promote the development of digitalization as a whole. *Administration Reform*, (1), 4-7. doi:10.14150/j.cnki.1674-7453.2022.01.002

Wang, S., Jiang, X., & Wang, X. (2019). *Countries launch national digital development strategies, global "digital" education in action.* https://mp.weixin.qq.com/s/0FyKF3g8J3YTfVw5lwdrUg

Wang, Y. (2018). Digital economy reshapes the global economic pattern-- differentiation and integration driven by policy competition and economies of scale. *Global Review*, *10*(4), 60-79, 154-155. doi:10.13851/j.cnki.gjzw.201804004

Wei, C., & Guo, C. (2021). Empowering and reshaping: The reform of government governance in the era of digital economy. *Theory Journal*, (5), 51-58. doi:10.14110/j.cnki.cn-37-1059/d.2021.05.006

Wu, F. (2000). The global and local dimensions of place-making: Remaking Shanghai as a world city. *Urban Studies (Edinburgh, Scotland)*, *37*(8), 1359–1377.

Wu, J., Zhang, F., Sun, X., Zhu, Y., & Liu, C. (2020). Anti-epidemic promotes China's Digital Transformation: Opportunities and challenges. *Journal of the Chinese Academy of Sciences*, *35*(03), 306–311.

Wu, W. (2021). Beijing has completed 47,000 5G base stations. *The Beijing News*. http://epaper.bjnews.com.cn/html/2021-11/26/content_811575.htm?div=-1

Xia, X., Li, Z., Liang, Y., Bi, F., Zheng, J., & Tao, L. (2020). *Heavyweight! The country's first official announcement of the scope of the "new infrastructure": 3 major aspects, 7 major areas of exposure.* http://www.china-cer.com.cn/xinjijian/202004214081_7.html

Xu, J., & Yeh, A. G. O. (2005). City repositioning and competitiveness building in regional development: New development strategies in Guangzhou. *China International Journal of Urban and Regional Research*, *29*(2), 283–308.

Xu, Y., & Sun, W. (2021). *Shenzhen-Hong Kong cooperation in the perspective of metropolitan area.* https://mp.weixin.qq.com/s/_qzHSWgK1w38UNH88gNMdw

Yao, Y., & Ye, Z. (2021). Government and Enterprise in Digital Transformation: Role orientation and relationship Construction. *Journal of Zhengzhou University*, *54*(04), 26–31. https://www.cnki.net

Yu, P., Chen, D., & Ahuja, A. (2022). Smart and Sustainable Economy: How COVID-19 Has Acted as a Catalyst for China's Digital Transformation. In S. Kautish & G. Kaur (Eds.), AI-Enabled Agile Internet of Things for Sustainable FinTech Ecosystems (pp. 106–146). IGI Global. https://doi.org/10.4018/978-1-6684-4176-3.ch006.

Yu, P., Chen, J., Sampat, M., & Misuko, N. (2022). The Digital Transformation of Rural Agricultural Business Management: A Case Study of China. In S. Bilgaiyan, J. Singh, & H. Das (Eds.), Empirical Research for Futuristic E-Commerce Systems: Foundations and Applications (pp. 23–52). IGI Global. https://doi.org/10.4018/978-1-6684-4969-1.ch002.

Yu, P., Ge, Y., Mandizvidza, K., & Mulli, J. (2023). How Can Small and Medium Enterprises in the Chinese Market Achieve Sustainable Development Goals Through Blockchain? In D. Taleb, M. Abdelli, A. Khalil, & A. Sghaier (Eds.), Examining the Vital Financial Role of SMEs in Achieving the Sustainable Development Goals (pp. 52–85). IGI Global. https://doi.org/10.4018/978-1-6684-4834-2.ch004.

Yu, P., Gong, R., & Sampat, M. (2022). Blockchain Technology in China's Digital Economy: Balancing Regulation and Innovation. In P. Tehrani (Ed.), Regulatory Aspects of Artificial Intelligence on Blockchain (pp. 132–157). IGI Global. https://doi.org/10.4018/978-1-7998-7927-5.ch007.

Yu, P., Gu, H., Sampat, R. M., Lin, Q., & Chen, Z. (2022). Chinese EdTech Economy in the COVID-19 Era. In S. Fazzin (Ed.), EdTech Economy and the Transformation of Education (pp. 114–137). IGI Global. https://doi.org/10.4018/978-1-7998-8904-5.ch007.

Yu, P., Gu, H., Zhao, Y., & Ahuja, A. (2022). Digital Transformation Driven by Internet Data Center: Case Studies on China. In D. Piaggesi, H. Landazuri, & B. Jia (Eds.), Cases on Applying Knowledge Economy Principles for Economic Growth in Developing Nations (pp. 203–230). IGI Global. https://doi.org/10.4018/978-1-7998-8417-0.ch011.

Yu, P., He, K., & Sampat, M. (2022). COVID-19's Impact on the Chinese Tourism and Hospitality Sector. In V. Costa & C. Costa (Eds.), Sustainability and Competitiveness in the Hospitality Industry (pp. 23–66). IGI Global. https://doi.org/10.4018/978-1-7998-9285-4.ch002.

Yu, P., Kwok, S., & Jiang, Z. (2022). How COVID-19 Has Stimulated Innovation in the Chinese Education Sector. In J. Saiz-Alvarez (Ed.), Handbook of Research on Emerging Business Models and the New World Economic Order (pp. 343–364). IGI Global. https://doi.org/10.4018/978-1-7998-7689-2.ch017.

Yu, P., Kwok, S., & Jiang, Z. (2023). How COVID-19 Has Stimulated Innovation in the Chinese Education Sector. In I. Management Association (Ed.), *Research Anthology on Remote Teaching and Learning and the Future of Online Education* (pp. 1612-1634). IGI Global. doi:10.4018/978-1-6684-7540-9.ch080

Yu, P., Liu, Z., & Hanes, E. (2022). Supply Chain Resiliency, Efficiency, and Visibility in the Post-Pandemic Era in China: Case Studies of MeiTuan Waimai, and Ele.me. In Y. Ramakrishna (Ed.), Handbook of Research on Supply Chain Resiliency, Efficiency, and Visibility in the Post-Pandemic Era (pp. 195–225). IGI Global. https://doi.org/10.4018/978-1-7998-9506-0.ch011.

Yu, P., Liu, Z., Hanes, E., & Mumtaz, J. (2022). Integration of IoT and Blockchain for Smart and Secured Supply Chain Management: Case Studies of China. In S. Goyal, N. Pradeep, P. Shukla, M. Ghonge, & R. Ravi (Eds.), Utilizing Blockchain Technologies in Manufacturing and Logistics Management (pp. 179–207). IGI Global. https://doi.org/10.4018/978-1-7998-8697-6.ch010.

Yu, P., Lu, S., Hanes, E., & Chen, Y. (2022). The Role of Blockchain Technology in Harnessing the Sustainability of Chinese Digital Finance. In P. Swarnalatha & S. Prabu (Eds.), Blockchain Technologies for Sustainable Development in Smart Cities (pp. 155–186). IGI Global. https://doi.org/10.4018/978-1-7998-9274-8.ch009.

Yu, P., Lu, Y., Hanes, E., & Gu, H. (2022). Digitized Education: Enhancement in Teaching and Learning – China Case Study. In C. Krishnan, F. Al-Harthy, & G. Singh (Eds.), Technology Training for Educators From Past to Present (pp. 1–35). IGI Global. https://doi.org/10.4018/978-1-6684-4083-4.ch001.

Yu, P., Tang, H., Tang, H., & Hanes, E. (2022). Using "Digitalization + Intellectual Property" Management to Realize Cultural Economy: Case Study of Chinese Museums. In R. Pettinger, B. Gupta, A. Roja, & D. Cozmiuc (Eds.), Handbook of Research on Digital Transformation Management and Tools (pp. 236–264). IGI Global. https://doi.org/10.4018/978-1-7998-9764-4.ch011.

Yu, P., Wang, Y., & Hanes, E. (2022). Innovative Management Strategy of Wine Tourism in the COVID-19 Era: A Case Study of China. In R. Kovid & V. Kumar (Eds.), Cases on Emerging Market Responses to the COVID-19 Pandemic (pp. 59–89). IGI Global. https://doi.org/10.4018/978-1-6684-3504-5.ch004.

Yu, P., Xu, S., Cheng, Z., & Sampat, M. (2023). Does the Development of New Energy Vehicles Promote Carbon Neutralization?: Case Studies in China. In A. Pego (Ed.), Climate Change, World Consequences, and the Sustainable Development Goals for 2030 (pp. 109–131). IGI Global. https://doi.org/10.4018/978-1-6684-4829-8.ch006.

Yu, P., Xue, W., & Mahendran, R. (2022). The Development and Impact of China's Digital Transformation in the Medical Industry. In M. Rodrigues & J. Proença (Eds.), Impact of Digital Transformation on the Development of New Business Models and Consumer Experience (pp. 97–128). IGI Global. https://doi.org/10.4018/978-1-7998-9179-6.ch006.

Yu, P., Yu, M., & Sampat, M. (2022). Smart Management for Digital Transformation in China. In B. Barbosa, S. Filipe, & C. Santos (Eds.), *Handbook of Research on Smart Management for Digital Transformation* (pp. 411-438). IGI Global. doi:10.4018/978-1-7998-9008-9.ch019

Yu, X. (2021). Analysis of policies related to "Internet + government services" in the context of digital government construction. *Chinese Engineering Consultants*, *2021*(1), 63–67.

Yu, K. (2021). *Shanghai was awarded the first batch of "gigabit cities" in the country, and 5G network led the country.* https://www.thepaper.cn/newsDetail_forward_15991886

Zhai, Y., Jiang, M., & Wang, W. (2021). The theoretical interpretation and operating mechanism of China's digital transformation. *E-government*, (6), 67-84. doi:10.16582/j.cnki.dzzw.2021.06.007

Zhang, L. (2020). The Integration of industrialization and Informatization has entered a new stage of Digital Transformation of Manufacturing Industry. *Cybersecurity & Informatization*, *2020*(6), 28-31.

Zhang, X., Chen, S., Luan, X., & Yuan, M. (2020). Understanding China's city-regionalization: Spatial structure and relationships between functional and institutional spaces in the Pearl River Delta. *Urban Geography*, 1–28.

Zhang, X., & Sun, Y. (2019). Investigating institutional integration in the contexts of Chinese city-regionalization: evidence from Shenzhen–Dongguan–Huizhou. *Land Use Policy*, *88*. doi:10.1016/j.landusepol.2019.104170

Zhang, Y. (2021). The "27" to stimulate the dynamic power of digital transformation. *Jiefang Daily*. doi:10.28410/n.cnki.njfrb.2021.004857

Zhang, Y., Huang, Y., & Zhao, Z. (2020). *How Digital Reinvents Real Estate in the Age of Inventory.* https://ifenxi.com/research/content/5558

Zhao, H., & Su, P. (2020). Understanding the structure and determinants of city network through intra-firm service relationships: The case of Guangdong-Hong Kong-Macao Greater Bay Area. *Cities*, *103*. doi:10.1016/j.cities.2020.102738

Zhongguancun Alliance for the Integration and Development of Information Technology and Real Economy (AIITRE) & China Enterprise Federation. (2021). *2021 White Paper on the Development Index and Method Path of Digital Transformation of State-owned Enterprises*. Digitalization Think Tank.

Zhou, X. (2021). *The digital economy will be sounded in 2021, and Zhejiang, Shanghai, Beijing and Guangdong intend to do so.* https://m.21jingji.com/article/20210128/herald/ba1b9070cdcb2e9022f71e788d48a7f7_zaker.html

ENDNOTES

1 JD.com is the largest online retailer in China.

2 Compound annual growth rate.

3 Time Division Duplex.

Compilation of References

Abdulkhaliq, S. S., & Mohammadali, Z. M. (2019). The Impact of Job Satisfaction on Employees' Performance: A Case Study of Al Hayat Company-Pepsi Employees in Erbil, Kurdistan Region-Iraq. *Management and Economics Review*, *4*(2), 163–176. doi:10.24818/mer/2019.12-07

Abrahamsson, A. (2007). Sustainopreneurship - business with a cause. Conceptualizing entrepreneurship for sustainability [Master's thesis, Växjö University, School of Management and Economics]. https://www.diva-portal.org/smash/get/diva2:205051/FULLTEXT01.pdf

Acquaah, M., Amoako-Gyampah, K., & Jayaram, J. (2011). Resilience in family and nonfamily firms: An examination of the relationships between manufacturing strategy, competitive strategy, and firm performance. *International Journal of Production Research*, *49*(18), 5527–5544. doi:10.1080/00207543.2011.563834

Acquisti, A., Taylor, C., & Wagman, L. (2016). The Economics of Privacy. *Journal of Economic Literature*, *54*(2), 442–492. doi:10.1257/jel.54.2.442

Acs, Z. J., & Szerb, L. (2007). Entrepreneurship, Economic Growth and Public Policy. *Small Business Economics*, *28*(2-3), 109–122. doi:10.100711187-006-9012-3

Advanced Manufacturing. (2021). *Global digital transformation in major countries.* https://mp.weixin.qq.com/s/bCm-x0h5XHuwbsm2yzrnjA

AfDB. (2014) *Green growth Sierra Leone: investing in environmentally sound economic growth.* African Development Bank, Tunis (www.afdb.org/fileadmin/ uploads/afdb/Documents/Project-and-Operations/Sierra_

Afsar, B., Badir, Y., & Kiani, U. S. (2016). Linking Spiritual Leadership and Employee Pro-Environmental Behavior: The Influence of Workplace Spirituality, Intrinsic Motivation, and Environmental Passion. *Journal of Environmental Psychology*, *45*, 79–88. doi:10.1016/j.jenvp.2015.11.011

Ahmed, N., Ashraf, M., & Mangi, R. A. (2019). Relationship of working environment, employee empowerment, training & development and organizational commitment. *Pakistan Business Review*, *21*(3), 113–125.

Akgün & Halit Keskin. (2014). Organizational resilience capacity and firm product innovativeness and performance. *International Journal of Production Research*, *52*(23), 6918–6937.

Albuquerque, R., Koskinen, Y., & Zhang, C. (2019). Corporate social responsibility and firm risk: Theory and empirical evidence. *Management Science*, *65*(10), 4451–4469. doi:10.1287/mnsc.2018.3043

Aleksić, A., Stefanović, M., Arsovski, S., & Tadić, D. (2013). An assessment of organizational resilience potential in SMEs of the process industry, a fuzzy approach. *J Loss Prevent Proc*, *26*, 1238–1245. doi:10.1016/j.jlp.2013.06.004

Alesi, P. (2008). Building enterprise-wide resilience by integrating business continuity capability into day-to-day business culture and technology. *Journal of Business Continuity & Emergency Planning*, *2*(3), 214–220.

Al-Hawari, M. A., Bani-Melhem, S., & Shamsudin, F. M. (2019). Determinants of frontline employee service innovative behavior: The moderating role of co-worker socializing and service climate. *Management Research Review*, *42*(9), 1076–1094. doi:10.1108/MRR-07-2018-0266

Ali Research Institute & 21st Century Institute of Economics. (2020). *Guangdong-Hong Kong-Macau Greater Bay Area Digital Integration Innovation Report*. https://yuegangao.cn/news/3672.html

AlKindy, A. M., Shah, I. M., & Jusoh, A. (2016). The impact of transformational leadership behaviors on work performance of omani civil service agencies. *Asian Social Science*, *12*(3), 152. doi:10.5539/ass.v12n3p152

Allen, C. (2012). *A green economy knowledge sharing platform: Exploring options*. UNCSD Secretariat.

Al-Shaibani, H., Lasla, N., & Abdallah, M. (2020). Consortium Blockchain-Based Decentralized Stock Exchange Platform. *IEEE Access: Practical Innovations, Open Solutions*, *8*, 123711–123725. doi:10.1109/ACCESS.2020.3005663

Alsop, R., & Heinsohn, N. (2012). *Measuring empowerment in practice: Structuring analysis and framing indicators* (Vol. 3510). World Bank Publications.

Alvarez, S. A., & Barney, J. B. (2007). Discovery and creation: Alternative theories of entrepreneurial action. *Strategic Entrepreneurship Journal*, *1*(1-2), 11–26. doi:10.1002ej.4

Alzalabani, A. H. (2017). Antecedents of job satisfaction in Saudi Arabia: Impact of industrial sector. *International Journal of Business and Management*, *12*(11), 61–72. doi:10.5539/ijbm.v12n11p61

Amin, A., & Thrift, N. (1995). Institutional issues for the European regions: From markets and plans to socioeconomics and powers of association. *Economy and Society*, *24*(1), 41–66. doi:10.1080/03085149500000002

Amin, F. A. B. M. (2021). A Review Of The Job Satisfaction Theory For Special Education Perspective. [TURCOMAT]. *Turkish Journal of Computer and Mathematics Education*, *12*(11), 5224–5228.

Anand, S., Vidyarthi, P., & Rolnicki, S. (2018). Leader-member exchange and organizational citizenship behaviors: Contextual effects of leader power distance and group task interdependence. *The Leadership Quarterly*, *29*(4), 489–500. doi:10.1016/j.leaqua.2017.11.002

Anderson, A. R. (1998). Cultivating the garden of Eden: Environmental entrepreneuring. *Journal of Organizational Change Management*, *11*(2), 135–144. doi:10.1108/09534819810212124

Anderson, K., Nelgen, S., & Pinilla, V. (2017). *Global wine markets, 1860 to 2016: A statistical compendium*. University of Adelaide Press. doi:10.20851/global-wine-markets

Anser, M. K., Shafique, S., Usman, M., Akhtar, N., & Ali, M. (2021). Spiritual leadership and organizational citizenship behavior for the environment: An intervening and interactional analysis. *Journal of Environmental Planning and Management*, *64*(8), 1496–1514. doi:10.1080/09640568.2020.1832446

Antheaume, N., Robic, P., & Barbelivien, D. (2013). French family business and longevity: Have they been conducting sustainable development policies before it became a fashion? *Business History*, *55*(6), 942–962. doi:10.1080/00076791.2012.744583

Antunes, P. (2011). BPM and exception handling: Focus on organizational resilience. *IEEE Transactions on Systems, Man, and Cybernetics*, *41*, 383–392. doi:10.1109/TSMCC. 2010.20625 04

Aouadi, A., & Marsat, S. (2018). Do ESG controversies matter for firm value? Evidence from international data. *Journal of Business Ethics, 151*(4), 1027–1047. doi:10.100710551-016-3213-8

Argote, L., & Greve, H. R. (2007). A behavioral theory of the firm: 40 years and counting: Introduction and impact. *Organization Science, 18*(3), 337–349. doi:10.1287/orsc.1070.0280

Aryee, S., Walumbwa, F. O., Zhou, Q., & Hartnell, C. A. (2012). Transformational leadership, innovative behavior, and task performance: Test of mediation and moderation processes. *Human Performance, 25*(1), 1–25. doi:10.1080/08959285.2011.631648

As'Ad, M. (2004). *Seri ilmu sumber daya manusia: Psikologi rganiza. Edisi Keempat. Cetakan Kesembilan [Human resource science series: Organiza psychology, fourth ed., ninth printing].* Liberty.

Ates, Ö. T., & Ihtiyaroglu, N. (2019). Analysis of the Relationship between Stress and Organizational Commitment in Employees: A Meta-Analysis Study. *Journal of Education and Training Studies, 7*(1), 94–106. doi:10.11114/jets.v7i1.3702

Aupperle, K. E., Carroll, A. B., & Hatfield, J. D. (1985). An empirical examination of the relationship between corporate social responsibility and profitability. *Academy of Management Journal, 28*(2), 446–463. doi:10.2307/256210

Avey, J. B., Avolio, B. J., Crossley, C. D., & Luthans, F. (2009). Psychological ownership: Theoretical extensions, measurement, and relation to work outcomes. *J. Org. Behav. Int. J. Indus. Occup. Org. Psychol. Behav, 30*(2), 173–191. doi:10.1002/job.583

Avgouleas, E., & Kiayias, A. (2019). The Promise of Blockchain Technology for Global Securities and Derivatives Markets: The New Financial Ecosystem and the 'Holy Grail' of Systemic Risk Containment. *European Business Organization Law Review, 20*(1), 81–110. doi:10.100740804-019-00133-3

Awazu onsen Houshi ryokan. (2017). *Welcome.* Awazu onsen Houshi ryokan. https://www.ho-shi.co.jp/en/

Baharlo, M., Beshlideh, K., & Naami, A., & Hashemi Sheikh Sabaani S.E. (2015). Analysis of the relationship between ethical leadership and organizational citizenship behavior. *Ethics Sci Technol, 10*, 19–27.

Bai, C. A., Cordeiro, J., & Sarkis, J. (2020). Blockchain technology: Business, strategy, the environment, and sustainability. *Business Strategy and the Environment, 29*(1), 321–322. https://ideas.repec.org//a/bla/bstrat/v29y2020i1p321-322.html. doi:10.1002/bse.2431

Bai, C., & Sarkis, J. (2017). Improving green flexibility through advanced manufacturing technology investment: Modeling the decision process. *International Journal of Production Economics, 188*(C), 86–104. https://ideas.repec.org//a/eee/proeco/v188y2017icp86-104.html. doi:10.1016/j.ijpe.2017.03.013

Bai, X. J., Yan, W. K., & Chiu, Y. H. (2015). Performance Evaluation Of China's Hi-Tech Zones In The Post Financial Crisis Era— Analysis Based On The Dynamic Network SBM Model. *China Economic Review, 34*, 122–134. doi:10.1016/j.chieco.2015.04.001

Baker, M., Bergstresser, D., Serafeim, G., & Wurgler, J. (2018). Financing the response to climate change: The pricing and ownership of US green bonds (No. w25194). National Bureau of Economic Research.

Bamisile, O., Obiora, S., Huang, Q., Okonkwo, E. C., Olagoke, O., Shokanbi, A., & Kumar, R. (2020). Towards a Sustainable and Cleaner Environment in China: Dynamic Analysis of Vehicle-To-Grid, Batteries and Hydro Storage for Optimal Re Integration. *Sustainable Energy Technologies and Assessments, 42*, 100872. doi:10.1016/j.seta.2020.100872

Banbury, C. M., & Mitchell, W. (1995). The effect of introducing important incremental innovations on market share and business survival. *Strategic Management Journal, 16*(S1), 161–182. doi:10.1002mj.4250160922

Bandinelli, R., Acuti, D., Fani, V., Bindi, B., & Aiello, G. (2020). Environmental practices in the wine industry: An overview of the Italian market. *British Food Journal, 122*(5), 1625–1646. doi:10.1108/BFJ-08-2019-0653

Banz, R. W. (1981). The relationship between return and market value of common stocks. *Journal of Financial Economics, 9*(1), 3–18. doi:10.1016/0304-405X(81)90018-0

Barbier, E. B. (2014). *Whither the green economy?* Triple Crisis. (http:// triplecrisis.com/whither-the-green-economy/)

Barbier, E. B. (2013). The green economy postRio+20. *Science, 33*, 887–888.

Barnett P (2015) If what gets measured gets managed, measuring the wrong thing matters *Corporate Finance Review.*

Barnett, M. L., & Salomon, R. M. (2006). Beyond dichotomy: The curvilinear relationship between social responsibility and financial performance. *Strategic Management Journal, 27*(11), 1101–1122. doi:10.1002mj.557

Barney, J. (1991). Firm resources and sustained competitive advantage. *Journal of Management, 17*(1), 99–120. doi:10.1177/014920639101700108

Bassey, M. (2003). Case study research. In J. Swann & J. Pratt (Eds.), Educational research in practice: Making sense of methodology (pp. 111 123). Continuum.

Basu, S. (1983). The relationship between earnings' yield, market value and return for NYSE common stocks: Further evidence. *Journal of Financial Economics, 12*(1), 129–156. doi:10.1016/0304-405X(83)90031-4

BauerR.HannD. (2010). Corporate environmental management and credit risk. *Available at* SSRN 1660470.

Bauer, R., Koedijk, K., & Otten, R. (2005). International evidence on ethical mutual fund performance and investment style. *Journal of Banking & Finance, 29*(7), 1751–1767. doi:10.1016/j.jbankfin.2004.06.035

Bavik, A., Bavik, Y. L., & Tang, P. M. (2017). Servant leadership, employee job crafting, and citizenship behaviors: A cross-level investigation. *Cornell Hospitality Quarterly, 58*(4), 364–373. doi:10.1177/1938965517719282

Beasley, J. E., Meade, N., & Chang, T. J. (2003). An Evolutionary Heuristic for the Index Tracking Problem. *European Journal of Operational Research, 148*(3), 621–643. doi:10.1016/S0377-2217(02)00425-3

Bebbington, J., & Unerman, J. (2018). Achieving the United Nations sustainable development goals: An enabling role of accounting research. *Accounting, Auditing & Accountability Journal, 31*(1), 2–24. doi:10.1108/AAAJ-05-2017-2929

Bebchuk, L. A., & Hamdani, A. (2009). The Elusive Quest for Global Governance Standards. *University of Pennsylvania Law Review, 157*, 1263–1317.

Bechky, B. A., & Okhuysen, G. A. (2011). Expecting the unexpected? How SWAT officers and film. *Academy of Management Journal, 54*(2), 239–261.

Becker, P., Abrahamsson, M., & Tehler, H. (2014). An emergent means to assurgent ends: societal resilience for safety and sustainability C.P. Nemeth, E. Hollnagel (Eds.), Becom. Resilient, pp. 1-12. Ashgate Publishing, Ltd.

Bello, Z. Y. (2005). Socially responsible investing and portfolio diversification. *Journal of Financial Research, 28*(1), 41–57. doi:10.1111/j.1475-6803.2005.00113.x

Bell, S. J., Tracey, P., Jan, B., & Heide, J. B. (2009). The organization of regional clusters. *Academy of Management Review, 34*(4), 623–642.

Belt, A., & Kok, S. (2018). *A Reality Check for Blockchain in Commodity Trading.* Boston Consulting Group.

Benbasat, I., Goldstein, D., & Mead, M. (1987). The case research strategy in studies of information systems. *Management Information Systems Quarterly*, *11*(3), 369–386. doi:10.2307/248684

Bendell, J. (2017). Currency Innovation for Sustainable Financing of SMEs: Context, Case Study and Scalability. *Journal of Corporate Citizenship*, *67*(67), 39–62. https://www.jstor.org/stable/26629178. doi:10.9774/TandF.4700.2017.se.00005

Bernstein, S. (2013). Rio+20: Sustainable development in a time of multilateral decline. *Global Environmental Politics*, *13*(4), 1312–1321. doi:10.1162/GLEP_e_00195

Bevan, G., & Hood, C. (2006). What's measured is what matters: Targets and gaming in the English public health care system. *Public Administration*, *84*(3), 517–538. doi:10.1111/j.1467-9299.2006.00600.x

Bhandari, L. C. (1988). Debt/equity ratio and expected common stock returns: Empirical evidence. *The Journal of Finance*, *43*(2), 507–528. doi:10.1111/j.1540-6261.1988.tb03952.x

Bhandarkar, V. V., Bhandarkar, A. A., & Shiva, A. (2019). Digital stocks using blockchain technology the possible future of stocks? *International Journal of Management*, *10*(3). doi:10.34218/IJM.10.3.2019/005

Bhatti, M. H., Bhatti, M. H., Akram, M. U., Hashim, M., & Akram, Z. (2016). Relationship between job stress and organizational commitment: An empirical study of banking sector. *Journal of Business Management and Economics*, *7*(1), 29–37.

Bilge, S. (2010). Recent feminist outlooks on intersectionality. *Diogenes*, *57*(1), 58–72. doi:10.1177/0392192110374245

Bina, O., & La Camera, F. (2011). Promise and shortcomings of a green turn in recent policy responses to the 'double crisis'. *Ecological Economics*, *70*(12), 2308–2316. doi:10.1016/j.ecolecon.2011.06.021

Black, B. S., De Carvalho, A. G., & Gorga, É. (2012). What matters and for which firms for corporate governance in emerging markets? Evidence from Brazil (and other BRIK countries). *Journal of Corporate Finance*, *18*(4), 934–952. doi:10.1016/j.jcorpfin.2011.10.001

Bliese, P. D., & Ployhart, R. E. (2002). Growth modeling using random coefficient models: Model building, testing, and illustrations. *Organizational Research Methods*, *5*(4), 362–387. doi:10.1177/109442802237116

Bocken, N. M., de Pauw, I., Bakker, C., & van der Grinten, B. (2016). Product design and business model strategies for a circular economy. *Journal of Industrial and Production Engineering*, *33*(5), 308–320. doi:10.1080/21681015.2016.1172124

Bocken, N. M., Schuit, C. S., & Kraaijenhagen, C. (2018). Experimenting with a circular business model: Lessons from eight cases. *Environmental Innovation and Societal Transitions*, *28*, 79–95. doi:10.1016/j.eist.2018.02.001

Bodas-Freitas, I. M., & Corrocher, N. (2019). The use of external support and the benefits of the adoption of resource efficiency practices: An empirical analysis of European SMEs. *Energy Policy*, *132*, 75–82. doi:10.1016/j.enpol.2019.05.019

Boin, A., & van Eeten, M. J. B. (2013). The Resilient Organization—A critical appraisal. *Public Management Review*, *15*, 429–445.

Bolino, M. C. (1999). Citizenship and impression management: Good soldiers or good actors? *Academy of Management Review*, *24*(1), 82–98. doi:10.2307/259038

Bolino, M. C., Hsing, H.-H., Harvey, J., & LePine, A. (2015). "Well, I'm tired of tryin'." Organizational citizenship behavior. *The Journal of Applied Psychology*, *100*(1), 56–74. doi:10.1037/a0037583 PMID:25111252

Bollen, N. P. (2007). Mutual Fund Attributes and Investor Behavior. *Journal of Financial and Quantitative Analysis*, *42*(3), 683–708. https://www.jstor.org/stable/27647316. doi:10.1017/S0022109000004142

Borel-Saladin, J. M., & Turok, I. N. (2013). The green economy: Incremental change or transformation? *Environmental Policy and Governance*, *23*(4), 209–220. doi:10.1002/eet.1614

Borgatti, S. P., Everett, M. G., & Johnson, J. C. (2018). Analyzing social networks. *Sage (Atlanta, Ga.)*.

Borgatti, S. P., Mehra, A., Brass, D. J., & Labianca, G. (2009). Network analysis in the social sciences. *Science*, *323*(5916), 892–895. doi:10.1126cience.1165821

Borges, F. M., & Menegon, N. L. (2012). Different roles in the quest for system resilience. *Work (Reading, Mass.)*, *41*, 3238–3245.

Bourdage, J. S., Goupal, A., Neilson, T., Lukacik, E. R. E.-R., & Lee, N. (2018). Personality, equity sensitivity, and discretionary workplace behavior. *Personality and Individual Differences*, *120*, 144–150. doi:10.1016/j.paid.2017.08.018

Bouslah, K., Kryzanowski, L., & M'zali, B. (2013). The impact of the dimensions of social performance on firm risk. *Journal of Banking & Finance*, *37*(4), 1258–1273. doi:10.1016/j.jbankfin.2012.12.004

Bowen, A., Fankhauser, S., Stern, N., & Zenghelis, D. (2009) *An outline of the case for a 'green' stimulus Grantham Research Institute on Climate Change and the Environment*, London E-Prints. (http://eprints.lse.ac.uk/24345/1/An_outline_of_the_case_for_a_green_stimulus.pdf)

Bowler, W. M., Halbesleben, J. R. B., & Paul, J. R. B. (2010). If you're close with the leader, you must be a brownnose: The role of leader–member relationships in follower, leader, and coworker attributions of organizational citizenship behavior motives. *Human Resource Management Review*, *20*(4), 309–316. doi:10.1016/j.hrmr.2010.04.001

Branch, M., Goldberg, L. R., & Hand, P. (2019). A guide to ESG portfolio construction. *Journal of Portfolio Management*, *45*(4), 61–66. doi:10.3905/jpm.2019.45.4.061

Brand U (2012) Green economy – the next oxymoron? No lessons learned from failures of implementing sustainable development GAIA - *Ecological Perspectives for Science and Society*, *21*, 28–32

Brayfield, A. H., & Rothe, H. F. (1951). An index of job satisfaction. *The Journal of Applied Psychology*, *35*(5), 307–311. doi:10.1037/h0055617

Briggs, S. A., & Ward, S. (2012). Earth observation from satellites: Supporting the outcomes of UNCSD (Rio+20). *Environmental Policy and Law*, *42*, 357–364.

Brinck, P. (1992). Our Common Future and Beyond: Interpretations of Sustainable Development. In U. Svedin & B. H. Aniansson (Eds.), *Society and the Environment: A Swedish Research Perspective* (pp. 3–12). Springer Netherlands., doi:10.1007/978-94-011-2799-8_1

Brockington, D. (2012). A radically conservative vision? The challenge of UNEP's towards a green economy. *Development and Change*, *43*(1), 409–422. doi:10.1111/j.1467-7660.2011.01750.x

Brock, W. A., Mäler, K. G., & Perrings, C. (2002). Resilience and Sustainability: The Economic Analysis of Nonlinear Dynamic Systems. In L. H. Gunderson & C. S. Holling (Eds.), *Panarchy: Understanding Transformations in Human and Natural Systems* (pp. 261–289). Island Press.

Brown, E., Cloke, J., Gent, D., Johnson, P. H., & Hill, C. (2014). Green growth or ecological commodification: Debating the green economy in the global South. *Geografiska Annaler. Series B, Human Geography*, *96*(3), 245–259. doi:10.1111/geob.12049

Brown, M. E., & Treviño, L. K. (2006). Ethical leadership: A review and future directions. *The Leadership Quarterly*, *17*(6), 595–616. doi:10.1016/j.leaqua.2006.10.004

Brown, M. E., Treviño, L. K., & Harrison, D. A. (2005). Ethical leadership: A social learning perspective for construct development and testing. *Organizational Behavior and Human Decision Processes, 97*(2), 117–134. doi:10.1016/j.obhdp.2005.03.002

Brüggemann, H., Stempin, S., & Meier, J. M. (2020). Consideration of digitalization for the purpose of resource efficiency in a learning factory. *Procedia Manufacturing, 45*, 140–145. doi:10.1016/j.promfg.2020.04.085

Bruneau, M., Chang, S. E., Eguchi, R. T., Lee, G. C., O'Rourke, T. D., Reinhorn, A. M., Shinozuka, M., Tierney, K., Wallace, W. A., & von Winterfeldt, D. (2003). A framework to quantitatively assess and enhance the seismic resilience of communities. *Earthquake Spectra, 19*(4), 733–752. doi:10.1193/1.1623497

Bruni, R., Cesarone, F., Scozzari, A., & Tardella, F. (2015). A Linear Risk-Return Model for Enhanced Indexation in Portfolio Optimization. *Spectrum (Lexington, Ky.), 37*(3), 735–759. doi:10.100700291-014-0383-6

Brzoska, P., & Razum, O. (2010). *Validity issues in quantitative migrant health research: The example of illness perceptions* (Vol. 58). Peter Lang.

Buchari, E., & Basri, H. (2015). The importance of human resources development and its impact in increasing of national port productivity. *Procedia Engineering, 125*, 519–525. doi:10.1016/j.proeng.2015.11.049

Buterin, V. (2015, August 7). *On Public and Private Blockchains*. Ethereum Foundation Blog. https://blog.ethereum.org/2015/08/07/on-public-and-private-blockchains

Butler, C. D. (2016). Sounding the Alarm: Health in the Anthropocene. *International Journal of Environmental Research and Public Health, 13*, 665.

Calvo, J. (2022). Kongo Gumi, la empresa en activo más antigua del mundo [Kongo Gumi, the oldest active company in the world]. *Eleconomista*. https://www.eleconomista.es/podcasts/noticias/12002183/10/22/Kongo-Gumi-la-empresa-en-activo-mas-antigua-del-mundo.html

Canakgoz, N. A., & Beasley, J. E. (2009). Mixed-integer Programming Approaches for Index Tracking and Enhanced Indexation. *European Journal of Operational Research, 196*(1), 384–399. doi:10.1016/j.ejor.2008.03.015

Cancino, C., Merigó, J. M., Coronado, F., Dessouky, Y., & Dessouky, M. (2017). Forty years of Computers & Industrial Engineering: A bibliometric analysis. *Computers & Industrial Engineering, 113*, 614–629. doi:10.1016/j.cie.2017.08.033

Cañete. (2022). *Bodegas Juan Gil apuesta por el respeto al medio ambiente y la calidad sostenible* [Bodegas Juan Gil is committed to respect for the environment and sustainable quality]. Laverdad. https://www.laverdad.es/economia-region-murcia/empresa/bodegas-juan-apuesta-20220409001917-ntvo.html?ref=https%3A%2F%2Fwww.google.com%2F

Caprotti, F., & Bailey, I. (2014). Making sense of the green economy. *Geografiska Annaler. Series B, Human Geography, 96*(3), 195–200. doi:10.1111/geob.12045

Carhart, M. M. (1997). On persistence in mutual fund performance. *The Journal of Finance, 52*(1), 57–82. doi:10.1111/j.1540-6261.1997.tb03808.x

Carpenter, S., Walker, B., Anderies, J. M., & Abel, N. (2001). From metaphor to measurement: Resilience of what to what? *Ecosystems (New York, N.Y.), 4*, 765–781.

Carrillo-Higueras, F., Prajogo, D., & Smith, L. (2018). Environmental commitment and its drivers in the Australian wine industry: A behavioural approach. *Australasian Journal of Environmental Management, 25*(4), 439–458. doi:10.1080/14486563.2018.1460630

Carstensen, L. L. (1992). Social and emotional patterns in adulthood: Support for socioemotional selectivity theory. *Psychology and Aging, 7*(3), 331–338. doi:10.1037/0882-7974.7.3.331 PMID:1388852

Carvalho, F. A., Koren, O., & Goodrich, J. K. (2012). Transient Inability to Manage Proteobacteria Promotes Chronic Gut Inflammation in TLR5-Deficient Mice. *Cell Host & Microbe, 12*(2), 139–152. https://www.sciencedirect.com/science/article/pii/S1931312812002272. doi:10.1016/j.chom.2012.07.004

Casanueva, C., Castro, I., & Galán, J. L. (2013). Informational networks and innovation in mature industrial clusters. *Journal of Business Research, 66*(5), 603–613. doi:10.1016/j.jbusres.2012.02.043

Castillo-Merino, D., & Rodríguez-Pérez, G. (2021). The effects of legal origin and corporate governance on financial firms' sustainability performance. *Sustainability, 13*(15), 8233. doi:10.3390u13158233

Castleden, M., McKee, M., Murray, V., & Leonardi, G. (2011, September). Resilience thinking in health protection. *Journal of Public Health, 33*(3), 369–377. doi:10.1093/pubmed/fdr027

Caves, R. E. (1998). Industrial organization and new findings on the turnover and mobility of firms. *Journal of Economic Literature, 36*(4), 1947–1982.

CBRE. (2022). *Guangdong-Hong Kong-Macau Greater Bay Area: China's pioneer urban agglomeration, the first bay in the world in the future.* http://www.199it.com/archives/774509.html

Cefis, E., Bettinelli, C., Coad, A., & Marsili, O. (2021). Understanding firm exit: A systematic literature review. *Small Business Economics*. doi:10.100711187-021-00530-4

Cefis, E., & Marsili, O. (2006). Survivor: The role of innovation in firms' survival. *Research Policy, 35*(5), 626–641. doi:10.1016/j.respol.2006.02.006

Centobelli, P., Cerchione, R., Esposito, E., & Oropallo, E. (2021). Surfing blockchain wave, or drowning? Shaping the future of distributed ledgers and decentralized technologies. *Technological Forecasting and Social Change, 165*, 120463. doi:10.1016/j.techfore.2020.120463

Cerne, M., Babic, K., Connelly, C. E., & Skerlavaj, M. (2015). Team—Level knowledge hiding, social leader-member exchange, and PM. In Academy of management proceedings. (Vol. 1, p. 16302). Academy of Management, Briarclif Manor.

Chandani, A., Mehta, M., Mall, A., & Khokhar, V. (2016). Employee engagement: A review paper on factors affecting employee engagement. *Indian Journal of Science and Technology, 9*(15), 1–7. doi:10.17485/ijst/2016/v9i15/92145

Chang, H., & Meyerhoefer, C. (2020). COVID-19 and the Demand for Online Food Shopping Services: Empirical Evidence from Taiwan. *American Journal of Agricultural Economics, 103*(2), 448–465. doi:10.1111/ajae.12170

Chan, J. K. (2011). Enhancing Organisational Resilience: Application of Viable System Model and MCDA in a Small Hong Kong Company. *International Journal of Production Research, 49*(18), 5545–5563. doi:10.1080/00207543.2011.563829

Château de Goulaine. (2022). *The history.* Château de Goulaine. http://www.chateaudegoulaine.fr/english-informations/opening-hours-admission-prices/the-history

Chatzistamoulou, N., & Tyllianakis, E. (2022). Commitment of European SMEs to resource efficiency actions to achieve sustainability transition: A feasible reality or an elusive goal. *Journal of Environmental Management, 321*, 115937. doi:10.1016/j.jenvman.2022.115937 PMID:35988398

Chauhan, Y., & Kumar, S. B. (2018). Do investors value the nonfinancial disclosure in emerging markets? *Emerging Markets Review, 37*, 32–46. doi:10.1016/j.ememar.2018.05.001

Chava, S. (2014). Environmental externalities and cost of capital. *Management Science, 60*(9), 2223–2247. doi:10.1287/mnsc.2013.1863

Chellappandi, P., & Vijayakumar, C. S. (2018). Bibliometrics, Scientometrics, Webometrics/Cybermetrics, Informetrics and Altmetrics—An Emerging Field in Library and Information Science Research. *Shanlax International Journal of Education, 7*(1), 5–8.

Chen, H. (2021). *SAIC Group: seeking results in the process of change to promote SAIC's high-quality development through digital transformation.* http://www.sasac.gov.cn/n4470048/n13461446/n15927611/n15927638/n16135043/c16574872/content.html

Chen, J. C. (2017). Innovative Practice and Thinking on the Construction of Zizhu Innovation and Entrepreneurship Corridor. *China Journal of Commerce,* 6.

Chen, L. (2021). Guangzhou High-tech Zone: Strive to Build an Important Engine for High-Quality Development of the Guangdong-Hong Kong-Macao Greater Bay Area. *Guangdong Science and Technology.*

Chen, C.-H. V., & Kao, R.-H. (2011). A multilevel study on the relationships between work characteristics, self-efficacy, collective efficacy, and organizational citizenship behavior: The case of Taiwanese Police Duty-Executing Organizations. *The Journal of Psychology, 145*(4), 361–390. doi:10.1080/00223980.2011.574168 PMID:21834327

Chen, L., Feldmann, A., & Tang, O. (2015). The relationship between disclosures of corporate social performance and financial performance: Evidences from GRI reports in manufacturing industry. *International Journal of Production Economics, 170*, 445–456. doi:10.1016/j.ijpe.2015.04.004

Chen, S.-L., Shih, C.-T., & Chi, N.-W. (2018). A multilevel job demands–resources model of work engagement: Antecedents, consequences, and boundary conditions. *Human Performance, 31*(5), 282–304. doi:10.1080/08959285.2018.1531867

Chen, Y., & Volz, U. (2022). Scaling up sustainable investment through blockchain-based project bonds. *Development Policy Review, 40*(3), e12582. doi:10.1111/dpr.12582

Chewning, L. V., Lai, C.-H., & Doerfel, M. L. (2013). Organizational resilience and using information and communication technologies to rebuild communication structures. *Management Communication Quarterly, 27*, 237–263. doi:10.1177/08933 18912 46581 5

Chiaburu, D. S., Oh, I.-S., Berry, C. M., Li, N., & Gardner, R. G. (2011). The five-factor model of personality traits and organizational citizenship behaviors: A meta. *J.L. Pletzer Personality and Individual Differences, 173* (2021), 110550

Chien, F., Chau, K. Y., Ady, S. U., Zhang, Y., Tran, Q. H., & Aldeehani, T. M. (2021). Does the Combining Effects of Energy and Consideration of Financial Development Lead to Environmental Burden: Social Perspective of Energy Finance?, pp. 1-14. Environmental Science and Pollution Research. doi:10.100711356-021-13423-6

Chien, F., Ajaz, T., Andlib, Z., Chau, K. Y., Ahmad, P., & Sharif, A. (2021). The Role of Technology Innovation, Renewable Energy and Globalization in Reducing Environmental Degradation in Pakistan: A Step Towards Sustainable Environment. *Renewable Energy, 177*, 308–317. doi:10.1016/j.renene.2021.05.101

Chien, F., Anwar, A., Hsu, C. C., Sharif, A., Razzaq, A., & Sinha, A. (2021). The Role of Information and Communication Technology in Encountering Environmental Degradation: Proposing an SDG Framework for the BRICS Countries. *Technology in Society*, *65*, 101–115. doi:10.1016/j.techsoc.2021.101587

China Academy of Information and Communication Technology (CAICT). (2021). *White Paper on Global Digital Governance*. http://www.caict.ac.cn/kxyj/qwfb/bps/202012/P020201215465405492157.pdf

China Business Network (CBN). (2022). *China's 5G network deployment for three years, the scale of application into a critical period.* https://www.sohu.com/a/554771719_114986

China Center for Information Industry Development (CCID). (2020). *White Paper on the Development of New Infrastructure*. https://v1.cecdn.yun300.cn/site_1801180113/%E2%80%9C%E6%96%B0%E5%9F%BA%E5%BB%BA%E2%80%9D%E5%8F%91%E5%B1%95%E7%99%BD%E7%9A%AE%E4%B9%A6.pdf

China Central State-Owned Companies Digital Development Academy. (2021). *White Paper on Development Index and method path of Digital Transformation of State-owned Enterprises*. http://www.clii.com.cn/lhrh/hyxx/202112/P020211215020914.pdf

China Development Institute. (2022). *Shared Innovation-accelerating towards the Global Top Science and Technology Bay area*. Author.

China Environmental Protection Industry Research Institute. (2020). *Policy Suggestions on Promoting the Formation of Green Consumption and Lifestyle in the 14th Five Year Plan*. CEPIRI. http://www.zghbcyyjy.cn/?p=21564

China Information and Communication Research Institute. (2021). *White Paper on Vehicle Networking*. CEPIRI. https://my.mbd.baidu.com/r/CIiYSYgucw?f=cp&u=c98d9d27995e162d

China Internet Network Information Development Association (CNNIA). (2021). *China Internet Development report (2021)*. https://mp.weixin.qq.com/s/H-Zl9avqjJp_zYBcwwuvEQ

China Software Research Institute. (2022). *White Paper on the Integration of Operation and Management of Central Enterprises in the Digital era (2022)*. http://www.199it.com/archives/1365318.html

Choi, D. I., & Gray, E. R. (2008). The venture development processes of sustainable entrepreneurs. *Management Research News*, *31*(8), 558–569. doi:10.1108/01409170810892127

Choi, J. K., Thangamani, D., & Kissock, K. (2019). A systematic methodology for improving resource efficiency in small and medium-sized enterprises. *Resources, Conservation and Recycling*, *147*, 19–27. doi:10.1016/j.resconrec.2019.04.015

Choi, W., Yoo, E., Seol, E., Kim, M., & Song, H. (2020). Greenhouse Gas Emissions of Conventional and Alternative Vehicles: Predictions Based on Energy Policy Analysis in South Korea. *Applied Energy*, *265*, 114754. doi:10.1016/j.apenergy.2020.114754

Cichorzewska, M., & Rakowska, A. (2017). Organizational citizenship behavior of Polish and Ukrainian civil servants – a comparative study. In *Management Challenges in a Network Economy: Proceedings of the MakeLearn and TIIM International Conference* (pp. 393–394). ToKnowPress.

Clark, D. (2022a). Estimated number of companies worldwide from 2000 to 2021. *Statista*. https://www.statista.com/statistics/1260686/global-companies/#:~:text=There%20were%20estimated%20to%20be,were%20around%20328%20million%20companies.%20

Clark, D. (2022b). Oldest 20 companies still operating worldwide in 2021. *Statista.* https://www.statista.com/statistics/1259761/oldest-companies-worldwide/

Clarke, K. R. (1993). Non-parametric multivariate analyses of changes in community structure. *Austral Ecology, 18*(1), 117–143. doi:10.1111/j.1442-9993.1993.tb00438.x

Clark, H. (2013). What does Rio+20 mean for sustainable development? *Development, 56*(1), 16–23. doi:10.1057/dev.2013.13

Clémençon, R. (2012). Welcome to the Anthropocene: Rio+20 and the meaning of sustainable development. *Journal of Environment & Development, 21*(3), 311–338. doi:10.1177/1070496512457289

Clement, V., & Rivera, J. (2017). From adaptation to transformation: An extended research agenda for organizational resilience to adversity in the natural environment. *Organization & Environment, 30*, 346–365. doi:10.1177/10860 26616 65833 3

Cohen, B., Smith, B., & Mitchell, R. (2008). Toward a sustainable conceptualization of dependent variables in entrepreneurship research. *Business Strategy and the Environment, 17*(2), 107–119. doi:10.1002/bse.505

Cohen, B., & Winn, M. I. (2007). Market imperfections, opportunity and sustainable entrepreneurship. *Journal of Business Venturing, 22*(1), 29–49. doi:10.1016/j.jbusvent.2004.12.001

Coles, E., & Buckle, P. (2004). Developing community resilience as a foundation for effective disaster recovery. *Australian Journal of Emergency Management, 19*(4), 6–15.

Colli, A., Howorth, C., & Rose, M. (2013). Long-term perspectives on family business. *Business History, 55*(6), 841–854. doi:10.1080/00076791.2012.744589

Connell, J., & Voola, R. (2013). Knowledge integration and competitiveness: A longitudinal study of an industry cluster. *Journal of Knowledge Management, 17*(2), 208–225. doi:10.1108/13673271311315178

Corresponsables (2022). Somos una de las bodegas más grandes de Europa energéticamente sostenibles [We are one of the largest energy-sustainable wineries in Europe]. Corresponsables. https://www.corresponsables.com/entrevistas/juan-gil-bodegas-grandes-europa-energeticamente-sostenibles

Corresponsables. (2022). *Debemos romper con la visión errónea de que el medio ambiente lo soporta todo* [We must break with the erroneous view that the environment supports everything]. Corresponsables. https://www.corresponsables.com/entrevistas/matarromera-romper-vision-erronea-medio-ambiente

Corrocher, N., Lamperti, F., & Mavilia, R. (2019). Technological Forecasting and Social Change Do Science Parks Sustain or Trigger Innovation? Empirical Evidence from Italy. *Technological Forecasting and Social Change, 147*, 140–151. doi:10.1016/j.techfore.2019.07.005

Coutu, D. L. (2002). How resilience works. *Harvard Business Review, 80*(5), 46–55.

Crédito y Caución. (2020). *La pandemia incrementa la mortalidad entre las empresas con tres años de vida. [The pandemic increases mortality among companies with three years of life].* Iberinform. https://www.iberinform.es/noticias/detalle/La-pandemia-incrementa-la-mortalidad-entre-las-empresas-con-tres-anos-de-vida

CRIC in Shenzhen. (2022). *White Paper on Guangdong-Hong Kong-Macau Greater Bay Area's Investment in 2022.* https://mp.weixin.qq.com/s/uc1ZozjFzD9ph1uRSdHjww

Crichton, M. T., Ramsay, C. G., & Kelly, T. (2009). Enhancing organizational resilience through emergency planning: Learnings from cross-sectorial lessons. *Journal of Contingencies and Crisis Management, 17*, 24–37.

Croo, A. D. (2015, March 20). *Why digital is key to sustainable growth.* World Economic Forum. https://www.weforum.org/agenda/2015/03/why-digital-is-key-to-sustainable-growth/

Ćulibrk, J., Delić, M., Mitrović, S., & Ćulibrk, D. (2018). Job satisfaction, organizational commitment and job involvement: The mediating role of job involvement. *Frontiers in Psychology, 9*, 132. doi:10.3389/fpsyg.2018.00132 PMID:29503623

Cunha, P., Neves, S. A., Marques, A. C., & Serrasqueiro, Z. (2020). Adoption of energy efficiency measures in the buildings of micro-, small- and medium-sized Portuguese enterprises. *Energy Policy, 146*, 4215. doi:10.1016/j.enpol.2020.111776

Cuthill, M., Ross, H., Maclean, K., Owens, K., & Witt, B. (2008). Reporting Social Outcomes of Development: An Analysis of Diverse Approaches. *The International Journal of Interdisciplinary Social Sciences: Annual Review, 3*, 145–158.

Da Ponte, E., Fleckenstein, M., Leinenkugel, P., Parker, A., Oppelt, N., & Kuenzer, C. (2015). Tropical forest cover dynamics for Latin America using Earth observation data: A review covering the continental, regional, and local scale. *International Journal of Remote Sensing, 36*(12), 3196–3242. doi:10.1080/01431161.2015.1058539

Dalal, R. S., Bhave, D. P., & Fiset, J. (2014). Within-person variability in job performance a theoretical review and research agenda. *Journal of Management, 40*(5), 1396–1436. doi:10.1177/0149206314532691

Dallyn, S. (2017). Cryptocurrencies as market singularities: The strange case of Bitcoin. *Journal of Cultural Economics, 10*(5), 462–473. doi:10.1080/17530350.2017.1315541

Danaei, A., & Iranbakhsh, F. (2016). Key drivers of innovative behavior in hotel industry: evidence from a developing country. Iran. J. Manage. Stud., 9(3): 599-625.

Dane, F. C. (1990). *Research methods.* Thomson Brooks/Cole Publishing Co.

Danes, S. M., Lee, J., Amarapurkar, S., Stafford, K., Haynes, G., & Brewton, K. E. (2009). Determinants of family business resilience after a natural disaster by gender of business owner. *Journal of Developmental Entrepreneurship, 14*(4), 333–354. doi:10.1142/S1084946709001351

Dansereau, F. Jr, Graen, G., & Haga, W. J. (1975). A vertical dyad linkage approach to leadership within formal organizations: A longitudinal investigation of the role making process. *Organizational Behavior and Human Performance, 13*(1), 46–78. doi:10.1016/0030-5073(75)90005-7

Das, L. (2015). Work participation of women in agriculture in Odisha. *IOSR Journal of Humanities and Social Science (IOSR-JHSS), 20*(7), 66-78.

Daskon, C. (2010). Cultural resilience – the roles of cultural traditions in sustaining rural livelihoods: A case study from rural kandyan villages in central Sri Lanka. *Sustainability, 2*(4), 1080–1100.

Davidescu, A. A., Apostu, S. A., Paul, A., & Casuneanu, I. (2020). Work flexibility, job satisfaction, and job performance among Romanian employees—Implications for sustainable human resource management. *Sustainability, 12*(15), 6086. doi:10.3390u12156086

Davies, A. R. (2013). Cleantech clusters: Transformational assemblages for a just, green economy or just business as usual? *Global Environmental Change, 23*(5), 1285–1295. doi:10.1016/j.gloenvcha.2013.07.010

Dawson, C. S. (2010). *Leading culture change: what every CEO needs to know.* Stanford University Press.

De Bakker, F. G., Groenewegen, P., & Den Hond, F. (2005). A bibliometric analysis of 30 years of research and theory on corporate social responsibility and corporate social performance. *Business & Society*, *44*(3), 283–317. doi:10.1177/0007650305278086

de Oliveira Teixeira E, Werther WB (2013) Resilience: continuous renewal of competitive advantages. *Bus Horiz 56*, 333–342. https://doi.org/ r.2013.01.009 doi:10.1016/j.busho

Death, C. (2015). Four discourses of the green economy in the global South. *Third World Quarterly*, *36*(12), 2207–2224. doi:10.1080/01436597.2015.1068110

Dehghan, H., Mobinyzadeh, V., & Habibi, P. (2016). The effects of heat stress on job satisfaction, job performance and occupational stress in casting workers. *Jundishapur Journal of Health Sciences, 8*(3).

Dekker, J. M., Funahashi, T., & Nijpels, G. (2008, April 1). Prognostic Value of Adiponectin for Cardiovascular Disease and Mortality. *The Journal of Clinical Endocrinology and Metabolism*, *93*(4), 1489–1496. doi:10.1210/jc.2007-1436

del Río, P., Carrillo-Hermosilla, J., & Könnölä, T. (2010). Policy Strategies to Promote Eco-Innovation: An Integrated Framework. *Journal of Industrial Ecology*, *14*(4), 541–557. doi:10.1111/j.1530-9290.2010.00259.x

Deloitte. (2021). *The Great Bay area under the New Development pattern-- the focal Point of Guangdong-Hong Kong-Macau Greater Bay Area's Development during the 14th five-year Plan period.* https://www2.deloitte.com/cn/zh/pages/about-deloitte/articles/gba-new-develop-with-dtt.html

Deluga, R. J. (1995). The relationship between attributional charismatic leadership and organizational citizenship behavior. *J. Appl. Soc. Psychol. 25*, 1652–1669. doi:. 1995.tb02638.x doi:10.1111/j.1559-1816

Deng, X., Kang, J. K., & Low, B. S. (2013). Corporate social responsibility and stakeholder value maximization: Evidence from mergers. *Journal of Financial Economics*, *110*(1), 87–109. doi:10.1016/j.jfineco.2013.04.014

Denyer, D. (2017). *Organizational Resilience: A summary of academic evidence, business insights and new thinking.* BSI and Cranfield School of Management.

Department for Digital Culture, Media & Sport. (2017). *UK Digital Strategy 2017.* https://www.gov.uk/government/publications/uk-digital-strategy/uk-digital-strategy

Derwall, J., & Verwijmeren, P. (2007). Corporate governance and the cost of equity capital: Evidence from gmi's governance rating. *European Centre for Corporate Engagement Research Note, 6*(1), 1-11.

Derwall, J., Guenster, N., Bauer, R., & Koedijk, K. (2005). The eco-efficiency premium puzzle. *Financial Analysts Journal*, *61*(2), 51–63. doi:10.2469/faj.v61.n2.2716

DesJardine, M., Bansal, P., & Yang, Y. (2017). Bouncing back: Building resilience through social and environmental practices in the context of the 2008 global fiscal crisis. *Journal of Management*, *26*, 014920631770885. doi:10.1177/0149206317 70885 4

Dey, A., & Orton, B. (2016). Gender and caste intersectionality in India: An analysis of the Nirbhaya case, 16 December 2012. In gender and race matter: Global perspectives on being a woman. Emerald Group Publishing Limited.

Dhaliwal, D. S., Li, O. Z., Tsang, A., & Yang, Y. G. (2011). Voluntary nonfinancial disclosure and the cost of equity capital: The initiation of corporate social responsibility reporting. *The Accounting Review*, *86*(1), 59–100. doi:10.2308/accr.00000005

Dimara, E., Skuras, D., Tsekouras, K., & Tzelepis, D. (2008). Productive efficiency and firm exit in the food sector. *Food Policy*, *33*(2), 185–196. doi:10.1016/j.foodpol.2007.08.003

Dimitriou, T., & Karame, G. (2013). Privacy-friendly tasking and trading of energy in smart grids. *Proceedings of the 28th Annual ACM Symposium on Applied Computing*, (pp. 652–659). ACM. 10.1145/2480362.2480488

Dobbs, R., Oppenheim, J., Thompson, F., Brinkman, M., & Zornes, M. (2011). *Resource revolution: meeting the world's energy, materials, food, and water needs*. McKinsey Global Institute.

Doern, R. (2016). Entrepreneurship and Crisis Management: The Experiences of Small Business during the London 2011 Riots. *International Small Business Journal*, *34*(3), 276–302. doi:10.1177/0266242614553863

Dooley, B., & Ueno, H. (2020). This Japanese shop is 1,020 years old. It knows a bit about surviving crises. *The New York Times*. https://www.nytimes.com/2020/12/02/business/japan-old-companies.html

Drempetic, S., Klein, C., & Zwergel, B. (2020). The influence of firm size on the ESG score: Corporate sustainability ratings under review. *Journal of Business Ethics*, *167*(2), 333–360. doi:10.100710551-019-04164-1

Drescher, D. (2017). *Blockchain Basics: A Non-Technical Introduction in 25 Steps*. Springer. https://link.springer.com/book/10.1007/978-1-4842-2604-9

Drucker, P. (2012). *Management*. Routledge. doi:10.4324/9780080939063

Ducuing, C. (2019). How to Make Sure My Cryptokitties Are Here Forever? The Complementary Roles of Blockchain and the Law to Bring Trust. *European Journal of Risk Regulation*, *10*(2), 315–329. doi:10.1017/err.2019.39

Duit, A. (2016). Resilience thinking: Lessons for Public Administration. *Public Administration*, *94*, 364–380.

Dumas, C., & Louche, C. (2016). Collective beliefs on responsible investment. *Business & Society*, *55*(3), 427–457. doi:10.1177/0007650315575327

Dunbar, R. I. M., Marriott, A., & Duncan, N. D. C. (1997). Human conversational behavior. *Human Nature (Hawthorne, N.Y.)*, *8*(3), 231–246. doi:10.1007/BF02912493 PMID:26196965

Dussault, M. (2006). Teachers' self-efficacy and organizational citizenship behaviors. *Psychological Reports*, *98*(2), 427–432. doi:10.2466/pr0.98.2.427-432 PMID:16796098

Dutta, A. (2017). Modeling and Forecasting the Volatility of Carbon Emission Market: The Role of Outliers, Time-Varying Jumps and Oil Price Risk. *Journal of Cleaner Production,* doi:10.1016/j.jclepro.2017.11.135

Du, W., Pan, S. L., Leidner, D. E., & Ying, W. (2019). Affordances, experimentation and actualization of FinTech: A blockchain implementation study. *The Journal of Strategic Information Systems*, *28*(1), 50–65. doi:10.1016/j.jsis.2018.10.002

Eccles, R. G., Ioannou, I., & Serafeim, G. (2014). The impact of corporate sustainability on organizational processes and performance. *Management Science*, *60*(11), 2835–2857. doi:10.1287/mnsc.2014.1984

Eck, N. J. V., & Waltman, L. (2014). Visualising bibliometric networks. In *Measuring scholarly impact* (pp. 285–320). Springer.

Eiadat, Y., Kelly, A., Roche, F., & Eyadat, H. (2008). Green and Competitive? An Empirical Test of the Mediating Role of Environmental Innovation Strategy. *Journal of World Business*, *43*(2), 131–145. doi:10.1016/j.jwb.2007.11.012

Eichholtz, P., Kok, N., & Quigley, J. M. (2010). Doing well by doing good? Green office buildings. *The American Economic Review*, *100*(5), 2492–2509. doi:10.1257/aer.100.5.2492

Eichholtz, P., Kok, N., & Quigley, J. M. (2013). The economics of green building. *The Review of Economics and Statistics, 95*(1), 50–63. doi:10.1162/REST_a_00291

Eisenhardt, K. M. (1989). Building theories from case study research. *Academy of Management Review, 14*(4), 532–550. doi:10.2307/258557

Ekienabor, E. E. (2016). Impact of job stress on employees' productivity and commitment. *International journal for research in business, management, and accounting, 2*(5), 124-133.

El Ghoul, S., Guedhami, O., Kwok, C. C., & Mishra, D. R. (2011). Does corporate social responsibility affect the cost of capital? *Journal of Banking & Finance, 35*(9), 2388–2406. doi:10.1016/j.jbankfin.2011.02.007

Elentably, A. (2015). Strategic and Operational Plan Implementation of Seaports (Utilization Jeddah Port). TransNav. *International Journal on Marine Navigation and Safety of Sea Transportation, 9*(4).

Elkington, J. (1999). *Cannibals with Forks: The Triple Bottom Line of 21st Century Business.* Capstone.

Eltantawy, R. A. (2016). The role of supply management resilience in attaining ambidexterity: A dynamic capabilities approach. *Journal of Business and Industrial Marketing, 31*(1), 123–134. doi:10.1108/JBIM-05-2014-0091

EnjoyZaragoza. (2021). *Bodegas Borsao, un referente europeo de sostenibilidad* [Bodegas Borsao, a European benchmark in sustainability]. EnjoyZaragoza. https://www.enjoyzaragoza.es/instalaciones-borsao/

Enzmann, P., & Moesli, M. (2022). Seizing opportunities: ASEAN country cluster readiness in light of the fourth industrial revolution. *Asia and the Global Economy, 2*(1), Article 100021. doi:10.1016/j.aglobe.2021.100021

Eriksson, P., & Kovalainen, A. (2015). Qualitative methods in business research: A practical guide to social research. *Sage (Atlanta, Ga.).*

Essiam, J. O., Mensah, M. E., Kudu, L. K., & Gyamfi, G. D. (2015). Influence of job stress on job satisfaction among university staff: Analytical evidence from a public university in Ghana. International Journal of Economics. *Commerce and Management, 3*(2), 1–15.

European Commission. (2005). *Thematic strategy on the sustainable use of natural resources.* EC. https://ec.europa.eu/environment/archives/natres/index.htm

European Commission. (2010). *Europe 2020: A strategy for smart, sustainable and inclusive growth.* EC. https://eur-lex.europa.eu/LexUriServ/LexUriServ.do?uri=COM:2010:2020:FIN:EN:PDF

European Commission. (2011). *Roadmap to a resource efficient Europe.* EC. https://eur-lex.europa.eu/legal-content/EN/TXT/?uri=CELEX:52011DC0571

European Commission. (2012). *Ethical and Regulatory Challenges to Science and Research Policy at the Globle Level.* European Commission.

European Commission. (2013). *The opportunities of business of improving resource efficiency - final report.* EC. https://ec.europa.eu/environment/enveco/resource_efficiency/pdf/report_opportunities.pdf

European Commission. (2018). *A clean planet for all: A European strategic long-term vision for a prosperous, modern, competitive and climate neutral economy.* EC. https://eur-lex.europa.eu/legal-content/EN/TXT/?uri=CELEX%3A52018DC0773

European Investment Bank. (2022). *Small and medium enterprises: overview.* EIB. https://www.eib.org/attachments/lucalli/smes_overview_2022_en.pdf

Eurostat (2009). *The environmental goods and services sector: a data collection handbook.* Eurostat, Luxembourg.

Eurostat. (2013). *Resource Efficiency Scoreboard: Thirty indicators to measure resource efficiency in the EU.* Eurostat. https://ec.europa.eu/environment/resource_efficiency/news/up-to-date_news/11122013_en.htm

Eurostat. (2022). *Sustainable development in the European Union - 2022 edition.* Eurostat. https://ec.europa.eu/eurostat/web/products-flagship-publications/-/ks-09-22-019

Evangelista, R., Guerrieri, P., & Meliciani, V. (2014). The economic impact of digital technologies in Europe. *Economics of Innovation and New Technology, 23*(8), 802–824. doi:10.1080/10438599.2014.918438

Fabozzi, F. J., Ma, K. C., & Oliphant, B. J. (2008). Sin stock returns. *Journal of Portfolio Management, 35*(1), 82–94. doi:10.3905/JPM.2008.35.1.82

Fama, E. F., & French, K. R. (1993). Common risk factors in the returns on stocks and bonds. *Journal of Financial Economics, 33*(1), 3–56. doi:10.1016/0304-405X(93)90023-5

Fama, E. F., & MacBeth, J. D. (1973). Risk, return, and equilibrium: Empirical tests. *Journal of Political Economy, 81*(3), 607–636. doi:10.1086/260061

Fan, G. (2022). *Sharing Innovation.* In Science and Innovation Bay Area Seminar.

Fan, Y. Y., & Zhang, D. (2018). Review of Research on Responsible Innovation and Its Enlightenment to Innovation Management. *Science-Technology and Management,* 20.

Fan, Y., Fang, C., & Zhang, Q. (2019). Coupling Coordinated Development between Social Economy and Ecological Environment in Chinese Provincial Capital Cities-Assessment and Policy Implications. *Journal of Cleaner Production, 229*, 289–298. doi:10.1016/j.jclepro.2019.05.027

Faraj, S., & Sproull, L. (2000). Coordinating expertise in software development teams. *Management Science, 46*, 1554–1568.

Feinberg, M., Willer, R., & Schultz, M. (2014). Gossip and ostracism promote cooperation in groups. *Psychological Science, 25*(3), 656–664. doi:10.1177/0956797613510184 PMID:24463551

Ferguson, P. (2014). The green economy agenda: Business as usual or transformational discourse? *Environmental Politics, 24*(1), 17–37. doi:10.1080/09644016.2014.919748

Figueroa-Armijos, M. (2017). Women's Entrepreneurship in Global and Local Contexts, Growth and Change, 48(3), 487-489.

Filippi, C., Guastaroba, G., & Speranza, M. (2016). A Heuristic Framework for the Bi-Objective Enhanced Index Tracking Problem. *Omega, 65*, 122–137. doi:10.1016/j.omega.2016.01.004

Financial Food. (2019). *Bodegas Campo Viejo avanza en sostenibilidad* [Bodegas Campo Viejo advances in sustainability]. Financial Food. https://financialfood.es/bodegas-campo-viejo-avanza-en-sostenibilidad/

Fioramonti, L. (2014). The world's most powerful number: An assessment of 80 years of GDP ideology. *Anthropology Today, 30*(2), 16–19. doi:10.1111/1467-8322.12098

Flammer, C. (2020). Green bonds: Effectiveness and implications for public policy. *Environmental and Energy Policy and the Economy*, *1*(1), 95–128. doi:10.1086/706794

Fleet, G. (2003). Yeast interactions and wine flavour. *International Journal of Food Microbiology*, *86*(1-2), 11–22. doi:10.1016/S0168-1605(03)00245-9 PMID:12892919

Fletcher, G., & Griffiths, M. (2020). Digital transformation during a lockdown. *International Journal of Information Management*. doi:10.1016/j.ijinfomgt.2020.102185

Fontana, R., & Nesta, L. (2009). Product innovation and survival in a high-tech industry. *Review of Industrial Organization*, *34*(4), 287–306. doi:10.100711151-009-9210-7

Foody, G. M. (2007). Editorial: Ecological Applications of Remote Sensing and GIS. *Ecological Informatics*, *2*(2), 71–72. doi:10.1016/j.ecoinf.2007.06.001

Forsberg, E. M., Thorstensen, E., Casagrande, F. D., Holthe, T., Halvorsrud, L., Lund, A., & Zouganelic, E. (2021). Is RRI a New R&I Logic? A Reflection from an Integrated RRI Project. *Journal of Responsible Technology, 5*.

Fosse, J., & Petrick, K.. (2016). *Towards a Green Economy in the Mediterranean - Assessment of National Green Economy and Sustainable Development Strategies in Mediterranean Countries. eco-union, MIO-ECSDE*. GEC.

Foster, S., & Dye, K. (2005). Building continuity into strategy. *Journal of Corporate Real Estate*, *7*(2), 105–119.

Francisco, K., & Swanson, D. (2018). The Supply Chain Has No Clothes: Technology Adoption of Blockchain for Supply Chain Transparency. *Logistics*, *2*(1), 1. doi:10.3390/logistics2010002

Friede, G., Busch, T., & Bassen, A. (2015). ESG and financial performance: aggregated evidence from more than 2000 empirical studies. *Journal of sustainable finance & investment, 5*(4), 210-233.

Friede, G., Busch, T., & Bassen, A. (2015). ESG and Financial Performance: Aggregated Evidence From More Than 2000 Empirical Studies. *Journal of Sustainable Finance & Investment*, *5*(4), 210–233. doi:10.1080/20430795.2015.1118917

Friedman, M. (1970). A Friedman doctrine: The social responsibility of business is to increase its profits. *The New York Times Magazine, 13*(1970), 32-33.

Friedman, M. (1962). *Capitalism and Freedom*. University of Chicago Press.

Fuentes-Fernández, R., Martínez-Falcó, J., Sánchez-García, E., & Marco-Lajara, B. (2022). Does Ecological Agriculture Moderate the Relationship between Wine Tourism and Economic Performance? A Structural Equation Analysis Applied to the Ribera del Duero Wine Context. *Agriculture*, *12*(12), 2143.

Fugas, C. S., Silva, S. A., & Meliá, J. L. (2013). Profiling safety behaviors: Exploration of the sociocognitive variables that best discriminate between different behavioral patterns. *Risk Analysis*, *33*(5), 838–850. doi:10.1111/j.1539-6924.2012.01913.x PMID:23078368

Gabryelczyk, R. (2020). Has COVID-19 Accelerated Digital Transformation? Initial Lessons Learned for Public Administrations. *Information Systems Management*, *37*(4), 303–309.

Galbreath, J., & Tisch, D. (2020). The effects of women in different roles on environmentally sustainable practices: Empirical evidence from the Australian wine industry. *Australasian Journal of Environmental Management*, *27*(4), 434–451. doi:10.1080/14486563.2020.1838351

Gallopín, G. C. (2006). Linkages between Vulnerability, Resilience and Adaptive Capacity. *Global Environmental Change*, *16*(3), 293–303.

Galvez, J. F., Mejuto, J. C., & Simal-Gandara, J. (2018). Future challenges on the use of blockchain for food traceability analysis. *Trends in Analytical Chemistry*. https:// doi:10.1016/j.trac.2018.08.011

Gan, Q., Lau, R. Y. K., & Hong, J. (2021). A critical review of blockchain applications to banking and finance: A qualitative thematic analysis approach. *Technology Analysis and Strategic Management*, *0*(0), 1–17. doi:10.1080/09537325.2021.1979509

Gans-Morse, J., Kalgin, A. S., Klimenko, A. V., Vorobyev, D., & Yakovlev, A. A. (2020). Public service motivation and sectoral employment in Russia: New perspectives on the attraction vs. socialization debate. [Paper presentation]. *Higher School of Economics Research Paper No. WP BRP, 26.*

Gao, H. W., & Zhang, Y. L. (2020). Research on Ways to Improve Innovation Ability of High-Tech Zones. *Economic Research,* 5.

García-Rodríguez, J. (2019). Beronia es premiada por su apuesta enoturística basada en la sostenibilidad [Beronia receives award for its commitment to wine tourism based on sustainability]. *La Gaceta del Vino*. https://lagacetadelvino.com/nuestras-firmas/reconocimiento-a-beronia-rioja-por-sus-buenas-practicas-medioambientales/

Garrido-Prada, P., Lenihan, H., Doran, J., Rammer, C., & Perez-Alaniz, M. (2021). Driving the circular economy through public environmental and energy R&D: Evidence from SMEs in the European Union. *Ecological Economics*, *182*, 106884. doi:10.1016/j.ecolecon.2020.106884

Gast, J., Gundolf, K., & Cesinger, B. (2017). Doing business in a green way: A systematic review of the ecological sustainability entrepreneurship literature and future research directions. *Journal of Cleaner Production*, *147*, 44–56. doi:10.1016/j.jclepro.2017.01.065

Gaver, W. W. (1991). Technology affordances. *Proceedings of the SIGCHI Conference on Human Factors in Computing Systems Reaching through Technology - CHI '91*, (pp. 79–84). ACM. 10.1145/108844.108856

Geissdoerfer, M., Vladimirova, D., & Evans, S. (2018). Sustainable business model innovation: A review. *Journal of Cleaner Production*, *198*, 401–416. doi:10.1016/j.jclepro.2018.06.240

Gephart, R. P., Van Maanen, J., & Oberlechner, T. (2009). Organizations and risk in late modernity. *Organization Studies*, *30*(2–3), 141–155.https://doi.org/ doi:10.1177/0170840608101474

Geroski, P. A. (1995). What do we know about entry? *International Journal of Industrial Organization*, *13*(4), 421–440. doi:10.1016/0167-7187(95)00498-X

Gertler, M. S. (2003). Tacit knowledge and the economic geography of context, or the undefinable tacitness of being (there). *Journal of Economic Geography*, *3*(1), 75–99.

Gibson Brandon, R., Krueger, P., & Schmidt, P. S. (2021). ESG rating disagreement and stock returns. *Financial Analysts Journal*, *77*(4), 104–127. doi:10.1080/0015198X.2021.1963186

Gibson, J. J. (1979). *The Ecological Approach to Visual Perception.* Psychology Press. doi:10.4324/9781315740218

Gibson, J., Ivancevich, J., & Konopaske, R. (2011). *Organizations: Behavior, structure, processes.* McGraw-Hill Higher Education.

Giebels, E., de Reuver, R. S. M., Rispens, S., & Ufkes, E. G. (2016). The critical roles of task conflict and job autonomy in the relationship between proactive personalities and innovative employee behavior. *The Journal of Applied Behavioral Science*, *52*(3), 320–341. doi:10.1177/0021886316648774 PMID:27536008

Gimenez, R., Hernantes, J., Labaka, L., Hiltz, S. R., & Turoff, M. (2017). Improving the resilience of disaster management organizations through virtual communities of practice: A Delphi study. *Journal of Contingencies and Crisis Management*, *25*, 160–170. doi:10.1111/1468-5973.12181

Gittell, J. H., Cameron, K., Lim, S., & Rivas, V. (2006). Relationships, layoffs, and organizational resilience: Airline industry responses to September 11. *The Journal of Applied Behavioral Science*, *42*, 300–329.

Giungato, P., Rana, R., Tarabella, A., & Tricase, C. (2017). Current Trends in Sustainability of Bitcoins and Related Blockchain Technology. *Sustainability*, *9*(12), 12. doi:10.3390u9122214

Glavanits, J. (2020). Sustainable Public Spending Through Blockchain. *European Journal of Sustainable Development*, *9*(4), 4. doi:10.14207/ejsd.2020.v9n4p317

Global Sustainable Investment Alliance. (2018). *Global sustainable investment review.* GSI. http://www.gsi-alliance.org/wp-content/uploads/2019/03/GSIR_Review2018.3.28.pdf

Global Sustainable Investment Alliance. (2020). *Global sustainable investment review.* GSI. http://www.gsi-alliance.org/wp-content/uploads/2021/08/GSIR-20201.pdf

Gnägi, M., & Strub, O. (2020). Tracking and Outperforming Large Stock-Market Indices. *Omega*, *90*, 101999. doi:10.1016/j.omega.2018.11.008

Godfrey, P. C., Merrill, C. B., & Hansen, J. M. (2009). The relationship between corporate social responsibility and shareholder value: An empirical test of the risk management hypothesis. *Strategic Management Journal*, *30*(4), 425–445. doi:10.1002mj.750

Goss, A., & Roberts, G. S. (2011). The impact of corporate social responsibility on the cost of bank loans. *Journal of Banking & Finance*, *35*(7), 1794–1810. doi:10.1016/j.jbankfin.2010.12.002

Government, H. M. (2011). *Enabling the transition to a green economy: government and business working together.* HM Government.

Govindji, R., & Linley, P. A. (2007). Strength's use, self-concordance and well-being implications for strengths coaching and coaching psychologists. Int. Coach. *Psychological Review*, *2*, 143–153.

Grant, D. E. (2000). *The impact of mentoring and gender -specific role models on women college band directors at four different career* [Dissertation, University of Minnesota]. ProQuest Dissertations Publishing, 9966225.

Grant, A. M. (2008a). Does intrinsic motivation fuel the prosocial free? Motivational synergy in predicting persistence, performance, and productivity. *The Journal of Applied Psychology*, *93*(1), 48–58. doi:10.1037/0021-9010.93.1.48 PMID:18211134

Grant, A. M. (2008b). The significance of task significance: Job performance effects, relational mechanisms, and boundary conditions. *The Journal of Applied Psychology*, *93*(1), 108–124. doi:10.1037/0021-9010.93.1.108 PMID:18211139

Grant, L. (2014). Hearts and minds: Aspects of empathy and wellbeing in social work students. *Social Work Education*, *33*(3), 338–352. doi:10.1080/02615479.2013.805191

Gray, H. M., Gray, K., & Wegner, D. M. (2007). Dimensions of mind perception. *Science*, *315*(5812), 619–619. doi:10.1126cience.1134475 PMID:17272713

Green Economy Coalition (2012). *Principles for a green, fair and inclusive economy.* .

Green Economy Coalition (2012). *The Green Economy Pocketbook – The case for action.* Green Economy Coalition.

Green Growth Knowledge Platform (GGKP). (2013). Moving towards a common approach on green growth indicators: Green Growth Knowledge Platform scoping paper. Green Growth Knowledge Platform, Geneva.

Greenberg, J. (2010). Organizational injustice as an occupational health risk. *The Academy of Management Annals, 4*(1), 205–243. doi:10.5465/19416520.2010.481174

Greer, C. R. (2021). *Strategic human resource management.* Pearson Custom Publishing.

Guangdong Guangdong-Hong Kong-Macau Greater Bay Area Research Institute. (2022). *Guangdong-Hong Kong-Macau Greater Bay Area's digital "accelerated run": speed up the construction of a new digital infrastructure "base", cluster transformation and reshape industrial advantages.* https://mp.weixin.qq.com/s/QAXrsKRXC2ZphPoGRzMZWQ

Guangzhou Government. (2017). *Policies and Measures for Promoting Green Finance Development in Huangpu District and Guangzhou High-tech Zone.* Author.

Guangzhou Government. (2021). *Measures for Promoting hydrogen Industry development of Guangzhou Development Zone and Guangzhou Huangpu District, 202107.* Author.

Guastaroba, G., & Speranza, M. G. (2012). Kernel Search: An Application to the Index Tracking Problem. *European Journal of Operational Research, 217*(1), 54–68. doi:10.1016/j.ejor.2011.09.004

Guerras Martín, L. Á., & Navas López, J. E. (2016). *La dirección estratégica de la empresa: Teoría y aplicaciones [The strategic direction of the company: theory and applications]* (5th ed.). Thomson Reuters Civitas.

Guiness World Records. (2022). *Oldest hotel.* https://www.guinnessworldrecords.com/world-records/oldest-ho tel

Guo, Y., Li, B., & Han, Y. (2020). Dynamic network coupling between high-speed rail development and urban growth in emerging economies: Evidence from China. *Cities, 105.* doi:10.1016/j.cities.2020.102845

Hair, J. F., Anderson, R. E., Babin, B. J., & Black, W. C. (2010). *Multivariate data analysis: A global perspective* (*Vol. 7*). Pearson.

Halbritter, G., & Dorfleitner, G. (2015). The wages of social responsibility—Where are they? A critical review of ESG investing. *Review of Financial Economics, 26*(1), 25–35. doi:10.1016/j.rfe.2015.03.004

Hale, A., & Heijer, T. (2006). Defining Resilience. In E. Hollnagel, D. D. Woods, & N. Leveson (Eds.), *Resilience Engineering: Concepts and Precepts* (pp. 35–40). Ashgate.

Halle, M. (2012) *Life after Rio: a commentary by Mark Halle*, IISD (https://www.iisd.org/sites/default/files/publications/com_li fe_ after_rio.pdf)

Hall, J. K., Daneke, G. A., & Lenox, M. J. (2010). Sustainable development and entrepreneurship: Past contributions and future directions. *Journal of Business Venturing, 25*(5), 439–448. doi:10.1016/j.jbusvent.2010.01.002

Hamel, G. and Välikangas, L. (2003). The quest for resilience. *Harvard Business Review, 81*(9), 52–63. 5.

Hamilton, S., Jo, H., & Statman, M. (1993). Doing well while doing good? The investment performance of socially responsible mutual funds. *Financial Analysts Journal, 49*(6), 62–66. doi:10.2469/faj.v49.n6.62

Hamrouni, A., Boussaada, R., & Toumi, N. B. F. (2019). Corporate social responsibility disclosure and debt financing. *Journal of Applied Accounting Research, 20*(4), 394–415. doi:10.1108/JAAR-01-2018-0020

Hansen, J. A., & Pihl-Thingvad, S. (2019). Managing employee innovative behavior through transformational and transactional leadership styles. *Public Management Review*, *21*(6), 918–944. doi:10.1080/14719037.2018.1544272

Hanson, A. (2019). Ecological Civilization in the People's Republic of China: Values, Action, and Future Needs. Asian Development Bank.

Hawlitschek, F., Notheisen, B., & Teubner, T. (2018). The limits of trust-free systems: A literature review on blockchain technology and trust in the sharing economy. *Electronic Commerce Research and Applications*, *29*, 50–63. doi:10.1016/j.elerap.2018.03.005

He, D., Enhai, Y., Xixi, Ch., Yanbin, L., & Kashif, A. (2020). Humble Leadership Affects Organizational Citizenship Behavior: The Sequential Mediating Effect of Strengths Use and Job Crafting *Journal Frontiers in Psychology, 11.* YEAR=2020URL=https://www.frontiersin.org/article/10.3389/fpsyg.2020.00065 DOI=10.3389/fpsyg.2020.00065

Heal, G. (2012). Reflections–defining and measuring sustainability. *Review of Environmental Economics and Policy*, 6147–6163.

Hedayat, A., Sogolitappeh, F. N., Shakeri, R., Abasifard, M., & Khaledian, M. (2018). Relationship between Organizational Commitment and Job Satisfaction. *International Letters of Social and Humanistic Sciences, 81.*

Hellstrom, T. (2003). Systemic Innovation and Risk: Technology Assessment and the Challenge of Responsible Innovation. *Technology in Society*, *25*(3), 369–384. doi:10.1016/S0160-791X(03)00041-1

Helwig, K. R. (2013). Resilience: A responsibility that can't be delegated. *Frontiers of Health Services Management*, *30*(2), 31–35. https://www.ache.org/pubs/Frontiers/frontiers_index.cfm

Henriques, I., & Sadorsky, P. (2008). Oil Prices and the Stock Prices of Alternative Energy Companies. *Energy Economics*, *30*(3), 998–1010. doi:10.1016/j.eneco.2007.11.001

Herndon, J. M., & Whiteside, M. (2019). Geophysical consequences of tropospheric particulate heating: Further evidence that anthropogenic global warming is principally caused by particulate pollution. *Journal of Geography. Environment and Earth Science International*, *22*(4), 1–23. doi:10.9734/jgeesi/2019/v22i430157

Herrera, I. A., Pasquini, A., Ragosta, M., & Vennesland, A. (2014). The SCALES framework for identifying and extracting resilience related indicators: preliminary findings of a go-around case study. *SIDs 2014-Proc. SESAR Innov. Days*. EUROCONTROL.

Herweijer, C., Waughray, D., & Warren, S. (2018). *Building Block(chain)s for a Better Planet*. World Economic Forum. https://www.weforum.org/reports/building-block-chain-for-a-better-planet/

Hiles, A. (2011). *The Definitive Handbook of Business Continuity Management*. Wiley.

Hirsch, P. M., & Levin, D. Z. (1999). Umbrella advocates versus validity police: A life-cycle model. *Organization Science*, *10*, 199–212.

Hoepner, A. G., Oikonomou, I., Sautner, Z., Starks, L. T., & Zhou, X. (2018). *ESG shareholder engagement and downside risk*. ECGI Global.

Hofstede Insights. (2022). *Compare Countries*. https://www.hofstede-insights.com/fi/product/compare-countries/

Hofstede, G. (1984). *Culture's consequences: International differences in work-related values*. Sage.

Hofstede, G. (2001). *Culture's consequences: Comparing values, behaviors, institutions and organizations across nations*. Sage publications.

Holland, T., & Smit, B. (2010). Climate change and the wine industry: Current research themes and new directions. *Journal of Wine Research, 21*(2-3), 125–136. doi:10.1080/09571264.2010.530095

Homer-Dixon, T., Walker, B., Biggs, R., Crépin, A.-S., Folke, C., Lambin, E., Peterson, G., Rockström, J., Scheffer, M., & Steffen, W. (2015). Synchronous failure: The emerging causal architecture of global crisis. *Ecology and Society*, 20.

Hong, H., & Kacperczyk, M. (2009). The price of sin: The effects of social norms on markets. *Journal of Financial Economics, 93*(1), 15–36. doi:10.1016/j.jfineco.2008.09.001

Hood, C. (2012). Public management by numbers as a performance-enhanced drug: Two hypotheses. *Public Administration Review, 71*, S85–S92.

Horne, J. F. (1997). The coming of age of organizational resilience. *Business Forum, 22*, 24–28.

Horne, J. F., & Orr, J. E. (1998). Assessing Behaviors that Create Resilient Organizations. *Employment Relations Today, 24*, 29–39.

Hua, Z. L. (2021). Exploration and Practice of Patent Navigation Theory in Universities -- A Case Study of North China Electric Power University. *Science and Technology in Chinese Universities, 3.*

Huang, W. (2021). *Investment outlook for the new infrastructure of the digital economy.* https://www.baogaoting.com/info/143751

Hughes, L., Dwivedi, Y. K., Misra, S. K., Rana, N. P., Raghavan, V., & Akella, V. (2019). *Blockchain research, practice and policy: Applications, benefits, limitations, emerging research themes and research agenda.* Brad Scholars. https://bradscholars.brad.ac.uk/handle/10454/17473

Hui, C., Li, X., Chen, T., & Lang, W. (2020). Deciphering the spatial structure of China's megacity region: A new bay area—The Guangdong-Hong Kong-Macao Greater Bay Area in the making. *Cities, 105*. doi:10.1016/j.cities.2018.10.011

Hu, J., & Liden, R. C. (2015). Making a difference in the teamwork: Linking team PM to team processes and effectiveness. *Academy of Management Journal, 58*(4), 1102–1127. doi:10.5465/amj.2012.1142

Hurley, R. F. (2011). *The Decision to Trust: How Leaders Create High-Trust Organizations* (1st ed.). Jossey-Bass.

Hu, W. (2018). Review and Prospect of the Development of Digital economy in China. *Civil-Military Integration on Cyberspace, 013*(06), 18–22.

Hyde, J. S. (1981). How large are cognitive gender differences? A meta-analysis using w2 and d. *The American Psychologist, 36*(8), 892–901. doi:10.1037/0003-066X.36.8.892

Iansiti, M., & Lakhani, K. R. (2017, January 1). The Truth About Blockchain. *Harvard Business Review.* https://hbr.org/2017/01/the-truth-about-blockchain

ICET. (2019). *Research Report on Dual Credits of China's Passenger Vehicles in 2018.* ICET. http://www.icet.org.cn/english/admin/upload/news/202003/977824.html

IgastroAragon. (2021). *Bodegas Borsao invierte 16,5 millones de euros en sus nuevas instalaciones, referente europeo en sostenibilidad* [Bodegas Borsao invests 16.5 million euros in new facilities, a European benchmark in sustainability]. IgastroAragon. https://www.igastroaragon.com/2021/10/bodegas-borsao-inviert e-165-millones-de-euros-en-sus-nuevas-instalaciones-referent e-europeo-en-sostenibilidad.html

Ignatiadis, I. and Nandhakumar, J. (2007). The Impact of Enterprise Systems on Organizational Control and Drift: A Human-Machine Agency Perspective, *International Journal of Enterprise Information Systems (IJEIS)*, *3*(3), 36-51. IGI Global. doi:10.1057/palgrave.jit.2000087

IIGCC. (2021). *The Institution Investors Group on Climate Change*. https://www.iigcc.org /about-us/our-members/

IMF. (2021). *G20 Note On Environmentally Sustainable Investment For The Recovery*. IMF. https://www.imf.org/en/Publications/Policy-Papers/Issues/2021/04/29/G20-Note-On-Environmentally-Sustainable-Investment-For-The-Recovery-460112

Indisa (2022). *Beronia es premiada por su apuesta enoturística basada en la sostenibilidad* [Beronia receives award for its commitment to wine tourism based on sustainability]. Indisa. https://www.indisa.es/al-dia/beronia-premiada-apuesta-enoturistica-basada-sostenibilidad

Industrial Internet Theory. (2021). *61 cases! SASAC release! Summary of digital transformation cases of state-owned enterprises!* https://mp.weixin.qq.com/s/ZEHsgdYBASl3Mlm_qgQGHQ

Institute for Global Industry & Tsinghua University. (2020). *Research report on Digital Transformation of Chinese Enterprises*. http://www.clii.com.cn/lhrh/hyxx/202101/t20210113_3947977.html

International Chamber of Commerce (2011) *Ten conditions for a transition toward a* "Green Economy", ICC.

International Chamber of Commerce. (2012). *Green Economy Roadmap*. ICC.

Irfan, U. (2017, December 2). *Bitcoin's price spike is driving an extraordinary surge in energy use*. Vox. https://www.vox.com/energy-and-environment/2017/12/2/16724786/bitcoin-mining-energy-electricity

Ishak, A. W., & Williams, E. A. (2018). A dynamic model of organizational resilience: Adaptive and anchored approaches. *Corporate Communications*, *23*, 180–196.

Işik, A. N. (2020). Ethical leadership and school effectiveness: The mediating roles of affective commitment and job satisfaction. *Int J Educ Leadersh Manag*, *8*(1), 60–87. doi:10.17583/ijelm.2020.4114

Ismail, A., & Razak, M. R. A. (2016). Effect of job satisfaction on organizational commitment. *Management & Marketing Journal, 14*(1).

Jaaron, A. A. M., & Backhouse, C. J. (2014). Service organisations resilience through the application of the vanguard method of systems thinking: A case study approach. *International Journal of Production Research*, *52*, 2026–2041.

Jain, M., Sharma, G. D., & Srivastava, M. (2019). Can sustainable investment yield better financial returns: A comparative study of ESG indices and MSCI indices. *Risks*, *7*(1), 15. doi:10.3390/risks7010015

Jänicke, M. (2012). Green growth: From a growing eco-industry to economic sustainability. *Energy Policy*, *48*, 13–21. doi:10.1016/j.enpol.2012.04.045

Jaoude, J., & Saade, R. (2019). Blockchain Applications – Usage in Different Domains. IEEE Access, (pp. 45360–45381). IEEE. doi:10.1109/ACCESS.2019.2902501

Jayaweera, T. (2015). Impact of work environmental factors on job performance, mediating role of work motivation: A study of hotel sector in England. *International Journal of Business and Management*, *10*(3), 271. doi:10.5539/ijbm.v10n3p271

Jeanbart, R., & Dahinden, D. Roitinger, A., & Kalberer, G. A. (2020). *Data, the Future of Financial Information* [A SIX White Paper.]. https://www.six-group.com/dam/download/company/report/whitepapers/six-whitepaper-future-of-financial-information-full-version-en.pdf

Jehangir, M., Kareem, N., Khan, A., Jan, M. T., & Soherwardi, S. (2011). Effects of job stress on job performance & job satisfaction. *Interdisciplinary Journal of Contemporary Research in Business*, *3*(7), 453–465.

Jensen, M. C., & Meckling, W. H. (1976). Theory of the firm: Managerial behavior, agency costs and ownership structure. *Journal of Financial Economics*, *3*(4), 305–360. doi:10.1016/0304-405X(76)90026-X

Jepsen, D. M., & Rodwell, J. J. (2006). A side by side comparison of two OCB models and their measures: expanding the construct domain's scope, *Proceedings of the 11th Annual Conference of Asia Pacific Decision Sciences Institute*, (pp. 670-674). Macquarie University.

Jessel, B., & DiCaprio, A. (2018). Can blockchain make trade finance more inclusive? *Journal of Financial Transformation*, *47*, 35–50. https://ideas.repec.org//a/ris/jofitr/1608.html

Jia, H. R., Liu, Z. X., & Xia, B. H. (2014). Research on Responsible Innovation in China Wireless Valley. *Natural Dialectics Research*, *33*(9), 55.

Jiao, C., Richards, D. A., & Zhang, K. (2011). Leadership and organizational citizenship behavior: OCB-specific meanings as mediators. *Journal of Business and Psychology*, *26*(1), 11–25. doi:10.100710869-010-9168-3

Ji, X., Zhang, Y., Mirza, N., Umar, M., & Rizvi, S. K. A. (2021). The Impact of Carbon Neutrality on the Investment Performance: Evidence from the Equity Mutual Funds in BRICS. *Journal of Environmental Management*, *297*, 113228. doi:10.1016/j.jenvman.2021.113228 PMID:34273643

Jones, K., Lanthier, Y., van der Voet, P., van Valkengoed, E., Taylor, D., & Fernández-Prieto, D. (2009). Monitoring and assessment of wetlands using Earth Observation: The GlobWetland project. *Journal of Environmental Management*, *90*(7), 2154–2169. doi:10.1016/j.jenvman.2007.07.037 PMID:18640766

Kabeer, N. (1999). Resources, agency, achievements: Reflections on the measurement of women's empowerment. *Development and Change*, *30*(3), 435–464. doi:10.1111/1467-7660.00125

Kahneman, D. (2003). Maps of bounded rationality: Psychology for behavioral economics. *The American Economic Review*, *93*(5), 1449–1475. doi:10.1257/000282803322655392

Kahneman, D., & Tversky, A. (1972). Subjective probability: A judgment of representativeness. *Cognitive Psychology*, *3*(3), 430–454. doi:10.1016/0010-0285(72)90016-3

Kahneman, D., & Tversky, A. (1979). Prospect Theory: An Analysis of Decision Under Risk. *Econometrica*, *47*(2), 263–292. doi:10.2307/1914185

Kahn, W. A., Barton, M. A., & Fellows, S. (2013). Organizational crises and the disturbance of relational systems. *Academy of Management Review*, *38*, 377–396. doi:10.5465/amr.2011.0363

Kahya, M., & Şahin, F. (2018). The effect of leader personality on follower behavior: The mediating role of leader–member exchange. *Leadership and Organization Development Journal*, *39*(1), 14–33. doi:10.1108/LODJ-08-2016-0206

Kaiser, L. (2020). ESG integration: Value, growth and momentum. *Journal of Asset Management*, *21*(1), 32–51. doi:10.105741260-019-00148-y

Kamp-Roelands, N. (2013). *Private sector initiatives on measuring and reporting on green growth.* OECD Publishing.

Kantur, D., & İşeri -Say. (2015). Measuring organizational resilience: A scale development. *Journal of Business. Economics & Finance*, *4*(3), 456–472.

Kao, R. H. (2017). Task-oriented work characteristics, self-efficacy, and service-oriented organizational citizenship behavior. *Personnel Review*, *46*(4), 718–739. doi:10.1108/PR-08-2015-0234

Kaplan, M.; Ö ˘güt, A.; Karayel, S. & Ilhan, ˙I. (2013). *The effects of ethical climate types on job satisfaction: The case of tourism industry.* Hacet. Üniversitesi ˙Iktisadi ˙Idari Bilimler Fakültesi Derg, *31*, 117–133.

Kattuah, S. E. (2013). *Workforce training for increased productivity in Saudi Arabia* [Doctoral dissertation, Victoria University].

Katz, D. (1964). The motivational basis of organizational behavior. *Behavioral Science*, *9*(2), 131–146. doi:10.1002/bs.3830090206 PMID:5888769

Kempf, A., & Osthoff, P. (2007). The effect of socially responsible investing on portfolio performance. *European Financial Management*, *13*(5), 908–922. doi:10.1111/j.1468-036X.2007.00402.x

Kendra, J. M., & Wachtendorf, T. (2003). Elements of Resilience after the World Trade Center Disaster: Reconstituting New York City's Emergency Operations Center. *Disasters*, *27*(1), 37–53.

Khan, S. A. R and Zhang Yu (March 25th 2019). *Introductory Chapter: Purchasing and Supply Management [Online First]*. IntechOpen, . https://www.intechopen.com/online-first/introductory-chapter-purchasing-and-supply-management doi:10.5772/intechopen.85380

Khan, S. A. R. (November 5th 2018). *Introductory Chapter: Introduction of Green Supply Chain Management [Online First]*. IntechOpen, . https://www.intechopen.com/online-first/introductory-chapter-introduction-of-green-supply-chain-management doi:10.5772/intechopen.81088

Khan, S. A. R., Dong, Q., & Zhang, Y. (2017). Role of ABC Analysis in the process of efficient order fulfillment: Case study. *Advanced Engineering Forum*, *23*(7), 114-121.

Khan, S. A. R. (2019). The nexus between carbon emissions, poverty, economic growth, and logistics operations-empirical evidence from Southeast Asian countries. *Environmental Science and Pollution Research International*, *26*(13), 13210–13220. doi:10.100711356-019-04829-4 PMID:30903475

Khan, S. A. R., & Dong, Q. (2017). Impact of green supply chain management practices on firms' performance: An empirical study from the perspective of Pakistan. *Environmental Science and Pollution Research International*, *24*(20), 16829–16844. doi:10.100711356-017-9172-5 PMID:28573559

Khan, S. A. R., Dong, Q., Zhang, Y., & Khan, S. S. (2017). The impact of green supply chain on enterprise performance: In the perspective of China. *Journal of Advanced Manufacturing Systems*, *16*(3), 263–273. doi:10.1142/S0219686717500160

Khan, S. A. R., Sharif, A., Golpira, H., & Kumar, A. (2019). A green ideology in Asian emerging economies: From environmental policy and sustainable development. *Sustainable Development*, *27*(2), 1063–1075. doi:10.1002d.1958

Khasawneh, S. (2011). Shared leadership and organizational citizenship behaviour in jordanian public universities: Developing a global workforce for the 21st century. *Educational Management Administration & Leadership*, *39*(5), 621–634. doi:10.1177/1741143211408447

Kim, M., Surroca Aguilar, J., & Tribo Gine, J. A. (2009). The effect of social capital on financial capital. *INDEM Working Paper Business Economic 09-02*.

Kimani, D., Adams, K., Attah-Boakye, D., Ullah, S., Frecknall-Hughes, J., & Kim, J. R. (2020). Blockchain, business and the fourth industrial revolution: Whence, whither, wherefore and how? *Technological Forecasting and Social Change*, *161*, 120254. doi:10.1016/j.techfore.2020.120254

Kim, I., & Venkatachalam, M. (2011). Are sin stocks paying the price for accounting sins. *Journal of Accounting, Auditing & Finance*, *26*(2), 415–442. doi:10.1177/0148558X11401222

Kim, S.-K., & Huh, J.-H. (2020). Blockchain of Carbon Trading for UN Sustainable Development Goals. *Sustainability*, *12*(10), 4021. doi:10.3390u12104021

Kish-Gephart, J. J., & Campbell, J. T. (2015). You Don't Forget Your Roots: The Influence of CEO Social Class Background on Strategic Risk Taking. *Academy of Management Journal*, *58*(6), 1614–1636. doi:10.5465/amj.2013.1204

Kohno, Y., Masuda, Y., Nagahashi, H., Tanaka, K., & Tashiro, K. (2012). Form development for self-rating an organization's vulnerability and resilience to disruption. *Journal of Disaster Research*, *7*(4), 392–407. doi:10.20965/jdr.2012.p0392

Kong, D. T., & Ho, V. T. (2016). A self-determination perspective of strengths use at work: Examining its determinant and performance implications. *The Journal of Positive Psychology*, *11*(1), 15–25. doi:10.1080/17439760.2015.1004555

Konovsky, M. A., & Pugh, S. D. (1994). Citizenship behavior and social exchange. *Academy of Management Journal*, *37*(3), 656–669. doi:10.2307/256704 PMID:10134637

Koshu Nishiyama Hot Spring. (2022). *The world's longest-standing hot spring inn.* Keiunkan. https://www.keiunkan.co.jp/en/

Kowalski, M., Lee, Z. W. Y., & Chan, T. K. H. (2021). Blockchain technology and trust relationships in trade finance. *Technological Forecasting and Social Change*, *166*(C), 120641. https://ideas.repec.org//a/eee/tefoso/v166y2021ics0040162521000731.html. doi:10.1016/j.techfore.2021.120641

Kreander, N., Gray, R. H., Power, D. M., & Sinclair, C. D. (2005). Evaluating the performance of ethical and non-ethical funds: A matched pair analysis. *Journal of Business Finance & Accounting*, *32*(7-8), 1465–1493. doi:10.1111/j.0306-686X.2005.00636.x

Krejcie, R. V., & Morgan, D. W. (1970). Determining sample size for research activities. *Educational and Psychological Measurement*, *30*(3), 607–610. doi:10.1177/001316447003000308

Kuckertz, A., & Wagner, M. (2010). The influence of sustainability orientation on entrepreneurial intentions. Investigating the role of business experience. *Journal of Business Venturing*, *25*(5), 524–539. doi:10.1016/j.jbusvent.2009.09.001

Kurniawaty, K., Ramly, M., & Ramlawati, R. (2019). The effect of work environment, stress, and job satisfaction on employee turnover intention. *Management Science Letters*, *9*(6), 877–886. doi:10.5267/j.msl.2019.3.001

La Porta, R., Lopez-de-Silanes, F., & Shleifer, A. (2008). The economic consequences of legal origins. *Journal of Economic Literature*, *46*(2), 285–332. doi:10.1257/jel.46.2.285

La Porta, R., Lopez-de-Silanes, F., Shleifer, A., & Vishny, R. W. (1997). Legal determinants of external finance. *The Journal of Finance*, *52*(3), 1131–1150. doi:10.1111/j.1540-6261.1997.tb02727.x

La Porta, R., Lopez-de-Silanes, F., Shleifer, A., & Vishny, R. W. (1998). Law and finance. *Journal of Political Economy*, *106*(6), 1113–1155. doi:10.1086/250042

La Porte, T. R., & Consolini, P. M. (1991). Working in practice but not in theory: Theoretical challenges of "high-reliability organizations". *Journal of Public Administration Research and Theory. J-PART*, *1*(1), 19–48.

La Porte, T. R., & Consolini, P. M. (1998). Theoretical and operational challenges of "high-reliability organizations": Air-traffic control and aircraft carriers. *International Journal of Public Administration*, *21*(6–8), 847–852. doi:10.1080/01900699808525320

La Porte, T. R., & Thomas, C. W. (1995). Regulatory compliance and the ethos of quality enhancement: Surprises in nuclear power plant operations. *Journal of Public Administration Research and Theory. J-PART*, *5*(1), 109–137.

Lampel, J., Bhalla, A., & Jha, P. P. (2014). Does governance confer organisational resilience? Evidence from UK employee-owned businesses. *European Management Journal*, *32*, 66–72.

Leana, C. R., & van Buren, H. J. III. (1999). Organizational social capital and employment practices. *Academy of Management Review*, *24*, 538–555.

Lederman, N. (2016). How pure is the beer in Germany? *BBC*. https://www.bbc.com/travel/article/20161027-how-pure-is-the-beer-in-germany

Lee, A. V., Vargo, J., & Seville, E. (2013). Developing a Tool to Measure and Compare Organizations' Resilience. *Natural Hazards Review*, *14*, 29–41. doi:10.1061/(ASCE)NH.1527-6996.0000075

Legovini, A. (2005). *Measuring women's empowerment and the impact of Ethiopia's women's development initiatives project.* The World Bank.

Leins, S. (2020). 'Responsible investment': ESG and the post-crisis ethical order. *Economy and Society*, *49*(1), 71–91. doi:10.1080/03085147.2020.1702414

Lejeune, M. A. (2012). Game Theoretical Approach for Reliable Enhanced Indexation. *Decision Analysis*, *9*(2), 146–155. https://pubsonline.informs.org/doi/abs/10.1287/deca.1120.0239. doi:10.1287/deca.1120.0239

Lengnick-Hall, C. A., & Beck, T. E. (2009). Resilience capacity and strategic agility: Prerequisites for thriving in a dynamic environment. In Christopher P. Nemeth, Erik Hollnagel, and Sidney Dekker (eds.) Resilience engineering perspectives, Volume 2. Preparation and restoration, 39–70. Aldershot: Ashgate Publishing.

Lengnick-Hall, C. A., & Beck, T. E. (2005). Adaptive fit versus robust transformation: How organizations respond to environmental change. *Journal of Management*, *31*, 738–757.

Lengnick-Hall, C. A., Beck, T. E., & Lengnick-Hall, M. L. (2011). Developing a capacity for organizational resilience through strategic human resource management. *Human Resource Management Review*, *21*, 243–255.

Lewis, D. (2010). Nongovernmental organisations, definition and history. *International encyclopedia of civil society*, *41*(6), 1056-1062.

Lewis, R., Donaldson-Feilder, E., & Pangallo, A. (2011). *Developing resilience*. Affinity Health at Work. https://www.cipd.co.uk/

Li, P., & Liao, M. (2021). Rethinking the Reflexivity of Responsible Innovation. *Journal of Dialectics of Nature*, 43.

Li, Q., Cao, S., & Wu, W. (2020). A systematic interpretation of the Digital Transformation of Governance in China: patterns and paths. *Chinese Public Administration*, (10), 44-51. doi:10.19735/j.issn.1006-0863.2020.10.06

Li, Z. G. (2017). Construction Experience and Enlightment to the Western Region of Wuhan East lake Hi- Tech Development Area Mass Entrepreneurship and Innovation Demonstration Base. Chongqing Academy of Science and Technology, 3, 629-635.

Liang, B. B., Chen, Y., Xie, K. F. & Liang, D. (2019). Analysis on the Influence Mechanism of Cooperative Innovation in High-tech Zone: A Case Study of East Lake National Innovation Demonstration Zone. *Science and Technology Management Research,* 15.

Liang, H., & Renneboog, L. (2017). On the foundations of corporate social responsibility. *The Journal of Finance*, *72*(2), 853–910. doi:10.1111/jofi.12487

Limnios, A. M., Mazzarol, T., Ghadouani, A., & Schilizzi, S. G. M. (2014). The Resilience Architecture Framework: Four Organizational Archetypes. *European Management Journal*, *32*(1), 104–116.

Lin, G. C. S. (2017). Planning for the development of the city-regions in the Guangdong-Hong Kong-Macao Greater Bay Area: What can and cannot be done. *Tropical Geography*, *37*(6), 755–756.

Linkov, I., Trump, B. D., Poinsatte-Jones, K., & Florin, M.-V. (2018). Governance Strategies for a Sustainable Digital World. *Sustainability*, *10*(2), 2. doi:10.3390u10020440

Linnenluecke, M. K. (2017). Resilience in business and management research: A review of influential publications and a research agenda. *International Journal of Management Reviews*, *19*(1), 4–30.

Linnenluecke, M. K., & Griffiths, A. (2012). Assessing organizational resilience to climate and weather extremes: Complexities and methodological pathways. *Climatic Change*, *113*, 933–947.

Li, T. T., Wang, K., Sueyoshi, T., & Wang, D. D. (2021). ESG: Research progress and future prospects. *Sustainability*, *13*(21), 11663. doi:10.3390u132111663

Liu, Z. X. (2015). A Review of Responsible Innovation Research: Background, Status and Trends. *Science and Technology Progress and Countermeasures*, *32*(11), 155.

Li, W., Chien, F., Hsu, C. C., Zhang, Y., Nawaz, M. A., Iqbal, S., & Mohsin, M. (2021). Nexus between Energy Poverty and Energy Efficiency: Estimating the Long-Run Dynamics. *Resources Policy*, *72*, 102063. doi:10.1016/j.resourpol.2021.102063

Li, W., Chien, F., Kamran, H. W., Aldeehani, T. M., Sadiq, M., Nguyen, V. C., & Taghizadeh-Hesary, F. (2021). The Nexus between COVID-19 Fear and Stock Market Volatility. *Econ. Ekonomska Istraživanja. Economic Research Journal*, 1–22.

Li, Y., & McKernan, J. (2016). Human rights, accounting, and the dialectic of equality and inequality. *Accounting, Auditing & Accountability Journal*, *29*(4), 568–593. doi:10.1108/AAAJ-07-2015-2142

Löbbecke, C., Lueneborg, L., & Niederle, D. (2018). *Blockchain Technology Impacting the Role of Trust in Transactions: Reflections in the Case of Trading Diamonds.* European Conference on Information Systems. https://www.semanticscholar.org/paper/Blockchain-Technology-Impacting-the-Role-of-Trust-L%C3%B6bbecke-Lueneborg/74037353be4d9f0e3312a1833b731b50ac29ccbe

Lorek, S., & Spangenberg, J. H. (2014). Sustainable consumption within a sustainable economy – beyond green growth and green economies. *Journal of Cleaner Production*, *63*, 33–44. doi:10.1016/j.jclepro.2013.08.045

Loureiro, P. M., & Conceição, C. P. (2019). Emerging Patterns in the Academic Literature on Responsible Research and Innovation. *Technology in Society*, *58*, 58. doi:10.1016/j.techsoc.2019.101148

Lu, Y. (2020). Fresh e-commerce demand surged Dada said vegetable sales during the Spring Festival increased fivefold compared with the same period last year. *The Beijing News*. https://baijiahao.baidu.com/s?id=1657402183597469100&wfr=spider&for=pc

Lundgren, L., & Jonsson, A. (2012). *Assessment of social vulnerability: A literature review of vulnerability related to climate change and natural hazards (CSPR briefing 9).* Linköping University Centre for Climate Science and Policy Research.

Luo, S. H. (2020). Zizhu High-Tech Park Promotes Sustainable Development Through Scientific And Technological Innovation. *China Sustainability Tribune,* 11.

Luo, S. Y. (2019). Industry and City Integration under the Requirement of High-quality Development Implementation Path Study. *East China Science & Technology,* 9.

Luu, T. T. (2017). CSR and organizational citizenship behavior for the environment in hotel industry: The moderating roles of corporate entrepreneurship and employee attachment style. *International Journal of Contemporary Hospitality Management, 29*(11), 2867–2900. doi:10.1108/IJCHM-02-2016-0080

Lu, X. H., Chen, D. L., Kuang, B., Zhang, C. Z., & Cheng, C. (2020). Is High-Tech Zone a Policy Trap or a Growth Drive? Insights from the Perspective of Urban Land Use Efficiency. *Land Use Policy, 95,* 95. doi:10.1016/j.landusepol.2020.104583

Mackey, A., Mackey, T. B., & Barney, J. B. (2007). Corporate social responsibility and firm performance: Investor preferences and corporate strategies. *Academy of Management Review, 32*(3), 817–835. doi:10.5465/amr.2007.25275676

Madsen, H., & Ulhøi, J. P. (2001). Greening of Human Resources: Environmental Awareness and Training Interests within the Workforce. *Industrial Management & Data Systems, 101*(2), 57–65. doi:10.1108/02635570110384320

Ma, F., Wang, H., Schandl, H., Fishman, T., Tan, X., Li, Y., Shi, L., Wang, P., & Chen, W. Q. (2022). Exploring the relationship between economic complexity and resource efficiency. *Resources, Conservation and Recycling, 186,* 106530. doi:10.1016/j.resconrec.2022.106530

Mahajan, S. (2011). Entrepreneurship among marginalised groups in India: an empirical study of scheduled castes with special reference to Maharashtra. Entrepreneurship and New Venture Creation: International Models and Benchmarks, Bangalore.

Maitlis, S. (2005). The social processes of organizational sensemaking. *Academy of Management Journal, 48,* 21–49.

Maitlis, S., & Christianson, M. (2014). Sense making in organizations: Taking stock and moving forward. *The Academy of Management Annals, 8,* 57–125. doi:10.1080/19416520.2014.873177

Malhotra, A., & Schuler, S. R. (2005). Women's empowerment as a variable in international development. *Measuring empowerment: Cross-disciplinary perspectives, 1*(1), 71-88.

Malla, D. G. B. (2020). An Economic Account of Innovation Policy in Canada: A Comparison of Canola, Wheat, and Pulses. *AgBioForum, 22*(1), 25–36. https://hdl.handle.net/10355/86604

Mallak, L. A. (1998). Measuring resilience in health care provider organizations. *Health Manpower Management, 24*(4), 148–152. doi:10.1108/09552069810215755

Malone, D., & O'Dwyer, K. J. (2014). *Bitcoin Mining and its Energy Footprint,* 280–285. IET. doi:10.1049/cp.2014.0699

Manfield, R. C., & Newey, L. R. (2017). Resilience as an Entrepreneurial Capability: Integrating Insights from a Cross-Disciplinary Comparison. *International Journal of Entrepreneurial Behaviour & Research.* doi:10.1108/IJEBR-11-2016-0368

Mansoor, M., Fida, S., Nasir, S., & Ahmad, Z. (2011). The impact of job stress on employee job satisfaction a study on telecommunication sector of Pakistan. *Journal of Business Studies Quarterly, 2*(3), 50.

Marco-Lajara, B., Falcó, J. M., Fernández, L. R., & Larrosa, P. S. (2022a). Evolución del pensamiento en la disciplina de dirección estratégica: la visión de la empresa basada en las capacidades dinámicas y en el conocimiento. [Evolution of thinking in the discipline of strategic management: the Dynamic capabilities and knowledge-based view of the enterprise] In Investigación y transferencia de las ciencias sociales frente a un mundo en crisis [Social science research and transfer in the face of a world in crisis], (pp. 1801–1826). Dykinson.

Marco-Lajara, B., Sáez, P. D. C. Z., Falcó, J. M., & García, E. S. (2022c). Las rutas del vino de España: el impacto económico derivado de las visitas a bodegas y museos. [Spain's wine routes: the economic impact of visits to wineries and museums] In Investigación y transferencia de las ciencias sociales frente a un mundo en crisis [Social science research and transfer in the face of a world in crisis]. (pp. 1774–1800). Dykinson.

Marco-Lajara, B., Zaragoza-Sáez, P. C., Martínez-Falcó, J., & Sánchez-García, E. (2022k). Does green intellectual capital affect green innovation performance? Evidence from the Spanish wine industry. British Food Journal.

Marco-Lajara, B., Zaragoza-Saez, P., & Martínez-Falcó, J. (2022g). Green Innovation: Balancing Economic Efficiency With Environmental Protection. In Frameworks for Sustainable Development Goals to Manage Economic, Social, and Environmental Shocks and Disasters (pp. 239-254). IGI Global.

Marco-Lajara, B., Zaragoza-Saez, P., & Martínez-Falcó, J. (2022n). Green Innovation: Balancing Economic Efficiency With Environmental Protection. In Frameworks for Sustainable Development Goals to Manage Economic, Social, and Environmental Shocks and Disasters (pp. 239-254). IGI Global.

Marco-Lajara, B., Zaragoza-Sáez, P., Falcó, J. M., & Millan-Tudela, L. A. (2022i). Corporate Social Responsibility: A Narrative Literature Review. In Frameworks for Sustainable Development Goals to Manage Economic, Social, and Environmental Shocks and Disasters (pp. 16-34). IGI GLOBAL. doi:10.4018/978-1-6684-6750-3.ch002

Marco-Lajara, B., Zaragoza-Saez, P., Falcó, J. M., & Sánchez-García, E. (2022j). COVID-19 and Wine Tourism: A Story of Heartbreak. In Handbook of Research on SDGs for Economic Development, Social Development, and Environmental Protection (pp. 90-112). IGI Global.

Marco-Lajara, B., Martínez-Falcó, J., Millán-Tudela, L. A., & Sánchez-García, E. (2023d). Analysis of the structure of scientific knowledge on wine tourism: A bibliometric analysis. *Heliyon (London)*, *9*, e13363.

Marco-Lajara, B., Martínez-Falcó, J., Sánchez-García, E., & Millan-Tudela, L. A. (2023a). Wine Tourism, Designations of Origin and Business Performance: An Analysis Applied to the Valencian Community Wine Industry. *Businesses*, *3*(1), 70–82. doi:10.3390/businesses3010006

Marco-Lajara, B., Sáez, P. D. C. Z., Falcó, J. M., & García, E. S. (2022b). El capital intelectual verde como hoja de ruta para la sostenibilidad: El caso de bodegas Luzón [Green intellectual capital as a roadmap for sustainability: the case of bodegas Luzón]. *GeoGraphos*, *13*(147), 137–146.

Marco-Lajara, B., Sánchez-García, E., Martínez-Falcó, J., & Poveda-Pareja, E. (2022o). Regional Specialization, Competitive Pressure, and Cooperation: The Cocktail for Innovation. *Energies*, *15*(15), 5346.

Marco-Lajara, B., Seva-Larrosa, P., Martínez-Falcó, J., & García-Lillo, F. (2022d). Wine clusters and Protected Designations of Origin (PDOs) in Spain: An exploratory analysis. *Journal of Wine Research*, *33*(3), 146–167. doi:10.1080/09571264.2022.2110051

Marco-Lajara, B., Seva-Larrosa, P., Martínez-Falcó, J., & Sánchez-García, E. (2021b). *How Has COVID- 19 Affected The Spanish Wine Industry? An Exploratory Analysis*. NVEO-Natural Volatiles & Essential Oils Journal.

Marco-Lajara, B., Seva-Larrosa, P., Ruiz-Fernández, L., & Martínez-Falcó, J. (2021a). The Effect of COVID-19 on the Spanish Wine Industry. In *Impact of Global Issues on International Trade* (pp. 211–232). IGI Global., doi:10.4018/978-1-7998-8314-2.ch012

Marco-Lajara, B., Zaragoza Sáez, P., & Martínez-Falcó, J. (2022m). Does Green Intellectual Capital Affect Green Performance? The Mediation of Green Innovation. *Telematique, 21*(1), 4594–4602.

Marco-Lajara, B., Zaragoza-Saez, P., Falcó, J. M., & Millan-Tudela, L. A. (2022h). Analysing the Relationship Between Green Intellectual Capital and the Achievement of the Sustainable Development Goals. In *Handbook of Research on Building Inclusive Global Knowledge Societies for Sustainable Development* (pp. 111–129). IGI Global. doi:10.4018/978-1-6684-5109-0.ch005

Marco-Lajara, B., Zaragoza-Sáez, P., Martínez-Falcó, J., & Millan-Tudela, L. A. (2023b). The Export Intensity of Spain's Autonomous Communities in Terms of the Marketing of Wine and Their Geographical Destinations. In *The Transformation of Global Trade in a New World* (pp. 1–21). IGI Global.

Marco-Lajara, B., Zaragoza-Sáez, P., Martínez-Falcó, J., & Ruiz-Fernández, L. (2022l). The effect of green intellectual capital on green performance in the Spanish wine industry: A structural equation modeling approach. *Complexity, 2022*, 2022. doi:10.1155/2022/6024077

Marco-Lajara, B., Zaragoza-Sáez, P., Martínez-Falcó, J., & Sánchez-García, E. (2022p). Las rutas del vino de España: el impacto económico derivado de las visitas a bodegas y museos. [Spain's wine routes: the economic impact of visits to wineries and museums] In *Investigación y transferencia de las ciencias sociales frente a un mundo en crisis* (pp. 1774–1800). Dykinson.

Marco-Lajara, B., Zaragoza-Sáez, P., Martínez-Falcó, J., & Sánchez-García, E. (2023b). The Internationalization of the Spanish Wine Industry: An Analysis of Trade Flows and Their Degree of Concentration. In *The Transformation of Global Trade in a New World* (pp. 22–46). IGI Global.

Martin-Barbero, S. (2020). COVID-19 has accelerated the digital transformation of higher education. *World Economic Forum*. https://www.weforum.org/agenda/2020/07/covid-19-digital-transformation-higher-education

Martínez-Falcó, J. M., Lajara, B. M., & Zaragoza-Sáez, P. (2023g). Analyzing the Evolution From Intellectual Capital to Green Intellectual Capital: A Literature Review. Intellectual Capital as a Precursor to Sustainable Corporate Social Responsibility, 72-90.

Martínez-Falcó, J., Lajara, B. M., & Zaragoza-Sáez, P. (2023f). Sustainable Intellectual Capital: A Comprehensive Construct for Understanding the Economic, Social, and Environmental Intangibles. In Intellectual Capital as a Precursor to Sustainable Corporate Social Responsibility (pp. 214-236). IGI Global.

Martínez-Falcó, J., Marco-Lajara, B. M., Zaragoza-Sáez, P., & Ruiz-Fernández, L. (2023h). Green Intellectual Capital as a Catalyst for the Sustainable Development Goals: Evidence From the Spanish Wine Industry. In Climate Change, World Consequences, and the Sustainable Development Goals for 2030 (pp. 163-182). IGI Global.

Martínez-Falcó, J., Marco-Lajara, B., & Zaragoza-Sáez, P. (2023i). Corporate Social Responsibility: A Comprehensive Analysis. In Positive and Constructive Contributions for Sustainable Development Goals (pp. 131-160). IGI Global.

Martínez-Falcó, J., Marco-Lajara, B., & Zaragoza-Saez, P. (2023j). Corporate Social Responsibility vs. Corporate Sustainability: Different Concepts for a Common Goal. In Positive and Constructive Contributions for Sustainable Development Goals (pp. 76-87). IGI Global.

Martínez-Falcó, J., Marco-Lajara, B., & Zaragoza-Saez, P. (2023k). Theoretical Perspectives on Corporate Social Responsibility: A Narrative Review. Positive and Constructive Contributions for Sustainable Development Goals, 96-113.

Martínez-Falcó, J., Marco-Lajara, B., Zaragoza Sáez, P., & Sánchez-García, E. (2023b). Wine tourism in Spain: The economic impact derived from visits to wineries and museums on wine routes. *Investigaciones Turísticas, 25*(25), 168–195. doi:10.14198/INTURI.21219

Martínez-Falcó, J., Marco-Lajara, B., Zaragoza-Sáez, P., & Sánchez-García, E. (2023a). Vino, Turismo y COVID-19: El impacto de la COVID-19 en las Rutas del Vino de España. *PASOS Revista de Turismo y Patrimonio Cultural, 21*(1), 83–97. doi:10.25145/j.pasos.2023.21.006

Martínez-Falcó, J., Marco-Lajara, B., Zaragoza-Sáez, P., & Sánchez-García, E. (2023c). Vino, Turismo y COVID-19: El impacto de la COVID-19 en las Rutas del Vino de España [Wine, Tourism and COVID-19: The Impact of COVID-19 on the Wine Routes of Spain]. *PASOS Revista de Turismo y Patrimonio Cultural, 21*(1), 83–97.

Martínez-Falcó, J., Sánchez-García, E., Millan-Tudela, L. A., & Marco-Lajara, B. (2023d). The Role of Green Agriculture and Green Supply Chain Management in the Green Intellectual Capital–Sustainable Performance Relationship: A Structural Equation Modeling Analysis Applied to the Spanish Wine Industry. *Agriculture, 13*(2), 425.

Mas, J. M., & Gómez, A. (2021). Social partners in the digital ecosystem: Will business organizations, trade unions and government organizations survive the digital revolution? *Technological Forecasting and Social Change, 162*. doi:10.1016/j.techfore.2020.120349

Masten, A. S., & Reed, M. J. (2002). Resilience in development. In C. R. Snyder and S. Lopez (Eds.). Handbook of positive psychology (pp. 74-88). Oxford Uk. Oxford. Oxford University Press.

Masterson, S. S. (2011). A trickle-down model of organizational justice: Relating employees' and customers' perceptions of and reactions to fairness. *The Journal of Applied Psychology, 86*(4), 594–604. doi:10.1037/0021-9010.86.4.594 PMID:11519644

Matos, P. (2020). *Esg and responsible institutional investing around the world. Literature review*. CFA Institute Research Foundation.

Mavilia, R., & Pisani, R. (2020). Blockchain and catching-up in developing countries: The case of financial inclusion in Africa. *African Journal of Science, Technology, Innovation and Development, 12*(2), 151–163. doi:10.1080/20421338.2019.1624009

Ma, Y., Cai, Y., & Chen, N. (2020). The influence and effect of Enterprise Digitalization Construction on COVID-19 's response to epidemic situation. *Review of International Economics, 2020*(05), 80–94.

Mayer, D. M., Kuenzi, M., Greenbaum, R., Bardes, M., & Salvador, R. B. (2009). How low does ethical leadership fow? Test of a trickle-down model. *Organizational Behavior and Human Decision Processes, 108*(1), 1–13. doi:10.1016/j.obhdp.2008.04.002

Mazer, J. (2021). *Demystifying Cryptocurrencies, Blockchain, and ICOs*. Toptal Finance Blog. https://www.toptal.com/finance/market-research-analysts/cryptocurrency-market

McAfee, K. (2016). Green economy and carbon markets for conservation and development: A critical view. *International Environmental Agreement: Politics, Law and Economics, 16*(3), 333–353. doi:10.100710784-015-9295-4

McCarthy IP, Collard M, Johnson M (2017) Adaptive organizational resilience: an evolutionary perspective. *Curr Opin Environ Sustain, 28*, 33–40. https://doi.org/ t.2017.07.005 doi:10.1016/j.cosus

McCarthy, L. (2017). Empowering women through corporate social responsibility: A feminist Foucauldian critique. *Business Ethics Quarterly*, *27*(4), 603–631. doi:10.1017/beq.2017.28

McDaniels, T., Chang, S., Cole, D., Mikawoz, J., & Longstaff, H. (2008). Fostering resilience to extreme events within infrastructure systems: Characterizing decision contexts for mitigation and adaptation. *Global Environmental Change*, *18*, 310–318.

McGuinness, M., & Johnson, N. (2014). Exploiting social capital and path-dependent resources for organisational resilience: Preliminary findings from a study on flooding. *Procedia Economics and Finance*, *18*, 447–455.

McManus, S., Seville, E., Vargo, J., & Brunsdon, D. (2008). Facilitated process for improving organizational resilience. *Natural Hazards Review*, *9*, 81–90. doi:10.1061/(ASCE)1527-6988(2008)9:2(81)

McShane, S., & Glinow, M. A. V. (2017). *Organizational behavior*. McGraw-Hill Education.

Mei, L., Chen, J., & Sheng, W. Z. (2014). Responsible Innovation-An Emerging Paradigm for Research and Innovation. *Natural Dialectics Research*, *30*(10), 83.

Merloni, E., Camanzi, L., Mulazzani, L., & Malorgio, G. (2018). Adaptive capacity to climate change in the wine industry: A Bayesian Network approach. *Wine Economics and Policy*, *7*(2), 165–177. doi:10.1016/j.wep.2018.11.002

Miao, R. T. (2011). Perceived organizational support, job satisfaction, task performance and organizational citizenship behavior in China. *Journal of Behavioral and Applied Management*, *2011*(12), 105. doi:10.21818/001c.17632

Michelson, G., Wailes, N., Van Der Laan, S., & Frost, G. (2004). Ethical Investment Processes and Outcomes. *Journal of Business Ethics*, *52*(1), 1–10. doi:10.1023/B:BUSI.0000033103.12560.be

Millan-Tudela, L. A., Marco-Lajara, B., Martínez-Falcó, J., & Poveda-Pareja, E. (2022). *Longevidad empresarial: revisión bibliométrica sobre la supervivencia y caída de las compañías [Buisness longevity: bibliometric review on the survival and fall of companies]*. Paper presented at the XXXVI AEDEM Annual Congress, Madrid, Spain.

Millan-Tudela, L. A., Marco-Lajara, B., Martínez-Falcó, J., & Sánchez-García, E. (2022). Pursuing Business Longevity: Ways to Enhance Sustainable Development. In Frameworks for Sustainable Development Goals to Manage Economic, Social, and Environmental Shocks and Disasters (pp. 79-95). IGI Global.

Millan-Tudela, L. A., Marco-Lajara, B., Poveda-Pareja, E., & Martínez-Falcó, J. (2022). Is business longevity a way of management success? Recepty na sukces w zarzadzaniu [Recipes for success in management] (pp. 308-311).

Ministry of Finance of the People's Republic of China. (2020). *Research report and case of Management Accounting Industry, Accounting Department of the Ministry of Finance of China*. http://kjs.mof.gov.cn

Miralles-Quirós, M. M., Miralles-Quirós, J. L., & Redondo Hernández, J. (2019). ESG performance and shareholder value creation in the banking industry: International differences. *Sustainability*, *11*(5), 1404. doi:10.3390u11051404

Mishra, L., & Kaushik, V. (2021). Application of blockchain in dealing with sustainability issues and challenges of financial sector. *Journal of Sustainable Finance & Investment*, *0*(0), 1–16. doi:10.1080/20430795.2021.1940805

Mishra, N. (2015). Empowering Women through Self Help Groups (SHGs) In Odisha–An Empirical Analysis. *International Journal of Novel Research in Humanity and Social Sciences*, *2*(3), 85–91.

Mitra, J. (2002). Consider Velasquez: Reflections on the development of entrepreneurship programmes. *Industry and Higher Education*, *16*(3), 191–202. doi:10.5367/000000002101296289

Miu, J. (2021). *China Merchants Group: using digitalization to create new competitiveness to promote the construction of world-class enterprises.* http://www.sasac.gov.cn/n4470048/n13461446/n15927611/n15927638/n16135038/index.html

Mohan, G. (2007). Participatory development: From epistemological reversals to active citizenship. *Geography Compass, 1*(4), 779–796. doi:10.1111/j.1749-8198.2007.00038.x

Mohanty, S. R., Das, B., & Mohanty, T. (2013). Empowerment of Women in Rural Odisha through Micro Enterprises. *IOSR Journal of Humanities and Social Sciences, 12*(1), 1–8. doi:10.9790/0837-1210108

Mohindra, N. (2011, February 16). *Transparent exchanges; As stock exchanges merge, regulators should remove the barriers to entry that stifle competition - Appeared in the Financial Post: Op-ed.* Fraser Institute. https://www.fraserinstitute.org/article/transparent-exchanges-stock-exchanges-merge-regulators-should-remove-barriers-entry-stifle

Monnaie de Paris. (2022). *La Monnaie de Paris.* Monnaie de Paris. https://www.monnaiedeparis.fr/fr/presentation-institution

Montecchi, M., Plangger, K., & Etter, M. (2019). It's real, trust me! Establishing supply chain provenance using blockchain. *Business Horizons, 62*(3), 283–293. https://ideas.repec.org//a/eee/bushor/v62y2019i3p283-293.html. doi:10.1016/j.bushor.2019.01.008

Moore, C., Mayer, D. M., Chiang, F. F., Crossley, C., Karlesky, M. J., & Birtch, T. A. (2019a). Leaders matter morally: The role of ethical leadership in shaping employee moral cognition and misconduct. *The Journal of Applied Psychology, 104*(1), 123–145. doi:10.1037/apl0000341 PMID:30221953

Mori, T. (2016). Financial technology: Blockchain and securities settlement. *Journal of Securities Operations & Custody, 8*(3), 208–227.

Morrow, K. (2012). Rio+20, the green economy and reorienting sustainable development. *Environmental Law Review, 14*, 279–297.

Mo, S., Wang, Z., Akrivou, K., & Booth, S. A. (2012). Look up, look around: Is there anything different about team-level OCB in China? *Journal of Management & Organization, 18*(6), 818–832. doi:10.5172/jmo.2012.18.6.818

Musakwa Wand Van Niekerk, A. (2014). Monitoring sustainable urban development using built-up area indicators: A case study of Stellenbosch, *South Africa Environment. Development and Sustainability, 17*(3), 547–566. doi:10.100710668-014-9560-7

Nagy, Z., Kassam, A., & Lee. L. E. (2017). Can ESG Add Alpha? An Analysis of ESG Tilt and Momentum Strategies. *The Journal of Investing, 43* (2APP), 28-32. doi:10.3905/joi.2016.25.2.113

Nassr, I. (2019). *Initial Coin Offerings (ICOs) for SME Financing.* OECD.

National Energy Administration. (2021). *Renewable Energy in China.* NEA. https://mi.mbd.baidu.com/r/CI0SrVaZQk?f=cp&u=f3673e088bb6486d

Nekhili, A., Boukadhaba, A., Nagati, H., & Chtioui, T. (2021). ESG Performance and Market Value: The Moderating Role of Employee Board Representation. *International Journal of Human Resource Management, 32*(14), 3061–3087. doi:10.1080/09585192.2019.1629989

Nellis, J. G., & Parker, D. (2004). *Principles of macroeconomics.* Pearson.

Neubert, M. J., Wu, C., & Roberts, J. A. (2013). The influence of ethical leadership and regulatory focus on employee outcomes. *Business Ethics Quarterly, 23*(2), 269–296. doi:10.5840/beq201323217

Newman, A., Kiazad, K., Miao, Q., & Cooper, B. (2014). Examining the cognitive and effective trust-based mechanisms underlying the relationship between ethical leadership and organizational citizenship: A case of the head leading the heart? *Journal of Business Ethics, 123*(1), 113–123. doi:10.100710551-013-1803-2

Ng, A. C., & Rezaee, Z. (2015). Business sustainability performance and cost of equity capital. *Journal of Corporate Finance, 34*, 128–149. doi:10.1016/j.jcorpfin.2015.08.003

Nguyen, Q. K. (2016). Blockchain—A Financial Technology for Future Sustainable Development. *2016 3rd International Conference on Green Technology and Sustainable Development (GTSD)*, (pp. 51–54). IEEE. 10.1109/GTSD.2016.22

Nitisemito, A. S. (2015). *Manajemen Personalia, Cetakan kedelapan [Personal Management, eighth edition]*. Ghalia Indonesia.

Niu, F., Chen, W., & Chen, X. (2021b). *Current process, challenges and ideas of digital transformation of SOEs*. https://mp.weixin.qq.com/s/AlzwYU1Cj7MExdtL68YyGw

Niu, F., Chen, W., & Wang, X. (2021a). *The core idea of digital transformation of SOEs: small mouth cut, open integration, rapid iteration.* https://mp.weixin.qq.com/s/HR1Iz4YXQfPRCxwC9zZqkg

Noble, D., & Patil, K. (2021). Blockchain in Stock Market Transformation: A Systematic Literature Review. *Revista Gestão Inovação e Tecnologias, 11*(4), 5088–5111. doi:10.47059/revistageintec.v11i4.2551

Novy-Marx, R. (2013). The other side of value: The gross profitability premium. *Journal of Financial Economics, 108*(1), 1–28. doi:10.1016/j.jfineco.2013.01.003

O'Brien, K., Sygna, L., & Haugen, J. E. (2004). Vulnerable or resilient? A multi-scale assessment of climate impacts and vulnerability in Norway. *Climatic Change, 64*, 193–225.

OECD (2018). *Environmental policy toolkit for SME greening in EU Eastern partnership countries*. OECD Publishing. . doi:10.1787/9789264293199-4-en

OECD. (2011). *Towards green growth: monitoring progress: OECD indicators Organisation for Economic Co-operation & Development OECD Publishing, Paris Pardee Centre. Beyond Rio+20: Governance for a Green Economy*. Boston University.

OECD. (2014) OECD green growth studies: green growth indicators 2014. Organisation for Economic Co-operation & Development OECD Publishing, Paris

Official website of Guangzhou HTZ. (2020). http://www.gddidg.com

Official website of Wuhan East Lake HTZ. (2020). http://www.wehdz.gov.cn

Official website of Zizhu High-Tech Zone. (2020). http://www.zizhupark.com

Olsen, A. L., Hjorth, F., Harmon, N., & Barfort, S. (2019). Behavioral dishonesty in the public sector. *Journal of Public Administration: Research and Theory, 29*(4), 572–590. doi:10.1093/jopart/muy058

Omidvar, M., Mazloumi, A., Mohammad Fam, I., & Nirumand, F. (2017). Development of a framework for resilience measurement: Suggestion of fuzzy resilience grade (RG) and fuzzy resilience early warning grade (REWG). *WOR, 56*, 463–474. doi:10.3233/WOR-17251 2

Operation Monitoring Coordination Bureau. (2022). *Interpretation of the statistical bulletin of the communications industry in 2021.* https://wap.miit.gov.cn/gxsj/tjfx/txy/art/2022/art_e2c784268cc74ba0bb19d9d7eeb398bc.html

Organ, D. W. (1988). *Organizational citizenship behavior: The good soldier syndrome.* Lexington Books.

Orlitzky, M., Schmidt, F. L., & Rynes, S. L. (2003). Corporate social and financial performance: A meta-analysis. *Organization Studies, 24*(3), 403–441. doi:10.1177/0170840603024003910

Oshio, S., Nakatani, M., Kaneko, M., & Nagamine, K. (2002). Negative na dekigoto karanotatchinaoriwomichibikushinritekitokusei; seishintekikaihukuryokusyakudo nosakusei. [The psychological properties that promote bounce back from negative states]. *Japanese Journal of Counseling Science, 35*, 57–65.

Ostern, N., Rosemann, M., & Moormann, J. (2020, December 14). *Determining the Idiosyncrasy of Blockchain: An Affordances Perspective.* Research Gate.

Ostrom, E., & Eggertsson, T. (1990). *Governing the Commons: The Evolution of Institutions for Collective Action.* Cambridge University Press. doi:10.1017/CBO9780511807763

Ouvrard, S., Jasimuddin, S. M., & Spiga, A. (2020). Does sustainability push to reshape business models? Evidence from the European wine industry. *Sustainability, 12*(6), 2561. doi:10.3390u12062561

Owens, B. P., & Hekman, D. R. (2012). Modeling how to grow: An inductive examination of humble leader behaviors, contingencies, and outcomes. *Academy of Management Journal, 55*(4), 787–818. doi:10.5465/amj.2010.0441

Owens, B. P., Johnson, M. D., & Mitchell, T. R. (2013). Expressed humility in organizations: Implications for performance, teams, and leadership. *Organization Science, 24*(5), 1517–1538. doi:10.1287/orsc.1120.0795

Özbuğday, F. C., Fındık, D., Özcan, K. M., & Başçı, S. (2020). Resource efficiency investments and firm performance: Evidence from European SMEs. *Journal of Cleaner Production, 252*, 119824. doi:10.1016/j.jclepro.2019.119824

Paech, P. (2017). The Governance of Blockchain Financial Networks. *The Modern Law Review, 80*(6), 1073–1110. doi:10.1111/1468-2230.12303

Paillé, P., Boiral, O., & Chen, Y. (2013). Linking environmental management practices and organizational citizenship behavior for the environment: A social exchange perspective. *International Journal of Human Resource Management, 24*(18), 3552–3575. doi:10.1080/09585192.2013.777934

Pandey, S. K., Wright, B. E., & Moynihan, D. P. (2008). Public service motivation and interpersonal citizenship behavior in public organizations: Testing a preliminary model. *International Public Management Journal, 11*(1), 89–108. doi:10.1080/10967490801887947

Parmentola, A., Petrillo, A., Tutore, I., & Felice, F. D. (2022). Is blockchain able to enhance environmental sustainability? A systematic review and research agenda from the perspective of Sustainable Development Goals (SDGs). *Business Strategy and the Environment, 31*(1), 194–217. https://ideas.repec.org//a/bla/bstrat/v31y2022i1p194-217.html. doi:10.1002/bse.2882

Pasteur, K. (2011). *From Vulnerability to Resilience: A Framework for Analysis and Action to Build Community Resilience.* Practical Action Publishing.

Paton, D., Smith, L., & Violanti, J. (2000). Disaster response: Risk, vulnerability, and resilience. *Disaster Prevention and Management, 9*(3), 173–179.

Patriotta, G. (2003). Sensemaking on the shop floor: Narratives of knowledge in organizations. *Journal of Management Studies*, *40*, 349–375.

Pearce, D. W., Markandya, A., & Barbier, E. B. (1989). *Blueprint for a green economy Earthscan.*

Pelling, M., & Manuel-Navarrete, D. (2011). From resilience to transformation: The adaptive cycle in two Mexican urban centers. *Ecology and Society*, *16*(2), 1–11. doi:10.5751/ES-04038-160211

Pelling, M., O'Brien, K., & Matyas, D. (2014). Adaptation and transformation. *Climatic Change*, *133*(1), 113–127. doi:10.100710584-014-1303-0

Pettit, T. J., Fiksel, J., & Croxton, K. L. (2010). Ensuring supply chain resilience: Development of a conceptual framework. *Journal of Business Logistics*, *31*(1), 1–21.

Ping An Securities. (2019). *Guangdong-Hong Kong-Macao Greater Bay Area Special Report-Speed up the construction of "rail + intelligent transportation" to create an integrated transportation network in the Greater Bay Area.* https://www.hibor.com.cn/docdetail_2556657.html

Ployhart, R. E., & Vandenberg, R. J. (2010). Longitudinal research: The theory, design, and analysis of change. *Journal of Management*, *36*(1), 94–120. doi:10.1177/0149206309352110

Podsakoff, P. M., MacKenzie, S. B., Moorman, R. H., & Fetter, R. (1990). Transformational leader behaviors and their effects on followers' trust in leader, satisfaction, and organizational citizenship behaviors. *The Leadership Quarterly*, *1*(2), 107–142. doi:10.1016/1048-9843(90)90009-7

Podsakoff, P. M., Paine, J. B., & Bachrach, D. C. (2000). Organizational citizenship behaviors: A critical review of the theoretical and empirical literature and suggestions for future research. *Journal of Management*, *26*(3), 513–563. doi:10.1177/014920630002600307

Pólvora, A., Nascimento, S., Lourenço, J. S., & Scapolo, F. (2020). Blockchain for industrial transformations: A forward-looking approach with multi-stakeholder engagement for policy advice. *Technological Forecasting and Social Change*, *157*(C), 120091. https://ideas.repec.org//a/eee/tefoso/v157y2020ics0040162520309173.html. doi:10.1016/j.techfore.2020.120091

Poly Investment Consultancy Research Institute, Jinghui Think Tank, Hexun, & 58 Anjuke Research Institute. (2019). *Guangdong-Hong Kong-Macau Greater Bay Area's Blue Book on Economic Development (2019).* http://www.199it.com/archives/978652.html

Pontificia Fonderia Marinelli. (2022). *Campane Marinelli.* Campane Marinelli http://campanemarinelli.com/en/

Pop, C., Pop, C., Marcel, A., Vesa, A., Petrican, T., Cioara, T., Anghel, I., & Salomie, I. (2018). Decentralizing the Stock Exchange using Blockchain An Ethereum-based implementation of the Bucharest Stock Exchange. *2018 IEEE 14th International Conference on Intelligent Computer Communication and Processing (ICCP).* IEEE. https://www.academia.edu/40383802/Decentralizing_the_Stock_Exchange_using_Blockchain_An_Ethereum_based_implementation_of_the_Bucharest_Stock_Exchange

Popescu, A.-D. (2020). Transforming Capital Markets by means of Financial Digital Assets. *Emulations - Revue de Sciences Sociales, 68*, 109–119.

Powers A. (2012) The Rio+20 process: forward movement for the environment? *Transnational Environmental Law,* 1403–12.

Powley, E. H. (2009). Reclaiming resilience and safety: Resilience activation in the critical period of crisis. *Human Relations*, *62*(9), 1289–1326.

Pritchard, A. (1969). Statistical bibliography or bibliometrics. *The Journal of Documentation, 25*(4), 348–349.

PwC. (2019). *The Core position of data Governance in the Digital Transformation of State-owned Enterprises*. https://www.pwccn.com/zh/blog/state-owned-enterprise-soe/core-position-data-governance-digital-transformation-soe.html

Quenson, Y. (2013). *The relationship between ethical leadership and individual directed organizational citizenship behavior: the moderating effect of leader-member-exchange*. Baptist University.

Ragin, C., & Schneider, G. (2011). Case-oriented Theory Building and Theory Testing. In M. Williams & W. Vogt (Eds.), *The Sage Handbook of Innovation in Social Research Methods* (pp. 150–166). Sage. doi:10.4135/9781446268261.n11

Rameshkumar, M. (2020). Employee engagement as an antecedent of organizational commitment–A study on Indian seafaring officers. *The Asian Journal of Shipping and Logistics, 36*(3), 105–112. doi:10.1016/j.ajsl.2019.11.003

Razak, N. A., Ma'amor, H., & Hassan, N. (2016). Measuring reliability and validity instruments of work environment towards quality work life. *Procedia Economics and Finance, 37*, 520–528. doi:10.1016/S2212-5671(16)30160-5

Razzaq, A., Wang, Y., Chupradit, S., Suksatan, W., & Shahzad, F. (2021). Asymmetric Inter-Linkages between Green Technology Innovation and Consumption-Based Carbon Emissions in BRICS Countries Using Quantile-On-Quantile Framework. *Technology in Society, 66*, 101656. doi:10.1016/j.techsoc.2021.101656

Rechtman, Y. (2017). Blockchain: The Making of a Simple, Secure Recording Concept. *The CPA Journal, 87*(6), 15–17. https://www.proquest.com/docview/2213055088

Redondo, M. (2019). Campo Viejo, viticultura integrada en el medio ambiente [Campo Viejo, viticulture integrated with the environment]. *Cinco Dias*. https://cincodias.elpais.com/cincodias/2019/11/27/companias/1574875847_496710.html

Refinitiv (2021). *Environmental, Social and Governance (ESG) Scores from Refinitiv* (issue February). Refinitiv. https://www.refinitiv.com/en/sustainable-finance/esg-scores#methodology

Renneboog, L., Ter Horst, J., & Zhang, C. (2008). Socially responsible investments: Institutional aspects, performance, and investor behavior. *Journal of Banking & Finance, 32*(9), 1723–1742. doi:10.1016/j.jbankfin.2007.12.039

Renneboog, L., Ter Horst, J., & Zhang, C. (2008). The price of ethics and stakeholder governance: The performance of socially responsible mutual funds. *Journal of Corporate Finance, 14*(3), 302–322. doi:10.1016/j.jcorpfin.2008.03.009

Republic of Rwanda. (2011) Green growth and climate resilience: national strategy for climate change and low carbon development. Republic of Rwanda, Kigali.

Resnick, D., & Birner, R. (2010). Agricultural Strategy Development in West Africa: The False Promise of Participation. *Development Policy Review, 28*(1), 97–115. doi:10.1111/j.1467-7679.2010.00476.x

Riaz, M., Ahmad, N., Riaz, M., Murtaza, G., Khan, T., & Firdous, H. (2016). Impact of job stress on employee job satisfaction. *International Review of Management and Business Research, 5*(4), 1370.

Richtnér, A., & Löfsten, H. (2014). Managing in turbulence: How the capacity for resilience influences creativity. *R & D Management, 44*, 137–151.

Rioux, S. M., & Penner, L. A. (2001). The causes of organizational citizenship behavior: A motivational analysis. *The Journal of Applied Psychology, 86*(6), 1306–1314. doi:10.1037/0021-9010.86.6.1306 PMID:11768072

RMB Trading and Research. (2020). *The central bank responded to the interview with Ant Group: to return to the origin of the payment to establish a financial control company in accordance with the law to ensure adequate capital.* https://mp.weixin.qq.com/s/zcV2GntTCyyMQ684XTQOrw

Robbins, S. P., & Judge, T. A. (2018). *Organizational Behavior* (18th ed.). Pearson Education.

Roberts, K. H. (1990). Some Characteristics of One Type of High Reliability Organization. *Organization Science*, *1*(2), 160.

Rossi, M., Mueller-Bloch, C., Thatcher, J., & Beck, R. (2019). Blockchain Research in Information Systems: Current Trends and an Inclusive Future Research Agenda. *Journal of the Association for Information Systems*, *20*, 1388–1403. doi:10.17705/1jais.00571

Ruizalba, J. L.; Guillermo, B.G.; Miguel, A. R.-M.; Blanca, M. J., (2014). Internal market orientation: empirical research in hotel sector. *Int. J. Hospit. Manage.*, *38*, 11-19.

Ruiz-Martin, C., Pérez Ríos, J., Wainer, G., Pajares, J., Hernández, C., & López-Paredes, A. (2017). The Application of the Viable System Model to Enhance Organizational Resilience. In Advances in Management Engineering (pp. 88–100). https://doi.org/ doi:10.1007/978-3-319-55889-9_5

Ruiz-Martin, C., López-Paredes, A., & Wainer, G. (2015). Applying complex network theory to the assessment of organizational resilience. *IFAC-PapersOnLine*, *48*(3), 1224–1229. doi:10.1016/j.ifacol.2015.06.251

Rule, P., & John, V. M. (2015). A necessary dialogue: Theory in case study research. *International Journal of Qualitative Methods*, *14*(4), 1609406915611575. doi:10.1177/1609406915611575

Russo, M. V., & Fouts, P. A. (1997). A resource-based perspective on corporate environmental performance and profitability. *Academy of Management Journal*, *40*(3), 534–559. doi:10.2307/257052

Ruzungunde, V. S., Murugan, C., & Hlatywayo, C. K. (2016). The influence of job stress on the components of organisational commitment of health care personnel in the Eastern Cape province South Africa. [IBER]. *International Business & Economics Research Journal*, *15*(5), 219–226. doi:10.19030/iber.v15i5.9780

Saberi, S., Kouhizadeh, M., Sarkis, J., & Shen, L. (2019). Blockchain technology and its relationships to sustainable supply chain management. *International Journal of Production Research*, *57*(7), 2117–2135. doi:10.1080/00207543.2018.1533261

Sabzipoor, M., Ahmadizad, A., & Ismaeel-Givi, M. (2012). Analysis of the relationship of organizational atmosphere with attitude variables and meta-role behaviors in the personnel of public libraries. [in Persian]. *Res Inf Sci Public Libr*, *17*, 581–602.

Sadhya, V., Sadhya, H., Hirschheim, R., & Watson, E. (2018). *Exploring Technology Trust in Bitcoin: The Blockchain Exemplar*. European Conference on Information Systems. https://www.semanticscholar.org/paper/Exploring-Technology-Trust-in-Bitcoin%3A-the-Exemplar-Sadhya-Sadhya/df10f099c7cecb 30d1dfa89dbe431f81ee868f27

Salaber, J. M. (2007, November). The determinants of sin stock returns: Evidence on the European market. In *Paris December 2007 Finance International Meeting AFFI-EUROFIDAI Paper*.

Salanova, M., Lorente, L., Chambel, M. J., & Martínez, I. M. (2011). Linking transformational leadership to nurses' extra-role performance: The mediating role of self-efficacy and work engagement. *Journal of Advanced Nursing*, *67*(10), 2256–2266. doi:10.1111/j.1365-2648.2011.05652.x PMID:21535088

Salvia, M., Reckien, D., Pietrapertosa, F., Eckersley, P., Spyridaki, N. A., Krook-Riekkola, A., Olazabal, M., De Gregorio Hurtado, S., Simoes, S. G., Geneletti, D., Viguié, V., Fokaides, P. A., Ioannou, B. I., Flamos, A., Csete, M. S., Buzasi, A., Orru, H., de Boer, C., Foley, A., & Heidrich, O. (2021). Will Climate Mitigation Ambitions Lead to Carbon Neutrality? An Analysis of the Local-Level Plans of 327 Cities in the EU. *Renewable & Sustainable Energy Reviews*, *135*, 110253. doi:10.1016/j.rser.2020.110253

Salwan, P., & Gada, V. P. (2018). Antecedents of resilience: An investigation into bharat forge. *Indian Journal of Industrial Relations*, *53*, 449–461.

Sánchez-García, E., Marco-Lajara, B., Seva-Larrosa, P., & Martínez-Falcó, J. (2022). Driving Innovation by Managing Entrepreneurial Orientation, Cooperation and Learning for the Sustainability of Companies in the Energy Sector. *Sustainability*, *14*(24), 16978.

Scheffer, M., Carpenter, S. R., Lenton, T. M., Bascompte, J., Brock, W., Dakos, V., Koppel, J. d., Leemput, I. A. d., Levin, S. A., & Nes, E. H. (2012). Anticipating Critical Transitions. *Science*, *2012*(338), 344–348.

Schlange, L. E. (2006). What drives sustainable entrepreneurs? *Indian Journal of Economics and Business*, (Special Issue), 35–45.

Schlechter, A. F., & Maharaj, I. (2007). Meaning in life and meaning of work: Relationships with organizational citizenship behavior, commitment, and job satisfaction. *Manag. Dyn.*, *26*, 24–4.

Schmalensee, R. (2012). From 'green growth' to sound policies: An overview. *Energy Economics*, *34*, S2–S6. doi:10.1016/j.eneco.2012.08.041

Schoch, K. (2020). Case study research. *Research design and methods: An applied guide for the scholar-practitioner*, 245-258.

Science and Innovation Bureau of SASAC. (2021). *Notice on the Release of Typical Cases of Digital Transformation of State-owned Enterprises in 2020.* http://www.sasac.gov.cn/n4470048/n13461446/n15927611/n15963955/c17505367/content.html

Scrimgeour, N., Nordestgaard, S., Lloyd, N. D. R., & Wilkes, E. N. (2015). Exploring the effect of elevated storage temperature on wine composition. *Australian Journal of Grape and Wine Research*, *21*, 713–722. doi:10.1111/ajgw.12196

Şenyurt, H., & Dinc, M. S. (2015). The Relationship among Ethical Leadership and Organizational Citizenship Behavior: a study of private primary and high school teachers in Bosubjective normia and Herzegovina. In: *International Conference on Economic and Social Studies - ICESoS'15*, (p. 138–44). International Burch University..

Sergio, E. S., Ana, V. J., Joaquim, R. S., & Carlos, A. G. (2020). Technological Forecasting and Social Change Open Innovation in Science Parks: The Role of Public Policies. *Technological Forecasting and Social Change*, 151.

Seva-Larrosa, P., Martínez-Falcó, J., & Ruiz-Fernández, L. (2022). Analizando las principales variables empresariales en los clusters vinícolas españoles teniendo en cuenta la localización de las empresas y su pertenencia a una marca colectiva. [Analysing the main business variables in Spanish wine clusters taking into account the location of the companies and their membership of a collective brand.] In *Miradas sobre el emprendimiento ante la crisis del coronavirus* (pp. 629–634). Dykinson.

Shang, Q. (2022). Why should State-owned Enterprises accelerate the Digital Transformation? *Lookout,* 6-7. http://lw.news.cn/2022-02/14/c_1310468941.htm

Sharfman, M. P., & Fernando, C. S. (2008). Environmental risk management and the cost of capital. *Strategic Management Journal*, *29*(6), 569–592. doi:10.1002mj.678

Sheffi, Y., & Rice, J. B. (2005). A supply chain view of the resilient enterprise. *MIT Sloan Management Review*, *47*, 41–48.

Shen, Z. P., Jian, X. B., & Zhao, J. (2018). Study on the Construction Modes of China's Overseas Cooperation Industrial Parks along the Belt and Road. *International Urban Planning*, 33.

Shen, J. (2014). Not quite a twin city: Cross-boundary integration in Hong Kong and Shenzhen. *Habitat International*, *42*, 138–146. https://doi.org/10.1016/j.habitatint.2013.12.003

Shepherd, D. A., & Patzelt, H. (2011). The new field of sustainable entrepreneurship: Studying entrepreneurial action linking "what is to be sustained" with "what is to be developed". *Entrepreneurship Theory and Practice*, *35*(1), 137–163. doi:10.1111/j.1540-6520.2010.00426.x

Shi, N. (2020). *Shenzhen takes the lead in achieving full coverage of 5G independent group network, many places accelerate the sprint to the 5G era*. https://company.cnstock.com/company/scp_gsxw/202008/4579088.htm

Shin, D., Zhong, B., & Biocca, F. A. (2020). Beyond user experience: What constitutes algorithmic experiences? *International Journal of Information Management*, *52*, 102061. doi:10.1016/j.ijinfomgt.2019.102061

Shin, J., Taylor, M. S., & Seo, M.-G. (2012). Resources for change: The relationships of organizational inducements and psychological resilience to employees' attitudes and behaviors toward organizational change. *Academy of Management Journal*, *55*, 727–748.

Shleifer, A., & Vishny, R. W. (1997). A survey of corporate governance. *The Journal of Finance*, *52*(2), 737–783. doi:10.1111/j.1540-6261.1997.tb04820.x

Siggelkow, N. (2007). Persuasion with Case Study. *Academy of Management Journal*, 50.

Singer, J. D., & Willett, J. B. (2003). *Applied longitudinal data analysis: Modeling change and event occurrence*. Oxford university press. doi:10.1093/acprof:oso/9780195152968.001.0001

Sinkovics, N., Sinkovics, R. R., & Yamin, M. (2014). The role of social value creation in business model formulation at the bottom of the pyramid–implications for MNEs? *International Business Review*, *23*(4), 692–707. doi:10.1016/j.ibusrev.2013.12.004

Sivarajah, U., Kamal, M. M., Irani, Z., & Weerakkody, V. (2017). Critical analysis of Big Data challenges and analytical methods. *Journal of Business Research*, *70*, 263–286. doi:10.1016/j.jbusres.2016.08.001

Skousen, C. J., & Sun, L. (2019). Do employee dimension ratings reflect employee performance? Evidence from MSCI's ESG database. *Applied Economics Letters*, *26*(14), 1182–1185. doi:10.1080/13504851.2018.1540843

Smith, C. A., Organ, D. W., & Near, J. P. (1983). Organizational citizenship behavior: Its nature and antecedents. *The Journal of Applied Psychology*, *68*(4), 653–663. doi:10.1037/0021-9010.68.4.653

Somers, S. (2009). Measuring resilience potential: An adaptive strategy for organizational crisis planning. *Journal of Contingencies and Crisis Management*, *17*(1), 12–23.

Sone, H. (2013). Tradition and Innovation in Japanese Long-Established Companies: Focus on E-Business. Paper presented at the *2013 Seventh International Conference on Innovative Mobile and Internet Services in Ubiquitous Computing*, (pp. 739-742). IEEE. 10.1109/IMIS.2013.156

Sonnenschein J and Mundaca L (2015). Decarbonization under green growth strategies? The case of South Korea. *Journal of Cleaner Production. 123*. 180–93

Spector, P. E., & Fox, S. (2002). An emotion-centered model of voluntary work behavior: Some parallels between counterproductive work behavior and organizational citizenship behavior. *Human Resource Management Review, 12*(2), 1–24. doi:10.1016/S1053-4822(02)00049-9

Spence, M. (2021). Government and economics in the digital economy. *Journal of Government and Economics, 3*. doi:10.1016/j.jge.2021.100020

Standing Committee of Hubei Provincial People's Congress. (2015). *Regulations on East Lake National Independent Innovation Demonstration Zone*. Author.

State Capital Jingjing. (2021). *Beijing Municipal State-owned Assets Supervision and Administration Commission Releases Implementation Opinions on Accelerating Digital Transformation of Municipal Enterprises*. https://mp.weixin.qq.com/s/Ld2UNKcR9CHkQ4E_8jUsRQ

State Council. (2020). *China's Energy Development in the New Era*. State Council. http://www.scio.gov.cn/zfbps/32832/Document/1695117/1695117.htm

Statman, M. (2000). Socially responsible mutual funds (corrected). *Financial Analysts Journal, 56*(3), 30–39. doi:10.2469/faj.v56.n3.2358

Statman, M. (2004). What do investors want? *Journal of Portfolio Management, 30*(5), 153–161. doi:10.3905/jpm.2004.442641

Statman, M., & Glushkov, D. (2009). The wages of social responsibility. *Financial Analysts Journal, 65*(4), 33–46. doi:10.2469/faj.v65.n4.5

Sternberg, E. (2000). The defects of stakeholder theory1. In R. I. Tricker (Ed.), *Corporate Governance* (pp. 391–400). Gower.

Stiglitz, J. E., Sen, A., & Fitoussi, J.-P. (2009). *Report by the Commission on the Measurement of Economic Performance and Social Progress*. Commission on the Measurement of Economic Performance and Social Progress.

Stigoe, J., Oven, R., & Machaghten, P. (2013). Developing a Framework for Responsible Innovation. *Research Policy, 42*(9), 1568–1580. doi:10.1016/j.respol.2013.05.008

Strategy. (2020). *Under the new situation, how do enterprises carry out digital transformation*. Strategy& Part of the PwC network. https://www.strategyand.pwc.com

Stuermer, M., Abu-Tayeh, G., & Myrach, T. (2017). Digital sustainability: Basic conditions for sustainable digital artifacts and their ecosystems. *Sustainability Science, 12*(2), 247–262. doi:10.100711625-016-0412-2 PMID:30174752

Suma, S., & Lesha, J. (2013). Job satisfaction and organizational commitment: The case of Shkodra municipality. *European Scientific Journal, 9*(17).

Sun, J. (2019). Path Identification of Government Promotion of Business Incubation: Multiple Case Studies in Zhangjiang, Zizhu and Wujiaochang. *Shanghai Economy*, 1.

Sun, Y. (2022). *10 trillion huge investments, where will the money for new infrastructure come from?* https://mp.weixin.qq.com/s/laRv5KsuswEMybmg3B6iNw

Sun, Y. J. (2019). Research on the Path of Establishing Science and Technology Service System in Industrial Park - Take Zizhu High-Tech Park as an Example. *Science & Technology Vision*, 8.

Sun, J., Yan, J., & Zhang, K. Z. K. (2016). Blockchain-based sharing services: What blockchain technology can contribute to smart cities. *Financial Innovation, 2*(1), 26. doi:10.118640854-016-0040-y

Sutcliffe, K. M., & Vogus, T. (2003). Organizing for resilience. In K. S. Cameron, J. E. Dutton, & R. E. Quinn (Eds.), *Positive organizational scholarship* (pp. 94–110). Berrett-Koehler.

Swa, M. (2015). *Blockchain: Blueprint for a New Economy*. O¢Reilly.

Tajeddini, K. (2010). Effect of customer orientation and entrepreneurial orientation on innovativeness: Evidence from the hotel industry in Switzerland. Tourism Manage., 31(2), 221-231.

Tajeddini, K., & Trueman, M. (2008). The potential for innovativeness: a tale of the Swiss watch industry. J. Market. Manage., 24(1-2), 169-184.

Tajeddini, K., & Trueman, M. (2012). Managing Swiss Hospitality: How cultural antecedents of innovation and customer-oriented value systems can influence performance in the hotel industry. Int. J. Hospital. Manage., 31(4): 1119-1129.

Tajeddini, K., & Trueman, M. (2014). Perceptions of innovativeness among Iranian hotel managers. J. Hospital. Tourism Technol., 5(1): 62-77. doi:10.1108/JHTT-12-2012-0036

Tajeddini, K., Trueman, M., & Larsen, G. (2006). Examining the effect of market orientation on innovativeness. J. Market. Manage., 22(5-6): 529-551. doi:10.1362/026725706777978640

Talay, M. B., Calantone, R. J., & Voorhees, C. M. (2014). Coevolutionary dynamics of automotive competition: Product innovation, change, and marketplace survival. *Journal of Product Innovation Management*, *31*(1), 61–78. doi:10.1111/jpim.12080

Taleb, N. N. (2012). *Antifragile: Things that Gain from Disorder* (Vol. 3). Random House.

Taleb, N. N., & Douady, R. (2013). Mathematical definition, mapping, and detection of (anti)fragility. *Quantitative Finance*, *13*(11), 1677–1689. doi:10.1080/14697688.2013.800219

Tallman, S., Jenkins, M., Henry, N., & Pinch, S. (2004). Knowledge, clusters and competitive advantage. *Academy of Management Review*, *29*, 258–271.

Tanaka-Iga. (2022). *納入実績 [Delivery Record]*. Tanaka-Iga. http://www.tanakaiga.com/works/

Tang, J., & Dai, X. (2021). Innovation Linkages in Digital Economy Industries - Evidence from Innovative Companies in Shenzhen. *Zhongshan Daxue Xuebao. Zhexue Shehui Kexue Ban*, *61*(06), 165–176. https://doi.org/10.13471/j.cnki.jsysusse.2021.06.017

Tan, L. P., Yap, C. S., Choong, Y. O., Choe, K. L., Rungruang, P., & Li, Z. (2019). Ethical leadership, perceived organizational support and citizenship behaviors: The moderating role of ethnic dissimilarity. *Leadership and Organization Development Journal*, *40*(8), 877–897. doi:10.1108/LODJ-04-2019-0160

Tapscott, D., & Tapscott, A. (2016). *Blockchain Revolution: How the Technology Behind Bitcoin and Other Cryptocurrencies is Changing the World*. Portfolio Penguin.

Tashakkori, A., Teddlie, C., & Teddlie, C. B. (2003). *Handbook of Mixed Methods in Social & Behavioral Research*. SAGE.

Tetlock, P. E. (1985, September). Accountability: A Social Check on the Fundamental Attribution Error. *Social Psychology Quarterly*, *48*(3), 227–236.

The Danish 92 Group Forum for Sustainable Development. (2012). *Building an Equitable Green Economy*. Danish 92 Group.

The Royal Mint. (2022). *The history of the Royal Mint*. The Royal Mint. https://www.royalmint.com/brand/our-story/

The World Bank. (2022). *Population, total.* The World Bank. https://data.worldbank.org/indicator/SP.POP.TOTL?end=2021&start=2012

Tierney, K. J. (2003). Conceptualizing and measuring organizational and community resilience: lessons from the emergency response following the September 11, 2001, attack on the World Trade Center. Univ. of Delaware, Newark, DE.

Tilley, F., & Young, W. (2009). Sustainability entrepreneurs: could they be the true wealth generators of the future? *Green Management International, 55*, 79-92. https://www.jstor.org/stable/greemanainte.55.79

TMT Post. (2021). *White Paper on Digital Capability Watch for Chinese Real Estate Companies in 2021.* https://www.tmtpost.com/base/report/5630989

Todd, S. Y., & Kent, A. (2006). Direct and indirect effects of task characteristics on organizational citizenship behavior. *North American Journal of Psychology*, *8*(2), 253–268.

Tompkins, J. A. (2007). 4 Steps to business resilience. *Industrial Management (Norcross, Georgia)*, *49*(4), 14–18.

Torri, M. C., & Martinez, A. (2014). Women's empowerment and micro-entrepreneurship in India: Constructing a new development paradigm? *Progress in Development Studies*, *14*(1), 31–48. doi:10.1177/1464993413504347

Tsai, S.-B., Chen, K.-Y., Zhao, H., Wei, Y.-M., Wang, C.-K., Zheng, Y., Chang, L.-C., & Wang, J. (2016). Using a Mixed Model to Explore Evaluation Criteria for Bank Supervision: A Banking Supervision Law Perspective. *PLoS One*, *11*(12), e0167710. doi:10.1371/journal.pone.0167710 PMID:27992449

Tsoukas, H. (1989). The Validity of Idiographic Research Explanations. *Academy of Management Review*, *14*(4), 551–561. doi:10.2307/258558

Tu, C., Tian, F., Li, L., Tan, W., Wang, X., & Liang, S. (2021). *Report of reform and innovation of Guangdong-Hong Kong-Macau Greater Bay Area in China (2021).* https://www.pishu.com.cn/skwx_ps/bookdetail?SiteID=14&ID=12719944

Tziperman, E. (2022). *Global Warming Science: A Quantitative Introduction to Climate Change and Its Consequences.* Princeton University Press.

Ugur, M., & Vivarelli, M. (2021). Innovation, firm survival and productivity: The state of the art. *Economics of Innovation and New Technology*, *30*(5), 433–467. doi:10.1080/10438599.2020.1828509

Umar, M., Ji, X., Mirza, N., & Naqvi, B. (2021). Carbon Neutrality, Bank Lending, and Credit Risk: Evidence from the Eurozone. *Journal of Environmental Management*, *296*, 113156. doi:10.1016/j.jenvman.2021.113156 PMID:34225048

UN E-Government. (2020). *Digital government in the decade of action for sustainable development. With addendum on COVID-19 Response. United Nations E-Government Survey.* https://publicadministration.un.org/egovkb/en-us/Reports/UN-E-Government-Survey-2020

UNCSD. (2012). *The Future we want, outcome of the United Nations Conference on Sustainable Development (Rio+20).* UNCSD.

UNCTAD. (2021). *Chapter 5—Capital Markets and Sustainable Finance.* World Investment Report. https://worldinvestmentreport.unctad.org/world-investment-report-2021/ch5-capital-markets-and-sustainable-finance/

Understanding the. 'E' in ESG (2019). SP Global. www.spglobal.com/en/research-insights/articles/understanding-the-e-in-esg

UNDESA. (2010). Progress to date and remaining gaps in the implementation of the outcoms of the major summits in the area of sustainable development, as well as an analysis of the themes of the Conference. Preparatory Committee for the UNCSD.

UNEP (United Nations Environment Programme). (2011). *Towards a green economy: Pathways to Sustainable Development and Poverty Eradication.* United Nations Environment Programme.

UNEP. (2012a). *Indicators: a UNEP green economy briefing paper.* United Nations Environment Programme.

UNEP. (2012b) *Measuring progress towards a green economy: draft working paper* United Nations Environment Programme, Nairobi.

UNEP. (2014b). *Using indicators for green economy policymaking United Nations Environment Programme.*

UNESCO. (2011*). From Green Economies to Green Societies.* UNESCO.

UNFCCC. (2015). *Paris Agreement Report of the Conference of the Parties on Its Twenty-First Session.* UNFCCC. https://unfccc.int/sites/default/files/paris_agreement.pdf

United Nations (2015) *Adoption of the Paris Agreement: FCCC/CP/2015/L.9/Rev.1.* UN.

United Nations Environment Programme. (2007). *The United Nations Environment Programme (UNEP) Developed a Guidance Document on Desalination.* UN. https://www.unep.org/resources/report/guidance-chemicals-control-contributing-national-progress-and-safety

United Nations Environment Programme. (2016). *Resource efficiency: Potential and economic implications. A report of the International Resource Panel.* UN. file:///C:/Users/ninas/Downloads/resource_efficiency_summary_report_english.pdf

United Nations Environment Programme. (2018). *Resource efficiency for sustainable development. Key messages for the group of 20.* UN. https://www.resourcepanel.org/resource-efficiency-sustainable-development-key-messages-group-20

United Nations Environment Programme. (2020). *Resource efficiency and climate change: Material efficiency strategies for a low-carbon future, A report of the International Resource Panel.* UN. https://www.unep.org/resources/report/resource-efficiency-and-climate-change-material-efficiency-strategies-low-carbon

United Nations. (1987). *Report of the World Commission on Environment and Development: Our Common Future.* UN. http://www.un-documents.net/our-common-future.pdf

US Department of Commerce. (2010a). *Measuring the green economy United States Department of Commerce.* Washington DC US Department of Commerce.

Usul, N., Özdemir, Ö., & Kiessling, T. (2017). Affect-based stock investment decision: The role of affective self-affinity. *Journal of Behavioral and Experimental Economics*, *68*, 97–109. doi:10.1016/j.socec.2017.04.004

Utz, S., & Wimmer, M. (2014). Are they any good at all? A financial and ethical analysis of socially responsible mutual funds. *Journal of Asset Management*, *15*(1), 72–82. doi:10.1057/jam.2014.8

Valastro, J. (2011), Organisational resilience: a position paper for critical infrastructure, pp. 1-41. Commonwealth of Australia.

Van Der Beek, D., & Schraagen, J. M. (2015). ADAPTER: Analysing and developing adaptability and performance in teams to enhance resilience. *Reliability Engineering & System Safety*, 141.

Van der Ploeg, R., & Withagen, C. (2013). Green growth, green paradox and the global economic crisis. *Environmental Innovation and Societal Transitions*, *6*, 116–119. doi:10.1016/j.eist.2012.11.003

van der Vegt, G. S., Essens, P., Wahlstrom, M., & George, G. (2015). Managing risk and resilience. *Academy of Management Journal*, *58*, 971–980.

Van der Voet, J., Steijn, B., & Kuipers, B. S. (2017). What's in it for others? The relationship between prosocial motivation and commitment to change among youth care professionals. *Public Management Review*, *2017*(19), 443–462. doi:10.1080/14719037.2016.1183699

Van Woerkom, M., & Meyers, M. C. (2015). My strengths count! effects of a strengths-based psychological climate on positive affect and job performance. *Hum. Resour. Manag. 54*, 81–103. doi:. 21623 doi:10.1002/hrm

Van Woerkom, M., Mostert, K., Els, C., Bakker, A. B., de Beer, L., & Rothmann, S. Jr. (2016a). Strengths use and deficit correction in organizations: Development and validation of a questionnaire. *European Journal of Work and Organizational Psychology*, *25*(6), 960–975. doi:10.1080/1359432X.2016.1193010

Vance, R. J. (2006). *Employee engagement and commitment*, 1-53. SHRM foundation.

VanDuuren, E., Plantinga, A., & Scholtens, B. (2016). ESG Integration and the Investment Management Process: Fundamental Investing Reinvented. *Journal of Business Ethics*, *138*(3), 525–533. doi:10.100710551-015-2610-8

Varriale, V., Cammarano, A., Michelino, F., & Caputo, M. (2020). The Unknown Potential of Blockchain for Sustainable Supply Chains. *Sustainability*, *12*(22), 22. doi:10.3390u12229400

Veithzal, R., & Sagala, E. J. (2004). *Manajemen sumber daya manusia untuk perusahaan [Human resource management for companies]*. PT Raja Grafindo Persada.

Venios, X., Korkas, E., Nisiotou, A., & Banilas, G. (2020). Grapevine responses to heat stress and global warming. *Plants*, *9*(12), 1754. doi:10.3390/plants9121754 PMID:33322341

Venkataraman, P., & Ganapathi, R. (2013). A Study of Job Stress on Job Satisfaction among the Employees of Small Scale Industries. *IOSR Journal of Business and Management*, *13*(3), 18–22. doi:10.9790/487X-1331822

Victor, P., & Jackson, T. (2011). Doing the maths on the green economy. *Nature*, *472*(7343), 295. doi:10.1038/472295a PMID:21512560

Vinetur (2018). *La apuesta sostenible de Matarromera obtiene cuatro certificados de AENOR [Matarromera's commitment to sustainability obtains four AENOR certificates]*. Vinetur. https://www.vinetur.com/2018101748520/la-apuesta-sostenible-de-matarromera-obtiene-cuatro-certificados-de-aenor.html

Vogus, T. J., & Sutcliffe, K. M. (2007). Organizational resilience: Towardsa theory and research agenda. Paper presented at *the Systems, Manand Cybernetics, ISIC*. IEEE.

Volkoff, O., & Diane, M. Strong. (2017). Affordance theory and how to use it in IS research. In The Routledge Companion to Management Information Systems (pp. 232–245). Routledge. doi:10.4324/9781315619361-18

Vossenaar, R. (2013). *The APEC list of environmental goods: an analysis of the outcome & expected impact*. International Centre for Trade and Sustainable Development.

Vranken, H. (2017). Sustainability of bitcoin and blockchains. *Current Opinion in Environmental Sustainability*, *28*, 1–9. doi:10.1016/j.cosust.2017.04.011

Walliman, N. (2010). *Research methods: The basics*. Routledge. doi:10.4324/9780203836071

Walumbwa, F. O., Wang, P., Wang, H., Schaubroeck, J., & Avolio, B. J. (2010). Psychological processes linking authentic leadership to follower behaviors. *The Leadership Quarterly*, *21*(5), 901–914. doi:10.1016/j.leaqua.2010.07.015

Wang, D., & Chen, R. S. (2019). Exploration and Practice of Patent Navigation Industry Development Model - Taking Wuhan East Lake High Technology Development Zone as an Example. *China Invention & Patent,* 16.

Wang, J. (2022). *Digital policy involution: Beijing, Shanghai, Guangzhou and Shenzhen, who is the leader?* https://mp.weixin.qq.com/s/aQlx4fUkBjlmJp-RzG98HQ

Wang, Q. (2022). Comprehensively build a digital government and promote the development of digitalization as a whole. *Administration Reform,* (1), 4-7. doi:10.14150/j.cnki.1674-7453.2022.01.002

Wang, Q., & Gao, X. (2019). Is It Possible To Build An Innovation Responsibility Community? The Necessity and Reality of the Western Theory of Responsible Innovation. *Journal of Nantong University,* 35.

Wang, S., Jiang, X., & Wang, X. (2019). *Countries launch national digital development strategies, global "digital" education in action.* https://mp.weixin.qq.com/s/0FyKF3g8J3YTfVw5lwdrUg

Wang, Y. (2018). Digital economy reshapes the global economic pattern-- differentiation and integration driven by policy competition and economies of scale. *Global Review, 10*(4), 60-79, 154-155. doi:10.13851/j.cnki.gjzw.201804004

Wang, Y., Singgih, M., Wang, J., & Rit, M. (2018, February 19). *Making sense of blockchain technology: How will it transform supply chains?* Wright, A., & De Filippi, P. (2015). Decentralized Blockchain Technology and the Rise of Lex Cryptographia. SSRN *Electronic Journal*. doi:10.2139/ssrn.2580664

Wang, C., & Zhao, H. (2016). The Assessment of Urban Ecological Environment in Watershed Scale. *Procedia Environmental Sciences, 36,* 169–175. doi:10.1016/j.proenv.2016.09.028

Wang, H., & Wen, K. (2020). The opportunity in danger of COVID-19 's epidemic situation-accelerating the Digital Transformation of our country. *Studies in Science of Science, 38*(03), 393–395.

Wang, L. C., Liu, L., & Wu, C. S. (2021). Research on Evaluation of High-quality Development of National High-tech Zones in the New Economic Environment: Empirical Research on 10 National High-tech Zones. *Science and Technology Management Research, 3,* 33–39.

Wang, P., Chu, P., Wang, J., Pan, R., Sun, Y., Yan, M., Jiao, L., Zhan, X., & Zhang, D. (2020). Association between job stress and organizational commitment in three types of Chinese university teachers: Mediating effects of job burnout and job satisfaction. *Frontiers in Psychology, 11,* 11. doi:10.3389/fpsyg.2020.576768 PMID:33132985

Wang, Y., Liu, J., & Zhu, Y. (2018). How does humble leadership promote follower creativity? the roles of psychological capital and growth need strength. *Leadership and Organization Development Journal, 39*(4), 507–521. doi:10.1108/LODJ-03-2017-0069

Wang, Z., & Dong, X. (2016). Determinants and Policy Implications of Residents' New Energy Vehicle Purchases: The Evidence from China. *Natural Hazards, 82*(1), 155–173. doi:10.100711069-016-2185-4

Wayne, S. J., & Green, S. A. (1993). The effects of leader-member exchange on employee citizenship and impression management behavior. *Human Relations, 46*(12), 1431–1440. doi:10.1177/001872679304601204

Wei, C., & Guo, C. (2021). Empowering and reshaping: The reform of government governance in the era of digital economy. *Theory Journal,* (5), 51-58. doi:10.14110/j.cnki.cn-37-1059/d.2021.05.006

Weick, K. E., & Sutcliffe, K. M. (2007). Managing the unexpected: Resilient performance in an age of uncertainty (2. ed.). San Francisco, CA: Jossey-Bass.

Weick, K. E., & Sutcliffe, K. M. (2001). *Managing the unexpected: Assuring high performance in an age of complexity.* Jossey-Bass.

Weick, K. E., Sutcliffe, K. M., & Obstfeld, D. (1999). Organizing for High Reliability: Processes of Collective Mindfulness. In R. S. Sutton & B. M. Staw (Eds.), *Research in Organizational Behavior* (Vol. 1, pp. 81–123). Jai Press.

Weihenstephan. (2022). *The World's Best Kristallweißbier is brewed in Weihenstephan!* Weihenstephan. https://www.weihenstephaner.de/en/news/the-world-s-best-kristallweissbier-is-brewed-in-weihenstephan

Wei, K. B., Rianne, A. M., Myriam, C., & Theo, A. (2019). Towards a Segmentation of Science Parks: A Typology Study on Science Parks in Europe. *Research Policy, 48*(3), 719–732. doi:10.1016/j.respol.2018.11.004

Welker, M., & Wood, D. (2011). Shareholder activism and alienation. *Current Anthropology, 52*(S3), S57–S69. doi:10.1086/656796

Weng Q, Xu B, Hu X and Liu H (2013) Use of earth observation data for applications in public health *Geocarto International, 29,* 33–16–16

Whalen, K. A. (2019). Three circular business models that extend product value and their contribution to resource efficiency. *Journal of Cleaner Production, 226*, 1128–1137. doi:10.1016/j.jclepro.2019.03.128

What Is the. 'G' in ESG? (2020). SP Global. www.spglobal.com/en/research-insights/articles/what-is-the-g-in-esg

What Is the. 'S' in ESG ? (2020). SP Global. www.spglobal.com/en/research-insights/articles/what-is-the-s-in-esg

Whitmee, S., Haines, A., Beyrer, C., Boltz, F., Capon, A. G., Dias, B. F. S., Ezeh, A., Frumkin, H., Gong, P., & Head, P. (2015). *Safeguarding human health in the Anthropocene epoch*: Report of The Rockefeller Foundation–Lancet Commission on planetary health. *Lancet, 386*, 1973–2028.

Wilbanks, T. J., & Romero Lankao, P. BaoMet al (2007) Industry, settlement, and society. In: Parry ML, Canziani OF, Palutikof JP, van der Linden PJ, Hanson CE (eds) Climate change 2007: impacts, adaptation, and vulnerability: contribution of Working Group II to the Fourth Assessment Report of the Intergovernmental Panel on Climate Change. Cambridge University Press, Cambridge.

Wildavsky, A. B. (1988). Searching for safety (3rd ed.) 2004. New Bruns-wick, London: Transaction Publishers.

Wilkinson, A., Elahi, S., & Eidinow, E. (2003). Section 2. Background and dynamics of the scenarios. *Journal of Risk Research, 6*, 365–401.

Williams, T. A., Gruber, D. A., Sutcliffe, K. M., Shepherd, D. A., & Zhao, E. Y. (2017). Organizational response to adversity: Fusing crisis management and resilience research streams. *The Academy of Management Annals, 11*, 733–769.

Williams, T., & Shepherd, D. (2016). Building resilience or providing sustenance: Different paths of emergent ventures in the aftermath of the haiti earthquake. *Academy of Management Journal*. doi:10.5465/amj.2015.0682

Woods, D. (2003). Creating Foresight: How Resilience Engineering Can Transform NASA' s Approach to Risky Decision Making. Testimony on the future of NASA for Committee of Commerce, Science and Transportation.

World Commission on Environment and Development. (1987). *Report of the World Commission on Environment and Development: Our common future*. United Nations. https://sustainabledevelopment.un.org/content/documents/5987our-common-future.pdf

Wu, W. (2021). Beijing has completed 47,000 5G base stations. *The Beijing News*. http://epaper.bjnews.com.cn/html/2021-11/26/content_811575.htm?div=-1

Wu, F. (2000). The global and local dimensions of place-making: Remaking Shanghai as a world city. *Urban Studies (Edinburgh, Scotland)*, *37*(8), 1359–1377.

Wu, J., Balliet, D., & Van Lange, P. A. M. (2016a). Gossip versus punishment: The efficiency of reputation to promote and maintain cooperation. *Scientific Reports*, *6*(1), 23919. doi:10.1038rep23919 PMID:27039896

Wu, J., Balliet, D., & Van Lange, P. A. M. (2016b). Reputation, gossip, and human cooperation. *Social and Personality Psychology Compass*, *10*(6), 350–364. doi:10.1111pc3.12255

Wu, J., Zhang, F., Sun, X., Zhu, Y., & Liu, C. (2020). Anti-epidemic promotes China's Digital Transformation: Opportunities and challenges. *Journal of the Chinese Academy of Sciences*, *35*(03), 306–311.

Wu, L.-Z., Birtch, T. A., Chiang, F. F. T., & Zhang, H. (2018a). Perceptions of negative workplace gossip: A self-consistency theory framework. *Journal of Management*, *44*(5), 1873–1898. doi:10.1177/0149206316632057

Wu, M., Liu, Y., Xu, Z., Yan, G., Ma, M., Zhou, S., & Qian, Y. (2020). Spatio-temporal Dynamics of China's Ecological Civilization Progress after Implementing National Conservation Strategy. *Journal of Cleaner Production*, *285*, 124886. doi:10.1016/j.jclepro.2020.124886

Wu, W., Wu, J. J., Wang, X., Zhong, B., & Yang, A. X. (2020). Ecological Environment Assessment for Greater Mekong Sub-Region Based on Pressure-State-Response Framework by Remote Sensing. *Ecological Indicators*, *117*, 106521. doi:10.1016/j.ecolind.2020.106521

Xia, X., Li, Z., Liang, Y., Bi, F., Zheng, J., & Tao, L. (2020). *Heavyweight! The country's first official announcement of the scope of the "new infrastructure": 3 major aspects, 7 major areas of exposure*. http://www.china-cer.com.cn/xinjijian/202004214081_7.html

Xie, J., Nozawa, W., Yagi, M., Fujii, H., & Managi, S. (2019). Do environmental, social, and governance activities improve corporate financial performance? *Business Strategy and the Environment*, *28*(2), 286–300. doi:10.1002/bse.2224

Xie, K. F., Song, Y., Zhang, W. Y., Hao, J. H., Liu, Z. M., & Chen, Y. (2018). Technological Entrepreneurship in Science Parks: A Case Study of Wuhan East Lake High-Tech Zone. *Technological Forecasting and Social Change*, *135*, 156–168. doi:10.1016/j.techfore.2018.01.021

Xiong, B. G., & Luo, Y. D. (2021). Promote the Innovative Development of My Country's Eco-Industrial Parks with "Responsible Innovation". *Ecological Economics*, *37*, 68–73.

Xu, Y., & Sun, W. (2021). *Shenzhen-Hong Kong cooperation in the perspective of metropolitan area*. https://mp.weixin.qq.com/s/_qzHSWgK1w38UNH88gNMdw

Xu, J., & Yeh, A. G. O. (2005). City repositioning and competitiveness building in regional development: New development strategies in Guangzhou. *China International Journal of Urban and Regional Research*, *29*(2), 283–308.

Yadav, V., & Unni, J. (2016). Women entrepreneurship: Research review and future directions. *Journal of Global Entrepreneurship Research*, *6*(1), 1–18. doi:10.118640497-016-0055-x

Yam, K. C., Fehr, R., Burch, T. C., Zhang, Y., & Gray, K. (2019). Would I really make a diference? Moral typecasting theory and its implications for helping ethical leaders. *Journal of Business Ethics*, *160*(3), 675–692. doi:10.100710551-018-3940-0

Yang, C. H., & Lee, W. H. (2021). Establishing Science Parks Everywhere? Misallocation in R&D and its Determinants of Science Parks in China. *China Economic Review*, *67*, 6. doi:10.1016/j.chieco.2021.101605

Yang, X. J. (2013). China's Rapid Urbanization. *Science*, *342*(6156), 310. doi:10.1126cience.342.6156.310-a PMID:24136949

Yan, Z., & Chen, C. C. (2013). Developmental leadership and organizational citizenship behavior: Mediating effects of self-determination, supervisor identification, and organizational identification. *The Leadership Quarterly*, *24*(4), 534–543. doi:10.1016/j.leaqua.2013.03.007

Yao, Y., & Ye, Z. (2021). Government and Enterprise in Digital Transformation: Role orientation and relationship Construction. *Journal of Zhengzhou University*, *54*(04), 26–31. https://www.cnki.net

Ye, Q., & Fan, M. L. (2021). Take the Lead in Layout to Support Guangzhou High-Tech Zone to Green Industry to Economic Benefits. *Science and Technology Daily*, 7.

Ye, Y., Zhu, H., Deng, X., & Mu, Z. (2019). Negative workplace gossip and service outcomes: An explanation from social identity theory. *International Journal of Hospitality Management*, *82*, 159–168. doi:10.1016/j.ijhm.2019.04.020

Yin, R. (2002). *Case study research: Design and methods*. SAGE Publications.

Yin, R. (2011). *Applications of case study research*. SAGE Publications.

Yiwei, L. (2022). *Series Research on Patent Situation of Strategic Emerging Industries New Energy Vehicles*. Sadie Think Tank. https://mp.weixin.qq.com/s/1l47qihqITCFbmkipXdt6A

Yu, K. (2021). *Shanghai was awarded the first batch of "gigabit cities" in the country, and 5G network led the country*. https://www.thepaper.cn/newsDetail_forward_15991886

Yu, P., Chen, D., & Ahuja, A. (2022). Smart and Sustainable Economy: How COVID-19 Has Acted as a Catalyst for China's Digital Transformation. In S. Kautish & G. Kaur (Eds.), AI-Enabled Agile Internet of Things for Sustainable FinTech Ecosystems (pp. 106–146). IGI Global. https://doi.org/10.4018/978-1-6684-4176-3.ch006.

Yu, P., Chen, J., Sampat, M., & Misuko, N. (2022). The Digital Transformation of Rural Agricultural Business Management: A Case Study of China. In S. Bilgaiyan, J. Singh, & H. Das (Eds.), Empirical Research for Futuristic E-Commerce Systems: Foundations and Applications (pp. 23–52). IGI Global. https://doi.org/10.4018/978-1-6684-4969-1.ch002.

Yu, P., Ge, Y., Mandizvidza, K., & Mulli, J. (2023). How Can Small and Medium Enterprises in the Chinese Market Achieve Sustainable Development Goals Through Blockchain? In D. Taleb, M. Abdelli, A. Khalil, & A. Sghaier (Eds.), Examining the Vital Financial Role of SMEs in Achieving the Sustainable Development Goals (pp. 52–85). IGI Global. https://doi.org/10.4018/978-1-6684-4834-2.ch004.

Yu, P., Gong, R., & Sampat, M. (2022). Blockchain Technology in China's Digital Economy: Balancing Regulation and Innovation. In P. Tehrani (Ed.), Regulatory Aspects of Artificial Intelligence on Blockchain (pp. 132–157). IGI Global. https://doi.org/10.4018/978-1-7998-7927-5.ch007.

Yu, P., Gu, H., Sampat, R. M., Lin, Q., & Chen, Z. (2022). Chinese EdTech Economy in the COVID-19 Era. In S. Fazzin (Ed.), EdTech Economy and the Transformation of Education (pp. 114–137). IGI Global. https://doi.org/10.4018/978-1-7998-8904-5.ch007.

Yu, P., Gu, H., Zhao, Y., & Ahuja, A. (2022). Digital Transformation Driven by Internet Data Center: Case Studies on China. In D. Piaggesi, H. Landazuri, & B. Jia (Eds.), Cases on Applying Knowledge Economy Principles for Economic Growth in Developing Nations (pp. 203–230). IGI Global. https://doi.org/10.4018/978-1-7998-8417-0.ch011.

Yu, P., He, K., & Sampat, M. (2022). COVID-19's Impact on the Chinese Tourism and Hospitality Sector. In V. Costa & C. Costa (Eds.), Sustainability and Competitiveness in the Hospitality Industry (pp. 23–66). IGI Global. https://doi.org/10.4018/978-1-7998-9285-4.ch002.

Yu, P., Kwok, S., & Jiang, Z. (2022). How COVID-19 Has Stimulated Innovation in the Chinese Education Sector. In J. Saiz-Alvarez (Ed.), Handbook of Research on Emerging Business Models and the New World Economic Order (pp. 343–364). IGI Global. https://doi.org/10.4018/978-1-7998-7689-2.ch017.

Yu, P., Kwok, S., & Jiang, Z. (2023). How COVID-19 Has Stimulated Innovation in the Chinese Education Sector. In I. Management Association (Ed.), *Research Anthology on Remote Teaching and Learning and the Future of Online Education* (pp. 1612-1634). IGI Global. doi:10.4018/978-1-6684-7540-9.ch080

Yu, P., Liu, Z., & Hanes, E. (2022). Supply Chain Resiliency, Efficiency, and Visibility in the Post-Pandemic Era in China: Case Studies of MeiTuan Waimai, and Ele.me. In Y. Ramakrishna (Ed.), Handbook of Research on Supply Chain Resiliency, Efficiency, and Visibility in the Post-Pandemic Era (pp. 195–225). IGI Global. https://doi.org/10.4018/978-1-7998-9506-0.ch011.

Yu, P., Liu, Z., Hanes, E., & Mumtaz, J. (2022). Integration of IoT and Blockchain for Smart and Secured Supply Chain Management: Case Studies of China. In S. Goyal, N. Pradeep, P. Shukla, M. Ghonge, & R. Ravi (Eds.), Utilizing Blockchain Technologies in Manufacturing and Logistics Management (pp. 179–207). IGI Global. https://doi.org/10.4018/978-1-7998-8697-6.ch010.

Yu, P., Lu, S., Hanes, E., & Chen, Y. (2022). The Role of Blockchain Technology in Harnessing the Sustainability of Chinese Digital Finance. In P. Swarnalatha & S. Prabu (Eds.), Blockchain Technologies for Sustainable Development in Smart Cities (pp. 155–186). IGI Global. https://doi.org/10.4018/978-1-7998-9274-8.ch009.

Yu, P., Lu, Y., Hanes, E., & Gu, H. (2022). Digitized Education: Enhancement in Teaching and Learning – China Case Study. In C. Krishnan, F. Al-Harthy, & G. Singh (Eds.), Technology Training for Educators From Past to Present (pp. 1–35). IGI Global. https://doi.org/10.4018/978-1-6684-4083-4.ch001.

Yu, P., Tang, H., Tang, H., & Hanes, E. (2022). Using "Digitalization + Intellectual Property" Management to Realize Cultural Economy: Case Study of Chinese Museums. In R. Pettinger, B. Gupta, A. Roja, & D. Cozmiuc (Eds.), Handbook of Research on Digital Transformation Management and Tools (pp. 236–264). IGI Global. https://doi.org/10.4018/978-1-7998-9764-4.ch011.

Yu, P., Wang, Y., & Hanes, E. (2022). Innovative Management Strategy of Wine Tourism in the COVID-19 Era: A Case Study of China. In R. Kovid & V. Kumar (Eds.), Cases on Emerging Market Responses to the COVID-19 Pandemic (pp. 59–89). IGI Global. https://doi.org/10.4018/978-1-6684-3504-5.ch004.

Yu, P., Xu, S., Cheng, Z., & Sampat, M. (2023). Does the Development of New Energy Vehicles Promote Carbon Neutralization?: Case Studies in China. In A. Pego (Ed.), Climate Change, World Consequences, and the Sustainable Development Goals for 2030 (pp. 109–131). IGI Global. https://doi.org/10.4018/978-1-6684-4829-8.ch006.

Yu, P., Xue, W., & Mahendran, R. (2022). The Development and Impact of China's Digital Transformation in the Medical Industry. In M. Rodrigues & J. Proença (Eds.), Impact of Digital Transformation on the Development of New Business Models and Consumer Experience (pp. 97–128). IGI Global. https://doi.org/10.4018/978-1-7998-9179-6.ch006.

Yu, P., Yu, M., & Sampat, M. (2022). Smart Management for Digital Transformation in China. In B. Barbosa, S. Filipe, & C. Santos (Eds.), *Handbook of Research on Smart Management for Digital Transformation* (pp. 411-438). IGI Global. doi:10.4018/978-1-7998-9008-9.ch019

Yuan, F., & Woodman, R. W. (2010). Innovative behavior in the workplace: The role of performance and image outcome expectations. *Academy of Management Journal*, *53*(2), 323–342. doi:10.5465/amj.2010.49388995

Yu, J., Liu, S. B., & Wang, Q. (2016). Research on the Innovation Evaluation Index System of Enterprise Leaders in Dalian High-Tech Zone. *Science and Technology Management Research*, *20*, 37.

Yu, P., Jiang, Z., Mandizvidza, K., & Chen, Z. (2022). Impact Investing and the Roles of Family Offices: Sustainable and Responsible Investment Strategies. In R. Sharma & K. Mehta (Eds.), *Handbook of Research on Stock Market Investment Practices and Portfolio Management* (pp. 244–268). IGI Global. doi:10.4018/978-1-6684-5528-9.ch013

Yu, P., Jiao, A., & Sampat, M. (2022). The Effect of Chinese Green Transformation on Competitiveness and the Environment. In P. Ordóñez de Pablos, X. Zhang, & M. Almunawar (Eds.), *Handbook of Research on Green, Circular, and Digital Economies as Tools for Recovery and Sustainability* (pp. 257–279). IGI Global. doi:10.4018/978-1-7998-9664-7.ch014

Yu, P., Liu, X., Mahendran, R., & Lu, S. (2022). Analysis and Comparison of Business Models of Leading Enterprises in the Chinese Hydrogen Energy Industry. In R. Felseghi, N. Cobîrzan, & M. Raboaca (Eds.), *Clean Technologies and Sustainable Development in Civil Engineering* (pp. 179–216). IGI Global. doi:10.4018/978-1-7998-9810-8.ch008

Yu, P., Tang, S., Ahuja, A., & Chang, X. (2022). Active Equity Investing: Post-COVID-19 Investment Strategies and Portfolio Construction Under the Unique Institutional Settings of China. In R. Sharma & K. Mehta (Eds.), *Handbook of Research on Stock Market Investment Practices and Portfolio Management* (pp. 301–328). IGI Global. doi:10.4018/978-1-6684-5528-9.ch016

Yu, P., Weng, Y., & Ahuja, A. (2022). Carbon Financing and the Sustainable Development Mechanism: The Case of China. In A. Rafay (Ed.), *Handbook of Research on Energy and Environmental Finance 4.0* (pp. 301–332). IGI Global. doi:10.4018/978-1-7998-8210-7.ch012

Yu, P., Xu, S., Cheng, Z., & Sampat, M. (2023). Does the Development of New Energy Vehicles Promote Carbon Neutralization?: Case Studies in China. In A. Pego (Ed.), *Climate Change, World Consequences, and the Sustainable Development Goals for 2030* (pp. 109–131). IGI Global. doi:10.4018/978-1-6684-4829-8.ch006

Yu, X. (2021). Analysis of policies related to "Internet + government services" in the context of digital government construction. *Chinese Engineering Consultants*, *2021*(1), 63–67.

Zanin, A., Dal Magro, C. B., Mazzioni, S., & Afonso, P. (2019, July). Triple Bottom Line Analysis in an Agribusiness Supply Chain. In *International Joint Conference on Industrial Engineering and Operations Management* (pp. 264-273). Springer.

Zehra, S. Z., Ather, M., & Zehra, B. (2017). A correlation between workplace stress and organizational commitment: Doctors response from public and private hospitals in Karachi, Pakistan. MPRA.

Zhai, Y., Jiang, M., & Wang, W. (2021). The theoretical interpretation and operating mechanism of China's digital transformation. *E-government*, (6), 67-84. doi:10.16582/j.cnki.dzzw.2021.06.007

Zhang, J., Chen, Y., & Liu, J. (2016). *Ethical leadership and OCBE: The influence of prosocial motivation and self-accountability.* Paper presented at the Academy of Management Proceedings, Briarcliff Manor, NY. 10.5465/ambpp.2016.15588abstract

Zhang, L. (2020). The Integration of industrialization and Informatization has entered a new stage of Digital Transformation of Manufacturing Industry. *Cybersecurity & Informatization*, *2020*(6), 28-31.

Zhang, L., & Huang, G. Q. (2015). Research on Collaborative Innovation Mechanism of In-Depth Integration of Industry, Education and Research in 'One-Zone, Multiple-parks' of East Lake National Independent Innovation Demonstration Zone. *Science Technology and Industry*, 15.

Zhang, X., & Sun, Y. (2019). Investigating institutional integration in the contexts of Chinese city-regionalization: evidence from Shenzhen–Dongguan–Huizhou. *Land Use Policy*, *88*. doi:10.1016/j.landusepol.2019.104170

Zhang, Y. (2021). The "27" to stimulate the dynamic power of digital transformation. *Jiefang Daily*. doi:10.28410/n.cnki.njfrb.2021.004857

Zhang, Y., Huang, Y., & Zhao, Z. (2020). *How Digital Reinvents Real Estate in the Age of Inventory*. https://ifenxi.com/research/content/5558

Zhang, L., Jiang, H., & Jin, T. (2020). Leader-member exchange and organisational citizenship behavior: The mediating and moderating effects of role ambiguity. *Journal of Psychology in Africa*, *30*(1), 17–22. doi:10.1080/14330237.2020.1721948

Zhang, T., Wang, L., Wang, H., Peng, L., & Luo, C. (2017). Assessment of Soil Salinization Ecological Environment Change in the Manas River Basin Using Remote Sensing Technology. *Acta Ecologica Sinica*, *37*(9), 3009–3018. doi:10.5846txb201601310225

Zhang, X., Chen, S., Luan, X., & Yuan, M. (2020). Understanding China's city-regionalization: Spatial structure and relationships between functional and institutional spaces in the Pearl River Delta. *Urban Geography*, 1–28.

Zhang, Y. X., & Hao, Y. (2020). Rethinking China's Environmental Target Responsibility System: Province-Level Convergence Analysis of Pollutant Emission Intensities in China. *Journal of Cleaner Production*, *242*, 118472. doi:10.1016/j.jclepro.2019.118472

Zhang, Y., Luo, H., & Wang, C. (2021). Progress and Trends of Global Carbon Neutrality Pledges. *Climate Change Research*, *17*, 88–97. doi:10.12006/j.issn.1673-1719.2020.241

Zhao, H., & Su, P. (2020). Understanding the structure and determinants of city network through intra-firm service relationships: The case of Guangdong-Hong Kong-Macao Greater Bay Area. *Cities*, *103*. doi:10.1016/j.cities.2020.102738

Zhao, J. L., Fan, S., & Yan, J. (2016). Overview of business innovations and research opportunities in blockchain and introduction to the special issue. *Financial Innovation*, *2*(1), 28. doi:10.118640854-016-0049-2

Zheng, Z., Xie, S., Dai, H.-N., Chen, X., & Wang, H. (2017, June 25). *An Overview of Blockchain Technology: Architecture, Consensus, and Future Trends*. IEEE. doi:10.1109/BigDataCongress.2017.85

Zheng, S. L., & Li, Z. C. (2020). Pilot Governance and the Rise of China's Innovation. *China Economic Review*, *63*, 63. doi:10.1016/j.chieco.2020.101521

Zhongguancun Alliance for the Integration and Development of Information Technology and Real Economy (AIITRE) & China Enterprise Federation. (2021). *2021 White Paper on the Development Index and Method Path of Digital Transformation of State-owned Enterprises*. Digitalization Think Tank.

Zhou, X. (2021). *The digital economy will be sounded in 2021, and Zhejiang, Shanghai, Beijing and Guangdong intend to do so*. https://m.21jingji.com/article/20210128/herald/ba1b9070cdcb2e9022f71e788d48a7f7_zaker.html

Zhuang, L., & Ye, C. (2020). Changing Imbalance: Spatial Production of National High-Tech Industrial Development Zones in China. *Land Use Policy*, 94.

Zolli, A., & Healy, A. M. (2012). *Resilience: Why Things Bounce Back*. Simon and Schuster, Inc.

About the Contributors

Bartolomé Marco-Lajara (PhD) is Professor at the University of Alicante. His research interests are strategic management and tourism management. He is the author of several books, book chapters and international articles related to the areas above mentioned. He is a member of the Tourism Research Institute at the University of Alicante since its foundation and the main researcher of the European project 'Next Tourism Generation Alliance' at his University, as well as of the public competitive project for the creation of the Tourist Observatory of the Valencian Community (Spain). He has taken part in others public and private projects, such as the development of the strategic plan of the Alicante province for the period 2010-2020. He is the Head of the Department of Management at the University of Alicante, and previously was the Assistant Dean of the Economics Faculty for the Business Degree.

Javier Martínez-Falcó is Assistant Professor in the Department of Management at the University of Alicante. In the field of research, he focuses his interest on issues related to the Strategic Management of the Company, specifically in the areas of Knowledge Management and Corporate Sustainability of wine companies, on which he has written several publications in the form of articles, book chapters and contributions to conferences. He has also participated in several national research projects and teaches Strategic Management on the ADE, TADE and DADE degree courses.

Luis A. Millán-Tudela is Assistant Professor in the Department of Management at University of Alicante. MBA and Bachelor of Mechanical Engineering, his research focuses on business longevity, and more specifically on the factors that influence the survival of companies. This activity is developed within the research group "Dirección Estratégica, conocimiento e innovación en una economía global (DECI-GLOBAL)". He also teaches strategic management in the Degree of Business Administration.

* * *

Pallavi Bhardwaj is a Research Scholar in the Faculty of Management Studies, Gurukula Kangri (Deemed to be University), Haridwar. She obtained her Bachelors and Masters in Commerce from the H.N.B. University. She has published her papers at UGC care list II. She has an experience of working as an Assistant Professor in BRD College of Management and Sciences, Roorkee. She has attended various national and international conferences.

Xiaochang Chang is an independent researcher. Her research interests include FinTech, Chinese economy and business analytics.

Yijun Chen is an independent researcher. Her research interests include Digital Transformation, RegTech, FinTech, Auditing and Cryptocurrencies.

Nicole dos Muchangos holds a bachelor's degree in Marine Sciences and a master's degree in Environmental Studies, both from the University of Aveiro. Her research interests focus mainly on entrepreneurship and go back to 2014 when she took part in a European summer program.

Emanuela Hanes is an independent researcher. Her cooperations include the Vienna University FH BFI Campus Wien, University of Graz and University of Salzburg. Her research interests include China-EU business strategies, RegTech, FinTech, Cryptocurrencies, Geopolitics, Chinese Strategic Planning and Development Policies.

Pankaj Madan is currently a Professor in the Faculty of Management Studies, Gurukula Kangri (Deemed to be University) Haridwar, and Dean in the Faculty of Engineering & Technology. He is Visiting Professor to Universities in China, Europe, and Latin America. His areas of teaching & Research are Decision Sciences and E-Commerce. His literary contributions to Emerald, Taylor, and Francis publications can be seen on Scopus.com, researchgate.net & Google Scholar. He has authored more than ten books and conducted more than 500 workshops and training sessions.

Kudzai Mandizvidza is an Economic Development professional who over time has worked in vast, multidisciplinary areas involving, Economic Research and Quantitative Analysis, Consultancy and Training, Agricultural Investment Management, Rural Economic Development, Agricultural Marketing, Project Management, Education and Food Security. He holds amongst other qualifications, a Master of Science in Agricultural Economics degree, as well as a Bachelor of Agribusiness Management degree. Kudzai has also worked with seasoned, multi- cultural and international researchers, at both academic and professional levels. He has contributed to the body of knowledge through publications, conference papers, desk studies, sector analysis, along with international investment reports.

Joaquín Martínez-Falcó holds a degree in History from the University of Alicante. He has a master's degree in Contemporary History from the Autonomous University of Madrid and a master's degree in Secondary Education from the University of Alicante. He has completed a mobility grant at the Andrés Bello University in Chile. He works as a history teacher in secondary education and is currently a PhD student at the University of Alicante on the relationship between the wine industry and historical heritage.

Joana Monteiro received her bachelor's degree in Tourism, Territory and Heritage from the University of Coimbra and a master's degree in Tourism Management and Planning from the University of Aveiro. She now works in managing of university residences. She is interested in management, entrepreneurship and sustainability.

Esther Poveda-Pareja holds a PhD in Economics, Business and Society and is an assistant professor of Management at the University of Alicante. Her research interests are mainly focused on corporate social responsibility and strategic management (concretely in agglomeration economies and tourism management). She is author of articles and book chapters related to these topics and has presented papers in national and international conferences. She has taken part in public and private projects related to these topics.

Anita Sable is a faculty in Symbiosis law school, Hyderabad, Symbiosis International (Deemed) University, Pune, India. She has more than 13 years of teaching experience. Currently she is serving as an assistant professor in the department of law.

Michael Sampat is an Independent Researcher working in Asian International Business and Biblical Studies.

Eduardo Sánchez García (PhD) is an Assistant Professor in the Department of Business Organization at the University of Alicante (Spain). His research is in the field of strategic management of the company. Specifically, he focuses on the study of the territorial agglomeration of companies in clusters and the absorptive capacity, and its influence on the innovative performance and entrepreneurial orientation of companies. He is co-author of several papers presented at conferences, both national and international, as well as several articles and book chapters related to his field of research.

Xiyan Shen is an independent researcher. Her research interests include RRI (responsible research and innovation), ESG (Environment, Social and Governance), token economy and Chinese business.

Ved Srinivas has nearly 8 years of experience in academia and the industry. An alumnus of the prestigious IIM Ahmedabad and Indore, his focus is on the arenas of Communication, Public Policy and Marketing. A geography graduate from SBSE College, University of Delhi (where he was adjudged the best student), he completed his MBA from Symbiosis College – a reputed institute based in Pune. He successfully cleared the NET exam, and is certified by the UGC in the subject of Management.

Nina Szczygiel (PhD) is a Professor of Management in the Department of Economics, Management, Industrial Engineering and Tourism (DEGEIT) of the University of Aveiro. Her research interests include topics of well-being and quality of life of societies, organizations, specific groups and individuals.

Naime Usul is a graduate of Business Administration from Bilkent University in 2007. She received her PhD in Finance from Bilkent University in 2017 with her thesis titled "Essays In Corporate Finance: An Analysis of Stock Market Investment Patterns in Emerging Countries From A Behavioral and A Traditional Perspective". She is interested in the areas of Corporate Finance and Behavioral Finance; in particular, in the investor behavior, investor psychology, corporate sustainability, and stock market anomalies. Her paper named "Affect-based stock investment decision: The role of affective self-affinity" was awarded with the first prize in Hakan Orbay Research Awards in 2017. After graduation, she taught courses in Başkent University for one semester. She has been working in Çankaya University since 2018.

Omar Vargas-González is Professor and Head of Systems and Computing Department at Tecnologico Nacional de Mexico Campus Ciudad Guzman, professor at Telematic Engineering at Centro Universitario del Sur Universidad de Guadalajara with a master degree in Computer Systems. Has been trained in Innovation and Multidisciplinary Entrepreneurship at Arizona State University (2018) and a Generation of Ecosystems of Innovation, Entrepreneurship and Sustainability for Jalisco course by Harvard University T.H. Chan School of Health. At present conduct research on diverse fields such as Entrepreneurship, Economy, Statistics, Mathematics and Information and Computer Sciences. Has colaborated in the publication of over 20 scientific articles and conducted diverse Innovation and Technological Development projects.

Işıl Sevilay Yılmaz received her BSc in Economics, a minor degree in City and Regional Planning, and an MBA degree from Middle East Technical University. After graduation, she worked at the Tax and Legal Services Department of PricewaterhouseCoopers İstanbul Office and received the title of Certified Public Accountant in 2005. After 2005, she worked in various private sector companies as a financial consultant. In 2016, she received her Ph.D. in Business Administration from Bilkent University with her thesis titled "Mergers and Acquisitions during Financial Crises". She has been working at TED University since February 2017. Her research interests include crowdfunding, corporate finance, sustainable finance, mergers and acquisitions, and financial crises.

Poshan (Sam) Yu is a Lecturer in Accounting and Finance in the International Cooperative Education Program of Soochow University (China). He is also an External Professor of FinTech and Finance at SKEMA Business School (China), a Visiting Professor at Krirk University (Thailand) and a Visiting Researcher at the Australian Studies Centre of Shanghai University (China). Sam leads FasterCapital (Dubai, UAE) as a Regional Partner (China) and serves as a Startup Mentor for AIC RAISE (Coimbatore, India). His research interests include financial technology, regulatory technology, public-private partnerships, mergers and acquisitions, private equity, venture capital, start-ups, intellectual property, art finance, and China's "One Belt One Road" policy.

Yanjuan Zhang is an independent researcher. Her research interests include management, FinTech and Chinese business.

Index

H

I

J

L

M

N

O

P

R

S

T

V

W

www.ingramcontent.com/pod-product-compliance
Lightning Source LLC
LaVergne TN
LVHW062137300926
849161LV00010B/2561